A SLOW BURNING FIRE

THE RISE OF THE NEW ART PRACTICE IN YUGOSLAVIA

A SLOW BURNING FIRE

MARKO ILIĆ

THE MIT PRESS
CAMBRIDGE, MASSACHUSETTS
LONDON, ENGLAND

This book was set in Arnhem Pro and Acumin Pro by The MIT Press. Printed and bound in the United States of America.

Library of Congress Cataloging-in-Publication Data
Names: Ilić, Marko, author.
Title: A slow burning fire : the rise of the New Art Practice in Yugoslavia / Marko Ilić.
Description: Cambridge, Massachusetts : The MIT Press, [2021] | Includes bibliographical references and index.
Identifiers: LCCN 2020007045 | ISBN 9780262044844 (hardcover)
Subjects: LCSH: New Art Practice (Art movement) | Art and society--Yugoslavia.
Classification: LCC N7248.5.N49 I45 2021 | DDC 709.497/09046--dc23
LC record available at https://lccn.loc.gov/2020007045

10 9 8 7 6 5 4 3 2 1

CONTENTS

ACKNOWLEDGMENTS **vii**

INTRODUCTION **1**

1 **A DRAFT DECREE ON THE DEMOCRATIZATION OF ART**
ZAGREB'S SC GALLERY (1966–1973) **15**

2 **A TASTER OF POLITICAL INSULT**
NOVI SAD'S YOUTH TRIBUNE (1968–1972) **69**

3 **THE INTERNATIONAL STRIKE OF ARTISTS**
BELGRADE'S SKC GALLERY (1971–1976) **115**

4 **ARTISTS AT WORK**
THE GROUP OF SIX AUTHORS AND RZU PODRUM (1975–1980) **167**

5 **WHAT IS THE ALTERNATIVE?**
LJUBLJANA'S ŠKUC GALLERY (1978–1984) **207**

6 **THE MIRACLE OF MIRACLES**
SARAJEVO AND THE LAST EPISODE OF THE "YUGOSLAV" CONTEMPORARY ART SCENE **251**

CONCLUSION **295**

NOTES **301**
BIBLIOGRAPHY **341**
INDEX **363**

ACKNOWLEDGMENTS

I have been writing this book for over a year now, but many years of research, reflection, and personal experience have, in one way or another, gone into it. The book began its life as a doctoral dissertation which was completed at the Courtauld Institute of Art in 2016 and funded by the UK's Arts and Humanities Research Council. I am particularly grateful to my PhD supervisor, Klara Kemp-Welch, for the patient and generous guidance she's provided me with throughout the years I've known her. I would also like to extend a huge thank you to my PhD examiners, David Crowley and Anthony Gardner, whose encouragement gave me the vital push I needed to adapt the thesis into a book. A lot of work was involved in developing the dissertation into a study that I hope can attest to recent global social and political transformations. I was given the opportunity to pursue this study by the Leverhulme Trust, which funded my Early Career Fellowship at University College London's School of Slavonic and East European Studies. I am very grateful to the Trust for its ongoing support, and for its generous contribution toward the book's publication costs.

Writing a book about art in a country that I barely knew, because it began unraveling a year after I was born, came with many challenges. I owe an enormous debt to several people who contributed to my understanding of a period which, although I never lived through it myself, has played a larger part in my life than I could ever have imagined. In particular, I would like to thank the following individuals for generously sharing their reflections, memories, and personal archives with me, especially those who agreed to be interviewed and who read through chapters of the manuscript: in Ljubljana, Barbara Borčić, Marina Gržinić, and Dušan Mandić; in Zagreb, Želimir Koščević, Branka Stipančić, and the late Mladen Stilinović; in Novi Sad, Slavko Bogdanović; in Belgrade, Zoran Popović, Jasna Tijardović, Biljana Tomić, and Raša Todosijević; in Sarajevo, Nermina Zildžo, Jusuf Hadžifejzović, and Saša Bukvić; in Priština, Shkëlzen Maliqi; and in Skopje, Suzana Milevska. I am very grateful to them all. With that, I would also like to acknowledge the more recent generation of scholars, curators, and theorists who either offered advice early on or whose work has been invaluable for my own: Ivana Bago, Branka Ćurčić, Lina Džuverović, Branislav Jakovljević, Jelena Vesić, and WHW.

For providing me with the images that have breathed life into this study, I would like to thank the following people: Sanja Iveković, Vladimir Jakolić, Braco Dimitrijević, Goran Trbuljak, Slavko Bogdanović, Karpo Godina, Raša Todosijević, Michael Corris, Goran Đorđević, Branka Stipančić, Sven Stilinović, Vlado Martek, Darko Šimičić, Bojana Švertasek, Zoran Popović, Laibach, Dušan Mandić, Barbara Borčić, Sadko Hadžihasanović, Saša Bukvić, Jusuf Hadžifejzović, and Jane Štravs. Thank you also to the following institutions for kindly granting me image permissions: Moderna Galerija, Ljubljana; the Croatian Academy of Sciences and Arts and the Museum of Contemporary Art, in Zagreb; the Museum of Contemporary Art in Vojvodina; the Matica Srpska Library in Novi Sad; the SKC Archive in Belgrade; as well as the National Gallery of Bosnia and Herzegovina, the Marinko Sudac Collection, the Richard Demarco Archive, and the NSK Archive.

I am extremely grateful to Victoria Hindley at the MIT Press for believing in this project and for accepting the manuscript. It is a tremendous honor to have my first book published by the Press—thank you for nurturing this project from its preliminary stages and for supporting early-career academics such as myself. Thank you to Paula Woolley for her careful editorial work on the manuscript and to Matthew Abbate, who saw the book to press, as well as to Margarita Encomienda, who designed it. It has been a pleasure working with such a brilliant team, and I am full of respect for the enthusiasm, precision, and professionalism shown by everyone at the Press.

Support from friends, colleagues, and family has provided a much-needed source of comfort and relief from what sometimes felt like a long and lonely writing process. Thank you to Josh Wood, Sofia Gotti, Yasmin El-Circy, Liz Storer, India Ross, Rosy Wiseman, George Hill, Will Leonardo, Toby Parker Rees, Emmett Roberts, Louisa Lee, Katarína Lichvárová, Serafina Bytyqi, Christina Novakov-Ritchey, Zoran Milutinović, and Sarah Wilson. Thank you also to Lila Božović, the Aleksandrović family, and to my family—Matija, Mila, Holly, and Max—for all of their love, care, and support.

Finally, thank you to my mother, Jovanka, for everything. This book is for her.

INTRODUCTION

Something in our world is dying, but what will be born in its place remains to be seen.[1] This feels like an era of annihilation, in which military conflicts continue to flare up throughout the world and the entire planet is en route to a capitalist-induced climate catastrophe. Living standards have been raised for millions in recent decades, but that has come at the cost of social cohesion and peaceful coexistence, and it has meant unimaginable poverty and persecution for millions more. An increasing number of countries worldwide are drifting to the right as economic and developmental inequality continues to widen at local, regional, and international levels. In North and South, East and West, youth are being left with few prospects. Gramsci's famous "pessimism of the intellect" is widespread, but his "optimism of the will" is, perhaps with good reason, in short supply.

In these times of annihilation and inequality, of war and poverty, Yugoslavia may once again have important lessons for us. How did this country founded on so-called workers' self-management—as well as a uniquely effective federal system—begin so well and yet end so catastrophically? And why, after years of peace and stability, did Yugoslav society take the turn it did at the end of the 1980s? This book argues that the four decades of Yugoslav socialism were far from a unilateral failure, and that mastering a balance sheet of its gains and losses is key to our understanding of global political and economic transformations in the second half of the twentieth century. It does so by focusing on one particular cultural legacy that emerged in many of the federation's republican capitals from the mid-1960s to the 1980s, known as the New Art Practice.

A term first coined in 1978, the New Art Practice has come to refer to forms of conceptual and performance art that emerged in the cities of Ljubljana, Zagreb, Novi Sad, Subotica, Belgrade, and Split, which, fueled by the youth movements of 1968, took on a more socially engaged form in the early 1970s. One of the richest chapters in recent art history, the phenomenon has received a significant amount of scholarly attention because of its many internationally renowned affiliates—Marina Abramović, Sanja Iveković, and Mladen Stilinović, among others. But it remains far from fully charted terrain. This book maps the New Art Practice's development alongside Yugoslavia's subversive search for a socialist political

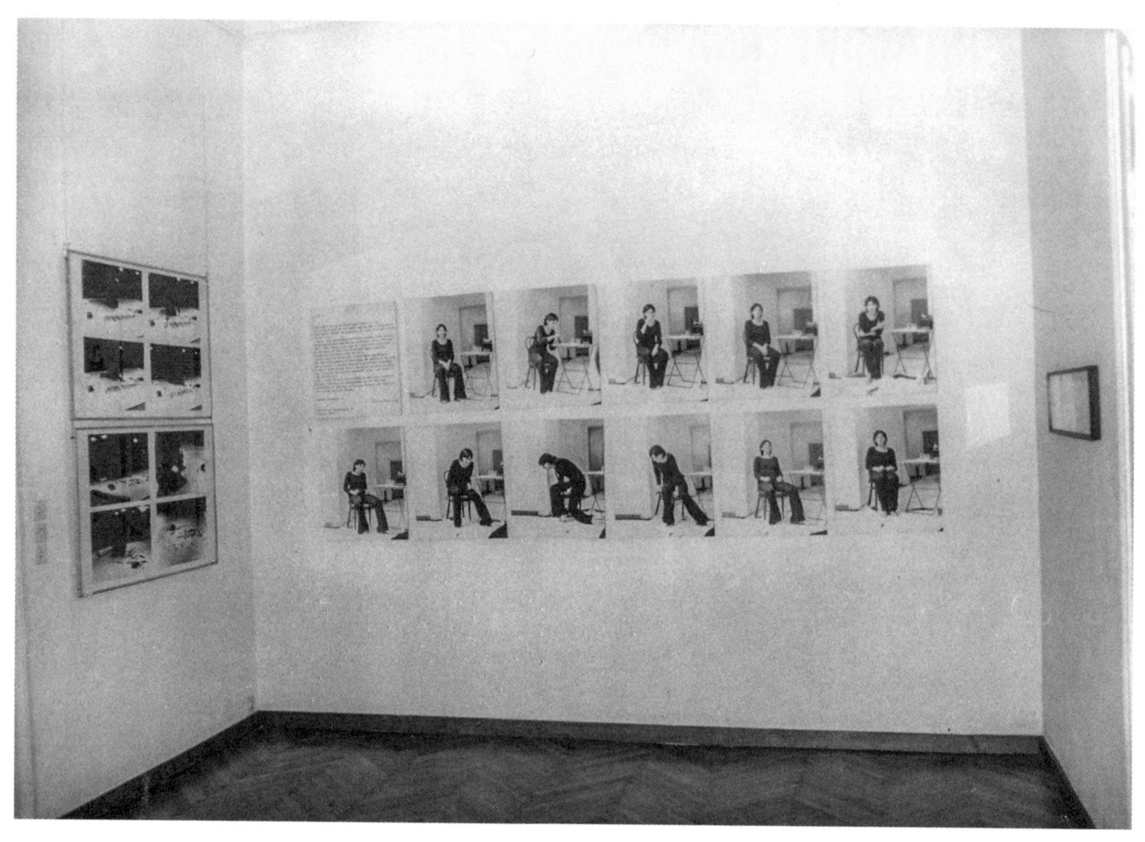

0.1. Installation view of the *Nova umjetnička praksa* [New Art Practice] exhibition, Galerija Suvremene Umjetnosti, Zagreb, 1978. Image courtesy of Muzej Suvremene Umjetnosti, Zagreb.

economy based on integral self-government from below in all human affairs. It proposes that the New Art Practice strove toward another world, one based on the principles of self-management and roiling beneath the conditions and processes that ultimately steered Yugoslavia's descent into ethnonationalism, destruction, and poverty. At the same time, this study seeks to amplify the New Art Practice's contradictions and inconsistencies in view of Yugoslavia's collapse in the 1990s and the wars of secession that raged for over a decade afterward. It does so by analyzing key actions, gestures, and propositions affiliated with the New Art Practice through the state-financed youth institutions known as Students' Cultural Centers, where many Yugoslav artists with prominent international profiles began their careers.

The genesis of the book was provided by a comprehensive catalogue that accompanied the first survey exhibition of conceptual and performance art in Yugoslavia: *The New Art Practice in Yugoslavia, 1966–1978*.[2] Organized by curator Marijan Susovski at Zagreb's Gallery of Contemporary Art in September 1978, this show was the first timely appraisal to recognize a singular thread in the work of young artists and collectives from many of the federation's republican capitals. It was also the first exhibition to introduce what became a locally accepted umbrella term. As Susovski summarized in the catalogue's introduction, what united artists of the New Art Practice was their "resistance to an inherited culture," their "conflict with tradition, pedagogic art canons, conventions, the institutionalized character of art," and their unrelenting urge to "develop art into an integral part of the criticism of the social praxis" by opposing the concept of an art based on "formal evolutionism."[3]

The *New Art Practice* exhibition arose out of a desire to document an all-Yugoslav movement. It was mounted in the midst of a social climate already scarred by years of political and economic instability that would eventually contribute to the country's disintegration. In that respect, it was pioneering, and it is therefore not surprising that most accounts of the New Art Practice continue to be shaped by this early appraisal and its contents. In its broadest possible definition, the New Art Practice has been understood as a form of engagement that, in the words of curator Bojana Pejić, allowed artists and critics "to distance themselves from the art production that surrounded them."[4] Recent work has similarly understood the New Art Practice's initial emergence as a critique of the "modernist paradigm of the 'autonomy of art.'"[5] As curator and theorist Jelena Vesić put it, the New Art Practice represented a "critical overturn that displaced the mimetic

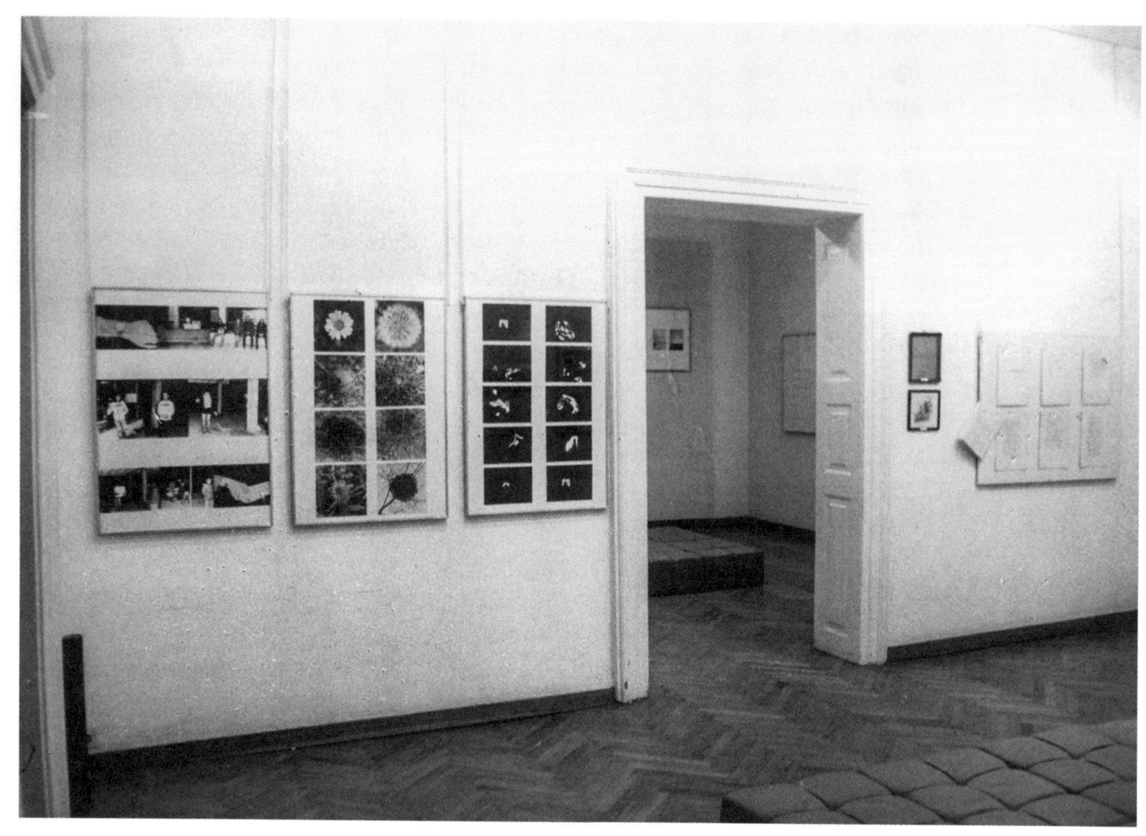

0.2. Installation view of the *Nova umjetnička praksa* [New Art Practice] exhibition, Galerija Suvremene Umjetnosti, Zagreb, 1978. Image courtesy of Muzej Suvremene Umjetnosti, Zagreb.

function of art from the field of 'representation' to the very ideological apparatus which set up the criteria for validating it."[6] Reaching a similarly overarching conclusion, MoMA curator Ana Janevski has noted that although "such activities developed quite independently of each other, they soon merged along a common artistic mentality, based mainly on the opposition to traditional and institutionalized forms of art and its presentation."[7]

To a reader unacquainted with Yugoslav art, these sweeping statements will most likely conjure up similarly general definitions of conceptual art and its "dematerialization," as a practice that, in the words of Blake Stimson, challenged the "authority of the institutional apparatus framing its place in society, and sought out other means for art to function in the world."[8] But while highlighting their clear points of convergence, accounts of the New Art Practice have emphasized its emergence within a socialist context, under a program that did not "function on the basis of a market premise, nor one fully controlled by the communist power apparatus."[9] Without a developed art market and corporate sponsorship, the New Art Practice could not adhere to Benjamin Buchloh's oft-cited argument about conceptual art's servitude to the "operating logic of late capitalism," by which "the insistence on artistic anonymity and the demolition of authorship produce[d] instant brand names and identifiable products."[10] Nor could it fit the familiar frame of "Eastern European Art," which positions artists as individuals suffering under totalitarian socialist regimes, because Yugoslavia was not a member of the Warsaw Pact but a nonaligned country, with a "third way" political and economic system. In the absence of either a "Western-style" art market or direct state control, definitions of the New Art Practice looked toward another clear adversary—neatly identifying the phenomenon as, in the words of art historian Miško Šuvaković, a "subversion of the moderate Socialist Modernism of that period."[11]

The term "socialist modernism" generally implies Yugoslavia's abandonment of socialist realist dogma and subsequent liberalization following its expulsion from the Communist Information Bureau in 1948. Needing to open itself up to Western Europe and America, for both military assistance and economic aid, and to develop a cultural system compatible with these geopolitical circumstances, Yugoslavia began to organize shows of modern American and European art as a way of involving the country in the international art world.[12] Works shown by artists abroad were of equal importance in this strategic sense, especially at the Venice Biennale, where Yugoslavia participated in its own pavilion starting in 1950. As the late art theorist Igor Zabel argued, no matter what the criteria were in choosing Yugoslav artists to be shown abroad, there was always an underlying effort in the postwar decades to match the standards of international art.[13]

The generally accepted narrative is that by the mid-1960s, the Yugoslav art world had become distinctly homogeneous. Those who had fought against socialist realism, and once represented the more "enlightened wings of the League of Communists," became leading figures in Yugoslavia's cultural life in the 1960s and 1970s.[14] They became professors at the Academies of Fine Art, museum directors, commissioners, and members of selection panels and purchasing committees. By the 1960s, socialist modernism had, so the master narrative goes, become a "semi-official art ideology."[15] In the words of Šuvaković, this "moderate modernism" was "a middle path between the abstract and the figurative, between the modern and the traditional, between regionalism and internationalism.... On the one hand this allowed artists to approach the mainstream of international Western modernism, while on the other it was a voice of resistance to more radical versions of modernism (from abstraction to the neo-avant-gardes)."[16]

Accounts of the New Art Practice have tended to adopt a stable definition of "socialist modernism" to establish its complementary opposition. Whereas socialist modernism was engaged "primarily with itself, with the quest for its own identity and for some 'autonomous,' uncontaminated space," the New Art Practice rejected the understanding of art as the production of "aesthetic objects, [by] using forms of work and activities that radically questioned the dominant artistic values and practices."[17] Yet Šuvaković's description of "moderate modernism" already gives a strong sense of the scattered, eclectic, and contradictory nature of this phenomenon—poised as it was between the "abstract" and the "figurative," and between the "modern" and the "traditional." It also provides a hint as to why polarities between the New Art Practice and socialist modernism are often tinged with one crucial oversight—that being that the latter was never an "official" cultural program or a monolithic construct in Yugoslavia. For socialist modernism clearly embodied a rather disparate field of practices, which were associated with a variety of individuals and encased within a wide range of institutions. Further complications arise from the fact that some of the institutions that promoted socialist modernism—including the Museums of Contemporary Art in Belgrade and Zagreb—were in fact occasional supporters of the New Art Practice, documenting and exhibiting the phenomenon in its earliest phase, and offering solo exhibitions to many of its main protagonists throughout the 1970s.[18]

In this book, I want to avoid such binaries, because they establish a division between "conformist" and "nonconformist" art and subsequently reassert the all too familiar scheme of setting dissident art in socialist Europe against critical art practices in the West. Put succinctly, I want to blur the boundaries between what constituted Yugoslavia's "official" and "unofficial" cultural spheres, by addressing the more complex and more relevant generational, political, and institutional factors that allowed for the emergence of the New Art Practice and secured its prolific development. Instead of framing the New Art Practice as an adversary to socialist modernism, this study situates it in the state institutions for youth, known as Students' Cultural Centers, which allowed artists to pursue new forms of artistic engagement.

Academic work on Yugoslavia's New Art Practice has already noted the galleries of the Students' Cultural Centers as the key sites for the introduction of new forms of self-organization in art and culture between the 1960s and the 1980s. It has also recognized that the Students' Cultural Centers themselves emerged as a result of the introduction of forms of self-management in Yugoslav society, which has broadly been understood as a system in which workers in factories, as well as other institutions in society, would have the final say over things that affected them. But for the most part, intepretations have focused on the marginal status of these spaces, which simultaneously guaranteed the New Art Practice's "relative autonomy [and] an extended field of possibilities."[19] In the words of Pejić, "the benefit—but also disadvantage—the New Art Practice experienced … was that it was promoted and regularly shown in the public galleries [that made up] parts of the universities or youth organizations."[20] The critical agency of the New Art Practice was tempered precisely by the status of the institutions that fostered it, linking its "contestational spirit" with "'experiments' otherwise characteristic of youth."[21] It is for this reason that Zagreb curator Ljiljana Kolešnik understood the "seemingly privileged position" of Students' Cultural Centers to be an attempt by the state to ghettoize critical art practices and thinking, thus "limiting their effects on a narrow segment of urban student youth, which, thanks to its education, collective sensibility, and resistance to [the] social and cultural values of the older generation, was ready to accept new cognitive paradigms."[22]

When we trace the landmark events and practices that emerged in the Students' Cultural Centers in Zagreb, Novi Sad, and Belgrade, such perspectives seem partially defensible. With no developed art market or direct state input, the artists affiliated with Students' Cultural Centers appeared to be working within an "interestless" space. Šuvaković has gone so far as to propose that Students' Cultural Centers represented "reservations in different social environments," through which "critical subversive practices from one context would be neutralized, without banning them, by transferring them to another."[23] Of course, such interpretations carry a lure: they once again rehearse the post-1989 stereotype bestowed on Eastern European artists as individuals struggling against repressive socialist regimes and their powerful systems of institutions. As with all matters regarding the exceptional Yugoslav case, however, the situation was not so straightforward, and although "alternative" artists working through official institutions did indeed have to make many compromises, there were also certain practical advantages to the arrangement.

Yugoslavia's experience with socialist self-management was a far more complex, gradual, and multifaceted phenomenon than might be apparent at first glance, with many of the elements that appeared to provide stability to the regime eventually contributing to, and precipitating, the country's violent disintegration. Acknowledging this, this study registers the many individuals who worked through Yugoslavia's youth spaces, and establishes a narrative of personal encounters and cultural dialogues between institutions. In other words, I map how artistic ideas circulated in the Yugoslav cultural space, and follow how they were recast, reinvented, and reinvigorated through various distribution channels. Far from being institutionalized margins or artistic "ghettoes," I argue, Students' Cultural Centers both laid the groundwork for a series of crucial self-organized initiatives in Yugoslavia, and allowed artists to step out from their immediate confines and into the international art arena.

How do we weave local histories into a global narrative of postwar art? What methodological tools do we have at our disposal to, as art historian Reiko Tomii recently put it, create a shared sense of history that "at once encompasses diverse localized stories and illuminates the complex state of contemporaneity, wherein diverse parallel phenomena exist at a given time and multiple stories tangle together"?[24] In Yugoslavia, it was the Students' Cultural Centers that allowed artists to pursue local interests by forging international alliances, and to register the intense presence of global forces within their immediate environment. By tracing the international networks of artistic exchange that these spaces solicited, this book analyzes how Yugoslav artists developed distinct practices that were parallel to, and very often critical toward, their counterparts in Western Europe and North America. Mapping this extended narrative of events, one that spans over two decades, I simultaneously examine how the New Art Practice was intimately tied to Yugoslavia's experience with socialist self-management, and the changes that this socioeconomic order underwent during this period.

Was the globalization of today's art world prefigured in the internationalization of art during the 1960s? Did it spread along the paths of capital, new media, and technologies? And if so, what was the role of local agencies? This book proposes that the New Art Practice emerged precisely at a time when Yugoslavia was integrating itself deeper into the world economy and beginning to succumb to the competitive logic dominant in global capitalism. Rather than being an alternative to this logic, Yugoslavia, I argue, was inextricably linked to it.

Yugoslavia was notorious for its constant economic reforms and new political constitutions, and the years between the mid-1960s and the early 1980s were particularly significant in the country's political development. This study takes as its departure point a series of economic reforms that were initiated during the mid-1960s, and which brought about a clear class stratification and consumerist tendencies in Yugoslavia. To this end, I examine how the New Art Practice both came out of, and was critical toward, the combination of workers' self-management and economic liberalization—along with its repercussions on the federation's previously guaranteed protections of social and economic equality and shared sovereignty. This entails reading the New Art Practice against the grain of the social and national tensions that weighed heavily in the background of the introduction of "market socialism," which culminated in the purging of liberal leaderships throughout the entire federation. This moment marked a crucial turning point not only for the political direction of self-management but also for the New Art Practice itself, driving some of its earliest proponents to stop making art at the same time as many of their counterparts around the world.[25]

These worldwide feelings of disillusionment and gestures of withdrawal provide a powerful indicator of how the combination of economic liberalism and political conservatism that took hold in Yugoslavia was by no means exclusive to the federation, but rather integral to the global transition to financialized capitalism and neoliberal policy regimes. Yugoslavia's rising deficits, its decline into a debt trap, and its political collapse in the late 1970s and 1980s were typical of the trajectory in many countries across the world, the key characteristics of which I highlight in the final three chapters. In chapter 4, I provide an extended narrative of events to reveal how the New Art Practice paved the way for two autonomous, artist-led projects in Zagreb. From the mid-1970s, these self-organized initiatives addressed the erratic and uneven implementation of self-management. While bearing obvious affinities with the politicization of artistic labor in North America at the beginning of the 1970s, these artist groups in Zagreb were formed precisely when self-management had aligned itself with the neoliberal idea of deregulation, and the "worker" was vanishing as a political subject in Yugoslavia. Seeking to salvage the idea of self-management, these artists paradoxically came to be burdened with the same nagging issues that shadowed federal politics at that time.

Central to the book's argument, then, is that Yugoslavia's decline not only occurred over a prolonged period of time but was inseparable from fundamental changes in the international environment. The 1970s were the last decade of growth in Yugoslavia, but this decade also set in motion the processes by which the majority of the country's successor states were "Balkanized" and rendered "southern" after the end of the Cold War. Like so many countries in the Second and Third World, Yugoslavia's growth during this decade was fueled through foreign borrowing; in 1983, it was revealed that the country had accumulated a foreign debt of over $20 billion, and was experiencing a massive decline in production, a worsening balance of trade, and hyperinflation. Austerity, declining living standards, and growing nationalist resentments provide the political backdrop for the final two chapters, which concentrate on the emergence of alternative art scenes in Ljubljana and Sarajevo.

In what might be described as the book's final section, I propose that the emergence of alternative art scenes in Ljubljana and Sarajevo, stemming from the rich legacy of the country's Students' Cultural Centers, resulted from and were reactions to the political decentralization and economic liberalization implied in self-management's later phase, along with Josip Broz Tito's death in 1980. As Yugoslavia's economy continued to spin out of control and deadlock began to set in, Ljubljana witnessed the rise of a so-called alternative scene which began to reflect on and adapt to the country's swiftly deteriorating social climate. Synchronously, Sarajevo experienced its own cultural awakening; in 1989, it even played host to the final and, in some respects, most decisive episode of Yugoslavia's art scene. But why did a highly sophisticated art scene, toying with antagonisms at the heart of Yugoslavia's political struggles, gain momentum only in the country's most developed and Westernmost republic, which would some ten years later exit the federation through an almost surgical secession? And why did the largest and most significant Yugoslav art event take place in Sarajevo, just a few years before Bosnia and Herzegovina would be subjected to the most prolonged, bloody agony during the country's disintegration? Although there are no straightforward answers to these questions, they carry important insights into the often overlooked center-periphery divide that plagued Yugoslav development and ultimately led to the disintegration of the federation.

In Yugoslavia, the key to the federation's long-term viability lay in its ability to overcome regional inequalities in a territory characterized by profound economic disparities. This involved a redistributive logic that was centralist at first, but ultimately succumbed to the pressures of richer republics following the market reforms that were given full rein in the 1960s. Never resolved, these uneven geographies resulted in enormous social and economic inequalities between Yugoslavia's richer republics and the provinces of the northwest (Slovenia, Croatia, Vojvodina, and Serbia), and the poorer ones in the southeastern regions (Bosnia and Herzegovina, Montenegro, Kosovo, and Macedonia); unsurprisingly, they also registered in the clearly unequal federal distribution of the New Art Practice itself. If, as Terry Smith has argued, contemporaneity consists of the "jostling contingency of various cultural and social mulitiplicities, all thrown together in ways that highlight the fast-growing inequalities within and between them," then there are many parallels to be drawn between the asymmetrical hierarchies in Yugoslavia's art scenes and our contemporary art world, which, in spite of its frequent claims to inclusivity, still denies access to those without the necessary privileges, languages, and technologies.[26] As Mladen Stilinović put it in one precise and pithy statement, "An Artist Who Cannot Speak English Is No Artist."[27] I hope this study alerts readers to how such "asynchronous temporalities" also bear the capacity to descend into nationalism, wars, and destruction.[28]

This point naturally leads to the challenges implicit in critically reconstructing a "Yugoslav" art history—challenges connected to the competition for prestige between national canons, and experiences of marginalization and marginality that are so painfully relevant to the Yugoslav experience. Because of the devastating obliteration of a common cultural memory that was set off by the Yugoslav wars, the majority of the federation's art histories have been structured around national borders, and organized into isolated, local narratives, by critics and scholars who have refrained from intervening in the interpretation of art from another country. Abroad, artists affiliated with the New Art Practice have largely been the subjects of individual monographs; rarely have they been considered alongside their neighboring and international counterparts. The clear result of these processes was the formulation of a Yugoslav art history consisting largely of three seemingly disparate and disconnected cities—Ljubljana, Zagreb, and Belgrade—as the only familiar locales in a territory that once consisted of eight constitutive parts. Conscious of the polemics that surround the competition for cultural capital in the (post-)Yugoslav space, this study aims to provide a balanced and transnational analysis of the New Art Practice. Some of the stories presented here will already be well known, others less known than they should be, but above all I have sought to bring artists and cultural workers together through a new critical frame—one that magnifies the New Art Practice's complex successes and failures, without recourse to nostalgia or reification.

Chapter 1 opens with the landmark events initiated by Zagreb's Students' Center (SC) Gallery—and the organic emergence of conceptual and "dematerialized" art practices within the space, following a series of developments that began with "environmental" works and innovative curatorial interventions. The new generation of artists working through the SC Gallery were among the first to problematize issues of authorship and direct communication. But while echoing similar shifts to dematerialization in Western Europe and America, the Zagreb artists' engagement was undoubtedly impacted by the vast series of economic reforms beginning in 1965, along with the political consequences of the so-called Croatian Mass Movement of 1971. Tracing the gallery's pioneering contributions to the New Art Practice, this chapter reflects on some of the challenges faced by artists working through the SC Gallery at a crucial moment in Yugoslavia's political development, and introduces some of the contradictions embedded in the country's cultural policy under self-management.

Chapter 2 traces a specific episode in the history of Novi Sad's Youth Tribune, when the city's New Art Practice crossed into political engagement and provocation. Beginning with the pioneering art collective from Ljubljana, OHO, and their visit to Novi Sad, the chapter follows the increased bureaucratization of the Youth Tribune, along with the events that drove its key players to appeal to an "Invisible Art." Although Yugoslavia is frequently characterized as a country that encouraged public debate, the important and often overlooked case of Novi Sad reveals the consequences of a direct confrontation with the city's cultural apparatus, at a moment marked by oppressive change and political turmoil.

To this day, Belgrade's Students' Cultural Center (SKC) Gallery continues to be the institution with which conceptual and performance art in Serbia (and, to an extent, Yugoslavia at large) has come to be identified, predominantly due to Marina Abramović's involvement in its early exhibitions. Mapping the extended networks fostered through the gallery's exhibitions, and most famously the April Meetings, chapter 3 follows the SKC Gallery's struggle to step out from its local context into the international art arena, beginning with the legendary *Drangularijum* exhibition, and tracing developments toward Goran Đorđević's *International Strike of Artists*, "a protest against the ongoing repression of the art system and the alienation of artists from the results of their work."[29]

Coming from the lessons learnt in Students' Cultural Centers, self-organized art collectives continued to address the conflicts within self-management. Building on the work of Ivana Bago and an extensive exhibition catalogue produced by Zagreb's Soros Center for Contemporary Art in 1998, chapter 4 considers two artist-led initatives in Zagreb that sought to establish autonomous collective organizations—the Grupa Šestorice Autora [Group of Six Authors] and Radna Zajednica Umjetnika (RZU) Podrum [Podrum: The Working Community of Artists].[30] While Bago has reflected on Podrum through the theoretical framework of "hospitality," I examine the development of these autonomous collectives in parallel with the decisive political and economic shifts that were taking place simultaneously in the Yugoslav Federation. In their own, individual ways, both illuminated the intricate political developments unfolding in Yugoslavia following the country's decentralization in 1974 and the Associated Labor Law of 1976, which essentially marked a very conservative turn from the founding principles of self-management.

Chapter 5 explores the significance of these initiatives in relation to the case of Ljubljana's Students' Cultural and Arts Center (ŠKUC) Gallery. While Ljubljana maintains a critical hegemony in the post-Yugoslav cultural space (courtesy of the city's neo-Lacanian School, which includes philosopher Slavoj Žizek), and though countless exhibitions and critical evaluations have canonized the subcultures supported by the ŠKUC Gallery, very few have focused on the emergence of the institution itself.[31] In this chapter, I examine the ways in which the gallery introduced conceptual art from Belgrade and Zagreb to what would become a key institution for the so-called alternative movement. In Yugoslavia's wealthiest and most ethnically compact republic, the gallery helped initiate an independent production and distribution system that directly challenged the cultural monopoly of the League of Communists in Slovenia.

The final chapter is devoted to the case of Sarajevo. In contrast to the capitals of the country's more developed regions, Sarajevo lacked a Students' Cultural Center for various political and economic reasons. For decades the city was perceived by Yugoslavia's most developed centers as a traditional and isolated city, dominated by a strict and conservative cultural policy. The 1980s were, however, decisive for the republic—following Yugoslavia's political decentralization, Bosnia and Herzegovina gained unprecedented state autonomy. In this chapter, I examine the emergence of the Zvono group in parallel with Sarajevo's celebrated "New Primitives" subculture, and alongside the practice of Jusuf Hadžifejzović.

In doing so, the chapter provides the first contextual consideration of the final episode of Yugoslavia's contemporary art scene—the Yugoslav *dokumenta*, which miraculously took place in Sarajevo in the wake of the country's disintegration.[32]

At a time when cultural institutions are becoming increasingly weighed down by forces greater than themselves in the shape of state reform and corporate power, I hope that this account of the New Art Practice's optimism and untenable inconsistences will invite us to think carefully about how art and culture can either preserve existing social structures or hold out for futures yet to come. Needless to say, the future that the New Art Practice saw for Yugoslavia never came, and this study is as much about delusions, failed projects, and painful legacies as it is about hopes and ideals. But if this book is to reach its horizon of intention, it will reopen unanswered questions about the contradictions between Yugoslavia's claims to an independent path to socialism and its ultimate collapse under the pressures of globalization, economic reform, and austerity. As it becomes increasingly clear that something in our world is dying, these are questions that any genuine internationalism will need to attend to, if it is to build a progressive, common world based on social justice and equality.

1 A DRAFT DECREE ON THE DEMOCRATIZATION OF ART

ZAGREB'S SC GALLERY (1966–1973)

LUXURY, WASTE, AND THE ORIGINS OF THE SC GALLERY

In January 1958, the Sixth Congress of the National Youth Organization of Yugoslavia convened in Belgrade to discuss the role of the young intellectual in socialist society. As part of the official policy on university education, they defined the young intellectual as exemplary of the new "socialist man, who would combine the courage, sincerity and self-sacrifice of a Partisan hero with the mastery of modern knowledge, and would follow the guidance of the League of Communists for the construction of society."[1] In a country that could afford "neither luxury nor waste," the graduate was expected to be a "socialist expert who would have a firm grasp of the essentials of Marxism, and devote their skills to the construction of the new order."[2] While in the old, prewar Yugoslavia the university had primarily served as a finishing school for the children of the privileged few, it now became key to the construction of a new society, open to a far broader demographic of youths.

Of course, Yugoslavia was not the only socialist country that considered the young a cornerstone of society. Yet in the Yugoslav case, the rapid expansion of the university system had emerged from its own particular set of circumstances, and within a period of unprecedented national independence, full employment, free social services, and a vast proliferation in schooling.[3] One immediate requirement of the new system was the further education of workers, to allow them to grapple with the complexities of factory management. This is why enterprises and trade unions helped fund over 200 workers' universities, which by 1968 had held almost 10,000 courses, in a country where two-thirds of the youth had received less than four years' schooling up to 1945.[4] In his *Histoire des démocraties populaires*, the Hungarian political scientist Ferenc Fejtö argued that this democratization of education, together with the agrarian reform and universal suffrage implemented in the 1950s, was being directed by nothing short of the first Enlightenment government in the Balkans, which would go on to produce the first modern proletariat and intelligentsia in this part of the world.[5]

In June 1950, the Federal People's Assembly passed a basic law on the management of state companies, agricultural companies, and economic enterprises by workers' collectives.[6] This initial introduction of workers' councils may not have resulted in a system of workers' control or a genuine democracy from below. But it did generate an unequaled amount of input by workers and of civic enthusiasm, which was reflected in exceptional economic results.[7] In 1952, to symbolize a new political direction, the party changed its name from the Communist Party to the League of Communists of Yugoslavia (LCY), in honor of Marx's Communist League of 1848.[8] Although a symbolic gesture, the name change signaled that the party's role was no longer to command citizens but to lead them, through persuasion, toward their socialist future.

Among manual workers and intellectuals alike, the introduction of workers' self-management raised hopes that the objects of social change could finally become its subjects. This enthusiasm was reflected in party membership, which by 1958 had the highest proportion of workers it would have in its entire history.[9] In the same year, the League of Communists announced a program that would transform "all state organs into organs of self-government," and effect the "emancipation of educational, scientific, artistic and all other cultural life from the administrative interference of governmental authorities."[10] For many of the party's members in 1958, the program's ambition for a "society in which classes and all traces of exploitation and the oppression of man by man will disappear," or in which individuals would have full responsibility in all spheres of society, may in fact have seemed an attainable ideal.[11]

In the same year that the League of Communists announced its ambitious program, the University of Zagreb was granted a center that would serve to guarantee the social security of the city's first postwar generation of students: the Studentski Centar [Students' Center, or SC]. Already in June 1957 a founding act had identified a location for the center, a site that had formerly served the Zagreb Fair on Savska cesta 25. By late 1958, adaptations to that space had begun. The renovated center was to include a restaurant, the SC Club, classrooms, the Students' Center Gallery (Galerija Studentskog Centra, or GSC), a Chamber Theater (Teatar & TD), and Students' Services, all claiming direct responsibility for the welfare of students.

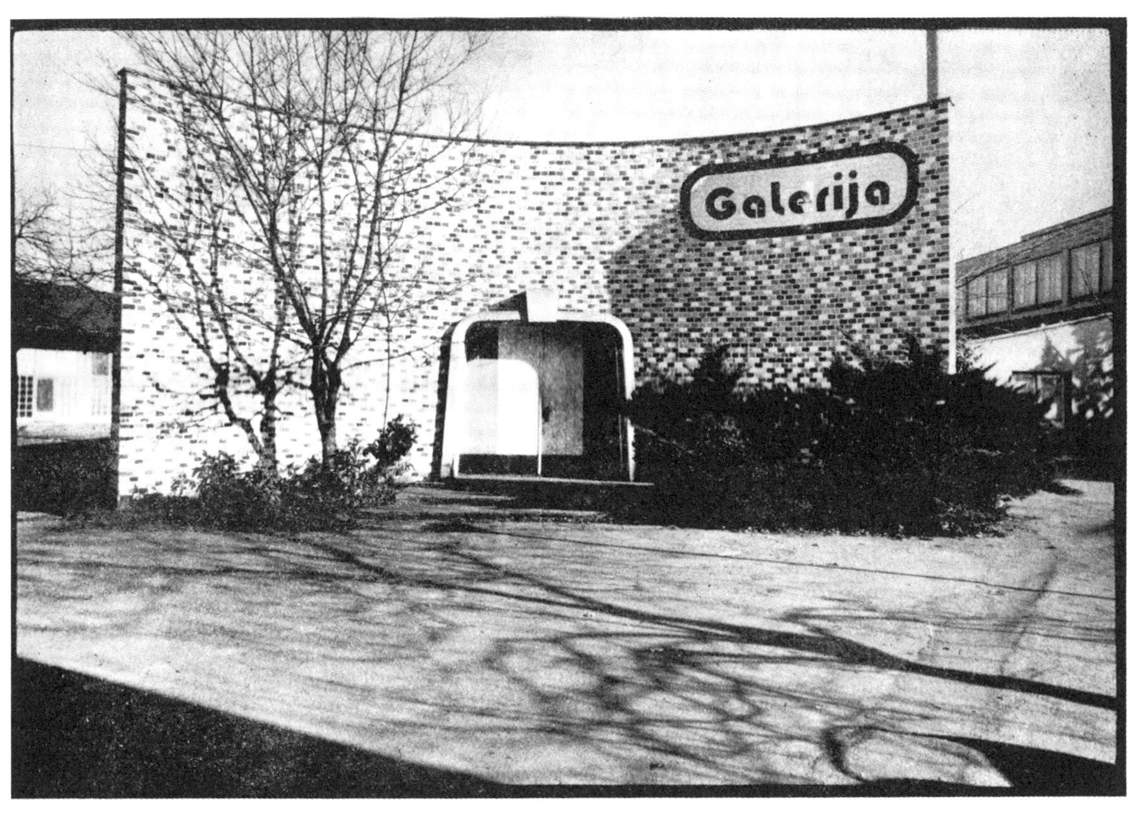

1.1. Exterior of Zagreb's SC Gallery, from *Novine GSC* [SC Gallery Newspaper], no. 52, 1975. Image courtesy of Arhiv za Likovne Umjetnosti HAZU, Zagreb.

At its opening, however, the SC Gallery left a fairly indistinguishable mark on the city's cultural scene, bound as it was to the "didactic, informative intentions" emphasized in its founding principles.[12] Instead, it was the city's Gallery of Contemporary Art—one of the first public institutions in the world to carry the term "contemporary art" in its name—that had become the key space for exhibiting the work of younger artists.[13] Overshadowed by the city's foremost contemporary art institution, the SC Gallery began, in the words of its first director, Dubravko Horvatić, "metaphorically in a position beneath zero ... in its first steps not really acting as a voice, but a mere exhibition space, with an improper purpose."[14] A lack of funding and poor physical conditions acted as further obstacles: according to Horvatić, the walls of the gallery were so damp that "mold stains blossomed around some exhibits," leading some to believe that in the time of Informel, the gallery was deliberately fostering them.[15]

By the mid-1960s, the SC Gallery had begun to fulfill its obligation of opening cultural activity up to a new generation of artists, largely because of its cooperation with Želimir Koščević. A young art historian, Koščević had previously worked in the city's Museum of Arts and Crafts, but his interests were largely shaped by Zagreb's New Tendencies art scene of the 1960s. As art historian Armin Medosch has rigorously detailed, New Tendencies was a movement that formed in Zagreb in 1961 with a common "desire to abolish the artist as creative genius and replace him or her with the notion of visual research."[16] Above all, this entailed disavowing the artist as a producer of commodities for the art market. It involved shattering the foundational myths of modernism, which privileged art's autonomy, and introducing the viewer as a coproducer of works. In a catalogue text from 1963, Matko Meštrović, a founding member of the movement, argued that New Tendencies wanted to

> nurture the seed of a general and encompassing revolutionary idea, which does not desire to express itself in a rebellious or destructive way.... The breaking down of social barriers, mental rigidity, routine schemes are by no means superfluous to performing this task. Art must perform a breakthrough into the extra-poetical and extra-human sphere, because today, without that action the human sphere cannot be enriched.[17]

In this text, Meštrović demanded that artistic activity break through individualism and established patterns of social behavior by exploring new media and technologies. From the outset, this was an influence that permeated Koščević's approach at the SC Gallery. In an essay from 1964, he had already argued for a "spatial imagination" that would harmonize the relationship between "technical and imaginative factors."[18] But whereas Meštrović proposed that visual research need not be rebellious, Koščević came to the SC Gallery with an awareness that the art institution would ultimately need to "act differently, to take its own stand," and act against the common premise that "a gallery should cater to the petty-bourgeois, who will enter its halls on a Sunday afternoon, feeling the greatest respect and piety for every moldy piece of rag, for every polished plank, for every carefully cleaned pebble.... Until this is changed there won't be any proper relations between art and society."[19]

In other words, Koščević was calling for new and experimental methods that could overcome society's passive and "petty-bourgeois" relationship to museums. He was demanding the introduction of new concepts that could shake up a settled institutional climate consisting of museums "already so mothy and dusty in their undisturbed following of provincial and bourgeois concepts."[20] This involved subjecting the ostensible neutrality of the art institution to scrutiny, a scrutiny that would steer the majority of the SC Gallery's activities in subsequent years.

THE SC GALLERY'S "SHAMELESS PROVOCATIONS"

The SC Gallery's first attempt to unsettle Zagreb's stable institutional climate took place in October 1967 with the exhibition *Hit-parada* [Hit Parade], which included the work of four painters from the same generation as New Tendencies: Mladen Galić, Ante Kuduz, Ljerka Šibenik, and Miroslav Šutej. According to the polemical catalogue introduction, the exhibition strove to "solve the space of the gallery through painting and illumination in a way that had not been previously attempted [in the republic of Croatia]."[21] Unlike New Tendencies, which largely sought to theorize the role of art in societies of advanced mass production, the artists shown in *Hit Parade* wanted to situate a series of "objects, or more accurately ideas, in a real urban space, in the frame of real life, and to sharpen the conflict between the space and the subject."[22] By creating site-specific installations, these artists were questioning the very basic foundations of art making, including the art object's mobility, which leaves it open to various manipulations.

The objects, or "ideas" as Koščević referred to them, included Šutej's small "forest of hanging multicolored plastic tape" at the entrance. These billowing threads of thin tape evoked the kind of plastic curtains placed at the entrances of Yugoslav barbershops. But in *Hit Parade*, the curtain was, according to one observer, wider, taller, longer, and more "pleasantly lyrical."[23] Galić displayed "long canvas worms," their cores filled with sawdust and their exteriors painted in various colors. Šibenik placed "500 or so blue and white pear-shaped helium balloons, floating and levitating in the center of the space."[24] The objects on display had one thing in common: they were all based on familiar forms from everyday life. To further animate the exhibition, a series of actions were performed by members of the SC's experimental theater, while live music played simultaneously, adhering to the exhibition's "parade theme."[25] In the supporting catalogue, *Hit Parade* announced itself as the first exhibition to successfully break through "the solid fence of 'lyrical abstraction,' 'Informel,' 'art brut,' and 'surrealism'—all the possibilities and styles which played a very significant role at a certain historical moment, but—here and now—have become the conservative force impeding new and fresh ideas."[26]

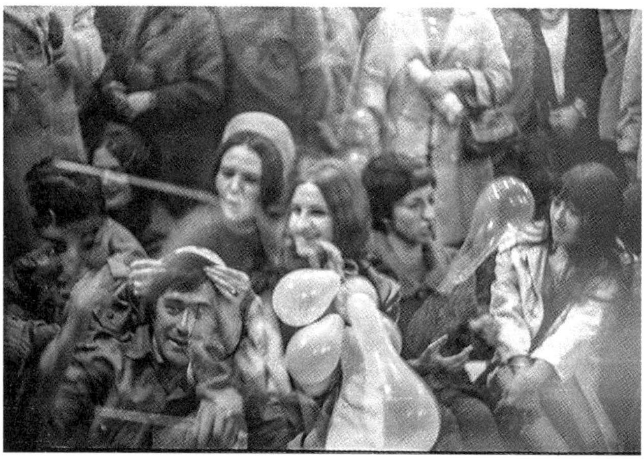

1.2. *Hit-parada* [Hit Parade] exhibition opening at Galerija Studentskog Centra, Zagreb, 20 October 1967. Photograph by Vladimir Jakolić. Image courtesy of Vladimir Jakolić and Arhiv za Likovne Umjetnosti HAZU, Zagreb.

For the artists participating in *Hit Parade*, the "solid fence" of Croatia's art scene seemed to consist of modernist painting, which had flourished as a result of the growing power of the more liberal wings of Yugoslavia's Communist Party in the 1950s. Yet, while being connected to the country's need to open itself to the West both economically and culturally, the dominance of modernist painting was by no means unique to the Yugoslav context. During the 1950s, Informel painting found echoes across the world as an existential cry against the atrocities committed in the Second World War; but in the following decade the individualism behind gestural, expressive painting had lost its creative potential for many younger artists, in Yugoslavia and beyond. Considering New Tendencies' pioneering attempts to nurture new relationships between the work and the viewer, *Hit Parade*'s self-declared triumph over the "solid fence" of modernist painting in Croatia may have seemed somewhat exaggerated. Yet it wasn't so much the work shown at *Hit Parade* that made it a watershed as it was the events that ensued on the night of its opening: the exhibition was destroyed by the public, provoking a wave of attacks on the SC Gallery from the national press.

Although it was intended primarily as an exhibition, *Hit Parade* was advertised as a "happening" in local newspapers, and attracted over 400 visitors to the opening. But even before the exhibition was set to open, a couple of "uniformed youths in hard hats," later identified as a group of students from the Academy of Fine Arts, stormed into the gallery and attempted to pull down the balloons in the center of the space. Instantly, the gesture spread: "through a strange, unreal laughter, as in some surrealist film, the destruction of the white and blue balloons began."[27] Some tossed their cigarette buts at them; others, making a "human ladder," climbed up to pull the balloons down, and after retrieving them began "pressing them between their palms, and bursting them with their nails."[28] Photographs taken at the opening attest to these press statements: the most iconic image, reproduced in several newspapers, captured a figure clutching at the balloons and pulling them off the ceiling. Then the crowd turned to the other "object ideas": some visitors slashed open the canvas worms and began throwing the sawdust on other visitors; others plucked the hanging threads at the entrance. Reportedly, the gallery became the scene of a "fierce struggle: women were screaming, laughter and shouting could be heard."[29] By 11 pm, the gallery resembled a "city dump."[30] In the end, all that remained among the debris of destruction was a series of photographs, along with a couple of eyewitness accounts. The "exhibition of ideas" had become a truly "dematerialized" phenomenon.

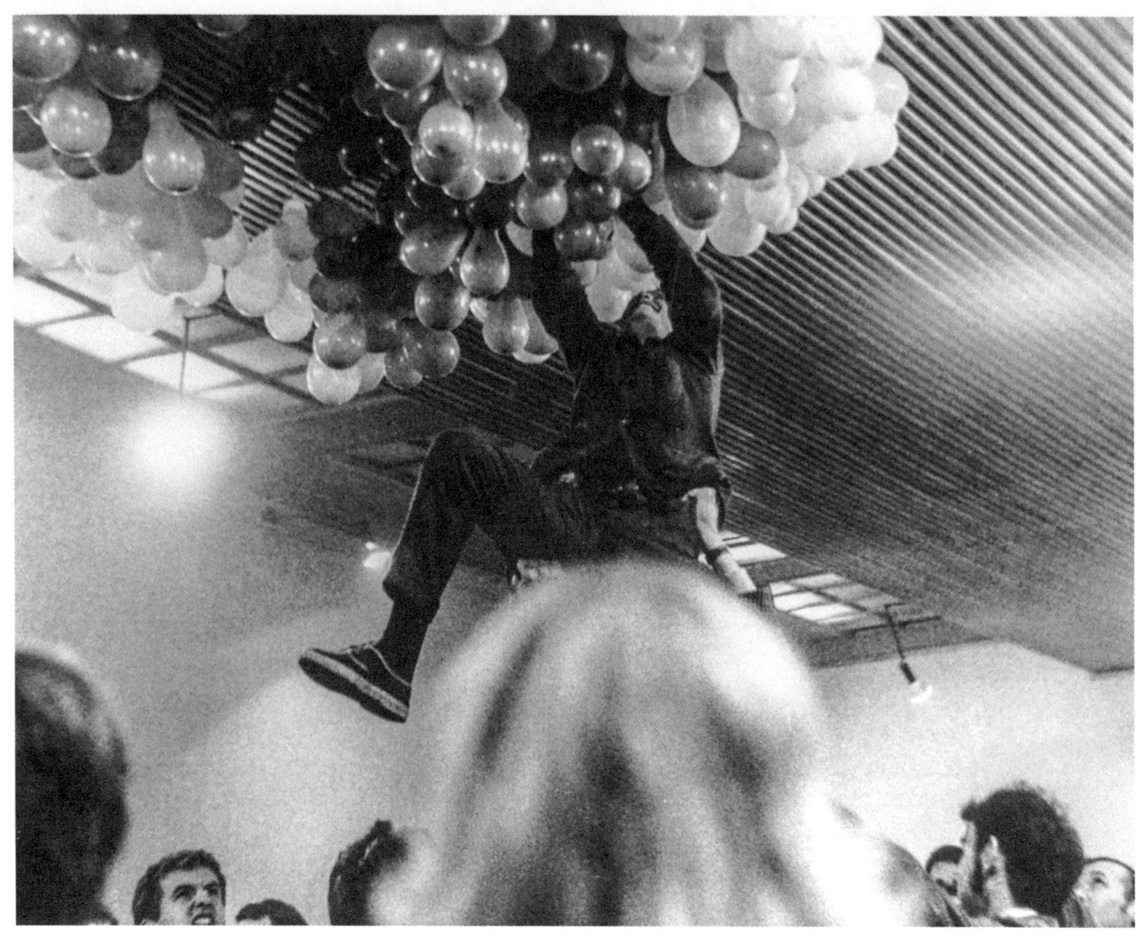

1.3. *Hit-parada* [Hit Parade] exhibition opening at Galerija Studentskog Centra, Zagreb, 20 October 1967. Photograph by Vladimir Jakolić. Image courtesy of Vladimir Jakolić and Arhiv za Likovne Umjetnosti HAZU, Zagreb.

By accident, *Hit Parade* became the first recorded example of spontaneous destruction in Zagreb's art scene. For the artists whose work was destroyed, this turn of events was nothing but a "miserable expression of a center that does not tolerate any kind of innovation."[31] Koščević, however, had a softer view of the nonsensical acts. As he recalls, "the fact that some saw it as an opportunity for destruction, which they then enacted, was a misunderstanding, but came out as charming, even silly!"[32] It served as an indicator of the "depth of misunderstanding and, at the bottom line, of intolerance on behalf of the conservative, bourgeois current, even among my generation at the time, which was infected by the virus from the Fine Arts Academy."[33] Despite the frivolity of the events that unfolded at *Hit Parade*'s opening, a general uproar from the press ensued: among the many accusations raised against the exhibition was that it was a "shameless provocation . . . a fad, exhibitionism."[34] For many of the critics reviewing the show, it provided an irresistible opportunity to take stock of the current condition of culture in Croatia.

In a review published in the Zagreb daily newspaper *Telegram*, one anonymous critic decried the decision made over a decade earlier to grant full freedom in artistic activity. He complained that this shift had resulted in a "whole series of dogmatisms" and "bigotry . . . violent separatism . . . waving the flag against orthodoxy . . . art stripped of its sense."[35] This review was even featured on the newspaper's front cover, under the heading "From dogmatism to vandalism."[36] Another newspaper published a caricature of a drunken bar brawl, in which two critics stand by, remarking, "You see, in our country art trends are all over the place, even the opening of a simple bistro needs to be a happening!"[37] In its review of the event, the official Party paper *Borba* questioned whether the "SC Gallery could not have found a more rational way of spending their endowed funds, especially in view of the fact that fairly serious discussions have been made on raising the price of student board and lodging in the hostels of the establishment that subsidized it."[38]

The final critique was particularly telling, in that it highlights how the hostility directed toward *Hit Parade* may have been the result of a particularly tense economic climate, as Yugoslavia began developing a more liberal and world-dependent economy. In 1965, two years before the SC Gallery staged *Hit Parade*, the League of Communists had announced a massive economic reform that aimed to remove political involvement from economic decision making and to open the country up to a market economy.[39] Although the use of market forces had already begun in the mid-1950s, these reforms gave enterprises almost complete autonomy over the management of their profits, while credit became more accessible. As a result, Yugoslav socialism was becoming increasingly profit-oriented.

After 1965, socialist enterprises stopped being neutral spaces regulated by the respect of the law of self-management, as new incentives for profitability took priority over workers' rights. The reform dismantled investment funds and centralized planning, and subsequently enlarged the market's role in the formation of prices. The banking system itself was transformed, in order to allocate resources according to profitability, which was perceived as a turn away from planning to enterprise-by-enterprise management, bound together by a market that was both neutral and effective. Placed under a tight investment squeeze, self-managed enterprises tried to avoid firing existing workers but stopped hiring new ones. Subsequently, what used to be a guarantee of a relatively prosperous life in a socialist society, including stable employment and housing, became less secure; unemployment levels rose to 20 percent in some regions.[40]

In a climate where the devaluation of the national currency, the dinar, had led to a sharp rise in prices, the issue of financing, and more specifically the students' material situation, was used to discredit *Hit Parade*. But it is ironic, if not revealing, that one critic accused the exhibition of being a "decadent import," at a time when growing youth unemployment had led to an unprecedented rise in economic migration. Until 1962, it was neither popular nor desirable to work abroad, but with economic liberalization, the policy of open borders came to be identified as an official part of the party's political program. Yet it was not the unrestricted flow of people that was threatening to the regime; rather, it was an openness to Western influences, trade, and consumerist culture. As one Yugoslav reporter from Radio Free Europe put it: "The ideological influence ... is—as it now seems—impossible to stop. This is also true in relation to Yugoslavia's manpower export, since more than one million Yugoslav citizens live and work in Western 'capitalist' countries, and thus fall under the influence of a non-socialist way of life."[41]

To an extent, the reporter who accused *Hit Parade* of being a "decadent import" may have had reasonable concerns, given that the origins of the New Art Practice were intimately connected to the country's opening up to world markets. After all, it was these significant economic shifts that provided the backdrop for the emergence of the phenomenon's pioneers, the OHO group from Ljubljana. In 1965, the same year that the market reform was launched, the group's founding members, Marko Pogačnik and Iztok Geister, moved to Ljubljana to study at the Academy of Fine Arts. Initially joined by the filmmaker Naško Križnar, their circle of collaborators expanded rapidly, largely through their involvement in several youth publications, including the university newspaper *Tribuna*, which enabled them to circulate their ideas more widely. Within the narrow space of five years, the artists were internationally embraced as pioneers of the "dematerialization of art" in Yugoslavia. Not only did the group participate in the landmark *Information* show at MoMA—largely because of an accidental encounter in Germany between the exhibition's curator Kynaston McShine and Taja Vidmar, an art history student from Ljubljana who was working at the Nuremberg Kunsthalle in 1969—but they were also the only group from socialist Europe to be featured in Lucy Lippard's canonical book *Six Years: The Dematerialization of the Art Object*.[42] In her retrospective essay "Escape Attempts," Lippard enthusiastically announced that "by 1970 Yugoslavia had also kicked in" as part of the worldwide turn to "post-object" or "idea" art; in parentheses, she attributed this achievement to the OHO group exclusively.[43]

OHO's unprecedented ascent to international recognition was undoubtedly connected to Yugoslavia's growing openness to the West and its markets, although their work would become increasingly critical of the influences that accompanied this new orientation. Part of the new generation born in the 1940s, the like-minded students at the Fine Art Academy who formed OHO foreshadowed the trajectory through which many of the artists affiliated with the New Art Practice began their careers. Their involvement with Ljubljana's student publications enabled them to circulate their ideas more widely, and facilitated their recognition in other republics. By 1971, the leading Yugoslav critic Ješa Denegri declared that the spread of "conceptual art in Ljubljana, Zagreb, and Novi Sad was conditioned by the impression left by OHO exhibitions on young artists."[44] OHO successfully made their mark on these "young" artists by exhibiting in the country's expansive network of state-funded youth cultural institutions, with the group's first exhibition outside of Slovenia being shown at the SC Gallery in April 1968.

It was through the works shown at the so-called *Izložba cipela* [Exhibition of Shoes], together with an accompanying lecture and series of happenings, that Zagreb's new generation of young artists and critics were introduced to OHO's unique intellectual framework of "reism." In its broadest possible definition, reism has been understood as a philosophical project aimed at discovering the radical independence of "things" from humans.[45] In Zagreb, this intellectual approach was most evident in the display of Marko Pogačnik's *Bočice* [Flasks]: a multitude of industrial bottles transformed into ghostly, pastel-colored plaster casts, molded from products of everyday consumption, such as plastic bottles and containers, and strewn across a series of white pedestals of varying heights.

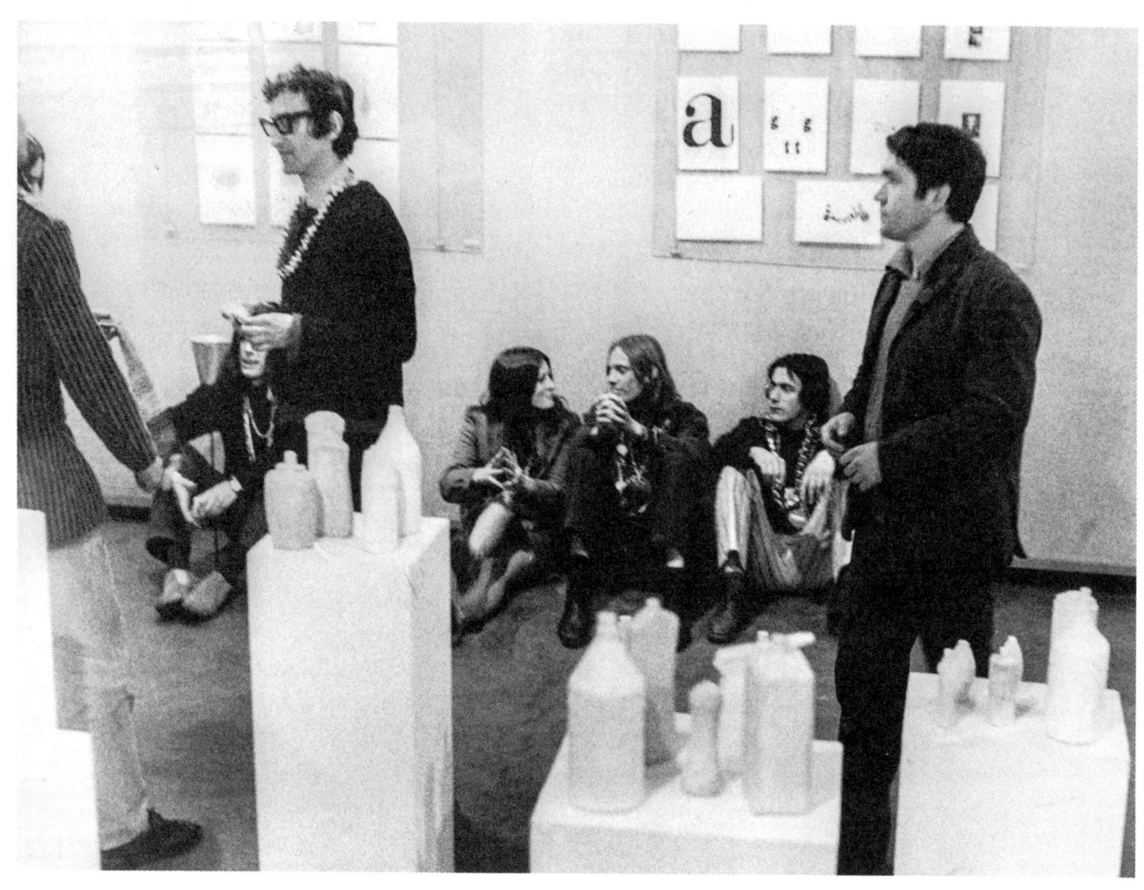

1.4. OHO's *Izložba cipela* [Exhibition of Shoes], Galerija Studentskog Centra, Zagreb, April 1968. Photograph by Vladimir Jakolić. Image courtesy of Vladimir Jakolić and Arhiv za Likovne Umjetnosti HAZU, Zagreb.

According to Tomaž Brejc, OHO's earliest historian, the *Flasks* were intended to be "viewed in light of their actual existence that has been obliterated because of their utilitarian function."[46] In other words, as simulacra of commodity items, these objects encouraged spectators to extract information from them visually, by looking at them, and not through their use or brand value.

OHO's use of commodity items was commonplace to 1960s neo-avant-garde practices throughout the world. But while OHO did certainly challenge the "modernist art mythology of the aura of uniqueness, autonomy, expression and existentialism" through these "neutral and disengaged" objects, as Piotr Piotrowski argued, locally their practice came out of the climate that accompanied the market reform.[47] In what would become an increasingly stratified society, OHO was formulating an artistic approach that sought to emancipate objects from their use value and to offer an "anti-commodity" model of seeing. Aimed at imagining new relationships between objects and humans, OHO's doctrine of reism could even be seen as an early warning against the dangers of consumerism for Yugoslav society at a time when economic reform continued to strengthen pro-capitalist tendencies, exacerbate power inequalities in socialist companies, and increase unemployment rates, while a universal rise in accessibility to consumer goods allowed large portions of society to enjoy a minor increase in living standards. Aligned with the countercultural currents of the New Left that penetrated Yugoslavia's youth through contacts with progressive student groups in the West, OHO's critique would also become an important stimulus for many of the younger generation of artists working through the SC Gallery.

A NEW GENERATION OF PLASTIC ARTISTS

In February 1969, OHO returned to Zagreb to mount their first exhibition at the Gallery of Contemporary Art. Their transfer from parallel youth spaces to a reputable contemporary art institution demonstrates the esteem that the collective had gained within the Yugoslav cultural space. Shortly after OHO had secured this institutional validation, the SC Gallery began to support a new, young and unknown group of artists by announcing, in June 1969, a competition intended to "encourage all explorations in the visual, or plastic, or any other field, to enable the realization of progressive ideas."[48] The aim of the competition was to turn the gallery into a shared space for visual research, one in which work operations were no longer autocratic, but based around more horizontal forms of collaboration.

All of the artists selected for the competition were then students at Zagreb's Academy of Fine Arts and, according to the young art critic Davor Matičević, used the competition as an opportunity to explore their "own development" rather than the "clichés fostered by old school tasks."[49] Matičević referred to the group as the "new generation of plastic artists" because of their approach to the gallery space.[50] This notion of "plasticity" figured prominently in theoretical accounts of the time, and according to Koščević implied the creation of the "total ambient [sic] by direct interventions in space."[51] In a similar vein to the events that spontaneously erupted at *Hit Parade*, plasticity also implied "the transformation of a passive viewer into an active participant of the realized work," as well as the "necessary correction of the function of art in society."[52] Because observing art from a distance was considered pedestrian, these artists sought to thrust the viewer into the middle of the work.

In this sense, the installations made during the SC Gallery's competition were intended to serve as "backgrounds" or "containers" that challenged the role of both the artist and the viewer. All of the installations were constructed from cheap industrial materials, and many of the participating artists presented these materials purely as they were, without recourse to illusion, narrative, symbolism, or personal expression. In the competition's second "environment," titled *Suma 680*, the young artist Braco Dimitrijević scattered 680 painted tin cans across the floor of the gallery. Like Pogačnik's *Flasks*, the environment invested everyday consumer items with a new, artistic value, but one that required active engagement from the audience, as they were invited to rearrange the cans as they desired. The newspaper *Telegram* likened the environment to a "surrealist four-colored landscape ... which constantly changes through the interventions of the visitors, and the occasional turning-off of the gallery lights."[53] For Matičević, *Suma 680* existed only as long as it was interacted with; he saw in the installation an echo of Johan Huizinga's definition of play in *Homo Ludens*, where he examined the conviction that civilization arises and unfolds in and around play: an activity that "adorns life, amplifies it and is a necessity"; "a stepping out of 'real' life into a temporary sphere of activity."[54] The artist was only the arranger of the environment, while the visitor became an active agent in the work's realization.

By introducing everyday objects into the sacrosanct space of the art gallery, *Suma 680* aimed to redefine the relationship of the hand and the head in art production. Circumventing the usual prohibitions against touching artworks and inviting audiences to interact with the objects on display, the work also embraced bodily participation. This attitude was further reinforced in the supporting *Novine Galerije SC* [SC Gallery Newspaper], which was published as a monthly broadsheet and often acted as an exhibition catalogue of sorts. In the November 1969 issue,

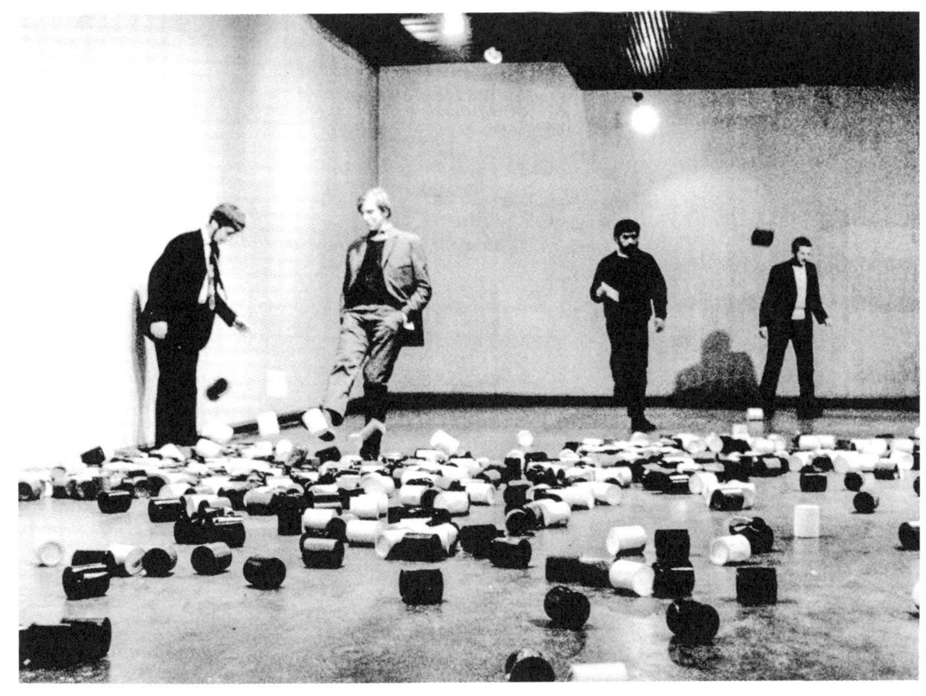

1.5. Braco Dimitrijević, *Suma 680*, Galerija Studentskog Centra, Zagreb, November 1969. Photograph by Vladimir Jakolić. Image courtesy of the artist, Vladimir Jakolić, and Arhiv za Likovne Umjetnosti HAZU, Zagreb.

the newspaper included photographs of the environment alongside other works produced by Dimitrijević at the time, which similarly sought to "democratize" art production through chance encounters. In one "experiment of communication" titled *Slika Krešimira Klike* [Painting by Krešimir Klika], Dimitrijević placed a Tetra Pak carton of milk on a busy street, and dashed from the site. After running over the carton, a car stopped, and "contact [was] made between the accidental author and the arranger," as the action's description printed in the *SC Gallery Newspaper* put it.[55] Through this gesture, the random driver was elevated to the accidental "author" of the flattened milk carton splattered on the asphalt. By bestowing this creative role on the random passerby, Dimitrijević hoped that such people would become interested in "the fragments of everyday life."[56]

Inevitably, Dimitrijević's early investment in the random passerby as a coproducer of art conjures up associations with what has come to be known as participatory art, primarily through the work of art theorist Claire Bishop. In her influential book *Artificial Hells*, Bishop proposed that participatory practices emerged in the Soviet Union and the Eastern Bloc because oppressive political regimes forbade such forms of engagement and deprived them of any kind of institutional support.[57] Emerging under varying degrees of state control in the 1970s, these discreet and playful forms of collaboration have often been analyzed as "political" gestures in the sense that they refused to "play politics."[58] In nonaligned Yugoslavia, however, it could be argued that participatory art practices carried a particular, local resonance, in the sense that they echoed self-management's promises of direct cooperation among self-managed associations linked together through a full-feedback democracy.

1.6. Braco Dimitrijević, *Slika Krešimira Klike* [Painting by Krešimir Klika], 1969. Photograph by Goran Trbuljak. Collection: Fond National d'Art Contemporain Limousin France. Image courtesy of the artist.

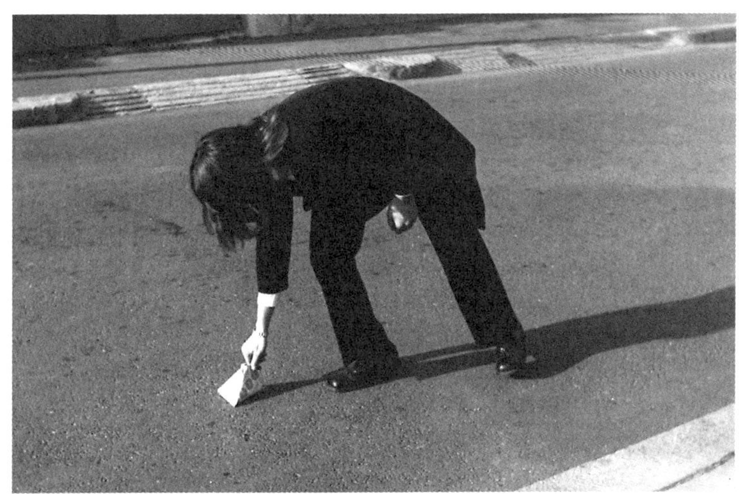

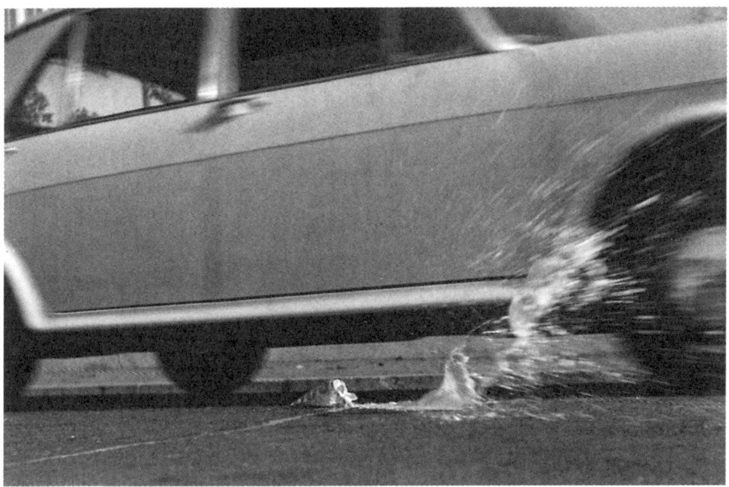

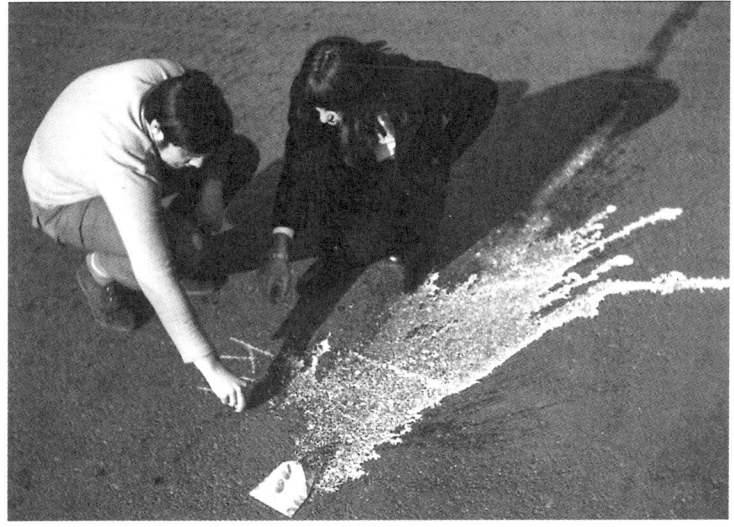

Far from being a mere economic alternative to capitalism and statist socialism, this project also involved a cultural dimension, with radically different relationships between people as well as relationships of people with their surroundings. Simply put, rather than the economy serving as a means to develop other human activities, human activities would become the means for developing the economy. As Josip Broz Tito, the leader of the Yugoslav People's Revolution and the president of Yugoslavia, explained in a speech from 1950, declaring that "Workers Manage Factories in Yugoslavia," self-management's principal aim was to fulfill Marx's "higher phase," in which the division of labor has vanished and labor has become not merely a means to live but itself the primary necessity of life:

> In a higher phase of communist society, after the enslaving subordination of the individual to the division of labor, and with it also the antithesis between mental and physical labor, has vanished, after labor has become not only a livelihood but life's prime want, after the productive forces have increased with the all-round development of the individual, and all the springs of co-operative wealth flow more abundantly—only then can the narrow horizon of bourgeois law be left behind in its entirety and society inscribe on its banners: from each according to his ability, to each according to his needs![59]

Just as self-management understood emancipation to lie in a system that was integrated vertically upward, from basic enterprises through various branch associations and up to federal decision centers, the new generation of artists working through the SC Gallery produced work that sought to overcome the boundaries between cultural elites and the broader masses, for society and within society.

The most significant unifying factor in SC Gallery's "environments" was that they were all produced from industrial materials donated to the gallery by manufacturers of concrete, electrical equipment, paint, and plastic. In some ways, this working relationship echoed parallel developments in American minimalism, which similarly incorporated mass-produced materials, to "'decompose' . . . mythified construction techniques," as Benjamin Buchloh put it.[60] Yet, unlike the growing trend toward sending art out to be made at a factory based on a blueprint that had taken hold in America by the late 1960s, the artists at the SC Gallery simply arranged materials donated to them in a manner that was transient, changeable, and interactive. These artists didn't have machinery and multiple assistants at their disposal, but working in this capacity enabled them to produce accessible, creative works, with very little or no financial means.

At the same time, these projects did share some common ground with process-based works produced concurrently in America, like Robert Morris's infamous 1970 solo exhibition at the Whitney Museum of Modern Art.[61] For the show, Morris simply directed a series of process pieces, spills of concrete and steel that filled a floor of the entire museum. In March of the same year, Sanja Iveković installed her *Untitled Environment* at the SC Gallery, which consisted of a kilometer's length of plastic tubes, densely clustered together, and colored blue, red, and yellow. Suspended from the gallery's ceiling and tangled and strewn around the space, the tubes produced a network of malleable forms, which the artist referred to as a "spatial drawing."[62] Like Morris's gesture, the work was wholly constructed in the gallery space. Yet, in a similar vein to the work of female artists like Eva Hesse, Lygia Clark, and Gego at this time, this installation evaded the clear sexism that American minimalism carried in its equating of oversized sculpture, manual labor, and masculinity. Composed of lightweight, hanging plastic tubes, Iveković's *Untitled Environment* encouraged visitors to pass through it, to bend the tubes and consequently change the shape and composition of the work, and to play with the infinite possibilities of curves and combinations. The installation experimented with inexpensive, mass-manufactured materials, and with the possibilities of the machine, so often associated with alienation and automation.

Through a more horizontal working partnership between artists and manufacturers, the SC Gallery's projects seemed, on the surface, to evade many of the conflicts of class interests implied by American minimalism, where artists both distanced themselves from production and insisted that they were factory producers. While possessing a deep resonance with the core principles of Yugoslav socialism, this synthesis between industries and artists was also aligned with the ideas of the International New Left of the 1960s, and in particular with Herbert Marcuse's critiques of alienation, first published in Yugoslavia in 1965.[63] It is not surprising that Marcuse's central idea that contemporary capitalist and technological society promoted "one-dimensional" thinking, reducing people's developmental opportunities, was embraced by the intellectual circles and Belgrade and Zagreb university professors associated with the Praxis School.[64] In the summer of 1968, Marcuse attended Praxis's Korčula Summer School for the second time. At the 1968 school meeting, which took place in August, with the theme of "Marx and Revolution," Marcuse's presentation was entitled "The Realm of Freedom and the Realm of Necessity: A Reconsideration," during which he emphasized:

> Human freedom in a true sense is possible only beyond the realm of necessity.... [Still another Marxian concept of the relation between freedom and necessity] envisages conditions of full automation, where the immediate producer is indeed "dissociated" from the material process of production, and becomes a free "Subject," in the sense that he can play with, experiment with the technical material, with the possibilities of the machine and of the things produced and transformed by the machines.[65]

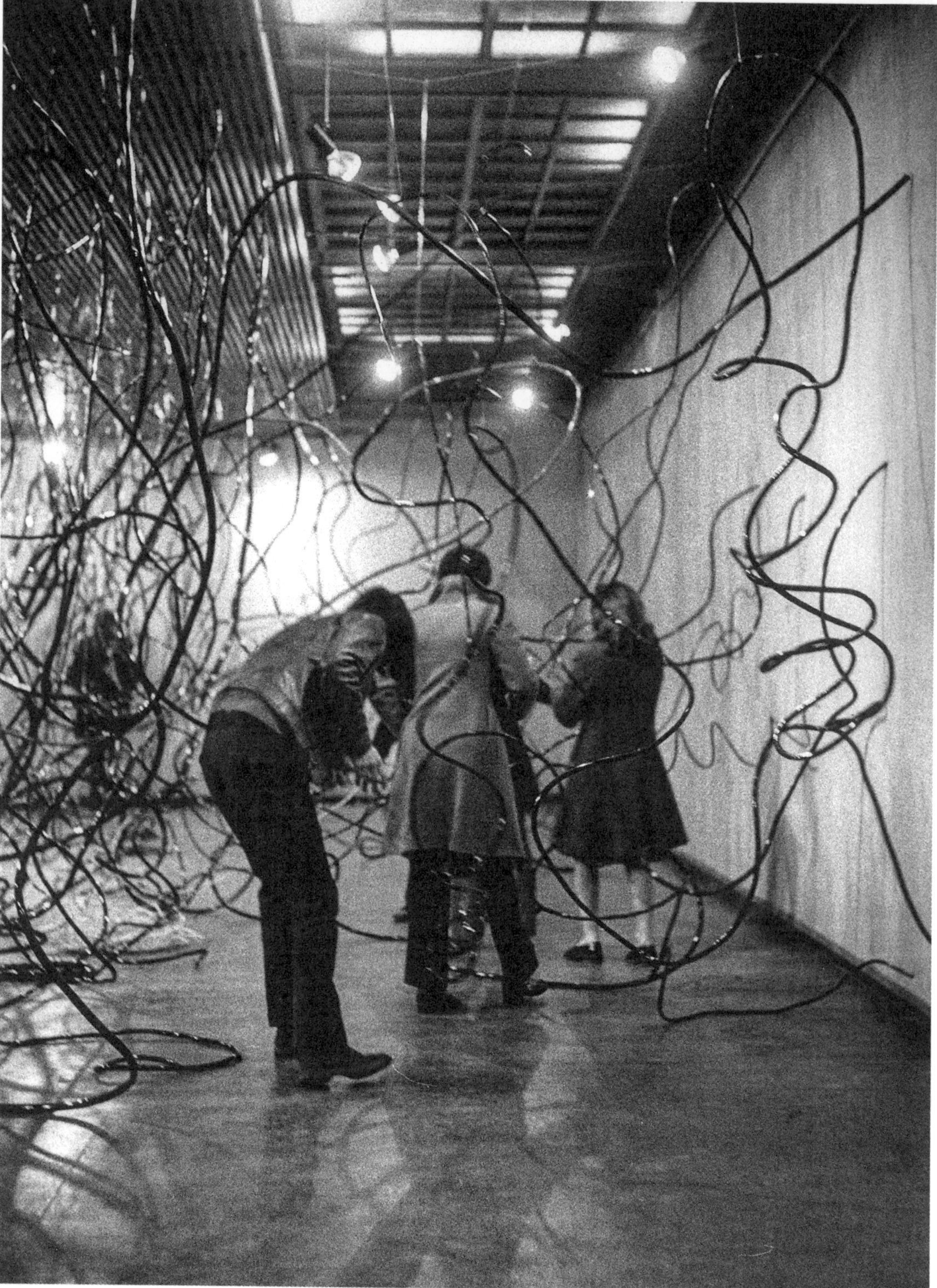

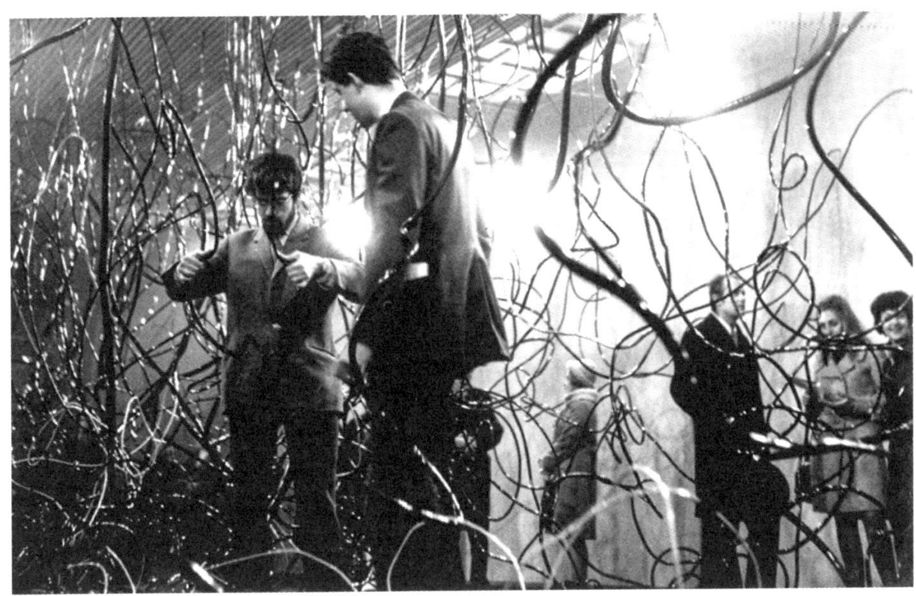

1.7. and 1.8. Sanja Iveković, *Bez naziva* [Untitled], Galerija Studentskog Centra, Zagreb, March 1970. Images courtesy of Sanja Iveković and Arhiv za Likovne Umjetnosti HAZU, Zagreb.

Just as the projects at the SC Gallery were driven by a collectivist and creative impulse, Marcuse was calling for a qualitatively different society based on new sensibilities. By the end of the 1960s, however, hopes that technological advances would make the world more humane for workers and artists alike had dimmed globally. It is striking, then, that artists working through the SC Gallery were celebrating machinery and mass-manufactured materials at the same time that many American minimalists had aligned themselves with the figure of the heroic factory worker. But it is certainly not coincidental. As art historian Jaleh Mansoor has asserted, the politicization of artistic labor emerged on both sides of the Atlantic at the very moment that "labor itself was changing such that the artist was bound to identify with a vanishing subject position."[66] For Mansoor, the work of American minimalists was less an inauthentic and elitist brand of artistic production than it was a "monument to the melancholic failure of the welfare state" that surfaced at a moment of "incipient globalization and financialization."[67] Seen through this analytical frame, the SC Gallery's environments could similarly be read as harbingers of the disconnect that would continue to grow between the optimistic apsirations of Zagreb's younger generation of artists and the manner in which they were both realized and received. Hidden away in the confines of a youth cultural space, viewed only by small, niche audiences, these environments were, after all, made in a period when self-management was already becoming subordinated to the uncontrollable capitalist elements introduced by market mechanisms. In hindsight, they appear as haunting monuments to a fading ideal, surfacing precisely when it was becoming increasingly apparent that self-management had became a secondary issue in the trend toward political decentralization that accompanied economic liberalization. This fateful shift became particularly evident shortly after the ousting of Aleksandar Ranković, the de facto head of the State Security Apparatus, vice president of Yugoslavia, and heir apparent to Tito, in 1966.

To many, Ranković was the embodiment of central state power and prewar Serbia's attempts at domination. His dismissal marked a watershed in Yugoslav politics and triggered a major reassessment of national rights in almost every republic. It carried a range of enormously positive outcomes, including broader cultural freedoms and a greater influence of the republics and autonomous regions in federal decision making. But the system of secret infiltration may have paradoxically been one of the few forces working to strengthen the government against disintegrative tendencies in republican leaderships. By removing all obstructions impeding the reform program, Ranković's ousting resulted in the growing erosion of a common Yugoslav platform on which to build federal policies. During the 1960s, the republics' and autonomous provinces' congresses became more important than the central government, and their representatives began to protect the interests of their republics more vigorously.[68]

Retrospectively seen as the tolerant years, and a kind of "golden age" in literature and the visual arts, the 1960s also marked the emergence of regional political elites, increased foreign leverage, and market relations that undermined any kind of solidarity between Yugoslavia's working classes. Decentralization gave more control to republican and local leaders, but, as Darko Suvin has argued, confined self-management to the enclosure of basic enterprises.[69] Self-management became a "minor economic sop to working people in compensation for their disempowerment, for the denial of effective and permanent democratic control from below."[70] It also remained both ineffective and unjust, while financing continued to be driven primarily by the logic of market competition. The young artists and cultural workers at the SC Gallery may have sensed the damaging impact that capitalist elements had wrought on Yugoslav socialism at the time, when they began to express their early disillusionment with the revolutionary potential of conceptual art in Western Europe and America.

CONCEPTUAL ART AND "ROTTEN CAPITALISM"

In the same month that the SC Gallery initiated its competition, it announced in local newspapers the opening of a new exhibition that would, according to the press release, "close immediately after the opening."[71] On 27 June at 9 pm, visitors waited at the gallery's entrance to be allowed into the *Izložba žena i muškaraca* [Exhibition of Women and Men]. Outside, copies of the *SC Gallery Newspaper* were distributed, proclaiming that the exhibition they were about to enter would give them the "opportunity to look at themselves."[72] The text informed confused and bewildered visitors of what was expected from them: "For God's sake, be the exhibition itself! At the exhibition, you are the work, you are the figuration, you are the social realism.... Art is not outside of you. Either there is no art, or that art is you ... live here intimately with your ideas, even if you don't have any."[73]

The existing photographic documentation captures a sequence of events, which begins with a large crowd of over a hundred visitors waiting outside of the Gallery's entrance and shows them entering a bright, floodlit space and gradually realizing that they themselves were the subject of the exhibition. At that point, they slowly began to move away from the center toward the wall to minimize their exposure. But it was too late. Visitors found themselves staring "eye-to-eye, face-to-face, all united in a unique exhibit, where the exhibitions move, sounds resonate, and heat is formed."[74] Soon an element of frivolity swept in: while some visitors transformed the distributed newspaper into paper airplanes and launched them into the gallery space, others turned the sheet into paper masks.

By placing an emphasis on social relations, the *Exhibition of Women and Men* challenged the passive relationship between the art gallery and its public. Acting in his role as the gallery's director, Koščević requested that his audience "become the exhibition," and by accepting this invitation, the audience participated with the institution in redefining the social function of the exhibition.[75] Yet the accompanying statement reveals that the *Exhibition of Women and Men* was more than just an exercise in rethinking gallery conventions. Demanding that the visitor become not only the "exhibition itself" but also, through this transformation, "the figuration" and "social realism," the exhibition asserted Yugoslavia's "non-aligned" geopolitical position between the two superpowers and their spheres of cultural influence.[76] This demand, along with the accompanying statement's attack on the images of nudity "imported from rotten capitalism," hint at how the *Exhibition of Women and Men* may have in fact been an expression of concern over Yugoslavia's supposed neutrality, at a moment when its political and economic independence from the two dominant power blocs was becoming increasingly jeopardized.

1.9. and 1.10. *Izložba žena i muškaraca* [Exhibition of Women and Men], Galerija Studentskog Centra, Zagreb, 27 June 1969. Photographs by Vladimir Jakolić. Images courtesy of Vladimir Jakolić and Arhiv za Likovne Umjetnosti HAZU, Zagreb.

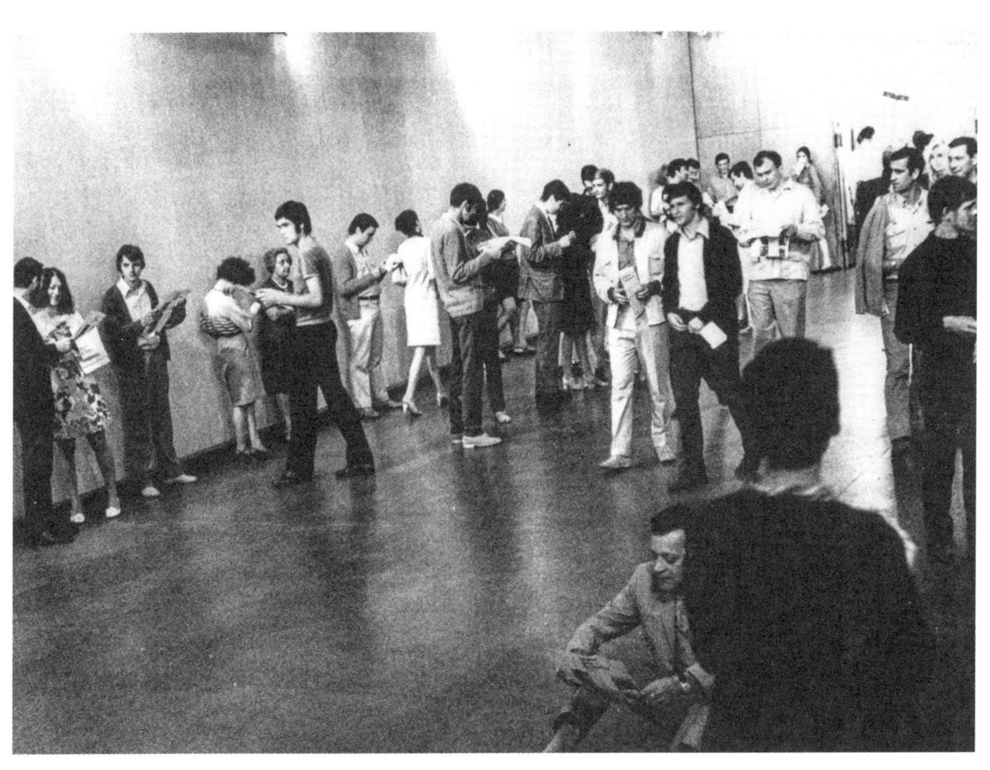

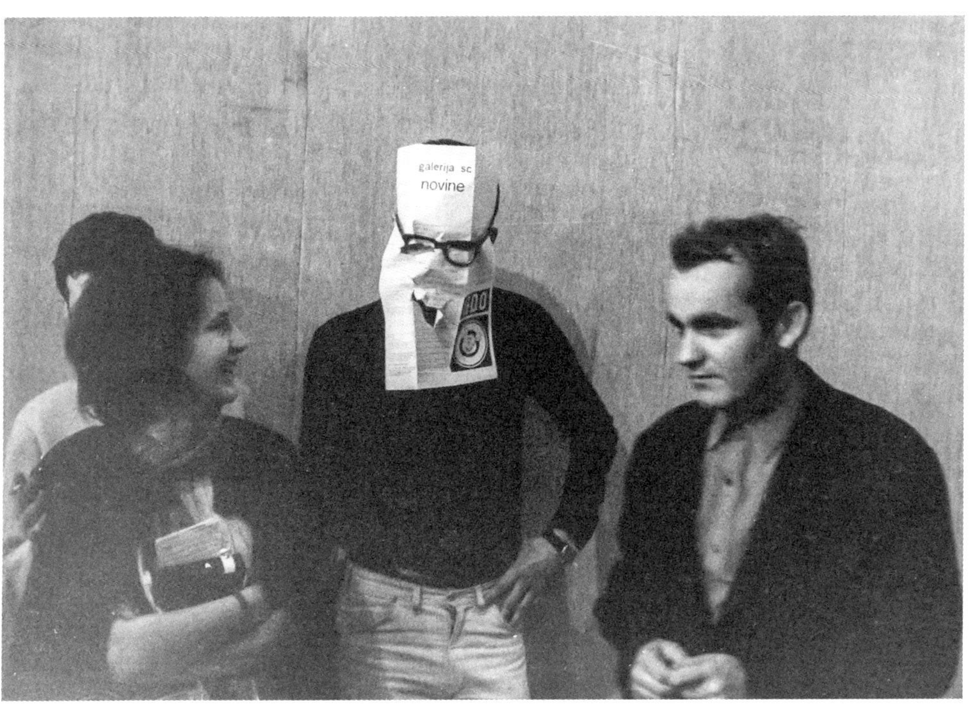
galerija sc
novine

Throughout much of the 1960s, Yugoslavia staunchly protected its anti-imperialist, nonaligned position and promoted its unique form of socialism. In 1967, it denounced Israel and its Western allies for their preemptive strike in the Six Day War; in the following year, it approved Aleksander Dubček's pro-reform policy in Czechoslovakia and understood the short period of political liberalization as a confirmation of self-management's growing support across the Eastern Bloc. But after the Warsaw Pact invasion of Czechoslovakia in August 1968, the Yugoslav leadership began signing economic agreements with the European Economic Community and the World Bank in order to avoid an economic meltdown similar to that of 1948. At this time, nonalignment also began to be seen by the younger politicians in Croatia, Serbia, and Slovenia as an enormous economic burden without results, while the opening of the country's economy began aggravating preexisting economic disparities between the developed northwestern republics and the rest of the country.[77] Although subtle, the allegations of *Exhibition of Women and Men* against the abuses of "rotten capitalism" were nevertheless prescient: they anticipated the role that the capitalist outside would play in Yugoslav society. A year after OHO introduced local audiences to the reist approach, the SC Gallery seemed to also glimpse the forces that would begin to fuel economic disputes between Yugoslavia's regional party leaderships.

Staged one year before Lippard's estimated date for Yugoslavia's entry into the global shift to "idea" art, the *Exhibition of Women and Men* is today considered a pioneering gesture of dematerialization, which played out in Zagreb when there was little critical understanding of conceptual art. At a time when Yugoslavia was integrating itself deeper and deeper into the Western capitalist world system, it should come as no surprise that the artists in the SC Gallery were participating in international artistic debates regarding the commodity character of art and the role of public art institutions. Yet they were clearly doing so from their own political context. In November 1971, the artist Goran Trbuljak demonstrated this stance with his solo exhibition at the SC Gallery. For the first major public presentation of his work, he chose to exhibit nothing except for a poster, mass-printed in the accompanying edition of the *SC Gallery Newspaper*. The poster consisted of a simple headshot of the artist, along with a caption in large script mimicking the font of advertisements, giving the artist's name along with the statement, "Ne želim pokazati ništa novo i originalno" [I do not wish to show anything new or original].[78] Through this bold gesture, Trbuljak rejected the pursuit of the new, innovative art that later came to be viewed in Western Europe and America as a symbolic ally of corporate ideology. At the same time, he offered no alternative,

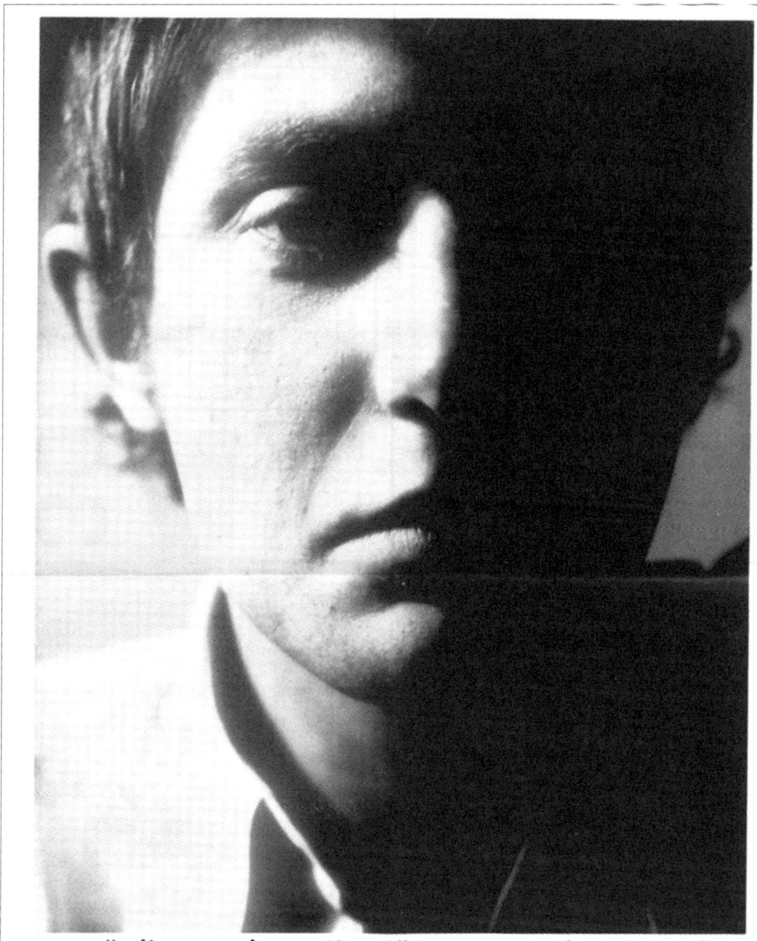

1.11. Goran Trbuljak, *Ne želim pokazati ništa novo i originalno* [I Do Not Wish to Show Anything New or Original], printed in *Novine GSC*, no. 30, November 1971. Image courtesy of the artist.

as by declaring that he didn't wish to show anything new or original, he managed to produce something that was precisely that—a work that was as new as it was original.

Had Trbuljak's work been shown in a commercial gallery in New York, for instance, it would have had an altogether different significance. But displayed in a state-financed youth institution, in a country without a developed art market and no corporate sponsorship, it captured what art historian Ivana Bago has described as the New Art Practice's anchoring in its "Yugoslav situatedness—towards the production and reception of art in the West, after it had become evident that dematerialized art was subject to cooptation by the art market and institutions that were becoming increasingly corporate."[79] Refusing the expectation that an artist should produce something new or original, Trbuljak's work anticipated what Alexander Alberro would later describe as conceptual art's "contradictory nature," "in which the egalitarian pursuit of publicness and the emancipation from traditional forms of artistic value were as definitive as the fusion of the art-works with advertising and display."[80] By playing with an advertising format and using his own headshot to accompany his declaration, Trbuljak was commenting on how Western conceptual art's experimentation with novel methods was, from the outset, inextricably linked to the unprecedented careerism of its key protagonists as well as to an art market booming from corporate investment during the 1960s which elevated a select few, while most artists scrambled for money and lived in poor conditions. In the following year, Lippard would publish her highly influential "Postface" for *Six Years* in which she similarly expressed her doubts about conceptual art's negation of the commodity status of the art object. "For the most part," she reflected in retrospect, "artists have been confined to art quarters, usually by choice."[81] They had little choice but to maintain their "resentful reliance on a very small group of dealers, curators, critics, editors and collectors, who are all too frequently and often unknowingly bound by invisible apron strings to the real world's power structures."[82]

1.12. Galerija Studentskog Centra, *Poštanske pošiljke* [Postal Packages], Zagreb, April 1972. Photograph by Petar Dabac. Image courtesy of Arhiv za Likovne Umjetnosti HAZU, Zagreb.

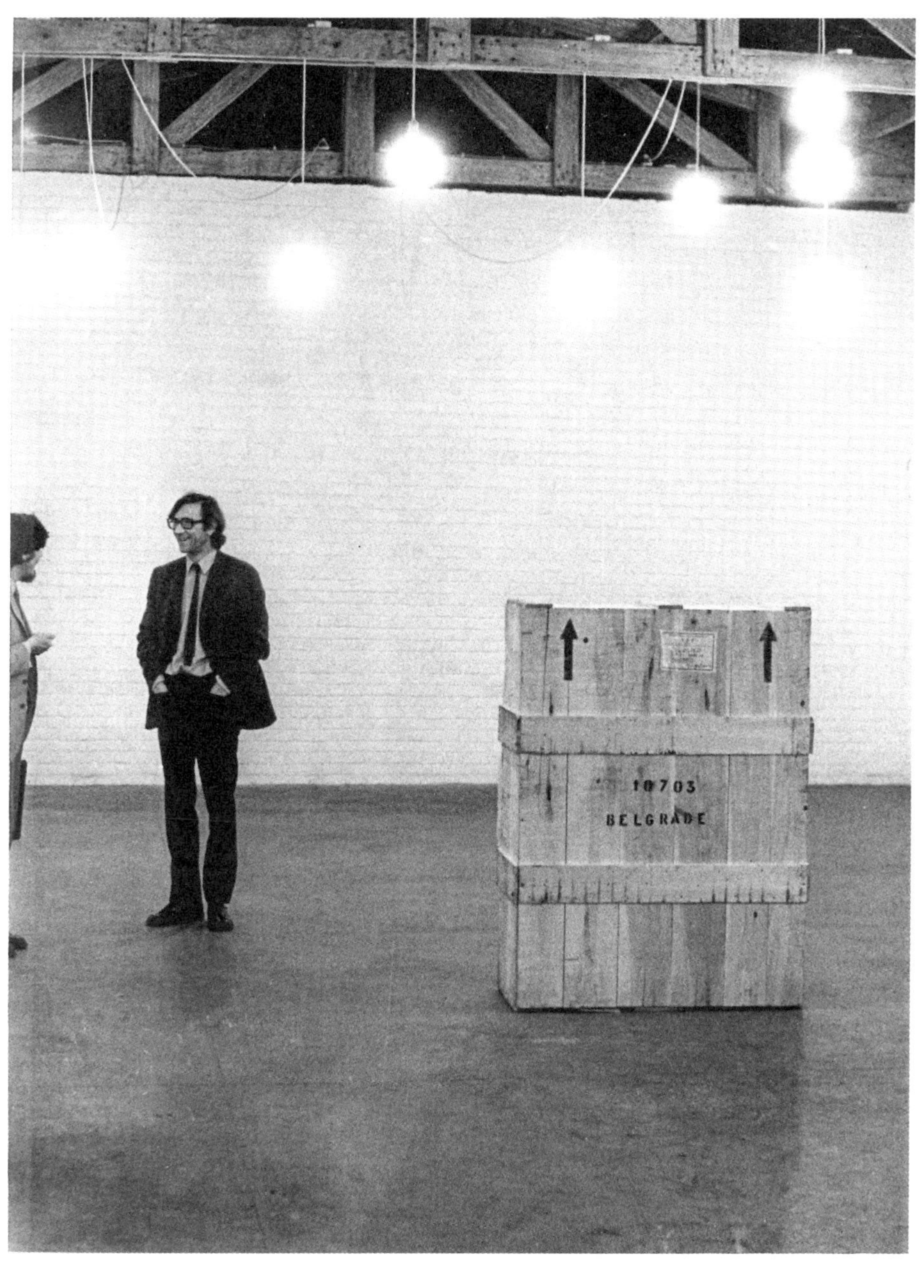
10703
BELGRADE

Whether or not conceptual artists were resentful of their patrons remains a huge subject of contention to this day. What is certain, though, is that artists working at the SC Gallery were well aware of the movement's ultimate subservience to, and co-optation by, the market. In the same year that Lippard penned her reservations, the SC Gallery was supposed to display work from the now-celebrated mail art section of the seventh Biennale des Jeunes in Paris curated by the young critic Jean-Marc Poinsot. Traveling from Paris via Belgrade's Students' Cultural Center, the exhibition was meant to introduce local audiences to the latest international trends. But in a decision that resembled the conviction underpinning the *Exhibition of Women and Men*, Koščević decided to simply present the sealed wooden crate in which the works had arrived. Rather than displaying the show as it was intended, hung on the gallery's walls, he exhibited them literally as a mail item packed in a box. Identifying the mail art movement through its means of transport, Koščević made a gesture of disobedience that rejected the contradictory commercialization of conceptual art, which by 1972 had become so mainstream that it was being shown in the most conventional of exhibition contexts—the biennial. As the exhibition's accompanying statement explained:

> Instead of contributing to the further commodification of conceptual art, and instead of helping in its ruin under the spotlights of the galleries and the museums, we have exhibited here the content of this exhibition in its genuine, unadulterated state. We have exhibited what is in our view the [reduction] of conceptual art: postal consignments. We are aware that such a concept for an art exhibition will be accepted very reluctantly in our environment, which still longs for basic information [on conceptual art abroad]. But it is not our responsibility to adjust to these defects. Or even to multiply them, by shrugging our shoulders, and by agreeing to exhibit works which were never intended to be presented under a glass cover (so as to not damage them).[83]

In a socialist society where capitalist elements were becoming increasingly visible and pervasive, the SC Gallery grew increasingly critical of Western conceptual art's political economy, or its "defects" as the *Postal Packages* exhibition statement described it. The gallery's growing disenchantment with conceptual art was, however, connected to deeper fears of the failures of Yugoslav socialism at the time. This becomes clear when examining the SC Gallery's activities alongside a series of seismic events that took place in Zagreb—beginning with the institution's failure to effect its "Draft Decree on the Democratization of Art" in 1970, and ending with the disastrous cultural consequences that accompanied a crisis in federal politics in 1972, the same year in which the *Postal Packages* were (not) shown.

POSSIBILITIES FOR 1971

Between 1970 and 1972, the SC Gallery was less concerned with the "dematerialization of the art object" than it was with advocating the idea that art should leave the museum entirely and engage with the city and its inhabitants directly. As Koščević explained retrospectively, the early projects installed in the gallery were merely experiments, because "we envision [those objects and ideas] in the urban space, in the real flow of life."[84] For him, art in the urban sphere was the only way to break out of the art world's narrow field of influence, because when art takes to the streets, it can no longer be ignored. Although it has some obvious parallels with the ideas of many Western conceptual artists, this position was less aligned with conceptual art than it was with the Soviet avant-garde. It took direct inspiration from Vladimir Mayakovsky's famous declaration in 1918, when Moscow artists initiated their own struggle to bring art into society, that "the streets [are] our brushes, the squares our palettes."[85] At the SC Gallery, the first attempt to take to the streets took place in June 1970 by way of a collaboration with the artists Boris Bućan and Davor Tomičić. For their *Akcija total* [Total Action], the artists pasted posters featuring a monochrome print, consisting of white geometric and symmetrical abstract forms, on advertising pillars, boxes, and billboards at various locations throughout the city. These locations became "action spaces," in which the artists distributed leaflets featuring a "Draft Decree on the Democratization of Art," inspired by Vladimir Mayakovsky, Vasily Kamensky, and David Burliuk's 1918 "Decree No. 1 on the Democratization of Art."

Just as the Decree of 1918 called for a revolution through which the streets would become a "place for everyone to celebrate art," *Akcija total* similarly sought to surpass institutional barriers which, according to the "Draft Decree," "distorted, obscured, and hindered any discussion of the very idea of art."[86] The "Draft Decree" was driven by an awareness of how art circulated, and ultimately targeted art's claims to autonomy by detailing its servitude to ideological and economic ends within Yugoslavia's larger political system. As the declaration emphasized, the action was a protest against the "representatives of disciplines like painting, graphic and applied arts [who] consciously make their work mystifying in order to be able to continue to produce lies ... persistently trying to persuade us not to believe what we see, but to rely on their clairvoyant guidance."[87] It opposed the current status of art disciplines in Yugoslavia—a "monstrous fabrication of thousands and thousands of paintings, and sculptures, countless luxury designs in applied arts, stupid architectural and urban projects and realizations, and even more stupid 'critical' interpretations of all this"—which was impeding the

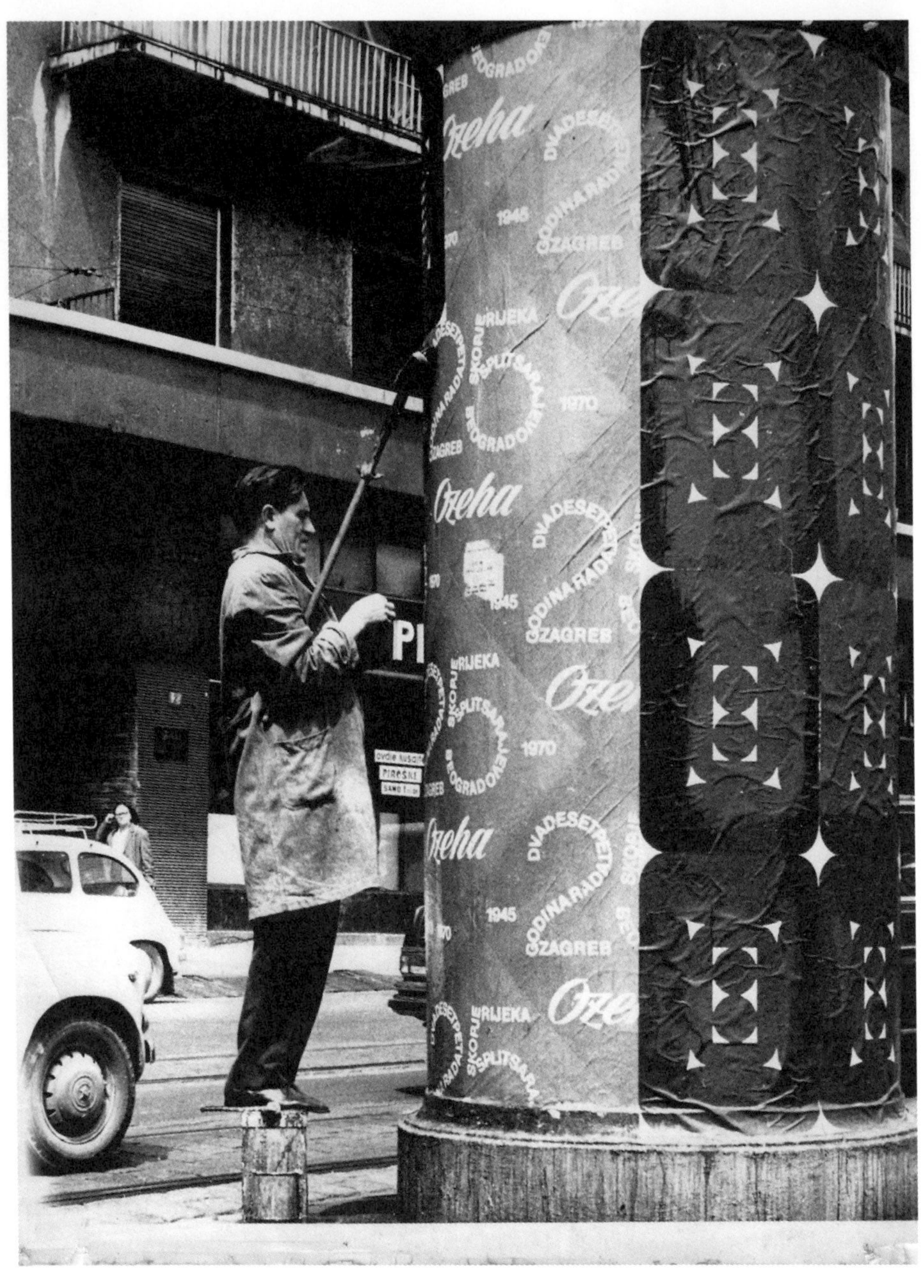
Ozeha
DVADESETPET
GODINA RADA
ZAGREB
RIJEKA
SKOPJE
SPLIT
SARAJEVO
BEOGRAD
1945
1970

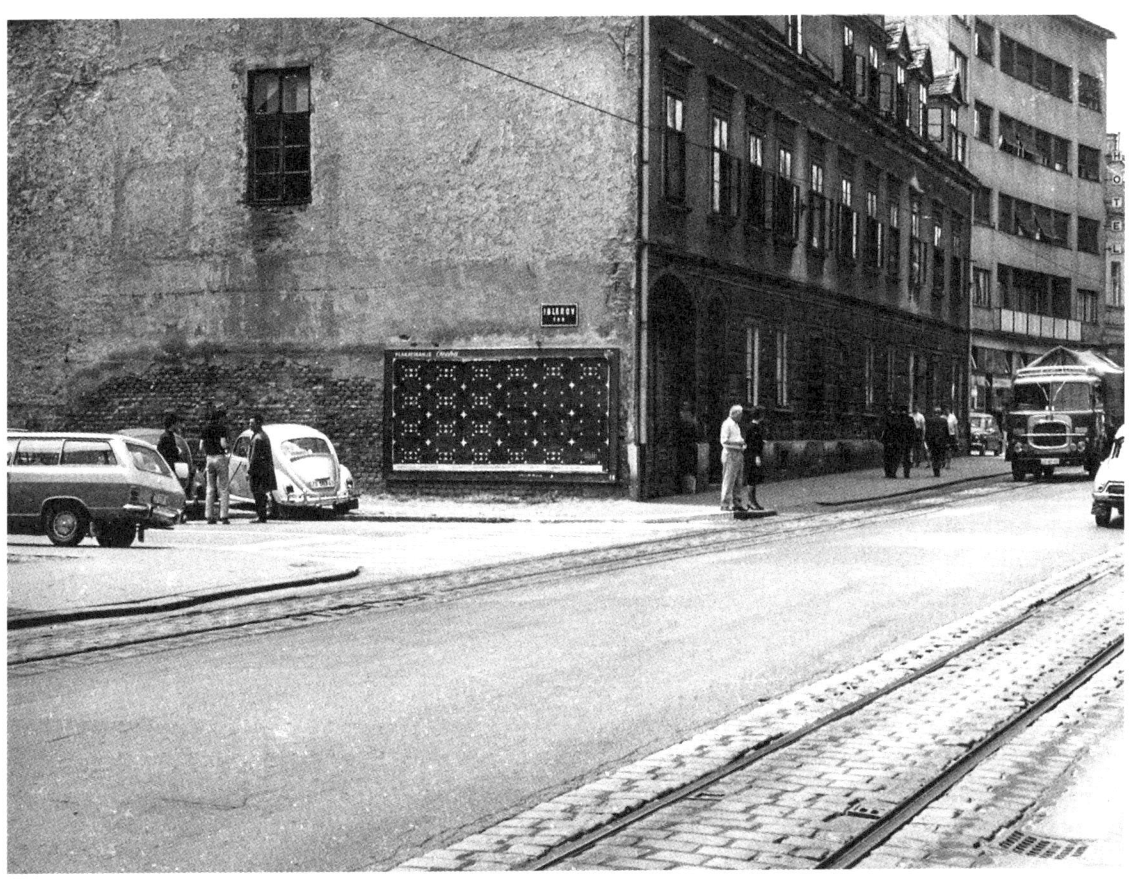

1.13. and 1.14. Boris Bućan and Davor Tomičić, *Akcija total* [Total Action], Zagreb, 16 June 1970. Photographs by Enes Midžić. Images courtesy of Arhiv za Likovne Umjetnosti HAZU, Zagreb.

possibility of "broader social dimensions."[88] More than ever, "the conceptual strength of art" was necessary, and could be enacted only through an extreme abolition of all artistic disciplines; as they outlined:

1. the following are hereby abolished: painting, sculpture, graphic art, applied arts, industrial design, architecture, and urban planning.
2. A ban is hereby placed on the following: all activity in the history of art and especially so-called art criticism.
3. There shall be no exhibitions in galleries, museums, or art pavilions.[89]

All of these criticisms pointed toward a significantly nepotistic Yugoslav art system, marked by domination and exploitation: from the discipline of "art history" ("a hobby for leisurely professors," who purely serve the interests of a limited elite, which in turn "accepts and tolerates this discipline, not because of its spiritual needs, but for decorative needs") to the applied arts, which, as the decree stressed, were conditioned by class interests:

> In a society which does not struggle anymore to secure the bare minimum, but which fights hard to achieve a higher standard of living, the products of applied artists fit perfectly into the pattern of society's development. The by-product of this development is the ever-increasing number of workers in tertiary activities, whose needs are exactly on the level of their luxury-seeking neighbors, and the luxury-seeking neighbor's neighbor. Such needs are again matchlessly satisfied through the industry of numerous artificiers [sic] who are faithfully following the taste of their chosen clientele.[90]

The "Draft Decree" raised the following question: how had such high standards and luxury needs arisen in an allegedly "democratic" society founded on the material basis for the "broadest masses of the working people"?

Following the reforms that ensued from 1965, state investment planning and price reform were largely abandoned in favor of placing profits wholly at the discretion of enterprises. Without the central determination of wages, wages were no longer allocated according to "work done" but according to the "results of work." In a country where conditions for earning income were rarely equal, this was bound to encourage competition among workers and between workplaces.[91] Combined with the pressures of market competition and a commitment to wage differentials in order to secure skilled labor, self-management actually increased inequality, as workers' councils tended to empower managers, engineers, and white-collar workers over the lower-skilled working class. By the end of the 1960s, the leading Croatian politician Stipe Šuvar estimated that 2 percent of the Yugoslav population had reached the living standard of the capitalist "middle class" and another 10 percent were close to it, while 20 percent of citizens lived on a bare minimum.[92]

Disparities rose across the board, not only between workplaces, different skill categories, and industries, but also between regions and republics. As soon as wages depended less on the work done and more on sale in the market, pressures grew from regions with a strong position in the world market, largely Slovenia and Croatia, for more economic autonomy. As the forces of federal cohesion began to corrode under the centrifugal pull of the market, struggles over state investment and economic policies became increasingly contested at the regional level. This meant that workplaces often identified their interests with their enterprise management or the governments of their republics rather than with other workplaces or the other republics of the federation. As a result, Yugoslavia's working class became atomized and regionally fragmented. They were sidelined in what was becoming a fierce struggle over investment and the accumulation of capital between a new technocratic class of local functionaries and regional political and economic elites—consisting of managers, directors, and other leaders of business enterprises and financial institutions—and the old, centralized federal authority. During the 1960s, both became the core of a rising middle class, consciously disassociating themselves from lower social groups through their higher incomes and individualized attitudes and lifestyles.

Akcija total attempted to confront the conditions of alienation and commodification in what it perceived to be a stratified Yugoslav society. It interrupted the regular ebb and flow of life to engage with the everyday citizen. The posters pasted over advertisements consisted of abstract, clean, and functionless forms, placed where they were least expected, in situations where images usually had explicitly commercial roles, to "indicate the beautiful possibilities that arise by freedom from terror and function."[93] Consisting of white specks floating on a blue ground and then pasted on a series of small sheets aligned together, the posters produced a symmetrical pattern that challenged the objectivity and neutrality often associated with formalist art. With its clearly outlined program, the action was directed against a society that had declared itself to be run in the interest of the overwhelming majority of working people, but was in fact conditioned by confrontations between various social tiers and interest groups.

At the time that the SC Gallery wrote its "Draft Decree on the Democratization of Art," however, many of Zagreb's citizens may have felt as though "democratic" tendencies were in fact flourishing, following the rise of a younger and more reform-minded generation of Croatian communists. After the ousting of

Ranković, a liberal majority in the League of Communists of Croatia (LCC) rose through the ranks and won Tito's support.[94] Led by Miko Tripalo, these figures played a crucial role in implementing the liberalizing economic reforms. In 1968, Savka Dabčević-Kučar was appointed the head of the party in Croatia, and two years later, in January 1970, called for the Tenth Session of the League of Communists in Croatia, seen as a turning point in the republic's efforts to redefine the federal system.

In this meeting, demands driven by an aspiration for a fairer deal in the federation were raised. Dabčević-Kučar stressed that the greatest threat to the development of socialist Yugoslavia was "unitarism," often linked to greater Serbian chauvinism and the prewar period or the federation's attempts to reduce the autonomy of the republics.[95] The meeting not only called for "adequate proportional representation" in Croatia's social and political organizations, but also identified the continuing concentration of finance capital in Belgrade as a factor impeding the republic's development.[96] Broadcast on television, the meeting became central to Croatia's liberal movement and the revival of the national cause. Elsewhere, it was received negatively: in Serbia, politicians, the media, and the public alike were offended by the suggestion that unitarism was a bigger threat to Yugoslav cohesion than nationalism and separatism.[97] Many intellectuals argued that the introduction of decision making by consensus between the federal units was bound to cripple the federal system, and would threaten Yugoslavia's common market. In other republics, unease was felt over the Croatian leadership's persistence in further pursuing economic reforms, particularly those concerning the distribution of foreign currency and the need for a separate banking system. The republic's traditional partners in the more developed regions like Slovenia approached the Croatian developments with suspicion, while less-developed regions like Macedonia, though fully supporting the fight against unitarism, expressed concerns about how the economic reforms might threaten their share of the federal funds.[98] To varying degrees and for various reasons, republican leaderships throughout the federation began voicing their feelings of doubt and deprivation.

Nevertheless, Tito agreed that the high profile of Serbs was a problem, and amendments to the federal constitution based on the concerns raised at the Tenth Session were passed in the following year. By limiting federal responsibilities to the areas of defense, foreign affairs, the single market, and funds for underdeveloped regions, Tito hoped to make the idea of Yugoslavia more acceptable to non-Serbian nations. In effect, this meant further decentralization, as republics were given de facto control over the federal assembly, which oversaw the work of the federal government. It ensured that republics could now use their newly acquired powers to block the government's economic decisions; "republican particularism" would begin to stifle the work of the federal administration. For the Croatian Party liberals, however, the 1971 constitution was simply a return to the "true principles" of revolution abandoned after the war, which sought to carve out maximum autonomy for the Croatian Party governmental organizations in relation to central political authorities.[99]

Akcija total raised some challenging questions about the role of culture in Yugoslavia at a time when the liberal tone of the Tenth Session was being experienced throughout many aspects of society. It also set a precedent for future art developments in Zagreb. A year after the SC Gallery first declared its "Draft Decree," the most discussed subject among the city's younger generation of artists and theorists became art projects that somehow addressed the urban environment. The outcome of these discussions was particularly felt in the organization of the exhibition *Mogućnosti za 1971* [Possibilities for 1971], which took place at Zagreb's Gallery of Contemporary Art and assembled the new generation of Zagreb's plastic artists who had first been introduced to the public through the environments at the SC Gallery. *Possibilities for 1971* built on the SC Gallery's previous activities and invited interventions that would facilitate the "enrichment or rearrangement" of Zagreb's Gornji grad (Upper City). The exhibition's catalogue announced that the participating artists were ultimately motivated by

> [the] social role of art in the present time. The significance of such works is that they are not made for sale, namely, since they don't have the character of goods, they cannot become a means for gaining profit.
>
> They ought to be the common property of all citizens; and socialist society, which, in striving for other aims in addition to material well-being, should be the promoter and buyer of artistic activity.[100]

As with the SC Gallery's earlier environments, most of the works installed in the oldest part of the city were made from materials provided free of charge by industrial producers (listed on the back page of the exhibition catalogue). This relationship defined the physical composition of the works, which also had to comply with the "simple technical conditions in the environment."[101] Much like the SC Gallery's "Draft Decree," *Possibilities for 1971* aimed to facilitate a "democratic form of communication with audiences."[102] Arguably the work that most effectively achieved the constructive goal was Iveković's *Prolaz* [Passage]: a series of curved neon tubes placed across the Zakmardijev passage, rhythmically

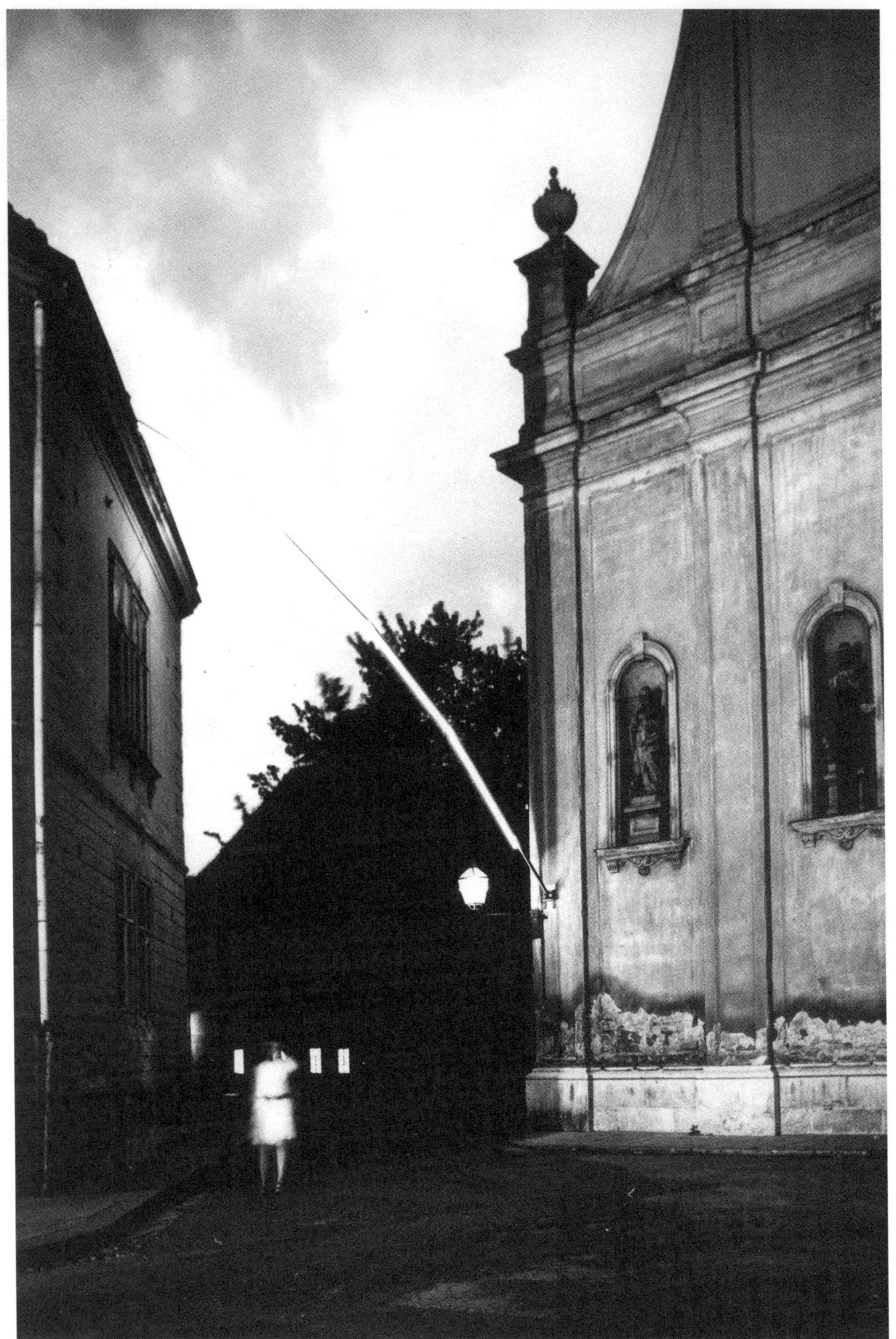

arranged in the area between two squares to produce an illuminated "rainbow." As Iveković recalls, she initially chose the passage because "traffic is always quite lively, but [she] wanted in some way to thematize the urban motion":

> The operation was pretty expensive and complicated. It was difficult to install all those neon tubes, and our contractor warned us of potential safety risks. When we finally assembled everything, the thing only lasted two days. The next day a notice was announced in the comments section of *Vjesnik*. In that article, the author emphasized how important it was that the passage was finally lit up, considering that girls from the local high school pass through there, and have experienced encounters of an uncomfortable kind. This comment led me to think about the social role of such interventions.[103]

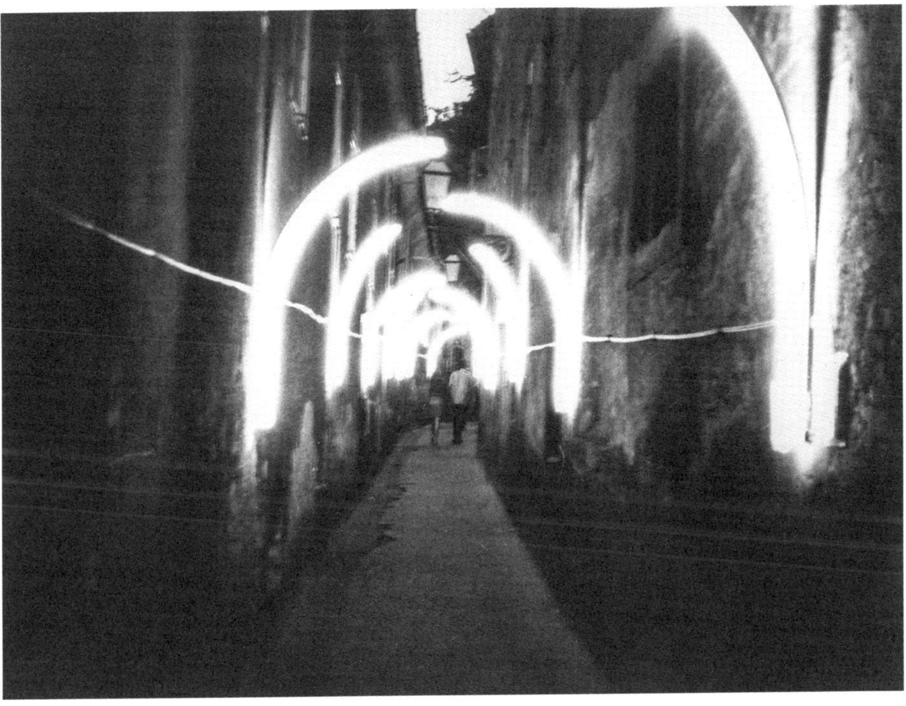

1.15. and 1.16. Sanja Iveković, *Prolaz* [Passage], part of *Mogućnosti za 1971* [Possibilities for 1971], Galerija Suvremene Umjetnosti, Zagreb, 1971. Images courtesy of the artist.

Iveković's work demonstrates, although perhaps inadvertently, the kind of social aims these interventions possessed; or as the exhibition catalogue foreword romantically described it, the "euphoria of combining art with the machine for the general benefit of all citizens."[104] The irony, however, is that soon after this project, commissions for urban environmental projects ceased to appear. For Iveković, it seemed that such initiatives, "suspended on an understanding of art which communicated 'with the people,' close to the socialist concept, applied an artistic language that was so radically new that the audience was really limited."[105] At the time, many of the critics initially enthusiastic about art's interaction with the urban space began to express their doubts. They complained of art's failure to successfully "reach the people"—in spite of its anti-elitist and egalitarian aims—and criticized the public's indifference to the artist's offer to act in the public good. Many of the artists previously working with environments began instead to critically examine the circumstances that may have been driving the public's apathy. This included a turn from urban interventions to what Davor Matičević described as the "basic criteria of modern urban life": "the false myths or pseudo-needs imposed on the consumer by mass media."[106]

These "false myths or pseudo-needs" had infiltrated Yugoslav society through the Western cultural influences that came with the opening of the country's borders. By the end of the 1960s, self-management was experiencing a serious crisis, not only because it was taking an increasingly capitalist form, but also because it turned a large part of the population into guest workers of the capitalist West. In the words of art historian Branislav Dimitrijević, this shift in policy resulted in nothing short of an "aestheticization of Western cultural representations of glamorized consumer lifestyles," in which the "image of capitalist production as inhumane" and of work in capitalism as "alienated" disappeared in the "bright light of shop windows and advertisements," and the "West" became "a place of well-being, with crystal clear swimming pools, modern cars, nice-looking well-groomed people, a space where there is no work, but only leisure and fun."[107] As Yugoslavia became an increasingly divided society toward the end of the 1960s, historian Dušan Bilandžić observed that "the masses were caught up in a fever of consumption and money making: in every part of the country, peasants and workers were building houses and buying durable consumer goods, while the richer people were getting vacation houses, ever more expensive cars, and so forth."[108]

In February 1973, the SC Gallery installed an exhibition by Boris Bućan which placed advertising at the service of art making. In his *Bućan Art* series, the artist covered each standardized canvas with the logo of a global corporation, including

Coca-Cola, Marlboro, Swiss Air, and BMW, and replaced its name with the word "Art." One reporter from a city newspaper was puzzled by the artist's intentions, concluding, perhaps sneeringly, that "to at least free us from the frustrating dilemma of whether or not it is 'art,' Bućan has added the single word 'art' in front of familiar signs, companies and distributors."[109] Deeply ambivalent, the works manipulated a series of contradictions, including the individual, hand-painted "auratic" canvas against the mass-printed corporate logo—art versus advertisement—in a "semantic play" that both "comment[ed] on the commodification of art" and questioned art's ability to compete with the visual culture of commodity capitalism.[110]

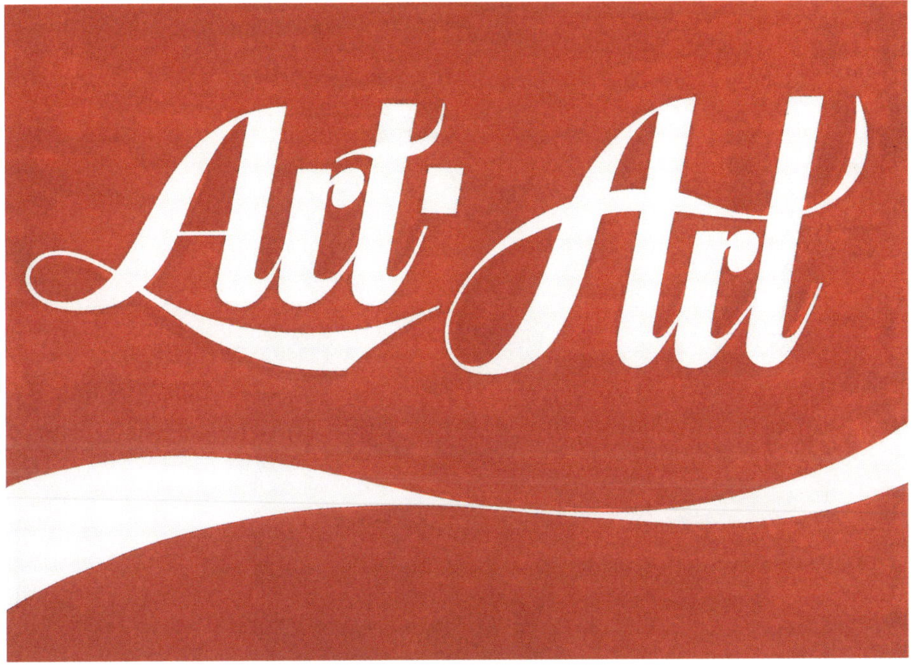

1.17. Boris Bućan, *Art (According to Coca-Cola)*, 1972, from the *Bućan Art* series. Image courtesy of the Marinko Sudac Collection.

A few months later, Bućan more forthrightly inscribed the word *Laž* [Lie]—on a silk banner and displayed it on the facade of a house in Zagreb. For him, this word had become a pillar of Yugoslav society, at a time when rising foreign credit, unsustainable imports, and a runaway consumerism were substituting for genuine democracy from below. The causes of this substitution become clear when we consider a series of events that occurred at the SC Gallery in 1971 alongside a serious crisis in federal politics that together would cast a dark and lingering shadow over the gallery's future activities.

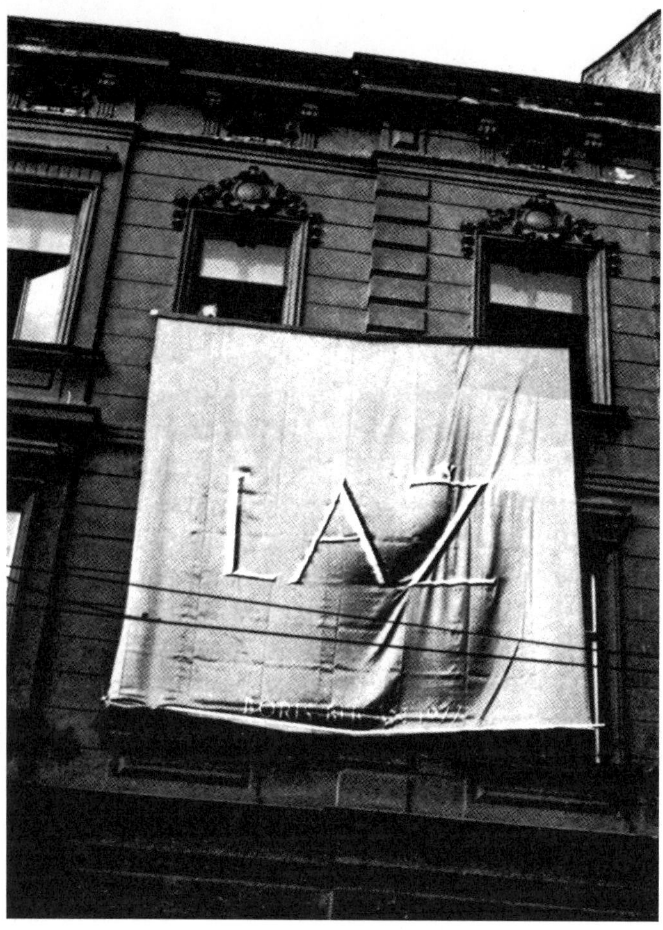

1.18. Boris Bućan, *Laž* [Lie], Zagreb, 1973.

NEW ART IN THE CROATIAN SPRING

Paraphrasing the legendary French filmmaker Jean-Luc Godard, Iveković retrospectively explained that these early projects were concerned not with "making political art," but with "making art in a political way."[111] Yet, while the general activities of the SC Gallery were primarily committed to fostering an art that "communicates with 'the people,'" they emerged at a time when local popular agitation for expanding Croatian autonomy was beginning to spin out of control. Escalating demands emerged primarily through the activities of one ancient Croatian cultural institution, the Matica Hrvatska, which became an aggressive defender of Croatian national sentiment and the nucleus of a new, nationalist policy beyond party control. By the beginning of the 1970s, the Matica Hrvatska had fully transformed from a cultural institution to a political organization with ambitions to counterpose the LCC.[112]

In a society faced with acute social problems, the pressure grew greater to solve them not through self-management but in some other way. In Croatia, the "other way" favored nationalism over Marxism and grew into an expansive mass movement, later named the Croatian Spring.[113] Spearheaded by the Matica Hrvatska, this movement politically co-opted science and art to spread the idea that the Croatian nation was superior to the other nationalities in Yugoslavia. It understood sovereignty to reside in a particular ethnic community, and offered the concept of a national economy as a salvation for the republic's alleged economic exploitation. Even though this demand contradicted the principle of Yugoslavia's single market, the Matica Hrvatska proposed that Croatia should have its own central bank, an autonomous military, currency, and separate UN seat. All the while, expressions of nationalism were occurring with greater frequency, ranging from "the midnight destruction of an advertising sign in the Cyrillic alphabet by a gang of youths wearing armbands inscribed with the Croatian national emblem" to huge political rallies, in which Zagreb "folk singers belted out the patriotic ballads ... [and] the old red-and-white chequerboard flag, which had been rarely displayed since the early 1950s, was hoisted once more," straying beyond the lexicon of self-managing socialism.[114]

In the unstable political situation of 1971, marked by frequent protests and political rallies, the desire to produce work in the urban environment was itself mired in complications, as was especially the case of the Sixth Zagreb Salon. A yearly survey exhibition of visual and applied arts, founded in 1965 by the city's Association for Fine Arts, the Salon was the first exhibition in Zagreb to take artistic interventions in the urban sphere as its central theme. Conceived by art

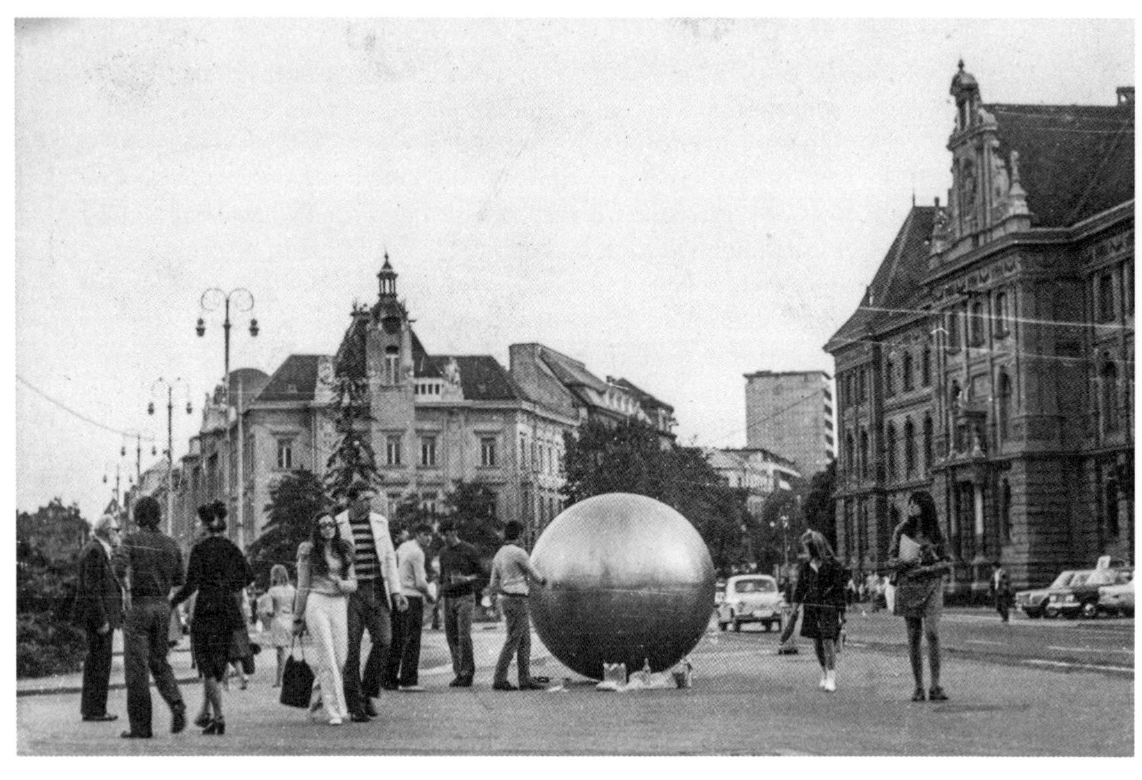

1.19. Ivan Kožarić, *Prizemljeno sunce* [Grounded Sun], Zagreb, 1971. Image courtesy of Muzej Suvremene Umjetnosti, Zagreb.

historian Željka Čorak, "The City as a Site of Plastic Happening" was the first theme of the newly established Proposal section of the Sixth Zagreb Salon. It called for proposals based on the "problems of our everyday living space," and recognized the "problematics of the city and its functioning as a local and global priority."[115] Twenty-four proposals were submitted, all of which were displayed in an exhibition at the SC Gallery, while four were realized in the city center.

One of the selected projects was Ivan Kožarić's *Prizemljeno sunce* [Grounded Sun]—a large, abstract fiberglass sphere two meters in diameter, covered in gold paint, and placed in one of the busiest areas of the city, in front of the National Theatre on Marshal Tito Square. The first noncommemorative sculpture to be erected in Zagreb, the work was as abstract as it was figurative, both a representation of the sun and a simple, spherical form. A video recording of the sculpture in its urban setting captures the immense curiosity it solicited from passersby.[116] Some stopped to inspect it for a brief moment, and approached it and touched its surface; others knocked on it to assess it density, and tried to test their physical strength by attempting to roll it forward. But despite its playful and even innocuous dimensions, the work became the target of hostility from the city's older and more conservative generation of critics. One member of the Board of Culture for the Socialist Committee of Zagreb, Rene Hollos, penned an attack on the Proposal section in the student journal *Studentski list*, complaining that he found it "surprising that some of these 'artists' claim such a 'freedom of creativity' to attack the citizenship with their degenerative and hysterical statements, and call for works that are able to be presented anywhere, just as a dog can find any tree or corner to cock its leg at. How long will we be terrorized by such '*Croatian*' artists?"[117]

In his letter, Hollos not only attacked what was in his view a "degenerative" sculpture but also demanded that "all those who poison our environment" be held accountable for their crimes.[118] Soon after Hollos made this crude demand, the *SC Newspaper* printed a series of responses from the younger generation of critics, who addressed the "tragic meaning" which the Board of Culture had "for culture, public and political life," at a moment "marked by deep social and political transformations."[119] The "tragic meaning" these authors were alluding to was the opportunistic position the Board had assumed at a "suitable moment for forming its own private ambitions"—these being to manipulate the programs of the city's Art Academy.[120] Zvonko Maković even identified in Hollos's demands "the darkest past of our civilization … solely dark, fascist, Stalinist dogmas."[121] These younger critics, in contrast, were fighting a "battle for the freedom of thought, of socialist thought."[122] The same issue of the *SC Newspaper* included a letter from the Secretariat for Communal Matters, which had ordered the removal of Kožarić's sculpture. Their justification was that the sculpture had "become the target of mindless citizens, who chose to vent their feelings with paint, fire and graffiti, all of which had disfigured the environment."[123] *Grounded Sun* had been attacked with black paint on two occasions, and was almost set on fire on another.

Yet, contrary to the account outlined in the letter from the city's board, the work had not been vandalized by "mindless citizens." Instead, many suspected that the attack was perpetrated by a group of figurative painters called Biafra, which believed that "nonfigurative art could not deal with issues of humanity, which should be the main concern of artistic creation."[124] According to Koščević, Biafra's activities came from a position that was "definitely right wing" and arose from the "national" question.[125] Their position was fortified by the growing influence of the Matica Hrvatska, which at the time was pouring out pamphlets and booklets advocating for the renewal of Croatia's nationhood, culture, and economy.

For Košćević, the fate of *Grounded Sun* was indicative of what was at the time a highly divided Croatian art scene. These divisions had already surfaced following the destruction of *Hit Parade*, but had now become representative of two different "'political orientations': 1968 against 1971."[126] As chapter 3 discusses in detail, the politics of 1968 was connected to the student movements which protested against the "embourgeoisement" of Yugoslav socialism and the failure of self-management to create an egalitarian society. In contrast, the political scene in 1971 was fueled by nationalism and stemmed from the Croatian leadership's efforts to strengthen the republic's position within the Yugoslav federation, as opposed to securing equality among its citizens. Translated into Zagreb's art scene, these competing positions manifested themselves as the "traditional, conservative and bourgeois civil milieu" set against the "free, open, explorative, and avant-garde experimental line," both of "which were equally strong."[127] Whereas the SC was fostering engagement based on the principles of self-managing democracy, Biafra was aligning itself with what was becoming a populistic nationalist movement.

In his contribution for the Proposal section, Braco Dimitrijević captured the spirit of the "1968" position by directly addressing the "ordinary citizen." For *Casual Passerby I Met at 1:15 pm, 4:23 pm, and 6:11 pm in Zagreb, 1971*, he installed large, blown-up photographs of three pedestrians, selected at random, on the building of the Writers' Club in Republic Square, in which political rallies were traditionally held. As in his 1969 *Painting by Krešimir Klika*, in which the driver of a car accidentally became an artist by running over a milk carton, so here were random people endowed with an importance usually reserved for those in the highest positions of power. The work placed the president on a par with an ordinary citizen. It replicated self-management's founding goal to accomplish Lenin's precept, quoted by Tito in 1950, that "to fight against bureaucracy until the end, to gain victory over it, is only possible if the whole population takes part in it."[128]

Just a day before "The City as a Site of Plastic Happening" was set to open, a mass political rally took place in which Dabčević-Kučar addressed a crowd of 200,000 people in front of the facade on which Dimitrjević's works were later installed. At this public mass gathering, the stage was decorated with a large Croatian tricolor and checkered coat of arms, along with the words of the new constitutional amendment that defined Croatian autonomy within the federation. According to American diplomats who witnessed the event, several members of the audience wept when the Croatian national anthem was played, and Dabčević-Kučar's speech was interrupted nearly forty times by frantic cheers and chants, triggered by catchphrases like "provocateurs," "Informbiro-ists," "statists," and "Serbian greater state hegemonists."[129] When the prime minister castigated "deaf and blind nationalists" for endangering the reform by their extremism, however, the crowd remained largely silent. In a society where big decisions were made in a way that few people could see or understand, nationalism had become the only way to protest against a feeling of disempowerment.

THE SC GALLERY'S "FINAL ISSUE"

A few months later, in November 1971, the political crisis in Zagreb reached its breaking point after over thirty thousand university students in the city boycotted classes and organized a strike that lasted twelve days. Initially driven by the constitutional amendments and the goal of altering the disadvantageous laws on hard currency, the striking students attempted to force Dabčević-Kučar and Tripalo into taking a more aggressive stance. By then, however, nationalist tendencies had spread through many of the city's key institutions, including the university and the mass media.[130] According to the diplomat Cvijeto Job, the culmination of the Croatian Mass Movement represented "the most serious event [in Yugoslavia's postwar history], mixing anti-centralist, nationalist, extreme nationalist, pro-Ustaše [the Croatian Fascist, ultranationalist organization active between 1929 and 1945], anti-communist, reformist, democratic, democratic socialist, liberal and non-libertarian elements."[131] Once the students went on strike, and the leaders confessed that they empathized with the "strike's 'progressive' motives," the removal of Croatia's liberal faction appeared inevitable.[132]

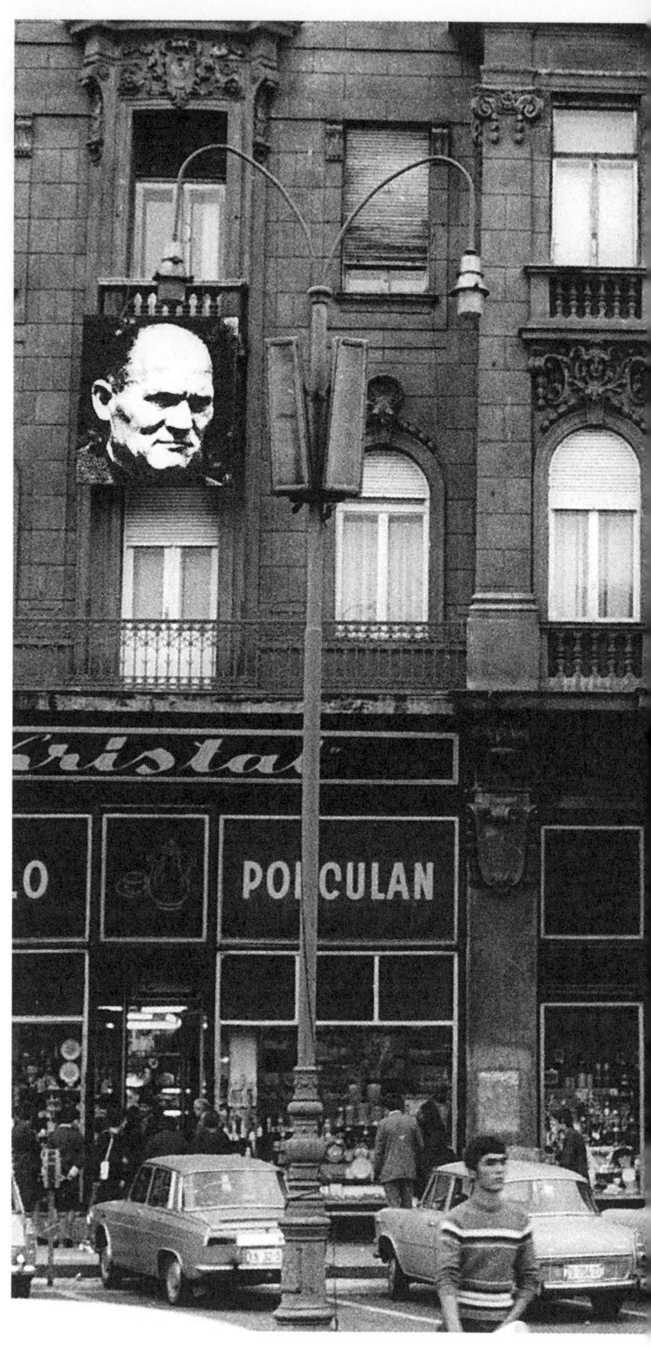

1.20. Braco Dimitrijević, *Casual Passerby I Met at 1:15 pm, 4:23 pm, and 6:11 pm in Zagreb, 1971*. In the collection of Museum Moderner Kunst, Vienna. Photograph by Enes Midžić. Image courtesy of the artist.

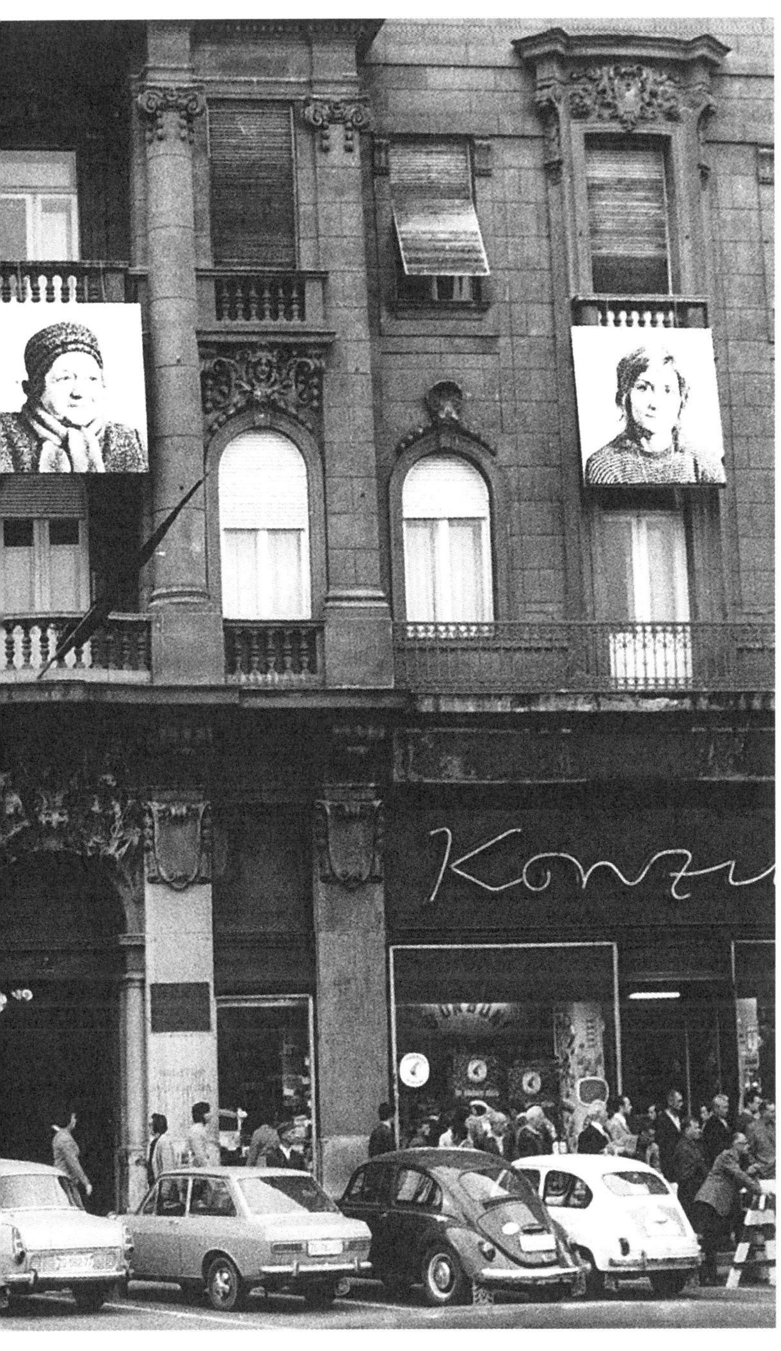

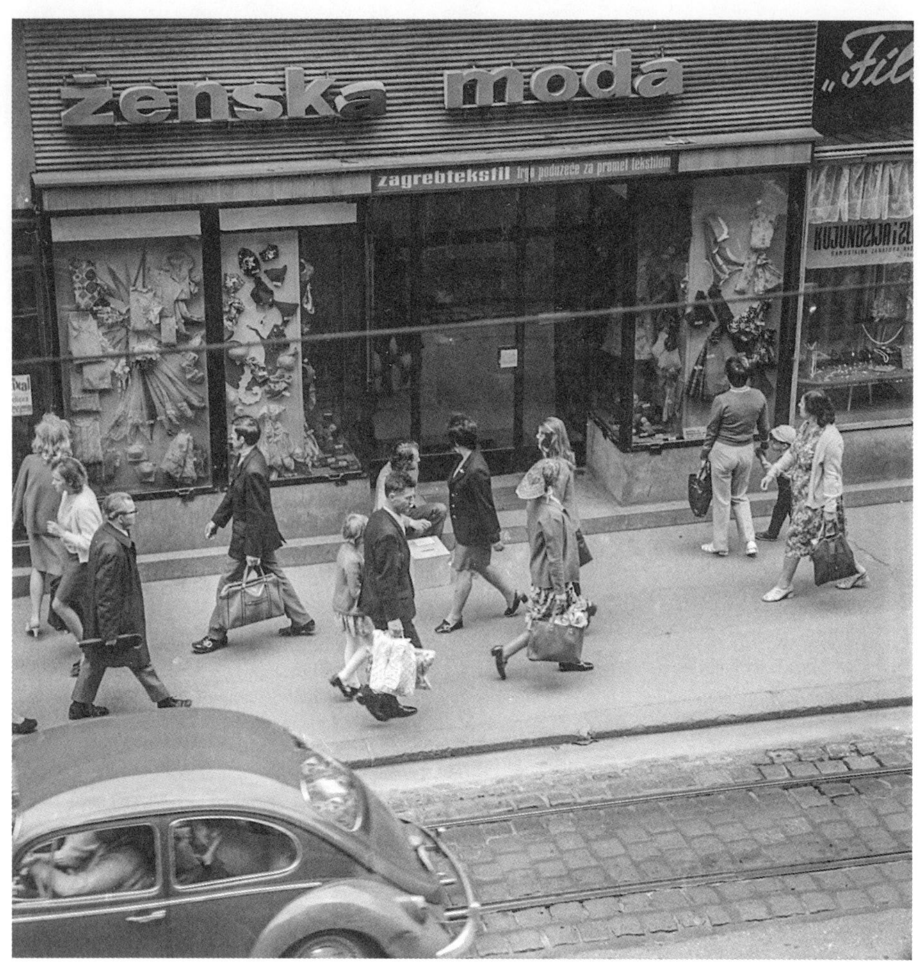

1.21. Goran Trbuljak, *Referendum*, Zagreb, July 1972. Image courtesy of the artist.

On the afternoon of 2 December 1971, Yugoslav radio stations interrupted their regular programs to broadcast a speech made by Tito at a closed party conclave the previous day. In his speech, Tito conceded that there were a "good number of reasons which led such a development as a massive strike of students, a strike which had a tendency towards growing into a general strike ... bringing our whole life to a standstill."[133] Nevertheless, he criticized the Matica Hrvatska and the student strikes, and ultimately charged Croatia's Party leadership with pandering to nationalists and separatists, and with "liberalism" in the face of a "counter-revolution."[134] Within ten days of the meeting, the LCC leadership, along with several of their closest collaborators—all together, around two thousand people—had resigned. Having removed the top two layers of the Croatian leadership, along with an entire political and administrative class, the purge ushered in a period in which Croatia was often described as the "sullen republic."[135]

The purges would spread to Serbia in the following year, in the wake of the leadership's refusal to support Tito's measures against Croatia. At precisely the same moment that Tito began removing the liberal leaderships in the rest of the republics, the *SC Gallery Newspaper* announced Goran Trbuljak's *Referendum*, completed on 14 July 1972. Driven by the assumption that "an artist is anyone who is given the opportunity to be one," the artist stood in the middle of a busy pedestrian street in Zagreb's city center, stopping random passersby to ask them to vote on whether or not Goran Trbuljak was an "artist." According to the action's documentation in the *SC Gallery Newspaper*: "By their own choice, citizens had to proclaim whether a person whose work and name they had never seen or heard of before was an artist.... Out of 500 ballots, 257 were positive, 204 negative, and 37 were spoilt votes, so the person selected as an artist was that person whose work and name had not been known before by the voters."[136]

Like many of the early activities that took place at the SC Gallery, Trbuljak's *Referendum* was a self-reflexive attempt to ascribe artistic activity a structural position within society at large. The work harnessed the participation of viewers, who became active agents in the work's realization as they cast their vote. The work itself rested on the registry of these acts of participation. But although echoing the SC Gallery's early commitment to participation, Trbuljak's *Referendum* took place at a moment when Yugoslavia had once again returned to a coercive and firm-hand rule. What might have seemed to be a merely artistic action mimicking the procedures of voting in fact offered a latent reflection on the lack of participatory decision making in Yugoslavia. As this chapter has revealed, it was the lack of opportunities for pluralist evaluation based on the principles of self-management

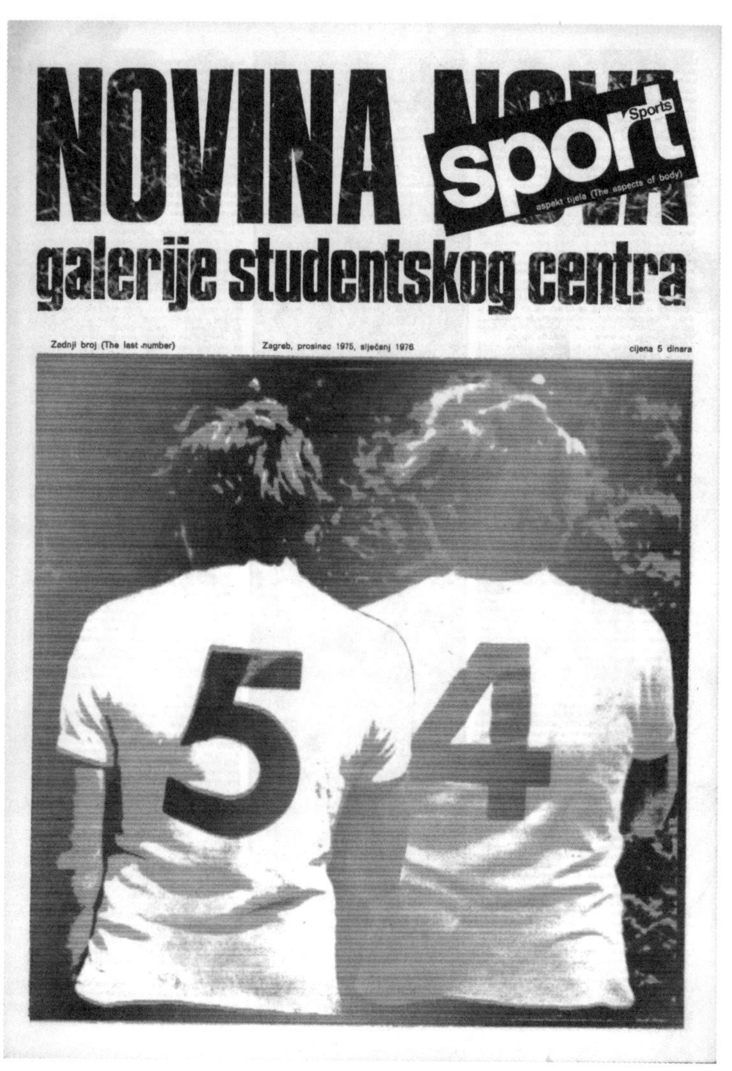

1.22. Cover of *Novine GSC*, "The Last Number," December 1975, edited by Vladimir Gudac. Image courtesy of Arhiv za Likovne Umjetnosti HAZU, Zagreb.

that had hindered all attempts throughout the 1960s to measure the advantages and side effects of the market reforms. Without a radical associative democracy, the crisis escalated into political disorientation and eventually nationalism. Instead of containing nationalist tendencies, the repression of 1971 would also help to fuel extremism some decades later, and to create the future "postcommunist" heroes.

Yet the very bitter irony of 1971 was that many of the Croatian Mass Movement's demands were in fact met by Tito in the constitution of 1974, discussed at length in chapter 4. Although perhaps ironic, this result was typical of the Janus-faced character of the regime, which sought simultaneously to divide and rule, and to unite and rule.[137] Concessions were made from above, while all independent movements and any real chance for political pluralism were repressed. Many of the Croatian Mass Movement's demands were indeed met in 1974, but no further effort was made in the 1970s or 1980s to bring a new generation of progressive leaders back into political life. And while the constitutions of 1974 and 1976 effectively dismantled the banking system and technocratic power in large factories, they did so under pressure from richer republics that wanted to control their foreign trade without the meddling of federal institutions. Despite its popularity among workers, self-management remained ineffectual in the face of a system that was incoherent at a macroeconomic level, while a combination of repression and increasing economic liberalization encouraged a mentality of everyone looking out for themselves.

By 1975, the SC Gallery had just about given up. In December of that year, it released the last number of its *Newspaper*: a special issue dedicated to sports, treated as an analogy to the lack of popular participation in the field of culture.[138] The theme was chosen due to its widespread popularity, having found its "way to all fields of human behavior."[139] Unlike cultural activity, "it is easier to gather money for sports"—the lack of special "monographs or 'collected works' is compensated for by newspapers and magazines that provide detailed and extensive daily reports from sports fields." The declaration continued:

> It seems as if there is nothing else happening from day to day, nothing else that should be noticed and pointed out. When we consider the values respected in sports, which are based on COMPETITION, we struggle to understand what makes these values so important. If we are to speak honestly about sports, we should make clear that it is the ELITE's chosen amusement, in spite of the millions of people who "participate" from the audience. A handful of players are able to maintain the people's attention: playing not only with a ball but also with people's nerves. While we believe in work that enables mass participation, we cannot support a theory that favors individual efforts and includes certain rules and a system of propaganda. Lately sports have become the site of political struggle.[140]

The analogy to sports served to demonstrate the kind of apathy that came to replace the SC Gallery's initial commitment to democracy and public participation. In the same year as this proclamation, the gallery released a self-published monograph marking a ten-year anniversary of sorts. Consisting of extensive photographic documentation and chronologies, the book identified itself as a contribution toward the "future critical study of the gallery, its activity, and artists."[141] In a sense, it was a kind of archiving of the pioneering events organized through the gallery.

In an increasingly stratified political climate, the once youthful optimism that drove the gallery's programs was abandoned. Starting in the mid-1970s, and at the height of self-management's crisis, artists previously working through the SC Gallery would begin to take matters into their own hands by seeking out new models of self-organization. Their initial idealism was to be substituted with an unwavering pessimism. In Novi Sad, by contrast, the cultural struggle for self-management would result in severe political repercussions.

2 A TASTER OF POLITICAL INSULT

NOVI SAD'S YOUTH TRIBUNE (1968–1972)

TRANSLATING THE NEW ART PRACTICE

On 20 September 1970, the artist Bogdanka Poznanović realized her *Akcija srce-predmet* [Action Heart-Object] in the center of Novi Sad, the largest city of the multinational Socialist Autonomous Province of Vojvodina. She asked four young participants to carry a giant styrofoam heart—two meters tall, twenty centimeters thick, and covered in a glossy red polyvinyl film—from the Marshal Tito Bridge, through the city center's bustling streets, and into the arts salon of the Youth Tribune. There, the object was placed above a square white tablecloth with an immaculately arranged table setting, and remained on display for nine days, while a fixed metronome, set inside its core, ticked at a regular rhythm of seventy-six beats per minute. While the heart was being carried through the streets of the city, this spontaneous and unfamiliar action had intercepted the city's evening rush hour, disrupting the daily routine of Novi Sad's inhabitants. Hung inside the intimate confines of the gallery space, the heart became a static object for display, still pulsating from within the atrium of the city's experimental art scene.[1]

Devised by a pioneer in the exploration of new media and an influential figure for the city's new generation of experimental artists, Poznanović's *Action Heart-Object* was performed in the heat of the Youth Tribune's programmatic development, and playfully characterized the space's principal role and intentions. Founded a few years before Zagreb's Students' Center, in 1954, the Youth Tribune was nevertheless the outcome of a similar climate, when the League of Communists began the process of extending self-management from the workplace into the political sphere. Perhaps not coincidentally, the space also opened in the same year as the signing of the historic Novi Sad Agreement by Serbian, Croatian, and Bosnian cultural organizations, writers, linguists, and intellectuals.[2] At a time when the still-centralized party set to work on fostering a shared national consciousness of "Yugoslavness," or *jugoslovenstvo*, this agreement aimed to build unity across ethnic and linguistic divisions within the country by establishing a Serbo-Croatian language standard. Emphasizing the similarities between the language spoken in Serbia and Croatia, the agreement further stated that the groups of linguists from these nations would work together toward a single dictionary for their language, as well as other forms of cultural cooperation which would contribute to the development of a single, harmonious, and federalized Yugoslavia.

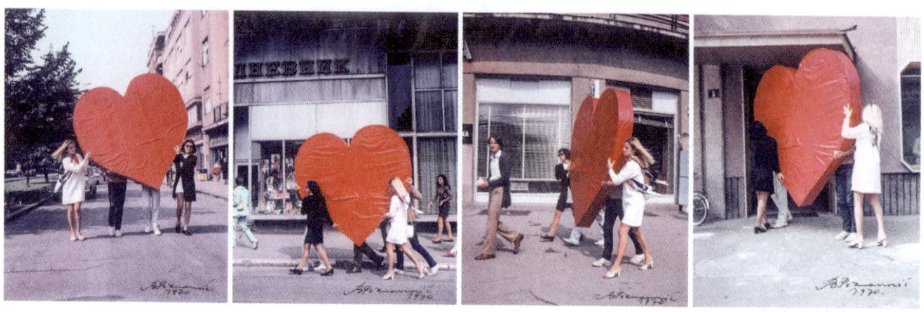

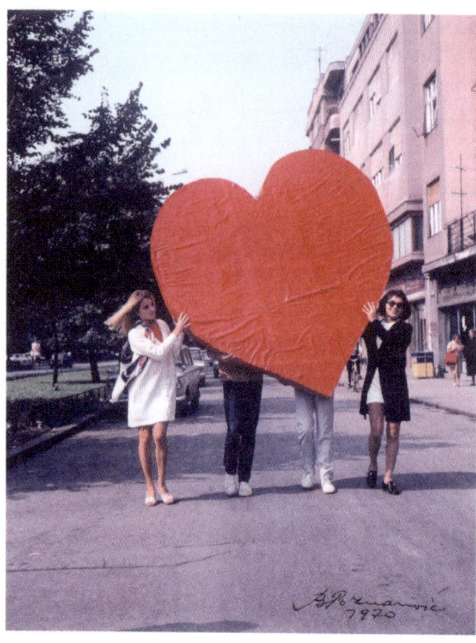

2.1. and 2.2. Bogdanka Poznanović, *Akcija srce-predmet* [Action Heart-Object], Novi Sad, 1970. Images courtesy of the Marinko Sudac Collection.

If the Novi Sad Agreement aimed to encourage mutual tolerance among Yugoslavia's national communities, the founding of the Youth Tribune could similarly be seen as an attempt to cultivate a shared sense of "Yugoslav socialist patriotism" in the city's first postwar generation. Established by the Provincial and Municipal Youth League of Vojvodina, the space was originally intended to serve as a social base for the city's youth and students enrolled at the newly opened People's University. In the 1960s, it swiftly became a gathering place for a new generation of social and cultural workers from the city's university, which opened in 1960, together with a number of artists and journalists aiming to raise the cultural awareness of the city's youth. By the time Poznanović staged her action in 1970, these developments had led to a clustering of cultural phenomena in Novi Sad that was unparalleled in the rest of Yugoslavia, not only in the field of visual arts but also in literature as well as film production, through the city's renowned, state-supported Neoplanta Film Company, founded in 1966.[3]

As with the SC Gallery in Zagreb, the Youth Tribune had secured a pivotal role in Novi Sad's cultural awakening in the 1960s, at the height of the loosening of cultural policy in Yugoslavia. Ignited by the student uprisings of 1968, the space, under the direction of Judita Šalgo, who became the Tribune's editor-in-chief in the same year, maintained a steadfast commitment to fostering an "atmosphere of spontaneous discussion and thought."[4] As Šalgo explained in a public statement in 1970, the Tribune's staff were above all determined to ensure that the space never become a mere entertainment spot for youth—that the standard of its programs never be disputed through the position of "certain mass social structures, groups, local interests or the so-called interests of the youth."[5] In other words, the Tribune's aim was not to simply "entertain the youth with socialist ideas alongside beat music," but rather to "establish a context with fresh ideas and nonconventional thoughts, here and around the world."[6] Only by "overcoming local surroundings" would the Youth Tribune be able to commit itself to an invigorating dialogue with the public.[7]

If the fulfilment of remaining "open" rested on an expanded, intercultural dialogue, it was the Tribune's editorial boards that successfully facilitated a vibrant network of cultural exchange between writers and artists throughout Yugoslavia. The center's framework included two editorial offices: for *Polja* [Fields], a magazine for art and literature, inaugurated in 1955, and *Új Symposion* [New Symposium], a magazine for culture, art, and politics in Hungarian, begun in 1965. Publishing and translating important works of both Serbian and Hungarian historical avant-gardes, as well as the contemporary advocates of new writing and art from the multiethnic and multilinguistic Yugoslav cultural space, the Youth Tribune's magazines enabled a cross-fertilization of dialogue.

Dejan Poznanović, one of the Tribune's founding members and editor-in-chief of *Polja* between 1958 and 1962, played a crucial role in these dialogues, by contemporaneously translating a significant number of Slovenian texts into Serbo-Croatian.[8] Apart from translating several texts for the journals surrounding the Youth Tribune, Poznanović also contributed translations of Slovenian authors to the first issue of *Rok*, a magazine that was vital for the Yugoslav experimental art scene, gathering within its three issues some of the most important names in the country's art world. Edited by the experimental prose writer Bora Ćosić in Belgrade in early 1969, the first issue of *Rok* promoted the concept of mixed-media art, and conveyed a new creative sensibility that transcended the academic orientations of painting and sculpture. Self-defined as a "periodical for literature and the aesthetic study of reality," and announcing a fight against writing that increasingly "'took the wrong tack' . . . by pleasing individuals and making them happy," *Rok* called for the construction of "new forms of consciousness, multi-dimensional, sublime, and liberating."[9] Within the local context, the issue was also pivotal in introducing OHO's texts and events to a Serbo-Croatian audience, through the prism of the "OHO movement in the space of mixed media." *Rok*'s first issue included a translation of the OHO manifesto, first published in Ljubljana's student newspaper *Tribuna* in 1966, which ardently declared:

> To observe, to see oneself, means to be free. To observe, to look elsewhere further from oneself, means to be in a relationship or a dichotomy. The absolute and the relative have nothing in common. The one excludes the other. Free perception is the absolute perception. Conquerors of space stand in a certain relationship to space. Thus they are situated neither in themselves nor the space they have taken up.[10]

Rok illustrated OHO's reist attitude by publishing the textual instructions for actions that were performed by the group during their visit to Zagreb.[11] In these conceptual programs, or "ideas," "everyday scenes" of eating and drinking, winding yarn, and reading were divided into smaller actions and transferred into an artistic context. In *Jabuka* [Apple], the act of eating an apple was separated into schematic movements: "the apple travels toward the mouth; biting is heard; movements of jaws are seen"; in *Ritual*, the gesture of drinking wine was fragmented into the simplified operations of the "hand taking a bottle, wine flows into a glass."[12] When splintered and separated, eating and drinking were no longer processes of human nourishment, but mechanical actions—"rituals," as proposed by the action's title. They echoed much of OHO's work at this time, which, as Igor Zabel has argued, was directed at transforming consciousness "into a permanently open and attentive reistic vision."[13]

While *Rok*'s first issue introduced OHO's "Reistic" approach to audiences beyond the group's immediate confines in Ljubljana, it also invested the group with a powerful countercultural charge. On the pages of *Rok*, OHO's early works and texts were printed alongside various Fluxus manifestoes, letters and plays by Ay-O, the work of George Brecht, Hi-Red Center, and George Maciunas, and a discussion between Pierre Cabanne and Marcel Duchamp. These were in turn interspersed with photographs of battered and bleeding students from the protests of May 1968 in Paris, and processions in Prague commemorating the death of the young Czech student Jan Palach, who died in January 1969 after setting himself alight in protest of the end of the Prague Spring. Through *Rok*, OHO's fleeting and ephemeral gestures, largely staged in Ljubljana, were able to reach larger and unanticipated audiences in Zagreb, Belgrade, and Novi Sad, and were contextualized alongside a complex range of ideas that emerged in and around the watershed year of 1968, not only in Yugoslavia but throughout the world. This eccentric array of influences also became central to Novi Sad's New Art Practice scene, which first awakened following OHO's seminal visit to the Youth Tribune in 1969.

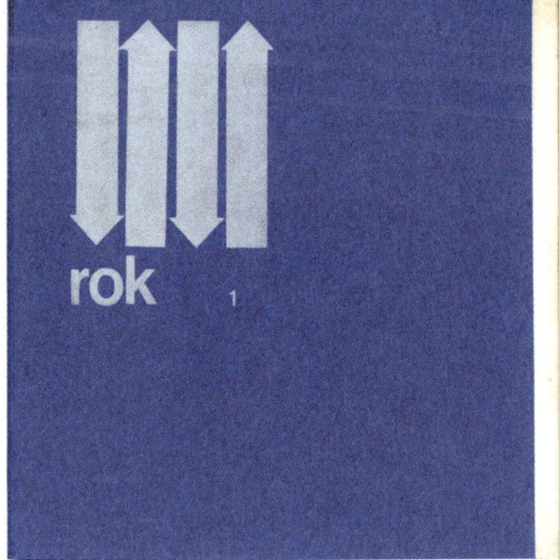

2.3. Front cover of *Rok*'s first issue, Belgrade, 1969. Image courtesy of Bora Ćosić.

"GREAT-GREAT-GRANDFATHERS": OHO IN NOVI SAD

OHO first came to Novi Sad on 1 November 1969, at the invitation of Šalgo and the technical advisors for the fine arts salon, Bogdanka Poznanović and Biljana Tomić, to mount an exhibition at the Youth Tribune.[14] During their stay, they reenacted their *Triglav* project, first performed at Ljubljana's Zvezda Park on 30 December 1968, as a culmination to a tumultuous year loaded with student demonstrations. In Ljubljana, OHO members Milenko Matanović, David Nez, and Drago Dellabernardina had positioned themselves in the center of the city square, cloaked in a black cloth that enveloped their bodies, leaving only their long-haired heads visible. Together, they arranged their silhouetted figures to replicate the craggy outline of Mount Triglav, the highest peak of the Julian Alps. With the title of their work displayed in an inscription placed at their feet, the artists were not only recreating the crags of the peak, but also creating a literal representation of "tri-glave," translated into English as "Three Heads."

According to *Triglav*'s principal author Milenko Matanović, the idea behind the work was simple: it was intended to be a late December gift to the citizens of Ljubljana by bringing the mountain to the city, particularly for the benefit of those who were not able to visit it themselves.[15] But regardless of the artist's own personal motivations, there is still an undeniably ironic element in this action. Triglav is not only the highest mountain in Slovenia but it was, and still remains, a constant symbol of the Slovene nation. An emblem of the republic's national pride, Triglav was also used as a branding name during this period. In Ljubljana, OHO's action was first performed when the country's political and economic decentralization during the 1960s had reopened the question of "national identity," with the Slovene press becoming increasingly centered on issues pertaining to the republic's sovereignty and Slovene statehood.[16] This was also a moment when leaders of Yugoslavia's wealthiest republic became openly critical of the federal tax system, which aimed to fund the less developed southern republics' growth by redistributing profits from the wealthier northwestern regions. One year later, OHO performed *Triglav* for the second time in Novi Sad, just months after the situation in Slovenia had reached a breaking point, when dissatisfaction over the Federal Executive Council's failure to submit to the World Bank a funding proposal for road construction projects in that republic erupted in protests that threatened the collapse of the federal government, and even prompted the personal intervention of Tito himself.[17]

Dubbed the "Slovene road-building crisis," these protests were a clear symptom of the country's decentralizing economic reforms, which had made the

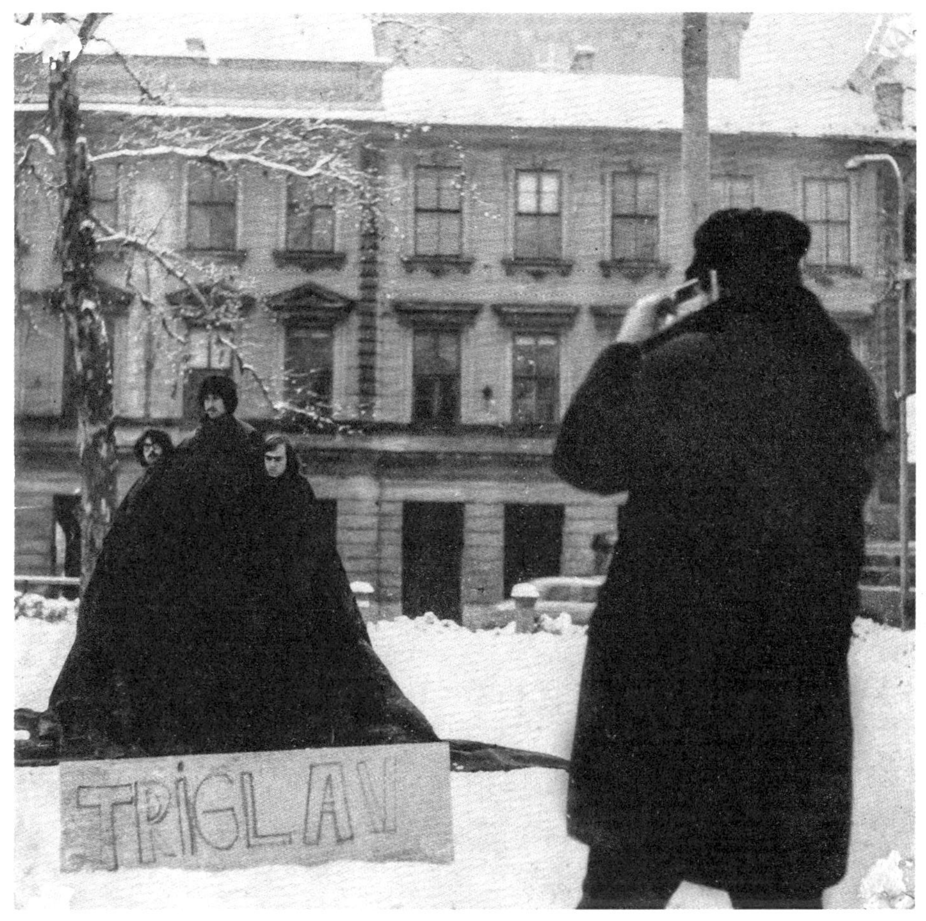

2.4. OHO, *Mount Triglav*, conceived by Milenko Matanović and performed by Drago Dellabernardina, Milenko Matanović, and David Nez, Zvezda Park, Ljubljana, 30 December 1968. Image courtesy of Moderna Galerija, Ljubljana.

federal government vulnerable to attacks from various local, republican, ethnic, and economic forces. The crisis revealed how, as the acceleration of economic reforms continued to increase existing disparities between the levels of development in the republics and provinces, the points of contention between Yugoslavia's nationalities were beginning to shift from historically determined cultural issues to economic priorities. As Yugoslavia's "national question" began to resurface in the 1960s, OHO's reenactment of the three-peaked mountain behaved as a subtle reflection on the complex intersections between consumerism, nationalism, and political conservatism which, as discussed in the previous chapter, followed the turn to market reform. In Novi Sad, the happening was reenacted on the city's Katolička Porta Square, outside of the Tribune. This time wrapped in white shrouds, *Triglav*'s actors introduced local artists to the philosophical tenets of the reist approach. At the same time, the action captured some of the individual faces caught in the abstractions that accompany any notion of collective national or political identity. Seen through the developments that peaked in the road-building crisis of 1969, *Triglav* seemed both to inhabit Slovenia's national symbol and to claim it for itself, replacing the anonymous peaks of the mountain with the scruffy and unshaven faces of the 1960s counterculture.

If *Triglav* performed, and subsequently activated, the core principles of reism while potentially carrying a veiled political critique, the *Prapradedovi* [Great-Great-Grandfathers] exhibition at the Youth Tribune itself was, according to Tomaž Brejc, OHO's earliest historian, governed by the collective's turn to "arte povera, land art, body art, process art and conceptual art."[18] It was the first public showing of OHO's *Summer Projects* from 1969, published in the adjoining exhibition catalogue. For these projects, the group left the gallery space and began to work in the open air, first the city and then the landscape—and to turn their focus away from things and toward the relations between people in natural settings. In Novi Sad, the group arrived a few days before the show, and according to Marko Pogačnik, "immediately started scouring the scrapyards and stores for the elements each of us needed for his installation. And by the time the show opened the exhibition was mounted."[19]

2.5. Marko Pogačnik, *Project: Water Oozing from the Lower into the Upper Bucket on a Woolen Yarn*, Novi Sad, 1969. Image courtesy of Moderna Galerija, Ljubljana.

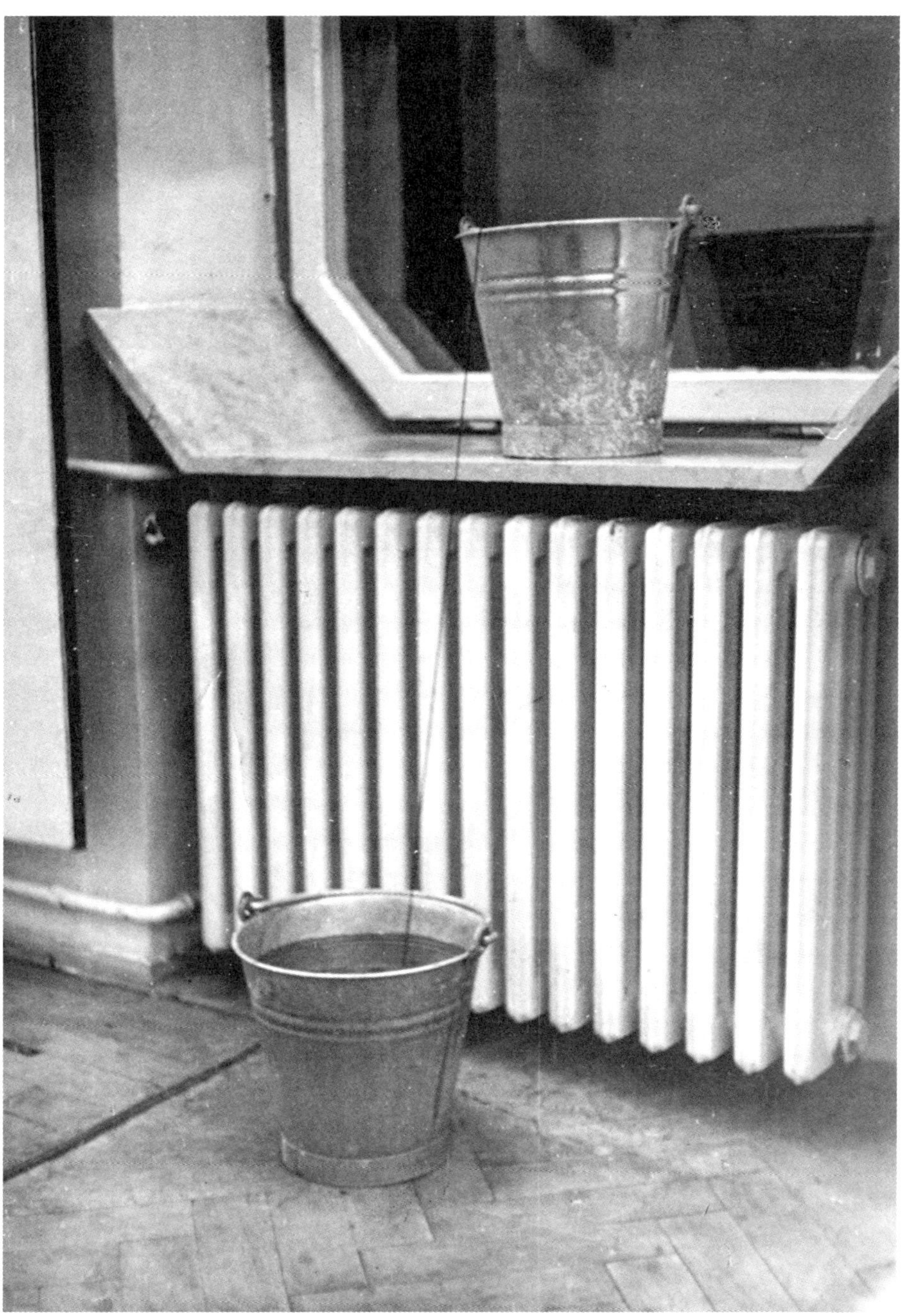

For their exhibition at the Youth Tribune, the group took the explorations begun with the *Summer Projects* a step further, choosing to interrogate and emphasize the height, weight, and measurements of the materials displayed, and to stress natural processes through sculpture. In one of Pogačnik's works, titled *Project: Water Oozing from the Lower into the Upper Bucket on a Woolen Yarn*, the artist positioned a metal bucket filled with water on a window shelf, and another on the parquet floor of the exhibition hall, connecting them together with a piece of wool thread. In the installation, Pogačnik recalls that he wanted to show "the crucial difference between the possible and the actual. Theoretically, water should travel from the lower bucket to the upper bucket due to osmosis; in practice, this does not happen. What interested me here was how I could visibly demonstrate something invisible, namely, the difference between a theoretical possibility and the actual state of affairs."[20]

Works such as Pogačnik's *Project* sought to expose the tension between conflicting positivist and metaphysical tendencies, which was a preoccupation that ran through much of OHO's early work. They also shared the raw materiality found in arte povera, to which the group had a personal connection through its member Tomaž Šalamun, who had lived in Paris and Rome a few years earlier. But although they shared a sense of the material qualities characteristic to arte povera, the titles of their works, including *Project: Water Oozing* . . . , hinted at a driving preoccupation with natural processes, and more broadly at art's ability to communicate ideas that went beyond formal concerns.

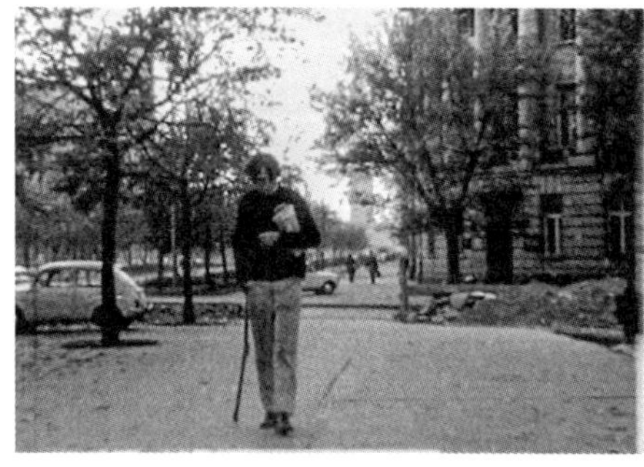

2.6. Tomaž Šalamun, *Marking the Line to Petrovaradin*, Novi Sad, 1969. Image from Naško Križnar's film, *OHO: Novi Sad II*, 1969. Image courtesy of Moderna Galerija, Ljubljana.

Great-Great-Grandfathers was also accompanied by a series of actions, including Tomaž Šalamun's *Marking the Line to Petrovaradin*. In this action, Šalamun walked from the entrance of the Tribune's gallery toward the city's Petrovaradin Fortress, carrying a large box of chalk and a pair of school compasses in his arms, and carefully drawing a white line behind him. Much like the installations assembled at the exhibition, this action was aimed at interrogating relations, with the artist connecting two respective territories through drawing. In its engagement with the "outside"—that is, with passersby—the predetermined scheme also involved an element of unpredictability.[21] Reaching the end of the designated path, Šalamun recited a poem, titled "Why I Drew the Line," intended to resolve the bewilderment of unsuspecting passersby. It explained: "a line: you can touch it with your hands; you can place a tree upon it; you can wet it; you can lie on it; you can shut your eyes so that you do not see it.... The relationship between can and cannot is art, which is why the line is art."[22] Replacing imitation with process, *Marking the Line to Petrovaradin* marked a continuation of OHO's artistic concern with spatial perception and sensuous experiences. By crossing the borders between "can" and "cannot," it was one of many attempts to traverse the sharp distinctions between art and life, with which OHO would become increasingly interested in the subsequent phase of their activities.

DECODING GRUPA KÔD

No longer relying on what Brejc described as the "visual, rational logic of the picture," OHO's "new sensibility" was a vital precursor to the activities of Novi Sad's New Art Practice scene, which to an extent modeled itself on the "ideas and experience of the collective."[23] Grupa KÔD [code] was an art group founded in April 1970 by six young people associated with the Youth Tribune and the culture section of the city's university broadsheet, *Index: Magazine of the Students' Association of Vojvodina*. The six were Slobodan Tišma, Janez Kocijančić, Mirko Radojičić (then culture editor of *Index*), Miroslav Mandić, Branko Andrić, and Slavko Bogdanović. Unlike Zagreb's generation of "plastic artists," the group's members were not academically trained artists but students at the city's university from a variety of disciplines, mostly literature. This is why the group was predominantly concerned with structural linguistics, semantics, and semiology, using media and materials as a "background" for the "mental components of the artistic work."[24] But like Zagreb's new generation of artists, the collective favored "direct communication" and sought out interactive audiences for their work.[25] The name of the group itself stood as a metaphor for its activities—a "code" being a system of signs that enables

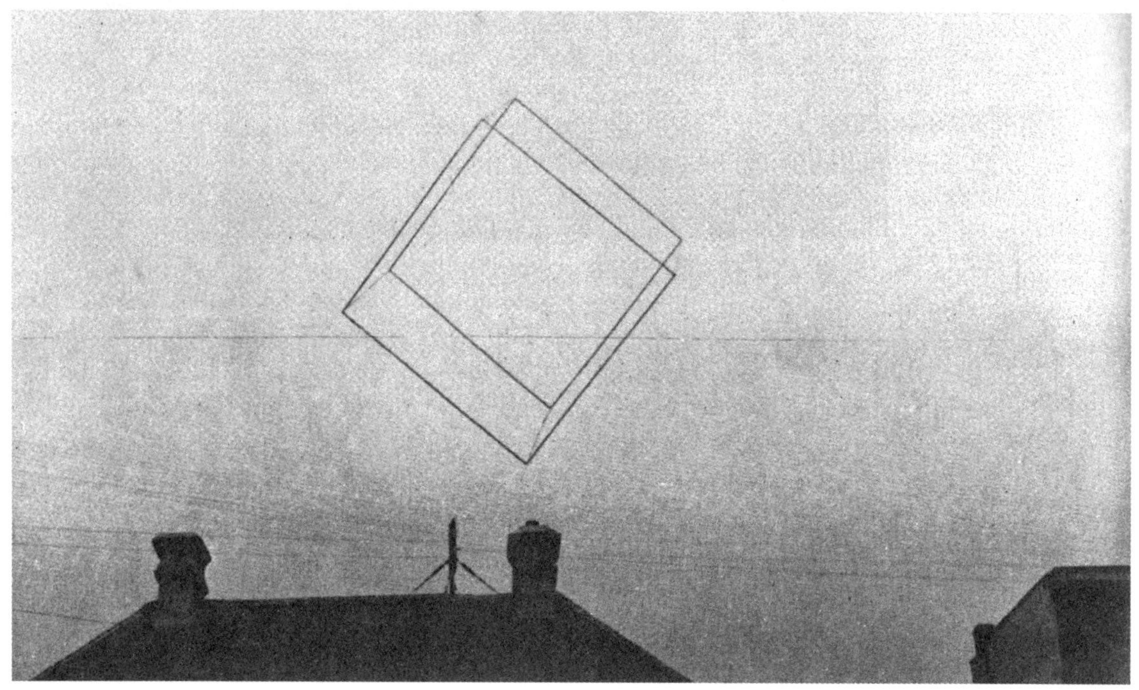

2.7. Slobodan Tišma, Grupa KÔD, *Kocka* [Square], Katolička Porta, Novi Sad, 18 April 1970. Image courtesy of Slavko Bogdanović and Muzej Savremene Umetnosti Vojvodine.

2.8. Grupa KÔD, Mirko Radojičić, *Estetika* [Aesthetics], Novi Sad, 1970. Image courtesy of Slavko Bogdanović and Muzej Savremene Umetnosti Vojvodine.

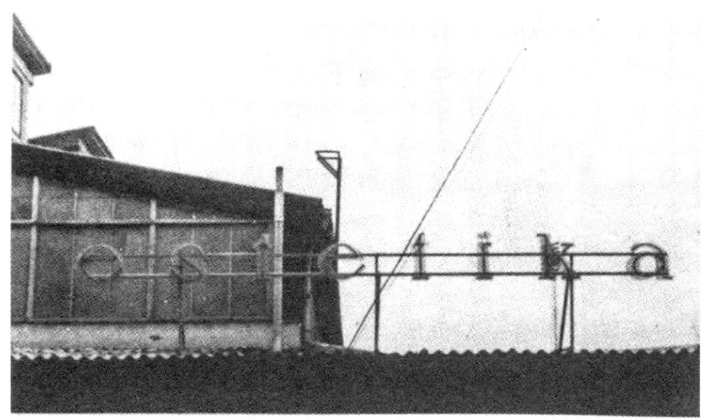

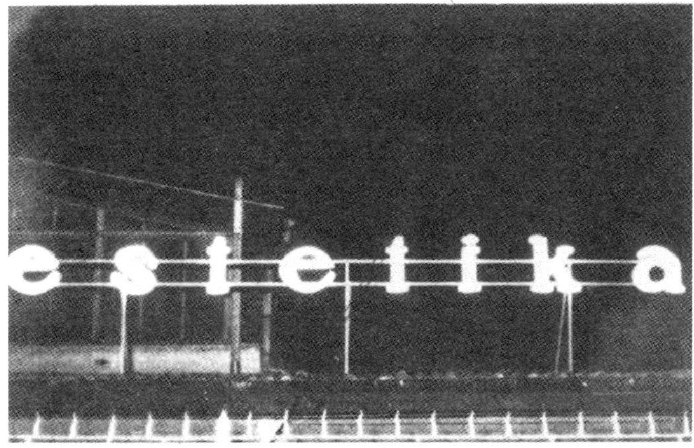
estetika

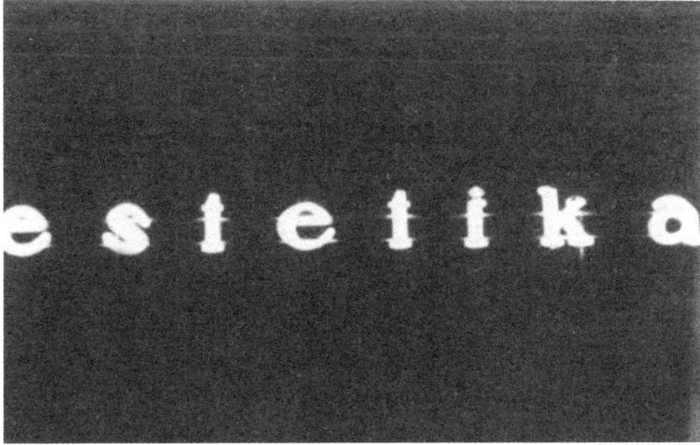
estetika

communication, and carries messages from one system to another. Significantly, KÔD was able to carry out some of its first actions and works only through the financial assistance of the Tribune, and particularly Šalgo's support. Working at *Index*'s culture section further allowed the group to disseminate some of its most important works, including manifestos, visual poetry, and the documentation of actions and interventions. Although *Index* was only a student newspaper, it was in many respects decisive for Yugoslavia's neo-avant-gardes, gathering and publishing work by some of the most important names in the country's intellectual and artistic scenes.

KÔD's methodical approach was first introduced to the public with an appearance at the Youth Tribune's small visual arts space—the "parquet salon"—on the evening of 9 April 1970. That night, the group produced a spatial intervention akin to those previously executed by OHO, in which two corners of the gallery were diagonally linked by a rope, while a number of ropes hung vertically from the room's ceiling. Nine days later, Tišma hung an iron wire construction in the city's Katolička Porta Square. Shaped to form the outlines of a perfect cube, and raised nine meters above ground level by a nylon thread, the construction was meant to represent a symbol of absolute form. This concrete object in real space favored an objective, elementary model over the traditionally hand-crafted art object. As a stripped-down, neutral, and skeletal construction, it eschewed the expressive indexicality of painting and traditional sculpture. Taken on the same day, Radojičić's photograph of a neon-light advertisement for the construction firm Aesthetics further advanced this rejection of traditional "aesthetics." The photograph reduced a term associated with the philosophical investigation of beauty and taste in art to a company's name. It called for a stepping out from what was considered "art" into an "aesthetics" that embraced everyday human activity. Both works deflated the importance allotted to "aesthetics," and in doing so echoed Lucy Lippard and John Chandler's enthusiastic announcement, two years earlier, that the shift from art as product to art as idea would emancipate the artist from both economic and technical limitations.[26] The works further followed the internationally influential demands made by Marcuse in 1969, that art "lose its privileged and segregated dominion over the imagination" and perform the "material and intellectual reconstruction of society, creating the new aesthetic environment."[27]

From the outset, KÔD wanted to make art "an integral part of life" and to free "art of all the functions ascribed to it, starting from the educational and cognitive functions to the religious and ideological ones."[28] Just as artists working through

Zagreb's SC Gallery were intent on fostering an art that "communicated with the people," KÔD set its sights on the hierarchical nature of Yugoslavia's art scene, which the group's members perceived as catering to a limited audience. In the essay "Galleries," published in *Index*, Miroslav Mandić targeted the conventional functioning of an art gallery, which was frequently used as a "cultural representative for the policy of a given state apparatus."[29] In opposition to the politically submissive role of galleries, KÔD began to produce work that could escape the art system's self-imposed isolation. Audience participation was the only factor that could liberate the gallery from total fetishization: a gallery would become a "stable in which we [the public] will create the gallery space ... so that it become[s] a part of us, of our perceptive consciousness [and so that] we are no longer integrated into it as 'passive consumer.'"[30]

KÔD's ambition to create an art that communicated with the public was first realized in their *Javni čas umetnosti* [Public Art Class]: an event held on the quays by the banks of the river Danube on 18 October 1970, in which Goran Trbuljak also participated. During the so-called class, Tišma traced the outline of his shadow with white paint on the surface of the concrete slabs set by the edge of the river, while Miroslav Mandić began a series of tautological works, including the huge letters *T-R-A-V-A* [Grass], printed on a colorless celluloid and placed on the lawn, and the polystyrene letters *D-U-N-A-V* [Danube] thrown into the waters of the river. Bogdanović and Radojičić carried out works titled *Apotheosis to Jackson Pollock*, by pouring durlin-enamel lacquer onto the ground, and placing paper on top to obtain an image from the asphalt's rough and irregular surface. As implied by the action's title, it produced an indexical image from paint splattered on the surface of tarmac which became an ironic idolization of Jackson Pollock's drip paintings. If Pollock's paintings were, according to American art critic Harold Rosenberg, not a picture "but a gesture of liberation, from Value—political, aesthetic, moral," Bogdanović's and Radojičić's action sought to undermine the concept of art as a self-satisfying, hedonistic action whereupon artists realized themselves.[31] Here the "drip paintings" weren't being produced by the artist's hand, but as a result of the random and unpredictable patterns and marks made on the asphalt's surface.

As a "class" that invited participation, the action paralleled the social goals that George Maciunas had established for the Fluxus movement. Writing in 1964, Maciunas explained that Fluxus was fueled by "a step by step elimination of the Fine Arts," and a desire to "redirect the use of materials and human ability into socially constructive purposes."[32] For this reason, Fluxus was against "art as a medium for the artist's ego," and opted instead for the "spirit of the collective, ... anonymity,

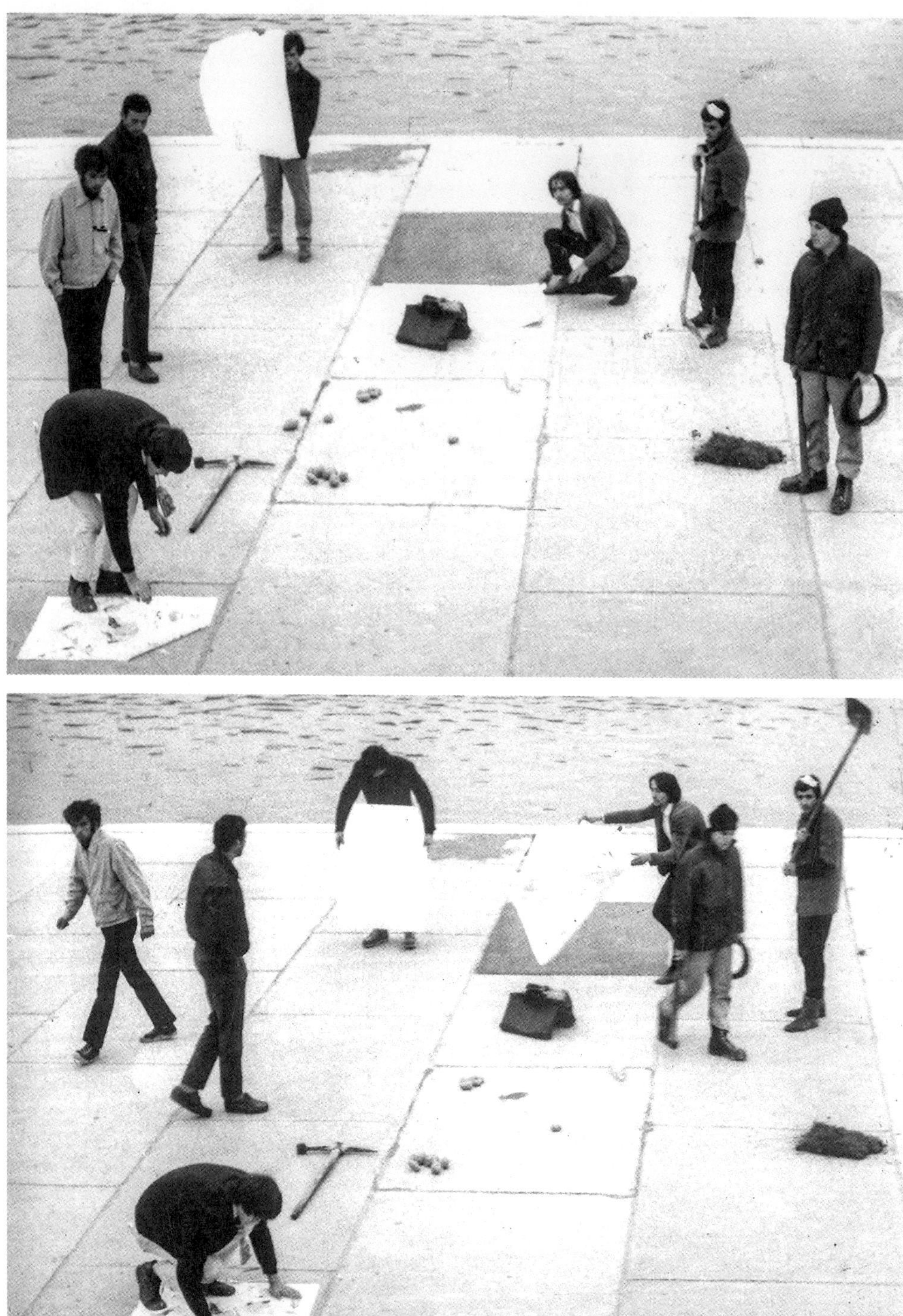

and anti-individualism."[33] Seeking to free creativity from its confinement within the "artistic" field, Fluxus declared that creativity was inherent to all human activity. The impersonality of collective organization, seen by Maciunas as a means of abolishing the barriers between the "artistic" and "non-artistic," permeated all of KÔD's activities. It was further invoked in Slavko Bogdanović's hand-written thesis of 1970: *ART (TODAY); ARTIST (CREATOR); PARTICIPANT (AUTHOR)*, which stressed the importance of the New Art Practice's opening up to the viewer—seeking to convert the viewer into participant with "a readiness to not only finalize the artist's idea, but to actually expand, add, change, perfect it."[34]

2.9. Grupa KÔD, with Goran Trbuljak, Božidar Mandić, and Vladimir Mandić, *Javni čas umetnosti* [Public Art Class], Danube Quay in Novi Sad, 18 October 1970. Image taken from Slavko Bogdanović, *Inventar Discernacije* (Belgrade: Orion Art, 2018), 214, with the permission of Slavko Bogdanović.

2.10. Grupa KÔD, with Goran Trbuljak, Božidar Mandić, and Vladimir Mandić, *Javni čas umetnosti* [Public Art Class], Danube Quay in Novi Sad, 18 October 1970.

From left to right: Two active participants from the general public moving between Miroslav Mandić and Slavko Bogdanović; Slavko Bogdanović making a print from colors poured onto the concrete pavement (*Apotheosis to Jackson Pollock*); Miroslav Mandić holding up a sheet of white paper; Mirko Radojičić spreading a sheet of white paper; Božidar Mandić holding a bunch of metal wire, and Vladimir Mandić with a shovel. Image taken from Slavko Bogdanović, *Inventar Discernacije* (Belgrade: Orion Art, 2018), 214, with the permission of Slavko Bogdanović.

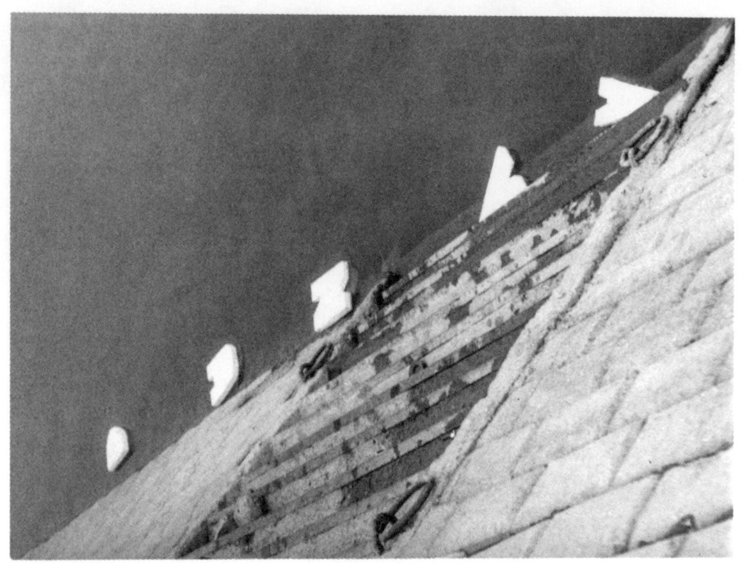

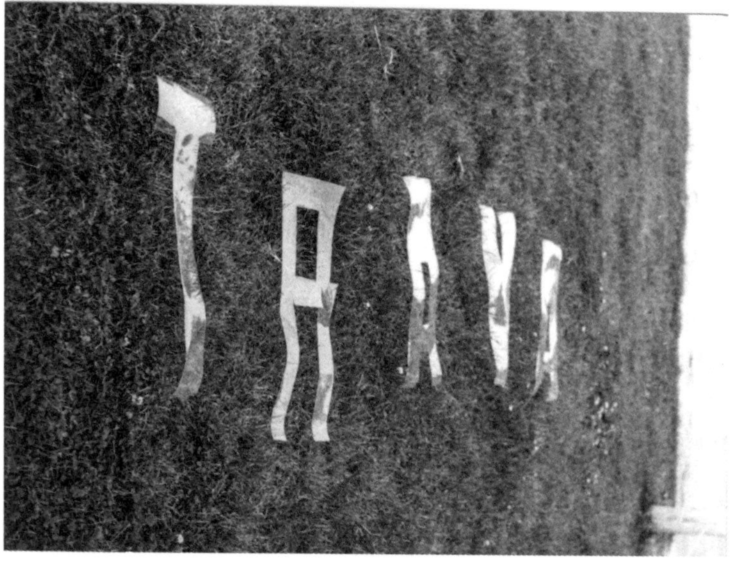

2.11. Miroslav Mandić, Grupa KÔD, *Trava; Dunav* [Grass; Danube], part of *Javni čas umetnosti* [Public Art Class], Danube Quay in Novi Sad, 18 October 1970. Image courtesy of Slavko Bogdanović.

JANUARY'S MESSAGES OF INSOLENCE

Throughout KÔD's brief but critical history, their work represented a form of engagement aimed not at politicization but rather at the "democratization" of art. The most significant part of their activities pivoted on reducing the importance of authorship, as a way to undermine what they perceived as the generally uncritical and unreflective distribution of art in Novi Sad. Acting as a counterpoint to a complacent "art system," KÔD was beginning to highlight the inert functioning of cultural consumption in Yugoslavia. The fervor with which its members carried out work at *Index* came to an abrupt halt with their dismissal, as a result of long-lasting tensions between Vojvodina's Association of Students and the city's Communist Alliance. As happened with the SC Gallery's activities, this was a clear confrontation between a new generation of free-thinking and progressive cultural workers and local state organizations.[35] The last issue of *Index* to be edited by the group members was published on 29 November 1970; the conservative new staff who replaced them did not favor experimental art practices.[36] According to Želimir Žilnik—Novi Sad's celebrated filmmaker and previous editor-in-chief of the Tribune—the disbanding and replacement of the staff at this time was enforced because the local party organizations "knew what the power of the magazine was: though *Index* was a student newspaper, it was well edited in its time, and was pointing out anomalies in politics and offering alternatives, which resulted in the banning of several issues."[37]

At the same time, the Youth Tribune had come into conflict with the municipal sociopolitical organizations of Novi Sad, which had little understanding of its programs and frequently complained that the Tribune did not "fulfil the interests of a wide circle of youth … and, especially recently, insists too much on the so-called avant-garde currents, experiments neglecting the affirmative majority."[38] An essay published in *Index* entitled "What Will Become of the Youth Tribune?" reported on the conflicting interests that existed in the management of the institution.[39] A month earlier, a local paper had declared that the founders of the Tribune, the Municipal Youth League, were intending to take the institution and its editorial boards under its patronage to ensure that its basic function remain "education and discipline."[40] This newspaper report was the first that the Tribune's editorial team had heard of this plan. Though such stringent action had yet to be taken on the programmatic orientation of the Tribune, it marked the beginning of interventions by local sociopolitical leagues.[41]

In certain respects, the infringement that was implemented at the editorial office of *Index* and eventually at the Youth Tribune resembled political tendencies that Yugoslavia's earliest critics had begun to voice in the 1950s.[42] Already in 1957, Milovan Đilas, Yugoslavia's most famous dissident and leader of Agitation and Propaganda for the League of Communists of Yugoslavia (LCY) until his expulsion in 1954, observed in his book *The New Class: An Analysis of the Communist System* that the party bureaucracy had effectively become the "new ruling class" in the Soviet Union and other socialist states, including his native Yugoslavia.[43] In Yugoslavia's case, while the LCY had proclaimed that the creation of an "association of direct producers" was to lead to the "withering away of the state" in the near future, self-management had continued to exist at the base under the control of strong statism at all higher levels of social organization. In its 1958 *Program*, the LCY even emphasized that to be "in the interest" of the majority does not necessarily mean "to be supported by [that] same majority."[44] For this reason, the LCY argued, a vanguard was needed to educate the masses to "think and act in a socialist manner until the very last citizen has learned to manage the affairs of the community."[45] In Novi Sad, the experimental practices that occurred through the cooperation of *Index* and the editorial organizations of the Youth Tribune seemed to be tempered in their agency through their institutionalized status. The local administrations prevailed and oversaw events, just as Đilas had argued in 1957: "authority [continued to be] the basic aim and means of Communism and every true Communist. The thirst for power [was] insatiable and irresistible.... Careerism, extravagance, and love of power [were] inevitable, and so [was] corruption."[46]

Of course, more than a decade had passed since Đilas first made his damning indictment, and by 1970 the organization and operation of Yugoslavia's political system had changed dramatically. During the 1960s, Yugoslav politics had become, as discussed in the previous chapter, completely dominated by attempts to introduce economic reforms into the federal system. But though the new socioeconomic system emerged out of a reform that formally conceptualized a combination of market socialism and a self-managed economy, the political outcome was "republican particularism." Questions about the position and status of various national groups rapidly began to overshadow Yugoslavia's political life, which in turn began to reignite national grievances. In the multinational province of Vojvodina itself, a conflict between Serbian and Croatian nationalists was being stoked by two cultural institutions—the Matica Hrvatska and Matica Srpska—while Serbian nationalist groups became very active at Novi Sad's university.[47] By the end of 1970, the inability of the government to overcome interrepublican conflicts had led Tito to declare the need for authoritative measures. During a speech delivered in Priština in November 1970, the president delivered a warning to the leaderships of all republics, and announced that the time had come for action to end conflicts impeding the functioning of the party and the government. He warned:

> I never was a supporter of such liberalism.... We decisively approached those who did not stand on the line of the Party and who did not support its decisions. We have to act that way today, too, without regard [for the fact] that such a broad democratization of our life has come to pass. Because even under conditions of democracy there must exist some factor which regulates relations in society.[48]

In Priština, Tito made clear the urgency of the situation and the necessity of a strong and firm response to uncontrolled liberalization. "Administrative measures" were once again needed to overcome the rise of interregional conflicts and economic nationalisms, and to restore central authority in the party, much like those noted by Đilas at the end of the 1950s.[49] KÔD's dismissal from *Index* happened in the same month that Tito made his exceptionally direct warning. In Novi Sad, it would seem that efforts to reimpose control (or, as Tito put it, "regulate relations in society") were already well under way, as the Youth League embarked on revoking the Youth Tribune's right to self-managing autonomy.

As a platform that was able to reach wider audiences, in its most critical period *Index* represented an important channel for KÔD's experimental activities. After their dismissal from *Index*, the only locus that remained open to those in pursuit of experimental art practices was the Youth Tribune itself, and its small visual arts space—the "parquet salon"—despite the fact that its "programs continued to be conceived in a traditional way."[50] Joining forces with other marginalized members of Novi Sad's cultural scene, under the leadership of Vujica Rešin Tučić—an experimental writer and the editor-in-chief of *Polja* from 1967 to 1971—KÔD's members participated in a collective whose name would be changed every month after that particular month. Working together represented a combination of efforts to create a space for their artistic activities, of which they had all been deprived.[51]

The January Group first appeared together at the Youth Tribune on 21 January 1971, in an action documented in the Tribune's diary as the "Work Day of the January Group," between noon and 9 pm.[52] During the event, former KÔD members investigated issues that had prevailed in their earlier practice. Bogdanović nailed several books together and exhibited them, to produce art out of matter, where the book was no longer a text to be read but an immediate presence. Tišma made a legend of signs from a geographical atlas on a wall, while on the floor

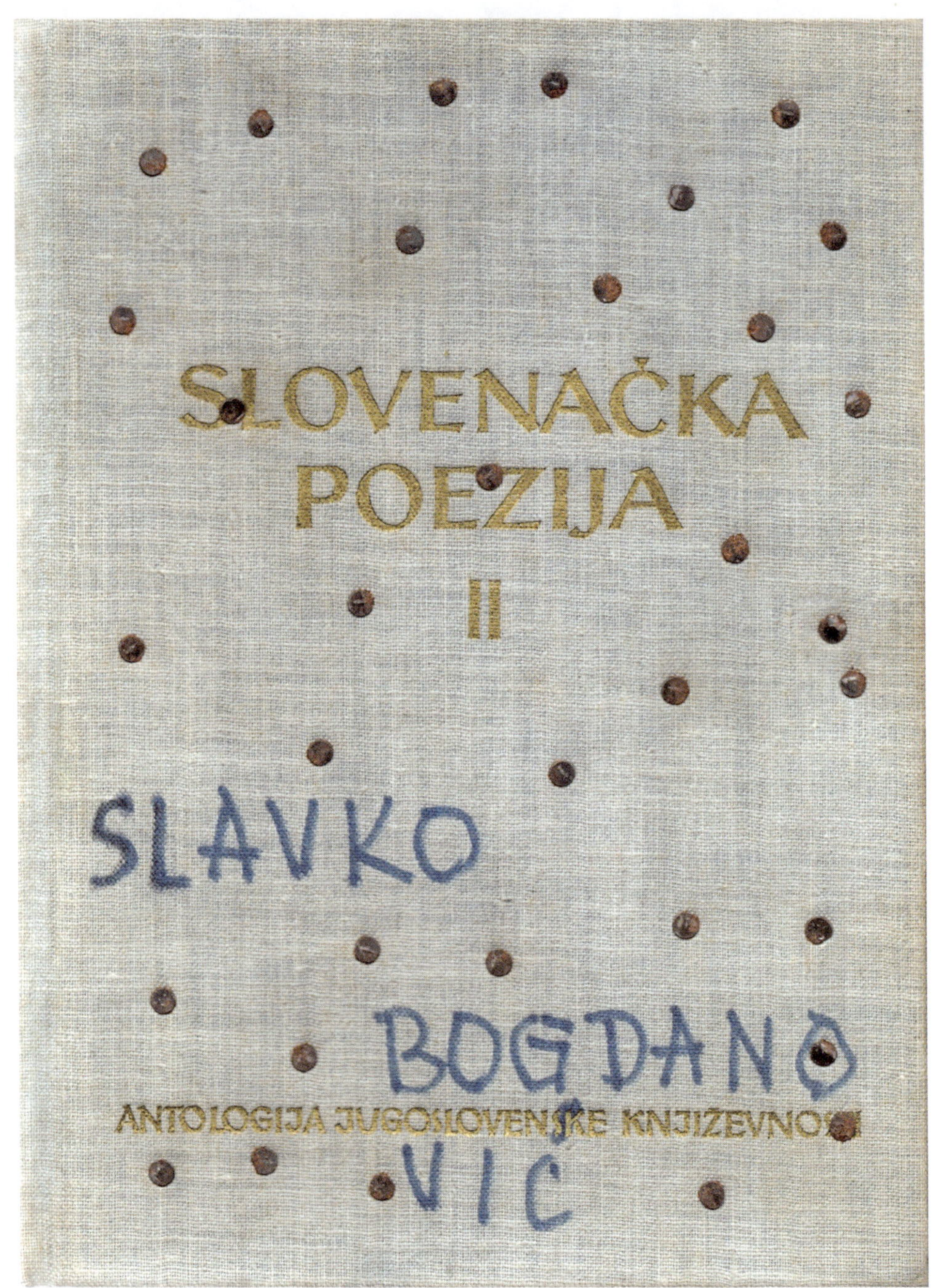
SLOVENAČKA
POEZIJA
II
SLAVKO
BOGDANO
ANTOLOGIJA JUGOSLOVENSKE KNJIŽEVNOSTI
VIĆ

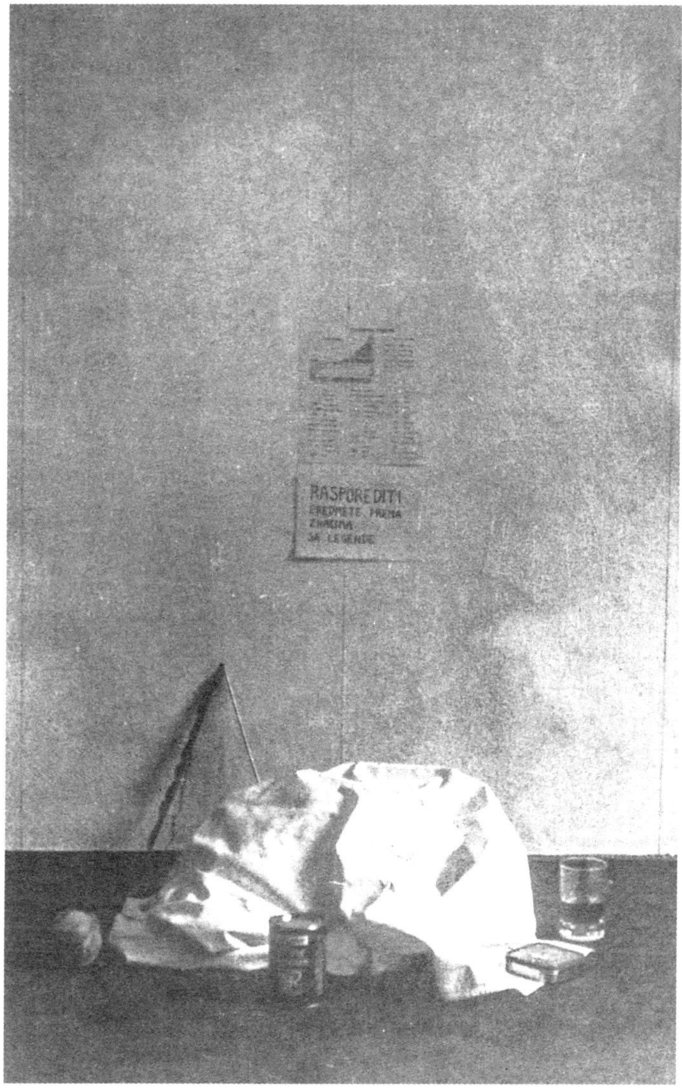

2.12. Slavko Bogdanović, *Zakovana knjiga* [The Riveted Book], 1971. Image courtesy of Slavko Bogdanović.

2.13. Slobodan Tišma, *Rasporedite predmete prema priloženoj legendi* [Arrange the Subjects According to the Signs of the Legend], 1971. Image courtesy of Slavko Bogdanović and Muzej Savremene Umetnosti Vojvodine.

he put a crumpled white canvas along with other objects. In an accompanying text he stipulated that the objects should be arranged according to the legend—another play on the index, disrupting the autonomy of the sign.[53] Yet these more "objective" pieces were overshadowed by the most controversial work shown—a poster featuring a real ten-dinar note, inscribed with the caption "How we are," beneath which were featured numerous swear words, paired with their authors' signatures. These words of a "ludic-political" nature were hastily interpreted by local citizens as qualifications "directed against our society and system"—"false avant-gardism," calling for "opposition to the politics of the Communist Party."[54] A week later, a newspaper referred to the heterogeneous January Group display exclusively as the "exhibition of swear words," and reported that it had brought into question the continued existence of the Youth Tribune.[55] Apparently this gesture had provoked one group of Novi Sad's workers to complain to the Municipal Committee for Culture, and demand that the space, due to its "open-mindedness, have its funds cut."[56] When asked whether this exhibited ten-dinar note would be the last social dinar paid into the account of the Tribune, Dragan Kosanović, the secretary for the Municipal Committee for Culture, responded that the committee would refuse to continue funding activities of a "sensationalist character," including "improvised and unprepared programs of suspicious ideological worth."[57]

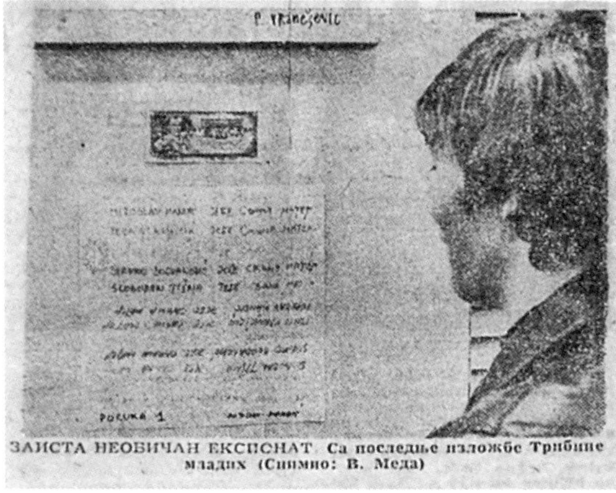

2.14. January Group, *Kako smo* [How We Are], photograph from *Novosti* (Belgrade), 30 January 1971. Image courtesy of Slavko Bogdanović and Matica Srpska Library Novi Sad, Serbia.

Triggering a threat of the potential liquidation of the Tribune, these "antisocial" four-letter expletives had penetrated a deeper taboo in Yugoslav society. Writing for Zagreb's *Studentski list* [Student Paper], Hrvoje Turković recognized that this gesture had happily "coincided with the day of an announced devaluation of the new dinar."[58] By appropriating a symbol of the Yugoslav economy, the action had intersected with real social concerns—real economic conditions. The new dinar had been introduced in 1965 through the broad economic reform that resulted in the increased liberalization of self-management. Never very stable, and suffering from an inflation rate of 15 to 25 percent per year, this currency emblematized the beginning of self-management's transformation into an increasingly profit-oriented system, which had replaced "egalitarian criteria" with "economic rationality."[59] Its general instability embodied the behavior of a new technocratic class of local functionaries and regional political elites, which had temporarily supplanted the old, centralized federal authority in matters regarding the control over investment and the accumulation of capital. The fighting of these new economic elites and political leaders to enhance their power over central policies was the key catalyst reigniting Yugoslavia's "national question." Though seemingly irreverent in both its means and content, the January Group's gesture encapsulated the many contradictions that emerged from socialist modernization after market reform, including the worsening of power relations within socialist firms and organizations. Charged with containing "antisocialist ideas," their simple gesture had awakened the insufficient or even nonexistent participation of the broad masses in political life.[60] It raised accusations of which the LCY were themselves guilty, including "false avant-gardism" and "suspicious ideologies and distorted values."

Praxis author Rade Bojanović pointed out that intellectuals in socialist countries were frequently condemned for the very deviations they were fighting against. He observed: "out of the desire to dominate and idealize their personalities, bureaucrats try to represent all the prevailing principles of society in all its institutions and finally even society itself."[61] In Novi Sad, the January Group's "farce" had reflected unfavorably on political realities, showing that "Stalinism and its methods of disqualification" remained in the form of "ideological-social purges."[62] At the beginning of the 1970s, "purges" had in fact returned to Yugoslavia's political life. At the Congress of Self-Managers in Sarajevo in 1971, Tito candidly announced that those who did not conform to the actions of leadership would be forcibly removed from their positions. Responding to press reports from abroad that claimed he had made similar threats before but that this was "all an empty gun in the past," he reassured his audience that this time "it will not be an empty gun, we have plenty of ammunition ... we will know how to stop people who confuse us and disrupt our socialist development."[63] In the case of the Youth Tribune, the implications of this threat of violence would come to light after a series of artistic provocations in the following months.

THE FEBRUARY GROUP'S "OPEN LETTER TO THE YUGOSLAV PUBLIC"

Condemned in Novi Sad, the Youth Tribune collaborators were forced to seek a new audience, and organized another political happening at Belgrade's Dom Omladine [Youth House]. On 9 February 1971, between 5 pm and midnight, the group "for new art, February from Novi Sad" invited the public to a "Taster of the New Art," consisting of "verse, painting, songs, plays and film projections." The display included some twenty panels of KÔD's conceptual works, on which documentation is sparse. Yet again the most memorable aspects of the evening rested in the open attacks on Novi Sad's cultural and political establishments—forcing the public to "demonstratively abandon the hall," and creating negative feedback from the media. According to press reports, the public and the organizer of the event had been brazenly deceived: under the guise of "new," "conceptual," "poor," or "neuro-art," as publicized by the event's program, the February Group carried out an open political demonstration against the "Party management of Vojvodina and against one leading politician of that Province."[64] Reporting on this "fault at the Youth House," a member of the then-current editorial board of the Tribune, Miroslav Antić, claimed that this disgrace had "blackened, spat [on], and spoiled the culture of [Novi Sad], and there was no epilogue in sight. Novi Sad remains silent."[65] Pero Zubac, editor of *Polja*, further added that the events left a "bitter taste, like mud had been stuffed in [his] mouth."[66]

These two members of the Youth Tribune's new editorial team had clearly denigrated what they understood as "acts of political reckoning."[67] Yet, having been mentioned by Antić as one of the witnesses who "ran away from the disgrace of the Youth House in Belgrade," Želimir Žilnik offered his thoughts on the implications of this "tastelessness and insolence."[68] Žilnik had remained until the termination of the "taster," because he was bothered by "what was really the disgrace"—not that "young people write slogans, shout, play and swear," but rather the "shame that in the city where we ourselves live, there is a lot of truth in what the youth speak in agitation."[69] As he testified, the editorial team of *Polja* had been paralyzed in fear before its own staff and editors, so there was no way for the Youth Tribune to reach self-managing rights, and most disturbingly, "young people [were] being manipulated by various forums and being cheated."[70]

Though there remain only a few photographs of the event, all of which barely testify to the levels of destruction mentioned in official press statements, one detail was frequently observed in the news accounts. Throughout the course of the night, the group proclaimed the slogan, "We love the Russians, the Russians love us, the Russians will save us."[71] Certainly it was a proclamation that in itself would have caused severe contention, considering Yugoslavia's complex and often strained relationship with the Soviet Union.[72] The USSR had provided a constant threat to Yugoslavia's independence, especially following the Warsaw Pact invasion of Czechoslovakia in August 1968. Because the Soviet justification for invading Czechoslovakia was founded on the premise that socialism in that country was at risk of collapse, it also carried a strong resonance in the context of Yugoslavia's growing national crisis. Responding to the rise in nationalism in Croatia in July 1971, for instance, Tito made clear that foreign countries were waiting to see "whether the process of disintegration would be halted," and he proposed that a failure to establish order could spark Soviet intervention.[73] No wonder, then, that one newspaper chose to refer to this specific feature of the "taster" as an "imbecilic song-melody."[74] Within the specific frame of events, this slogan carried a more subtle significance, being a reference to Karpo Godina's 1971 film *Zdravi ljudi za razonodu* [Healthy People for Fun], produced by Novi Sad's Neoplanta Film company.[75]

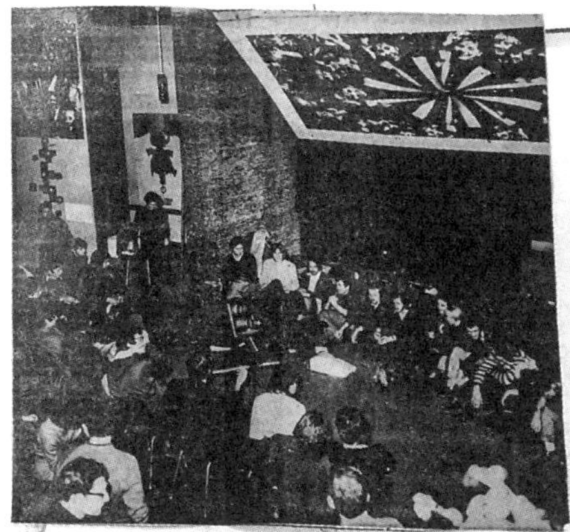

2.15. Grupa za Nove Umetnosti "Februar" [The February Group for New Art], *Zakusku novih umetnosti* [A Taster of New Art], Youth House, Belgrade, 9 February 1971, Photograph from *Vjesnik* (Zagreb), 2 March 1971. Image courtesy of Slavko Bogdanović and Matica Srpska Library, Novi Sad, Serbia.

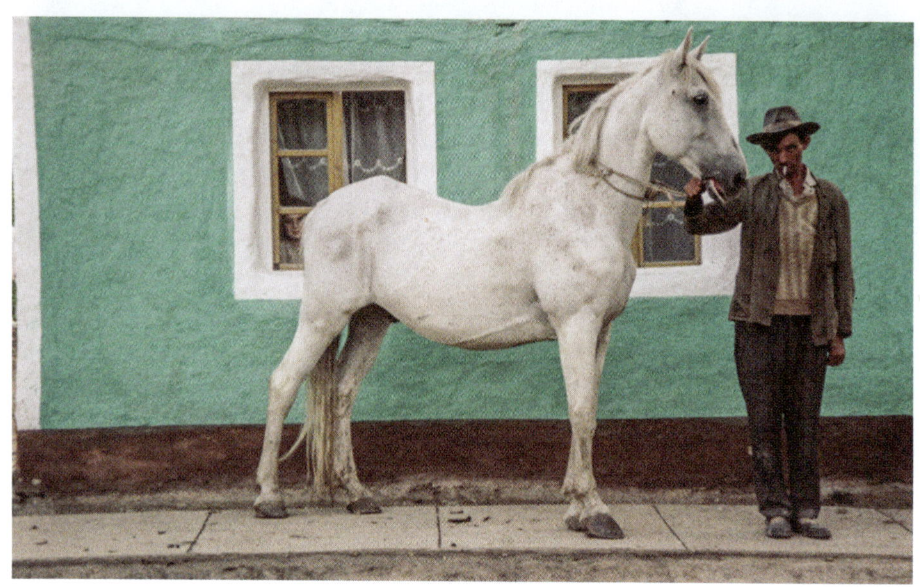

2.16. Still from Karpo Godina's *Zdravi ljudi za razonodu* [Healthy People for Fun], Neoplanta Film, Novi Sad, 1971. Image courtesy of Karpo Godina.

Healthy People for Fun depicted the multiethnic diversity of the Autonomous Province of Vojvodina by filming the harmonious coexistence of nations and ethnic groups. While the short film documented the tradition of each ethnic group painting the facades of their houses in the same color (Croats, red; Hungarians, green; Slovaks, blue), it did so through a playful and humorous approach, receiving acclaim from critics and winning a prize at its premiere at Belgrade's Documentary and Short Film Festival. The film's scenes were structured by announcements from the respective ethnic groups, followed by the repeated song lyrics, written by Predrag Vranešević, "we love the Russians / Croats / Hungarians / Slovaks / Gypsies" (finally concluding with the line "we love them all!"). Still, the film was soon withdrawn from public screening due to its potentially subversive elements, because the Film Review Commission was not clear whether Godina had remained dedicated to the concept of Brotherhood and Unity, Yugoslavia's founding ideological pillar, adopted during the National Liberation Struggle as a radical transformative moment that triumphed over all ethnic diversities. To the Film Review Commission, it was unclear whether the director had, through the film's emphatically simple message of harmonious coexistence, chosen to glorify or ridicule it. Not being "readable" enough, *Healthy People for Fun* was considered an attack on one of the key emblems of Yugoslav society, and consequently an attack on the state itself, and received almost immediate censorship. Perhaps this is not surprising, considering that at the time of the film's release, growing economic resentments were beginning to unsettle Brotherhood and Unity's founding premise of equality and peaceful coexistence among Yugoslavia's many nations and ethnicities.

The origin of the song that was chanted at the February Group's happening reveals the general motivation behind the event, which was directed not against "self-managing society" explicitly but rather at the cultural potential of Novi Sad, which had experienced a constant "arbitration of political organs and functionaries in art and culture."[76] The significance of the event was further clarified by the February Group in their "Open Letter to the Yugoslav Public," dated 12 February 1971. Addressing the public was a bold gesture; it represented a plea for protection from local political organs. The text spoke out about the situation surrounding the Youth Tribune and endeavored to clarify the events in Belgrade. Appealing to an "artistic language," it raised in advance its reservations about any political readings that could be extrapolated from the text. But despite this strategic and prophetic petition, it was taken as another object of political suspicion. Writing in the Croatian daily paper *Vjesnik*—in itself demonstrating how widespread news of Novi Sad had become—Sava Dautović used the letter to denounce, rather than illuminate, the events in Belgrade in order to ridicule the "young rebels," ending his article with words quoted from Mirko Čanadanović, secretary of the Provincial League of Communists in Vojvodina:

> There is a distorted understanding of cultural creativity and political activism. Freedom is, rightfully, understood as something which is given, provided, or inhibited from others, and not as a result of just creating—something which is given through real and consistent efforts. In the future there will be fewer of those who will credulously assign these public forums to these provocateurs, who have nothing to show other than their creative impotence and primitivism.[77]

The tone of Čanadanović's declaration reveals the kind of "repressive tolerance" that was being enacted at the Youth Tribune—identifying freedom as "something which is given," that is, a gift.[78] These "warnings" did not go unaddressed, however. Writing in Zagreb's *Tjedni list omladine* [Weekly Youth Newspaper], Zvonko Maković responded to these declarations in an essay titled "When Will the Pumpkins Blossom," in which he sought to retaliate against Dautović's mockery and Čanadanović's slogans, by complaining that the words of the letter had been distorted and taken out of the context in which they had been written, in order to be denigrated.[79] The essay's title referenced Dragoslav Mihailović's celebrated novel of 1968, *Kad su cvetale tikve* [When the Pumpkins Blossomed], which initially received popular and critical acclaim, and was reworked into a play, only to be banned after a few performances.[80]

When the Pumpkins Blossomed depicted the violent and crime-ridden milieu of Belgrade's suburbs through the story of one young hooligan, Ljuba Šampion, a boxing champion whose life is unsettled by the imprisonment of his father and brother as Cominformists (Yugoslav Communists who took Stalin's side in the 1948 break).[81] Written by a victim of Goli Otok (Mihailović had spent fifteen months of his early twenties in the concentration camp, and experienced subsequent years of exclusion and poverty), *When the Pumpkins Blossomed* was instantly suspicious because of its focus on a Cominformist family. The detail that led to the play's banning was a line in which Ljuba's father tells his son: "They are worse than the Germans." Comparing the Yugoslav Communists to Nazi occupiers even provoked the personal intervention of Tito himself. By referencing Mihailović's novel, Maković was alluding not only to another instance of the violation of freedom of speech, but also, by analogy, to the destructive effects and underside of the "Communist Revolution," which had arguably deprived Yugoslavia's postwar generation of an active political voice.

Did the "pumpkins" ever blossom at Novi Sad's Youth Tribune? Following the events of Belgrade and the "Open Letter," an article entitled "February Sentenced in March" announced that four Novi Sad Cultural Associations had sent a letter to the Municipal Cultural Committee with 1,200 signatures of high school and university students, distancing themselves from the activities of the Tribune.[82] The letter announced a "unanimous condemnation of the newest orientation of the group at the Youth Tribune," and demanded that the Municipal Cultural Committee and Municipal Youth League "take the necessary social measures to ensure the program of this youth cultural institution does not alienate the general living and cultural interests of workers, high school youth, and university students of our city."[83] Clearly, the Belgrade events were the final straw—having confronted the local state institutions so directly, the February Group's actions had entered the sphere of broad public knowledge.

Why did the February Group's appeals to the public, which they sought to engage from the outset, go unheard to the extent that their dismissal was even demanded? The public's hostility can partially be explained by the disinformation that was filtering through media outlets, which portrayed the serious, purposeful endeavors of the Tribune as "self-serving," with members of February accused of attempting to seek "monopolization," in collaboration with Šalgo, who was "interfering with the view of this youth institution" and "bringing it to a critical situation, [provoking an] intervention from the side of the Youth League."[84] The youth of Novi Sad were being manipulated by various official organs, most notably the Municipal Communist Youth League. Their authority continued to be maintained through what *Praxis* author Ivan Kuvačić described as forms of "voluntary obedience," upheld by the "press editor replacing the role of the gendarme or jailer."[85] Once the Youth League had defined its values, adhering to the LCY leadership, it ensured these norms were to be followed.

Initially granted "self-managing autonomy" from its founder, the Youth Council of Vojvodina, the Youth Tribune had now become completely subordinated to its interests. On 17 October 1971, a local paper announced that "Novi Sad [Is] Waiting for a Director": "faced with the extreme activities of the Tribune, the Youth League of Vojvodina was forced to interrupt [them, and so] a new program and new council will be constructed."[86] In the same year, the city's Neoplanta Film Company had also come into conflict with the Executive Committee of the Province of Vojvodina. The production house was accused of not "fulfilling its social mission," and of digressing from its "obligation of working with young amateurs and providing cinematic experiences for ordinary people."[87] In spite of being successfully "self-managed"—largely self-reliant and operating on little state subsidy—Neoplanta became one of the first production houses to be accused of not abiding by the principles of socialist self-management. In March 1972, the studio's director, Svetozar Udovički, was dismissed from his position by the Provincial Executive Committee, and replaced with a diligent "communist," Draško Ređep. A few months later, those previously working at the Youth Tribune would face a similar plight, as local youth organizations continued to campaign against those who refused to adhere to the party line.

GOING "UNDERGROUND"

With the Youth Tribune now closed to the city's experimental artists, Bogdanović and Mandić began to seek different channels through which to engage in their activities. In May 1971, they formulated a proposal for a magazine to be called "L.H.O.O.Q." which was to be committed to the "development of interpersonal relations."[88] Alluding to Duchamp's *L.H.O.O.Q.*, a "correction" or "restoration" of *La Gioconda* (the *Mona Lisa*), the magazine was to appear only as a part of "other official reviews," mainly for logistical reasons, as it was impossible for the artists to publish independently.[89] It first appeared in the May 1971 issue of the Youth Tribune's *Új Symposion*—which, thanks to the support of the magazine's editor, Ottó Tolnai, was the only journal that remained accessible to them—as a proposal requesting the Yugoslav public and institutions to approve funds and normalize the work of the proposed journal.[90] This first issue contained texts that dealt with its theorization alone, indicating its political requirements and structural underpinnings, and above all emphasizing that "the editorial board which wishes to print a number of *L.H.O.O.Q.* can't condition the terms of printing, eject some texts or correct ideas, inasmuch as they are significant for that number or the general orientation and profile of *L.H.O.O.Q.*"[91]

Again, this project represented an attempt to overcome institutional intervention and to enable "progressive thinking and freedom of creation."[92] While the first issue of *L.H.O.O.Q.* appeared in *Új Symposion*, the other twelve were hand-typed and produced in limited print runs of one to four copies. It appeared six times subtitled as a "paper for the permanent destruction of everything existing"; three times as an "underground paper for developing interpersonal relations"; and three times as an "underground paper for [a] new revolution."[93] Already apparent in these titles is a kind of opposition, in the sense of George Schöpflin's oft-cited definition as a readiness "to establish organizations which reject the leading role of the party to create information networks."[94] The magazine's oppositional nature was further conveyed through its rebellious content—one issue, for instance, included Bogdanović's *Stripa o grupi KÔD* [Comic about the Group KÔD], where among other symbols he appropriated the semantically charged sign of the swastika, clockwise and counterclockwise, to present the history of the group, posing a polemical question toward public values. Other issues included political-ludic texts, such as "Drugs and Revolution: Junkies of All Countries, Unite!," which adopted the form of party revolutionary speech to discuss drugs, another highly taboo topic of discussion in socialist society.[95] Nomadically tying together the seemingly incompatible—irony, paradox, provocation, rebellion, revolution—the text even directly insulted what it described as the "radical extremists" of Serbia.[96]

L.H.O.O.Q.'s ultimate aim was to breach the information monopoly of the city's municipal leagues. But the journal's existence came to an inevitably premature halt after the publication of Miroslav Mandić's "Song on Film: Sonnet or Fourteen Stanzas," originally featured in the final issue of the "Underground Paper for [a] New Revolution" and reprinted in the *Új Symposion* of September 1971.[97] Written in defense of Dušan Makavejev's film *WR: misterije organizma* [Mysteries of the Organism], the text also included a discussion on the creation of films based on the National Liberation Struggle, and, most provocatively, a "script for Josip Broz Tito," which simply read: "to capture Josip Broz Tito, in color, in one shot, which lasts two hours. The camera is static. Along with the inscription 'The End,' the announcer says 'it was Josip Broz Tito.'"[98] Despite the text's seemingly inert critical position toward the president, Tito's cult of personality remained an untouchable topic. No matter how innocent the comments might have been, confronting Tito represented a breach—and as a result, Mandić was held in court. Within a week of the publication's dissemination, the Serbian national newspaper *Novosti* commented:

> Miroslav Mandić seriously offends our nation, state, and the President of the Republic … through various comparisons of an offensive, ironic, and distasteful nature (executed in his words through a "clearly defined aesthetic-ethical stance"). The author argues that the relation between "Yugoslav film and Yugoslav society is very bad," and specifically attacks the figure of the President of the Republic, Josip Broz Tito, with an apparent intent to degrade his personality as much as possible, to insult and represent our society in a wicked light, and turn the Yugoslav community into a mockery.[99]

Distorted as "antisocialist excesses and vulgarisms," Mandić's words further resulted in the temporary closure of *Új Symposion* by the Youth League, which had already been "confronted with similar tendencies of exhibitionistic expression at the Youth Tribune through the January and February Groups."[100] But they had not fully succeeded in eradicating these "unacceptable tendencies," as the latter

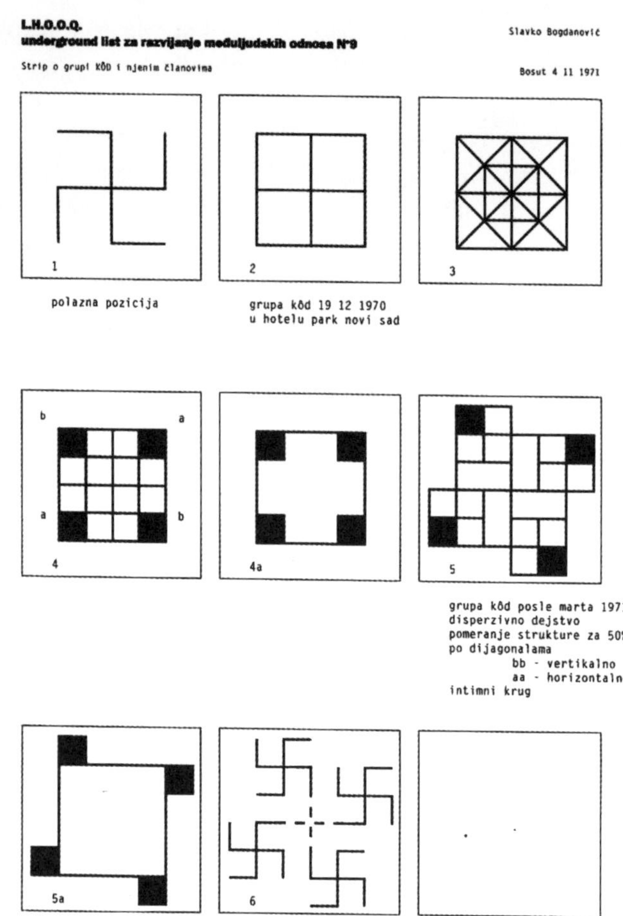

2.17. Slavko Bogdanović, *Stripa o grupi KÔD* [Comic about the Group KÔD], *L.H.O.O.Q.: Underground Paper for the Development of Interpersonal Relations*, no. 9, Bosut, 4 November 1971. Image courtesy of Slavko Bogdanović.

continued their destructive activity through the pages of *Új Symposion.*[101] This time the district attorney's office of Novi Sad intervened—the banning came after Čanadanović, secretary to the Provincial League of Communists in Vojvodina, demanded the Serbian original copy from the editorial staff. The original objective of Mandić's text was to compel the party to undertake a dialogue with society. Breaching the information monopoly of the city's Youth League, by attacking Tito's iconic status as Partisan and lifelong president his text insisted that the state abide by its own formal legality—"direct democracy"—which, of course, would have undermined the system completely. As a result, he received a nine-month prison sentence, and was banned from further publishing until 1984.[102]

L.H.O.O.Q. was forced to continue its activities deep underground, "restricted to independent acts of defiance or disagreement."[103] Outside these intimate projects, Bogdanović began to criticize the unfavorable cultural conditions in Novi Sad, including through a letter to Jaša Zlobec, a Slovenian intellectual and the editor of the city's student magazine *Tribuna*, who had participated in a discussion at the Youth Tribune in January 1971. Initially intended for publication, the letter was withdrawn by the author at the last moment. In this letter, Bogdanović addressed Zlobec's suggestion of the "possibility of acting through the party in forming some oppositional force," by noting the regional differences in political climates.[104] In Ljubljana, working within institutional frames appeared a "real and acceptable exit," since it seemed the "Slovene Party left more space for free breath"; in Novi Sad, however, "arguments were [exclusively] handled through force ... and any kind of divergence resulted in a purge."[105]

These practices that dominated Novi Sad, and "South of the Sava (except Belgrade)," can more generally be explained by the reaffirmation of party control over society, following the Croatian Mass Movement in the spring of 1971.[106] In Vojvodina itself, the reassertion of central authority similarly entailed the removal of all those "who came into conflict with the revolution, revolutionary practice and the line of the LCY."[107] As in Zagreb and Belgrade, the Tito-led coalition conducted a struggle against certain currents of "anarcho-liberalism and opportunism [with] fractionalism" in the League of Communists of Vojvodina. After six weeks of political struggle, the central leadership successfully mobilized veterans and other sociopolitical organizations in the province to demand the resignation of the president and secretary of the Provincial Party Committee, until they had sufficient support to force them out at a meeting in December 1972.[108] No wonder, then, that Bogdanović's letter specifically referenced the fact that Čanadanović,

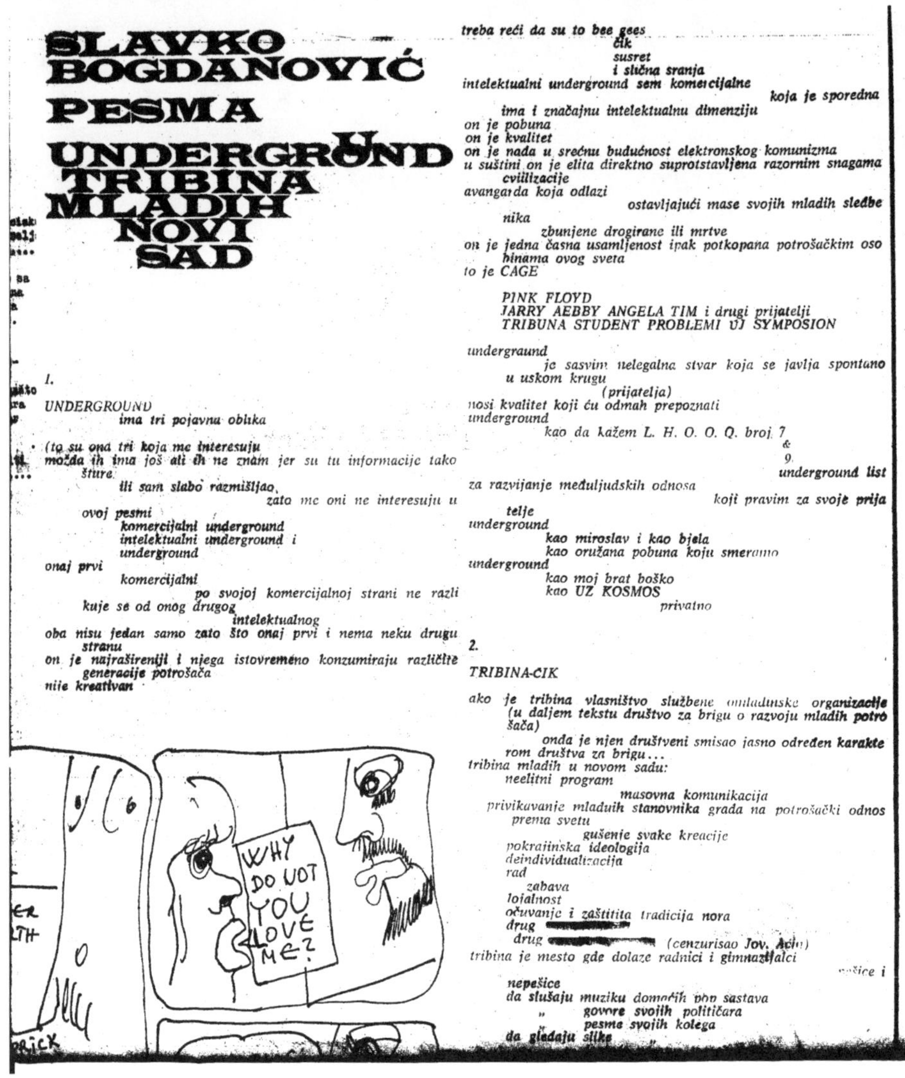

SLAVKO BOGDANOVIĆ

PESMA

UNDERGROUND

TRIBINA MLADIH NOVI SAD

1.

UNDERGROUND
ima tri pojavna oblika

(to su ona tri koja me interesuju
možda ih ima još ali ih ne znam jer su tu informacije tako
šture
ili sam slabo razmišljao,
zato me oni ne interesuju u
ovoj pesmi
komercijalni underground
intelektualni underground i
underground
onaj prvi
komercijalni
po svojoj komercijalnoj strani ne razli
kuje se od onog drugog
intelektualnog
oba nisu jedan samo zato što onaj prvi i nema neku drugu
stranu
on je najrašireniji i njega istovremeno konzumiraju različite
generacije potrošača
nije kreativan

treba reći da su to bee gees
čik
susret
i slična sranja
intelektualni underground sem komercijalne
koja je sporedna
ima i značajnu intelektualnu dimenziju
on je pobuna
on je kvalitet
on je nada u srećnu budućnost elektronskog komunizma
u suštini on je elita direktno suprotstavljena razornim snagama
cviilizacije
avangarda koja odlazi
ostavljajući mase svojih mladih sledbe
nika
zbunjene drogirane ili mrtve
on je jedna časna usamljenost ipak potkopana potrošačkim oso
binama ovog sveta
to je CAGE

PINK FLOYD
JARRY AEBBY ANGELA TIM i drugi prijatelji
TRIBUNA STUDENT PROBLEMI UJ SYMPOSION

undergraund
je sasvim nelegalna stvar koja se javlja spontano
u uskom krugu
(prijatelja)
nosi kvalitet koji ću odmah prepoznati
underground
kao da kažem L. H. O. O. Q. broj 7
&
9.
underground list
za razvijanje međuljudskih odnosa
koji pravim za svoje prija
telje
underground
kao miroslav i kao bjela
kao oružana pobuna koju smeramo
underground
kao moj brat boško
kao UZ KOSMOS
privatno

2.

TRIBINA-CIK

ako je tribina vlasništvo službene omladinske organizacije
(u daljem tekstu društvo za brigu o razvoju mladih potro
šača)
onda je njen društveni smisao jasno određen karakte
rom društva za brigu...
tribina mladih u novom sadu:
neelitni program
masovna komunikacija
privikavanje mladuih stanovnika grada na potrošački odnos
prema svetu
gušenje svake kreacije
pokrajinska ideologija
deindividualizacija
rad
zabava
lojalnost
očuvanje i zaštitita tradicija nora
drug [censored]
drug [censored] (cenzurisao Jov. Acin)
tribina je mesto gde dolaze radnici i gimnazijalci
pešice i
nepešice
da slušaju muziku domaćih pop sastava
" govore svojih političara
" pesme svojih kolega
da gledaju slike "

2.18. Slavko Bogdanović, "Pesma underground tribina mladih Novi Sad" [Underground Song for the Youth Tribune, Novi Sad], *Student*'s "Underground" issue, Belgrade, 16 December 1971. Image courtesy of Slavko Bogdanović.

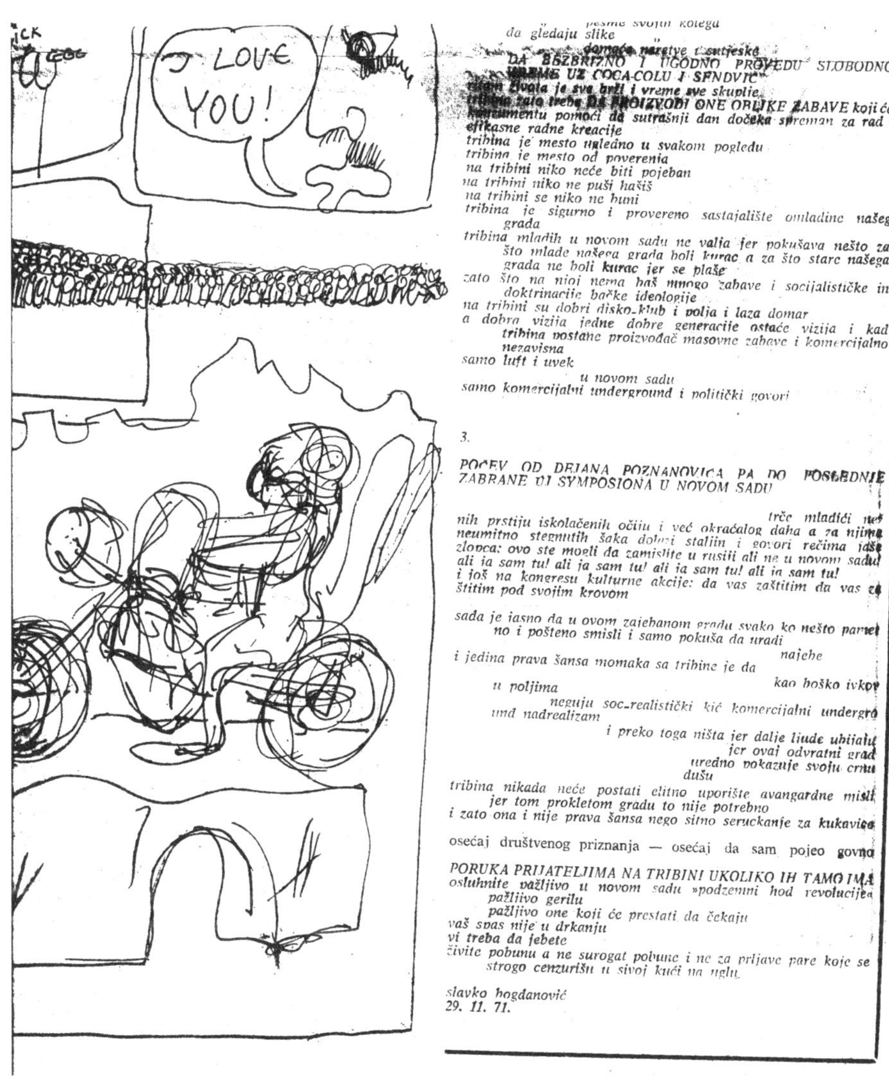

pesme svojih kolega
da gledaju slike
domaće naretve i sutjeske
„DA BEZBRIZNO I UGODNO PROVEDU SLOBODNO VREME UZ COCA-COLU I SENDVIČ"
[illegible] života je sve brži i vreme sve skuplje
tribina zato treba DA PROIZVODI ONE OBLIKE ZABAVE koji će ...mentu pomoći da sutrašnji dan dočeka spreman za rad i efikasne radne kreacije
tribina je mesto ugledno u svakom pogledu
tribina je mesto od poverenja
na tribini niko neće biti pojeban
na tribini niko ne puši hašiš
na tribini se niko ne buni
tribina je sigurno i provereno sastajalište omladine našeg grada
tribina mladih u novom sadu ne valja jer pokušava nešto za što mlade našega grada boli kurac a za što stare našega grada ne boli kurac jer se plaše
zato što na njoj nema baš mnogo zabave i socijalističke in doktrinacije bačke ideologije
na tribini su dobri disko-klub i polja i laza domar
a dobra vizija jedne dobre generacije ostaće vizija i kad tribina postane proizvođač masovne zabave i komercijalno nezavisna
samo luft i uvek
u novom sadu
samo komercijalni underground i politički govori

3.

POČEV OD DEJANA POZNANOVIĆA PA DO POSLEDNJE ZABRANE UJ SYMPOSIONA U NOVOM SADU

trče mladići ne...
nih prstiju iskolačenih očiju i već okraćalog daha a za njima neumitno stegnutih šaka dolazi staljin i govori rečima jaše zlopca: ovo ste mogli da zamislite u rusiji ali ne u novom sadu! ali ja sam tu! ali ja sam tu! ali ja sam tu! ali ja sam tu!
i još na kongresu kulturne akcije: da vas zaštitim da vas zaštitim pod svojim krovom

sada je jasno da u ovom zajebanom gradu svako ko nešto pametno i pošteno smisli i samo pokuša da uradi

najebe

i jedina prava šansa momaka sa tribine je da

u poljima

kao boško ivkov

neguju soc-realistički kić komercijalni undergro und nadrealizam

i preko toga ništa jer dalje ljude ubijaju
jer ovaj odvratni grad
uredno pokazuje svoju crnu dušu

tribina nikada neće postati elitno uporište avangardne misli jer tom prokletom gradu to nije potrebno
i zato ona i nije prava šansa nego sitno seruckanje za kukavice

osećaj društvenog priznanja — osećaj da sam pojeo govna

PORUKA PRIJATELJIMA NA TRIBINI UKOLIKO IH TAMO IMA
osluhnite važljivo u novom sadu »podzemni hod revolucije«
pažljivo gerilu
pažljivo one koji će prestati da čekaju
vaš spas nije u drkanju
vi treba da jebete
živite pobunu a ne surogat pobune i ne za prljave pare koje se strogo cenzurišu u sivoj kući na uglu

slavko bogdanović
29. 11. 71.

2.19. Slavko Bogdanović, "Pesma underground tribina mladih Novi Sad" [Underground Song for the Youth Tribune, Novi Sad], *Student*'s "Underground" issue, Belgrade, 16 December 1971. Image courtesy of Slavko Bogdanović.

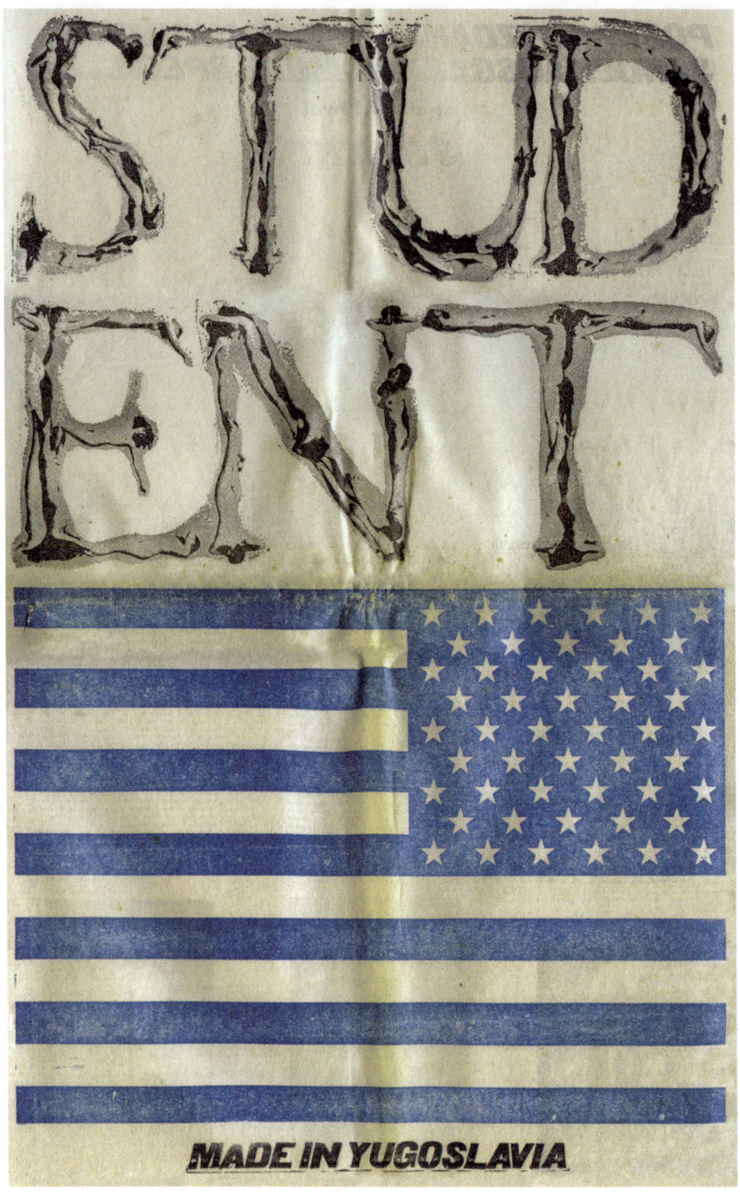

2.20. Bálint Szombathy, cover of *Student*'s "Underground" issue, Belgrade, 16 December 1971. Image courtesy of Slavko Bogdanović.

who had previously stipulated that freedom was something "given," was thanked on the 21st session of the representatives of the LCY by Tito for the "firm stance which he expressed there."[109] Quoting Zlobec's observation made during his trip to the Youth Tribune, Bogdanović concluded: "Something like that could be imagined in Russia, but not in Novi Sad."[110]

At a moment when mass media and institutions remained inaccessible, Bogdanović pleaded in the same letter for "revolutionary action [to] unfold outside the institution" and go underground in order to "DESTROY the Youth League and the Council of Students ... conservative and counterrevolutionary organizations which actually don't exist, but vegetate in the forms of bulky, bloated bureaucratic organizations, and represent a sclerotic mind which thinks, and works, in the name ... of the party."[111] His "underground" task culminated in the censored "Underground" issue of Belgrade's *Student* newspaper, printed on 16 December 1971, where he published his "Pesma underground tribina mladih" [Underground Song of the Youth Tribune]. Printed in Belgrade's leading youth publication, this text directly addressed cultural stagnation in Novi Sad.[112] It noted the current conditions at the Youth Tribune, which, being the "official property of the youth organization (hereinafter to be referred to as the council for the concerns of young consumers)," had just become an "adaptation of young inhabitants of the city with a consumerist stance to the world ... [a] suffocation of all creation, [an exponent of] provincial ideology, deindividualization, a preservation and conservation of new tradition."[113] These accusations were subtly reinforced through the issue's cover, designed by a Bosch + Bosch group member, the artist Bálint Szombathy: a reversed blue-and-white print of the American flag, supplemented with a simple caption, stating "Made in Yugoslavia." Taken in conjunction with Bogdanović's "Song," the cover seemed to imply that in the country often dubbed "America's communist ally," a softer style of engagement was distracting from the urgent work needed to nurture a healthy political culture that could sustain "self-managing" relations—a tendency that was beginning to deprive Novi Sad's principal youth institution of its political agency.

Written in 1971, Bogdanović's text anticipated many of the issues that have become central to recent political histories on the former Yugoslavia—namely that, because it was linked with the market from its inception, self-management was, in the words of historian Vladimir Unkovski-Korica, "devoid of emancipatory potential from the beginning."[114] Following the removal of the liberal leaderships in 1971–1972, a new and strengthened Federal Executive Bureau was introduced, and democratic centralism was, for a brief moment, reasserted as the first principle of political life. But while clearly coercive measures were being taken in the political sphere, softer and more dispersed means were employed to preserve public compliance. At the beginning of the 1970s, austerity measures were lifted, and material comforts once again began to cushion the heavy hand of the LCY. All the while, consumerist tendencies distracted people's attention from a growing crisis in federal politics and the system of self-management itself. Already in 1971, Bogdanović complained of how the previously progressive Youth Tribune had become a "distributor of mass entertainment," simply promoting "commercial underground and political talks"—"disco clubs and socialist indoctrination."[115] The Tribune's programs had been steered away from a healthy, active, and engaged understanding of culture to a totally conformist direction—far removed from the state's ideological pillar of commercial relations theoretically grounded upon the "social ownership of the means of production." Serving a society consumed with consumption, the new program represented a kind of commercial compensation for the lack of genuine popular participation in the guidance of the Tribune's affairs. Regarding those who attempted to change this situation, Bogdanović concluded:

> **BEGINNING WITH DEJAN POZNANOVIĆ AND TO THE LAST BANNING OF ÚJ SYMPOSION IN NOVI SAD**
>
> Young men with gentle fingers are running, their eyes goggled, already short of breath, and behind them inevitably follows Stalin, with clenched fists, saying the words of Jaša Zlobec, "this could be expected in Russia, but not in Novi Sad. But I am here! I am here! I am here!"
>
> And also on the Congress of Cultural Action: to protect you, to protect you under my roof.
>
> Now it is clear that in this fucked-up city, everyone who thinks of something smart and is honest or dares to do it,
> is fucked over
> and the only change for the boys from the Tribina Mladih is to,
> like Boško Ivkov
> in *Polja*,
> foster socialist kitsch, commercial underground,
> surrealism
> and nothing beyond that, because beyond it people get killed,
> because this disgusting city
> shows its black soul every time.
> The Tribune will never become a stronghold of avant-garde thought,
> since there is no need for it in this fucked-up city
> and therefore it doesn't stand a real chance.[116]

Following the purging of the Croatian liberal leadership and in the wake of the Serbian leadership's dismissal, Tito vigorously denied that he was attempting to return the party to its Stalinist past.[117] But while from the outset Tito's government emphasized the risk of making the same error "being made by the leading communists in many countries" (including the Soviet Union's failure to put the slogan "the factories for the workers" into practice even thirty-one years after the October Revolution), the LCY seemed once again to be relying on certain methods of authoritarian rule at the beginning of the 1970s. Could it be that Yugoslavia had entered an affair similar to the fatal romance Makavejev depicted in *WR* between Vladimir Ilyich (a Russian ice-skater visiting Yugoslavia with his ice ballet troupe, whose words in the film are often direct quotations of his namesake, Lenin) and Milena (a young Yugoslav communist)? According to Vladimir: "We Russians appreciate your efforts to find your own way. You are a proud and independent nation. However, we are sure you will find out yourselves that the course we've chosen is the best one." For Makavejev himself, the film's two leading figures stood for two types of socialism—self-management and autocratic—with their tumultuous relationship exploring the dilemmas of spontaneity and organization: "How to allow spontaneity without destroying organization, and how to organize without killing spontaneity?"[118] In Novi Sad, 1972 was the year in which spontaneity was ceded for organization and control. For Bogdanović, this was now a city which followed Stalin with "clenched fists," and remaining loyal meant completely identifying with the leadership.[119] Breaching the party's goal of securing order and preserving its strong central authority, Bogdanović's "Song" had exposed the real, base foundations of power. As a result, the artist received an eight-month prison sentence.

TOWARD AN "INVISIBLE ART"

After the reaction of the local state apparatus, former KÔD members Slobodan Tišma and Čedomir Drča withdrew from the practice of public art. According to Tišma, the only solution that remained was to "go around institutions (that had become occupied by state apparatchiks), to leave the state and society out of everything, [so] everything [would] be strictly private, intimate."[120] In this compromised situation, they created the time-based action called *THE END*, including works like *Nevidljiva umetnost* [Invisible Art], *Invisible Band*, and *Invisible Artist*, between 1972 and 1977. In that time, Tišma and Drča drank American Coca-Cola and Russian kvass every day with friends in front of a local store. Today, these "invisible" actions exist only through sparse photographic documentation: framing still-life displays composed of detailed reproductions of ancient Greek imagery, or empty Coke bottles and Coke pencil holders perched on a storefront window or on the front windshield of the nationally produced Fića automobile. In other images, the protagonists are captured wearing T-shirts embossed with the caption "The End," while clutching empty Coca-Cola bottles. Yet, rather than acting as documents of an artistic performance, these photographs are visual residues of a way of thought and reflection that, at the time, occupied a tiny place in the larger scheme of things. For these artists, the gesture represented an "end" to their art, but one that was by no means unprecedented; it paralleled Duchamp's famous renunciation of art in favor of chess, and his refusal to work as a way of freeing himself from the art world's productivism.[121] It marked the inevitable termination of their involvement with cultural institutions in general so that they could avoid the institutionalization that went hand in hand with critical and experimental art practices at that time, both locally and internationally.

Asked why he chose not to publish anything until 1995, Tišma recently revealed that the "reason consisted of a great disenchantment with what happened in the early Seventies. The great illusions were crushed. The idea that life equals art was definitely dead. I didn't want to deal in any way with strategies, i.e. politics. I started to doubt everything we did and I simply quit."[122] Certainly, such feelings of disillusionment resonated with many of the key practitioners of "global conceptualism" around that time.[123] But in Novi Sad, these private acts also emerged in response to the utter disappointment sensed by artists over being abandoned by the Youth Tribune. Even the gesture of drinking Coca-Cola and kvass in their free time could be perceived as an ironic imitation of the Tribune's newly assigned function, as a location where, according to Bogdanović's account,

> workers and high schoolers; literate and illiterate [come] to listen to local pop bands; speeches by their politicians; music of their colleagues; to look at pictures ... TO SPEND THEIR TIME CAREFREE AND PLEASANTLY WITH A COKE AND SANDWICH.... The rhythm of life is all the quicker and time all the costlier. The Tribune therefore needs to DISTRIBUTE FORMS OF ENTERTAINMENT which will help the consumer to greet the next day with a readiness to work and with effective work creativity [sic].[124]

2.21. Slobodan Tišma and Čedomir Drča, *Primeri nevidljive umetnosti* [Examples of Invisible Art], Novi Sad, 1976. Image courtesy of Muzej Savremene Umetnosti Vojvodine.

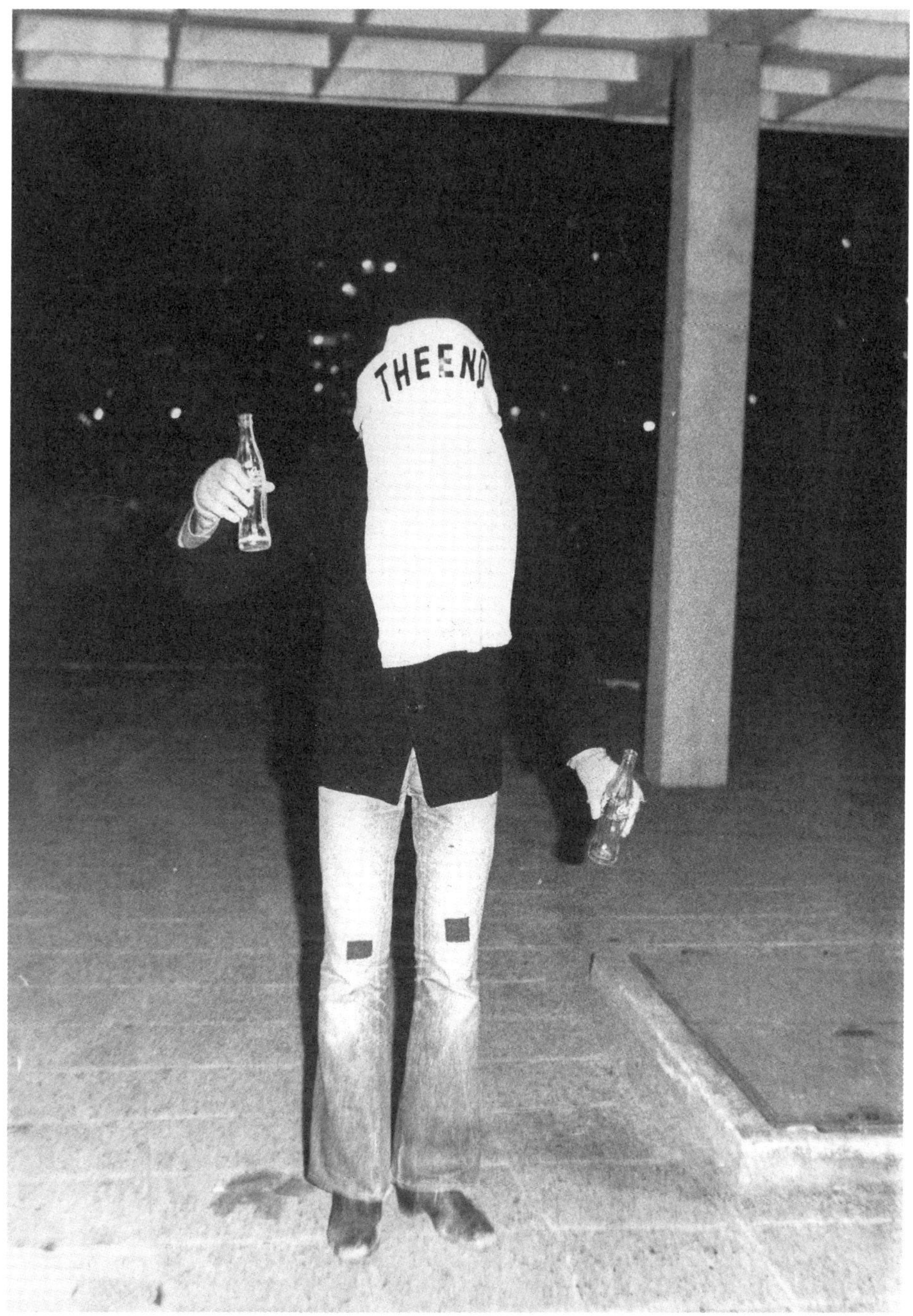
THEEND

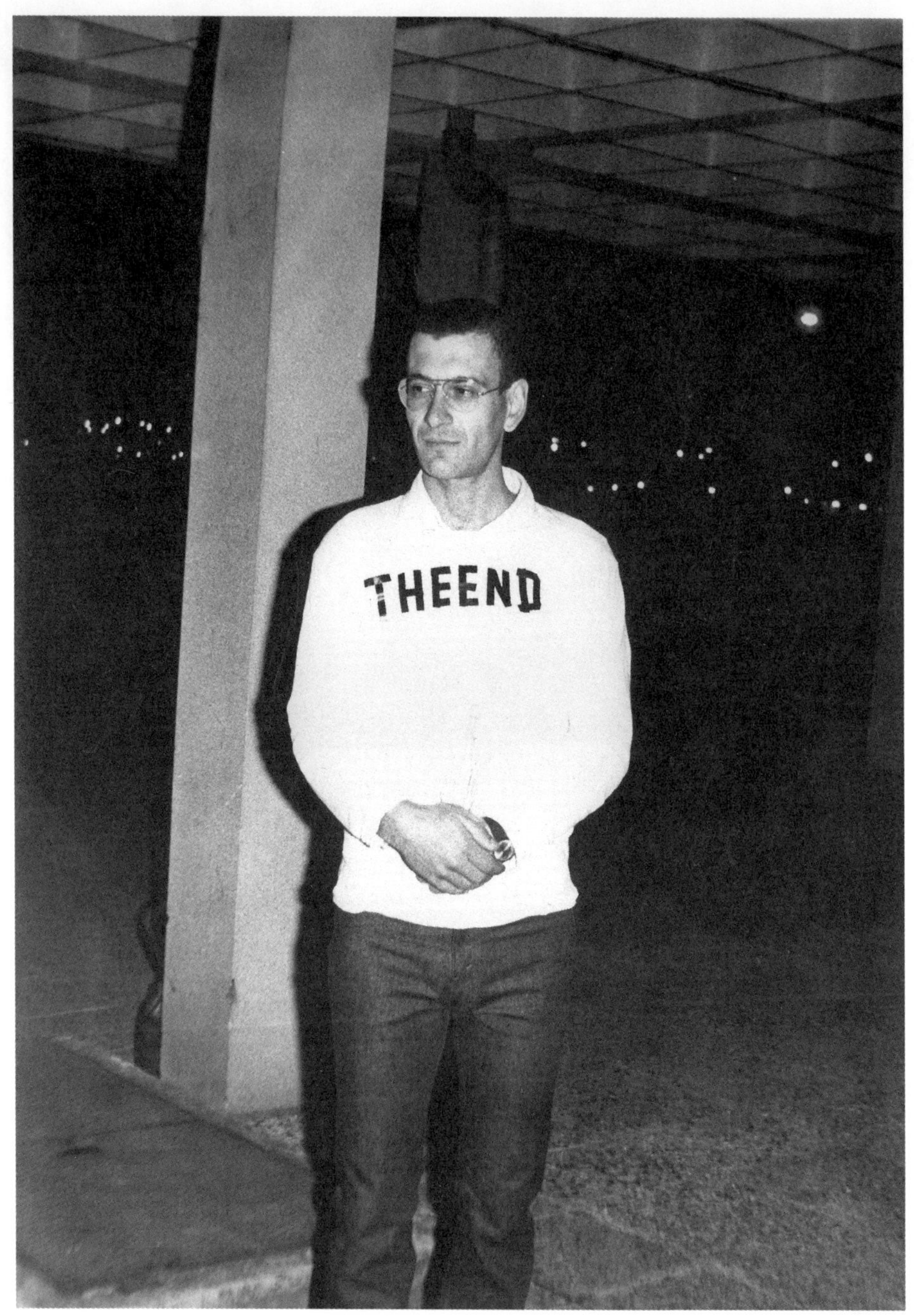
THEEND

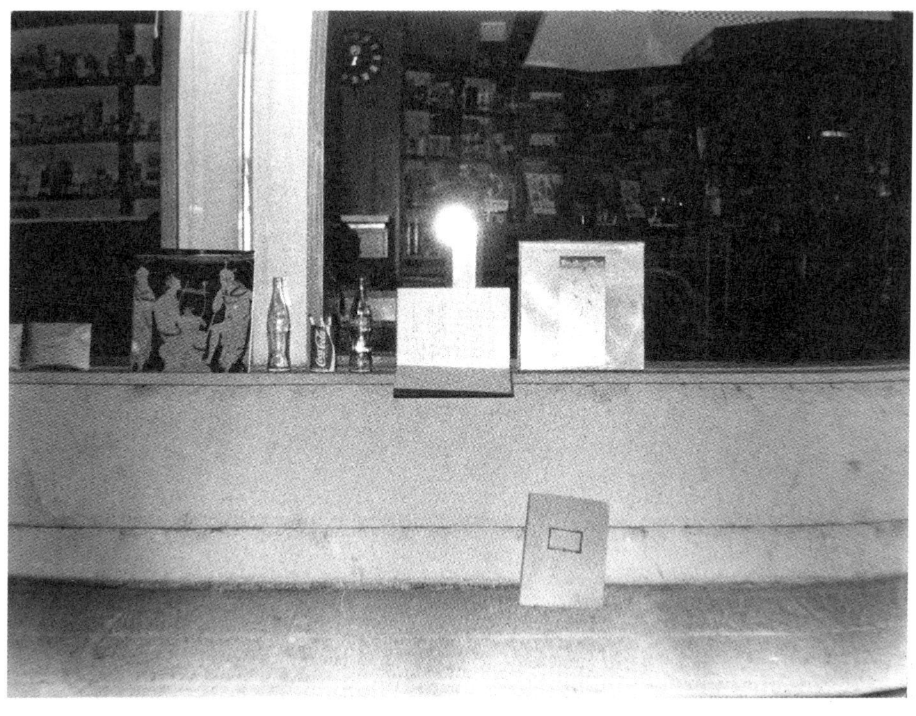

2.22. and 2.23. Slobodan Tišma and Čedomir Drča, *Primeri nevidljive umetnosti* [Examples of Invisible Art], Novi Sad, 1976. Images courtesy of Muzej Savremene Umetnosti Vojvodine.

For these artists, *THE END* became the only viable form of artistic engagement in a socialist society that was unable to integrate difference; it thus marked the cessation of the New Art Practice in Novi Sad's official cultural institutions. At a moment of oppressive change and political turmoil, escapism became the only form of artistic engagement available to these artists. In the same year that Tišma and Drča began to pursue *Invisible Art*, OHO also dropped all public performances and embarked on a "period of silence," forming a commune in an abandoned farmhouse in Šempas instead.[125]

Beginning in 1971, Belgrade's newly opened Students' Cultural Center and its gallery, founded in reaction to events in that city in 1968, would inherit the struggle to establish new forms of cultural engagement—concluding in similar disillusionment, albeit under very different political and cultural circumstances.

3 THE INTERNATIONAL STRIKE OF ARTISTS

BELGRADE'S SKC GALLERY (1971–1976)

JUNE TURMOIL

It started on what was scheduled to be an evening of light entertainment. On 2 June 1968, a dress rehearsal for a traveling show called *Caravan of Friendship* was set to take place in a large outdoor amphitheater on the outskirts of New Belgrade, but was moved to the cinema hall of the nearby Workers' University because of a rain forecast.[1] A large crowd of Belgrade University students from the nearby complex of dormitories, popularly known as Studenski Grad [Student City], gathered in front of the venue, alongside members of the general public. At one point, party officials and a large group of Volunteer Youth Brigade workers were allowed in, while the students were denied access. Some of them tried to force their way in, but security guards intervened. A fierce struggle ensued: over forty policemen used batons and water cannons to disperse the crowd of students. Many were injured; rumor had it that one of the students had been shot.

In one of their first official statements from the protest, students noted that the police had "waited for students at the underpass in New Belgrade and both times dispersed us with violence, the use of firearms, and because of that a great number of our colleagues were injured."[2] In their view, civil rights had been violated by the police violence, and so this became the overarching concern of the protest: a call for increased social justice and more institutional protection for civil rights. The following morning, a neighborhood student action committee was formed to discuss further action. In the afternoon, around ten thousand students occupied all the faculties of Belgrade University, proclaiming a strike that lasted over a week in the institution they had renamed "Red University–Karl Marx."[3] By the next day, protests in support of Belgrade students' demands had spread to Niš, Zagreb, Ljubljana, and Sarajevo.[4] In Sarajevo, thousands of students attended a rally in front of the Philosophy Faculty building and later marched toward the city center, where they staged a sit-in, clashed with the police, and organized a protest in front of the Communist League Executive Committee building.[5] In Zagreb, three thousand students and supporters attended assemblies at the Students' Center and declared "we are the truth."[6]

Although Yugoslavia's 1968 encompassed voices from a broad ideological spectrum—ranging from those "who adhered to the idea of socialism with a human face to those who were antisocialist," as Kemal Kurspahić, then an editor at Belgrade's *Student* newspaper put it—it has largely been historicized as sparked by a resentment of the country's rising "red bourgeoisie," along with growing social inequality and unemployment that accompanied the country's turn to market reform.[7] Students lashed out against "socialist barons" and "enrichment at the expense of the workers," and demanded: "bureaucrats, stay away from the working class."[8] As in Paris, they made efforts to link their cause to the working class. In Zagreb, students tried to recruit passing workers to take part in their assembly, stressing that "we students are fighting for you"; in Belgrade, they sent emissaries to local factories.[9] At the Philosophy Faculty, students chanted "from the heart," "workers ... we are not the opposition but the negation of everything false."[10] Besides expressing solidarity with the workers, students formed an all-Yugoslav front: at rallies in Zagreb, police reported chants of "Zagreb-Belgrade!" and "Belgrade-Zagreb!"; in both Zagreb and Sarajevo, placards expressed support of their counterparts in Belgrade, "because their problems are the same as our problems."[11]

On 3 June, Belgrade students issued a Political Action Program demanding "measures that will rapidly reduce the great social inequality in our community."[12] These measures included the implementation of the "socialist principle of distribution according to one's work"; the abolition of "differences in personal incomes based on nonsocialist, privileged positions"; and action against the "accumulation, in nonsocialist fashion, of private property."[13] The program called for the "systematic development of self-management, not only in the workplace but at all levels, from communal to federal, so that producers can exercise real control over organs of production."[14] Alongside these calls for the further development of self-management, students demanded that "all social and political organizations, including the League of Communists, be democratized, through means of public expression," along with the "creation of a proviso that would outline how the university could become a truly free, critical, and veritable self-managing institution":

> The system of self-governing relations needs to be developed not only in organizing labor, but in all layers of our society, from the commune to the federation.... It is necessary [not only] to improve the material situation of the students, but to further develop the institutions of student standards. According to the principle of self-governing relations, in our society the administration of these institutions has to be laid in the hands of the students.[15]

In short, students denounced privilege and demanded self-management from below. They sought to expand social justice, to reform the economy, and to spark an ideological reorientation from within the framework of self-management. But, according to several accounts, they lacked a clearly articulated "alternative" vision. While the students insisted that their program was the "program of the Yugoslav Communist Party," Tito used this lack of ideological differentiation from the party's official politics to put an end to the protests through a skillful, conciliatory televised speech. The almost immediate suppression of the protests not only resulted in numerous arrests, trials, and prison sentences for some of its participants, but also, for performance studies scholar Branislav Jakovljević, marked a clear historical point from which to trace the "beginning of the end of Yugoslavia."[16]

Looking back at the events of 1968 today, it seems reasonable to conclude that the students failed to hold the League of Communists accountable for the lack of egalitarianism, self-management, and solidarity in Yugoslav society. Yet although it feels fitting to read the apparent pitfalls of the student demonstrations through the lens of Yugoslavia's disintegration, the 1968 moment signaled a temporary strengthening of artistic and cultural freedoms in the country, which, as the previous chapters have shown, reached a high point in the years 1968 to 1971. For the younger Praxis member Nebojša Popov, the lasting impact of the demonstrations was their inherent demand for the freedom of expression, association, and demonstration beyond party control, along with the joining of different forces within Belgrade's critical intelligentsia.[17] Ten years after the events of that summer, Ješa Denegri similarly observed that the emergence of "new attitudes in art took place at the same time as broader social and spiritual events in and immediately after 1968."[18] Nowhere in Yugoslavia was this shift in artistic attitudes as profoundly felt as in Belgrade, where a new generation of artists who had received a political awakening through the events of June were able to take advantage of a new institution that would support their practice: Belgrade's Students' Cultural Center.

Several testimonies identify that the founding of the Students' Cultural Center (Studentski Kulturni Centar, or SKC) was a concession to the students' demands for the "immediate" improvement of living conditions, and a result of institutional reforms implemented at Belgrade University after the demonstrations.

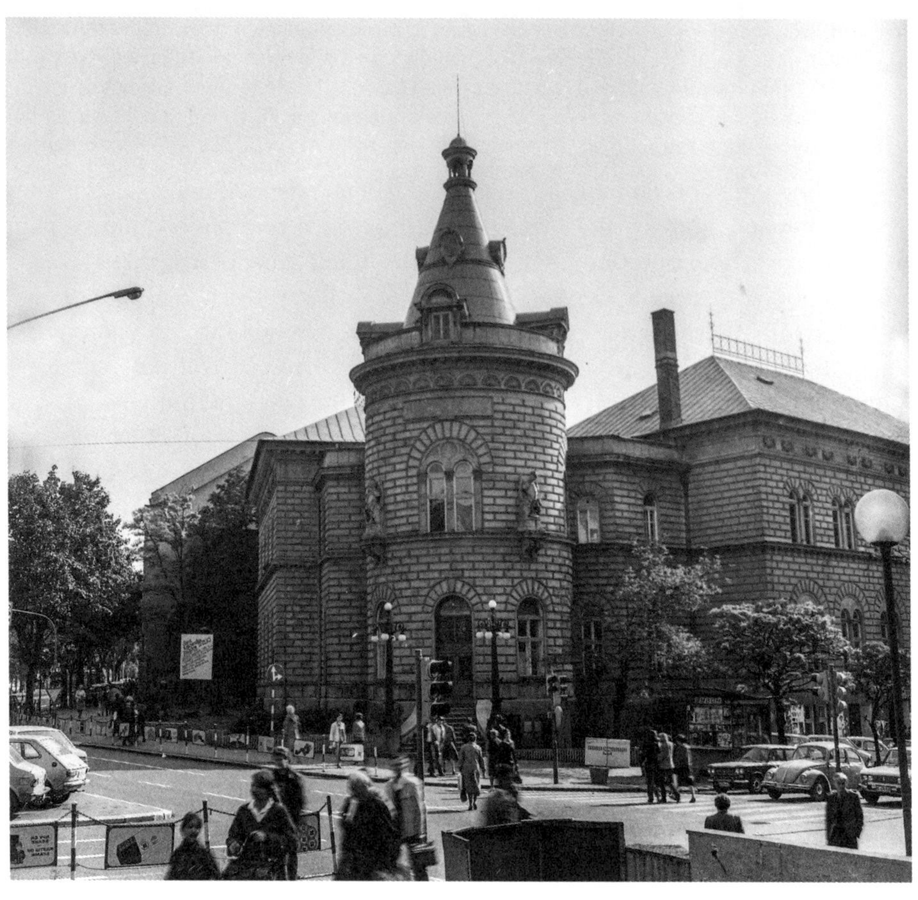

3.1. The Belgrade SKC exterior. Image courtesy of the SKC Archive, Belgrade.

Located in the historic Northern Vračar area and overlooking Ulica Maršala Tita, the allocated building had formerly served as the social club for the secret police until Ranković's dismissal in 1966. Having fallen into disrepair, the building was handed over to the newly formed student cultural institution in 1969.[19] Immediately plans were made to transform the space, along with all of its previous affiliations with central state power, into a cultural center that "would seek its audience among those students that have been, to a certain extent, excluded from Belgrade's cultural curriculum."[20] Equipped with two halls that would host a film forum, music events, and roundtable discussions, along with two galleries, a club space, a restaurant, and a lounge, the newly renovated space was officially opened on 4 April 1971, on the Day of Students, commemorating the death of Žarko Marinović—a student killed in the 1936 conflict between the progressive student communists and the right-wing Organization of Yugoslav Nationalists.[21]

According to its founding program, the Students' Cultural Center would become "integral to the culture of our socialist society"—a statement that in many respects echoed the demand of the 1968 demonstrations that the "commercialization of culture must be rendered impossible and the possibility of creative cultural activity be opened to all."[22] Božidar Zečević, director of the center's Film Forum, argued that before 1968 the university had failed to define a clear concept for cultural activity:

> Admittedly, many societies worked ... plays, choirs, and folklore, several of which were affirmed. But, all of those were seen, from above, through some demagogic or festive conceptions; folklore, celebrations, anniversaries ... clichés of socializing which 1968 had altogether overthrown. Exhausted and dried up, that national, populist inertia still prevailed in the consciousness of the university and student leadership.... They didn't know what they would do with such a center. Even if they proposed something, albeit with good intentions, they were just populist fantasies ... without cultural, and much less historical reason.[23]

For this reason, the center's new cultural program emphasized the importance of contemporary cultural developments. As in Novi Sad, the new staff made a serious effort to ensure that the SKC did not simply become a "clubbing space, appealing to 'mass' or 'consumerist' culture," boiling down to the usual "dancing and folklore activity."[24] Each of its departments would confront debates from the "perspective of Marx's social theory in the broadest sense," with a clear aim of "contributing to the growth of a critical, self-managing conscience of the youth," and to developing a "democratic culture, so significant for successful self-managing communication."[25]

In this respect, the newly articulated program of the SKC paralleled the broader social atmosphere of Serbia between 1968 and 1971, which included the softening of censorship in the media and growing tolerance for cultural and literary activities. This softening began in November 1968, when a new Serbian Party leadership headed by Marko Nikezić and Latinka Perović was elected at the Sixth Congress of the League of Communists of Serbia (LCS). They represented a popular liberal double act in Serbian political life, comparable to Tripalo and Dabčević-Kučar. Adopting a strict principle of noninterference in the affairs of other republics, they limited their attention to critiquing Serbian nationalism and Serbian hegemonic tendencies within Yugoslavia. Nikezić in particular felt that nationalist tendencies in Serbia could only be self-destructive: "We cannot expect unity within this country, if the feeling continues that Serbs are the foundation of Yugoslavia.... If Yugoslavia is necessary, then it is necessary for all, and not just Serbs."[26] Although the Serbian Party leadership was still divided between liberals and conservatives, the new Serbian leadership repudiated the sort of policies associated with Ranković—emancipating Belgrade from its associations in the popular consciousness with Serbian domination and the locus of a highly centralized power in the prewar monarchist Kingdom of Yugoslavia.

Similarly, the SKC Gallery sought a style of radical will that would abandon the local provincialism that had hitherto defined many of the university's cultural programs. Dunja Blažević, daughter of an eminent representative of the LCY, was appointed as director of the gallery, granting her a certain amount of immunity and enabling her to mount projects that others might not have been able to accomplish. Coming from Zagreb, she brought with her connections and conceptual relations with the New Tendencies, as well as the currents of the New Art Practice being fostered by the SC Gallery. In part due to these expanded affiliations and connections, the SKC Gallery's founding principles identified the crucial priority of keeping "up-to-date [with] new, original and significant art developments.... Collaboration with other galleries, museums and art institutions, accompanied by the exchange with artists from all over our country and the world, represent the main prerequisites of that policy."[27]

Unlike Zagreb, with its pedigree of avant-garde practices, including Gorgona, EXAT 51, and New Tendencies, and Ljubljana, where the OHO group realized their first projects starting in 1966, Belgrade was, according to Raša Todosijević, a key artist working with the gallery, a space without "gravitation, sensible judgement, analogies or daring compilations."[28] He further elaborated that in Belgrade the historical avant-gardes were left aside: "no Duchamp, but Bonnard; no Malevich, but Chagall; no Pop, but New Figuration," no legacy to inherit, except for the reception of a stagnant, "second class modernist abstraction and its diluted Parisian echoes."[29]

The "diluted Parisian echoes" Todosijević referred to would certainly fall under the banner of what is often labeled as socialist modernism. But these influences have often been overlooked because of the overemphasis placed on the first exhibition of American modern art in Belgrade, organized by New York's Museum of Modern Art in 1955.[30] As the first exhibition of American modern art in a socialist country, featuring works by De Kooning, Pollock, Gorky, Rothko, and Motherwell, *Modern Art in the United States* has often been understood as an expression of America's "soft power" approach to cultural diplomacy, and its efforts to deploy abstract expressionism as a "weapon of the Cold War" at a time of the McCarthyist "Red Scare."[31] Yet the impact this exhibition exerted on Belgrade's art scene was almost unnoticeable. Instead, it was the legacy of European modernism that bore a lasting influence on the city's art scene. As early as 1950, the first comprehensive exhibition of modern art was organized in Belgrade under the heading of *New French Fine Art*, including works by Van Gogh, Matisse, and Picasso, among others.[32] Referring to the works on display, at the show's opening a leading communist named Veljko Petrović explained that those "pure bourgeois artists"

> opened the eyes of humanity to the grace and subtle pathos of the stature and movements of the little man, the man of the masses, during work, relaxation, play.... This so-called "decadent art" is full of technical inventions, ideas, coloristic and linear subtleties ... that will be used in decorative painting in the future, in some more ordered and healthier times. We are not preventing ourselves from exhibiting the works of these artists. We want our man, our working socialist man, not to be deprived of anything that is human.[33]

In Belgrade, models of the École de Paris, cubism, expressionism, early abstraction, and later Informel were considered styles that could represent the needs of socialism.[34] European modernism was received enthusiastically because it reflected a lineage of developments in Yugoslav art that predated the Second World War, survived the socialist revolution, and was maintained in education institutions and artists' associations throughout the 1950s.[35]

Driven by the goal of bringing Belgrade up to scratch with the more recent international art developments that had already taken hold in Ljubljana and Zagreb, the SKC Gallery operated in a nonhierarchical way, without the traditional divisions between cultural producers and their audience.[36] Although it was a professional cultural institution with paid employees, under the provision of Blažević and Biljana Tomić (curator of Belgrade's Atelje 212 Gallery), the SKC Gallery was run through a combination of volunteer work and professional, paid labor.[37] Based on cooperation between those who worked in the gallery and people from the outside—artists, art historians, designers, philosophy and sociology students—the gallery was a space where "everyone could decide the programs together."[38] The informality of this arrangement was crucial for young artists, as there was no obligation to apply for exhibitions or screenings as there were in other galleries. What was usually obtained by manifestos, proposals, and set programs was, in this case, acquired by a "shared confidence in each other's sensibilities."[39]

EXHIBITING THE "CURRENT SITUATION"

According to Blažević, the SKC Gallery was envisioned as an open institution that would essentially approach art, culture, and education "in relation to society."[40] Like Zagreb's SC Gallery, which in 1969 opened itself up to collaboration and cooperation through its competition, the SKC Gallery offered not only a new exhibition space but also a key stimulus for a generation of younger artists training at the Academy of Fine Arts. Immediately after its inauguration in 1971, an informal group of artists began to gather at the gallery, consisting of Marina Abramović, Era Milivojević, Neša Paripović, Zoran Popović, Raša Todosijević, and Gergelj Urkom. This was a group of friends who had known each other even before the SKC was opened. Their intense friendship consisted of frequent discussions and culminated in joint exhibitions, actions, and works. But while exhibiting together, the members of the group subscribed to no common artistic program beyond a unanimous rejection of the training they had received at the Academy of Fine Arts. As Urkom explained in 1972: "What we obviously have in common today does suggest that what brought us together was more than mere formality. It's not that we share the same attitude toward art, so much as we would say that the closeness of our views originated from similar viewpoints toward life."[41]

At the SKC Gallery, the collaboration between these artists was further supported by a group of young art historians who were to systematically follow their work. Curators that are today internationally recognized, including Bojana Pejić, began their careers within the SKC Gallery, promoting its earliest collaborators, both locally and abroad.

A defining moment in the group's rejection of their academic training was their exhibition in June 1971 entitled *Drangularijum* (vaguely translated as "a collection of small and curious things," or literally as "trinket-arium"), staged less than two months after the SKC opened. After a stormy meeting between the young artists and critics, it was decided that the exhibition would "aim to demystify

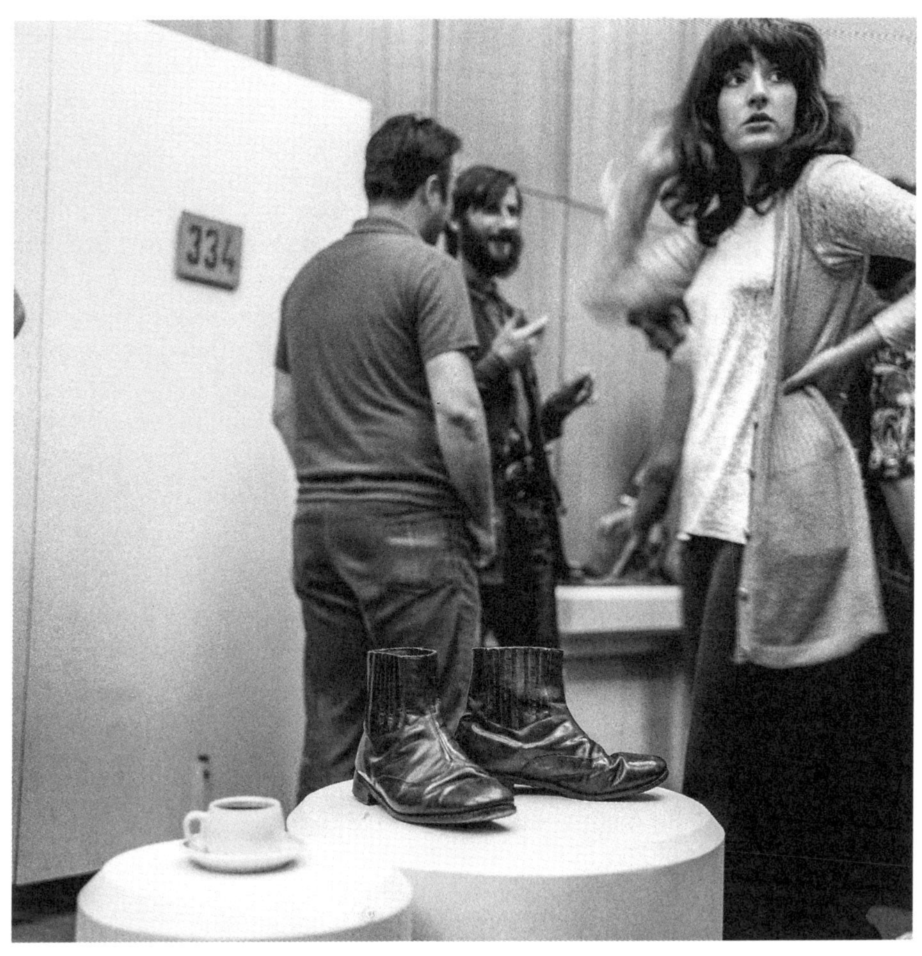

3.2. Installation view of *Drangularijum*, SKC Gallery, Belgrade, June 1971. Image courtesy of the SKC Archive, Belgrade.

the symptoms of the prevalent plastic arts," taking Duchamp's readymades as a departure point.[42] Just as the SC Gallery's *Hit Parade* had announced an end to the dominant "illusionistic approach" in Zagreb, *Drangularijum* became the SKC's first exhibition attempting to "deskill" art making and to undermine the individualism inherent in expressive painting.

Photographs of the installation reveal a cluttered and disorganized array of random objects, including a basket, placed ironically on a towering pedestal, and a functionless door propped up in the center of the exhibition space. Gergelj Urkom brought an old blanket—an "object not exceptionally dear to him"—but one which would, against his will, immediately acquire an unintended meaning within the frame of the exhibition, "nonetheless only one green blanket."[43] The most radical contribution to the exhibition was from Todosijević, who brought his partner, Marinela Koželj, and "displayed" her within a still life set-up, on a chair, beside a "blue night table with bottle."[44] In the exhibition catalogue, he explained his motivations behind this gesture: "Marinela is not an exhibit. She is in constant relation with all things. She passes by them, touches them. I wished to note down their mutual relations, not as a photograph or a dead museum exhibit. Marinela moves, she speaks."[45]

3.3. Raša Todosijević, *Marinela, plava natkasna sa flašom, stolica za maleckog Kaldera* [Marinela, Blue Night Table, Chair for Little Calder], *Drangularijum*, SKC Gallery, Belgrade, June 1971. Image courtesy of Raša Todosijević.

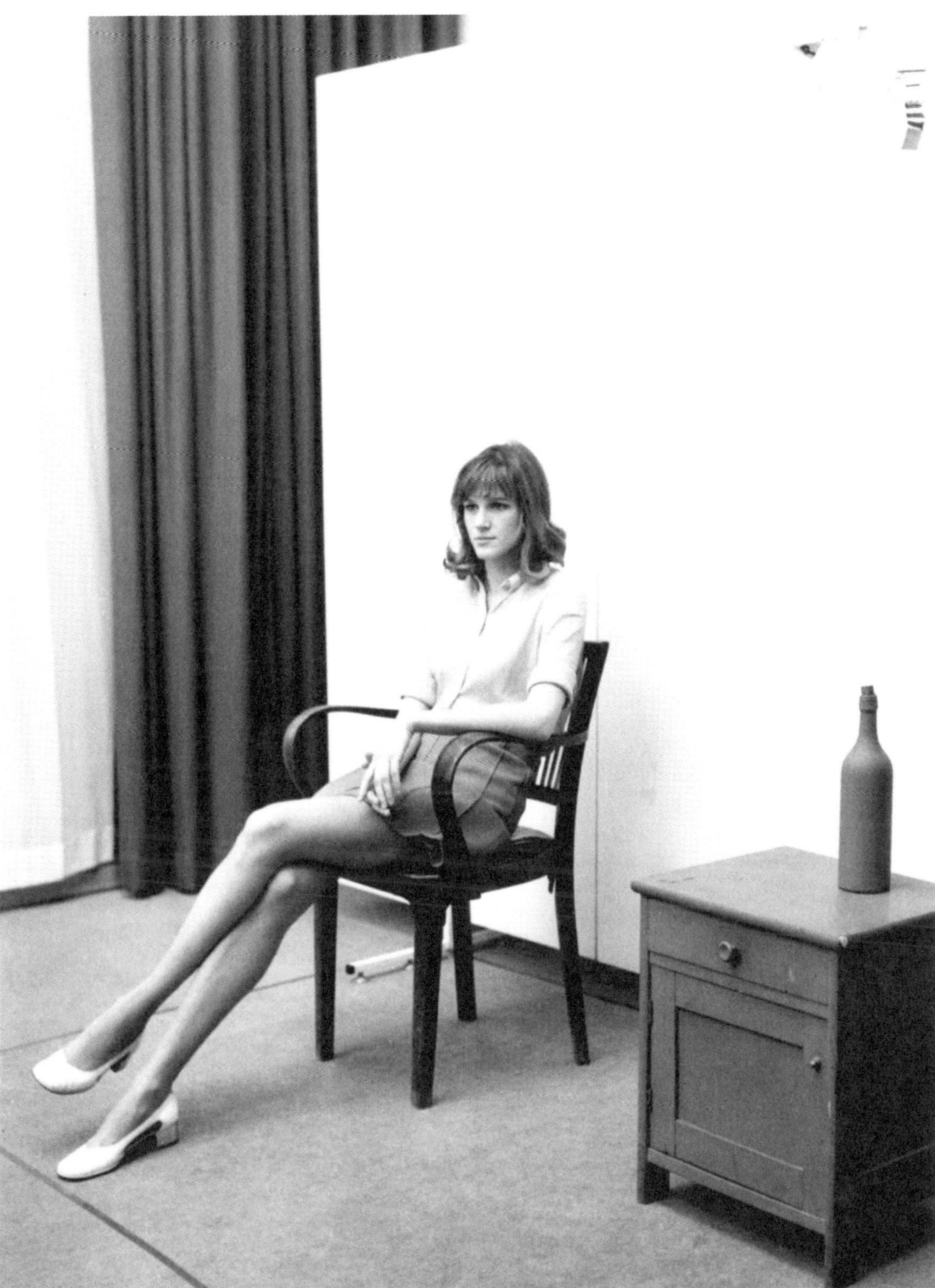

Yet, while this exhibition moved to process-based work, Belgrade's landmark gesture still lagged behind its counterparts. After all, two years prior to *Drangularijum*, a new generation of artists in Zagreb, such as Trbuljak, had succeeded in completely cutting ties with the art object itself. But, as Bojana Pejić explained in her short contribution to the exhibition catalogue, *Drangularijum* was not, and did not aspire to be, "original," because "similar exhibitions are being held around the world and individual attempts of this kind exist locally as well."[46] It was, nevertheless, the first serious "presentation of this kind which should have appeared earlier [in Belgrade], but had not due to perennial problems of financing, which are constant associates of our 'cultural life.'"[47] The exhibition presented a challenge to the static atmosphere of Belgrade's gallery scene: "In the sea of standard exhibitions this is a glove being slapped in the face of a city used to the monotonous presentation of affirmed, rather than new, names."[48] As such, it represented a cornerstone in the SKC group's resistance to the dominant artistic trends in Belgrade, and its attempts to redefine the relationship of the hand and the head in art making.

Todosijević recalls the accusations these initial experiments aroused among professors at the city's Academy of Fine Arts where the artists had studied, who he said preferred a "cowardly, provincial art."[49] According to Todosijević, the new generation of artists who began working through the SKC were frequently accused of being "lazy" and "trying to intellectualize things."[50] Their professors told them that what they were doing were "passing experiments … [and] that they would soon return to the good old painting ground."[51] They were left with one option: "Our only strategy was not to work; in our last year in the Academy we gave up going to school everyday. Soon after the Academy we started going to the Students' Cultural Center and we said we were coming to bring new things. We were going to make new art in Belgrade. Really, believe me, we wanted to change things—killing the father, which I enjoy."[52]

With all of its oedipal undertones, "killing the father" meant fostering a shared opposition to what artists at the SKC considered Belgrade's isolated art scene. Starting in 1971, the gallery began organizing a response to the October Salon, an annual exhibition which for decades featured mainstream and modernist-oriented Yugoslav art. Named after the October Revolution, this manifestation could be seen as yet another example of Yugoslavia's oxymoronic art scene, fusing commemoration and revolutionary symbolism with the quintessential bourgeois institution of the salon. Yet the SKC Gallery's "Octobers" were not intended to act simply as confrontations between "alternative" and "official" established art scenes. In 1972, the informal group of artists at the SKC announced the opening of *Oktobar '72* in the national newspaper *Politika ekspres* under the heading "Exhibition Instead of Protest."[53] They explained that their aim was not to "provoke scandal" but in some way to complete the October Salon, as the "exhibition's jury had stopped being interested in contemporary art developments."[54] By restricting their attention to "local exhibitions in the city, without any analysis or deep thought," the jury had largely ignored experimentation due to their "classical understanding of art, where everything that isn't produced on a woven canvas with oil paints in the hands of a worthy master isn't art."[55] The exhibition catalogue for *Oktobar '72* similarly announced that the project's fundamental goal was "to critically analyze the existing artistic practice and position the function of visual culture in the wider context in our society."[56] This is why so many of the projects installed at *Oktobar '72* emphasized "the conscious abandonment of the 'privileges' of the status of an artist, the kind that is still produced by our school, ... and the problematization of comprehending the role and meaning of art today."[57]

Yet this new form of artistic engagement was developing precisely at a political moment that, in the words of Jasna Tijardović, a young critic and curator at Belgrade's Museum of Contemporary Art, turned "out to be one of the most difficult times since the state ideology of self-management started to control all forms of intellectual freedom."[58] These processes had already begun in 1969, when the Serbian authorities began to target those responsible for 1968, both within the student community and among the professors of Belgrade University. But, as the previous chapters have revealed, the main repression took place only after the 1968 critiques were accompanied by two other forces of contestation: nationalism and liberalism. In Serbia, nationalist tendencies had already surfaced in May 1968, in part through a speech made by the famous writer Dobrica Ćosić on the "Kosovo question" at the Fourteenth Plenum of the Central Committee of the League of Communists of Serbia (LCS).

In the midst of a growing national movement among Albanians in the autonomous province of Kosovo, Ćosić came into conflict with LCS's Central Committee after denouncing the use of self-management as a cover for what he believed to be a "particularist," "bureaucratic nationalism."[59] He accused the decentralizing reforms of fueling anti-Serbian sentiments in other republics, and of simultaneously reviving an "anachronic, retrograde, primitive Serbianism."[60] Two months later, he left the party, and in 1969 took over the presidency of an ancient cultural organization called the Serbian Literary Cooperative, where he created a coalition for his new national program of Serbian "cultural and spiritual" unity "regardless of the existing republics or state borders."[61] In the 1980s, it would provide the core platform for Serbia's wider nationalist movement.[62]

The Croatian Mass Movement led many Serbian intellectuals to conclude that Yugoslavia was in a pronounced state of crisis. Whereas in Croatia the constitutional amendments fell short of what was being advocated, Serbian intellectuals argued that granting the autonomous provinces powers equal to those of the republics placed Serbia on an unequal footing with the other republics. In parallel with these "national" condemnations of the amendments, certain intellectuals criticized the way in which they were being adopted, and argued that the biggest threat to Yugoslavia was not the proposed constitutional reforms, but the lack of constitutionality itself, where decisions were being made behind closed doors.[63] With the suppression of the Croatian Mass Movement, however, all criticism, irrespective of its political orientation, became unacceptable. At this time, pressure mounted on the Serbian leadership to suppress any challenges to the regime, leading to the extreme political decisions made in Novi Sad in 1971. In October 1972, the same month that the SKC Gallery staged its alternative *Oktobar*, the Serbian leadership would face its own dismissal, after denying that Serbia had a nationalist problem and refusing to support the political trials taking place throughout Yugoslavia.

By October, the LCS leadership's refusal to establish closer control over the republic's social, economic, and political organizations led Tito to accuse them of being "more liberal, both in ideopolitical confrontation and with respect to the policy of criminal prosecution, pronouncement of sentence, and even presentation in the mass media," and of tolerating "ultraleftists" on the basis of "the theory that these are people who ideologically are for self-management but just are unrealistic and have illusions."[64] On 9 October 1972, Tito met with the political leadership of Serbia and accused them of insubordination and "unsocialist" economics. Soon after this meeting, both Nikezić and Perović submitted their resignations. By the end of the campaign to restore the principles of "democratic centralism," over one thousand people had been removed from the party.[65]

Like Zagreb's and Novi Sad's youth cultural centers, the SKC Gallery's pursuit of artistic experimentation at the beginning of the 1970s stood at odds with a political climate dominated by coercive control over intellectual freedoms. It is no coincidence that precisely at a moment marked by extreme cultural intolerance, the artists at the SKC Gallery began to look abroad and to foster networks with Western artists and critics. At the same time as *Oktobar '72*, and as part of

Belgrade's International Theatre Festival 6 (BITEF), French conceptual artist Daniel Buren installed his characteristic vertical red and white stripes on the screen of the large theater hall of Dom Omladine [Youth House], and gave a talk about his practice at the SKC Gallery. In the same month, Richard Demarco, Scottish promoter of visual arts, visited the SKC Gallery because he had "long wanted to compare the contemporary art scene in Yugoslavia with what [he] had discovered in numerous visits, since 1968, to Poland and Romania."[66] As a result of this meeting, he invited eight Yugoslav artists to participate in Edinburgh Arts '73.

CONCEPTUALISM'S "ALLEGED MARXISTS"

Held at Edinburgh's Melville College, the exhibition *Eight Yugoslav Artists* consisted of some documents chosen by the artists and brought to Edinburgh by Tomić. The exhibition's most notable element, however, was its culmination in a set of performances enacted inside the college's gymnasium. The four-hour-long *ART EVENT* of 19 August 1973 consisted of actions delivered concurrently (due to time restrictions), by Todosijević, Urkom, Abramović, and Popović. During the "art event," Urkom upholstered a chair in front of an audience, ironically translating the artistic act into a form of everyday manual craft. Abramović performed her *Rhythm 10*—a piece in which she rhythmically stabbed the spaces between the fingers of her splayed hand with a sharp pointed knife on a ground of plain white paper, changing the knife every time she cut herself, until all the knives set out in front of her had been used and the sequence had been brought to an end. The unnerving "knife game" was recorded and then played back, while the artist attempted to mimic the first arrangement of the action. At their core, both pieces maintained an uncompromising insistence on no other reality than their own—on concrete, as opposed to illusory, information. In the words of Abramović: "The painter uses color to paint blood. As a performer I do not use my blood as a color but as blood. During the performance, I am inside reality: blood is blood, pain is pain, the body is the body."[67] In a similar vein, Todosijević performed his *Odluka kao umetnost* [Decision as Art], while his partner, Marinela Koželj, sat passively beside him. For the action, he stripped to the waist and applied paint to four small plants placed at the corner of the stage. Then, after covering his torso with salt, the artist picked a live carp from a water tank and positioned it on the floor, during which he began to gulp large quantities of water, until the fish died.

It was also in Edinburgh that the group first met Joseph Beuys, who was invited by Demarco to give his *12 Hour Lecture* in the same gymnasium where *Eight Yugoslav Artists* was held. Beuys had already exhibited *The Pack* at the Edinburgh

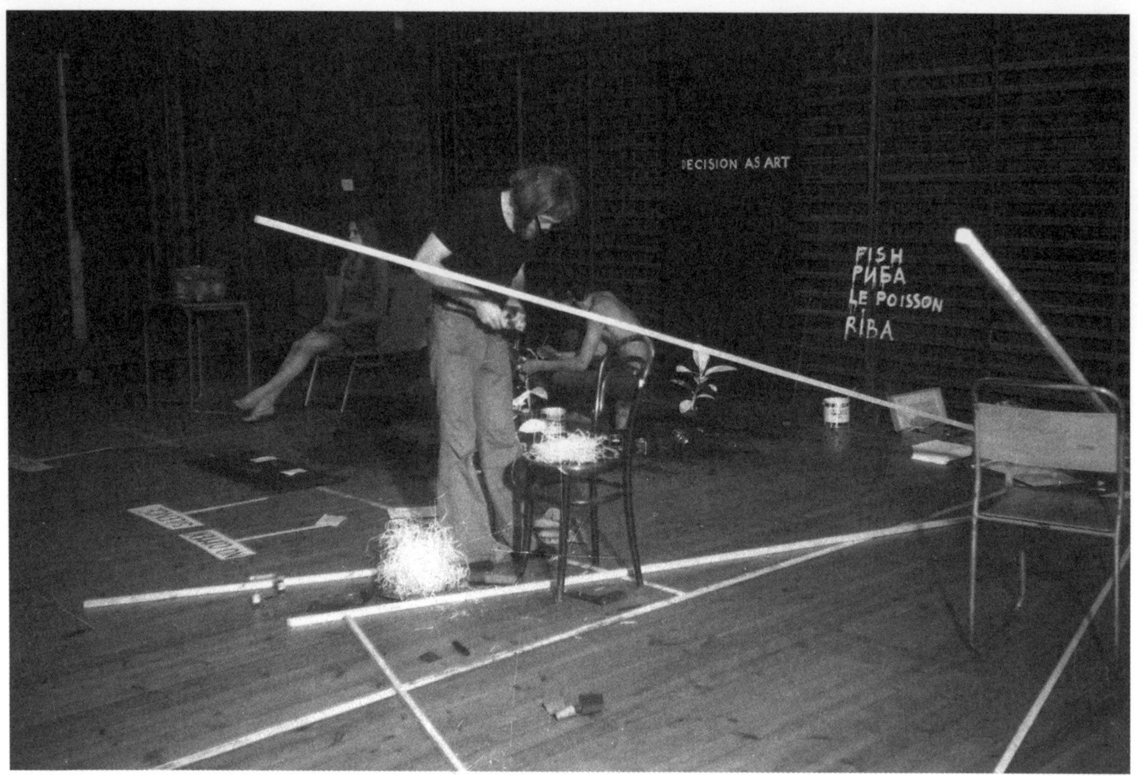

3.4. Gergelj Urkom, event for the Richard Demarco Gallery at Melville College, Edinburgh, 19 August 1973. *Eight Yugoslav Artists*. Edinburgh Arts 1973. Image courtesy of Demarco European Art Foundation and Demarco Digital Archive, University of Dundee.

3.5. Marina Abramović, *Rhythm 10*, Edinburgh, 19 August 1973. *Eight Yugoslav Artists*. Edinburgh Arts 1973. Image courtesy of Demarco European Art Foundation and Demarco Digital Archive, University of Dundee. © Marina Abramović. Courtesy of Marina Abramović and Sean Kelly Gallery, New York. DACS 2020.

3.6. Raša Todosijević, *Odluka kao umetnost* [Decision as Art], Edinburgh, 19 August 1973. *Eight Yugoslav Artists*. Edinburgh Arts 1973. Image courtesy of Demarco European Art Foundation and Demarco Digital Archive, University of Dundee.

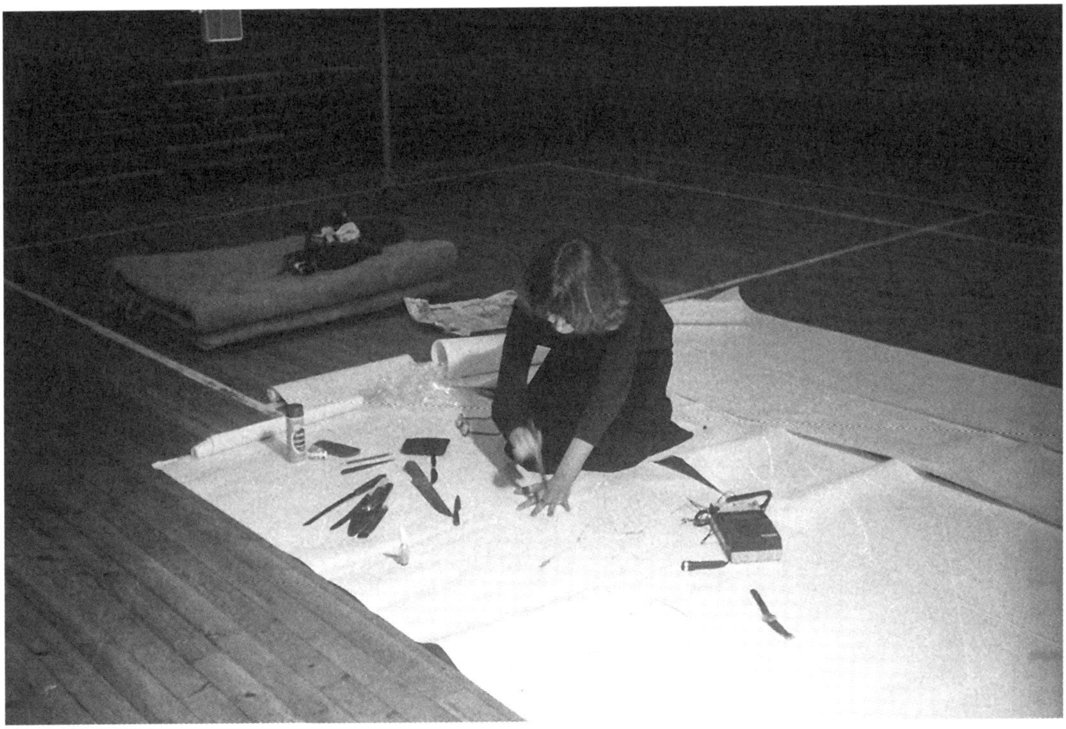

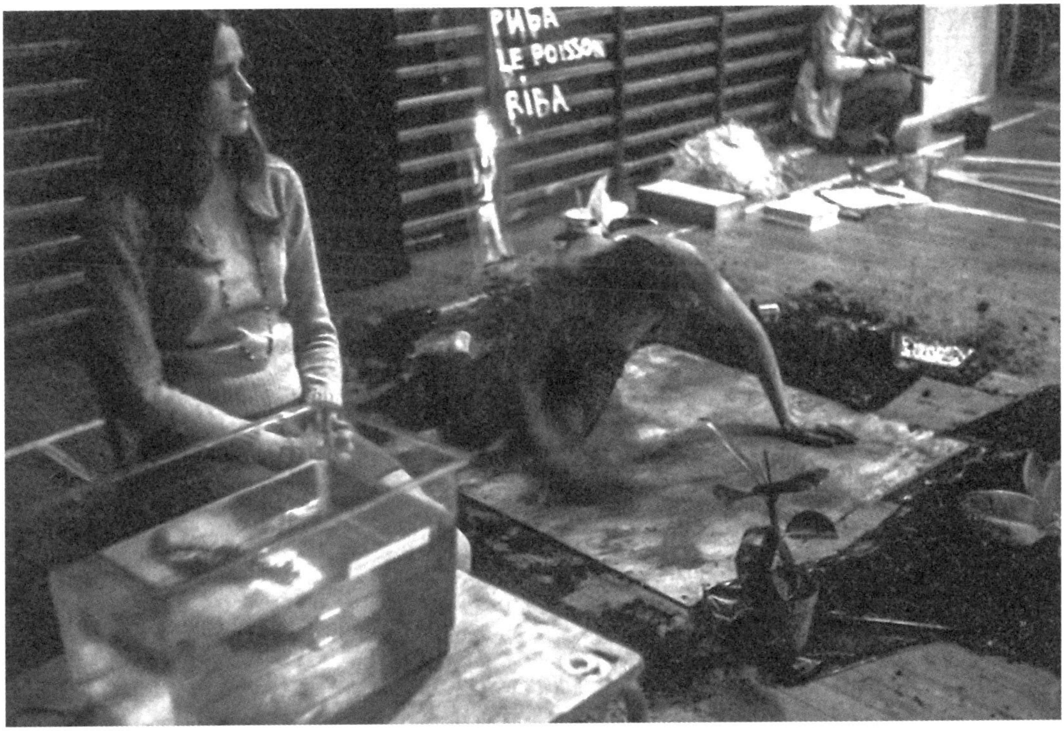

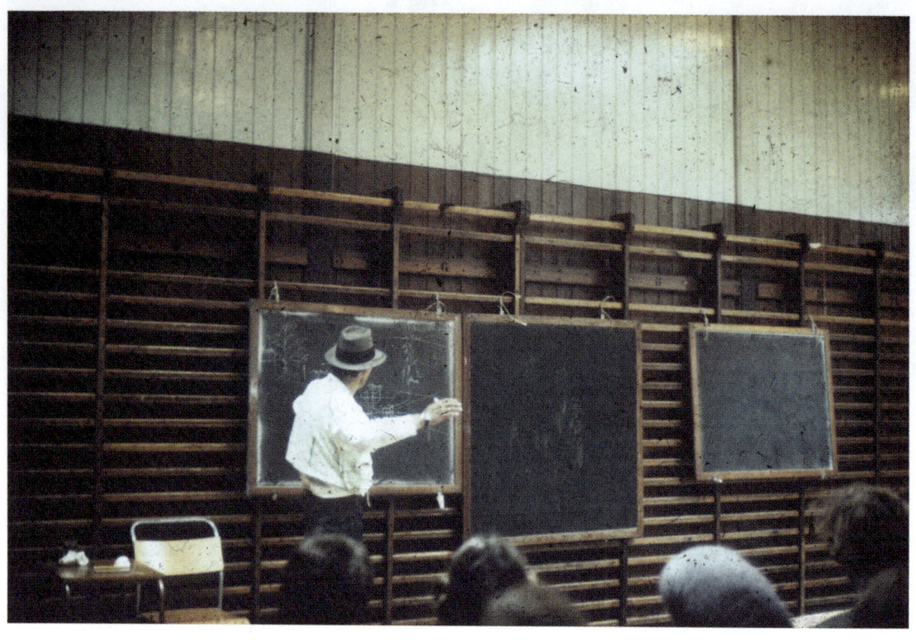

3.7. Joseph Beuys, *Twelve Hour Lecture: A Homage to Anacharsis Cloots.* The Richard Demarco Gallery at Melville College, Edinburgh, 20 August 1973. Edinburgh Arts 1973. Image courtesy of Demarco European Art Foundation and Demarco Digital Archive, University of Dundee.

College of Art in 1970 for *Strategy: Get Arts*—an exhibition that Demarco believed had emphasized "the artist's role as a powerful defender of the truth inherent in fairy tales and as a magician able to revive our sense of wonder."[68] Beuys also performed *Celtic (Kinloch Rannoch) Scottish Symphony*, in which he made and erased a series of drawings on a single blackboard, maneuvering it with a shepherd's crook and holding it aloft as if it were a sacred piece of equipment. One contemporary observer, Alistair Mackintosh, described the performance as "much too rich and too personal, and this points to the main difficulty in dealing with Beuys—his art is so individual that current art language cannot describe it without distorting its essential character."[69] Mackintosh acknowledged that he was assessing the man himself rather than his work, but only because "Joseph Beuys' greatest work is Joseph Beuys, or rather the presentation of Joseph Beuys."[70] Still, the performance was "electrifying"—"everyone who sat through its entirety was converted to the Beuys cult, although everyone, needless to say, had a different explanation."[71] In 1973, Beuys performed one of his blackboard lectures, again propagating a romantic and personal narrative based on a mythology of healing.

Amid this atmosphere of hysterical fanaticism, Todosijević used a children's John Bull printing set to produce ten copies of a work consisting of just the inscription "Josephine Beuys," accompanied by the author's signature. This simple gesture was meant to ironically debunk the auratic notion behind Beuys, and attacked the field of meaning generated around the private "Beuys" mythology. While many of the artists working at the SKC Gallery revered and respected Beuys, including Todosijević himself, this ultimately Duchampian translation challenged Beuys's decision to fill Duchamp's silence with a flood of words. The mute and reduced gesture confronted Beuys's private and quasi-symbolic authorial system, attacking the "curious sectarianism" that surrounded his work.[72] Intending to sell the prints for £5 each, Todosijević sparked contention among Beuys obsessives, even provoking one gallery owner from Minneapolis to purchase almost the entire print run, just to prevent it from being spread across Edinburgh.[73]

Todosijević's work offers a subtle insight into the "negatively catalytic" reactions of Belgrade artists toward the supposed spirit of unbridled creativity abroad.[74] In Yugoslavia, these sentiments roughly coincided with the collapse of several art groups, which were similarly disappointed with conceptual art's commercialization. In 1971, two years before the Belgrade artists participated in Edinburgh Arts, such disillusionment had led OHO to stop working as a group and to form a commune in Šempas. Combined with a repressive political climate, this skepticism also led to the dismantling of Grupa KÔD, who, confronted with "conceptual"

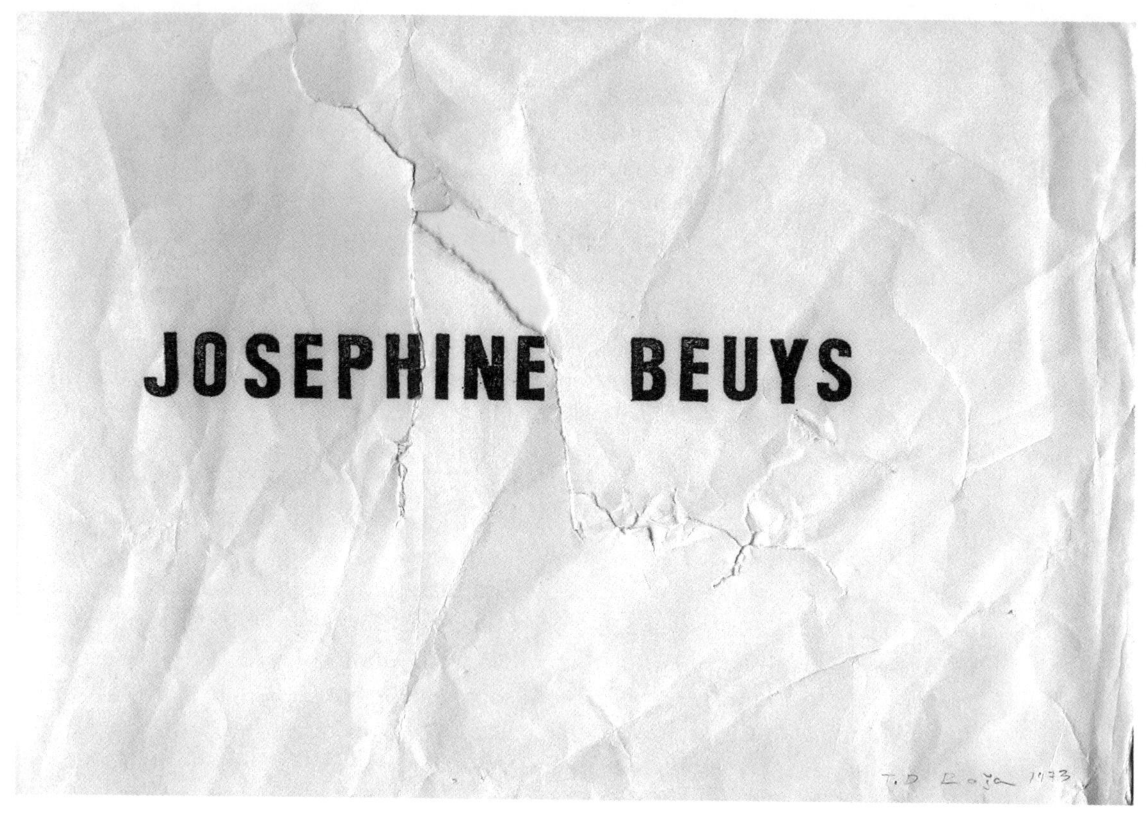

3.8. Raša Todosijević, *Josephine Beuys*, Edinburgh, 1973.
Image courtesy of the artist.

works priced in the range of $10,000 at the Biennale des Jeunes in 1972—works which Koščević refused to unpack at the SC Gallery—also ceased further public activity upon their return to Yugoslavia.[75]

As in many of Yugoslavia's other capitals, experiences abroad led Belgrade's new generation of artists to become highly cynical of Western artists, "mainly because of the amount of money associated with each artist."[76] Writing in 1975 for the New York artists' magazine *The Fox*, Jasna Tijardović summarized the skepticism that was felt by Yugoslav artists, who simply couldn't understand what "made them [as visiting artists]—and they were allegedly Marxists—so powerful and important. A lot of Yugoslav artists did similar work but received no money, no accolades. So we all thought, given the notion of the Yugoslav self-management system, that we could make something of our own, which really belongs within our society and our culture."[77]

Within this artistic climate, artists working through the SKC began to interpret contemporary Western art through their own particular cultural circumstances. Whereas for artists in Zagreb this initially meant fostering an "art which left the institution and communicated with 'the people,'" as Iveković put it, Belgrade's new generation of artists began to think about relations between art and politics in a "nonaligned" way.[78] While Western conceptual art had initially challenged "liberal ideology and the logic of capital," Belgrade artists preferred to "confront and undermine the imperialism of [Western] art, or at least try to link art with class consciousness."[79] It was at the notorious Third April Meeting of 1974 that this standpoint was most explicitly declared.

"INVERSIONS, IMITATIONS, AND CONTRASTS"

In Belgrade, expanded networks of exchange were above all cultivated through the famous *Aprilski susreti* [April Meetings], organized in the SKC Gallery since 1972 as an "open competition dedicated to experiments in the areas of art, film, theater, music, architecture, and design."[80] In the bulletin issued during the First April Meeting in 1972, the organizers declared that their intention was to depart from the "existing form of April festivities, from spectacle, revelry and Avala outings, and to give the manifestations related to 4 April a character that is oriented toward work and research."[81] With this aim in mind, the First April Meeting was announced throughout Yugoslavia as a competition on the theme of "expanded media" that would support younger artists in their "explorations of the possibilities of interdisciplinary ties in different areas of expression."[82]

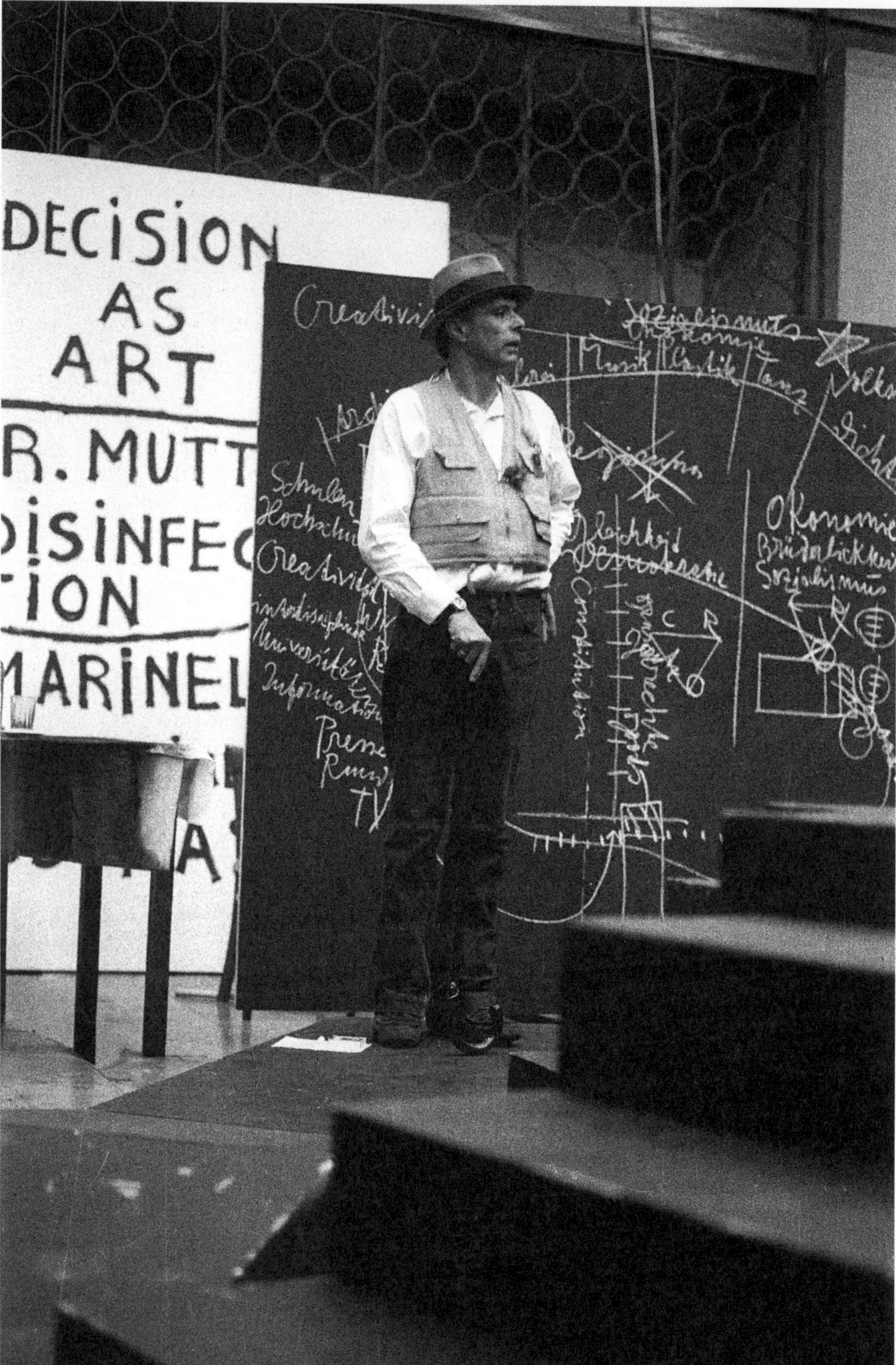
DECiSiON
AS
ART
R. MUTT
DiSINFEC
TION
MARiNEL
Ökonomie
Tanz
TV

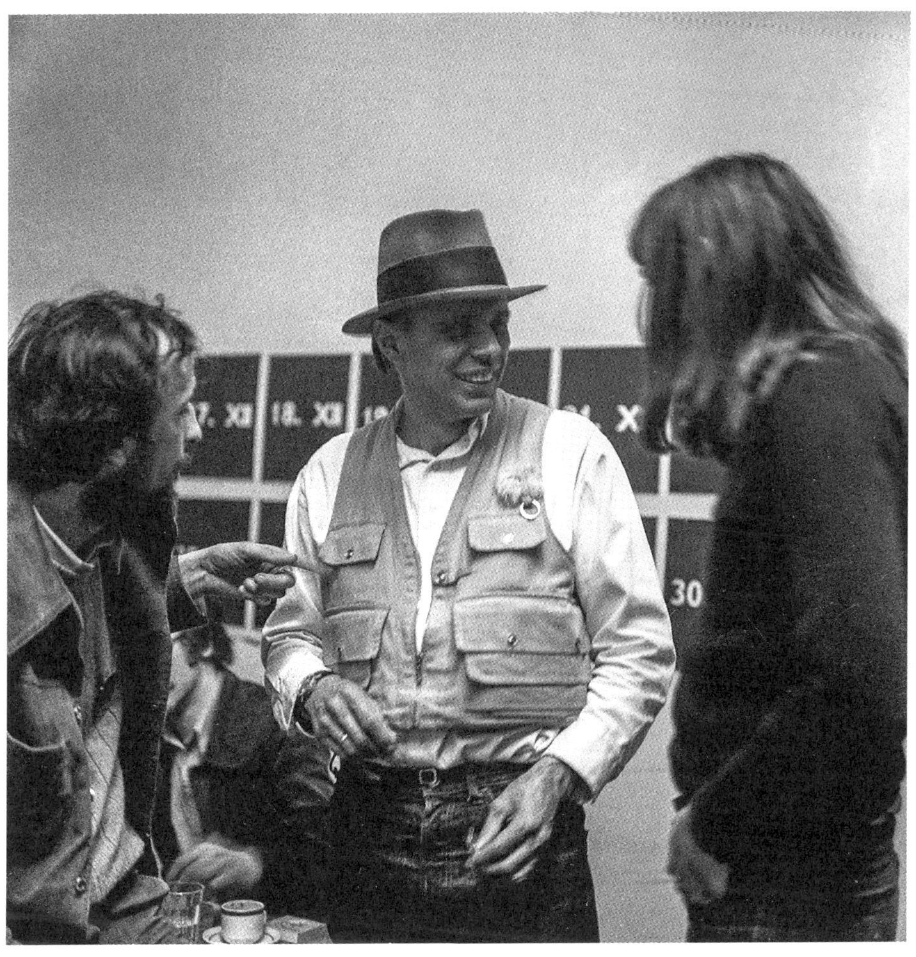

3.9. Joseph Beuys delivering a lecture at the Third April Meeting on 19 April 1974. Photograph by Nebojša Čanković. Image courtesy of the SKC Archive, Belgrade.

3.10. Joseph Beuys at the Third April Meeting, Belgrade, 18 April 1974. Photograph by Nebojša Čanković. Image courtesy of the SKC Archive, Belgrade.

According to Matko Meštrović—one of the key figures of Zagreb's New Tendencies Movement—the April Meetings were intended to "stimulate those who were not professionally dealing with art, in that independent creative activity was encouraged rather than copying the work of 'professionals.'"[83]

With the aim of overcoming the "classical limits of the specialized arts," the Third April Meeting of 1974 lasted six days, and included in its programs a diverse array of theater performances, film screenings, happenings, and art "events."[84] The most notable aspect of the Meeting, however, was Beuys's attendance, by invitation from the group of Belgrade artists and Biljana Tomić.[85] Beuys stayed for almost a week at the city's Hotel Moskva, where he regularly met local artists and engaged in daily discussions. At the SKC he lectured on his ideas about the interaction between the artist and society, and presented the concept of an "artistic/anarchistic counter-culture and a revolutionary reinterpretation of history."[86] Beuys's invitation seemed to underline the general intentions of the April Meetings—his preference for direct communication and his utopian goal of democratizing art into "social sculpture" correlated with several of the actions performed at the event. In fact, Denegri identified public participation as the defining achievement of the April Meetings: "the successful communication with a much wider audience, including those who do not fall within the circle of professionally formed artists, ... removed art from ubiquitous metaphysics and abandoned art's autonomy."[87]

Speaking retrospectively, Denegri noted that Beuys's Belgrade visit was not only spectacular but also "emblematic, insofar as it advanced the programmatic politics of those who subscribed to his expanded concept of art."[88] Removed from purely formalist concerns, Beuys's pedagogical and real-time political actions—his formation of the Organization for Direct Democracy by Referendum and the Free International University in 1972—reflected his effort to press the direction of art practice toward the very "spirit of the collective."[89] His lecture given at the SKC expounded his theory of art as social sculpture: "Art that no longer refers solely to the modern art work, to the artist, but comprehends a notion of art relating to everyone and to [the] very question and problem of the social organism in which people live. Without doubt, such a notion of art would no longer refer exclusively to the specialists within the modern art world, but extend to the whole work of humanity."[90]

Beuys's social idealism was based on the presupposition that creative potential is universal—the assumption that "in principle every person is then an artist."[91] His presence and participation resonated through all of these events, now historicized through photographic documentation. In several photographs he is shown sipping cocktails and dressed in his staple long fur coat, which perpetuated his origin myth, in others wearing his hat and hunter's vest which were so inextricably linked to the Beuys brand. Looking through these snapshots, one could conclude that Beuys's call for the "victory of socialist warmth and self-determination over materialist greed and alienation" resonated in a socialist country, and adhered to an event fostering an art driven by participation.[92] Todosijević, however, believed that "somehow this general feeling of jubilant liberalism was a fraud: the goal was to show the West that there exists a kind of art here that is as modern and progressive as similar tendencies in America, Italy, or England."[93] Despite what ultimately seemed a festival of free-thinking tendencies, in line with the idealistic global push toward the "democratization of art," a cynical reasoning still prevailed in two performances at the Meeting—radical gestures that reduced art to a form of hostile action.

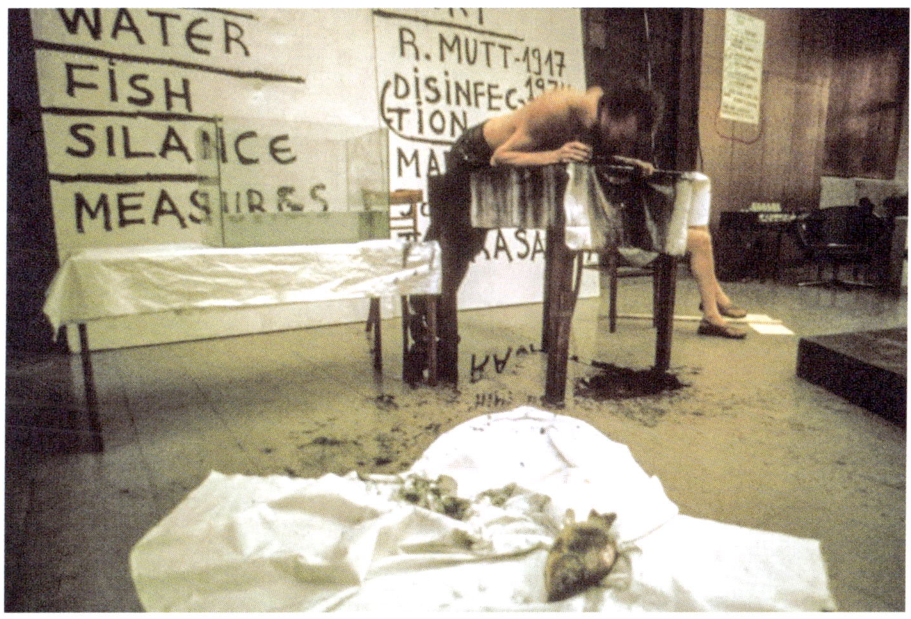

3.11. Raša Todosijević, *Pijenje vode—inverzije, imitacije, i kontrasti* [Drinking Water: Inversions, Imitations, and Contrasts], Third April Meeting, Belgrade, 19 April 1974. Image courtesy of the artist.

Just an hour before Beuys's scheduled lecture, Todosijević began his complex *Pijenje vode—inverzije, imitacije, i kontrasti* [Drinking Water: Inversions, Imitations, and Contrasts], by throwing a fish in front of his audience, waiting for it to struggle for breath. Over the course of thirty-five minutes, he drank twenty-six glasses of water, in synchronicity with the fish's spasms. Artist and fish were bound in a dialogue of suffering; external suffering was inverted back onto the artist himself. As a result of the high quantity of water in his body, Todosijević said he

> had to vomit periodically on the table in front of me. In order to determine the duration of the whole piece, I poured, under the white tablecloth, violet pigment powder easily dissoluble in water. I thought to interrupt the piece at the moment the cloth was completely soaked by violet color due to the poured water.... I've not had any intention to describe some state of facts or relations in nature, but to show and define by means of thought-out inversion, or simple act, the artistic gesture, that is art.[94]

All the while, Marinela Koželj sat by stoically, overdressed in contrast to Todosijević's seminude body. Her static stance was an important feature of the action, further compromising the spectator's coherent perception of the individual author/artist. The events took place in front of large white sheets of paper on which Todosijević had written the key words (in English):

PRESUMPTION ABOUT ART	DECISION AS ART
IMITATION	R MUTT—1917
WATER	DISINFEC—1974
FISH	-TION
SILANCE [sic]	MARINELA
MEASURES	JOSEPHINE BEUYS
	RAŠA

Writing of "lists," Briony Fer identified in the indexical trace a "deadpan banality" within which lurks a "kind of terrifying and comic extravagance."[95] Todosijević's "list" acted as a semantic anchor—a "verbal correlative" to the performative character of the event, transposing it into the mental sphere. As Peggy Phelan has argued, performance art—as a move from the grammar of words to the grammar of the body—represented a transferral from the traditional clarity of metaphor to the realm of metonymy. Additive and "associative," metonymy works to secure a horizontal axis of contiguity and displacement.[96] In one sense, *Drinking Water* presents the relations between the primary powers of the artist's subjectivity—establishing a conceptual model of the "artist's decision" to treat "something" or "anything" as art, even drinking excessive amounts of water. As "R Mutt" proved, the performative act, the gesture that announces "I intend X as a work of art," is always dependent on the figure of the artist—the agent is always there. The performing body is metonymic of self, of character, of voice, of "presence." But in the plenitude of its apparent visibility and availability, the performer actually disappears and represents something else—"Marinela," "fish," "disinfection"—"art."

If Beuys and the general current of the April Meetings had privileged the majority and assumed that "every person is an artist," Todosijević wanted to act as the catalyst that exhausted viewers, ambushed and deceived them. Of the objects he chose to present, he made it clear that he did "not wish them to be interpreted as symbolic, associative or for them to be given attributes."[97] *Drinking Water* was inspired by his performance at Edinburgh, where he had thrown a goldfish on the floor, waiting for it to die. People pleaded for the artist to put the fish back into the aquarium, making Todosijević question the audience's hypocrisy: "They eat so many chickens every day, why are they crying about fish?"[98] Furthermore, the artist put his own body at jeopardy to trigger a threatening feeling of anxiety. In the words of the artist himself: "My performance does not want to demystify; it is intended to irritate all that is negative in man in order to reveal it—the bitterness you feel after my performance is the negative in you. It triggers off a referential system which is immediately related to either fascism or aggression, but it's not my aggressiveness that's the problem, it's yours."[99]

Whereas Beuys proliferated the recurring theme of an individual origin myth, based on his plane crash in the Crimea and rescue by Tatars, Todosijević's event challenged closed systems and generated the conditions of the creative act, where no work of art is finished until completed by the spectator. Todosijević did not rely on "communicative clichés" to endow his artistic event with elements of symbolic meaning aimed at some form of active criticism; rather, the very act of artistic behavior became devoid of any socially authorized role. And while Beuys's practice was almost entirely dependent on the signifying capability of the metaphor, metonymic processes permeated Todosijević's performance. In one sense a "disinfection" and in another a contagion, *Drinking Water* was unreproducible and nonmetaphorical. Within this impossible system, the author was marked as loss; "SILENCE" prevailed.

In a way, Todosijević's indirect interrogation of Beuys's practice anticipated the criticisms that Benjamin Buchloh would raise in his 1980 essay "Beuys, the Twilight of the Idol: A Preliminary Critique," in which he argued that Beuys invoked mythical forms of experience in a way that reversed the liberation of art from ritual and cult. In Buchloh's words:

> Visual ideology ... immerses its viewers in "meaning" as much as the discourses of religion and neurosis do: to the extent that literally everything within these belief systems is "meaningful." Reaffirming the individual's ties to such systems, the actual capacities of individual development are repressed. Beuys keeps insisting on the fact that his art-object and dramatic performance activities have "metaphysical" meaning, transcending their actual visual concretion and material appearance within their proper discourse.[100]

Taking Buchloh's scathing critique into consideration, one could argue that many local artists attending the April Meetings saw through Beuys's facade because it mirrored the myriad contradictions shaping Yugoslav society at the time of his visit. By basing his practice on a private mythology, Beuys remained consciously oblivious to the conditions that determined his work and its reception. Put succintly by Buchloh, his espousal of the "integration of art, science and politics," which he referred to as a "totalized concept of art," was nothing more than "simple-minded utopian drivel."[101] Just as Beuys's practice relied on a combination of ahistorical, "utopian drivel" and a passive reliance on the art world's financial system, Yugoslavia's claims to autonomy had ultimately given way to its total dependence on the world economy dominated by the West, while self-management was quickly devolving into a mere caricature of the original ideal. After Tito's split with Stalin, the country gave itself a new orientation by developing notions of self-governance aimed at building a horizon of direct cooperation between "self-managed associations." By 1974, however, the country's aspiration to abolish exploitation had ultimately succumbed to two types of neoconservatism: one internal, connected to the reintroduction of "firm hand" repressive policies by the old-guard party members; the other external, linked to international money markets in the late 1960s and early 1970s. Simply put, self-management had been distorted into a hybrid combination of regressive socialism and market deregulation. It was this conservative climate, further discussed in chapter 4, that provided the political backdrop for the most canonical event that took place at the April Meeting that year.

One day after Beuys's and Todosijević's actions, Abramović performed her career-defining *Ryhthm 5*, by staging a highly routinized, ritualistic cleansing process. In the courtyard of the SKC, Abramović built a huge five-pointed star, and poured a hundred and fifty liters of petrol on it, then cut her hair, her nails, and her toenails. She lay down inside the star and had someone light it. Lasting for over an hour and a half, until the artist passed out from low oxygen levels (and had to be carried out by Urkom and Radomir Damnjan), *Rhythm 5* represented (to Abramović, at least) a symbol of the postwar generation's frustrations:

> I had to exceed the heroism of my parents with a heroic deed, bringing myself to the physical boundaries of the possible. They were ready to sacrifice their own lives for freedom and for revolution. That cult of sacrifice for an idea, for the people, was present in the psychological make-up of our parents, in their stories about the Second World War and the Partisan movement. I had to show them I am ready for sacrifice.[102]

Born in 1946 into a family of the postwar communist elite, Abramović was the daughter of revolutionary Partisan leaders during the Second World War. After the war, her mother became director of the Museum of the Revolution in Belgrade, and her father, a career military man, became a general. As such, the family represented the "new class" of secular Partisans who established a high social position within what was supposed to be a nonhierarchical society. Abramović's statement locates *Rhythm 5* within her biography, reflecting on her irritation as a member of the postwar generation that was being kept far from power and responsibility by their parents. Her retrospective testament defines the performance as a kind of "self-sacrifice" (in which she placed herself inside the "red" star—the official state emblem of the "communist state"), or as "a redemptive process," as Bojana Pejić put it.[103] Whether or not one is willing to accept this reading of the now mythicized event, the gesture was undeniably subversive in relation to the general premise of the April Meetings. Rather than possessing any determined significance, it is perhaps the abstract nature of *Rhythm 5*—its refusal to adhere to any practical or sanitized criteria—that granted it a canonical position at the event. Completely self-contained and self-concerned, it acted as an antithesis to the utopian belief that "expanded art" could actually "democratize" society.

What resonance did Todosijević's and Abramović's actions have within the immediate context of the Meetings? The most revealing aspect of the festival appears to have been a moderated discussion on the theme of "Expanded Media or New Art?," where visiting (Western) and local critics disagreed on the broader political and economic conditions that determine art production. Here Italian critic and curator Achille Bonito Oliva raised his concept that art's basis is dependent on three elements: the propositions of artists, the market, and the public. In this structure, it was the market system that adduced art as a required good rather than an excess. The scheme raised serious disagreement among local participants,

3.12. Marina Abramović, *Rhythm 5*, 1974. Image courtesy of the SKC Archive, Belgrade.

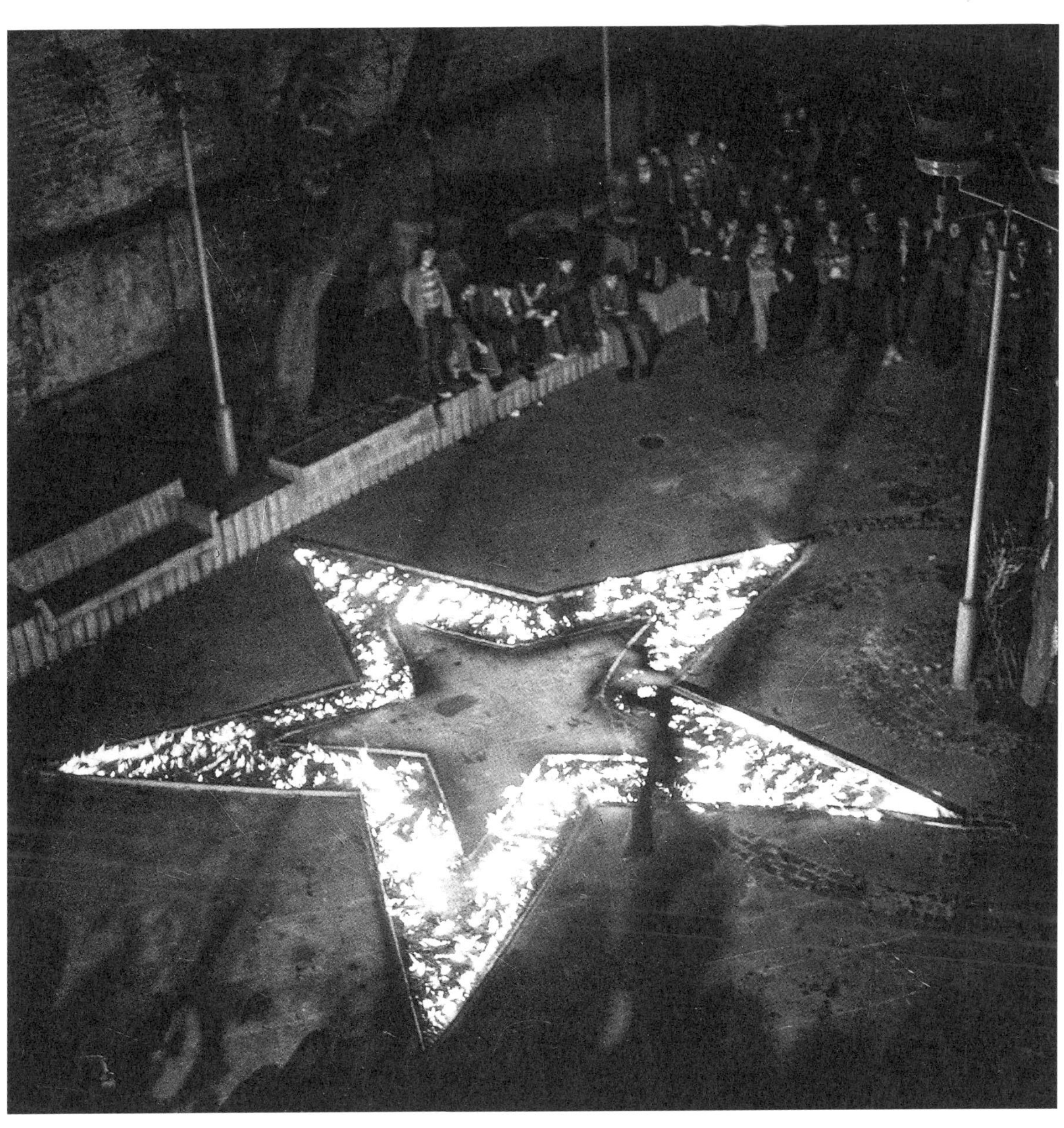

triggered by Blažević's question of how such a formulaic appraisal is altered when the "market" criterion is eliminated. In response, Bonito Oliva proposed that in socialist societies, "ideological criteria" replace the external pressures of commercial forces. Consequently, he said, "the Students' Cultural Center [was] marginal, since it [did] not correspond to the values of the state apparatus."[104] In this view, although woven together by their undoubtedly defiant, violent, and insurgent nature, performed within the program of a festival committed to the theme of "expanded media," and linked with "experiments" otherwise characteristic of "youth," Todosijević's and Abramović's events could not belong to an alternative culture. Despite being performed in public, at a state-funded gallery, and based on an unflinching provocation, these gestures could never have been perceived as "political" acts.

ART WITHOUT A MARKET

Achille Bonito Oliva's remark sparked serious contention among other critics participating in the discussion. In particular, Barbara Reise, the London-based art historian and close friend of the Art & Language group, was strongly opposed to Bonito Oliva's formula, which suggested all art outside of Western circuits was less valuable than Western art. In her words: "In talking about what we've called new media, directly in relation to what is considered art, we have an international culture, but instead we are arguing about some ideology."[105] The "ideology" Reise was referring to had failed to register Yugoslavia's particular positioning on the Cold War geopolitical and cultural fault lines, and assumed that socialist realism still prevailed there. Regardless of the country's complex political identity, for many Western visitors Yugoslavia meant communism; it meant somewhere in the "East," though perhaps not quite of it. Divided by Cold War configurations, Europe's contemporary art scene was established on a system of difference, one which predetermined the interpretation of works.[106]

The disagreement anticipated several of the challenges that Popović and his wife, Jasna Tijardović, would raise during their trip to New York, in February 1974, where they immediately made contact with Joseph Kosuth and began to lecture on "Art in Serbia/Yugoslavia" at several universities. Their visit coincided with a seminal moment in Art & Language's development, as the collective began to rigorously expand their critical awareness of the social preconditions of art production. *The Fox* was a "political" journal by members of the group, with a self-proclaimed aim of considering "art, and the lives of artists in relation to (a) social philosophy."[107] Substituting analytical philosophy with a Marxist reading of concrete conditions in the cultural system, members explained the motives behind their ideological standpoints. In the majority of texts, an obsession with communal organization prevailed as a resistance to the bureaucratization of art. Popović and Tijardović collaborated with the group by contributing an essay on "Art in Serbia/Yugoslavia" for the first issue. But rather than launching directly into a self-critical evaluation of their practice in relation to the social and economic base upon which they operated, they first needed to make a crucial clarification, addressing preconceptions of Yugoslav art similar to those raised at the April Meeting discussions:

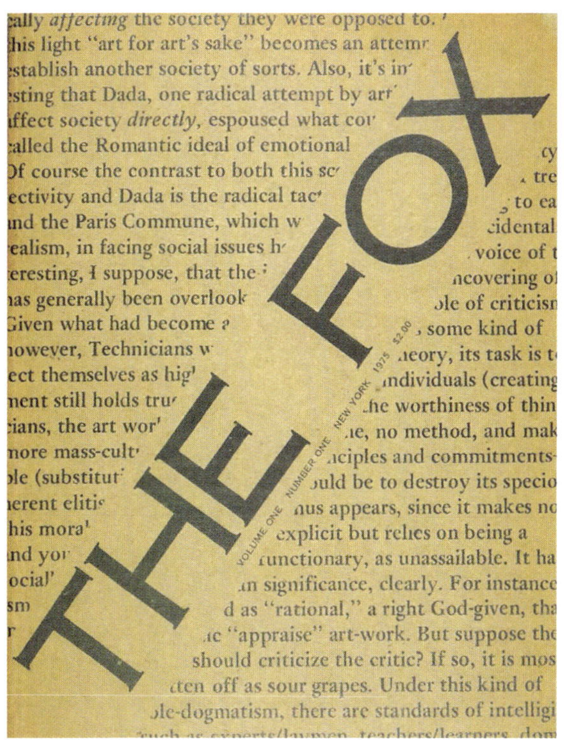

3.13. Art & Language, front cover of *The Fox 1*, New York, 1975. Image courtesy of Michael Corris.

> During our stay in New York, we tried to talk with as many artists and students as we could. We talked about what we saw and what we know of the galleries as well as our experiences in Yugoslavia. That meant we spoke somehow differently and perhaps sometimes more fundamentally. We have the feeling that this sort of "deeper" talk was thought to be inappropriate or strange, or looked on as a reflection of something having its sources in the socio-political system that we come from—as if we were expressing not our opinion but merely the official opinion of our state. It seemed to be considered that what we thought or did was not of ourselves, but somebody else, that we were mere products, finally, of a communist ideology—and it is well known what that means. It is equated, for one thing, with Social Realism, and that means "poverty" in art. In New York it seems that everybody believes they are thinking freely, democratically, as if this thinking has no connection with the society they live in.[108]

In such a situation, with the Yugoslav artist preconceived as a communist Other, some artists initially associated with the activities of the SKC Gallery nevertheless chose to pursue an international career—including, most famously, Abramović, who from 1975 worked almost exclusively abroad. For other artists, who continued to collaborate with the SKC Gallery, a natural development was to behave in a more consciously strategic way. Since the art system had predetermined the perspective of these artists, they felt it was essential to reflect on this position and adopt it as a kind of starting point. For Belgrade's artists, this position constituted a reflection of the system of "self-managing democracy." Although Popović and Tijardović were the first to pursue this stance with their essay for *The Fox*, in the following year it became a driving force in the SKC Gallery's activities.

SELF-MANAGEMENT OR SELF-PROTECTION?

Returning from their trip to New York, in October 1975, Popović and Tijardović invited Jill Breakstone, Michael Corris, and Andrew Menard, members of New York's Art & Language group, to conduct a four-day seminar on "Cultural Imperialism" at the SKC Gallery. This visit resulted in the production of a series of nine-meter-square panels, with photos of the meeting and excerpts from the seminar transcripts, as well as other items the visitors discovered through their research into socialist self-management.[109] In a letter about the trip to Belgrade published in *Left Curve* magazine, Michael Corris wrote that "self-management may be working better in Yugoslavia than in most socialist countries, but it is constantly diluted, reified by the state bureaucracy," and consequently had the "tendency to get too heavy—[due to] the power of administration."[110] According to Corris, the best work, while paralleling "international art" practices, acknowledged the

DOES BEING A CONSUMER EVER ALLOW YOU TO HAVE A DIALECTICAL RELATIONSHIP TO YOUR CULTURE?

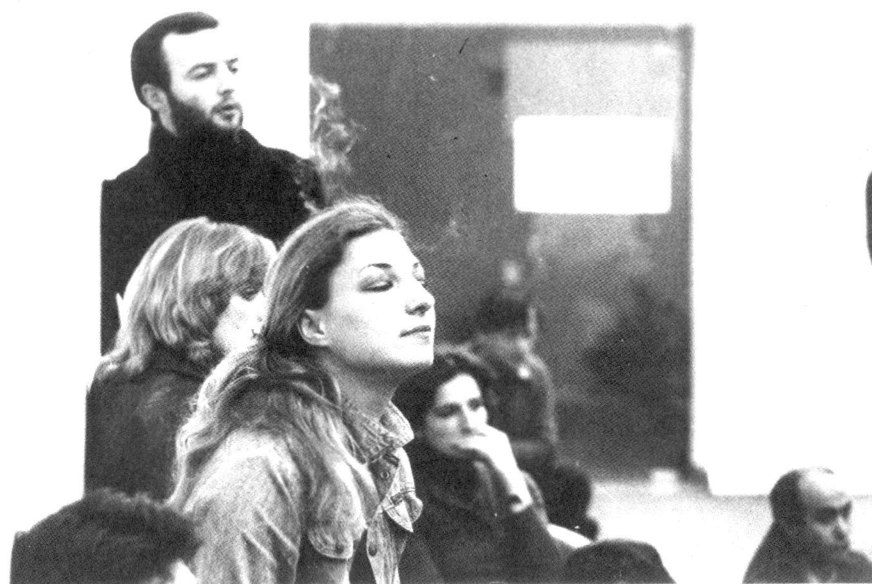

J. Tijardović **Part of my job at the Museum of Modern Art here in Belgrade is meeting with worker representatives, and trying to explain to them about recent art. This is a very difficult problem. They say I am too "abstract", and I think they need to be educated more, but I can't do it because they think I'm too "abstract". I think the Museum should be accountable to the workers, but sometimes I feel they are not willing to make much effort to understand something different from what they are used to. They are used to French Impressionism and "naive" or "intimist" art from Yugoslavia. Yet this kind of art helps detach them from a more dialectical relation to their own culture—it isn't about the self-management of culture but about imperialism, and style, and art appreciation.**

3.14. Art & Language, panel from *The Organization of Culture under Self-Management Socialism*, Belgrade, 1975–1976. Image courtesy of Michael Corris.

strengths of the local cultural context. Corris concluded that the artists working with the gallery

> aren't in fact supported by the bureaucracy. Because of their work they have been excluded from this privilege—as are most artists doing newer kinds of art (bureaucracy makes little distinction among newer kinds of art, thereby lending credence to the idea that the avant-garde has "revolutionary" potential, even if it's bourgeois art)—though they do get an occasional prize (they know some of the right people), and they do get to lecture occasionally.[111]

These were preoccupations that were again discussed in the Art & Language seminars—regarding the distribution of culture in relation to the "workers." As with the activities of Zagreb's SC Gallery and Novi Sad's Youth Tribune, the SKC's collaborators complained of the inadequacy of self-management relations in what they described as "curbing the role of state activities."[112] For Todosijević, the problem lay in the fact that in "90% of cases those who talk about workers are not from workers' families," and subsequently, although enterprises had independence, they were still dominated by councils of educated and higher-skilled workers that took over management and decision making. In short, the system had produced only a semblance of participation.[113] Regarding the SKC Gallery itself, Michael Corris reached a similar conclusion in his letter to *Left Curve*, labeling it an "institutionally (financially) sanctioned means for students, and particularly artists (most of whom are no longer students) to register some kind of dissent, but as a means which virtually excludes all other means."[114] He continued:

> With the center then, they now have a place to show their work fairly regularly and they have a generally receptive audience as well, even if not too many "workers" show up. Not that their work can change very much, of course. Which is the overwhelming impression we've been left with: something is better than nothing, yes, how true, but it's all so frustrating, the same ground covered time and again, the same discussions, the same exhibitions, "art and revolution," "art and revolution." (The art in factories is generally Impressionism, or so we've been told, the universal cultural solvent).[115]

3.15. SKC Gallery, cover for *Oktobar '75*, Belgrade, 1975.
Image courtesy of the SKC Archive, Belgrade.

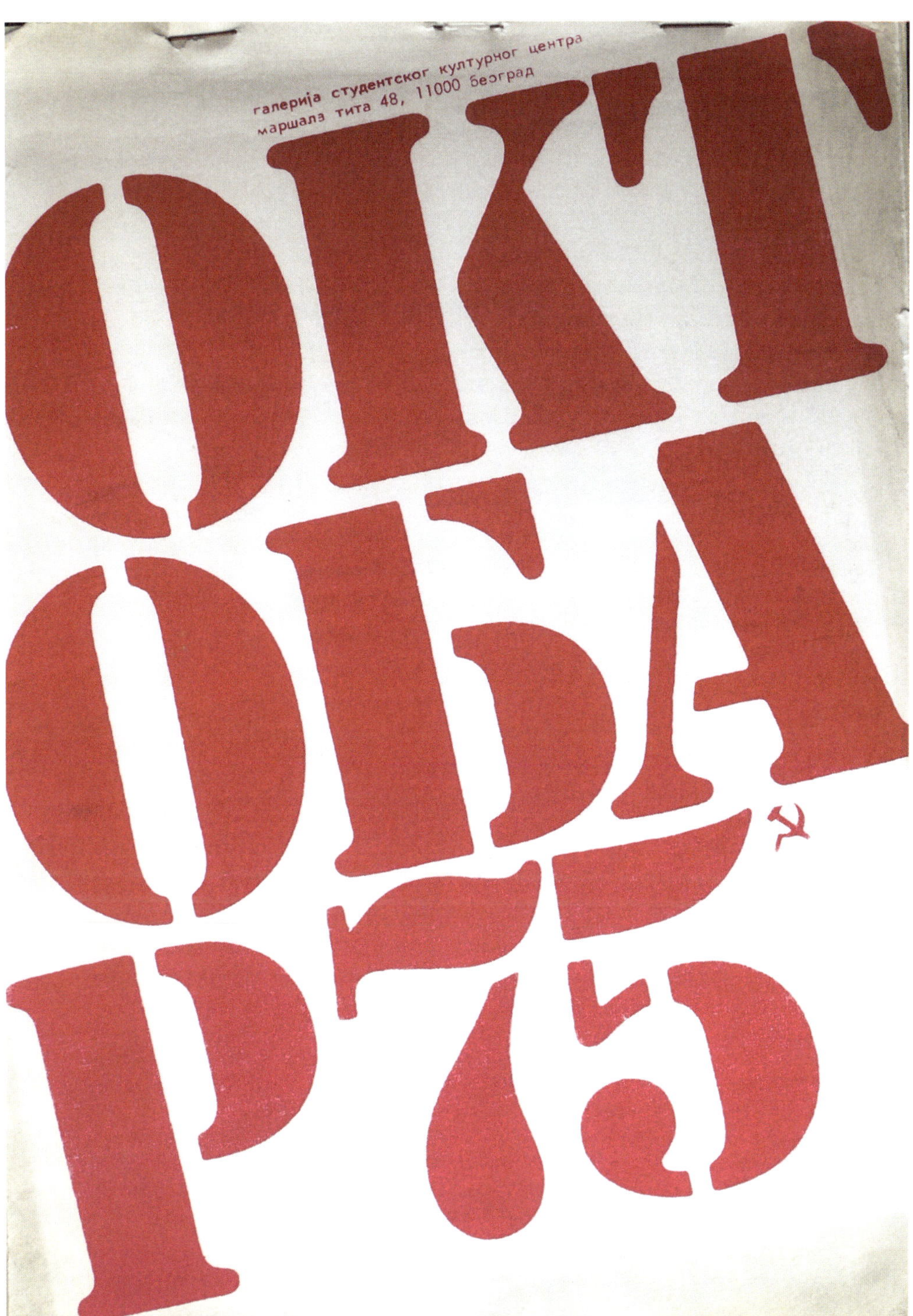
галерија студентског културног центра
маршала тита 48, 11000 београд
ОКТ
ОБА
Р 75

Following the discussions of the possibilities for modern art in a socialist society, the SKC Gallery organized the event *Oktobar '75*, during which the gallery remained closed. Instead of hosting an exhibition, the gallery produced a fifty-odd-page stapled booklet printed on rough paper, containing essays dealing with the relationship between art and society, art and the market, and art within Yugoslav self-management. According to Jelena Vesić, some saw the gesture as imposing "homework" that fell in line with the party-line propaganda of Yugoslav socialism.[116] For the majority of participants, however, *Oktobar '75* presented a vital opportunity to question the relationship between artists and institutions under self-management. For example, in her essay "Art as a Form of Ownership Awareness," Dunja Blažević wrote of the impossibility of linking art to a social base under a markedly bureaucratic structure, except as a "mechanistic and formalist inclusion," or as a strictly guided, propagandistic, and apologetic art. She affirmed:

> Art should be changed! As long as we leave art alone and keep on transferring works of art from studios to depots and basements by means of social regulations and mechanisms, storing them, like stillborn children, for the benefit of our cultural offspring, or while we keep on creating, through the private market, our own variant of the nouveau riche or kleinbürgers, art will remain a social appendage, something serving no useful purpose, but something it is not decent or cultured to be without.... Is it not extremely comical to build a self-managing social system using the political means of a feudal or bourgeois structure?[117]

For Blažević, culture in Yugoslavia remained trapped within petit-bourgeois frameworks because of a political economy in which the main consumers of high art remained national museums, factories, and institutions. Under what Blažević termed Yugoslavia's "own variant of the nouveau riche or kleinbürgers," the art produced in the SKC, or in the other youth cultural institutions in Yugoslavia, clearly never entered this economy, despite being exhibited occasionally in the country's larger and more prestigious contemporary art institutions. The other texts in *Oktobar '75*, including contributions from Todosijević, Denegri, and Pejić, subsequently called for a move away from tautologies, and a resistance to art that excluded its own dialectical mechanism. Popović most explicitly supported the politicization of art in his essay "For a Self-Managing Art":

> Art must be negative, critical, both towards the external world and in relation to its own language, its own (artistic) practice. It is pointless and hypocritical to be engaged, to speak and act in the name of some humanity or mankind, political and economic freedoms, and to remain passive, on the other hand, in relation to the system of "universal" artistic values, the system that is the basic prerequisite of the existence of artistic bureaucracy.... By way

of its monopoly of information and education, the bureaucracy creates an inert artist and a passive consumer of art—it produces "merry robots."[118]

The texts from *Oktobar '75* were also presented by the same protagonists in *Kino beleške* [Cinema Notes]—a film directed by British-German filmmaker Lutz Becker, with the assistance of Popović. Following the 1975 April Meeting, Becker was invited to make an art newsreel about the SKC. Taking its theme from Dziga Vertov's revolutionary theory of *kino-pravda* [film truth], *Kino beleške* was filmed and edited in November 1975.

In *Kino beleške*, Abramović chose to articulate her critical position through performance. She first appeared in the film seated by an office desk, working at a typewriter. She assumed the role of the office bureaucrat, miming the operations of a culture which she was opposed to. The following scene cuts into a raw version of her piece *Umetnost mora biti lepa—umetnik mora biti lep* [Art Must Be Beautiful—Artist Must Be Beautiful], in which she combed her face and hair in close-up while repeating the phrases "art must be beautiful—artist must be beautiful." In this performance by the only female member of the SKC's informal group of six artists, she violently criticized the general understanding of art in Yugoslavia, and the conventional expectations of its public. Assuming that the woman artist was expected by society to simply "be beautiful," Abramović's action moreover reflected on the clearly phallocratic status of Yugoslavia's art scene, in which men continued to dominate.[119]

The final scene invoked the whole society in a cultural depravation. Over shots of a snow-covered Belgrade, Abramović read the program listing of *TV Beograd* from 29 November 1975, the Day of the Yugoslav Republic. Republic Day represented a major national holiday, celebrating the foundations of postwar Yugoslavia as a federal republic. It was the day on which elementary school first-graders were inducted into the "Pioneer" Movement. The date "29.XI.1943" featured prominently on the Yugoslav coat of arms. Despite these origins, the vapidity of the television programs, targeted at the general public on a national holiday, reflected the ideological poverty of the cultural effort under self-management, constantly fragmented by short news broadcasts, programs aimed to improve farming knowledge, Partisan television series and Partisan songs in modern arrangements, etc. In this simple gesture of appropriation, Abramović invoked not just the state of art in a "self-managing" society, but further its implications for culture at large.

Another sequence, filmed in Popović and Tijardović's private apartment, focused on the arrangement of books on a table, featuring a book on Malevich

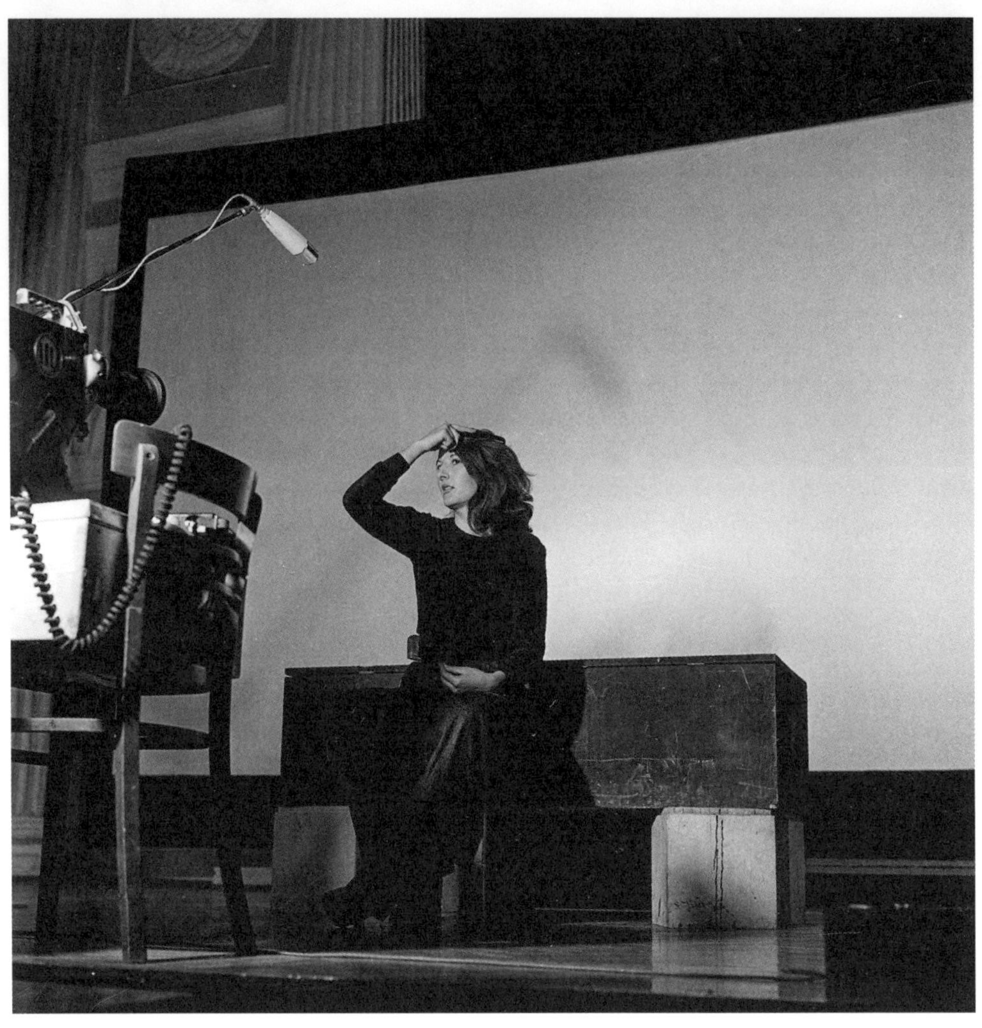

3.16. Marina Abramović, *Umetnost mora biti lepa—Umetnik mora biti lep* [Art Must Be Beautiful—Artist Must Be Beautiful], 1975. Image courtesy of the SKC Archive, Belgrade. © DACS. / © Marina Abramović. Courtesy of Marina Abramović and Sean Kelly Gallery, New York. DACS 2020.

and texts by Art & Language and Antonio Gramsci. The following image cut in to a close-up of a poster of Marx's image, with a quotation from his 11th Thesis on Feuerbach written below: "Philosophers have hitherto only interpreted the world in various ways; the point, however, is to change it." This montage suggests that if art were no longer to be an apologetic and servile reflection of the existing reality, it would have to involve itself in broader trends of social change. Such an urge was further registered in the final scene of the film, in which Blažević read directly from her *Oktobar '75* essay over aerial views of the SKC, calling for a literal perspective on the SKC's position from the outside.

The struggles implicit in this self-critical outside viewpoint were suggested in Tijardović's contribution to the newsreel. She appeared in the film reclining on a divan, while voicing a simple request: "I would like this film to have no symbolism regarding anything or anyone. It seems it's always easiest to speak about something else than about oneself." Finishing her sentence, she creased her face and grit her teeth. Her simple gesture invoked several of the difficulties she shared in her correspondence with Michael Corris following the trip to New York: "One can talk about anything generally, because it is not opposed to the main ideology. Talking about your experience is something different, could be danger [sic]."[120]

Founded as a direct consequence of the 1968 student demonstrations, and intended as a cultural forum through which the city's university could become a "truly free, critical, and veritable self-managing institution," the SKC Gallery had maintained the possibility of developing self-management from within itself.[121] Yet it became reluctant to address issues of self-management, as Tijardović would explain in her essay for the third issue of *The Fox*, "The 'Liquidation' of Art: Self-Management or Self-Protection?" The title immediately invokes a repressive political rhetoric—"liquidation" being a violent, corporate term of dissolution—a theme she continued to evaluate in her estimation of the SKC Gallery's "political" behavior toward art and politics. Though envisioned as an open, public institution when it was founded, the gallery became driven by the assumption that art, as an expression of the individual, could never act more widely, "never be aimed at general social use."[122] In contrast, architecture and design could be adapted to specific social processes, since they were always devoted to the wider public. For this reason, huge amounts of funding were spent on the interior design of the SKC, forcing its programs to mesh with its financial priorities. Just as the country's institutions and financing structures privileged modernism, in the SKC's administration interior design was employed as a means of evading the urgent work needed to establish a truly self-critical model of artistic engagement.

Certain artists were isolated, and in fact the center began to "use the programs of architecture, design and expanded media as a weapon against art."[123] Tijardović concluded: "I can now understand why some art groups and many individuals in this country have stopped working, become silent, or chosen mysticism instead of activism."[124]

By 1975, both funding the center's gallery and internal struggles for dominance over the direction of programs had become crippling concerns. According to Popović, the center became isolated because, at its conception, it "never worked out its sources of finances, so the bureaucracy doesn't know who's responsible for financing us, and because it isn't in black and white, bureaucracy is trying to avoid its obligations to finance us."[125] Additionally, although initially established with a "shared confidence in each other's sensibilities," the gallery was beginning to show internal conflicts of interest. According to Branislav Dimitrijević, the staff of the gallery had split into two factions: the neo-Marxist group associated with *Oktobar '75*, led by Blažević and steered by an approach that was either "emancipatory or manipulative, depending on the angle from which it is viewed"; and the newly formed conceptualist collective Grupa 143 [Group 143], founded by Tomić.[126] The first of these tendencies was oriented toward the idea of the SKC as a "meeting point" of radical youth culture and the political establishment, and advocated for a critical role. The second tendency emerged as an intertextual examination of art, among artists and thinkers tired of the fact that continuous debates about the geopolitical circumstances of artistic production prevented them from dealing with art itself.

Founded in March 1975, Grupa 143 focused their research primarily on epistemological and theoretical questions about the "art world" in general, and the critical potential of intellectualized art-thinking, shaped by structuralist and post-structuralist theory as well as British and American conceptualism. Their first activities included talks of "a pedagogic nature," such as, for example, an "analysis of the documentation of the OHO group," and texts on the theme of "the character of work as representing a document in the cognitive process."[127] Clearly, the SKC Gallery was failing to achieve self-managing interests internally. By 1975, it had arguably become a space lacking any clear articulation or attitude. According to the statements of witnesses, the running of the gallery changed in 1976 when a radical position of cultural criticism was abandoned—Blažević had ceased to be interested in art, and had instead become director of the center itself, leading to a depoliticization of artistic practices in the gallery.[128]

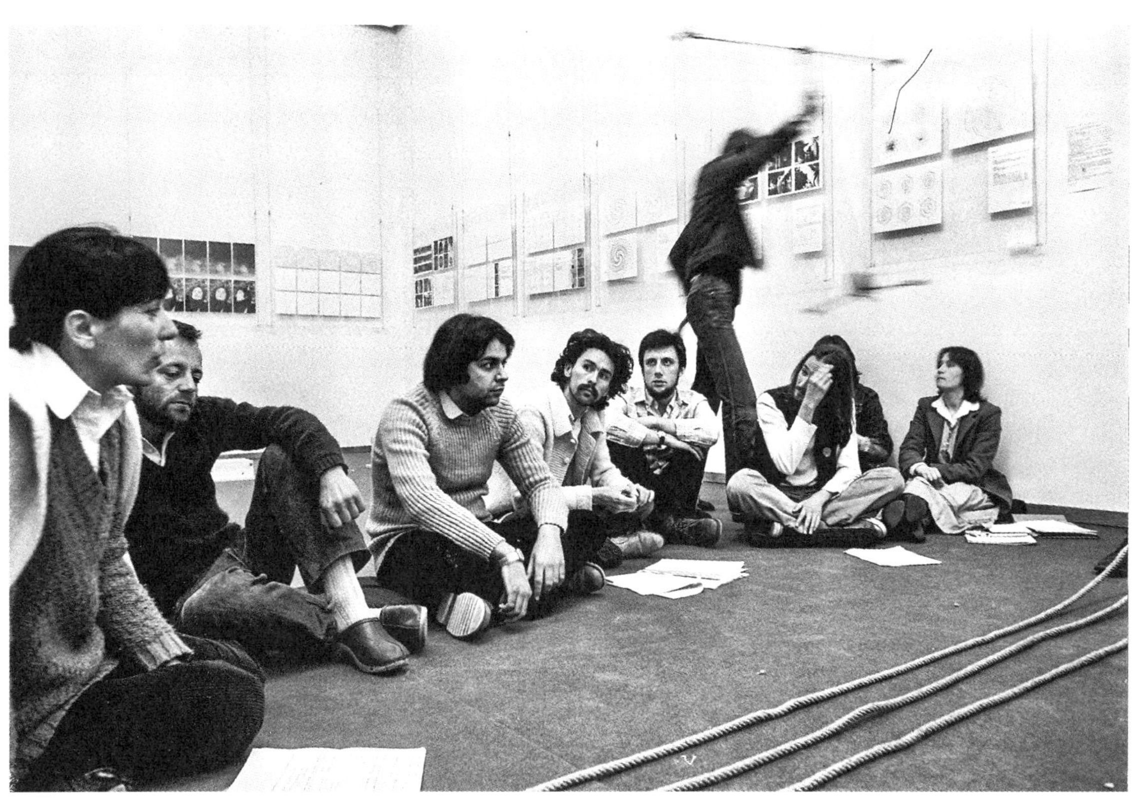

3.17. Grupa 143 at Belgrade's Students' Cultural Center. Image courtesy of the SKC Archive, Belgrade.

ART AGAINST THE NEW ART

In October 1976, Raša Todosijević deconstructed the myth of artistic freedom being promoted by the likes of Grupa 143 in the performance *Was ist Kunst, Marinela Koželj?* This work consisted of the artist touching, slapping, and smearing paint over the face of Marinela Koželj, while demanding an answer to his interrogation, "What is art?" In the performance's video, Todosijević whispers, shouts, screams, rants, pleads, and begs the same question over and over again at the silent woman impassively facing him. The artist's authoritarian tone of voice parodied the repressive manner of a police interrogation, constituting a kind of masculine theater of brutality. The fact that it was a man enacting a clearly aggressive act against a submissive and passive woman rendered the action all the more shocking, evoking not only misogyny and women's subjugation but also domestic violence.[129] Yet despite the uncomfortable, unsettling, and disturbing dimensions of this work, *Was ist Kunst?* was ultimately a satirical investigation into the nature of art itself. Rather than making a statement on authoritarianism or misogyny, Todosijević was reflecting not only on the local situation with regard to the rise and fall of the New Art Practice, but also on the global ending of a golden era that started with groundbreaking propositions, including Kosuth's "Art as Idea as Idea" of 1969.[130] If conceptual art began with such heroic statements, it ended with one tormenting question: "*Was ist Kunst?*"

By the mid-1970s, it was not only the SKC Gallery that was struggling to overcome conceptual art's institutionalization. In New York, Art & Language similarly identified that conceptual art's radicalism had reached an "impasse through aestheticization, inflation and institutionalization."[131] Writing in 1975, Joseph Kosuth had made a categorical distinction between "theoretical conceptual art" and "stylistic conceptual art," the latter of which had by then come to represent "superstructure begetting superstructure: a formalistic hypostatization of cultural sleepwalking."[132] Similarly, Mel Ramsden observed that conceptual art was destined to become an "insular and boring spectacle of fads ... professionalized, specialized, and essentially 'quaintly harmless' to the operation of the market structures."[133] Ultimately, the daring art of the 1970s had become a diversion of "intoxications, infatuations, and even the odd pseudo-revolution," because artists continued to separate their private lives from political social life, producing art under the platitudinous guise of the "massive evidence of 'creativity' and 'artistic freedom.'"[134] Artists continued to avoid responsibility for, or action against, the everyday complicities and compromises of institutional manipulation.

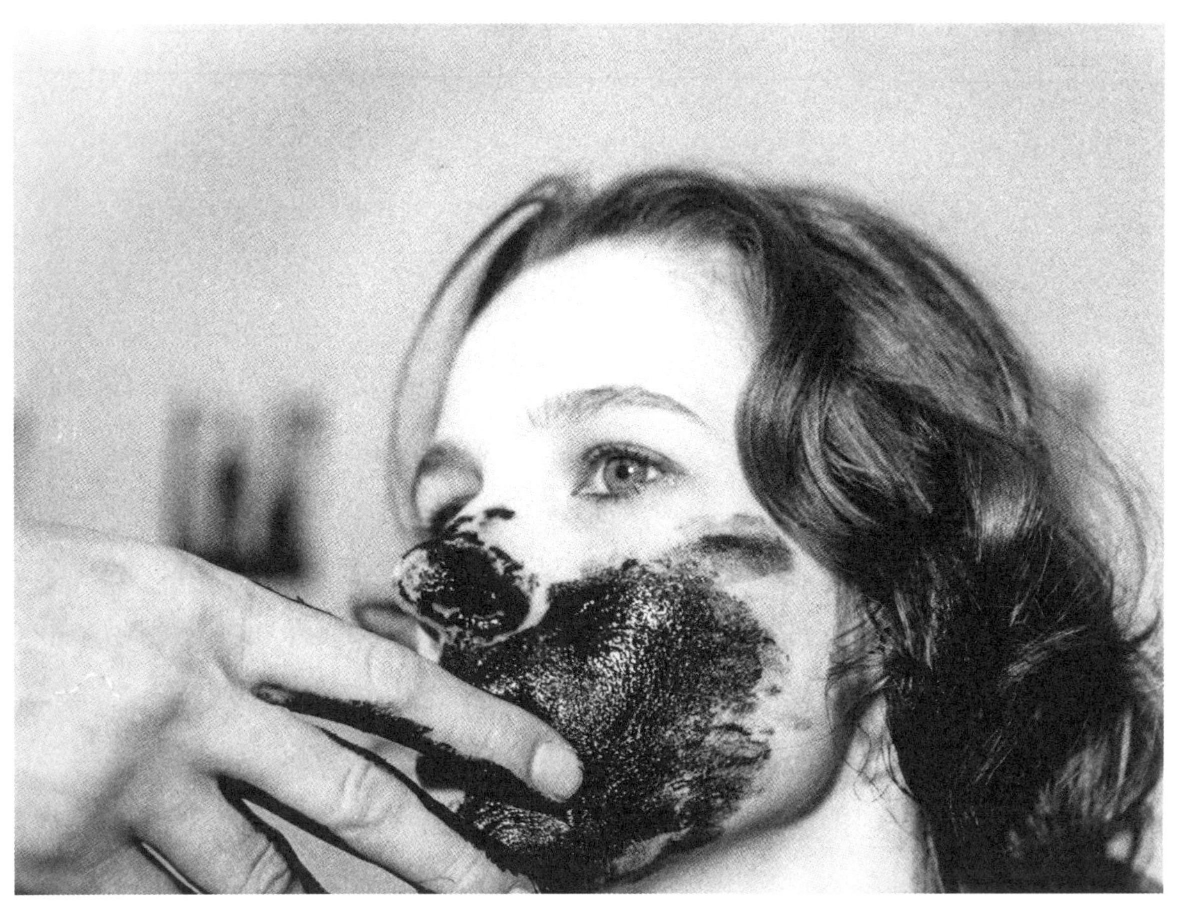

3.18. Raša Todosijević, *Was ist Kunst, Marinela Koželj?*, Belgrade, 1977. Image courtesy of the artist.

Just as Novi Sad's younger artists were forced to resort to an "invisible art," a deep skepticism began to dominate the work of artists who continued to work in the SKC. In April 1977, during the Sixth April Meeting, Todosijević invited "all friends and acquaintances of art" to visit the SKC Gallery and to sign *Art's Condolence Book*. In the same month, the gallery also exhibited *Umetnost, ironija itd.* [Art, Irony, etc.], a documentary exhibition of international artists including figures such as Gilbert & George and Trbuljak, along with the familiar associates of the SKC.[135] For the show, Todosijević included his *Edinburgh Statement*, based on the group's participation in Edinburgh Arts '73, a text that systematically revealed the wider power structures that determine art production. His eight pages of text diligently listed all those who profited from the art world, to illustrate the contiguity between the cultural and social sphere and to uncover the political and economic rhizomes emanating from the cultural system, including the countless profiteers. Todosijević excoriated "all those who use liberal language to disguise their decadent, dated, reactionary, chauvinist and bourgeois models of art and culture with verbal liberalism, that they might attain positions outside the world of art and culture, thus being both above and beyond art and culture."[136] Of course, the artist did not exclude himself from this scrutinizing critique; he admitted he had written the text to "somehow profit from the good and bad in art."[137]

By the late 1970s, Goran Đorđević, an electrical engineering student and collaborator with the SKC Gallery, had become equally disillusioned with conceptual art. From his first appearance at the Second April Meeting in 1973, he had pursued the so-called analytical line of Belgrade conceptualism, with works aligned with the "rigorous methods applied in science."[138] After a couple of years he came to the conclusion that, locally, conceptual art had ended in what he described as "white kitsch"—elementary, minimal, process-based conceptual works.[139] In trying to resolve his own critical position, Đorđević sought to organize an *International Strike of Artists* in 1979. In a gesture that echoed Lee Lozano's 1971 *General Strike Piece* in New York, which announced the artist's total withdrawal from the art world and a turn to a "personal revolution," Đorđević sent out an appeal, in letter form, to thirty-nine artists and cultural workers around the world. In the letter, he called for a "protest against the ongoing repression of the art system and the alienation of artists from the results of their work," as an attempt to coordinate activity independent of art institutions at an international level.[140] Could a strike—generally understood as a means of mobilizing workers and pressuring institutions to change policies—be adopted in the international art scene?

The majority of the thirty-nine responses from artists and critics expressed serious doubts about the possibility of organizing such a complex international action. Hans Haacke, for example, refused the offer on the basis that rather than withholding socially critical works from the art system, "every trick in the book should be employed to inject such works into the mainstream art world, particularly since they are normally not well received there."[141] Similarly, Lucy Lippard wrote that it was necessary to subvert the system internally: "rather than strike I spend all my energy on striking *back* at the art system by working around and outside of it and against it and letting it pay for my attempts to subvert it.... As you can see, I place my faith in action, organization, networking, rather than making voids which I fear would be invisible."[142] Like Lippard and Haacke, other former members of the 1969 Art Workers' Coalition in New York—who had picketed museums into taking a moral stance on the Vietnam War, and had fought to pressure the city's museums to implement reforms, such as a more open and inclusive exhibition policy to include more female, Black, and Puerto Rican artists, along with a free admission day—had also continued to commit themselves to undermining the mechanisms of the art world from within.

What was the alternative, if one could work only from within the art world? After his failed attempt to organize the strike, Đorđević entered the new and final phase of his work, in which he began to use the copy as a means of turning art against itself. On 29 January 1980, he staged a show called *Against Art* in the SKC Gallery, with the exhibition's subheading explaining that "the works displayed at the exhibition are not works of art. They are only attitudes towards art."[143] The display included his *Kratka istorija umetnosti* [A Short History of Art]: a series of twenty drawings, all in the same format, representing well-known icons of art history from the prehistorical period to conceptual art. All of "canonical" Western art history was translated into a traditional medium—drawing on paper—in order to establish a connection between "high art" and what the artist termed "kitsch." Đorđević had chosen to revert to the manual craft of drawing in order to compromise the semantic value of the original works, and to threaten the linear development of avant-garde work. According to the artist, art of the 1970s, dominated by the need to apply "new media," had harnessed "no guarantee of immunity from stupidity. It was enough for anyone to make any kind of performance, film, video, or series of photos, draw some diagrams which look exact, to be new and avant-garde."[144] Replicating the Western art historical canon through the manual craft of drawing had enacted a vacillating cultural subversion, counterbalancing the ideological servitude of the New Art Practice, which had encountered a total

July 9,1980
138 Prince St.
NYC 10012 NY
USA

Dear Goran Dordevic,

Sorry to take so long, but rather than strike I spend all my energy on striking <u>back</u> at the art system by working around and outside of it and against it and letting it pay for my attempts to subvert it. While I am well aware of the dangers of such a position, I have tried others over the last 12 years and have found this to be the one that is most effective. It permits me to work collectively with a large number of people, to set up small independent organizations which do their best to resist co-option by not becoming too unwieldy or too ambitious. The three that I am most active in now are <u>Heresies: A Feminist Publication on Art and Politics</u>, Printed Matter Inc. (distributor of artists' books), and P.A.D.—a newly formed international archive ("Political Art Documentation"), about which I enclose an info sheet. Another and far more ambitious organization is in the works now, intended to be a kind of "De-Center" beginning at the roots of art education to channel art toward social change.

As you can see, I place my faith in action, organization, netowrking, rather than in making voids which I fear would be invisible. At the same time, I am heartily in favor of communication between artists in all countries who are rebelling against the repression (economic and political) and institutionalization of the idea of art, since the sterilization process that is under way must be stopped by some relatively drastic means. I hope that you will let Middle European artists know about PAD in particular; eventually we plan to find a way to reproduce the material we receive and send it back out in exchange to artists' groups all over the world. The actions that could arise from such coordinated efforts will be, I think, far more effective than withdrawing from a system that would have no trouble attracting "scabs" to replace us.

All best,

Lucy R. Lippard

P.S. I'd be very interested to see the responses you've received.

3.19. Lucy Lippard's response to Goran Đorđević's *International Strike of Artists*, 1979. Image courtesy of the artist.

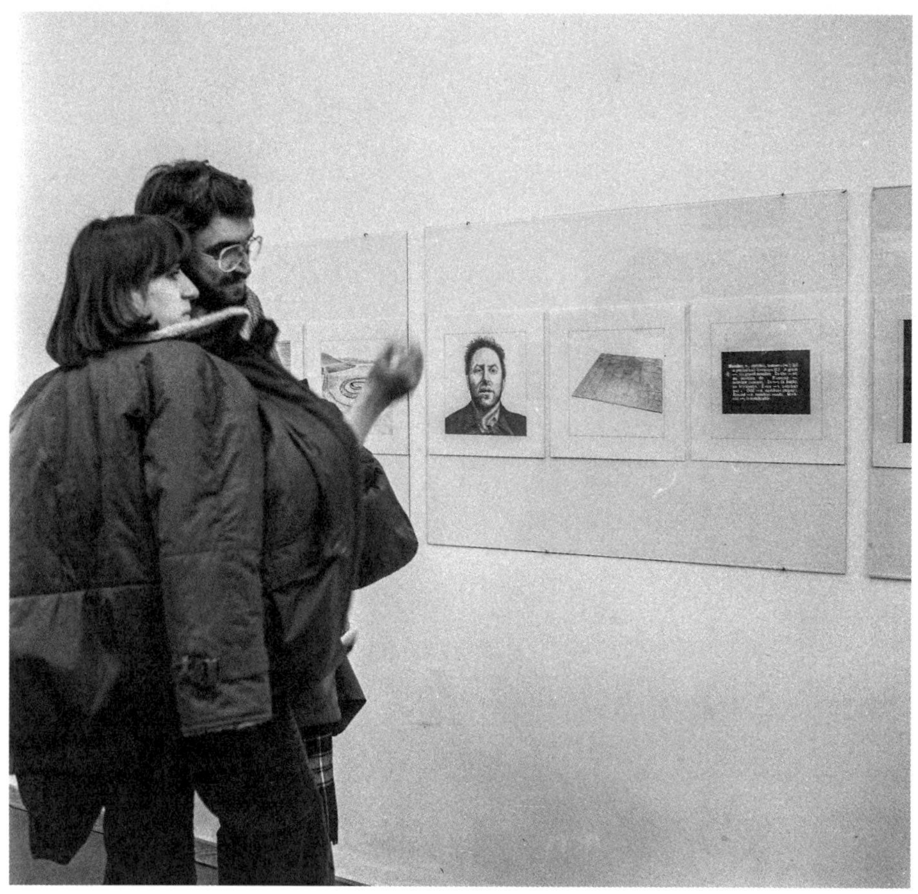

3.20. Goran Đorđević, *Kratka istorija umetnosti* [A Short History of Art], SKC Gallery, 1980. Image courtesy of Goran Đorđević and the SKC Archive, Belgrade.

3.21. and 3.22. Installation views of Goran Đorđević's exhibition *Glasnici Apokalipse—Kopije* [Harbingers of the Apocalypse—Copies] at the SKC's Srećna Galerija, Belgrade, April 1981. Images courtesy of the artist.

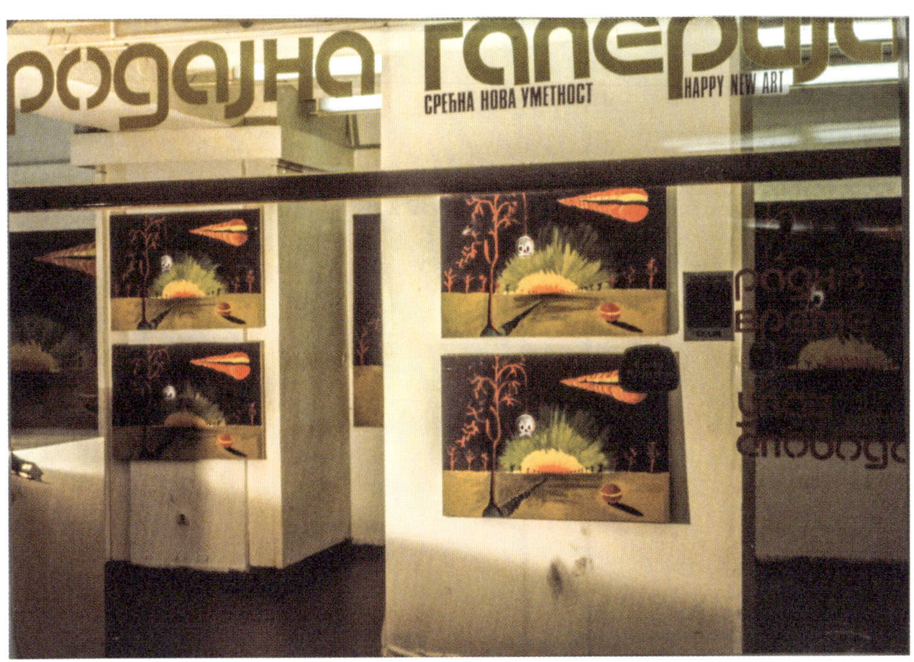
СРЕЋНА НОВА УМЕТНОСТ
HAPPY NEW ART

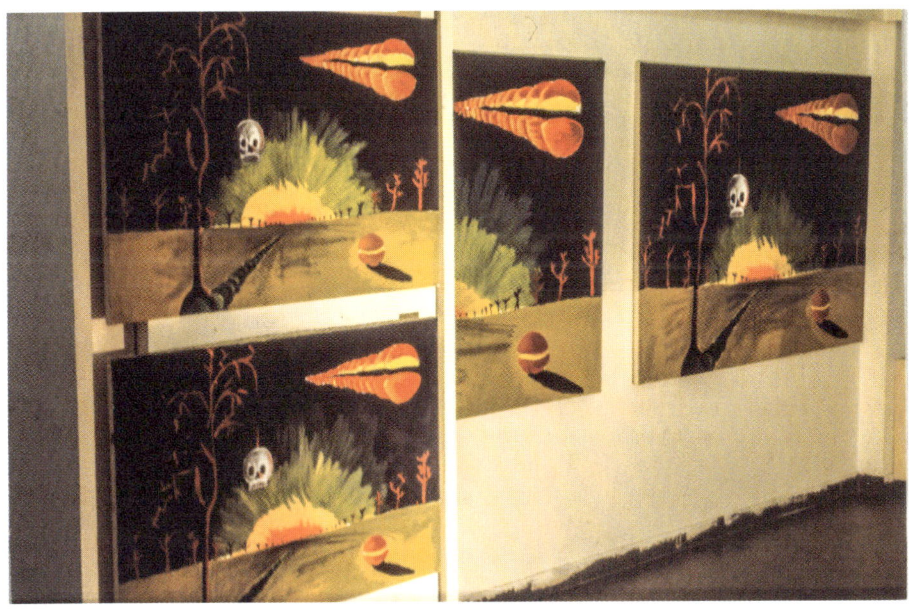

misunderstanding, or even denial, in the local art scene. The exhibition featured works that would become central to the concept of copying in Yugoslavia in the 1980s.

Between March and October of the same year, Đorđević also organized an exhibition in his apartment, consisting of fifty copies of his first ever painting, *Glasnici apokalipse* [Harbingers of the Apocalypse]. The original painting was, according to the artist, "an ugly, tasteless, and besides all that, dilettante painting, of which I was ashamed for years.... Ten years after it was done, I decided that the harbingers would become an important work of art."[145] Based on a painting that the artist was embarrassed of, the exhibition *Harbingers of the Apocalypse* involved inviting Yugoslav and international artists, including Todosijević, Popović, Dimitrijević, Mel Ramsden, Carolee Schneemann, and Lawrence Weiner, to make their own copies of the original work; the only instruction was that all participants make their copies as faithfully as possible, and only in the medium of painting. Sterile and unimaginative, copying made repetition and reproduction intrude into the features characteristic of contemporary art, such as the new, the original, and the authorial. The activities once almost exclusively associated with the SKC were now reduced to a multitude of handcrafted, tasteless copies.

Đorđević's *Harbingers* had declared, or even executed, the end of Belgrade's New Art Practice. In many ways, the work foreshadowed the experiences of two autonomous art collectives working in Zagreb at precisely the same time. Arising from the lessons learned in the Students' Cultural Centers, and collaborating with the artists working through the SKC, these collectives inherited the role of reflecting on the conflicts within self-management, and took on the task of illuminating the otherwise concealed shifting dynamics of state-society relations in Yugoslavia.

4 ARTISTS AT WORK

THE GROUP OF SIX AUTHORS AND RZU PODRUM (1975–1980)

1 MAY 1975

As socialist Yugoslavia entered its fourth decade, two of its most well-informed foreign observers took note of the country's state of affairs. For New York-based scholar Bogdan Denitch, the basic contradictions in Yugoslav society now seemed to rest between "the mundane possibilities of a relatively undeveloped, small, independent nation-state, and its heroic aspirations to solve the complex problem of multi-nationality, industrial democracy, egalitarianism, and social mobility in a way that ha[d] not yet been attempted anywhere in the world."[1] Whereas Denitch's prognosis mapped courageous ambitions against far less favorable circumstances, Dennison Rusinow, who had committed much of his career to writing about Yugoslavia with scrupulous care, was even more doubtful about the country's future path. Writing in 1977, he regretfully observed that it seemed "more likely that Yugoslavia would become another slovenly, moderately oppressive, semi-efficient, semi-authoritarian state run by an oligarchy of contending elites, a society in which many are free and participant, and many are not. Like most states."[2] For two of its most sympathetic supporters, this is what the Yugoslav experiment was now coming to: a disappointing descent into mediocrity, "like most states."

At a time when elegists for the country's founding hopes for self-management, fraternity, and solidarity could still grieve for mediocrity, an artist named Mladen Stilinović installed a work in Zagreb that seemed to capture the rising political apathy among Yugoslavia's younger generation. On 1 May 1975—internationally celebrated as Workers' Day, and a huge public holiday in Yugoslavia—the artist and his partner, Branka Stipančić, raised two banners in the center of the city. One was a frayed bandage carelessly pinned across a tree, with a message roughly

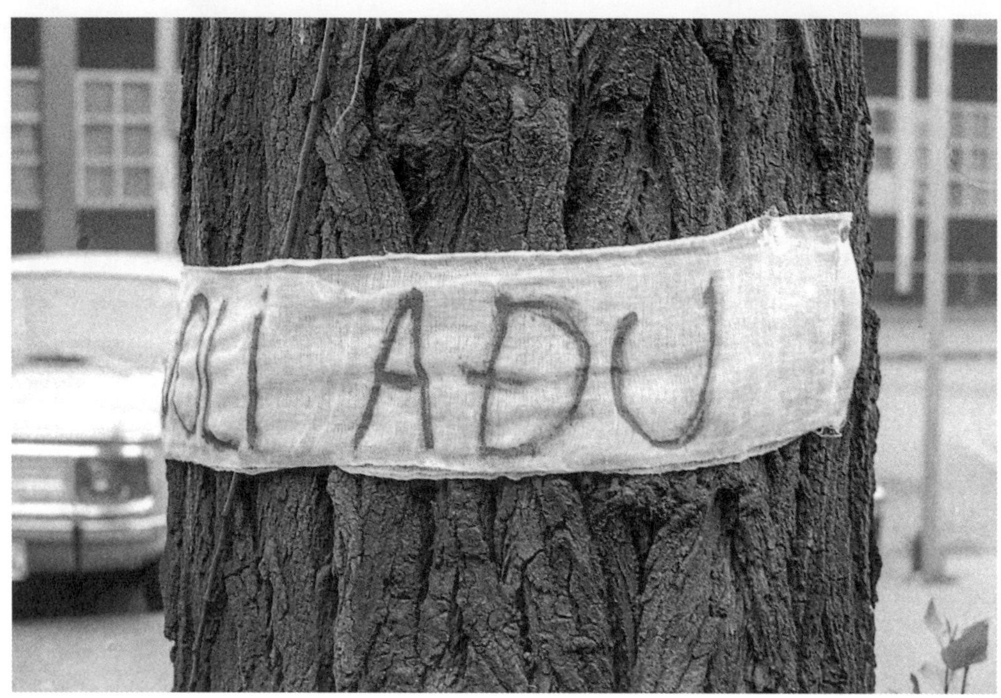
OLI AĐU

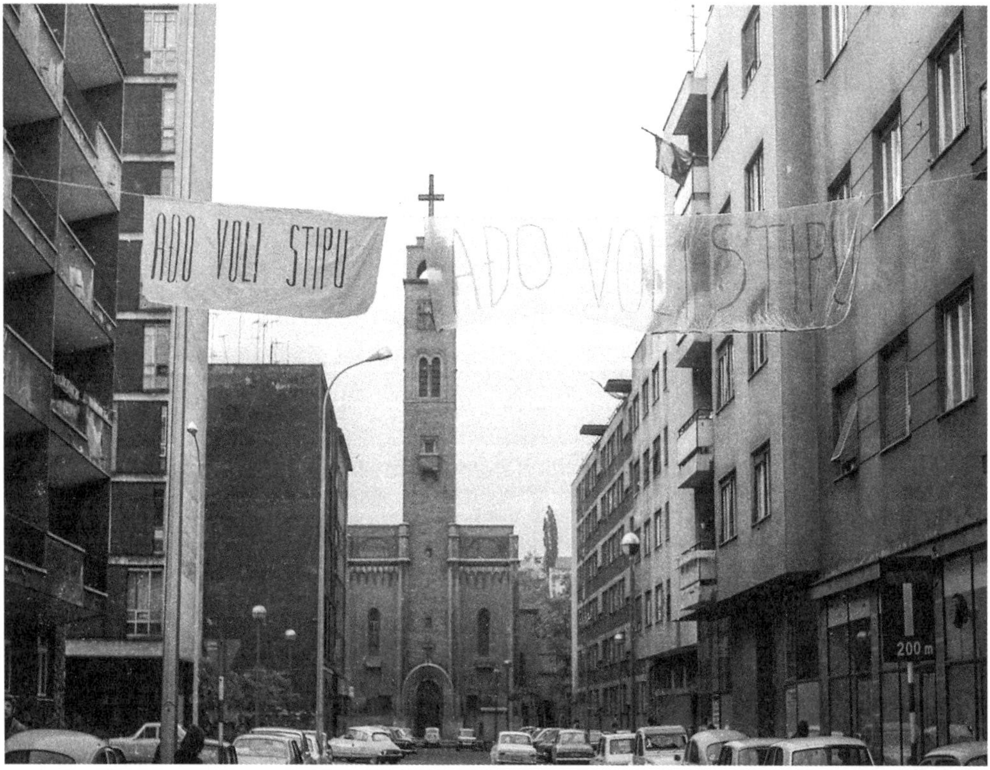

dabbed across its rough surface; the other, a tawdry, translucent sheet, hoisted from the windows of two adjacent apartment blocks and stretched across an entire road facing the historic St. Peter's Church. Although different in scale, the two banners were connected through their messages. Both contained handwritten declarations of love between Stipančić and Stilinović. Scrawled across the white ground, the seemingly irreverent statements "Ađo voli Stipu—Stipa voli Ađu" [Ađo Loves Stipa—Stipa Loves Ađo], using pet names for Stilinović and his partner, stood in stark contrast to the public nature of the May Day festivities, as the artist made abundantly apparent in his book of photographs, *1 Maj 1975*.

A tiny, staple-bound pamphlet, *1 Maj 1975* consists largely of snapshots documenting the decorations from the annual May Day parade, ranging from a giant banner depicting Tito in Republic Square, to flags hanging from lampposts and tiny printed stickers glued onto shop display windows. Flipping through the pages of the carelessly assembled, Lilliputian book, the reader finally reaches a photograph of the artist's intervention itself. Compared to the painstaking efforts invested in the decorations celebrating the parade—with their pristine presentation of government propaganda—Stilinović's and Stipančić's banners look rushed, haphazard, and clumsy. Unlike the various posters pasted inside of the city's shop displays, almost no care or effort seems to have been invested in either of them. Speaking retrospectively, Stilinović noted the clearly defined program of action that the May Day Parade involved: "Everyone knew what style should be followed in each case. You had to stick to the patterns: Tito—the flag—flowers and printed slogans. No one dared to write slogans by hand, sloppily."[3] With *Ađo voli Stipu*, Stilinović and Stipančić had dared to defy protocol. In a sea of disinterested socialist slogans declaring a common, collective program, the work's assertion of individual love and dignity may have seemed like a conscious renunciation of the parade.

4.1. and 4.2. Mladen Stilinović, *Ađo voli Stipu—Stipa voli Ađu*, from the artists' book *1 Maj 1975* [1 May 1975]. Images courtesy of Branka Stipančić, Zagreb.

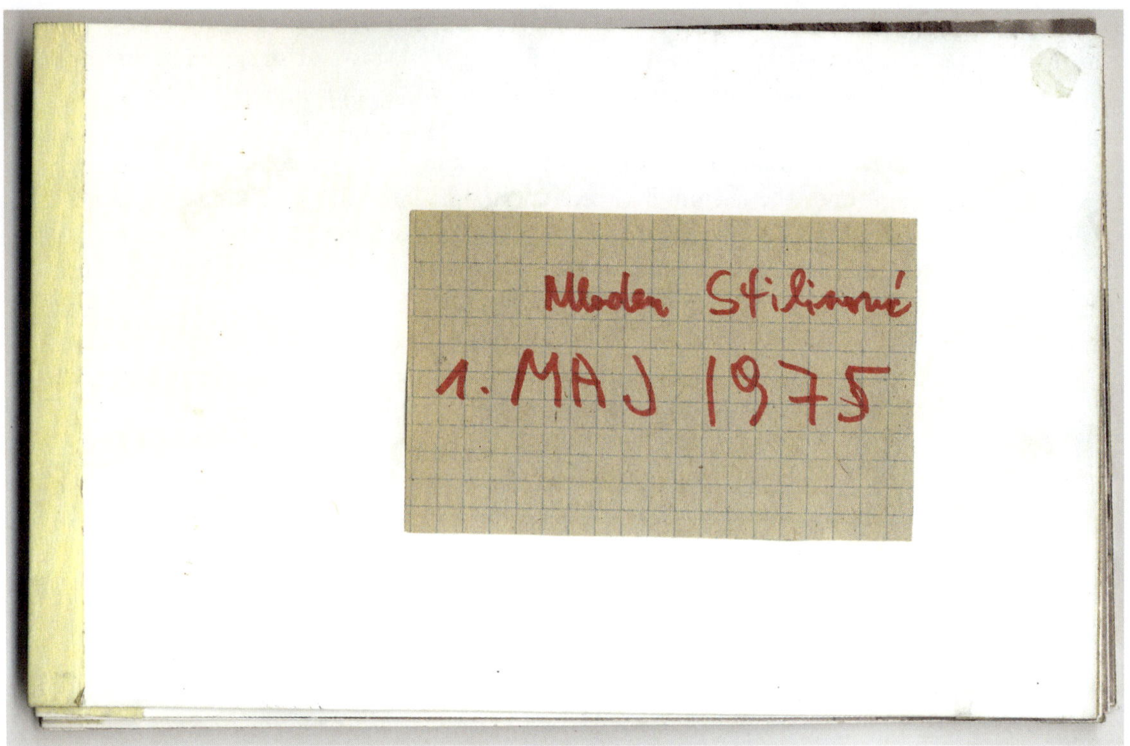
1. MAJ 1975

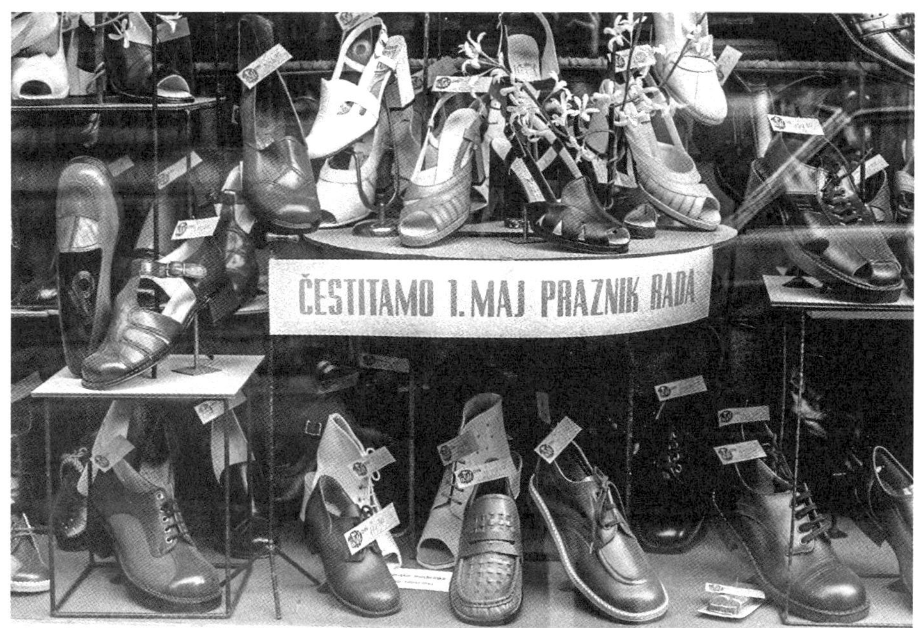

4.3. Mladen Stilinović, cover of *1 Maj 1975* [1 May 1975].
Image courtesy of Branka Stipančić, Zagreb.

4.4. Mladen Stilinović, *1 Maj 1975* [1 May 1975].
Image courtesy of Branka Stipančić, Zagreb.

Stilinović was not the first artist in Yugoslavia to address the type of ritualized discourse that had become numbingly dominant in the country's final quarter-century. In 1962, when Dušan Makavejev was commissioned to film a documentary on Belgrade's May Day march, he had decided to focus on the diligent preparations that went into the annual event instead of the semisacred spectacle itself. For seven days, Makavejev and his team filmed with a handheld camera, focusing entirely on backstage politics, including the primping of officials, disputes arising over convention, soldiers buffing up military vehicles, and individuals hoisting banners of Marx and Lenin onto the facades of apartment buildings. Makavejev believed *Parade* was the first political film in Yugoslavia without a propagandistic function because it lacked a narrative and employed a deadpan sarcasm, further accentuated by the choice of overly enthusiastic background music. Yet Makavejev's film did not challenge the event's premise; it certainly did not defy socialism as such. Stilinović's rejection of the May Day Parade would have been virtually unthinkable in 1962; it was, however, performed at a decisive moment when the League of Communists began to position itself away from the realm of politics proper and to implant itself into the very fabric of society.

A year before Stilinović and Stipančić announced their love on the state holiday, the Tenth Congress of the League of Communists had introduced its fourth constitution in less than thirty years. Retaining many of the characteristics of the system that had been developing since 1966, the 1974 constitution sought to define self-management as a new type of democratic system for regulating the national question in a multinational, socialist context. It defined Yugoslavia as an agreement among its federal units—between its republics and autonomous provinces. In his last testament on self-management in Yugoslavia, "Directions of Development in the Political System of Socialist Self-Management," the party's key ideologue, Edvard Kardelj, explained that following the 1974 constitution, the country was no longer a classical federation or confederation, but rather

> a self-management community of nations and nationalities of a new type, which is not based exclusively on a division of state functions, but above all on common interests determined by self-management and a democratic constitutional agreement among the republics and autonomous provinces.... In this way, the self-management system has given an entirely new, democratic quality to national relations as well.[4]

With the new constitution, the institution that held the country together—the Federal Executive Committee (FEC)—became fragmented into eight independent units, resulting in eight more or less strong and stable nation-states and a proportionately weaker central government. As will become evident, this arrangement transformed Yugoslavia into a contractual federation, in which all contractual parties were needed to consent to changes in the contract. It would render federal politics the almost impossible object of consensus between republics and autonomous provinces. Yet, in order to contain centrifugal tendencies, the new constitution simultaneously strengthened the role of the single party and the army, largely through its redefining of the very structure and role of self-management.

As Kardelj explained, the League of Communists was no longer to play the role of a "classical political party that rules over society," because the constitution had initiated a "new kind of democracy": a "self-managing socialist democracy."[5] In other words, the party no longer saw itself at the top of the social system, but instead wedged itself between various "decentralized" institutions: republics and communes, communes and enterprises, sociopolitical organizations and state institutions, etc.[6] Reputed to be the longest constitution in the world, the 1974 constitution served as the supreme statute of the federation, setting out the roles for social organizations of all kinds. It attempted to extend self-management into the realm of high politics, in which the Federal Assembly was itself a "body of socialist self-management," consisting of 220 delegates of self-managing organizations, communities, and sociopolitical organizations.

The sheer complexity of the structure made it dysfunctional at best and vulnerable to abuse at worst. In the words of Branislav Jakovljević, the new constitution essentially transformed the League of Communists into a "flowing and decentered medium: a universal mediator of all social exchanges, or a currency."[7] With the stockpiling of masses of legal documents, self-management began to conflate society and state, shifting the country's organizing principle of industrial democracy to the premise of state ideology. Paradoxically, judicial overregulation was supposed to facilitate the withering away of the state; instead, it ushered in continued federalization, less democracy, and an increased manifestation of party authority. By the latter half of the 1970s, the state administration had grown as much as eight to eleven times larger than administrations in countries of comparable size.[8]

A year after the constitution had declared supposedly "new" and "democratic" conditions, a group of artists came together in Zagreb with the common aim of circumventing art institutions. In April 1975, Mladen Stilinović and Željko Jerman returned to Zagreb from Belgrade's Fourth April Meeting, where they had agreed to organize an outdoor group exhibition.[9] On their return, they were joined by Vlado Martek, a literature and philosophy student; Boris Demur, a student of painting; and Mladen's younger brother, Sven Stilinović, and his friend from the

School of Applied Arts, Fedor Vučemilović. Together, they formed what would later be known as the Group of Six Authors, and began presenting their art on the streets, city squares, beaches, and riverbanks through their self-titled "Exhibition-Actions." For these artists, Exhibition-Actions offered an opportunity to talk about their work with a public that otherwise might never attend a gallery. According to art historian Nena Baljković, each site was selected according to its broader social significance. Organized under the patronage of Zagreb's Center for Film, Photography, and Television (CEFFT) between May 1975 and March 1977, the initial series of eleven Exhibition-Actions consisted of a carefully devised program in which each individual project sought to analyze the attitudes that various audiences in different spaces held toward less familiar, unconventional art practices.[10]

As a transcript of the people passing through the Exhibition-Action of Republic Square reveals, work by the Group of Six Authors tended to disturb the public or at least baffle them. While a handful of observations were positive—"this is fantastic," "the conversation is such that everyone is welcome," "it is beautiful, not only beautiful, but clever too"—the majority were distrusting and hostile—"this is shit, really awful," "instead of cleaning up the square, you're piling it up with rubbish," "if something like this were brought to me, I would throw it out of the window," "they are some kinds of lunatics," "this has got political connotations."[11] Clearly, the streets were a site of various contestations. But it was here that the artists could communicate with the public through their art as it was being made.

CHANGING THINGS SO THAT NOTHING CHANGES

What distinguished the Exhibition-Actions from the New Art Practice that preceded them was an eagerness to enter into direct discussion with the general public. Of equal significance was the fact that these artists refused to uphold a coherent, common aesthetic program. Instead, the Exhibition-Actions consisted of six artists with independent outlooks working side by side and presenting their work together. The term "group," then, indicated above all a sense of collaboration that did not prevent individual members from signing their respective works. For Mladen Stilinović, this framework of friendship, based on "plurality and an informal program of tolerance," rendered the Group of Six "democrats even before all those changes."[12]

Although Stilinović made this enigmatic observation three decades after the Group of Six Authors began presenting their work, his choice of words is striking, not least because of the weight they carried for discussions of "democracy" in the wake of the 1974 constitution. While the Group of Six Authors came together but simultaneously sought to preserve their autonomy as individuals, the Yugoslav Federation was still searching for a solution to the "democratic harmonization of various interest groups."[13] After 1971, Kardelj had come to believe that conflicts would continue to play a significant role in Yugoslav society, as they stemmed from the political pluralism under self-management. In "Directions of Development for Self-Management," he argued that the notion of "pluralism" was intrinsic to the concept of self-management. In his words, self-management was "not a system based on an ideal harmony, but rather a clash of opinions and criticism of practice, often even on a direct confrontation of particular interests.... In the process, partial interests should undergo the kind of ideological, scientific, and political synthesis which will open up new horizons and visions of socialist progress."[14]

In a sense, then, the new constitution paralleled the organizational structure of the Group of Six Authors, suspended as it was upon a loose association of artists, working together informally as a means of presenting their work to the public with greater ease. But whereas the Group of Six Authors worked without a common program, and understood the group arrangement as a channel through which to preserve their individual artistic ideas and identities, the Yugoslav constitution assumed the existence of shared goals and a minimum of potential conflict over significant issues of common concern.

For the bicameral federal parliament to function as a proponent of common (i.e., federal) interests, its members ought to have remained independent from republican and provincial leaderships. In reality, however, they were exposed to enormous pressures from their respective regions. Regional leaderships not only maintained a pivotal role in determining nominees for the Federal Committee, but also prioritized the loyalty of candidates to their republics or autonomous provinces over their qualifications. As such, the distribution of power stood in favor of the regions, which would come to act as an enormous handicap to countrywide policymaking. While subjecting the appointment of federal personnel to a strict regional and nationality "quota" system, the constitutional reform also gave republican and provincial representatives in state and government institutions a virtual veto over each stage of federal decision making.[15]

These political developments may contribute to a more nuanced analysis of why an obsession with accountability and ownership ran through both the organization of the Group of Six Authors, and many of their works presented at the Exhibition-Actions. For the first installment in the series, which took place in Zagreb's residential area of Sopot, Mladen Stilinović displayed two images, each vertically intersected with a straight line, with two words at opposite ends: *ja* / *ti*; *moje* / *tvoje* [me | you; mine | yours].[16] At the Jesuit Square Exhibition-Action, the artist projected the caption "*to je moje* [this is mine]" onto houses, people, cars, pavement, and trees. On first reflection, these gestures might seem like childish, disobedient declarations of ownership, nothing more than a game of greedy finger-pointing. Yet such a naïve method of appropriation, achieved through simple linguistic and spatial manipulations, represented a highly sophisticated reflection of the nagging problems of Yugoslavia's supposed "democratic decision making," where individual rights were being exercised exclusively through the right of regional autonomy and sovereignty (that is, individual rights delineated through territorial borders).

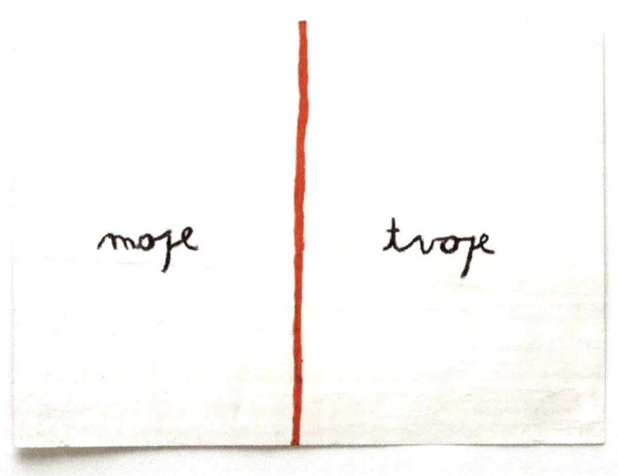

4.5. Mladen Stilinović, *Moje* | *tvoje* [Mine | Yours], Zagreb, 1974. Image courtesy of Branka Stipančić, Zagreb.

After 1974, both chambers of the Federal Assembly were composed of delegations chosen by territory. Announced as an important step toward direct democracy, this delegate system actually displaced decision making from the federal parliament to the private offices of local party leaderships. Delegations did not have to account for their actions publicly before a constituency, which should have determined their further political activity, thus affording the grounds for democratic accountability. As the power to determine personal, social, and economic policies still remained out of the reach of workers and citizens, two questions of accountability dominated: Who was entitled to what? And who was exploiting whom?

AUCTIONING RED

On 17 April 1976, the Group of Six Authors arrived in Belgrade to organize and perform an Exhibition-Action at the SKC Gallery's Fifth April Meeting. According to the exhibition catalogue documenting the first series of Exhibition-Actions, the aim of the Belgrade show was to examine the "relation between work prepared in sight of the occasion, and simultaneously executed works," or in other words, to produce works on site in response to those prepared in advance for the show.[17] As part of his contribution, Sven Stilinović performed *Akcija s toalet papirom* [Action with Toilet Paper]. Starting from the entrance door of the SKC, the artist unrolled two lines of toilet paper down the stairs, in parallel with each other. Previously, the artist had executed the same action at Zagreb's Jesuit Square. Together, they were, according to the artist, intended to represent "two white lines between two cities."[18]

In a way, Stilinović's action evoked the basic tenets of reism, along with Zagreb's rich history of urban interventions. In terms of its spatial configuration, the work could easily be aligned with Tomaž Šalamun's *Marking the Line to Petrovaradin* (1969), for example, which the artist performed in Novi Sad by carefully walking through the city and drawing white lines in chalk behind him. Yet Stilinović's action deliberately alluded to such pioneering gestures through the most lowly and most perishable of materials—through toilet paper. As such, his action could be seen as a kind of degradation of the heroic achievements of the New Art Practice, and the democratic ideals that accompanied them. Acting as an artistic depletion of sorts, playing with toilet paper also carried unsuspected political risks in 1976. According to the artist, the action was interpreted by passersby as being overtly political: "Namely, some people attacked me over how I could tie Zagreb and Belgrade together through toilet paper—with shit. How I could be breaking Brotherhood and Unity.... It was a sharp dispute ... but I didn't intervene."[19] These unexpectedly heated reactions from passersby raise the question: Why, in 1976, was the sophomoric gesture of rolling toilet paper down a building's steps suspected of being an attack on one of the principal pillars of Yugoslav socialism?

While there was nothing overtly political about *Action with Toilet Paper*, it was performed at a time when Yugoslavia's founding ideological pillar of Brotherhood and Unity was itself being contested. Following the economic decentralization of federal decision making, and the subsequent disintegration of governmental authority, a greater thrust toward autarchy—economic self-sufficiency—had defined interrepublican relationships, along with a stubborn resistance to interregional cooperation. The notion of "Brotherhood and Unity" was adopted by the League of Communists in response to the failures of the prewar Kingdom of Yugoslavia and the horrors of ethnic warfare during the Second World War. By 1976, the policy of peaceful coexistence, along with the slogans of the National Liberation Struggle, had been stripped of their political value, as the new constitution placed the burden of cooperation on a concept of decentralization that was underdeveloped in both theory and practice. As such, those ideological cornerstones upon which the Yugoslav Federation had been built were beginning to deteriorate, making them all the more delicate a subject in society.

In Belgrade, Mladen Stilinović similarly addressed the unstable political climate through a seemingly innocuous action. For his *Aukcija crvene* [Auction of Red], the artist staged an auction of paintings that carried the words "Auction of Red" painted on a white ground. Identifying the category "red" through words, materials, and actions, the *Auction* could have seemed like a purely tautological investigation—the familiar figure of Anglo-American conceptualism. Yet, for Stilinović, the color red was imbued with a deeper ideological significance, being the preeminent symbol of communism. As such, auctioning the color red was a way of highlighting the color's transformation from a "human structure, human material," into the unofficial property of the League of Communists. The effort to "desymbolize" the color proved impossible, however. Instead, the artist decided to profit from it, in a gesture that echoed Yves Klein's realization in 1955 that color could become a brand, when he signed his name to the Riviera sky and attempted to gain the official patent for the color "International Klein Blue." Similarly, Stilinović chose to sell off "red" as property, to become its sole entrepreneur, in a chaotic auction conditioned by no coherent set of rules: some pieces were sold from the starting price of five dinars, while others were gifted to the artist's friends, including Raša Todosijević.

Like the artist's earlier interventions in Zagreb, the *Auction of Red* once again raised questions of ownership. Self-management had stressed that its aim was the participation of workers and citizens in decisions about where they lived and worked. Although this may have seemed utopian, self-management nevertheless materialized in the organization of socialist firms, just as Kardelj's concept of "self-managing direct democracy" surfaced through the complex delegate system, and an intricate system of agency regulations that had penetrated every cell of society by the mid-1970s. For Stilinović, these regulations applied even to the abstract realm of color. Whereas Stilinović attempted to profit from the state's political monopoly, Željko Jerman chose to withdraw himself from it completely. On the pavement in front of the SKC Gallery, Jerman wrote the slogan "*Ovo nije moj svijet* [This Is Not My World]" with a photographic developer on a large roll of photographic paper. In many ways, the statement captured the dissatisfaction, disappointment, and frustration felt by many of the artists associated with the New Art Practice. Deeply nihilistic, the statement was exhibited on the facade of the SKC Gallery, only to be removed by the gallery's cultural workers a few hours later.

While in Belgrade, the Group of Six Authors also collaborated with Zoran Popović on *Untitled Film*, for which Mladen Stilinović submitted two stills. The first image was a photograph of Queen Elizabeth II, adorned in all her pomp and regalia, with a constellation of red stars carelessly drawn across her white gown. The second still captured the artist's sketch *Mine / Yours*. During the presentation of these images, Stilinović read out the following text:

> We in Yugoslavia, in politics, art, and writing, often hide behind the pronoun "WE." I have hidden behind it too, because it is easier to speak as if there is a big crowd of people behind you and to think that it supports you in what you are saying. But, in most cases, in political and art circles, I think that when someone speaks, it can happen, and it does happen very often, that no one supports what you are saying, wouldn't sign it, wouldn't confirm it. But it is done like that because one feels more secure. It is more secure to talk, think, write behind the pronoun as the responsibility is always ascribed to someone else, and not the person who actually speaks. "WE" is big, big, big—red. "WE" is in my works, and in my attitudes, and it is always repeated: WE are MINE—YOURS.[20]

Stilinović's statement seemed to point toward the role that collective speech played in the dispersal of power that had become synonymous with self-management's later phase. In theory, the 1974 constitution was supposed to ensure the fair and equal representation of citizens in the hierarchy of self-managing councils and committees, in the workplace and in all higher political structures. In practice, the League of Communists was continuing to define the terms of the agenda, while its unaccountable authority remained the subject

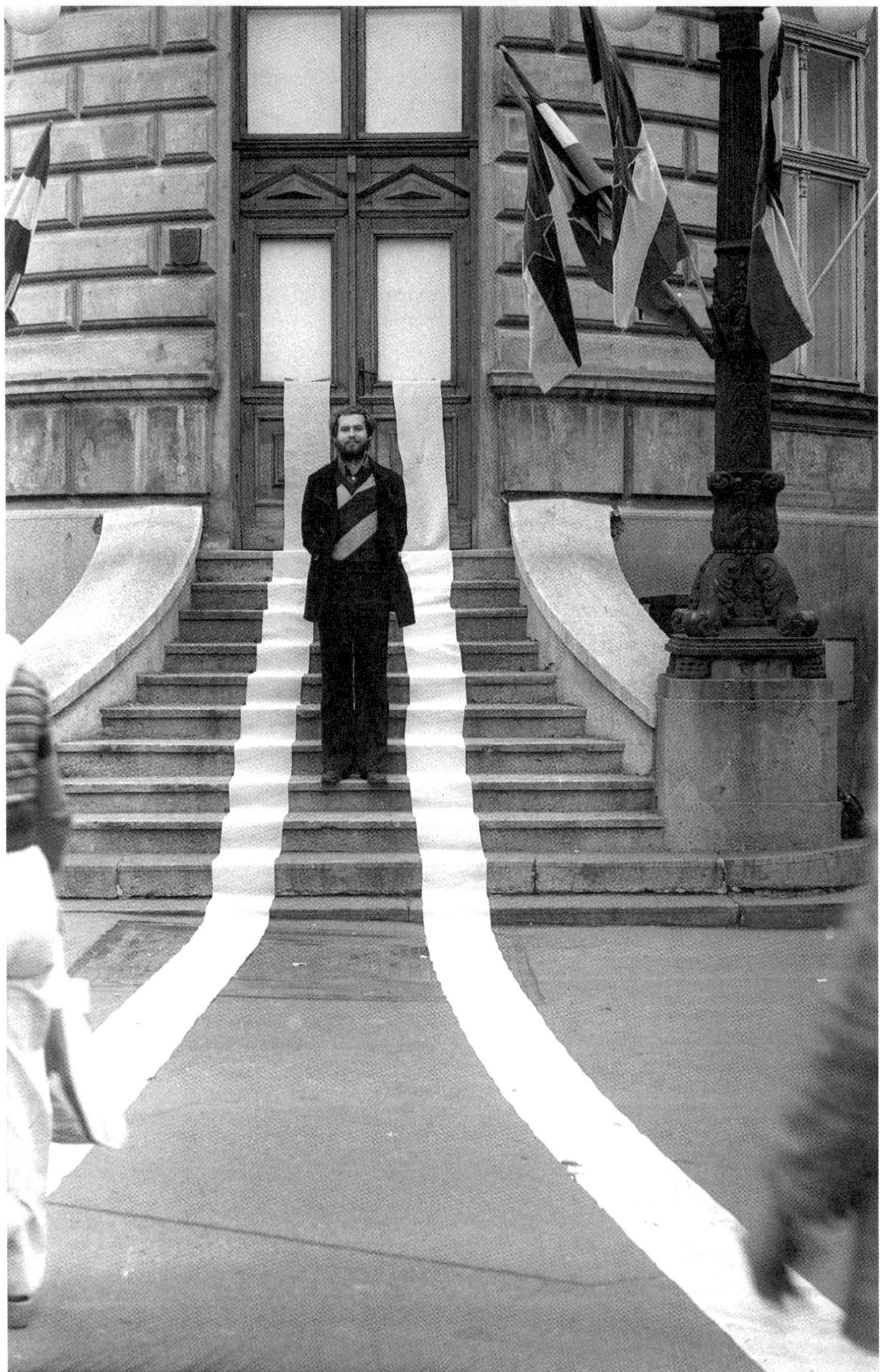

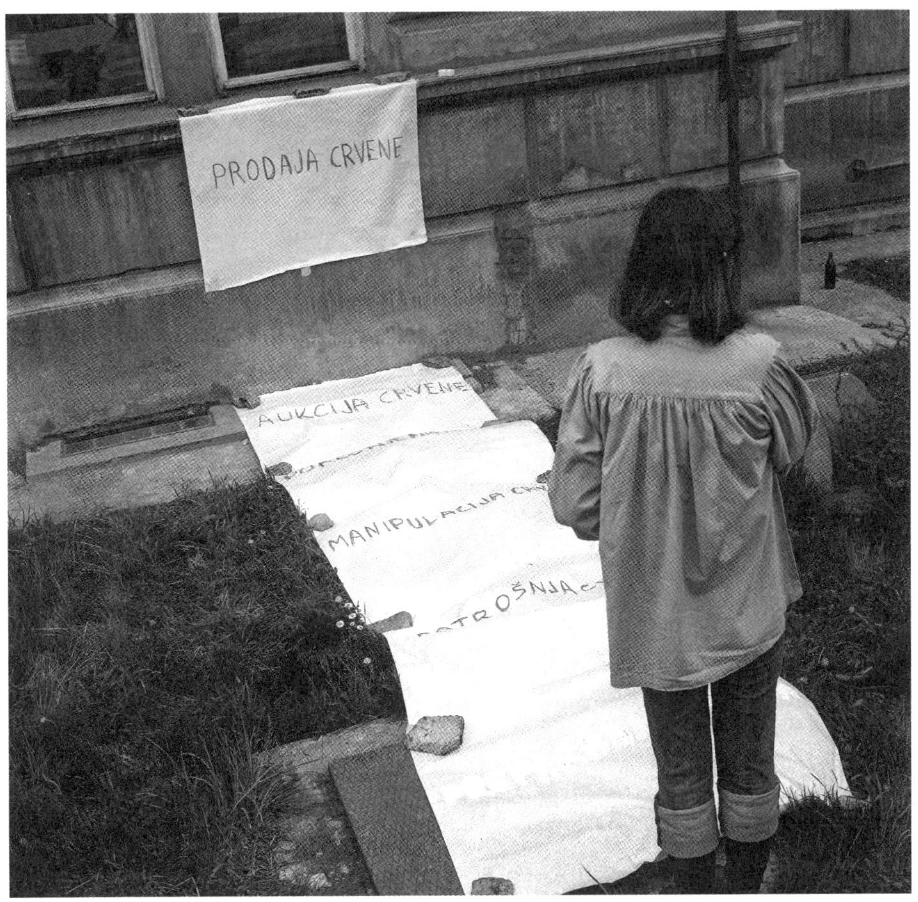

4.6. Sven Stilinović, *Akcija s toalet papirom* [Action with Toilet Paper], SKC Gallery, 1976. Image courtesy of the artist.

4.7. Mladen Stilinović, *Aukcija crvene* [Auction of Red], SKC Gallery, 1976. Image courtesy of the SKC Archive, Belgrade.

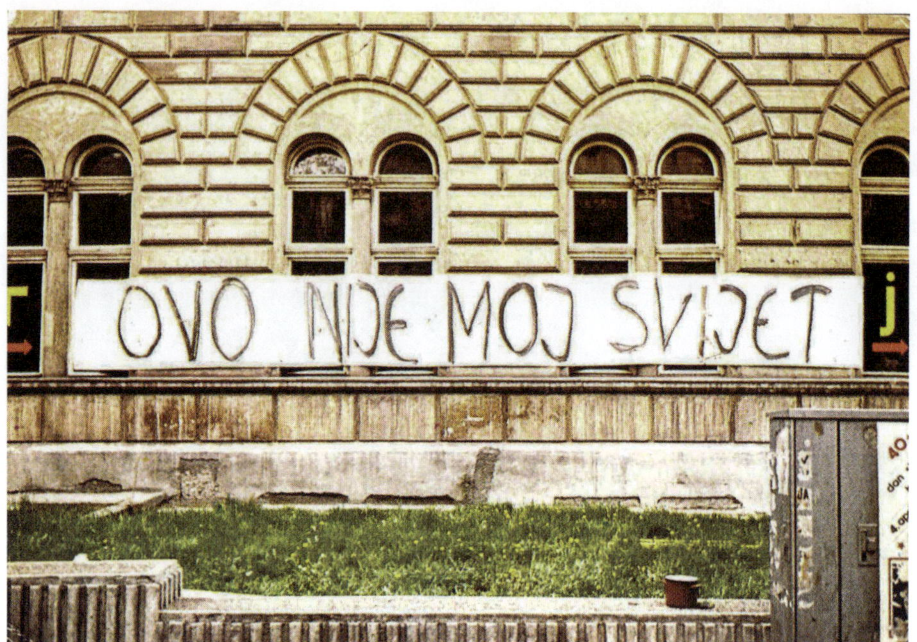

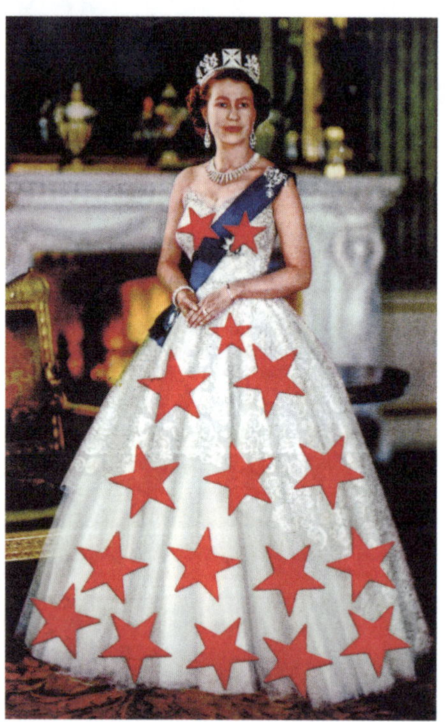

4.8. Postcard of Željko Jerman's *Ovo nije moj svijet* [This Is Not My World], SKC Gallery, 1976. Image courtesy of Bojana Švertasek and the SKC Gallery, Belgrade.

4.9. Mladen Stilinović, *Kraljica (2)* [Queen (2)], 1976 (detail of the installation *Red—Pink,* 1976–1981). Image courtesy of Kontakt Collection, Vienna.

of self-management. Stressing that maximum participation by the maximum number of citizens was its explicit goal, or as Stilinović summed up, that "WE" were all in it together, effectively served to neutralize criticisms against the self-management distortions. As Mark Thompson succinctly put it, it was "difficult to confront power that keeps dispersing itself, difficult to attack the monopoly of a system which has already denounced and, apparently, renounced its own monopoly." Hence, the 1974 constitution referred to citizens' "'inalienable right' to self-management."[21]

Later on in *Untitled Film*, Jasna Tijardović connected these political dynamics to the role of art and culture in Yugoslavia, along with art's support of what she described as the "status quo":

> The leopard can't change its spots. Traditional art ends with humanistic rhetoric, with corny complaints about human nature. It preaches humanism where it cannot be found. It often presents itself as something good for man. The recent new art, under the pretense of examining art, disputes the objectivity of the language of art. It believes that art is a thing in itself, tautological, supporting in this way the status quo. Its good point is that it doesn't present inhuman things as human. Art is elevated over and beyond our lives as an eternal, universal truth. We depend on such art; the point is that art should depend on us.... It often happens to me that I feel I'm living in an imagined society. I don't like this state of mind.[22]

In her statement, Tijardović proposed that the New Art Practice had failed to link itself to a social base and confined itself exclusively to the exploration of tautologies. Even though it had radically broken with the physical art object, little progress had been made—the leopard had not "changed its spots." In the same year that she voiced these doubts in *Untitled Film*, Zagreb's Gallery of Contemporary Art organized the exhibition *New Art Practice in Yugoslavia*. The first large-scale survey of conceptual and performance art in Yugoslavia, the show inaugurated the umbrella term used to describe the forms of artistic engagement that had emerged throughout many of Yugoslavia's capitals and taken on a more socially engaged form at the beginning of the 1970s. At the same time, it made a conscious effort to recognize the movement's many multiplicities and divergences.

As the show's curator, Marijan Susovski, noted, the New Art Practice emerged independently in many of Yugoslavia's largest cities, and in response to local art genealogies, which "represented the starting point for their different lines of development."[23] In her entry on the Group of Six Authors, Nena Baljković warned of the dangers implicit in analyzing avant-garde movements through their "formal characteristics" rather than their "revolutionary ideological potential."[24] Like

Tijardović, she noted that an overemphasis on formalism in art criticism had allowed the "lack of ideas" in a number of works to be "covered up by the use of the new art media." "Without the necessary ideological attitude," she argued, these works had retreated into the "practice of multiplication and [the] cosmetic treatment of worn-out artistic concepts."[25] Both Tijardović and Baljković noted the same conditions that had led to Goran Đorđević's disillusionment with the New Art Practice at roughly the same time: the general drive toward "new media" had failed to secure "immunity from stupidity. It was enough for anyone to make any kind of performance, film, video, or series of photos, draw some diagrams which look exact, to be new and avant-garde."[26]

Despite being shown at one of the country's most prestigious contemporary art museums, the 1978 *New Art Practice* exhibition did little to expand the narrow-minded understanding of conceptual art that dominated Yugoslav art criticism. This was particularly palpable in the lack of differentiation between the work of the Group of Six Authors and the work of those preceding them. Ultimately, the Group of Six Authors had discarded the tautology usually associated with Anglo-American conceptualism. They were producing poor, "dirty," carelessly executed, and unskilled works. Like Đorđević, they had disregarded the boundaries between artistic genres, treated exhibition standards with complete indifference, used perishable materials, and displayed their works in lowly settings. Yet, according to the group's members, the defining characteristics of their practice were largely overlooked by local art critics, who mockingly lumped their work together under the ambiguous term "conceptualism." Just months after the *New Art Practice* exhibition, Mladen Stilinović and Boris Demur gave an interview to *Polet* magazine—one of the most active and progressive youth publications in Zagreb—in which they complained that the term "conceptualism" was being manipulated so that "the whole effort is reduced to a sporadic and suspicious manifestation by critics in the general press."[27] More often than not, new work was being analyzed reductively, according to conceptual art's initial parting with the object; rarely was it recognized that a new system of methodologies was unfolding.[28]

What had prompted Stilinović and Demur to address these tendencies was a recent altercation between the Group of Six Authors and Zagreb's Youth Salon, an annual event organized by the Croatian Association of Visual Artists. Together with several other artists, the group submitted their work to the Youth Salon with an additional condition, stating that the rejection of one artist would result in all artists withdrawing their work. They explained that they were entering their work collectively in order to expand the salon's understanding of the "New Art Practice," which had until then always been presented in the press "under the wider plan of conceptualism."[29] Attempting to solicit a more thorough recognition of the New Art Practice, their gesture was perceived by one judge as "unlicensed pressure."[30] Writing in *Večernji list*, veteran Croatian art critic and member of the Youth Salon's panel Josip Depolo described the artists' letter as a "crude attempt at institutionalizing culture, opening the door to despotism and bureaucratic procedures."[31] Seeking to carve out a space for the New Art Practice at the city's "official" Youth Salon, the group of artists were perceived as saboteurs.

Responding to Depolo's accusations in *Polet*, Stilinović and Demur complained that many artists were being exhibited and supported abroad, while being neglected, criticized, and deprived of funding opportunities locally. Stilinović summarized the status of these artists with a proverb from Belgrade: "How long will artists be fed by their mothers?"[32] In the previous year, one artists' collective in Zagreb had already begun to address the deeper dynamics at play in this satirical question, by reflecting on the economic precariousness of artists affiliated with the New Art Practice.

HOW LONG WILL ARTISTS BE FED BY THEIR MOTHERS?

In 1978, Sanja Iveković and Dalibor Martinis invited a number of artists to collaboratively transform their studio into an independent exhibition space, where artists could also socialize and work together. Active for two years, Radna Zajednica Umjetnika (RZU) Podrum (literally translated as "The Working Community of Artists: Basement") was the first artist-run exhibition space in Yugoslavia. According to Iveković, the initiative originated from a time when "'nothing' happened, but during which heated discussions about the aims and potentials of an artist-run space took place."[33] It therefore came out of a readiness to enter into open and shifting discussions on what "the purpose and character of such a space—of what a 'working community of artists,' should be."[34] As with its indirect predecessor, *Oktobar '75*, Podrum attempted to salvage the idea of self-management in a working space that was based on equality and on an equal share of responsibilities among its members. In a broader sense, the working space occupied a position similar to the Marxist agenda of assuming control over the means of production.[35] As Stilinović emphasized in one crucial transcript of a conversation between its members, he alone wanted to be responsible for his work:

> When I work through other galleries or newspapers (and not [by] myself), they think they are responsible for my work. That bothers me and cannot be the truth. I would like, apart from that, for my work to be presented complete, i.e. how I imagined it—from the posters

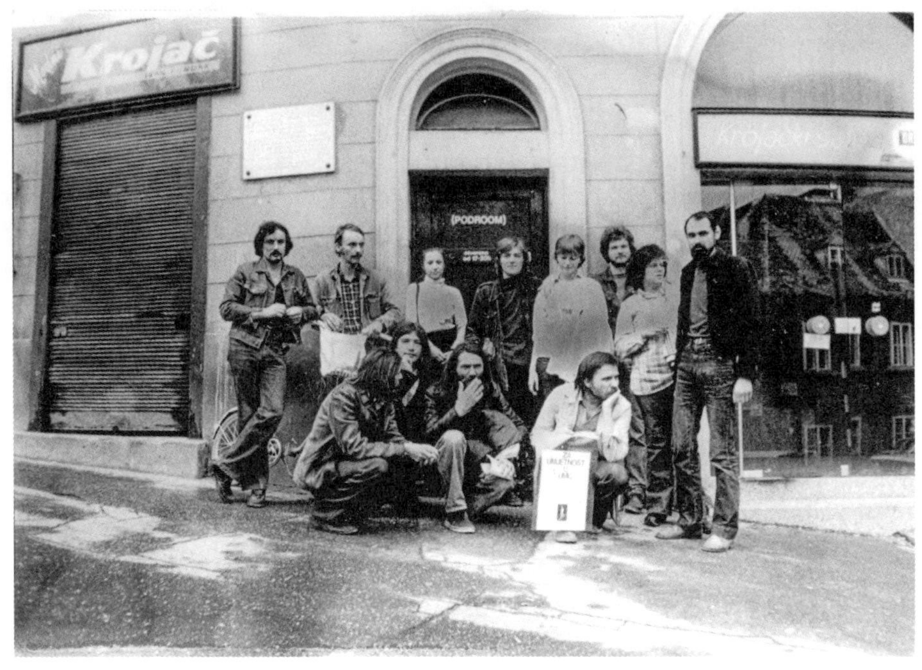

4.10. Podrum members outside of the exhibition *Za umjetnost u umu* [For Art in the Mind], RZU Podrum, 1978. Photograph by Sven Stilinović. Image courtesy of Sven Stilinović.

> and catalogues, to the duration of the exhibition and its preservation. I really like a sentence from Aretino: "life means not going to court." When I go through other institutions, I go to court, that's how I feel. When I go into Podrum, I go into Podrum.[36]

Podrum's preoccupation with gaining direct control over production emerged at the precise moment the Yugoslav government had made fundamental changes to the organization of firms, through the Associated Labor Law of 1976. To enable workers to manage their enterprises, the Associated Labor Law divided the Yugoslav economy into small functional units—a self-managed type of enterprise called the basic organization of associated labor (BOAL).[37] Although the BOALS could still operate as autonomous units (self-organized enterprises), they were usually too small to stay independent. Therefore, at least in theory, several BOALS "associated" into one work organization. A typical work organization had three or four BOALS and one work community—called a *radnička zajednica*. The highest level of association was the "complex organizations of associated labor" which sometimes had more than one hundred BOALS.

The Working Community of Artists represented a direct attempt to access and participate in the system of associated labor. Because it was an administrative hub for a group of artists set within a working community, issues related to labor were a central preoccupation from the outset, although for many of the artists this provoked a rebellion against the ideology of work as such. For other artists involved in Podrum, however, engaging with the immediate sociopolitical context that determined artistic production remained a core concern. Podrum's founding members, Iveković and Martinis, proposed the idea for launching a magazine as an "additional form of action" that would enable the group to reflect on the past and the future of the initiative.[38]

As Iveković explained later, the publication aimed to "really think about artists as workers, as political subjects."[39] *Prvi broj* [First Issue] was published in 1980, and members of Podrum were invited to participate in its development. Mladen Stilinović contributed a handwritten statement that discussed censorship and the lack of professionalism in the media and art institutions, while Marijan Molnar wrote on how artists continued to support dominant art trends, and Jerman confronted the problem of artists' low income in Yugoslavia. One page consisted of an invoice, split in the middle of the page, comparing the income of an independent artist and their real personal income against the personal income of staff employed by cultural institutions. It demonstrated the huge discrepancy between the two after all costs and expenditures were factored in. Another page directly copied a newspaper cut-out quoting state rhetoric about the relevance

PRVI BROJ

Trbuljak: Ovaj razgovor je u vezi ove publikacije, odnosno časopisa.
Stile: Ne, to je bilo prošli put.
Trbuljak: A sada je tema, šta?
Stile: Čekaj ovaj put mi smo se sastali, da svaki kaže nešto o Podrumu, i to bi išlo kao uvod u taj časopis, – katalog.
Sanja: Ali, ne da svaki drži monolog, nego da to bude razgovor.
Stile: Je pa dobro, ali neko mora početi, ne? Ja ću tebe pitati kaj ti misliš o Podrumu, a ovako ja odmah kažem mišljenje pa se onda neko nadoveže.
Trbuljak: Normalno počni.
Stile: A to kaj je meni napisano to je zato kaj sam si to napisao (čita tekst)
Zašto radim u Podrumu? Radim u Podrumu zato jer sam sâm odgovoran za ono što radim. Kad delujemo putem drugih galerija ili novina one (a ne ja) misle da su odgovorne za moj rad. To me smeta i to ne može biti istina. Volim, osim toga da moj rad bude kompletno prezentiran, tj. onako kako sam zamislio od plakata, kataloga do trajanja izložbe i čuvanja. Stvarno volim jednu rečenicu od Aretina: »Život znači ne ići na dvor«. Kada idem po ostalim institucijama, idem na dvor, tako se osećam (po cigarete). Kada idem u Podrum onda idem u Podrum.
Ovo što ću sada reći nije jedino iskustvo u vezi sa Podrumom ima i drugih ali im je najupečatljivije. Pošto sâm čuvam izložbe znam tko dolazi na izložbe (ovo nije stvar količine ljudi). Iz toga ko dolazi na izložbe proizlazi da nitko od ljudi iz galerija, novina, kulturnih institucija, fakulteta, nije zainteresiran... neću reći za nas koji radimo nego za kulturu, jer ako ovo nije za nekoga dobra umjetnost ili likovna umjetnost ovo sigurno spada u kulturu. Ljudi koji rade u institucijama misle da je ono mjesto gde rade kultura i da je drugdje nema. Svak od tih ljudi veže se za svoju instituciju i ne interesira ga da vidi bilo šta drugo (naravno kada se radi o inostranstvu to nije tako... mogu reći svi likovni kritičari iz Zagreba bili su u Kaselu ili Veneciji, nitko nije bio u Podrumu). Čast iznimcima.
Na osnovu jednog dolaženja u Podrum ili nijednog, kritičari a i umjetnici pisali su i davali izjave o Podrumu, uglavnom negativne i posprdne, a do sada je bilo tridesetpet (35) nastupa u Podrumu od dvadesetpetorice umjetnika.
Na osnovu izjave gospon Depola da se neoavangarda povukla u izolaciju ja izjavljujem sledeće: Nismo se mi povukli u izolaciju, vi ste nas stavili u izolaciju (s jedne strane vrlo teškom ekonomskom a konkretno – znam šta štampa, radio i televizija znače za javnost a i za vas. »OKO« do sada nije pisalo ni o jednoj izložbi održanoj u Podrumu (o jednoj), Vjesnik, Večernji List, radio i tv o ni jednoj itd... Ali ta izolacija me ne zanima, to je društveni fenomen koji zahtijeva drugačiju i podrobniju analizu... Ja mogu reći, ako vi dođete samo jedamput na izložbu i kažete da smo se povukli u izolaciju onda je očito da ste se vi povukli u izolaciju.
Martinis: To je jedno negativno iskustvo o tome kako sredina reagira.
Stile: To je pozitivno.
Martinis: Dobro kako ga shvaćaš, sad je pitanje da li, sad je to činjenica s kojom se mi moramo zadovoljiti ili jednostavno nastaviti raditi.
Stile: Ne možeš ti nekoga naterati da dođe u Podrum ako neće.
Martinis: Ne, hoću reći to ako to isto vredi ako izlažeš u Galeriji Suvremene s tim da će ti tamo biti, pazi tamo ti neće doći nitko iz galerije Moderne.
Stile: Pazi, to me ne zanima ovdje neće nitko doći, ali će s tim faktima svi baratati.
Martinis: Pa zato ti i velim to je samo negativno iskustvo jedno negativno određenje sredine prema ovom ovdje.
Petercol: Da ali i pozitivno.
Martinis: Mislim u ovaku konstalaciju onda se stvarno vidi da ne postoji nikakva, nikakva reakcija tj. da... neznam.
Trbuljak: Meni se čini da kad je on govorio šta je on dobio od Podruma u tom smislu šta Podrum njemu znači, više nego što mu znači jedna galerija, a ovo je on s jedne strane zadovoljan, razumeš jer je on u početku rekao zadovoljan sam zbog toga toga i toga a ovo je samo onako jedna opaska, mislim, usprkos toga što on ima kontrolu nad svim stvarima nad kojima oće imati, to je samo jedna digresija bila uz ono kaj taj sistem prati, a činjenica je ta kaj ti kažeš Marta da ovaj, to se ne mjenja ni u jednoj drugoj galeriji, mislim da ovaj...
Međutim samo jedno pitanje o kome bi se trebalo razgovarati da li ti, Stilinović je rekao kroz sebe samog znači on je zadovoljan... Možda je sad pitanje nad ostalima da oni to isto kažu kako su zadovoljni, u čemu su razočarani, u čemu misle ako su razočarani da se može nešto promjeniti.
G.P.: Radim tekst o Podrumu, pa sam naišao na problem kojeg bih izložio. Radi se o tome da mi nismo grupa, to je bilo osnovno polazište; nemamo jednu ideologiju, mislim, skupili smo se, na principu posebnog otklona od tradicionalnog. Postoji vrednovanje, jedan međusobni odabir na osnovu nekog povjerenja u rad ljudi koji su tu. Međutim, ima jedna druga stvar koja mi se čini jako problematičnom, a to je da se mi ponašamo ipak kao galerija prema onim umjetnicima koje pozivamo. U stvari, mislim da se nekako približavamo modelu galerije, samo što u ovom slučaju nije jedan galerist, nego grupa pojedinaca. Svatko od nas ima pravo pozvati nekog da održi ovdje izložbu, mi dajemo njemu prostor, a on sa svojim izlaganjem pomaže ideju Podruma. Međutim što se događa: kad on napravi izložbu, treba čekati da se netko sjeti, odnosno da ga zapita hoće li još, za godinu ili dvije, doći da ponovo napravi izložbu ili ne. Taj je odnos tipičan za galeriju: nudi mu se prostor i čast da izlaže, a ne nudi mu se suradnja. Mi bi ga trebali ravnopravno tretirati. Mislim da je ovdje došlo do izvjesne akumulacije moći koja se zasniva na prošlosti; to jest, na činjenici, zasluzi, da smo mi prije dvije godine, godinu i pol osnovali Podrum... i plus toga što posjedujemo prostor, odnosno da smo sticajem okolnosti dobili prostor. Time smo došli do zatvorene situacije u kojoj... koju bi trebalo prevladati. To je pitanje principa. Mislim da je to, u stvari, prikriveno nepovjerenje prema pozvanom umjetniku. Ukoliko smo ga mi jednom prihvatili, on treba biti upoznat s time da: ako želi može uzeti prvi slobodni termin da bi prezentirao rad, ili ako hoće može pozvati nekog, ne znam, desetog umjetnika.
Stile: To je pitanje kako se čovjek postavlja prema onom koga zove, ja sam Raši rekao, pitao sam ga da li želi nešto raditi u Podrumu, ne smatra se članom jer je u Beogradu, ali za svaku suradnju je otvoren.
Petercol: To treba ljudima reći, svakom tko je pozvan, pa neka on odluči sam: Kako, koliko, gost, član...
Dorogi: To je usko povezano sa organiziranjem i karakterom izložbi u Podrumu. Do sada su to bile mahom izložbe samostalne, a za to vrijeme nismo imali jednu ili dvije akcije koje su nekakav radikalni odklon od takvog načina prezentacije. Čovjek koji izvana dođe vidi da tu od nas netko sjedi, tu su ti radovi pet šest ljudi, možda nema nikoga i shvati to kao galeriju
Dorogi: I taj pojam da je podrum Galerija isključivo je vezan uz sam karakter načina rada i tu je problem
Martinis: Organizacija i prezentacija.
Dorogi: Kad bi mi mogli pronaći najidealniju formu prezentacije radova gdje bi sam autor bio uključen na jedan aktivniji način, onda on ne bi to shvaćao kao galeriju. Ako ga ti pozoveš i kažeš imaš termin tad i tad, pa imao on i performans i spavao tu tri sata ili tri dana, ali to je u biti samostalna izložba kao u bilo kojoj galeriji. Očito je problem u načinu rada i prezentiranja čovjeku koji dođe ovamo.
Maračić: Jebi ga ako čovjeku netreba prostor onda ne će ni tražiti da dođe...
Čekaj ne ćeš ti izmišljati neki novi sistem ukoliko radiš to i to
Dorogi: Ne, mislim.
Maračić: Sad ne ću ja koristiti prostor na neki drugi način samo zato da on ne bi funkcionirao kao
Martinis: Ne radi se o tome na koji način ćeš ti svoj rad prezentirati nego organizaciji i djelatnosti Podruma, bez obzira šta se unutra izlaže.
Maračić: Ali nitko nije bio ničim limitiran i radio je ono što hoće
Martinis: Dobro, ali govorimo o posljedicama toga... (nejasno) kakva je razlika od galerije Forum i Podruma osim u radovima... ali to je pitanje vremena za pet godina to može biti sve skupa etablirano i da netko kaže e znam njih oni su podrumaši, kao što mi kažemo forumaši, a to je grupa ljudi, jedan prostor koji afirmira jedan tip radova i unutra druge nema...
Dorogi: A to je povezano sa kriterijumima praktički
Sanja: Možda je dobro da se vratimo kad već govorimo o iskustvu kojeg imamo c tom prostoru
Stilinović: Da, inače bi o jednom problemu mogli
Sanja: Što se tiče Martinog i mog iskustva s Podrumom, ono se može odnositi na 76, 77. i samo djelomično na 78. (proljeće) i onda opet na 79. od veljače na dalje. Iako se 76. i 77. ovdje nije ništa događalo, mislim na izložbenu aktivnost, (pa se zato tek 1978. smatra početkom rada Podruma) za mene je to bilo značajno vrijeme jer smo se tada počeli okupljati oko ideje Podruma. Tada smo puno razgovarali, diskutirali, svađali se oko toga što bi trebala biti svrha i karakter takvog prostora, jedne radne zajednice umjetnika. Onda smo napravili i jednu koncepciju rada i aktivnosti koje bi se tu odvijale (o tome postoje još kod nas pismeni dokumenti) itd. Pa smo se opet nakon toga sastali, pa opet razgovarali, svađali. I naravno pokazalo se kako je strašno teško uskladiti naše stavove iako smo svi manje više spadali u istu generaciju, priroda našeg rada je bila ista, a i iskustva s institucijama u ovom gradu ista itd. Dakle, sve je u redu dok umjetnik postoji i radi sam, ali u trenutku kad on postaje član kolektiva onda stvar ne štima. To spada u najtradicionalniji stav o umjetnicima koji su, kao, izraziti »individualci« i koji nikako nisu u stanju da međusobno surađuju. A pokazalo se da je to kod nas i te kako još živo. I sad bez obzira što je to za nekog moglo biti jedno negativno iskustvo, ja mislim da smo mi u tom trenutku dobro napravili kad smo inzistirali na tome da prije nego što počnemo raditi u ovom prostoru pokušamo prvo ustanoviti neku zajedničku politiku. Jer tada nam se nije činilo dovoljno to što postoji taj prostor u kojem možemo izlagati naše radove, raditi si kataloge itd. I to što taj prostor je sam po sebi različit od galerija. Uostalom zato jer se i karakter našeg rada promijenio i svijest o tome koja je uloga umjetnika danas se promijenila, mi smo na neki način prestali biti samo »umjetnici«, a počinjemo biti i nešto više od toga...
Stile: Manje
Sanja: Više ili manje, po mom mišljenju više, kad kažem više mislim nije nam samo važno kako ćeš napraviti svoj rad, nego imaš i svijest o tome da djeluješ u jednom kontekstu i da umjetnici jesu neki činioci kulture i da prema tome imaš pravo da se kritički odnosiš prema tome a onda i da kreiraš tu, neku kulturnu politiku, ne znam... I kad smo mi u prvim planovima za Podrum bili naveli i te neke stvari kao što su Tribina (javne diskusije), tematske izložbe, predavanja, pa onda izdavanje biltena-časopisa, imali smo to na umu, tu jednu djelatnost koja nije po svom karakteru tradicionalno izložbena. Zato smo Marta i ja inzistirali više na tim nekim manifestacijama kao što je bio razgovor sa grupom CEAC iz Toronta, predavanje Lize Bear o alternativnom korištenju komunikacija, naš razgovor u Podrumu o alternativnim umjetničkim centrima u Kanadi i Americi, na biblioteci. Zato, recimo, ova odluka da se pokrene ovaj časopis mi se čini značajna, to je dobar znak.
d: Gle, nešto sam ti htio odgovorit'. Recimo, što ti kažeš, da smo se ovdje našli zato što je prije naš rad bio izvan tokova kulturne politike, da se mi sada, ovoga, nalazimo u toj poziciji da osim što smo umjetnici još stvarno otvaramo određenu kulturno političku problematiku, jer vidiš šta mislim ja povodom toga, mislim da sam rad pojedinog umjetnika u sebi već sadrži, i treba, se, kolko ja shvaćam takav rad, da on u sebi imanentno sadrži kulturnu politiku, samim tim što zahtijeva kontrolu prvo: nad načinom prezentacije, drugo: distribucije i treće: odnosa tog individualnog rada prema samoj kulturnoj situaciji, mjestu prezentacije i svim ostalim stvarima. E vidiš kolko ja razumijem te individualne radove, mislim da je to sve zajedno objedinjeno u svakom pojedinom radu ako

of culture to worker productivity in socialist society, along with a photograph of a woman, bejeweled and dressed in a fur gown, raising her fist. The photograph was accompanied by the strident declaration: "I advocate a new legislation on independent artists."

Responding to these issues, Iveković and Martinis drafted a proposal for a contract regulating financial responsibilities between artists and the institutions that presented their work. It demanded that the artist and institution take on a mutual responsibility for artworks, so that they would become a common good shared through public institutions with the wider community.[40] This, in turn, was how the artist was to earn his or her salary. Since grants for museums, galleries, and other cultural institutions were distributed by self-managing interest communities, Podrum was attempting to access state finances directly. This attempt to participate in Yugoslavia's highly atomized economic system would lead to future disagreements in the Working Community, echoing the conditions that were driving Yugoslavia's vast political and economic atomization.

PODROOM VS. PODRUM: LESS OR MORE?

According to *First Issue*, Podrum was a "form of artistic activity," in which the journal itself served as "one new alternative" to the gallery context.[41] Ultimately, the publication was intended to foster a sense of equality in the space. It emphasized absolute "respect for individual freedom and responsibility and the presentation of contributors ... governed on the principle of agreement among all interests."[42] As such, when Podrum applied for funding from municipal cultural organizations, the group stressed that they would prefer to receive funds individually, with each organizer personally responsible for their program, rather than as a "basic organization of associated labor." A letter from the Working Community of Artists sent to the City of Zagreb's "Self-Managed Interest Community" in January 1979 requested that each artist within the Working Community manage their own work, and that "every artist bear their expenditure for the organization of their action (poster, invitations, catalogues, etc.)."[43]

4.11. Radna Zajednica Umjetnika Podrum [Podrum: The Working Community of Artists], *Prvi broj* [First Issue], Zagreb, 1980. Image courtesy of Vlado Martek.

PRVI BROJ

PRVI BROJ je prvi broj kataloga radne zajednice umjetnika (RZU) PODROOM. Sam naslov ukazuje na neki niz brojeva to jest na ideju o kontinuiranom izdavanju ove publikacije.
RZU PODROOM nije galerija već jedan oblik umjetničkog djelovanja. Velik broj naših radova ne može se realizirati u galerijskom kontekstu jer je upravo njegova negacija i zato smo od početka nastojali otvoriti sve alternativne mogućnosti unutar kojih bi naš rad potpunije funkcionirao.
Brojevi kataloga trebaju biti jedna nova alternativa.
Kao i u radu PODROOMa, tako i u radu na Brojevima kataloga uvažavamo apsolutnu individualnu slobodu i odgovornost u radu i prezentiranju rada stvaraoca.
Brojevi kataloga su otvoreni svim potencijalnim suradnicima, a uređuju se na principu dogovora svih zainteresiranih.
Sadržaj svakog novog broja (kao i ovog Prvog) odražava aktualne probleme, interese i preokupacije umjetnika članova RZU PODROOM kao i onih koji će se uključiti kao suradnici.
Troškove tiska namirujemo iz uštedenih sredstava koje je SIZ kulture općine Centar dodijelio RZU PODROOM za 1979.
Prvi broj je besplatan.

(PODROOM)
12 mesnička, 41000 zagreb.YU

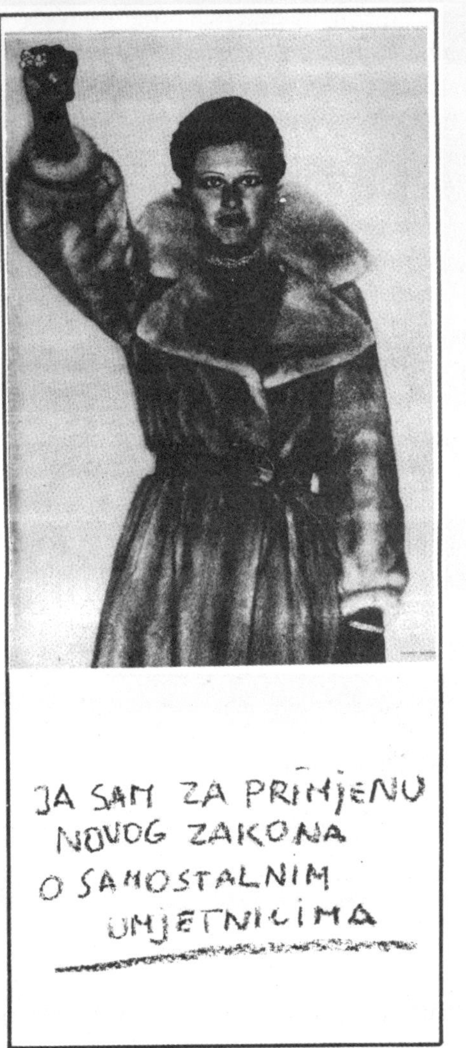

3

4.12. "I advocate a new legislation on independent artists," RZU Podrum, *Prvi broj* [First Issue], 1980. Image courtesy of Vlado Martek.

Yet the only recorded conversation between Podrum's founding members, published in *First Issue*, reveals that the initiative represented a constant debate over what it could be, rather than what it was. Two dominant and conflicting positions surfaced between the group's members: one that advocated self-sufficiency (the "not having to go to court" attitude, as Mladen Stilinović put it), and the claim that artists working in the space should strive to be "more than just artists," so that the Podrum could become a "base that coordinates a wider action on the level of cultural politics."[44] The conflict of interests was even expressed in disagreements over the name of the space itself. While Iveković and Martinis referred to it as "Podroom" (an anglicized spelling of the word *Podrum* [basement], and a pun that combined the Serbo-Croatian word *pod* ["under," "ground," or "floor"] with the English word "room"—to suggest a kind of organized base, with international leanings), many of the other group members referred to it as an ordinary basement or *podrum*—as a space locked away from public view. It was this disagreement over whether artists should strive to do more that precipitated Podrum's eventual dissolution:

> **Sanja [Iveković]:** For then it didn't seem enough to us that this space exists where we can exhibit our works, create our catalogues, etc. And besides, it was also because the character of our work had changed, along with the sense of what constituted the role of artists today; in a way, we ceased to be merely "artists," and are starting to be something more than that . . .
>
> **[Mladen] Stilinović:** Less.
>
> **Sanja:** More or less. In my opinion, it is more. When I say more I think that now it's not just important how you're going to make your work, but that you have the awareness of the fact that you are working in a context—that artists are some kind of cultural entity—and with that, that you have the right to critically relate towards that, and then to create there some kind of cultural politics.[45]

While most participants in the discussion opted for "less," Iveković and Martinis had larger ambitions for Podrum. They envisioned it as "a gathering space of artists with a non-traditional orientation. . . . Among other things, here we thought of open conversations, discussions, and a regular publication."[46] They were more invested in the "organization and activity of Podrum" than in its approach to presenting works, and emphasized the need to define a "collective politics" before beginning to work in the space.[47] This was, then, a call for "mutual cooperation" that could supersede the conventional notion of the artist as an isolated individual.[48]

According to Iveković, these initiatives were what would differentiate Podrum from the conventional art gallery and initiate the struggle against the marginalized "socio-economic status of the artist."[49] Along with fostering more international artistic networks of communication and exchange, and seeking to find common ground between local and international conditions, the tribune, lectures, bulletins and journals, and library would enable Podrum to become an "alternative social structure, rather than simply an exhibition space."[50] This aspiration was conveyed in *First Issue* through a photocopied photograph of a kitchen sink, piled up with used coffee cups, and a New Year's buffet table, full of leftovers and discarded crockery—traces of sociability that presented Podrum as a "gathering space, and not a gallery."[51] The tension between producing work and creating a space in which artists would reflect on the conditions of work attracted suspicion among other members of the group. Iveković and Martinis claimed that this tension solicited "severe criticism and allegations that we had usurped power within Podroom by organizing an event that didn't have the support of all of the Working Community's members. At the same time most members advocated that each member was free to organize, invest their own effort in, and be responsible for any action, exhibition, or manifestation."[52]

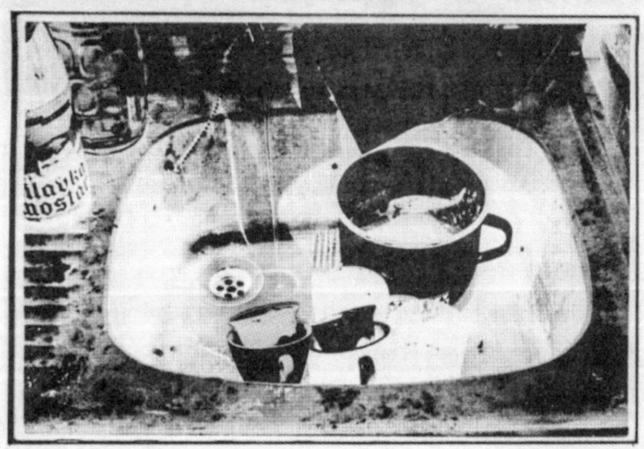

4.13. RZU Podrum, *Prvi broj* [First Issue], 1980.
Image courtesy of Vlado Martek.

As Podrum's key instigators and owners of the studio space that housed it, Iveković and Martinis remained the primary hosts, and their intentions began to arouse mistrust among other members. By emphasizing the need for consensus regarding a common program of action, Podrum's organization was beginning to mirror the sorts of struggles that had become central to Yugoslavia's political economy of associated labor. After 1976, enterprises became loose confederations of basic organizations of associated labor, linked together in production and planning through "self-management agreements" and "social compacts" concluded by workers in their basic organizations, and among basic organizations of self-management bodies.[53] The new notion of "social planning" was intended to serve as "an expression of the need for the coordination and harmonization of workers' interests."[54] While this economic arrangement repudiated the market as the coordinating mechanism, replacing it with negotiated contracts and incorporating social and aggregate economic goals, it decentralized economic decision making to the point that conscious coordination of any sort was rendered almost impossible. Although it was expected that the smaller units would be forced to cooperate to survive, the BOALs tended to act individually, each embarking on its own expansion plan. Both Podrum and the BOAL system, respectively, were subject to favoring individual interests, unable as they were to effect coherent programs.

If, as Branislav Jakovljević has argued, the history of socialist Yugoslavia is one of self-managing society slipping away from the control of the state and the state's attempts to regain control over society, then associated labor, and particularly its emphasis on the notion of "interest," served as a divisive tool in this struggle.[55] According to Kardelj, the notion of interest was central to associated labor: "the system of socialist self-management is not only a form of democratic rule by workers over conditions and means of production, but also the starting point of self-managing in the transformation of the entire society on the basis of the leading role of the interest of the working class."[56] In a system that had removed the financial incentives of a free market economy and the ideological drivers of a statist socialist economy, interest was to serve as an adhesive bonding workers together into a community, rather than spurring competition.

By ceding economic resources to individual firms, communities, and regions, associated labor aimed to empower the individual worker. Yet this move assumed that a system of social ownership of property would guarantee sufficient cooperation to construct self-management at the level of both the enterprise and society. Rather than uniting "working-class interests," the BOALs started to fight with one another to protect the smaller interests of their workers against the interests of those working in another BOAL of the same company.[57] Some firms were so divided that physical barriers were raised to separate workers from two BOALs. And while the working collective was able to participate in management and decision making, associated labor used over 976 articles to invent a norm for all economic, political, and cultural relationships. It thus foreclosed the political potential of self-management to facilitate the emergence of a spontaneous community. As Jakovljević has asserted, placing interest at the heart of associated labor denied other values "traditionally associated with proletarian struggle, such as solidarity or equality, [moving] self-management away from the modernist project of emancipation of labor in order to bring it closer to the neoliberal idea of its randomization and deregulation."[58]

Almost immediately after opening up their studio, Iveković and Martinis left Yugoslavia for Canada as visiting artists. Feeling trapped by their responsibility for instigating the project, they ended Podrum a year after their return, by sending a letter to the Working Community, informing them of their decision to revert the space back to its initial purpose (as their studio). The reasons they gave referred to the hostility of several Podrum members to a series of ideas and projects they had proposed. According to the letter, these tensions culminated with *First Issue*, because Iveković, as chief designer of the magazine, had failed to sign her visual and textual insertions in the publication:

> With the publication of *First Issue* we received, from RZU directly, sharp criticism and attacks toward the work carried out by Sanja Iveković, for not signing her interventions. On the basis of all of these experiences, we came to the conclusion that our activity within RZU causes distrust among the larger part of its members, which is expressed through the markedly aggressive statements of some people. We don't feel comfortable in that kind of atmosphere, and we find it unstimulating, the opposite of what we envisaged for the relations of RZU.[59]

The harmonious, self-managing relations of Podrum had collapsed over a missing signature, perceived as the "imposition of unwanted collective ownership and responsibility."[60] As was becoming ever more frequent in Yugoslavia, the social contract had been violated. Two years after it opened, Podrum had been liquidated.

NEGOTIATING "MY SPACE"

Insisting there was no such thing as a common program, and yet stubbornly sharing the same space based on equality, Podrum echoed the economic conditions that were driving Yugoslavia's fragmentation. In Podrum, maintaining the rights of each individual was imperative. For if there was ever even a suspicion that certain members were becoming dominant in the group and of hierarchies calcifying, Podrum would lose its purpose. Precisely this suspicion arose during their last meeting:

> **[Petercol]:** This kind of relationship is typical of a gallery: what's offered is the space, and the honor to exhibit, but cooperation isn't on offer. We should treat them on an equal basis.... I think what happened here is a certain accumulation of power based on the past; that is, on the fact, the merit, that two years, a year and a half ago, we founded Podrum ... and in addition to that, we own the space, that is, it so happened that we got the space.[61]

In Podrum, it was the space that remained a constant—one that was open to the public, but in fact was occupied predominantly by a fixed group of artists and a number of recurring visitors. It was also the space that became the ultimate obstacle in the initiative; for Iveković, it was "the weak point of the whole thing ... because this space existed, it prevented people from concentrating more on forming one concept of action, a program. Maybe we need to abolish the space, or forget that it exists."[62] Martinis added that the space's name alone could not guarantee that Podrum would not become "business as usual," and succumb to the conventional and exploitative relationship between galleries and artists.[63]

The struggle over the space itself was acutely expressed by Željko Jerman in his work *Moj prostor* [My Space]—a simple, handwritten note with those words, that declared ownership over a space that was supposed to be shared. In a Working Community of Artists where guests were invited to become hosts, this was the key factor stirring divisions: one permanent group was actively working on the development of the program, and the rest were simply treating it as an exhibition space. In another event held at Podrum, Vlado Martek invited renowned Belgrade critic Ješa Denegri to give a talk. Denegri came, but Martek wasn't there and so the talk couldn't begin.[64] After the audience had patiently waited for thirty minutes, Stilinović felt obliged to take over the responsibility of host, as Denegri's reputation, and the fact that he lived in Belgrade, made the visit noteworthy. The next day, when he was asked for an explanation, Martek admitted that he had planned for this scenario all along. With this gesture, what was effectively at jeopardy was the traditional reciprocity between guest and host. Hospitality was supplanted by hostility.

At precisely the same moment, Yugoslavia was experiencing its own internal negotiations over space, with domestic conflicts increasingly being defined in terms of sovereignty and independence. The declining effectiveness of federal decision making resulted in the growing reluctance of republics to compromise

moj prostor

their short-term economic interests, as well as a tendency toward localizing economic distribution. Recognized as sovereign states after 1974, Yugoslav republics significantly reduced their mutual trade. Not infrequently, one republic would import goods from abroad while another republic was exporting the same kind of goods. Thus, one republic would be paying more for imported goods that were already available on their domestic market.[65] Inevitably, economic self-sufficiency aggravated already burgeoning power imbalances. While the reforms of the 1970s responded to some of the more negative consequences of the economic developments of the 1960s, they in fact intensified these problems: the shelving of coherent and enforceable economic policies meant that, after a series of world financial shocks, the highest per capita "social product" of Slovenia compared to the lowest one in Kosovo had, by 1981, opened a gap equal to the one between the United Kingdom and Algeria.[66] In the 1980s, the richest 10 percent of Yugoslavians possessed more than the poorest 40 percent. Needless to say, this gap was no better than the one observed in capitalist countries.[67]

In Podrum, not only was cooperation beginning to be compromised, but so were the rules of competition. Podrum was a "Working Community of Artists," but what was constantly being contested was its horizontality, for "it implied the equality of goals and chances, and the existence of chances always implied competition."[68] Complete horizontality was impossible, however, as members of the community were always, as Bago has argued, "forging new alliances, agendas and secret aspirations."[69] Competition between individuals would come to jeopardize the group's sense of unity and the initiative's cohesiveness. Simultaneously, associated labor came to be connected with a ceaseless competition for resources. Competition was taking place both within republics—between more and less developed communes—and among republics and provinces. Many Yugoslav experts saw it as the root of the economic decline, paving the way for the "gradual shaping up of six 'national' economies within the system, which effectively excluded integrative and reintegrative forces."[70] In the midst of a deepening crisis, both the developed and underdeveloped regions alike now asked: What was left of the equality of nations in practical terms? Was it all just an ideal, an unfulfilled promise?

4.14. Željko Jerman, *Moj prostor* [My Space], RZU Podrum, 1978. Image courtesy of Bojana Švertasek.

By the beginning of the 1980s, two of the most important figures of the Yugoslav revolutionary leadership had died: Kardelj, creator of the four Yugoslav constitutions, in 1979, and Tito, the leader of the Yugoslav People's Revolution, the president of the LCY and state president, in May of the following year. Tito's death in particular marked a point of no return for Yugoslavia. Under a new collective presidency lacking a united purpose to address the challenges of the 1980s, the country would descend into further economic and political crisis. Compromising the delicate balancing act that had previously guaranteed governmental protection of social and economic equality, along with a shared sovereignty, the crisis would put an end to Brotherhood and Unity. In the same year, the Working Community of Artists dissolved. Unable to define a collective program of action, it had, according to Ljiljana Kolešnik, brought "all conflicts, aporias, and problems of self-managing socialism to daylight."[71] Not able to salvage self-management from the distortions of associated labor, Podrum marked an "end to all utopian projections of art as a vehicle of social changes and all illusions about the future of the socialist project."[72]

REFLECTIONS ON MONEY

While Podrum was struggling to establish an enduring feeling of equality among its members, the Group of Six Authors embarked on a project that sought an alternative form of collective engagement. Renouncing the struggle for recognition of independent artists in Yugoslav society, in autumn 1978 the group began publishing the magazine *Maj '75* [May '75]. The publication was made by binding together individual A4 sheets of paper which contained concepts, projects, and discussions about art. Either handwritten or screen-printed in Vlasta Delimar and Željko Jerman's studio, each issue was produced in no more than 150 copies. According to Stilinović, *Maj '75* represented a "free form ... everyone had their own sheets, and there were dialogues among different artists."[73] The journal represented the sum of works by individual artists who saw their allocated page as their personal space, completely under their control, with the distribution of the journal enabling them to break free from isolation.

Bound by cellophane tape, and replicated either manually or by photocopy, *Maj '75* was defined by its free and fluid form. As the introductory statement, printed on the first page of each issue, announced, the journal was initiated to allow artists to show their work outside of institutions, to supplement Exhibition-Actions, and to protect the individual stance of each artist. Its participants advocated "conceptualism with a human face," against the analytical line promoted by Art & Language. Ironically, the editions were catalogued alphabetically (A–LJ);

according to Martek, the "idea of bringing out the alphabet [represented] an adequate number and thus reveal[ed] the conceptualist obsession with linguistics."[74] He further noted that the journal advocated, above all, the following qualities: "brotherhood and greater individualism, history and timelessness, the local and the universal"; "vision and hopelessness"; "justice and subjectivity ... the energy of an eternal refusal to the mainstream culture and its tragic lightheartedness":

> Rhetorically or not, I always ask the following question: what is the use of liars in art (or ultra-aestheticians, as we art critics tend to say)? What followed most of the New Art Practice people like a shadow was the aura of ethics. That was also the case with the issues of *Maj '75* throughout the years of its publication. The way of participating, both spiritually and technically, the methods of distribution and feedback—all that was special, based on individual responsibility and intended for both expected and unexpected readerships.[75]

Issue Đ distinctly captures *Maj '75*'s unique spirit of collaborative critique. Three pages, representing the "work space" of three individual artists, are placed in a critical dialogue. The first is a contribution from Belgrade artist Zoran Popović, consisting of a small caption, stamped in the middle of the page. In bold, red capital letters, it commands: "GIVE ME YOUR MONEY." On the following sheet, Stilinović stuck a single dinar coin on the sheet with tape. Below it, he scribbled a statement in red crayon, ordering the reader to "Pljuni to iz usta" [Spit that out of your mouth]. A few pages later, Darko Šimičić submitted an invoice from a workers' club for the purchase of television equipment, along with a handwritten note, stating: "Ovaj rad govori nešto o meni" [This work says something about me].

Read together, these pages offered a nuanced reflection on the meaning of money in society, and the unappeasable passion for accumulation that it solicited, both "locally" and "universally," as Martek put it. A stern, tyrannical order, Popović's intervention characterized money as an object of worth and a measure of power. Almost in counterbalance to this reading, Stilinović refused to acknowledge money's exchange value, and chose instead to deflate it by framing the country's national currency alongside familiar jargon. If anything, "spit that out of your mouth!" sounds like a stern order from a parent disciplining a child, and a semantic play that presents the coin featured on the page through its ultimately material and unsanitary form. The final page in the sequence revealed how money was being dispensed in Yugoslav society—spent on the "worker" in the form of mass entertainment, to promote behavior that was at once engaged and obedient. As with much of the New Art Practice, Šimičić's simple contribution proposed that money in Yugoslavia was being invested in a socialist consumerism that, while possessing some external features of prosperity, was in fact preventing society from establishing an active political culture.

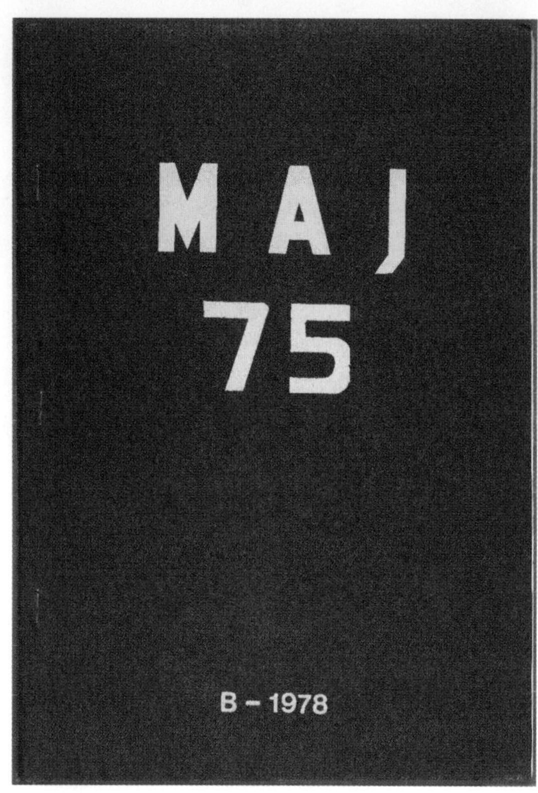

4.15. *Maj '75, Issue B*, cover, 1978. Image courtesy of Vlado Martek.

As inflation in Yugoslavia picked up in the 1970s and into the beginning of the 1980s, money appeared with greater frequency in the work of the Group of Six Authors. But what did money mean to the ordinary Yugoslav citizen at this time? During the 1970s, the Yugoslav government had fueled its growth with foreign borrowing. This decade ended with an extreme external economic shock, with Western Europe's economic recession following the second oil crisis in 1978 to 1979. The crisis contributed to Yugoslavia's balance-of-payment deficit, dried up the influx of "petrodollars" which were sustaining the economy, and stemmed the flow of "guest worker" remittances.[76] The interest rate for US dollars, in which the Yugoslav debt was calculated, rose into double digits. Burdened by years of economic mismanagement, the government had no choice but to turn to domestic resources to restore its ability to finance crucial imports.[77] By the end of 1979, the government had introduced austerity measures to cut domestic consumption and imported goods, and to increase exports.[78] Four years later, shortages of food and basic commodities would force the government to issue ration tickets. By 1985, the population living below the poverty line increased to 25 percent, unemployment reached 14 percent, and inflation escalated to 80 percent.[79]

Paradoxically, however, the late 1970s marked the greatest wave of public investment during the decade.[80] New roads, hotels, sports centers, and libraries were constructed, deluding the public into believing in a prosperity that in no way reflected the country's actual economic performance. Fear of being dependent on others in Yugoslavia seemed to result in republics increasing their dependence on international banks, a trend also supported by the government's encouragement of exporters, who were additionally looking for partners abroad, rather than within the country.[81] Various power centers refused to draw in their budgets, leaving the central government with no other choice than to constantly print new money. Austerity and declining living standards began to corrode the social fabric, rights, and securities that individuals and families had come to rely on. Not fully aware of the reasons behind these changes, people experiencing declining economic fortunes began to nurture political grievances.[82]

In the midst of growing political and economic paralysis, Mladen Stilinović began exploring the ways in which "politics contaminates language and means to avoid it."[83] In 1980, he began *O radu* [On Work], an installation composed of collages of photographs and captions cut out of newspapers and glued onto red-painted cardboard, with their crumpled edges framed in gold paint. The photographs captured political plenums, plenaries, and meetings dedicated to the

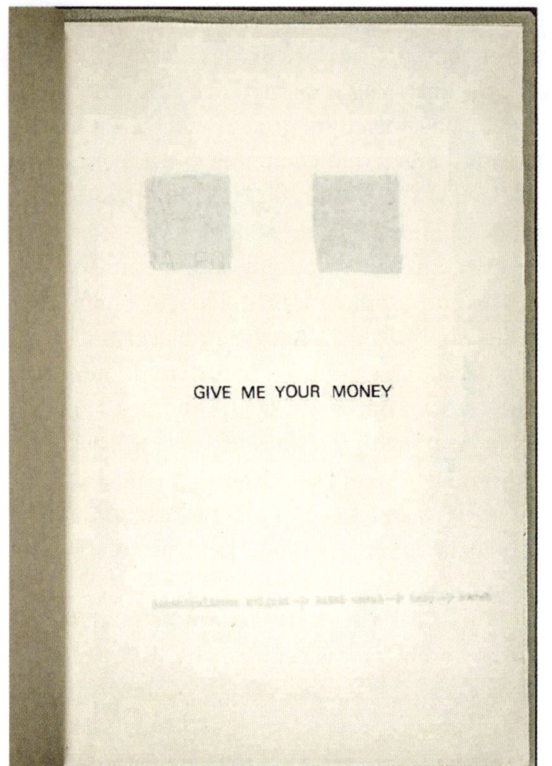

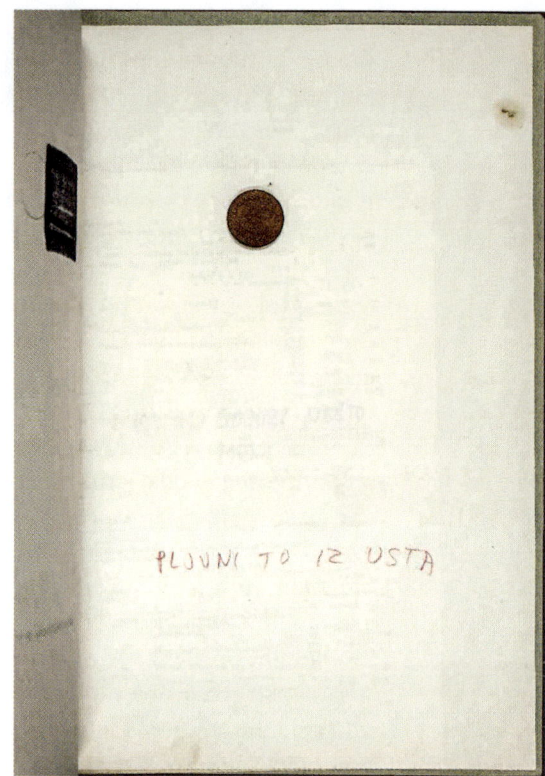

4.16. Zoran Popović, "GIVE ME YOUR MONEY," *Maj '75*, Issue Đ, 1980. Image courtesy of the artist.

4.17. Mladen Stilinović, "Pljuni to iz usta" [Spit That Out of Your Mouth], *Maj '75*, Issue Đ, 1980. Image courtesy of Branka Stipančić, Zagreb.

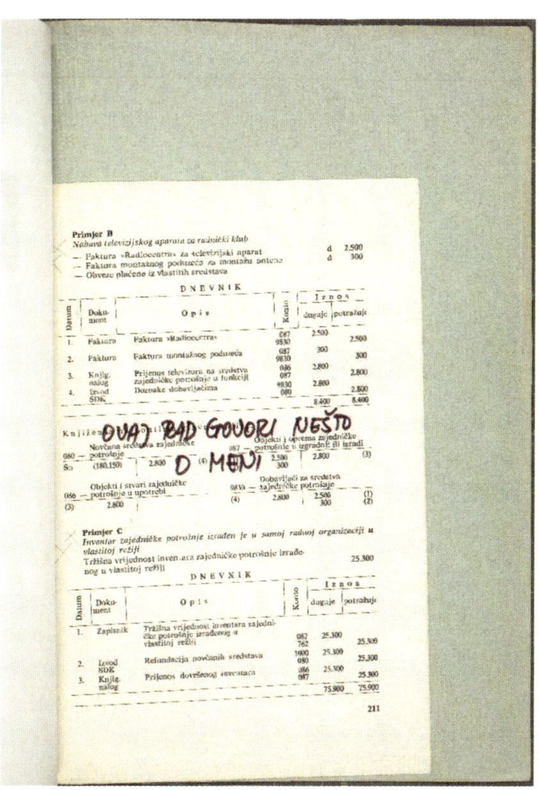

4.18. Darko Šimičić, "Ovaj rad govori nešto o meni" [This Work Says Something about Me], *Maj '75*, Issue Đ, 1980. Image courtesy of Darko Šimičić.

"working people," to whom the optimistic captions also referred. The following slogans appear:

> Better and more effective working methods from the base of the party to the central committee.
>
> Affirmation of work and self-government.
> Foreign currency creates work, and not the law.
> Proving oneself through work only.
> Order, work, and responsibility.
> Work more, complain less.
> Construction of associated labor as a precondition for social development.
> Labor surplus—to the workers.
> Shock work.

The installation captured the contradictory position of work in Yugoslavia's ideology of associated labor. Presented in the photographs were not, as might be expected, the working people, but rather their representatives, dressed strictly in suits. Proclaiming the rights of self-government and affirming that the working people had control, the slogans that accompanied the plenums were set in sharp contrast to the social reality of a resigned acceptance of growing inequality and class divisions. Those official catchphrases and official photographs from the plenums now gravitated to a background color that Stilinović had already deemed the property of the state (red), inside a shabby, hand-painted gold frame. Taken out of their original context, the noble declarations were displayed on recycled cardboard panels, suggesting the way prices are often scrawled on rough signs at food market stalls, a style that the artist called "cardboard design."[84] The installation was displayed with a single wooden chair placed in front of it, so that only one individual at a time could carefully reflect on the true implications of this political rhetoric.

On Work presented a sad picture of the Yugoslav project, which by the end of the 1970s had ultimately obscured the political dispossession of the working class. Though the League of Communists had not yet, at this time, denied the historical role that the struggles of the working class had played in the country's revolutionary gains, it had relegated this role firmly to the past. Class no longer played a foundational role in Yugoslav society. Instead, the working class had become mere "labor," while the idea of self-management had been hollowed out without anything to put in its place.[85] By the mid-1980s, this void would allow republican and provincial leaderships to establish themselves on a petty national basis, threatening the country's stability in the process. *On Work* anticipated these

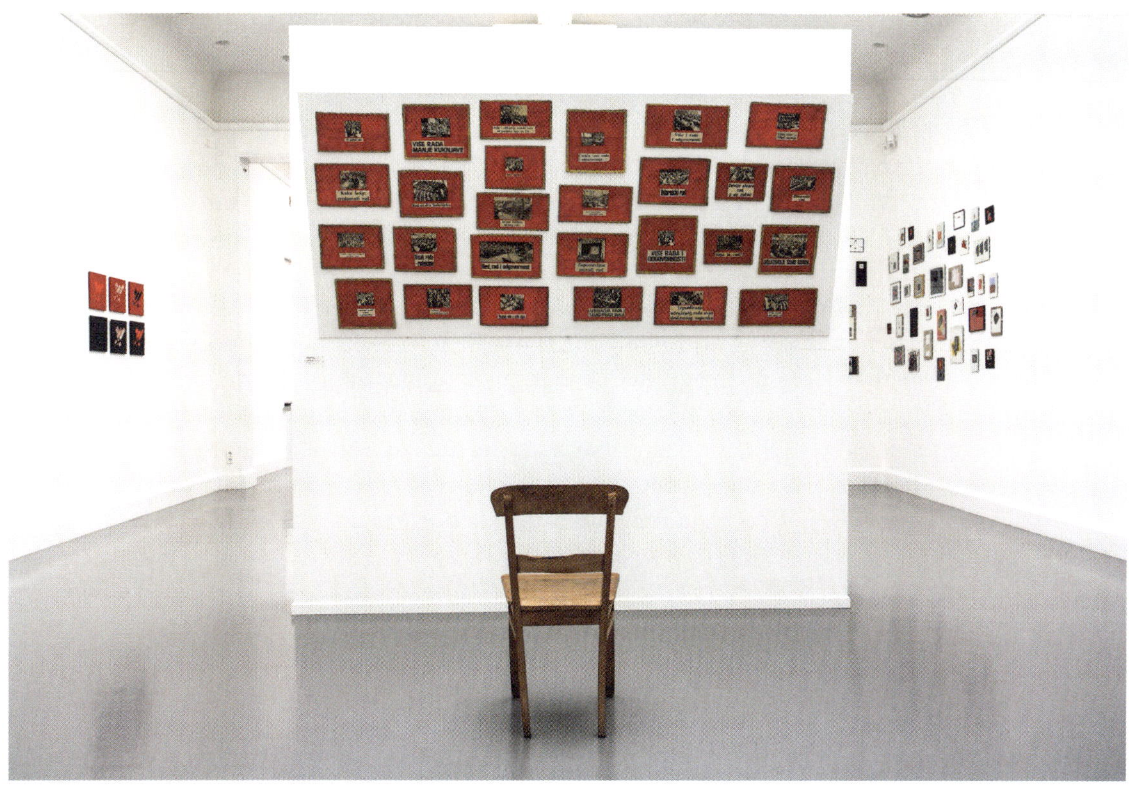

4.19. Mladen Stilinović, *O radu* [On Work], 1980–1984. Image courtesy of Branka Stipančić, Zagreb.

developments; it emptied the phrases of associated labor of all their meaning, if they even had any to begin with.

As it became increasingly apparent that associated labor marked another deeply conservative turn for Yugoslav socialism, many of the artists previously working through Podrum inevitably chose to pursue the "not having to go to court" option. While Podrum attempted to salvage the idea of self-management from associated labor, it had ultimately established the conditions for its own dissolution. Through its cessation, it simultaneously brought to light the measures that were driving Yugoslavia's economic downfall. In contrast, the Group of Six Authors found in *Maj '75* a channel through which to avoid all institutions. Closely entwined with the disintegrative change surrounding them, and defined by their autonomous organization, the work of the Group of Six Authors would play a decisive role in Ljubljana's alternative art scene. Zagreb's experience in establishing independent, small-scale initiatives would have a direct impact on Ljubljana's alternative art scene: anticipating its reactions to an economic and political crisis that would come to threaten Yugoslavia's very existence.

5 WHAT IS THE ALTERNATIVE?

LJUBLJANA'S ŠKUC GALLERY (1978–1984)

BASTARDIZING OHO

"Favorable" and "stable." These were the two words that the League of Communists of Slovenia used to describe the republic's national security situation when they met in Ljubljana in January 1979.[1] By then, economic stagnation, inflation, and labor unrest were all beginning to set in. Yet the only elements the leadership registered as threats to the republic's cohesion were a small group of intellectuals, propaganda centers abroad, and the institutions of foreign countries in Yugoslavia.[2] Certain philosophers and social scientists at the University of Ljubljana were branded as carrying "anarcho-liberal tendencies," an allegation that had been leveled against the city's youth movements a decade earlier.[3] In Ljubljana, students had managed to expand the arena for free speech following the tumultuous events of 1968; in the following year, they even established the first student-run radio station in Europe, Radio Študent. Nevertheless, the failed attempt to reform the party from within ushered in the so-called leaden years and a return to control. As in the rest of Yugoslavia, this entailed the purging of the Slovenian liberal leadership, along with the trial and conviction of all writers deemed "hostile."[4]

As the previous chapter showed, appearances were masking underlying tensions. While the 1974 constitution had enshrined the "freedom of thought and decision making," it simultaneously proscribed any type of "hostile propaganda," with a maximum prison sentence of ten years.[5] To further counteract any "malicious" or "untruthful" tendencies, as the constitution labeled them, the hard-line old guard of communists gave priority to cultural initiatives based on outdated symbols, particularly those celebrating the revolutionary achievements of the Second World War. On 8 February 1978, Slovene Culture Day, for example, a party plenary session for cultural workers of the National Liberation Front met for the first time since 1945.[6] The plenary session then met annually, restricting their conversations exclusively to the heroic achievements of the past, while steering away from any clear parallels to the crisis in national awareness that was beginning to surface throughout Yugoslavia in the 1980s. Meanwhile, several lengthy documentaries on the great role played by the National Liberation Struggle in the development of Slovenian culture were commissioned, along with other public projects such as the construction of a new Museum of the People's Revolution in the southern district of Ljubljana, which was, however, never realized.[7]

While a large proportion of funding for culture continued to be reserved for projects commemorating the achievements of the past, various initiatives outside of the mainstream began to surface at the beginning of the 1980s, largely due to the support of the republic's Socialist Youth Alliance (Zveza Socialistične Mladine Slovenije, or ZSMS). For three decades, the political direction of this organization was shaped by the demands of its parent party organization. Relatively autonomous in the 1960s, it was brought into line after the party's reform leadership was purged.[8] As the party became increasingly preoccupied with its own political and economic crisis toward the end of the 1970s, it once again began to loosen its grip. This growing flexibility in the Youth Alliance played a significant role in the founding of the city's Students' Cultural and Arts Center (ŠKUC) Gallery. In 1978, Taja Vidmar-Brejc, an art historian and curator of several OHO exhibitions, proposed that a small, empty space formerly operating as a bakery in the city's Stari Trg [Old Square] be converted into a gallery for the city's Students' Cultural Center.[9] Her request was approved by the city's Administration of Culture, but no funding was granted for the conversion of the premises. The venue's reconstruction began only when the Youth Alliance stepped in and guaranteed it would cover all the costs.[10] Although the cramped space offered modest possibilities in comparison to its counterparts in Belgrade and Zagreb, both of which had film forums, restaurants, and lounges, the allocation of a permanent premises did secure the promise of a continuous and flexible program of cultural activities.

The ŠKUC Gallery opened for the first time in September 1978 with an OHO retrospective, echoing both the SC Gallery's and the Youth Tribune's early presentation of the group's work in Zagreb and Novi Sad, respectively. But as Vidmar-Brejc herself noted, the decision to open the gallery with an exhibition of Ljubljana's pioneering art group was "slightly nostalgic, since OHO was already defunct at the time—although in fact, they initiated the whole thing."[11] What appeared to be a wistful gesture was, however, invigorated by the opening of the exhibition itself, which included a concert by Slovenia's first punk group, Pankrti [Bastards]. Pankrti had first performed at Ljubljana's Moste High School Gymnasium in 1977, shortly after punk had taken hold in Britain, America, and West Germany. Their music picked up on punk's themes of alienation and its association with anarchic narcissism, boredom, and nihilism, but directed these themes toward their immediate environment. According to the group's founding member, Gregor Tomc, Pankrti wanted to defy the League of Communists' attempts to "abolish the spontaneity of modern life." More specifically, they wanted to challenge "youth organization politicians," who "had their parents' tastes, had similar expectations in life, even the goal of their political activity was to realize the dreams of the older generation. For punks, taking any politics seriously was ridiculous, and taking 'youth' politics seriously would be piteous and a sign of bad taste."[12]

By the time Pankrti performed at ŠKUC, they had already experienced a series of altercations with the Youth Alliance. In the same year, they were prevented from playing at one high school in Ljubljana because the Youth Alliance branch sided with teachers' views that "Pankrti were obscene."[13] In the narrow confines of the ŠKUC Gallery, however, swarms of people turned up to see the band perform, climbing through the freshly painted windows into the back rooms. A photograph from the event testifies that various generations came to witness the event, adults and children alike, all perched within the low, hanging arches of the gallery space. According to Vidmar-Brejc, the event was cut short after "three mud-stained and disheveled people" were beaten up at the event by "some non-uniformed members of the UDV (internal State Security)."[14] Closed down prematurely, the event nevertheless inaugurated the ŠKUC Gallery's support of new youth subcultures, which would also come to define its art production in the following years. After the concert, the institution released the band's first double single against the ZSMS's orders; it contained the songs "Lepi in prazni" and "Lubljana je bulana" [Pretty and vacant / Ljubljana is sick], making a clear reference to the Sex Pistols' single "Pretty Vacant" released a year earlier. Over two thousand copies of Pankrti's record sold in a week.

Having emerged out of this unexpected fervor, the gallery nevertheless had its activities crippled in the following years by a chronic lack of funds. Only in 1980 was an agreement reached between various interest communities guaranteeing that they would share the cost of the gallery's expenses. Until then, the gallery's programs ran on meager resources, while the majority of its staff worked on a voluntary basis. It was even forced to close down on multiple occasions because of what one observer described as the "general public's understanding of the space as a host for excessive actions."[15] Starting in 1980, in the wake of Tito's death, the space would continue to court controversy due to its support for one anonymous art collective.

"THE BLACK-AND-WHITE SHOCK IN TRBOVLJE"

Twenty-seven days after Tito died at Ljubljana's Clinical Center on 4 May 1980, the group Laibach formed in the small mining town of Trbovlje. Four months later, in September 1980, they began to organize an exhibition in the town under the name *Alternativa slovenski umetnosti* [An Alternative to Slovene Art]. Supported by the ŠKUC Gallery, the exhibition was set to present films by the experimental filmmaker Davorin Marc, alongside pictures, engravings, and designs by ten young artists.[16] It was also to be accompanied by Laibach's first public concert, *Rdeči revirji*, or "Red Districts," the popular name for the Trbovlje region, where the Slovenian Communist Party was created in 1937. The event was publicized by a series of black-and-white posters pasted throughout the streets of Ljubljana and Trbovlje. The first, a white poster, featured a black cross that carried strong affinities to Kazimir Malevich's suprematist icon; it would later become a staple of Laibach's visual material. The second, a black print, contained a caricature of a man attempting to gouge a woman's eye out with a knife. Its subject was based on the Roman legend of the rape of Lucretia by Sextus Tarquinius, a popular theme in Renaissance painting. Both posters featured the German name for Ljubljana, "Laibach," on them. In an article published in the November 1980 issue of the student journal *Mladina* [Youth], one observer described the impression the posters left on the citizens of the small town:

> On Friday, 26 September, the black valley of Trbovlje was particularly dark, ... covered in black posters of bloodied black content. Pasted with the stickiest glue, they flanked the road and challenged the passers-by.... The public moral was threatened, the public service reacted, ... This time the strict whips that watch over public peace and order in the town that had found itself at risk declared both a week-long anti-smoking campaign, a prudent use of public resources campaign, and children's week. They came up with various posters and pasted them up over the blasphemous black patches that could not be removed and topped it all off with the splendid hair of the Slovenian pop singer Neca Falk, who that night desperately tried to entertain an audience at the Delavski dom venue in Trbovlje.[17]

Met with alarm, suspicion, and indignation, the posters resulted in the banning of the project before it even opened. Since then, the "black-and-white shock in Trbovlje" has become the stuff of legends, but has rarely been analyzed alongside the unstable political climate in which it mysteriously appeared. Carrying the name that many Slovenes equated with the country's occupation, both under the reign of the Austro-Hungarian Empire and the Nazi occupation during the Second World War, what made these posters menacing was their emergence at this point in 1980. Alluding to the republic's traumatic history, and inexplicably appearing in a small mining town (but nevertheless a significant one, where the first miners' strike in Yugoslavia took place in 1958) just months after Tito's death, the posters and the motives of their makers could not have appeared more suspect.

On the surface, Tito's death changed very little for Yugoslavia. The transition of power to the collective presidency seemed untroubled, and the federal leadership agreed that they would continue "along Tito's path." But as the previous chapter argued, the structural and symbolic pillars of Yugoslavia—nonalignment, self-management, and the revolutionary legacy of Brotherhood and Unity—had already begun to show the first signs of irreversible decay. After Tito's death, the largely confederate structure would be rendered almost unworkable; the system of decision making by consensus at the federal level and the locally controlled implementation of reforms blocked any effective way of addressing the economic crisis. To prevent the rise of autonomous criticism, however, the collective presidency once again began to emphasize cadre control, along with further censorship and repression.

following pages

5.1. Laibach Kunst, *Black Cross*, 1980. Exhibition poster for *Alternativa slovenski umetnosti* [An Alternative to Slovene Art], Trbovlje, 1980. Image courtesy of Moderna Galerija, Ljubljana.

5.2. Laibach Kunst, *The Deadly Dance*, 1980. Exhibition poster for *Alternativa slovenski umetnosti* [An Alternative to Slovene Art], Trbovlje, 1980. Image courtesy of Moderna Galerija, Ljubljana.

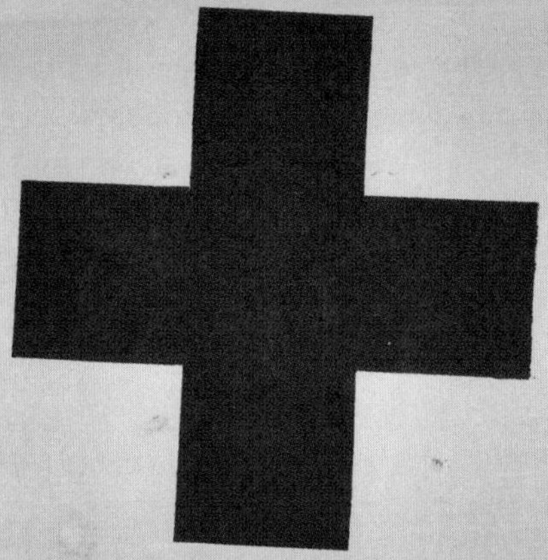
laibach

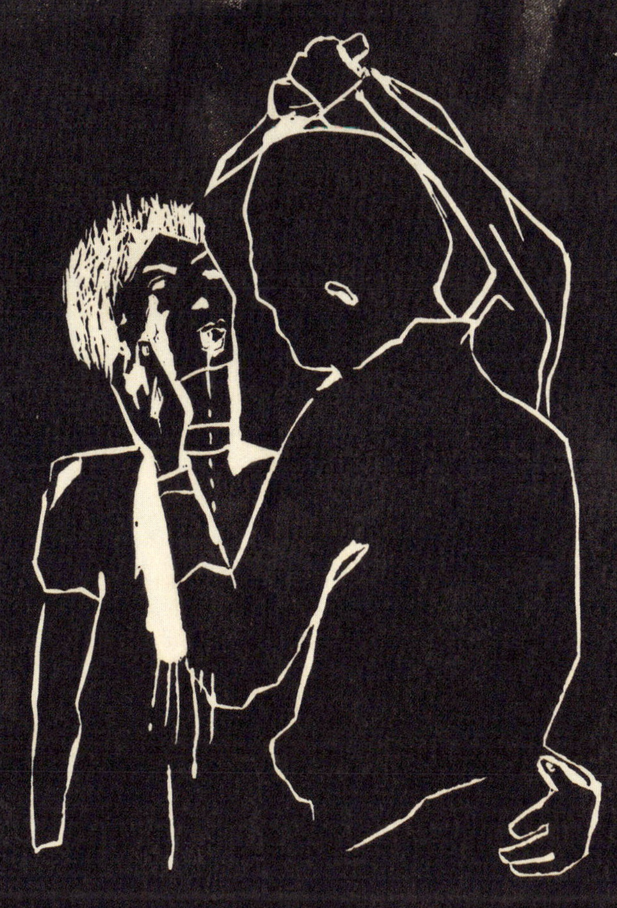
laibach

In the case of Slovenia itself, the return to repression included the forcible ousting of the republic's prime minister in June 1980.[18] A well-known figure in Yugoslav politics with reputed ties to the republic's managerial elites, he was replaced by a long-standing Slovenian police functionary. The official explanation behind this decision was to ensure the effective execution of "policy."[19] It was widely speculated, however, that the prime minister's ousting was directly tied to his opposition to federal import restrictions, spurred by managers of Slovenia's manufacturing industries concerned about the impact they would have on the republic's economy.[20] Either way, the appointment of a secret police functionary to the head of government would most certainly have trickled down to the lower levels of society, carrying an impact similar to the "top-level" purges effected in response to the Croatian Mass Movement. This tightening of official controls over independent activity may also partially explain why Trbovlje's Youth Alliance was swift to distance itself from the Laibach poster affair, and to align itself with the cause of "self-management" and the "working people's achievements."[21] In response to the *Mladina* report and the poster scandal itself, the Youth Alliance submitted the following letter to the journal in December 1980:

> Everything a young worker, peasant, miner, student is striving toward is present in all working people, in self-managers, in all of us who are building on the basis of our achievements. All these people who, in this rapid pace of life still find moments for relaxation, who search through and draw on our national tradition, were humiliated by these posters: their creativity, their past were all humiliated. They were surprised by the propaganda material that was supposedly inviting them to an art exhibition and a punk concert, and they publicly expressed their unwillingness to tolerate such things in their midst. In relation to this, we, the young people, feel that not all, especially not what our elders went through during the war, can be pasted on the walls behind the cover of the word "punk."[22]

At a time when the press continued to overflow with words such as "freedom," "decision making," and the "nonconflictual solving of social problems," the Youth Alliance remained committed to protecting the principles of the older guard of the LCY. The poster affair, in contrast, had cut through the ideological apathy that was still informing state discourse and general opinion at the time. Breaching the party's restrictions on accounts of Yugoslavia's prewar history, Laibach were, in the words of the Youth Alliance letter, "searching through and drawing on our national tradition." In many respects, this gesture anticipated the role that the past would increasingly come to play in the country's decline. It foreshadowed how a deepening crisis would clear space for new legitimizing myths of victimization throughout the entire federation. Two years later, Laibach labeled the scandal a "success since it was meant to be banned. The workers accepted in accordance with the police, confirming a high level of positive awareness."[23] Later, they renamed the poster affair the "First Banned Laibach Exhibition and Concert at the Trbovlje Workers' Center."[24] Although it never took place, "An Alternative to Slovene Art" would become a blueprint for the group's later exhibitions, and for its visual production at the ŠKUC Gallery.

TRIUMPHS OVER CONCEPTUALISM

By revealing a direct coalescence between art and politics, the "black-and-white shock in Trobvlje" was the first in a thread of actions to contest the political servitude of culture in Slovenia after Tito's death. A few months after the affair, a new generation of young cultural workers took over the ŠKUC Gallery's programs. Under the direction of Dušan Mandić, a student from the Academy of Fine Arts in Ljubljana, and codirectors Barbara Borčić and Marina Gržinić, the gallery began to exhibit works from Belgrade and Zagreb at the end of 1980, so as to offer "different approaches which aren't regular in our space."[25] In February 1981, the gallery invited Raša Todosijević to give a lecture alongside a photo-documentary exhibition of his actions. Although Todosijević had already been active in Belgrade for over a decade, this was the first time his work had been publicly shown in Slovenia. In its unshakeable interrogation of the agonizing question "Was ist Kunst?," Todosijević's work carried a double meaning in the local context. According to Mandić, it both "enabled a distance from Slovenian production, and triggered the question about the closed nature of the cultural milieu, which only today introduces a new practice not present in our space, in spite of the artist's many years of activity."[26] A month later, the ŠKUC Gallery installed Goran Đorđević's *Harbingers of the Apocalypse*. In retrospect, Gržinić recalled that the exhibition's visitors thought the organizers "were mad ... fill[ing] the gallery with a grammar school drawing in fifty variations, and to invite serious people to come and view the exhibition. How could they possibly think us sane, what else could they say but: 'Thank God we don't have to come to ŠKUC any more.'"[27]

A project as embedded in Belgrade's New Art Practice scene as it was in international developments in appropriation art, Đorđević's *Harbingers* resonated with the young artists gathering at the ŠKUC Gallery. Nine months after the exhibition, Laibach member Dejan Knez sent his friends a New Year's card of a Xeroxed collage based on René Magritte's famous 1933 painting *La Condition humaine* [The Human Condition]. He dedicated the work to to Đorđević, whom he regularly visited while serving in the military in Belgrade in 1981.[28] From the original Magritte painting, Knez cut out the landscape background behind the easel, and replaced it with a photograph of Hitler marching through rows of adoring troops carrying banners at the Bückeberg Harvest Festival, one of the many propaganda parades instrumental to the Nazi regime's pageant of power. In addition, he included the caption "artist condition" and "1934" at the bottom of the collage. In doing so, Knez drew attention to the political environment in which Magritte painted his work. He exposed what he understood to be the "artist condition," or the intersections between art and politics—between the surrealist symbolism of Magritte's painting, the artist's personal life, and Hitler's ascent to power at the time, all of which framed the painting. Revealing a new understanding of the relationship between art and politics, the work also introduced a completely novel approach to media. Until then, few works produced in Slovenia had shown such disregard for the boundaries between artistic genres, or for the distinctions between "high" and "low" culture, for that matter.

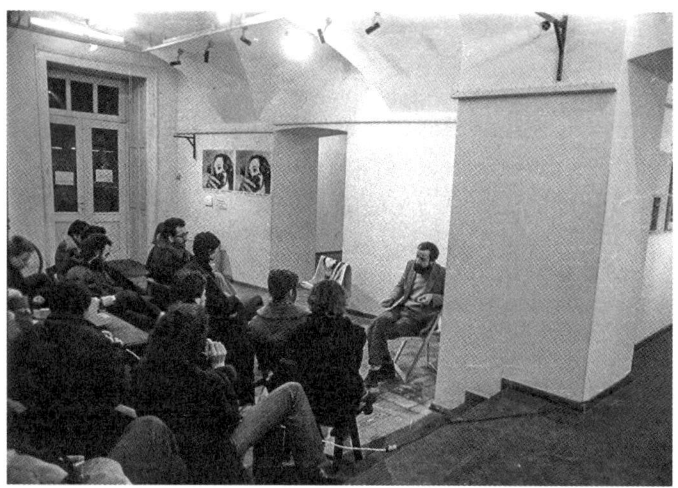

5.3. Raša Todosijević giving a lecture at the ŠKUC Gallery, Ljubljana, 1981. Photograph by Barbara Borčić. Image courtesy of Barbara Borčić.

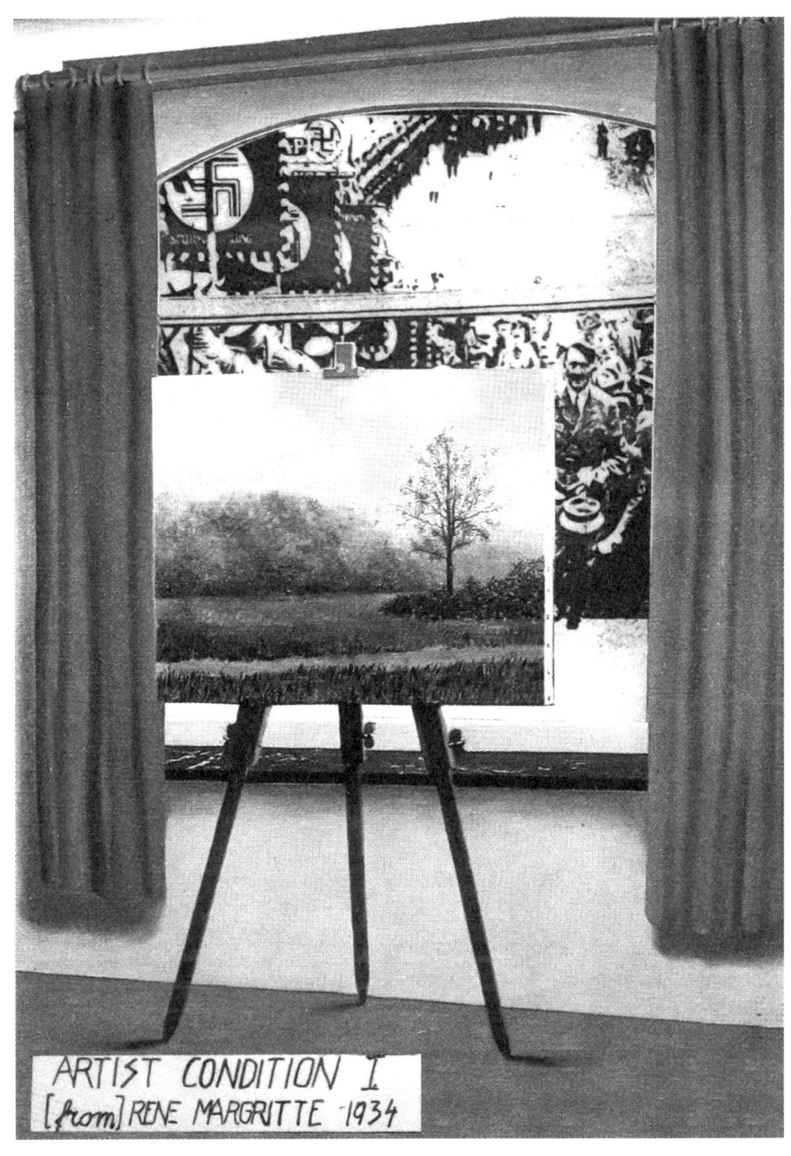

5.4. Dejan Knez, *Artist Condition I*, 1981, Xerox, A4 format. Image courtesy of Laibach.

Deeply indebted to Đorđević's practice of copying, Knez's decision to highlight the "artist condition" in Magritte's painting coincided with a significant moment in Yugoslavia's history, when the country once again stood at a crossroads between reform and repression. In April 1981, the conservative forces favoring the latter had shown their full force in Priština, the capital of Kosovo, where a series of student-led demonstrations demanding the status of republic for the province escalated into riots and were violently suppressed by police force. In an area of Yugoslavia burdened with the highest levels of unemployment and the lowest standards of living, the mass demonstrations revealed the Kosovo Albanians' feelings of discrimination because their province had not been promoted to the status of a republic.[29] The excessive measures taken to quell the protests, including mass purges and the temporary introduction of martial law, only served to confirm the Albanians' feeling of isolation from Yugoslavia's "south Slavic" nations. After the initial use of firearms against protesters and subsequent civilian deaths, over 1,600 Albanians were tried and imprisoned; a quarter of them were in their teens.[30] It was the first time since the Second World War that a member of the federation had been treated in such a violent way.

With Kosovo lying between delayed national emancipation and endemic poverty, the demand for an Albanian republic there shook the very foundations of the post-Tito regime. For many scholars, it was an event that would mark the beginning of Yugoslavia's end.[31] In the same year that the country had clearly entered a period of disintegrative change, the ŠKUC Gallery continued to revisit the experiences of the New Art Practice. Three months before Knez made his monumental artistic statement, Zagreb's Podrum, the Working Community of Artists, came to the gallery to show their work and discuss the collective dynamics of their organization. For Mandić, the group's visit to Ljubljana was important because it introduced the concept of a working community of artists that had not existed in the city until then. As he noted in an interview from 1982, Podrum were pioneering in the sense that they identified a range of "issues independently, organized themselves, and incorporated that form of inquiry into their actions and practice."[32] Gržinić similarly acknowledged the importance of Podrum's visit to ŠKUC, as introducing not a new institution per se, but a concept: "a way of thinking unknown in our surroundings."[33]

For Iveković, Podrum's ability to address the relationship between artists and their "immediate sociopolitical context" lay almost exclusively in the journal, the tribunes, and lectures, rather than the space itself. This emphasis on an expanded engagement became central to the ŠKUC Gallery's activities after Podrum's visit, and even provided the inspiration for the first issue of *Galerija ŠKUC izdaja* [ŠKUC Gallery Editions]. Edited by Borčić and Gržinić, the first issue included a typewritten transcript from the conversation with Podrum, along with a comic strip depicting a man with a gun and an axe destroying a house. It also featured photographs by Helmut Newton and an essay defining punk and sadomasochism as rebellions against totalitarian and consumer societies. Fusing text, drawing, and photography through Xerox, a medium that was both affordable and easily reproducible, the first *Galerija ŠKUC izdaja* marked the beginning of the gallery's idiosyncratic approach to the visual arts.

Shortly after Podrum's important visit to ŠKUC, the gallery began to collaborate with an entirely new kind of art collective: Laibach Kunst.[34] On 28 April 1982, between 6 and 10 pm, it hosted the exhibition *Ausstellung! Laibach Kunst*, which included an installation consisting of a grid of Xeroxed posters copied from a woodcut and pasted along an entire wall of the gallery space. All of the monochromatic prints depicted Laibach's *Metalec* [metal worker]: the shadow of an anonymous socialist worker, clutching a hammer and marching triumphantly from a heavily industrialized landscape. Based on a poster from the First Congress of the Metalworkers Association in 1945, it remains one of Laibach's most mysterious images. Simultaneously menacing and heroic, the colossal worker surfacing from a field of smokestacks conjures up associations with Soviet shock work, while clearly emulating a discarded artifact of socialist realism. Superimposed amid Laibach Kunst's wall of anonymous, archetypal laborers was a single painting depicting a stag, the source of which was in fact Edwin Landseer's *The Monarch of the Glen* (1851), an iconic Scottish image.[35] Because the stag was associated with Central European and Alpine contexts, the kitsch symbol also carried a salient significance in Slovenia. Even under Yugoslav socialism, Alpine symbolism remained present in Slovenian culture, which despite the official emphasis on "Brotherhood and Unity" still bore traces of its former Austrian rulers.

following pages

5.5. and 5.6. First issue of *Galerija ŠKUC izdaja* [ŠKUC Gallery Editions], edited by Barbara Borčić and Marina Gržinić, October 1981. Images courtesy of Barbara Borčić.

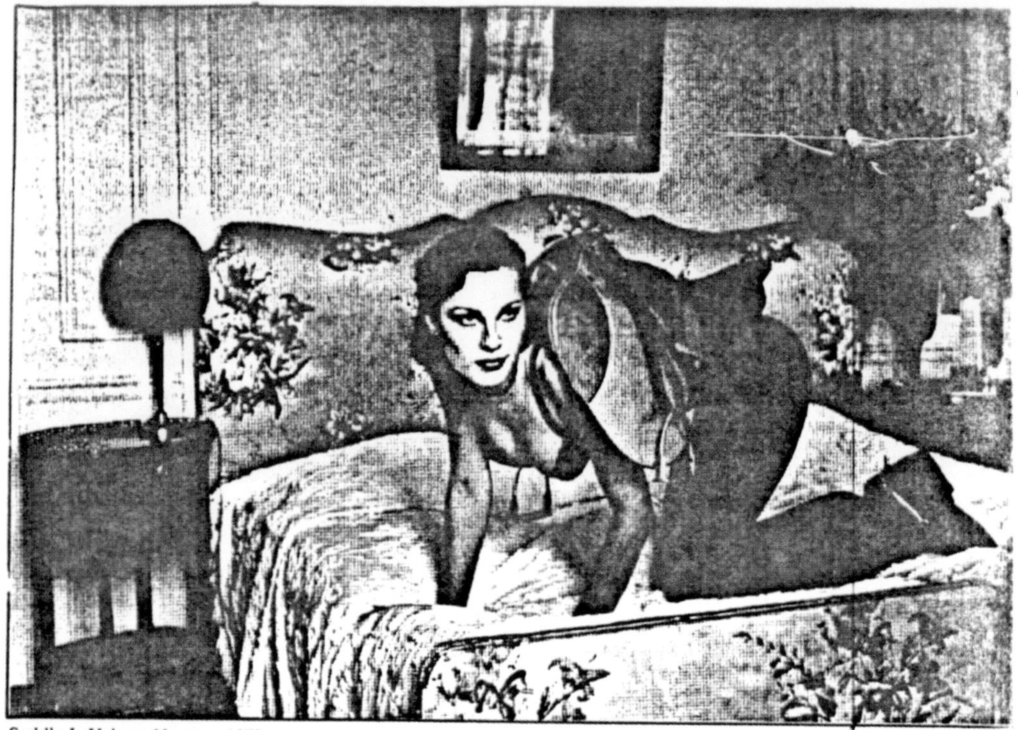

Saddle I: Helmut Newton, 1978

izpadel gnusen. To je drugi način zunanjosti - neprizanesljivo primerna koža, s katero pank predstavlja njega ali njo kot zunanje in odtujene samim sebi. To poenostavlja stik z zunanjim svetom (z drugimi), tako kot mrtva koža deluje na čutnem nivoju. Fetišist usnja se po eni strani zavaruje pred svetom, po drugi strani pa privede ta svet v bolj neposreden čutni stik z telesom. Na poti od fetišizma usnja do gume in v zadnjem času do plastike, posameznik vstopa v vrsto kulturnih izločitev/abstrakcij naše lastne kože.

Pank je povezan z drugimi kulturnimi abstrakcijami. Kot zmes stereotipov filmov groze, sci-fi tujcev (znanstvena fantastika) in obrabljenih asociacij iz stare pornografije, pank image vključuje tudi S/M kot združenje potlačenih (po pisanju časopisa Atomage), ki se privatno "oblačijo" z željo da jih pustijo na miru in v anonimnosti, tako da se lahko vdajajo neškodljivim željam. xxxxxxxxxx

Oblečen v usnje sadist lahko realizira domišljijo drugačnosti - telo kot dobro podmazana mašina realizira svojo neizprosno /kruto oblast/premoč nad žrtvijo (mazom). "Vrh" postane preko usnja izločitev/abstrakcija gospodarja. Toda, ali je to gospostvo Nietzche-anskega super heroja, ali pa je to domišljijska zveza z super moško ali super žensko kamejo? Kar je skupno celemu številu junakov in junakinj knjig za zabavo, so njihovi tesno oprijeti kostimi. To jih identificira z dejanjem (uniforma vrši podobno "obredno" vlogo). Toda usnjeno oblačilo je uniforma izločenca/outsider-a, ki prevzame nadčloveško kožo v svetosti nasilja. Misel, da usnjena oblačila fetišista in sadista izhajajo iz nekih arhetipnih poti kot napol standardni dizajni, videti kožo kot retorično nulto točko modnega dogovora, je zapeljiva.

Toda avtentična S/M moda je povezana tako s stereotipi iz filmov in knjig za zabavo kot s pank modo, samo da je njena stopnja polastitve bolj neškodljiva. Menjava stila ima opraviti s tem, da ne zaostaja za časom, in ne s tem, da je izven časa/izgubi stik z časom. Domišljija transformacije je za fetišista in sadista realizacija kulturne izločitve, prav tako kakor umik v prikrivanje in zadrego usnjenega abstrahiranega

S tem ko prevzamemo "drugo kožo" kulture vstopimo v namišljeno projekcijo nad njenimi mejami. Toda to je tudi način s katerim se mi kot posamezniki skrivamo kot naravni primerki/vzorci in se pojavimo da se soočimo s svetom kot primerki. Celotna dinamika mode je osredotočena na nasprotojoče impulze razodkrivanja in prikrivanja. Moda je oboje, preseganje tipičnega in mik v tipično. Znotraj pogleda kulture je naša povezanost z modo razdeljena med senzacionalno manifestacijo osebnosti in umik v senzacionalno anonimnost tipa. Prevladujoče smeri zadnjega desetletja so nadomestile obljube trenutne svobode z zagotovitvijo večne odvisnosti in aluzij na raj in utopijo, s peklom in distopijo. Toda bistvena dinamika mode je ostala nespremenjena. Referenčne točke za simboliko mode so se samo razširile. Od preproste navezanosti na stare kreposti, lepote, miline in narave je svet grdote, tesnobe in izumetničenosti, proizvedel novo bogatstvo simboličnemu beaednjaku mode. Negacija je vključena.

S/M par gospodar/suženj in aktiven/pasiven je skoraj simbol/znak kulturnega in izumetničenega. Predstavlja vloge in odnose ki jih vsiljujeta kultura in družba. Michel Foucault je videl S/M kot nekaj kar se je pojavilo v določenem trenutku zgodovine (pozno 18 stoletje) kot odraz nove kulturne zavesti/zavedanja seksualnosti, kot nekaj neodvisnega od ljubezni religije in nujnosti fizičnega razmnoževanja. Predstavljanje seksualnosti kot moči obenem povzroči da se razmerje družbenih sil pojavi kot zakoreninjeno v naravi seksualnosti in seksualnost kot zakoreninjena v razmerju družbenih sil (power relations of society). S/M predstavlja manipulacijo/zvijačnost gole seksualnosti. Redukcija seksa na enostavno družbeno opozicijo moči in nemoči, predstavlja nesvobodo. To je omejitev tistega kar mi vidimo ko najbližje sebi, izlaganosti kulture, in razmerja družbenih sil. Predstavlja grožnjo najbolj prisotnem dualizmu izkušnje ki jo doživljaš - privatno/družbeno (javno). Točno zaradi tega je S/M od nekdaj zauzemal prostor na meji tabuja znotraj socijalne zavesti. Zapletenost predstavlja omejitev seksualnosti na lažne odnose mestnega življenja in kulture. Eksplicitno govori "NI REŠITVE". Morda sprejetje S/M na nivoju mode predstavlja osnovno razveljavitev tega pomena, ali pa morda realizacijo tega kar sta domnevala/napovedala Adorno in Horkheimer kot neizbežna nesvoboda totalitarne potrošniške kulture v kateri je "povpraševanje" zamenjeno z preprosto poslušnostjo".

Rosetta Brooks

Prevod iz revije ZG/št.2/1980

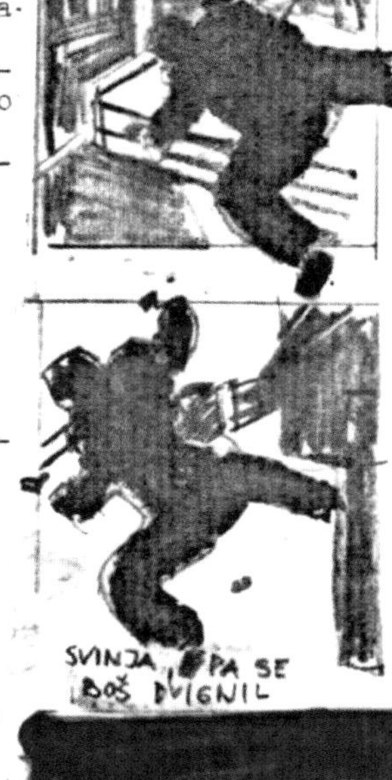

RZU Zagreb v ŠKUC-u

Galerija ŠKUC-a je seznanila "Slovensko občinstvo" s zagrebškim alternativnim likovnim dogajanjem. V treh tednih od 28.9. do 18.10. so se v ŠKUC-ovih prostorih predstavili umetniki "Radne zajednice umjetnika" iz Zagreba. ŠKUC-ev projekt predstavitve je zajemal kar 17 avtorjev tako da je vsak ponedeljek bila otvoritev nove razstave. V ŠKUC-u so se za razstavo ali/in akcijo predstavili naslednji avtorji:

28.9. D. Čada, Ž.Kipke, V.Martek, M.Stilinović, B. Ivandić, R.Radovanović in S. Stilinović;

5.10 M. Molnar, G.Petercol, D. Rakoci, D.Šimičić in F.Vučemilović;

12.10 V.Delimar, T.Gotovac, Z. Jerman,Z.Kutnjak in A.Maračić;

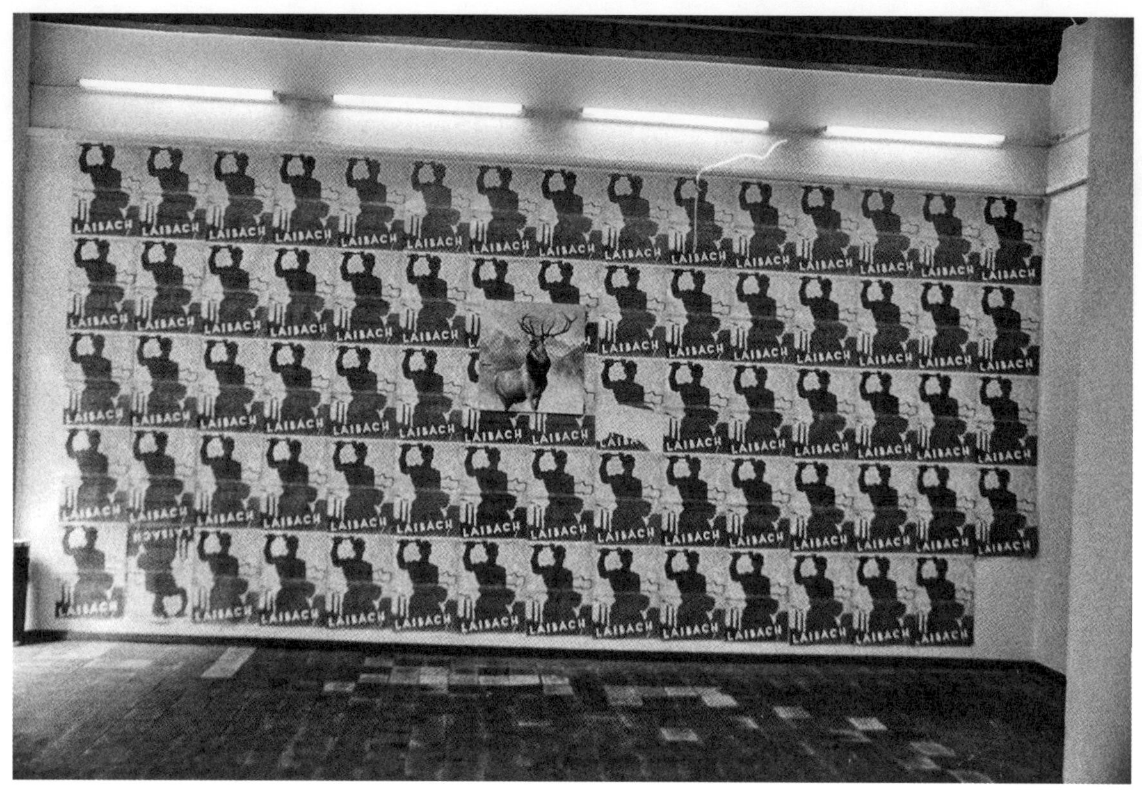

5.7. Installation view of *Austellung! Laibach Kunst*, ŠKUC Gallery, Ljubljana, April 1982. Photograph by Barbara Borčić. Image courtesy of Barbara Borčić.

Laibach's laborer first appeared at a time when there still remained hope that the Yugoslav system could be reformed through an increasingly combative working class. This effort would have required a stable relationship between the League of Communists and the working class, along with an uncompromising, all-Yugoslav commitment to national equality. But as commentator Branka Magaš noted some years later, the broader continental shifts in the 1980s were unfavorable to such an alliance.[36] In Laibach's installation at ŠKUC, the field of anonymous workers is dramatically supplanted by the lone portrait of the stag. As the workers regress into the background, the emblem of national identity takes center stage. Not only is the image in the center of the composition, it is unique amid an otherwise heavy, wallpapered field of repetitive, monochromatic forms. Through the jarring juxtaposition of the colossal worker and the kitschy national symbol, the Laibach Kunst installation at ŠKUC may have been commenting on the connection between the political dispossession of the working class and the growing investment in national identities throughout many of the republics at the time. Surfacing out of a mass of laborers, the Alpine symbol could even have alluded to the emphasis that Slovenia's intellectuals would later place on the republic's deeper connections to neighboring Austria, amid their growing sense that Yugoslavia's poorer regions were exploiting Slovenia. A few years later, these motifs would come to represent Slovenia's belonging to the "Central European space," and would offer solace against a rising influx of workers from the south and their threat to the republic's cultural identity.

This is just one of many possible interpretations of a highly complex work, which initiated the group's distinctive artistic approach to looping past traumas into present crises. Fusing traditional art, kitsch, and fine art with the contemporary art installation, *Ausstellung! Laibach Kunst* paved the way for the group's signature "monumental retro-avant-garde" method, defined by its use of quotation, appropriation, and recontextualization. According to an interview the group gave to the rock magazine *Džuboks* in the same year as the ŠKUC exhibition, this approach marked a "triumph over conceptualism":

> We are acquainted with the aberrations and contradictions of the disillusioned artistic avant-garde. We have no intention of reproducing or interpreting it. The ideology of "surpassing" has been surpassed and it must never happen again that the spectator-consumer confuses the packaging with art. All of our work, present and future, must leave behind all past works, regardless of their greatness. The dead past should be no match for us, who are alive![37]

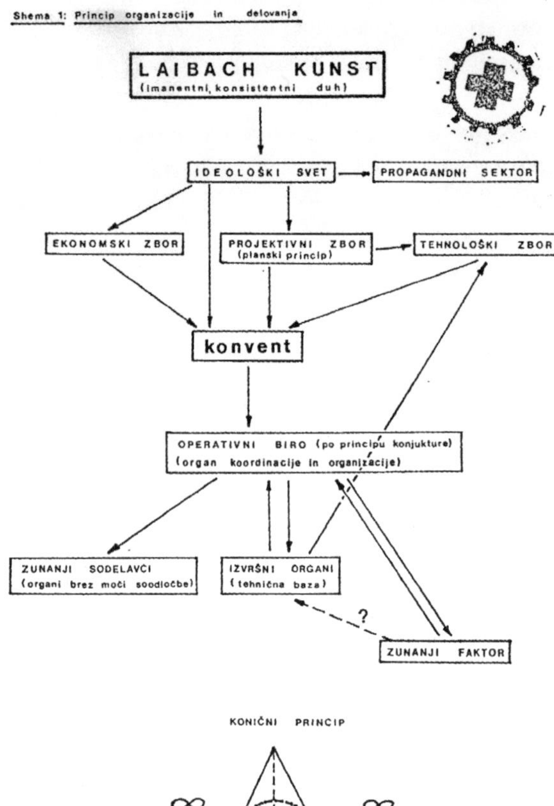

5.8. Laibach Kunst, *Principle of Organization and Work: Organigram*, 1982. Image courtesy of Laibach.

"Scheme 1: The principle of organization and operation / Laibach Kunst (immanent, consistent spirit) / Ideological Council / Propaganda Sector / Economic Assembly / Projective Assembly (planning principle) / Technological Assembly / Convent / Operative Bureau (according to the principle of conjuncture) (the authority of coordination and organization) / External collaborators (without decision-making power) / Executive Sector (technical base) / External factor / Conical principle"

"The ideology of 'surpassing' [had] been surpassed." While much of the work affiliated with the New Art Practice aimed to address the broader conditions that determined its production and reception, most of it had withdrawn into a hermetic world of self-reference. And whereas Podrum marked an attempt to participate in the system of associated labor—an effort which arguably led to its dissolution two years after it was established—Laibach Kunst staged a fanatical obsession with it. In 1982, the group released its first organizational diagram, known as the "organigram." It held as much resemblance to Alfred Barr's 1936 "Chart Illustrating the Development of Modern Art"—which famously attempted to map the genealogy of cubism and abstraction—as it did to diagrams representing Yugoslavia's complex system of political representation.[38] In the words of Alexei Monroe, it was a model that simply "recapitulated and attempted to transcend the institutional anarchy of the period and the fantastically complex, deliberately opaque web of state and parastate organizations within the Yugoslav system."[39]

With the "organigram," Laibach outlined a completely autonomous and anonymous organization whose individual bodies worked to maintain "the immanent, consistent spirit." More than their disturbing iconography, this commitment to anonymity and obsession with collective organization was what made Laibach threatening to the Yugoslav regime. As Branislav Jakovljević has argued, until then, no art movement had considered contesting the state's monopoly on secrecy.[40] A year after their first exhibition at the ŠKUC Gallery, in June 1983, the group consented to give an interview for Slovenian national television, on the current affairs program *TV tednik* [TV Weekly]. For their first major television appearance, they requested that the interview be held in the ŠKUC Gallery, with their own exhibition in the background, and that the journalist's questions be made available to them in advance. The group appeared on television wearing military fatigues and white armbands bearing their black cross, in front of graphic images of large political rallies. Their listless and stern expressions were illuminated by bright lights in a dark room, evoking an interrogation scene. Asked a series of questions by Jure Pengov, including "Can you tell us something about yourselves?" and "Who are you, and what do you do for a living?," Laibach responded with scripted statements such as: "We are the children of the spirit and the brothers of strength, whose promises are unfulfilled. We are the black phantoms of this world, we sing the mad image of woe. We are the first TV generation," and "Happiness lies in total negation of one's identity, deliberate rejection of personal tastes and beliefs. In depersonalization, sacrifice. In identification with a higher system, the mass, collective ideology."[41]

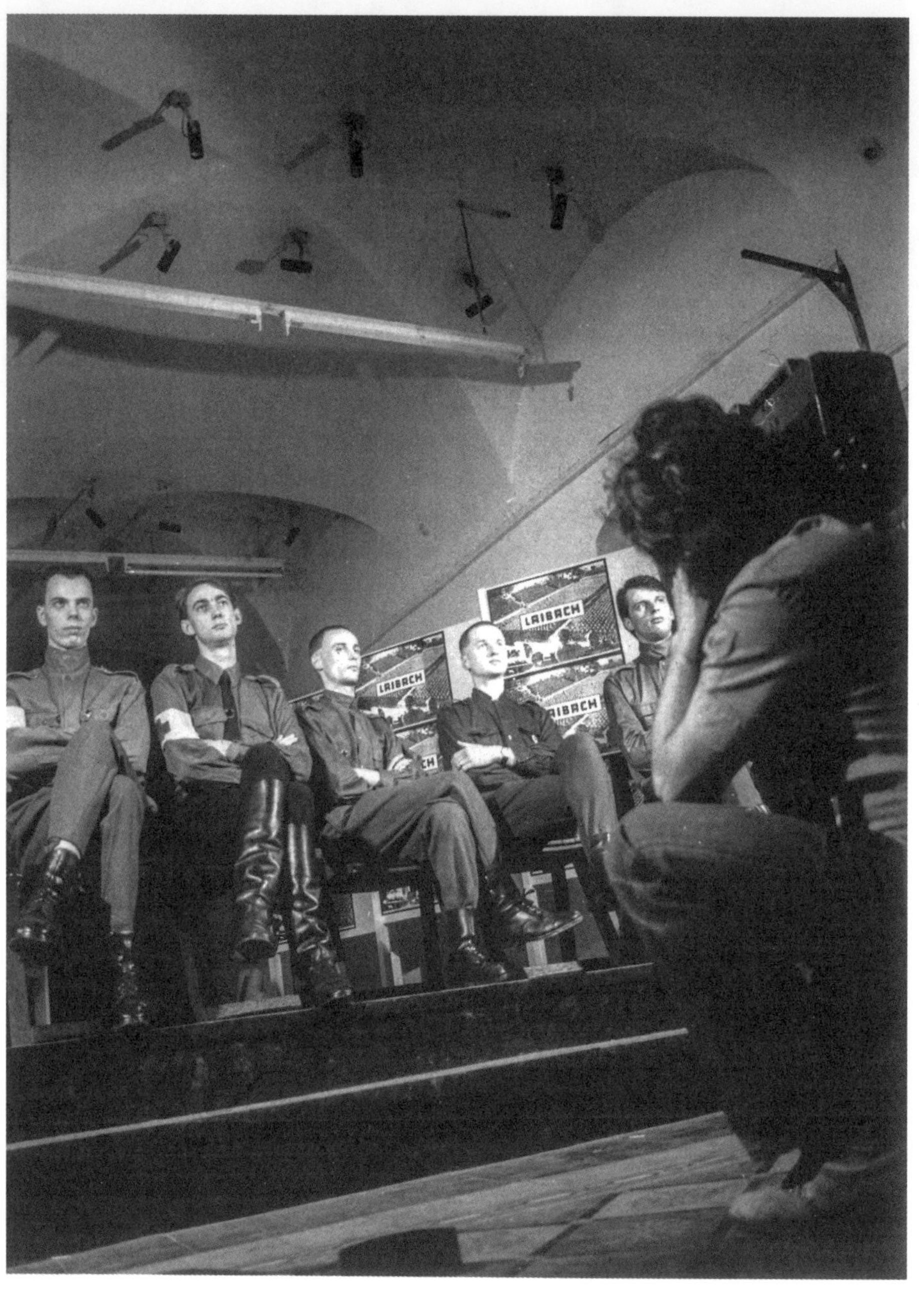

5.9. Laibach's *TV tednik* interview, Ljubljana, June 1983. Image courtesy of Laibach.

Without a doubt, the *TV tednik* interview was intended to spark public outrage. To an extent, it worked: at the end of the interview, the band's members were declared "enemies of the people," and an appeal was raised "to respectable citizens everywhere to intervene and destroy this dangerous group."[42] In 1983, the band's use of the name Laibach was outlawed. In a game of mutual manipulation, the group retrospectively appropriated the television interview as one of their "most successful projects."[43] Ironically, the group's banning would place them at the center of the republic's liberalizing initiatives, as voices from within the Youth Alliance arose strongly in their defense. Alongside other attempts to marginalize Ljubljana's punk scene, their banning would also lay the foundations for Laibach's ambivalent mainstreaming in the mid-1980s.

"PUNK IS A SYMPTOM"

Soon after it first arrived in Slovenia in 1977, punk grew in popularity with a youth population that was becoming increasingly disinterested in politics. Previously gathering in the suburbs, between 1980 and 1981 Ljubljana's punk youths established a mass presence in the city center, including the Plečnik Square, which they renamed "Johnny Rotten Square." Because of its growing visibility, the Slovenian leadership attempted to translate the trend's symbolic threat into an actual threat to Yugoslav socialism. In 1981, France Popit, the influential general secretary of the Slovenian Party, stated at a conference that punks "publicly throw up, take drugs, and in general behave in a tasteless manner."[44] At the same time, pro-regime journalists began to connect the subculture to Nazism. In November of the same year, Zlato Šetinc, the son of a high-ranking communist official and an editor of *Nedeljski dnevnik* [Weekly Diary], the newspaper with the largest circulation in the republic, published an article entitled "Who's Drawing Swastikas?" In the article, he arbitrarily connected three otherwise isolated events: the case of a group of high school students who had tortured a classmate, the fact that a couple of swastikas had appeared on walls in Ljubljana, and the circulation of a "fascist punk manifesto."[45] Among other things, Šetinc polemicized: "Those damned kids, where exactly do they come from? Who gave us these spurious seventeen-year-olds, who torture a schoolmate for the fun of it, and boys who kill their peers? Who steal cars, get drunk, and even take drugs? Where did the young people who draw swastikas, organize Nazi socialist parties, and who greet with a raised right hand come from?"[46]

Even before Šetinc's article was published, a "people's militia" had rounded up more than a hundred members of the city's punk scene during school time and in front of their professors and classmates, and taken them to the police station.[47] There, they were allegedly intimidated, occasionally beaten, and forced to sign statements accusing their acquaintances of Nazi activities. The repression peaked with the so-called Nazi punk affair, when members of a band called Četrti Reich [Fourth Reich] were arrested for writing a "Nazi manifesto."[48] In a recent interview, Pankrti's manager, Igor Vidmar, called the band's arrest and their trial a "show trial situation, totally misconstrued and [a] media blow-up: one of the three—a singer from Lublanski Psi [Ljubljana Dogs, a punk band]—had absolutely nothing to do with the 'Fourth Reich.' The other two had, but the so-called 'band' never even performed publicly."[49] In his view, the band's arrest essentially facilitated a "massive wave of heavy police oppression."[50]

Vidmar himself became embroiled in this wave of oppression when he was prosecuted for wearing two misconstrued lapel badges. One of them carried the slogan of the American hardcore punk group Dead Kennedys, "Nazi Punks Fuck Off." The other was a Campaign for Nuclear Disarmament (CND) "Crazy Governments" badge, depicting a crossed-out swastika, and a hammer and sickle with "crazy governments" written across them. In what was arguably the most absurd point in the punk scene's persecution for its supposed allegiance with fascism, Vidmar was sentenced to thirty days in prison for offending the "national and patriotic feelings of his citizens."[51] Later, he described his arrest as a "campaign for a 'final solution' of the punk question in Slovenia, for the removal of its ideologically impure foreign body from the healthy tissue of the Slovene nation."[52]

The "campaign for a 'final solution'" failed in the long run, however, as many prominent intellectuals began to defend punk against police harassment. Among the first to speak out in defense of the scene was the ŠKUC Gallery, largely through the production and distribution of its Xeroxed fanzines. The third issue of *Galerija ŠKUC izdaja*, published in December 1981, was dedicated to the "relation of the dominant ideology toward the subculture."[53] Alongside a copy of Šentic's original article, the issue brought together a series of essays which recorded instances of repression against the punk scene. Many of them also underscored the covert methods being employed to transform punk into a criminal offense. In her contribution, Gržinić described these processes as

> the deliberate closing of several establishments in which a "certain segment of young people" gather. The Tavern pod Skalco is closed; the Restaurant Rio has been "reorganized." At Medex, they sometimes decide arbitrarily not to serve "a certain kind of young person"; the police are summoned; there are provocations from the waiters at the Union Café. This is just one of the ways people make it impossible for this "certain segment of young people" to meet, to communicate with each other. This is a systematic pressure on

social forums, and has far-reaching consequences. In public, however, it is represented merely as the "policy" of certain establishments.[54]

Gržinić also noted that venues where punks gathered were being closed down for "technical reasons"—for renovation, because of complaints from neighbors, and due to unsanitary conditions. Her text implied that the eradication of such spaces was being projected as another type of "direct democracy," one being undertaken in the name of the "moral majority," as Tomaž Mastnak has argued.[55] The fanzine's graphic material served to underscore these tendencies. One sheet, designed by Borčić, is sliced through by bold vertical stripes, lines that evoke the bars of a prison cell. The design frames the central photograph of an act of bondage, in which a naked man has had his arms and legs bound by rope, and his mouth gagged with a handkerchief. Similarly, the fanzine's front cover featured an obfuscated and smudged image of a masked, listlessly hanging figure. Read alongside Gržinić's text, both images seemed to suggest an underlying connection between the attempts to stifle the thriving punk scene and the darker, even morbid, drives governing desire. Two years later, Gržinić explained that such transgressive images functioned as a form of critique, as "content that serve[d] the ideological function of the mass media (sexual repression, social control and manipulation, the use of banned symbols ...) so that they are meaningfully radicalised, [so that] the dark side of a set norm can be exposed, like 'graffiti on the walls of a prison.'"[56]

following pages

5.10. Third issue of *Galerija ŠKUC izdaja* [ŠKUC Gallery Editions], edited by Barbara Borčić and Marina Gržinić, December 1981. Page by Barbara Borčić. Image courtesy of Barbara Borčić.

5.11. Front cover of *Punk Problemi* no. 205/206, Ljubljana, February-March 1981. Image courtesy of Dejan Knez.

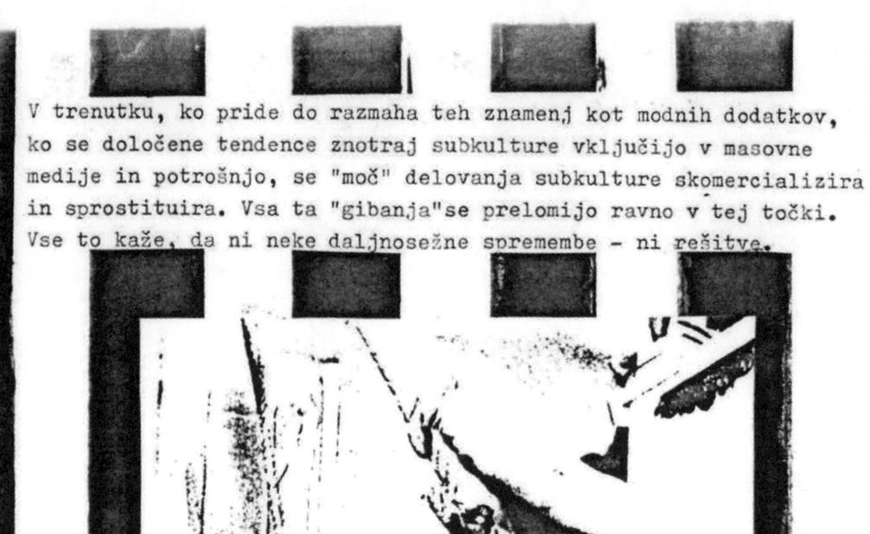

V trenutku, ko pride do razmaha teh znamenj kot modnih dodatkov, ko se določene tendence znotraj subkulture vključijo v masovne medije in potrošnjo, se "moč" delovanja subkulture skomercializira in sprostituira. Vsa ta "gibanja"se prelomijo ravno v tej točki. Vse to kaže, da ni neke daljnosežne spremembe - ni rešitve.

PUNK PROBLEMI

30-DIN

2-3/81

In other words, what is judged obscene—be it punk or sexual transgression—is not only a political issue; those ideological considerations become tangible when marked lines have been crossed.[57] A similar stance had also been advanced by the special "Punk" issue of *Problemi*, an important literary and philosophical journal in Slovenia since the 1960s. Edited at the time by Slavoj Žižek, *Problemi* gave punk a space to present itself alongside the ideas of the city's group of neo-Lacanian philosophers. In his editorial for the first issue in 1981, Žizek responded to the Socialist Youth Alliance's definition of punk as a "symptom, indicating underdeveloped self-managing relations, social alienation, the rule of commercial mass culture, and the inefficiency of our abstract ideological-political discourse."[58] He agreed that punk was a symptom, but disputed the actual diagnosis of the Youth Alliance. For him, punk was not a warning against the alarming dangers of "nihilist," "foreign," or even "anarchic" and "fascist" tendencies among a young generation.[59] It was not a contagious epidemic that needed to be cured, but rather a phenomenon that—

> viewed from the ordinary, habitual perspective—seems "foreign," "irrational," "an invasion of immorality." The symptom however, reveals an intrusion of the suppressed "truth" in the most calm, most normal everyday life, of exactly that life that is so shocked and annoyed by it. Symptom returns our suppressed truth in a perverted form ... punk literally enacts the suppressed aspect of "normality" and thereby "liberates," it introduces a defamiliarising distance.[60]

Žižek accepted that punk was a "symptom," but argued that the "symptom" should be allowed to speak. Since associated labor had completely dissolved the boundaries between the state and public life and private life, the only way to undermine the system was to attack the form of this politicization rather than dispute its ideological workings. Understanding punk as a "symptom" provided one such insight into the "normality" of social relations from a critical distance, while exposing what was being suppressed for this "normality" to function. Yet this timely defense of punk raises an important and often overlooked question: why did the "symptom" first surface in Slovenia's capital city, and not elsewhere in Yugoslavia?

It is not surprising that punk and its fierce support emerged in the federation's Westernmost, most developed and ethnically compact republic. After all, Slovenia was, in the words of political scientist Susan Woodward, always the "bellwether for change in the country and ... benefited most from Westernization."[61] When punk first surfaced as a "symptom," Slovenia was in fact experiencing pressures similar to other world-facing and full-employment economies, including a burgeoning youth press, a thriving civil society, and workers' resistance to austerity measures. Simultaneously, Slovenian economists began to perceive Yugoslavia more as a liability than an asset. Amidst growing public dissatisfaction, they expressed their unease over the republic's contributions to the federal budget—particularly for the Yugoslav National Army and federal funds directed to the less developed regions—and favored prioritizing market reforms that would support export trade to Western markets.[62] As a result of these economic arguments for reducing federal activity, the Slovenian Party also began to staunchly protect the republic's sovereignty at this time. In 1982, for example, the Slovenian Central Committee issued a direct warning to other republics and provinces that "any attempt to change anything in the present system would mean a grave danger for our unity."[63] The interconnections between Slovenia's dynamic youth subculture scene, the republic's push for liberalization, and Yugoslavia's deadlock will be central to my reading of ŠKUC's activities in 1982, the same year that the Slovenian Central Committee issued its stark warning to the federal government.

In 1982, the ŠKUC Gallery presented Dušan Mandić's work for the third time. Titled *Die Welt ist Schön* [The World Is Beautiful], the show was a direct reference to the 1928 photographic bestseller by Albert Renger-Patzsch, which was famously criticized by Walter Benjamin for obfuscating the brutal social and political realities of the time. As part of the exhibition, Mandić showed a series of "image-interventions" on commercial postcards, crosses, and letters he had collected during his one year of military service in the Serbian city of Niš. In some "interventions," soft pornographic photographs of women posing in lingerie were taken out of the context of their original surroundings and violently transplanted onto red-and-black-painted backgrounds. In others, sentimental portraits of men and babies were bloodied and tarnished by red scratches on the photographic surface. Such interventions not only spoiled the fallacy of the "beautiful, idyllic" worlds the postcards captured; they also translated them into the realm of violence. But to what end were these scenes from a "beautiful world" being violently degraded?

To mark the opening of the exhibition, the ŠKUC Gallery printed a fanzine which featured copies of the postcards on display alongside poems written by Brane Bitenc, frontman of the punk band Otroci Socializma [The Children of Socialism]. In the zine's introductory text, Mandić noted that the project came out of his personal experiences of subjugation during his military service: "the desire to paint, and a simultaneous awareness of total social control, total powerlessness, in which one finds a hold that extricates the surplus value in the form of the

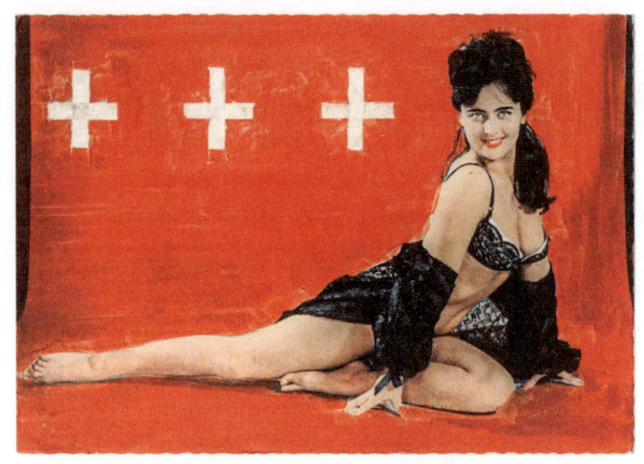

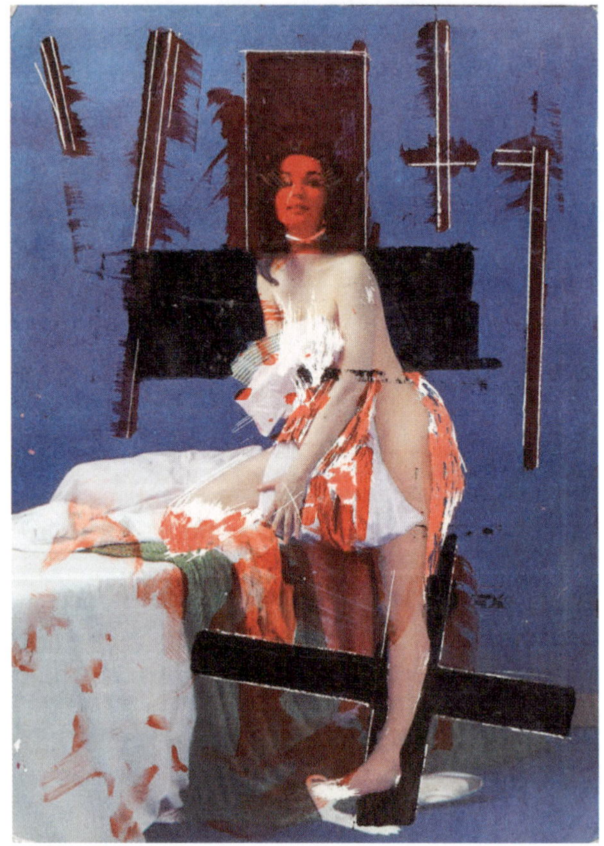

cross, the ceaselessly repeating cross."[64] These personal feelings of subjugation were further underscored by Bitenc's stories featured in the zine, including one called "Suicide I" which read: "there we lay ... you suddenly said you were a cop, out of the blue, no one was upset ... that year we spent together, everything was under surveillance."[65] Like many of the stories featured in the fanzine, this anecdote implied a fear of constant supervision; it also suggested that the stultifying conformity of military service prevented the artist from pursuing his "desire to paint." In the exhibition itself, Mandić included a hand-sketched self-portrait in his military gear, and an image of a cross covered in red barbed spikes. Projected side by side on a wall, these images alluded to how a feeling of constantly being monitored impacts an individual, preventing him, in this instance, from pursuing his desire to be an artist. In the exhibition invitation, Mandić referred to himself as "Vojak D. M." [Private D. M.], thereby renouncing his individual position as an artist for the military role forcibly imposed on him.

Mandić was not alone in feeling subjugated as a conscripted member of the Yugoslav People's Army. After the Second World War, the foundational myth of the Partisan victory granted the Yugoslav People's Army a legitimacy that no other army in a Communist country possessed other than the Soviet Red Army. Under Tito, its symbolic importance was carefully cultivated by official and popular culture, and although formally independent, the army remained closely entwined with the League of Communists. By the beginning of the 1980s, many youths were reluctant to join the armed forces, particularly in Slovenia, where it increasingly came under attack from a thriving and combative youth press. At this time, the army also became synonymous with the federal government, along with the secret police and restrictive measures against reform, while Slovenia was steadily transforming itself into a beacon for liberalizing initiatives.

5.12. and 5.13. Dušan Mandić, *Die Welt ist Schön*, 1981–1982. Images courtesy of the artist.

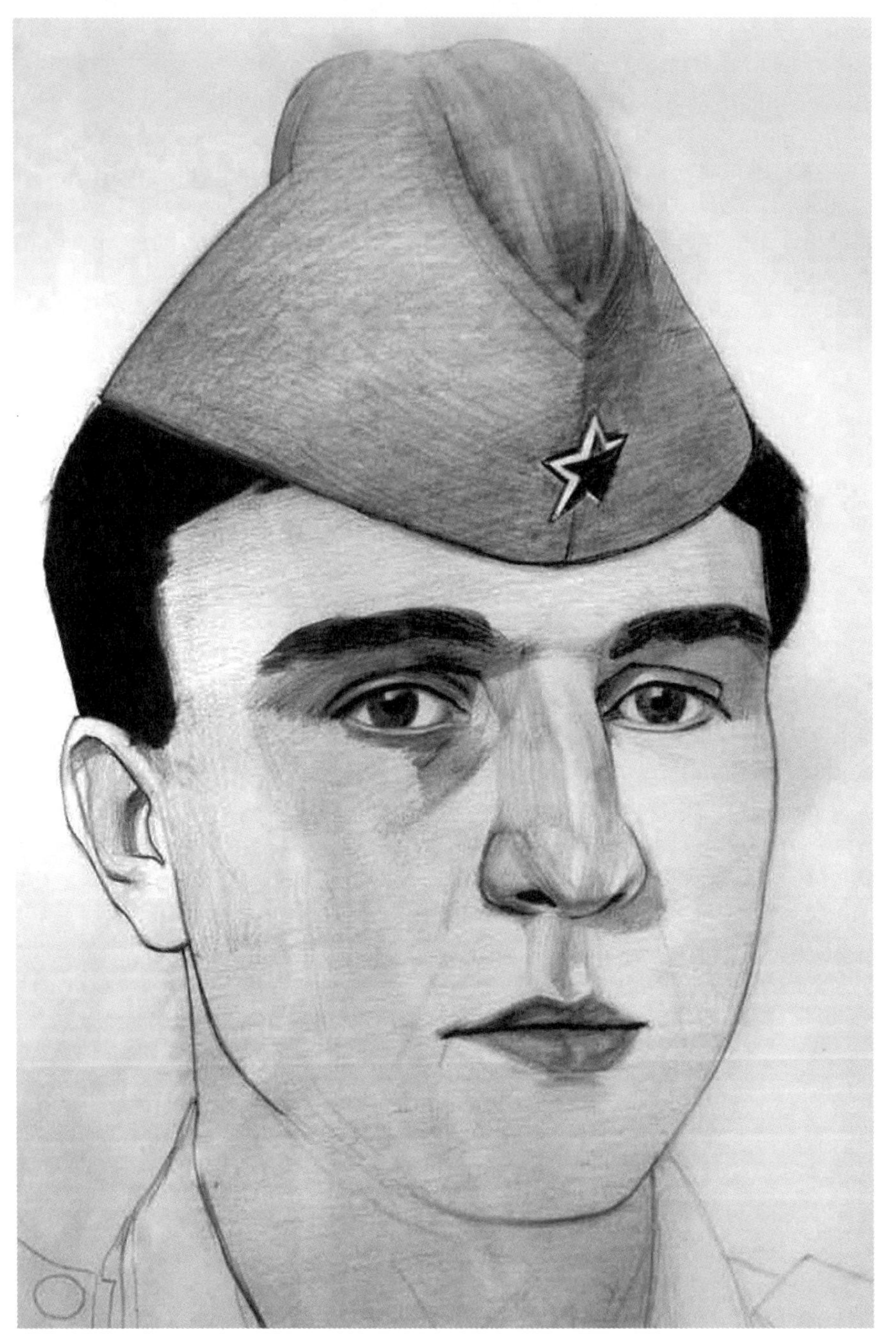

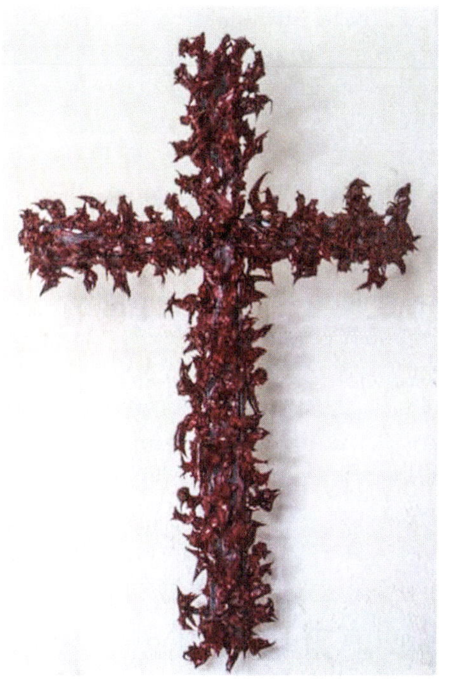

5.14. Dušan Mandić, *Portrait of a Private in the Barracks*, 1 December 1981. Image courtesy of the artist.

5.15. Dušan Mandić, *Cross*, 1981. Image courtesy of the artist.

Among the liberalizing initiatives taking place in Slovenia in the year that the ŠKUC Gallery presented *Ausstellung! Laibach Kunst* and *Die Welt ist Schön* was a new independent journal by critical intellectuals called *Nova revija*. Established in 1982, the journal was, according to one of its founders, Dimitrij Rupel, intended to support cultural modernization, to introduce Western-style democracy in Slovenia, and to promote it as an independent nation-state.[66] The journal would come to play a pivotal role in the republic's national question, and many of its contributors would become key political actors in independent Slovenia. Slovenia's "alternative" political scene was subsequently organized around two poles. One advocated a conservative program combined with demands for full democracy, while the other was structured around single-issue movements, including the introduction of civil instead of military service, the closure of nuclear power stations, and the abolition of "verbal crimes" and the death penalty. Whereas the critical intellectuals gathering around *Nova revija* addressed the question of nationhood as being equivalent to democratization, ŠKUC framed the practices it supported exclusively around social issues. Gregor Tomc bluntly described the aspirations of the initiatives associated with the ŠKUC Gallery as a confrontation not with "totalitarian socialism," but rather with the old guard without offering any alternative program, except a complete rejection of state power.[67]

By 1982, however, the conservative nature of the party had become so palpable that comparisons with Eastern European totalitarians seemed justified for the first time since 1948.[68] At a time when Slovenian urban youth began forging links with Central European groups on issue-oriented campaigns supporting civil liberties, *Die Welt ist Schön* could even be analyzed from the perspective of what the dissident György Konrad famously defined in 1984 as "antipolitics": the complete "anti-ideological, almost misanthropic distrust of collectivity, institutions and concepts embedded in society."[69] This stance was further underscored by the release of Otroci Socializma's new music cassette, whose sleeve featured a photocopy of one of Mandić's interventions. Both Mandić and the "Children of Socialism" attempted to demolish the apparent idyll of the established political order by showing irreverence for Yugoslavia's "sacred" symbols and myths, renouncing self-management's promises of a better, collective future, and focusing exclusively on the here-and-now. While the lyrics to Otroci Socializma's songs had previously been censored in the 1981 issue of *Punk Problemi*, which was forced to print blocks over the offending materials, the ŠKUC Gallery both published the lyrics in the exhibition's fanzine and made them available on audiocassette.

Merging art with popular culture, *Die Welt ist Schön* confirmed how closely the ŠKUC Gallery identified with punk's aesthetics, like the Lacanian thinkers who had readily accepted the subculture as their subject of study. The materials shown at the exhibition were united by their refusal to be politicized and their emphasis on individual freedoms. All of them could be understood as what Konrád described as "the political activity of those who don't want to be politicians and who refuse to share in power," and as being expressions of "independent forums that can be appealed to against political power."[70] By engaging in activities that fell outside of the more familiar and conventional duties of galleries, the ŠKUC Gallery was beginning to nurture a specific, "antipolitical" form of self-reflection. Advocating civil liberties, it would also begin to support a range of single-issue social movements, all of which were organized around particular campaigns, ranging from peace and ecology to feminism and gay rights, rather than according to broad ideological concerns. Starting in 1983, these movements in turn would come together as part of a vigorous "alternative scene."

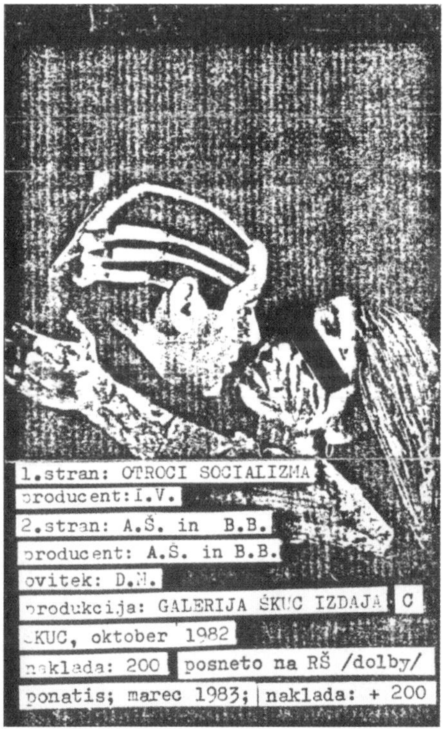

5.16. Dušan Mandić's design for the audiocassette cover of Otroci Socializma's self-titled debut album, released by *Galerija ŠKUC izdaja*, Ljubljana, October 1982. Image courtesy of the artist.

WHAT WAS "THE ALTERNATIVE"?

In autumn 1980, an amateur theater group took over the activities in the basement in Block IV of Ljubljana's university campus. The group went by the name of FV 112/15, later deciphered as the fifteenth entry on page 112 of France Verbinc's *Dictionary of Foreign Loan Words*: "C'est La Guerre" [It's war]. The group's name underlined its ambitions to create a theater in night clubs, where the entire club would become a stage and the audience would become actors. In 1981, the FV group began running the Tuesday night program of the city's student disco, based in the student dormitory complex. Before long, they were managing the entire club, later renamed Disco FV.

If Laibach were considered threatening because of their anonymity and their references to national socialism, FV was subversive because of its immense popularity. Disco FV introduced new technologies into the cultural field and combined the activities of a disco, concert hall, theater, and gallery. Alongside the ŠKUC Gallery, it was the only place where the city's more radical art practices were shown. The year 1982 was a watershed in the space's history: after acquiring video equipment, it soon began to organize regular video screenings of different music video clips, films, and video artworks. In the previous year, Disco FV had also begun encouraging young people to write graffiti across the city, and on the walls of the club itself. In the words of Nikolai Jeffs, guests were invited to contribute a multitude of "drawn, spray-painted, colored, lacquered and Xeroxed words, band names, coherent and nonsensical sentences, 'classic' urban, new anarcho-punk, and political appeals, slogans, symbols, and texts."[71] While the symbolic presence of subcultures was systematically being eradicated from public spaces—graffiti was being erased, and posters being torn down—the hallway of the FV Disco became a site for free expression. As Zemira Alajbegović noted in 1983:

> The openness of the FV scene allowed the inclusion of a large number of both regular and sporadic collaborators in developing the program, and for considerable equality in expression among the various tendencies within Ljubljana's alternative scene.... The walls of Disco FV, which with their graffiti and the remnants of photocopies and drawings represented a collective product by the disco's visitors ... articulated the younger generation's engaged production—emphatically alternative and indeed marginal in relation to traditional culture, the only "real," i.e. visible, culture, as well as the national, i.e. Slovene and Yugoslav, mass media culture.[72]

Alajbegović's contemporaneous account highlighted how Disco FV sought to overcome the usually hierarchical relationship between organizers and clientele. This was a space where actors and audience interacted, and where members of the audience became active agents in events. In May 1983, Igor Vidmar described the space as a "metaphor for the interaction and ghettoization of spontaneous, public, street communication: as a sort of marginal, underground bastion of democracy, a visual variant of punk as a symptom which has spoken out."[73]

The "symptom which [had] spoken out" found its ultimate voice in November 1983, when a group of small organizations including ŠKUC collaborated on the legendary conference *Kaj je alternativa?* [What Is the Alternative?] held at the FV premises in the Upper Šiška Youth Center. Much like *Punk Problemi*, the event gave the so-called alternative scene an intellectual space to present itself. The event featured some of Slovenia's most prominent philosophers, social scientists, artists, and cultural figures, debating issues that the alternative scene was grappling with at the time, including battles over public space, and the legal problems faced by Laibach and Vidmar. Mandić's poster for the event captured all of the burning issues addressed at the conference in a single image. The black-and-white photocopied print consisted of a couple caught in a loving embrace, wearing the "Disco FV" armband and the badges that had landed Vidmar in prison. Behind the idyllic scene of petit bourgeois romance was depicted the grid of Laibach's *Metalworkers*, along with the group's banned name.

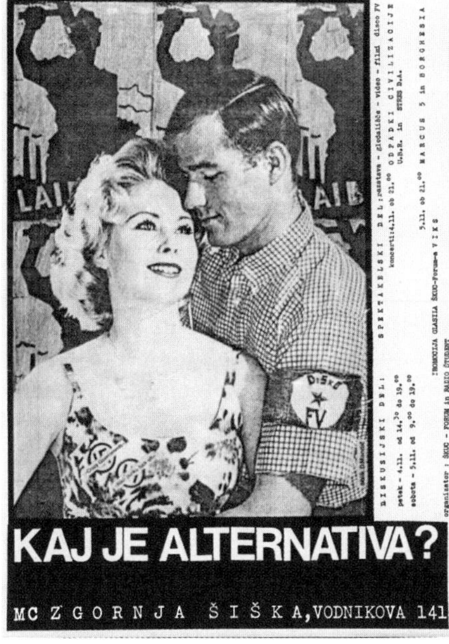

5.17. Dušan Mandić, Poster for *Kaj je alternativa?* [What Is the Alternative?], Upper Šiška Youth Center, Ljubljana, 1983. Image courtesy of the artist.

Like the majority of the participants at the conference, the poster was suggesting that the common ground of an otherwise heterogeneous phenomenon was its cutting through appearances to what was, at its core, a deeply conservative and oppressive environment. In the following year, Žižek would declare that the alternative scene had ultimately exposed the "cynical" nature of Yugoslav self-management, which had until then relied on the majority's "lack of interest and apathy," and sustained itself through an "extremely complicated network of relations among its delegates [which] thwarted any form of horizontal networking [and] any spontaneous 'initiative from below.'"[74] Because of the poster, Mandić received a visit from the police, who arrived at his house with a search warrant. He was, however, never prosecuted in court for it. Later, the work appeared in various youth publications, mostly in a censored form. *Mladina*, for example, published the poster with the swastikas covered in black blocks, revealing how forms of self-censorship were still at play in the city's more prominent youth publication. Once the "dull, official organ" of the Youth Alliance, *Mladina* would later reinvent itself as one of the most radical news magazines in Yugoslavia.

For the event itself, Mandić also produced a graffiti painting at the Youth Center. It consisted of a disembodied, floating barbed phallus surrounded by orderly rows of plain red crucifixes, along with the cryptic caption: "1968 IS OVER. 1983 IS OVER. FUTURE IS BETWEEN YOUR LEGS." The caption seemed to renounce the unquestioned sense of obligation and duty that the previous generation under socialism had felt and maintained. It implied that while the previous youth cultures connected to 1968 had shared a sense of confidence in their ability to change the world, and indeed felt an imperative to do so, the proponents of this new "alternative" culture were being driven by individual desires. Both 1968 and 1983 were over. And the "future"—the direction through which communism activated itself as something "not yet realized"—was now in the possession of the individual. It was right there, between their legs.

Mandić's graffiti work ultimately abolished the sense of responsibility associated with the New Art Practice in its earliest phase. In the artist's own words, it was an approach that was ultimately "comic instead of tragic," "popular instead of transcendent," and characterized by an impish humor.[75] The irreverence of his graffiti work permeated much of the cultural production at the FV, which also included videos that featured pornographic film interspersed with images of political figures such as Tito. At the same time, graffiti ascribed art production a new and undoubtedly more dynamic place in Ljubljana's social and cultural life. Asked by Zemira Alajbegović, "What drives you as an academically trained painter with a number of exhibitions in galleries to make graffiti paintings in Disco FV?," Mandić explained:

> It's about becoming a part of rock culture, mass culture, about not wanting to remain in some marginal bourgeois-culture position that at best reaches as far as theory—phenomenology—fetishisation of the object ... it's not about the alternative, actually, its about finding a place for one's practice in mass culture, in rock culture. A painting, a graffiti painting becomes a moment in the production of rock culture, like a record, music, image ...[76]

In other words, graffiti enabled Mandić to position himself as an artist within punk mass culture, and to go beyond the confined spaces of art galleries. At the end of November 1983, the visual art group Rrose IRWIN Sélavy (which eventually shortened its name, first to R IRWIN S, and then simply IRWIN) presented their graffiti work for the first time in the dance space of Disco FV.[77] Together with the group's distinctive approach to reactivating historic traumas, graffiti would play a central role in IRWIN's early work, particularly in one exhibition that took place in the ŠKUC Gallery in the following year.

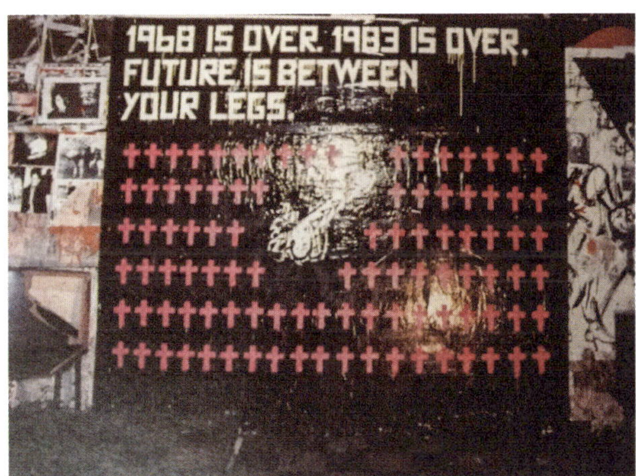

5.18. Dušan Mandić, graffiti work for *Kaj je alternativa?* [What Is the Alternative?], Upper Šiška Youth Center, Ljubljana, 1983. Image courtesy of the artist.

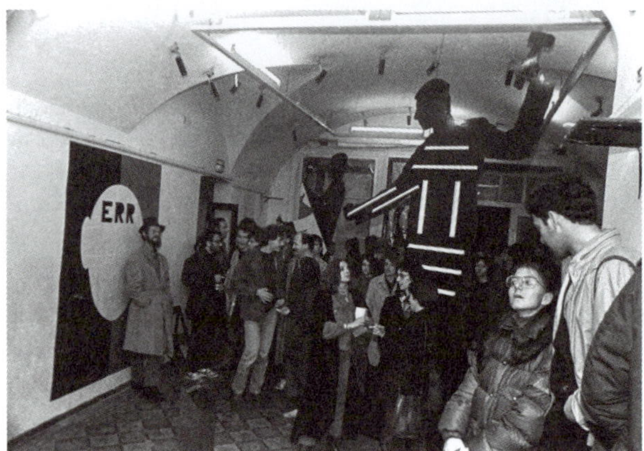

5.19. IRWIN, *Back to the USA*, ŠKUC Gallery, Ljubljana, 1984. Photograph by Barbara Borčić. Image courtesy of Barbara Borčić.

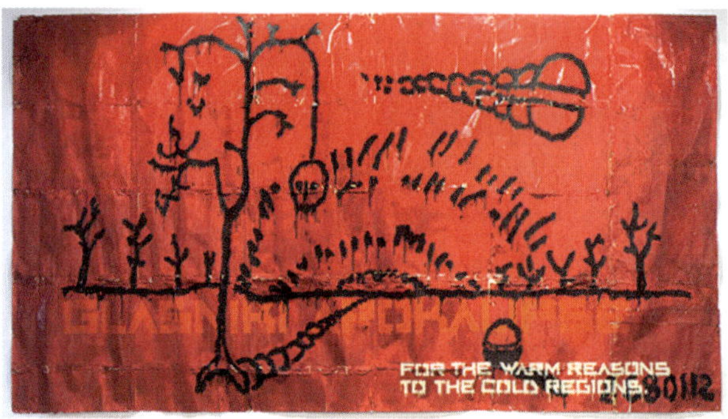

5.20. Dušan Mandić, *Untitled*, 1984. Graffiti paint and car lacquer. Photograph by Dejan Habicht. Image courtesy of the artist.

BACK TO THE USA

The entrance of FV and graffiti art into the ŠKUC Gallery was significant for the gallery's future activities, because it was from the FV scene that IRWIN first entered the exhibition space. In April 1984, the group presented their first major exhibition at the ŠKUC Gallery: *Back to the USA*. On first impression, IRWIN's project seemed to be a complete reconstruction of the paintings, photographs, and installations by American artists at an exhibition of the same name that had traveled to Switzerland and Germany in 1983 and 1984. Some of the artists in the exhibition, such as Nicholas Africano, Richard Bosman, Cindy Sherman, Matt Mullican, and Jonathan Borofsky, were already well known, and a quarter of them had participated in Documenta 7 in 1982.[78] Since the show was not destined to travel to Ljubljana, IRWIN decided to "bring" the exhibition to ŠKUC themselves. They recreated the works by copying the photographs in a catalogue from the original exhibition that two IRWIN members, Andrej Savski and Roman Uranjek, had brought back from Lucerne, where they saw the show.

In the fanzine accompanying the exhibition, Borut Vogelnik and Miloš Gregorič contributed a short text entitled "Back to the USA," in which they criticized the constant reduction of state subsidies for contemporary art, under which "art becomes both prohibited and simultaneously redundant."[79] Moreover, they located Slovenian art within the "sea of Western decadence, based on specific theories of humanism, progressiveness, rootedness, presence, etc."[80] For these artists, Slovenia's traditional art was characterized by an "uncritical combination of contrasting artistic styles and traditions."[81] Presenting a number of hand-painted "remakes" of works by American artists subsequently served as a critique of local art production as very often belated, and of the way the majority of prominent artists in Slovenia simply copied from their Western contemporaries, without acknowledging their sources and influences. As Tate curator Catherine Wood has argued, IRWIN "copied" and "remade the works of the American artists to draw attention to their frustrations with the false claims of 'originality' made by Yugoslav officials on the part of 'state' artists."[82]

Yet *Back to the USA* was more than just a one-dimensional critique, and the works displayed at the show were not simply faithful reproductions. Far from it, in fact—many of the "copies" were actually rooted in the fertile technical grounds that ensured the rapid proliferation of the alternative scene in Ljubljana. For his contribution, Mandić made a copy of Jonathan Borofsky's own version of Đorđević's *Harbingers of the Apocalypse*. Whereas Borofsky had made a miniature copy on transparent plastic film, reminiscent of an image slide, Mandić's "reproduction" enlarged the image to a five-meter-long painting, executed in graffiti stencils. By way of Borofsky's copy, Đorđević's self-declared "ugly, tasteless, and besides all that, dilettante painting" was transformed into an icon of the alternative scene. Its original composition was simplified and carelessly applied with black spray paint against a vividly monochromatic red background. The title of the work was featured in stenciled characters, along with the cryptic message: "for the warm reasons to the cold regions." Borofsky's work was thus filtered through the recent experiences of Ljubljana's thriving alternative art scene. In a similar vein, the invitation for *Back to the USA* featured Mandić's graffiti work for the *What Is the Alternative?* conference. With it, the graffiti from the FV scene was introduced to the gallery space, translated to a new medium and audience that allowed for new readings of the work.

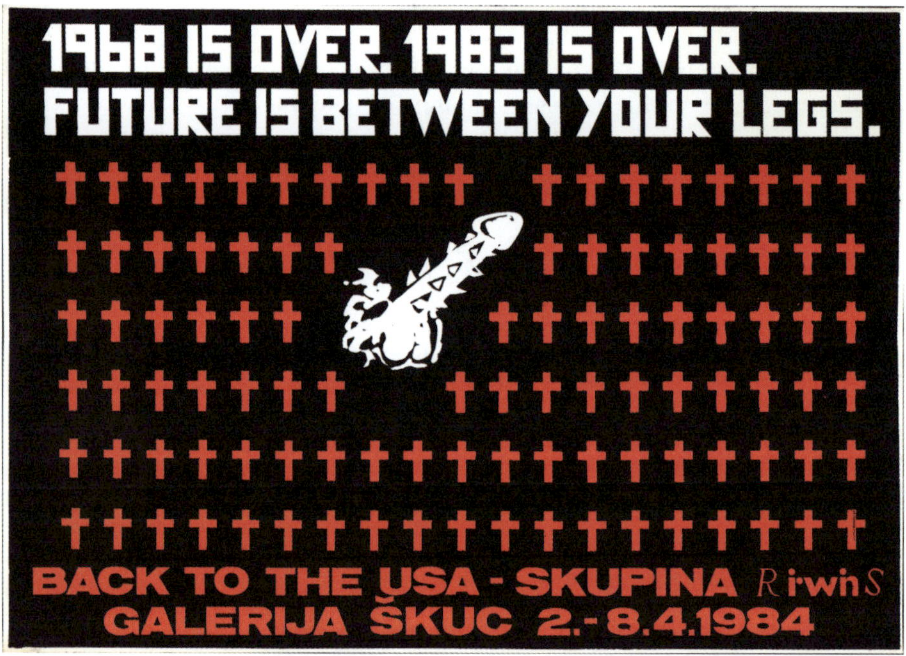

5.21. Invitation postcard for *Back to the USA*, 1984.
Image courtesy of Dušan Mandić.

Through such references, *Back to the USA* both rendered explicit the recent experiences of the alternative scene and offered new interpretations of their relevance to Slovenian art production. As such, the exhibition contained the basic postulates of IRWIN's "retroprinciple" concept, which implied using works by other artists and reinterpreting them in a way that reactivated them.[83] In another work shown at the exhibition, Mandić and Gržinić copied Cindy Sherman's *Untitled Film Stills* (1977–1980), but instead of taking photographs, Mandić recorded a four-minute video in which Gržinić imitated the artist's now famous film star poses. Sherman's original, voyeuristic works, defined by their grimy and quotidian spirit ("cheap and trashy," as the artist described them), were rendered animate and productively reimagined.[84] The figure of fictional femininity, pandering to stereotypes and prepackaged identities, was transformed into a living, blinking, and breathing person. Only the uncanny traces of Sherman's portraits remained in the work, executed in a medium that had been crucial to the Disco FV in its support of the alternative scene. In line with the gallery's unique approach to merging fine art with music, the video's sound track was provided by the FV's founders, Borghesia. Entitled "Cindy Sherman," the song was sampled from the group's audiocassette *Clones*, which was released by the ŠKUC Gallery to coincide with the opening of *Back to the USA*. These gestures emphasized the unique explosion in visual production that had emerged in Ljubljana at the time, which had transcended conventional gallery spaces and successfully made contact with a vivid subcultural youth scene.

Back to the USA captured the complexity of Ljubljana's alternative scene, in which activities were often loosely organized and dispersed, with no privileged actor or field of action. What remained important to the alternative scene was the fact that social issues were critically addressed through several channels at once, and through various models of articulation. In the words of Gržinić: "One suddenly started to feel the complexity of the scene, but one couldn't single out one facet, one trend. Each one of them was operating, and each had its own resonance."[85]

Yet, while the alternative movements regarded themselves as independent of, and opposed to, the state, their growing presence did have a major impact on future political developments. Although the general public's faith in self-management continued into the middle of the 1980s, by 1986 the alternative movements were nearing their peak, and were fully embraced by the Youth Alliance. Because of their growing popularity, the political leadership admitted that they were "serious" and examined their positions carefully. Simultaneously, social scientists in

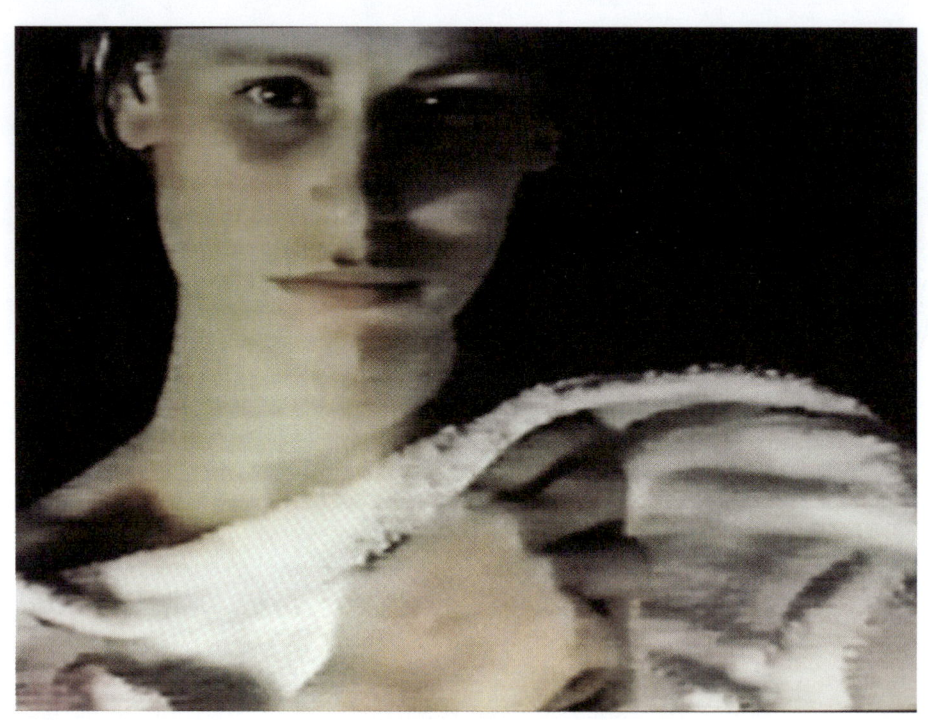

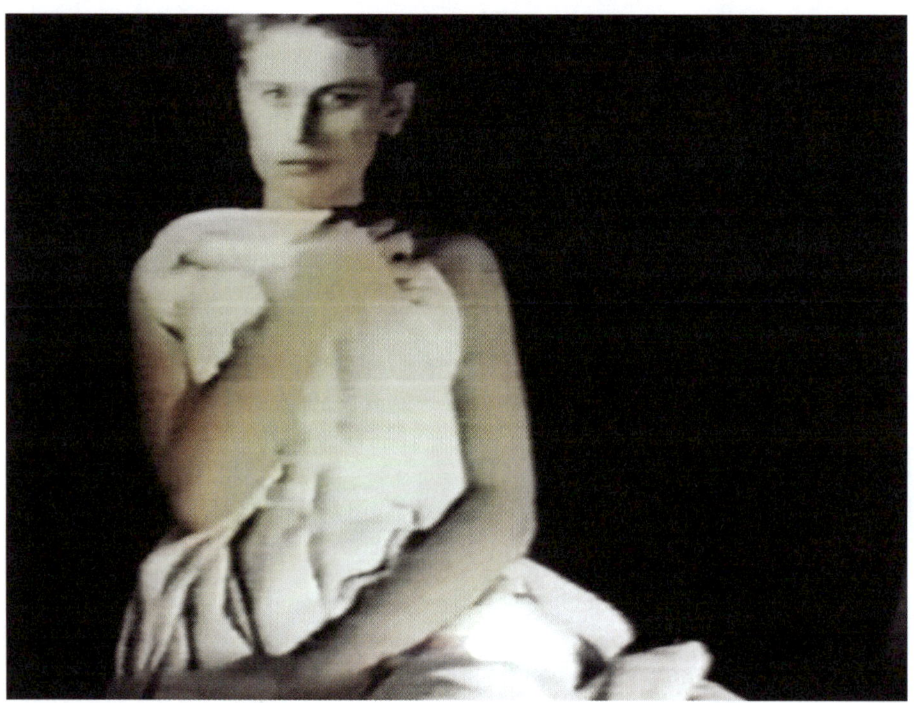

Ljubljana began developing a theory of "socialist civil society" to define the "new social movements" and "alternative scenes."[86] Initially these debates did not have much of a political impact, but later they become central to the Slovenian party's political aspirations for an independent Slovenia. By 1985, the term "civil society" first appeared in the rhetoric of the LCS, which understood the term as being "organically" linked to self-management.[87] With that, the leadership conceded that civil society was the party's programmatic aim, but refuted all of the movement's features that escaped integration and pacification. The effects of socialist civil society were therefore contradictory. While stimulating public debates around social issues, and therefore accelerating the process of abolishing the party monopoly, they arguably depoliticized these debates.

Amid growing power struggles within the institutions of the federal state, the new social movements were soon appropriated by Slovenian nationalist political figures—many of whom had been contributors to *Nova revija*—who safely followed the fresh path to secession. As Tomaž Mastnak has argued, "socialism was the collateral damage that came out of falling in love with civil society."[88] In his view, the new opposition "uncoupled democracy from socialism, dissociated itself from Marxist and Socialist ideology . . . and equated the state with non-democracy. Civil society became the embodiment of democracy whereas the state was denounced as totalitarian."[89] Similarly, Rastko Močnik has noted that it was the "apolitical effects of the ideology of 'civil society'" that permitted the Slovenian party to reestablish itself on a nationalist basis. These effects facilitated an independent Slovenia that would present itself as "'apolitical' with a 'civil societal' ideology, [while providing] the ground for a class (and therefore political) act par excellence—the reconstruction of capitalism."[90]

5.22. and 5.23. Dušan Mandić, Marina Gržinić, and Borghesia, *Cindy Sherman*, 1984. Images courtesy of Dušan Mandić.

Precisely when the Slovenian Party began to co-opt the "alternative," the groups previously working through ŠKUC formed an organization called Neue Slowenische Kunst (NSK). NSK began operating in 1984 as a union of three groups working in different mediums: the band Laibach, the visual arts collective IRWIN, and the Scipion Nasice Sisters Theatre.[91] Institutional and transparent in its appearance, but opaque and mutating in its behavior, NSK's ultimate goal was to appear from the outside as a real institution, by which it would conceptually substitute for and "correct" other institutions within the local context. According to Gržinić, "neither Slovenia nor Ljubljana had ever seen anything so shocking."[92]

At the same time that Slovenian authorities embraced the alternative and NSK was born, Sarajevo would begin to transform itself into one of the most important cultural capitals in Yugoslavia.

6 THE MIRACLE OF MIRACLES

SARAJEVO AND THE LAST EPISODE OF THE "YUGOSLAV" CONTEMPORARY ART SCENE

DAS IST SARAJEVO, THE "DARK VILAYET"

Following the Second World War, Yugoslavia realized it had inherited an economy characterized by profound disparities. Capitalist development was extremely uneven in the country, ranging from Slovenia, where commercial agriculture, roads, and manufacturing were already being developed in the mid-eighteenth century under Hapsburg rule, to parts of Bosnia and Macedonia, where Ottoman-style feudal relations had still cast a shadow on political, economic, and social life up until the 1930s. The party's initial response to these regional inequalities was to declare them unacceptable in a socialist country and to assign high priority to the fastest possible leveling of incomes. But in what was one of the most fateful political errors in Yugoslav history, the Federal General Investment Fund was abolished in 1963 and replaced by a smaller and inadequate "Fund for Accelerated Development." The market mechanisms that were given full rein in the 1960s continued to increase the gap in the standard of living between the richer republics and provinces of the northwest and the poorer ones in the southeastern regions. These regional gaps resulted not only in enormous economic disparities, but also in social and cultural inequalities among Yugoslav nations, with the systems of domination between more developed federal units (Slovenia, Croatia, and Serbia) and the less developed ones continuing to widen throughout the 1970s.[1]

Yet, contrary to popular belief, the record of regional development in Yugoslavia was more than a mere catalogue of failures. Under the League of Communists' leadership, a largely agrarian and peasant society was transformed into a middle-ranking industrial power in record time, and without many of the deformations characteristic of Stalinism.[2] Nowhere were these advances felt more profoundly than in the republic of Bosnia and Herzegovina. Associated for generations with the traumatic history of the region—with its complex Ottoman, Austro-Hungarian, Islamic, Orthodox, and Catholic legacies—after the war the republic witnessed unprecedented urbanization and industrialization, which should be counted among the success stories of Yugoslav socialism.[3] Of course, the republic's record rate of development carried a strategic value to the federation's integrity and was key to the broader political project of "Yugoslavism." An amalgam of faiths, nationalities, dialects, and histories, Bosnia and Herzegovina was the republic created most truly in Yugoslavia's image. As early as the birth of Tito's Yugoslavia, memories of the recent carnage were concealed beneath the veils of the Brotherhood and Unity discourse. As early as the decade after the war, the republic was reinvented as a thriving multicultural environment, and the perfect example of modern Yugoslavia.

As a multinational and religiously diverse model of Yugoslavia, Bosnia began to serve as a bulwark for democratic socialism. But precisely because its identity was inextricably linked to that of its neighboring republics, Bosnia was particularly vulnerable to nationalist forces. What was required was a delicate balancing act of national interests. As republics pushed for greater autonomy in the 1960s, the League of Communists granted Bosnian Muslims constitutional status comparable to that of Serbs and Croats, establishing a balance within the ethnically diverse republic and promoting it to equal status with the federation's other republics, all of which possessed national majorities.[4] This political milestone was secured by the prestige of the republic's leadership at this time, which achieved credibility with Tito by keeping nationalist hostilities in check during the 1960s, when the liberal leaderships in Belgrade, Ljubljana, and Zagreb were beginning to fall out of favor. The respect for this leadership was further heightened through economic results, and the republic developed manufacturing companies that functioned as monopolies in Yugoslavia's semiplanned economy. Helped by foreign credit, these companies seemed to work well in a republic that experienced great strides in economic growth during the 1970s, while its citizens enjoyed better living standards and its leaders enjoyed Tito's full confidence.

This confidence, however, came at a heavy price, and it was paid in the currency of political freedom. In reaction to Bosnia's multinational composition, the local cultural policy featured particularly strong and repressive propaganda; nowhere else in the federation was the cult of Tito as prominent as it was in this republic. Films made in Bosnia were often more submissive to socialist topics than those made in the rest of Yugoslavia, with pervasive efforts to emphasize the similarities and blur the differences between Serbs, Croats, and Muslims.[5]

The films completely denounced national themes, and very often centered on the Second World War. The most celebrated of these was Hajrudin Krvavac's *Valter brani Sarajevo* [Walter Defends Sarajevo] (1972), a film following a series of twists as the city's Partisans and their leader, a mysterious character known as Walter, resist German occupation. At the end of the film, a Nazi officer reflects on his inability to defeat his nemesis Walter. Standing on a hill, he points at Sarajevo below and remarks in German: "Sehen Sie diese Stadt? Das ist Walter! [You see that city? That's Walter!]." Also an alias of Tito, "Valter" represented a message of unity consistent with the republic's official politics. Following the film's release, the slogan "Das ist Walter" entered the realm of everyday speech, demonstrating how popular-cultural mythologies established a number of equivalences: "Tito-Partisans-Revolution-People," typified by the well-known maxim, "Tito, to smo mi" [Tito is all of us].

With the local administration maintaining a firm ideological grip over cultural production, the republic's capital, Sarajevo, was cast in the wider Yugoslav consciousness as a "dark vilayet" ("vilayet" being the Arabic-derived word for one of the chief administrative divisions of the late Ottoman Empire).[6] Until the early 1980s, the city's culture was associated with Bosnia's social and economic inferiority, as between 1952 and 1968 the republic continued to have the lowest growth rate of all the Yugoslav republics, along with high illiteracy and infant mortality rates.[7] In many ways, these cultural markers mirrored historical patterns of development. As Susan Woodward has argued, the dynamics of Yugoslav governmental policy were ultimately divided between two models, named after contrasting wartime administrations from 1941 to 1945: "Slovenia" and "Foča."[8] The first was a "liberal" approach to economic growth and was associated with the federation's northern, more developed regions, which benefited from neighboring markets, developed transportation, and the advantages of early industrialization. The second, dominant in Bosnia and Herzegovina, Kosovo, Macedonia, and Montenegro, where industries based on mining, metallurgy, and other basic manufacturing were dominant, was a "developmentalist" approach, and focused on the production of raw materials and food for home consumption. Even in the 1970s—a period when Bosnia experienced great strides in economic development—offshore processing and assembly continued to be concentrated in the regions closest to Western markets, namely Slovenia and Croatia, whereas energy, mining, and heavy industry sectors were in the southern regions and far from foreign markets. With its economies predominantly lying in agriculture and low-wage industries, Bosnia's cultural identity was also viewed as being inferior to that of Yugoslavia's northern regions. As the republic's capital, Sarajevo was seen by its northwestern neighbors as lacking the cultural sensibilities of an industrially developed Western society. Simply put, Sarajevo's cultural production was seen to lack the refinement of "progressive socialist culture"; it was perceived as something to be concealed from "Yugoslav" cultural visibility, or at least to be reshaped so as to conform to the recognized and accepted cultural mold.

Not only was Sarajevo's local culture considered a source of inferiority, but so was the city's colorful slang, which was viewed as a lesser deviation from the standardized Serbo-Croatian. Accordingly, the "dumb yokels" who were the target of Yugoslav jokes came from Bosnia. Sarajevo was known as much for the "aroma of ćevapi" (considered the national dish of Bosnia) as it was for the ethnic "jokes about Mujo and Haso." Based on dialogues between two fictive Bosnians, these jokes essentially cast the typical Bosnian as simple, uneducated, and misogynistic, implicitly identifying the republic's population as less sophisticated due to the region's economic and therefore (alleged) social inferiority. As Sarajevo-based writer Miljenko Jergović observed: "Of all the Yugoslav capitals, Sarajevo felt the least capital. On the beaches of the Dalmatian Coast, Sarajevans, unlike the inhabitants of Belgrade and Zagreb, strove to talk using standardized language. They were ashamed of their slang."[9] Sarajevan curator Nermina Zildžo elaborates:

> Sarajevo, i.e. Sarajevo's cultural scene, despised, and characterised as "primitive," any attempt to incorporate the linguistic realities of the city into the media, or even to use it in the spoken arts.... It was a kind of shame towards one's own distinctiveness, that was often so obvious that it could only be negated by a kind of "militant spirit." The writers were using "pure" literary language, or some form of the numerous home-grown variations.... Dialogues in prose were dry and empty as if they were conversations of idle native-language teachers rather than of literary heroes; simply, the language of the city was exiled from the public scene and, with it, its cultural specificities, with its rather rough features, anathematised.[10]

With even the local accent "exiled from the public scene," Sarajevo's sociocultural realm was relegated to the periphery. Not only was this the image through which the federation's other capitals framed their regard for Sarajevo's cultural presence, but it also pierced through the city's perception of itself.

By the beginning of the 1980s, however, the city's social climate was beginning to change. While Sarajevo's cultural activity had previously been determined by communist dogma, the death of Tito marked a loosening of the propagandist grip on the republic. The fragmentation of the political leadership and a weakened central government resulted in an awakening of various currents in the city's subcultural scene. Sarajevo began to strive for a cultural status that could overcome its long-lasting cultural domination by the country's largest and most developed capitals.

"WHO ARE THE BELLS RINGING FOR?": THE EMERGENCE OF CAFÉ-GALLERY ZVONO[11]

Writing on the "problem of cultural syncretism in Bosnia and Herzegovina," Nirma Moranjak-Bamburać explained "it is no wonder that the 'Bosnian paradigm' compels a storyteller such as Ivo Andrić, who, although in the negative sense of 'Bosnian cursedness,' caught something of the Bosnian 'slow being': of the eternal functioning of the regime of latency and delayed action."[12] With its cultural output echoing its belated economic and political development, according to curator Azra Begić, until the 1980s Sarajevo "barely existed on the distribution map of the New Art Practice in Yugoslavia, and innovations were, normally, accepted more easily with traditional forms of expression, rather than introduced through new media."[13]

Unlike Belgrade, Ljubljana, and Zagreb, Sarajevo did not possess its own Academy of Fine Art until 1972, which for the first time enabled students to train locally.[14] But from its founding, this institution offered a "traditional, ossified and pedagogical" model of academic training.[15] This is because throughout the 1970s, art in Bosnia and Herzegovina continued to be closely bound to the traditional disciplines of painting, sculpture, graphics, and drawing. Whereas in Zagreb and Belgrade conceptualism emerged almost simultaneously with Western Europe's contributions to the "dematerialization of art," the narrow and specialized elite engaging in theoretical debates on art in Bosnia and Herzegovina continued to struggle over the long-established conflict between "traditionalists" and "modernists."[16] According to art historian Aleksandar Adamović, local discourses on art stood between two competing groups: those who believed that "art should be closely linked with local culture, with a regional spiritual substratum (the most passionate of whom were the neo-romantics of the figurative school), versus their bitter opponents who continued to argue for 'internationalism' and 'contemporaneity.'"[17] Set between these two aesthetic dispositions, developments in local art production were frequently belated, with "popular" fine artists in Bosnia simply copying from Western trends, resulting in an indifferent combination of various artistic styles and traditions. In the words of Zagreb artist Antun Maračić:

> Sarajevo's art scene was marked by the stylistic pastiche of old movements. Elements of pop art, conceptual art and similar trends were aestheticized, along with a specific variant of misunderstandings derived from the use of Byzantine and Renaissance styles. An admiration of Renaissance-Daĺiesque techniques was combined with the charm of pop-artistic letters, conceptual sequences and tailored graphics: all interwoven with Informel tinges. It is this stylistic ruction that results in a fictive hermeticism and terrestrial pathos—in the most ordinary, and extremely valorized, kitsch.[18]

Of course, Bosnia and Herzegovina was not the only republic to be bypassed by the New Art Practice. Art production in the country's southernmost and poorest regions, Macedonia and Kosovo, followed similar patterns of development. As Skopje-based art theorist and curator Suzana Milevska has noted, throughout much of Yugoslavia's existence aesthetic debates in Macedonia continued to center on the issue of whether abstract and geometric art were suited "to traditional art practices . . . in the same way fresco painting, folk-costume embroidery and carpet weaving is."[19] In her view, "'flirtations' with national art and culture never completely disappeared, and were inevitably present even in most locally produced abstract work," because the New Art tendencies that dominated the art scenes of other Yugoslav republics "largely sidestepped the Macedonian art scene."[20] Shkëlzen Maliqi, a prominent philosopher from Kosovo, also observed recently that "visual art in Kosovo developed at a slower rate than in [the rest of] Yugoslavia, because of the scale of the art scene, along with the lack of professional galleries, institutions, criticism, and collectors, as well as a lack of an educated and art-loving public."[21] Like Milevska, he also noted that artists in Kosovo tended to fuse Informel and other international styles with local materials drawn from "daily life and Albanian folk art," and with "themes from Kosovar literature."[22] Although it would be a mistake to assume that this fusion of "socialist modernism" with local or national traditions was prominent only in Yugoslavia's less-developed regions, these retrospective reflections attest to the way regional inequalities played a significant role in the unequal federal distribution of the New Art Practice itself.[23]

Sarajevo had some notable exceptions to this pattern, however. One of the most radical oppositions to what art historian Meliha Husedžinović defined as "established ('middle-class taste') art" was Banja Luka's Četvorica [Group of Four]. Active from 1955 to 1961, in their first text they declared: "We are revolting against the academic inheritance of ideas about the pictorial craft and the functioning of painting in society."[24] In their second, they proclaimed their surroundings in Banja Luka an "aesthetically obsolete province," and complained of experiencing a series of "trials" initiated by local party organizations. Ten years later, in February 1972, members of the group 1+1+1 enacted the first piece of performance art in Sarajevo, at the opening of their group exhibition. Yet these developments were still fixated on "plastic categories," pushing toward an almost "minimalist restraint" and an inclination toward monochrome painting.[25] In 1975, four artists from Banja Luka formed the group Prostor-forma [Space-Form] to protest against the "pathetic rural and pastoral motifs, incomplete visual transcriptions of visual patterns and 'newly composed' folklore of all types which flood the mass media," as well as to oppose the "apathy, languor [and] fossilisation, once and for all, of established values and measures of these values."[26]

According to Aleksandar Adamović, contemporary art in Bosnia had lost a relevant social role at the beginning of the 1970s precisely because it lacked "well-defined substance for its concept":

> Art's so-called social value—its social substance—does not exist. [Contemporary art in Bosnia] has been excluded, first of all, from the process of technological progress, as a crucially important condition for social development, and barely survives in its marginal social position—being relegated instead to the realm of craft. Current criticism reinforces the numerous mystifications of this "craft," by applying aesthetic categories as the only relevant parameters of value.[27]

In other cities, the "classical limits of specialized arts" were surpassed through international manifestations that emphasized interdisciplinarity, experimentation with media, and "deprofessionalizing" art as a practice, including most notably Belgrade's April Meetings, which were even devoted to the theme of "expanded media."[28] The programs and initiatives directed by Students' Cultural Centers in the early 1970s enabled artists in other cities to break with the need to practice fine arts at all and to expand their engagement beyond the fields of painting and sculpture. A city "as much remote from the rest of Yugoslavia as it was from the rest of the world," Sarajevo did not experience the cultural advances secured by such programs, and throughout much of the 1970s did not possess a single gallery that concerned itself with new movements and media.[29]

At the same time, there were a handful of attempts to introduce conceptualism, and a "new kind of reasoning" in art, from other republics, including Azra Begić's valiant organization of an OHO exhibition in 1971. Years later, between 1978 and 1980, one of Sarajevo's rare exhibition spaces, the Collegium Artisticum, hosted a series of workshops, exhibitions, and lectures titled the "New Art Practice."[30] Established in 1975 under the alliance of the Association of Fine Arts, Association of Applied Arts, and the Association of Architects in Bosnia and Herzegovina, the Collegium Artisticum emerged just after Yugoslavia's decentralization of 1974. From its conception, it was intended for art that "was in accordance with the age in which it was created."[31] At first, this constituted a focus on the key protagonists of conceptual art in Yugoslavia, predominantly those who worked in Belgrade and Zagreb.

At the very least, the workshops at the Collegium Artisticum helped the first generation of artists training at Sarajevo's Art Academy realize that their city was missing something that their counterparts in other Yugoslav capitals had

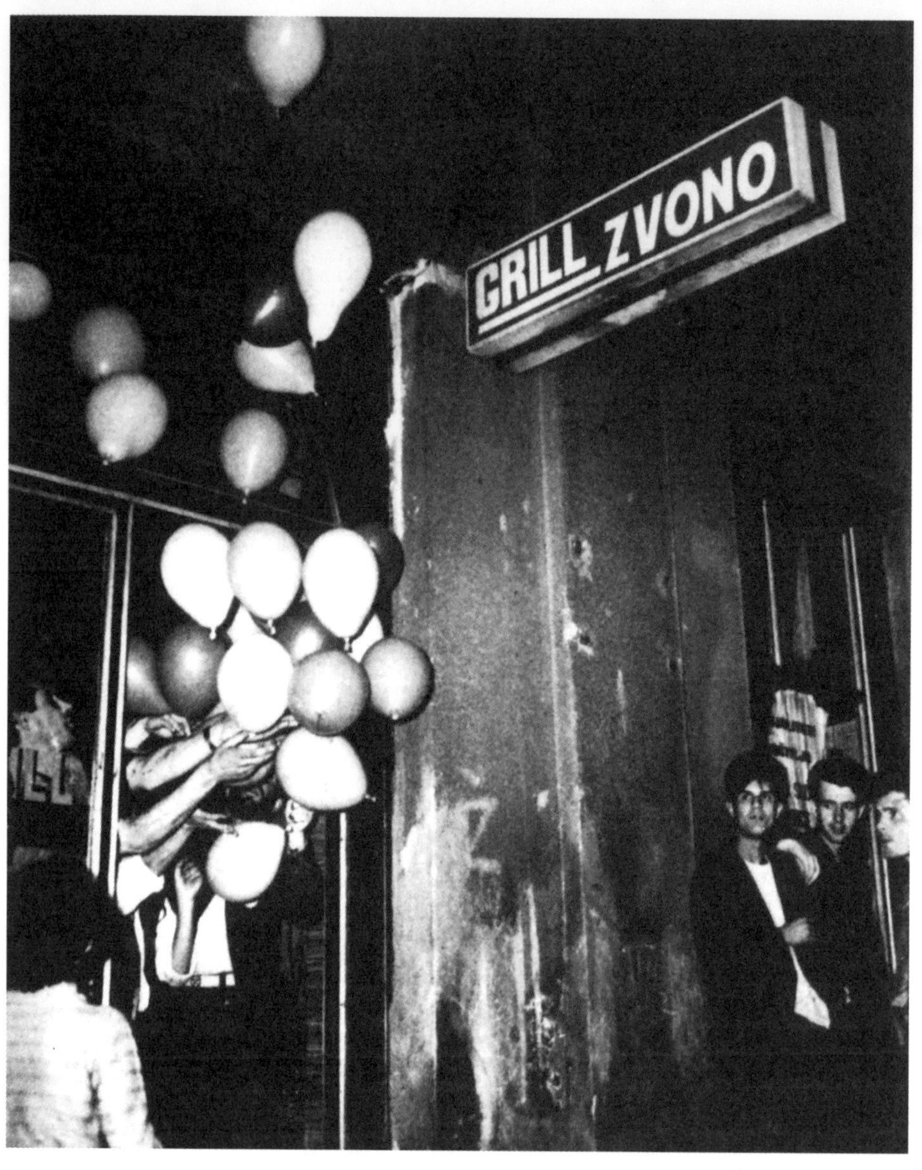

6.1. Café-Gallery Zvono, Sarajevo. Image courtesy of Aleksandar Saša Bukvić.

possessed for almost a decade—namely, a space in which to question the exhibition standards of mainstream institutions, a Students' Cultural Center. Unlike Belgrade and Zagreb, Sarajevo's fine art students did not have a space in which to exhibit while still training. As Aleksandar Saša Bukvić, a sculptor who studied at the city's Art Academy, recalls: "There was an 'unspoken rule' that prevented students from exhibiting publicly … a castrative regulation in the style of 'you are still just learning, but you want to exhibit?'"[32] Nor was there any space where artists could work collectively on projects and programs. Sarajevo did in fact have its own Youth House. Located in the Skenderija Cultural and Sports Center, it officially opened on 29 November 1969 (Republic Day) by hosting the premiere of the most expensive Partisan film ever made in Yugoslavia, *Bitka u Neretvi* [The Battle of Neretva]. But in line with its somewhat servile inauguration, the Youth House continued to be engaged with more populist forms of entertainment, mostly supporting folklore, amateur singing societies, and sports—not "so much a salient cultural center and gathering space for young creators, as it was a venue for entertainment and national music."[33] According to journalist Niazid Ahmić, the initial euphoria and enthusiasm for the Youth House had "deflated like a punctured football, to the point that along with other social clubs in the city, it resembled more of a 'retirement home' than a real cultural institute."[34]

At the beginning of 1979, the owner of a small bar called Zvono [Bell], located between the Skenderija Center and the Academy of Fine Arts, opened the doors of his venue to a young generation of artists training at the academy. Despite his advanced age, Mustafa Alijević—a lover of fine arts, with a "sophisticated taste and ear for youthful ventures"—allowed Jovan Maračić to install his "moth-eaten sound box" in the space and bring his own records to play.[35] With this modest gesture, young students from the fine art and music academies, along with students from the city's Architecture and Philosophy Faculties, gathered together to listen to jazz records. Two months later, students from the art academy began to present their works in the confines of the bar's cramped space.[36] For the first time, artists in Sarajevo no longer had to wait for a special occasion to exhibit and present themselves to the public. A new, self-organized model of artistic engagement in Sarajevo was hatched on the wall of this small local bar—only 40 meters long.

A commonplace "kafana"—a gathering space frequently synonymous in Balkan culture with decay, sloth, backwardness, and sorrow (where one "mourns, drinks, and mourns some more, while slowly contracting tuberculosis from the fumes of cigarettes")—was transformed into an independent and alternative gallery.[37] Previously a dormant space, attracting only "old pensioners" from the local vicinity, Zvono came to represent an extraordinary combination of a bar where one could drink coffee or an alcoholic beverage while exhibiting paintings on the wall. Completely self-financed, the exhibition programs of Zvono were not compromised by external interests. Rather, they were completely motivated by young enthusiasts who, since they earned nothing, had nothing to lose. As one of the café's most devoted volunteers and its eventual leader, Aleksandar Saša Bukvić, explained, "starting from nothing, there was no steam to lose."[38] The gallery's organization was driven above all by spontaneity, and a "small but mighty tempo."[39] Not only was this space smaller and more flexible than larger, established institutions, but as an informal venue, Zvono attracted a public that didn't necessarily go to official galleries and museums. After all, "it was far less intimidating for a passerby to walk into a café than a gallery."[40]

As Nermina Zildžo recalled: "Zvono was phenomenal. We didn't have a club in which we could all gather, talk amongst ourselves, hang out and drink coffee. In the whole of Bosnia and Herzegovina, we didn't have a single Students' Cultural Center."[41] With a new wave of young creators pouring out of the recently established academy, Zvono became a kind of unofficial student art center. For the first time, young artists were being introduced to a wider public. Changing exhibitions on a weekly basis, the space had launched over 550 shows by 1987; its reputation as a leading gallery space in the city had become so well established that not only did professors from the academy begin to show their work there, but also leading proponents of the New Art Practice, including Raša Todosijević and Tomislav Gotovac. The Café-Gallery Zvono had broken the ice. Throughout Sarajevo, the bells of an alternative art activity were beginning to ring.

"IF THE MOUNTAIN WON'T COME TO MUHAMMAD . . ."

It was from the modest organization of the Zvono bar that Sarajevo's most important art group emerged. In April 1982 five artists from Sarajevo's Academy of Fine Arts came together as a group with a desire to directly address the general public. Named after the café in which they frequently gathered, and on whose walls they had their first exhibitions, Zvono consisted of the sculptor Aleksandar Saša Bukvić and the four painters Sead Čizmić, Biljana Gavranović, Sadko Hadžihasanović, and Narcis Kantardžić, with the later addition of photographer Kemal Hadžić. They represented a new generation whose goal was to encourage ordinary people to engage with modern art, concerning themselves with the problem of "equalizing art with everyday life."[42] According to Bukvić, Zvono came from "fairly modest beginnings, thinking about how, as a group, we could attract a larger audience."[43] He continued: "We came to the idea that the only answer was to go out into the streets. It was pretty difficult to get people to enter the galleries to see an exhibition. So we operated on the saying: if the mountain won't come to Muhammad, Muhammad will go to the mountain."[44] These artists came together to communicate with an audience through an art that was accessible to everyone, even those who would only usually enter the gallery as a last resort for "escaping the rain."[45] Exhibiting on the streets and on the walls of cafés was the only means of presenting their ideas to everyone, of encouraging the casual passerby to establish an actual feeling toward art.

What is evident from the existing exhibition catalogues and press clippings from local newspapers is that these artists never stopped working as painters and sculptors, but rather set out to render their practice relevant and accessible to the public. Photographic documentation from their first exhibition on the boulevard of Vase Miskina captures the artists' large paintings installed on easels against the walls of building facades, with others carelessly placed on the ground. On one of Sarajevo's busiest streets, people paused for a moment to inspect the works at a closer glance. In other images, small children stand bewildered before Bukvić's large, curving, tentacle-like sculptures sprouting from the dull, gray pavement, carelessly splattered with spots evocative of Yayoi Kusama's obsessive polka dots. What was important in the first street exhibition was the model of presentation that the artists chose: sculptures left their pedestals and were casually scattered across the concrete slabs of the pedestrian path, to interrupt and intercept the regular ebb and flow of the city's circulation. They became interactive as people were able, and even encouraged, to touch the surfaces of these alien objects. In another photograph, the artists are shown distributing pamphlets to casual passersby, made to accompany the contents of the street exhibition. The photographs capture the artists' enthusiastic engagement with the public—their actions were not an attempt to change their practice as painters and sculptors, but rather were meant to act as a reflection on their status as artists, and on the potential ways that art could be involved more directly in the social environment. This simple realization paved the way for Zvono's future activities. In the words of Sadko Hadžihasanović:

> After the first exhibition in Vase Miskina, we realized that we could communicate directly with the public, with the ordinary citizen. Then we said: okay, we'll do everything that hasn't hitherto been done in Bosnia; everything that needs to be done. All the media which were formed in the world but which weren't practiced here, we need to experiment with ... which is why we did performances amongst other things. We used media that existed thirty years before us, but the ideas were totally unique, authentic and indigenous to this area. We always consciously wanted to have an idea that emerged from this region, but the media was what tied us to the international art scene.[46]

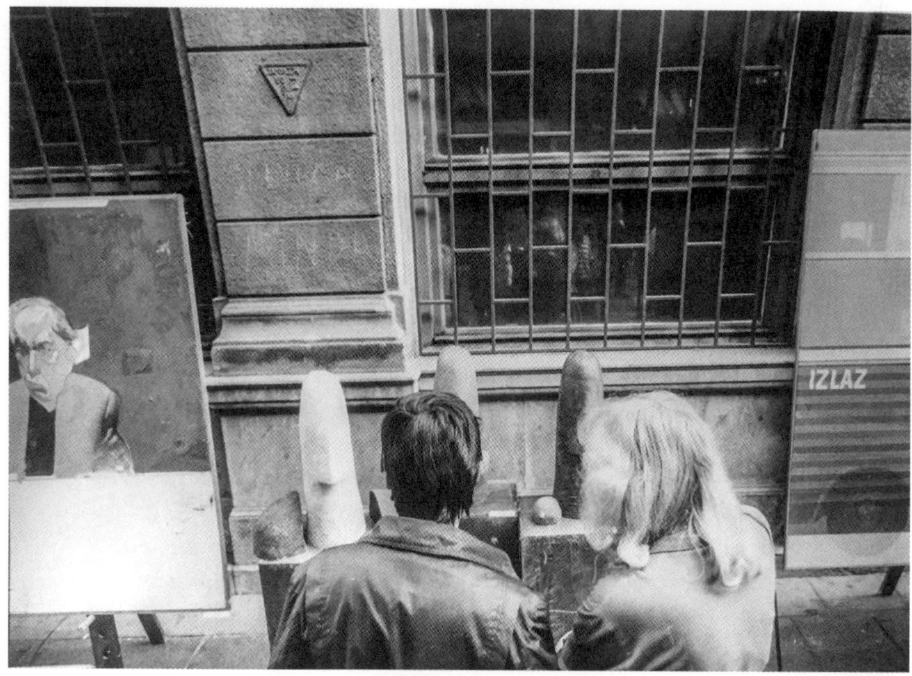
IZLAZ

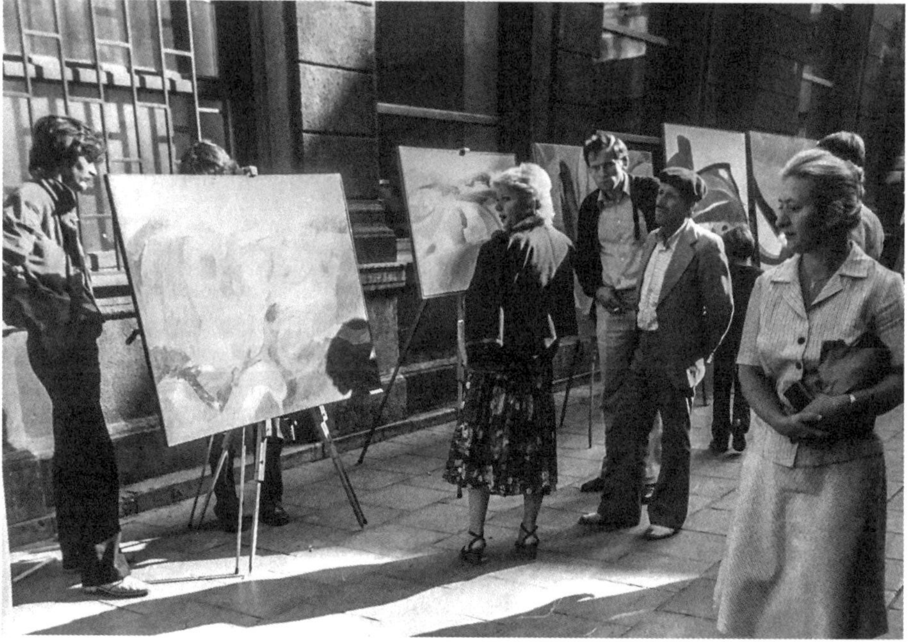

In the first stage of their activities, Zvono reserved their right to exhibit outside of established institutions, on the streets and in cafés. Very quickly, their practice expanded to the exploration of intertwining "traditional" and "new" methods of expression, irrespective of their academic orientation.

In several respects, such ambitions echoed those of Yugoslavia's preceding self-organized collectives, such as Zagreb's Group of Six Authors, who through their Exhibition-Actions similarly sought to supersede institutional limitations: to establish an art that identified its illustrations with the immediate environment and engaged with ordinary citizens. As with the Group of Six Authors, Zvono was formed with no strict postulates or rigid rules: the artists did not uphold a coherent, common aesthetic program, but held independent views while showing their work together. Their only common denominator was their opposition to traditional and institutional approaches to presenting art.

By 1982, the concept of working in a group might have appeared anachronistic, considering the number of Yugoslav collectives that had ended in bitter disagreement, dejection, and dissolution, including OHO, Grupa KÔD, and the informal group centered around Belgrade's *Oktobar '75*. Two years before Zvono's emergence, Zagreb's Working Community of Artists had stopped working together precisely because they refused to have a common program, with the end of the initiative marking, according to Ljiljana Kolešnik, an end to "all utopian projections of art as a vehicle of social changes."[47] Zvono was, moreover, established in the same year that IRWIN first appeared in Ljubljana, as an initiative that had consciously opted for a model of organization based on anonymity and collectivism, motivated by the eclecticism of the "retro-principle." But beyond these obvious distinctions, there was one unifying element between Yugoslavia's two newly formed art collectives. According to Bukvić, both were conceived on the grounds of "pushing out a single idea."[48] If IRWIN was established to analyze the formative moments of local (Slovene) culture—to render visible the ways in which local art production was frequently belated, by eclectically addressing the history of Slovenian art—the members of Zvono had similarly come together to address their local cultural situation. In a city without an understanding of art outside the paradigms of painting and sculpture, Zvono set themselves the task of changing the position of visual arts in Bosnia.

6.2. and 6.3. Zvono's street exhibition on Vase Miskina, Sarajevo, 1982. Images courtesy of Sadko Hadžihasanović.

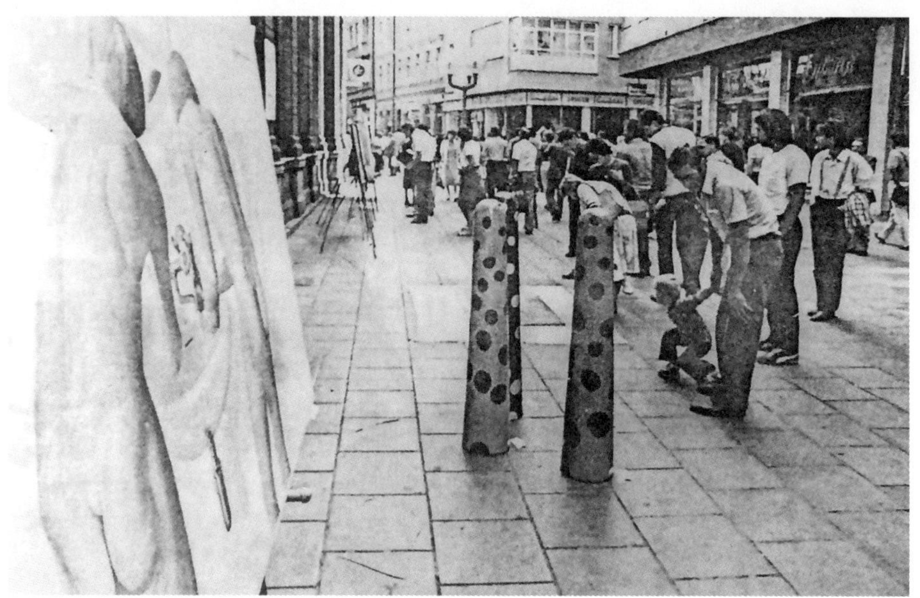

6.4. Aleksandar Saša Bukvić's sculptures at the street exhibition on Vase Miskina, Sarajevo, 1982. Image courtesy of the artist.

Yet the characteristics that united these two newly formed collectives also differentiated them. IRWIN emerged alongside a series of liberalizing initiatives in Slovenia, which, as the previous chapter showed, supported alternative culture from the mid-1980s. As part of the effort to build up the republic's profile as a beacon for democratization, this official support of alternative culture enabled artists to position themselves in relation to institutions. This official support would in turn lead to the eventual mainstreaming of the "alternative." In contrast, Zvono was self-reliant and financially self-sufficient, and operated in an artistic climate that lacked both a developed art market and any substantial state investment. For this reason, they faced challenges similar to the first generation of artists affiliated with the New Art Practice, who also felt as though they were working under the conditions of an "interestless space." As Sanja Iveković explained retrospectively, Yugoslavia's new generation of artists connected with Students' Cultural Centers had applied "an artistic language that was so radically new that the audience was really limited."[49] Zvono faced the same challenges felt by their predecessors. In a city where, according to Bukvić, "anyone who tried to do something different got smacked on the head" and lacked role models to emulate, Zvono set as their goal invigorating and awakening the existing foundations of the local art scene.[50]

In the summer of 1983 the group moved to the Ukrina Valley near Dervent, to experiment outside of the urban environment. There they made some of the first performance art in Bosnia and Herzegovina, including the sequence *Obitelj na vikendu* [Family on the Weekend], for which members of the group wrapped themselves in thick layers of toilet paper, until their bodies completely disappeared under thick white exoskeletons, packaged and bound by string. They renounced their corporeality in order to become absurd statues, standing listlessly behind their folding deck chairs like foreign intrusions in untamed and natural surroundings. The extensive documentation produced for this project suggests that the artists were using themselves to produce a kind of "synthesis between the domains of body art and fine art": positioning themselves as subjects in space with an emphasis on composition, on the symmetry of the arrangement, on their relation to water, to rocks, to the vegetation.[51] Yet, in a way, the action also evoked the legacy of the New Art Practice's "great-grandfathers," OHO, in its rejection of traditional techniques in favor of a new sensibility in experiencing the natural environment. *Family on the Weekend* represented a departure from a tradition burdened with meaning, just as much of OHO's practice was based on noticing and observing things as they "are," rather than through their function or man-made meanings. The critic Pavle Pavlović understood the work through this

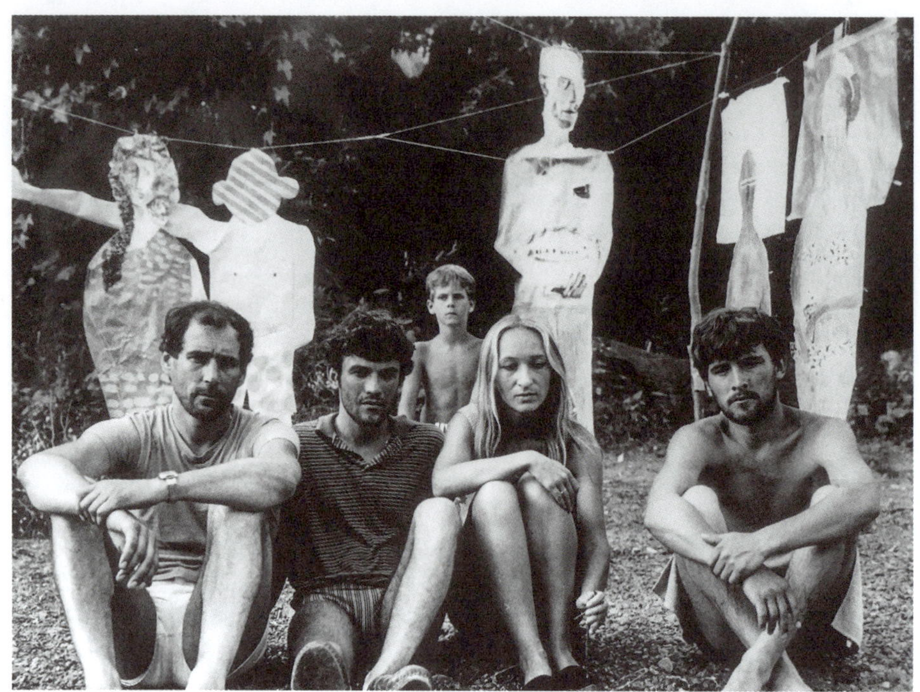

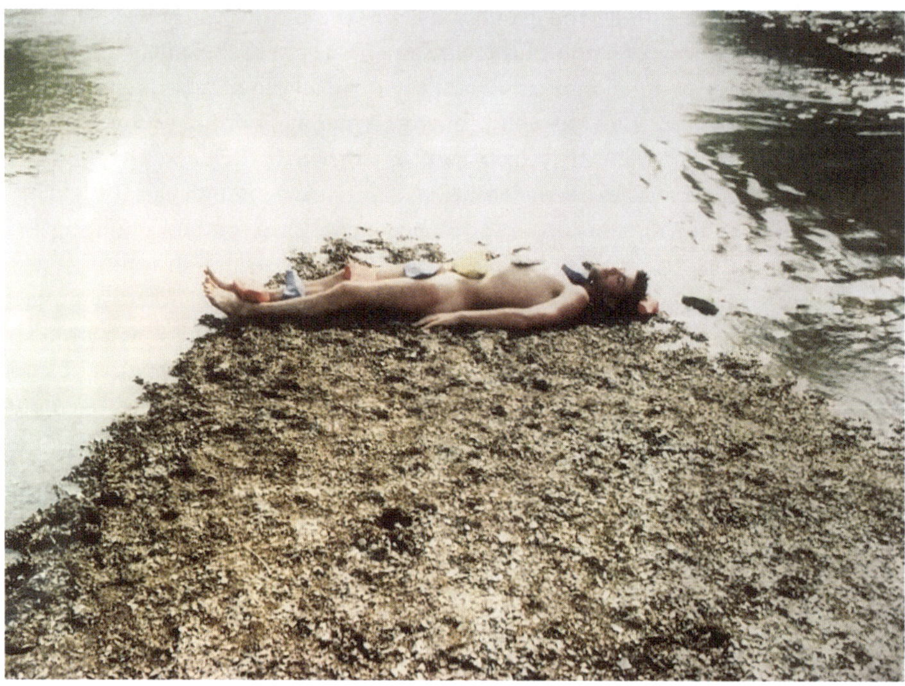

interpretive frame, as critiquing "urban man's alienation from nature. But with time, those shackles of urbanization in man wane, as he becomes closer to the natural environment: the liberation symbolized by the artists' gradual emancipation from their paper bones."[52] *Family on the Weekend* introduced an element of play and spontaneity as a counterpoint to the "alienation of people between one another, toward art, and nature."[53]

While Zvono continued to work within the domains of painting and sculpture, they aimed to shake up the passive relationship of art toward local realities. As in Zagreb, their provocations placed the artist in the role of an agitator, concerned no longer with producing works for museums, but with making art for and within society. In 1985, for instance, the group conceived one of their most well-known actions, *Izlog* [Shop Window], first performed as part of Belgrade's Yugoslav Meetings of Youth, and then in other cities throughout the federation. In the display window of Belgrade's largest department store, Beograd (situated on the city's busiest pedestrian street, Knez Mihailova), the artists stood completely still, transforming themselves into mannequins. Dressed in their own clothes, each artist assumed a certain pose and maintained it until the end of the store's opening hours. In doing so, they simultaneously placed themselves in the roles of a passive, silent witness and an object of observation—a subject who observes others from behind the glass pane of the display window, while also being observed. Hundreds of people stood in line to inspect these living mannequins. Making themselves the objects of scrutiny to an audience that didn't necessarily have a prerequisite knowledge of art, Zvono's action required a certain kind of bravery. In the words of Bukvić:

> It's not easy to stand, for example, in a display as we recently did. It isn't easy when you know that your neighbors and acquaintances pass through there, and it looks like a total circus to some people. But at least we know we've interested them—they see that something is happening. There, instead of some painted mannequins, they found themselves looking at living people in ordinary clothes. We showed that man's relation to, in this instance, clothing, is completely unnatural. Our city continues to waste its time with experiences in art that occurred over a hundred years ago, and that is what we want to change. Our group isn't fighting against people, but rather blocked perceptions.[54]

6.5. and 6.6. Zvono, *Obitelj na vikendu* [Family on the Weekend], 1983. Images courtesy of Sadko Hadžihasanović.

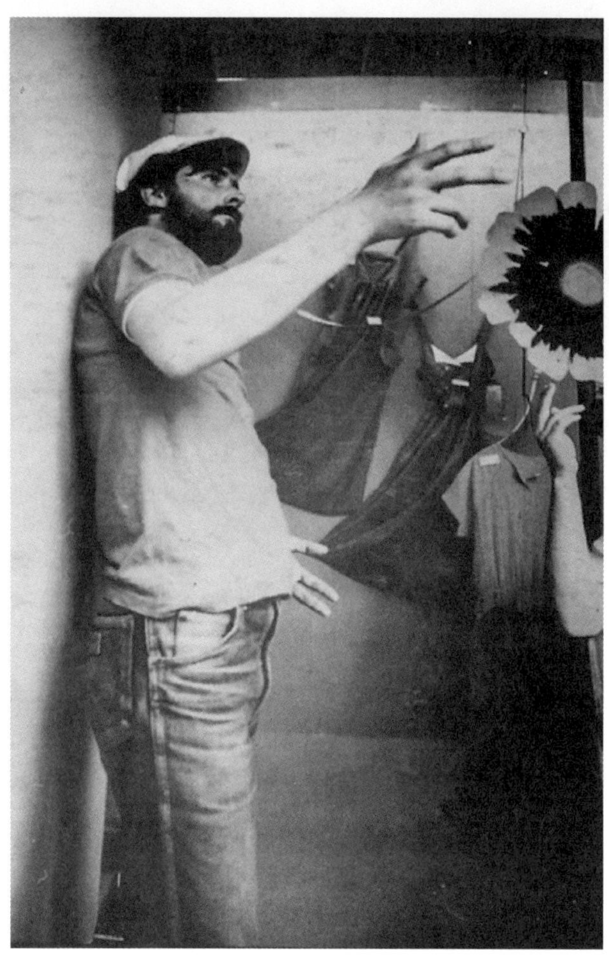

6.7. Zvono, *Izlog* [Shop Window], Belgrade, 1985. Image courtesy of Aleksandar Saša Bukvić.

Fighting against “blocked perceptions” involved reexamining notions of art in Bosnia and Herzegovina. It also called for an approach that was characterized by the principle of “serious play.” Zvono’s engagement lacked pretension and acted as a rejection of the more conservative values of the older generation of established artists. The group humorously toyed with art historical references and took an ironic stance toward what one contemporary critic called the “mystical arrogance of ‘large and serious’ art.”[55] In a performance from 1986 called *Passage through Painting* (also referred to as *Akcija Mondrian* [Mondrian Action]), the group placed a large screen of paper, evocative of Japanese folding screens, so that it completely obstructed a pedestrian sidewalk in the city center. Painted on the panels was one of Mondrian’s instantly recognizable and characteristic *Compositions*. To the confusion of passersby, the members began to forcefully walk through and tear the surface of the screen, opening up narrow incisions in the paper’s thin and delicate structure. Pedestrians were caught in a dilemma: whether or not to participate in ripping through this obstacle, and consequently violate the traditionally sheltered space of art. Almost immediately, several people joined in the destruction of the work, resulting in its complete “dematerialization.” Mondrian’s motif was shredded and torn into unrecognizable fragments of colored paper.

In a sense, *Mondrian Action* employed an approach to copying similar to that developed by Goran Đorđević, who in 1983 also copied a Mondrian painting in Belgrade’s National Museum, by simply placing an easel in the public institution and patiently replicating the image while a guard looked on. In Đorđević’s conceptually sophisticated gesture, copying was used to subvert the role of the author and artist, and to accentuate the tension between the original and the copy. Here, the copy superseded the significance of the original. With Zvono, copying was employed as an accompaniment to performance, and art history was referenced in order to ultimately bring art closer to a local public that might not possess an affinity for it. As *Mondrian Action* was realized only through the act of its own destruction, it represented an ironic mockery of the passive reception of modernist trends in the city. Mondrian was reactivated in a performative gesture aimed at creating an art that spoke to the person who was on the receiving end of it all—the ordinary citizen.

Above all, Zvono’s street exhibitions and group performances were steered by the principles of spontaneity and “unpretentious philosophy games.”[56] In 1986, Saša Bukvić, who before joining Zvono had been well known in Sarajevo as a pastry chef at both his father’s bakery and the Zvono café, decided to combine his

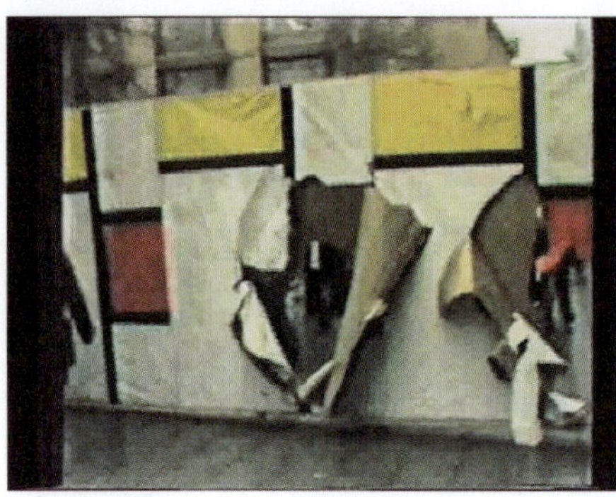

6.8. Zvono, *Akcija Mondrian* [Passage through Painting], Sarajevo, 1985. Image courtesy of Aleksandar Saša Bukvić.

6.9. Goran Đorđević, *Kako kopirati Mondrijana* [How to Copy a Mondrian], National Museum, Belgrade, 1983. Image courtesy of the artist.

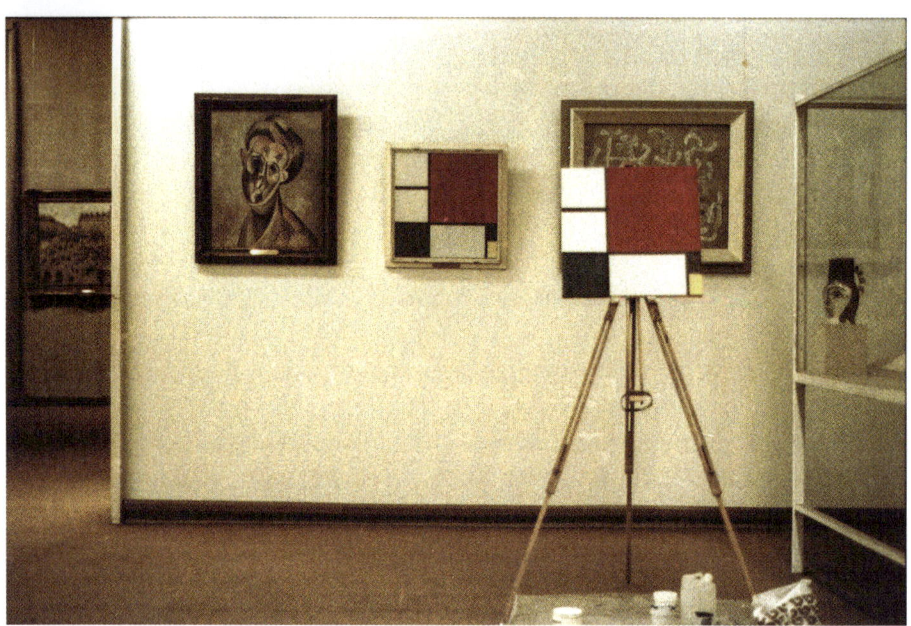

occupation as an academically trained sculptor with his experiences as an artisan-confectioner. At a retrospective exhibition marking four years of the group's activity, held at the Collegium Artisticum, he presented a sculpture embellished with flowers in the form of Tatlin's *Monument to the Third International,* while serving edible chocolate cakes to visitors. The *Wedding Cake à la Tatlin* transformed a symbol of the avant-garde into a sweet delicacy; referencing the tradition of constructivist sculpture and a symbol of utopian thought, it debased it into something traditionally served at celebrations—Tatlin's monumental iron skeleton now adorned and decorated with bulbous flowers. The only characteristic aligning these two disparate objects was their tall, tiered, and pyramidal constructions, along with their titles. In a sense, *Wedding Cake* is a distant evocation of Claes Oldenburg's body of work *The Store*, which similarly redefined the relationships between painting and sculpture and between subject and form, featuring brightly painted sculptures and sculptural reliefs shaped to evoke commercial products and comestibles—ice cream, oranges, cigarettes, hats, shoes—all things that could be found in surrounding stores. In *The Store*, Oldenburg hawked commonplace objects out of a storefront for two months, declaring in his famous manifesto that "I am for the art that a kid licks, after peeling away the wrapper. I am for an art that is smoked, like a cigarette, smells, like a pair of shoes. I am for an art that flaps like a flag, or helps blow noses, like a handkerchief. I am for an art that is put on and taken off, like pants, which develops holes, like socks, which is eaten, like a piece of pie."[57]

Bukvić's cake took Oldenburg's proposition one step further, by producing an art that *was* a "piece of cake." Playing on the local idiom *tatlı*—meaning "sweet" in Turkish—the *Tatlin Cake* registered sympathy for local everyday traditions, and marked a youthful turning point in Yugoslavia's art scene. There is an extremely blasphemous and petty-bourgeois element to Bukvić's sculpture—a kind of opposition to the hierarchy of values that had until then been sustained by art practitioners in Bosnia and Herzegovina, which further behaved as a humorous distancing from the seriousness and conviction associated with historical avant-gardes.

In the same year, IRWIN produced a stage replica of Tatlin's *Monument to the Third International* for the Scipion Nasice Sisters Theatre's "retro-garde event" *Krst pod Triglavom* [Baptism under Triglav], presented on the stage of Cankarjev Dom, the large conference and arts center in Ljubljana. Like IRWIN and Laibach, the theater group anchored their approach to existing symbols and motifs, basing the *Baptism under Triglav* on the poem "Krst pri Savici" [Baptism at the Savica Waterfall] by the Slovenian romantic poet France Prešeren. The replica of Tatlin's monument appeared on the stage at the beginning of the production. In the

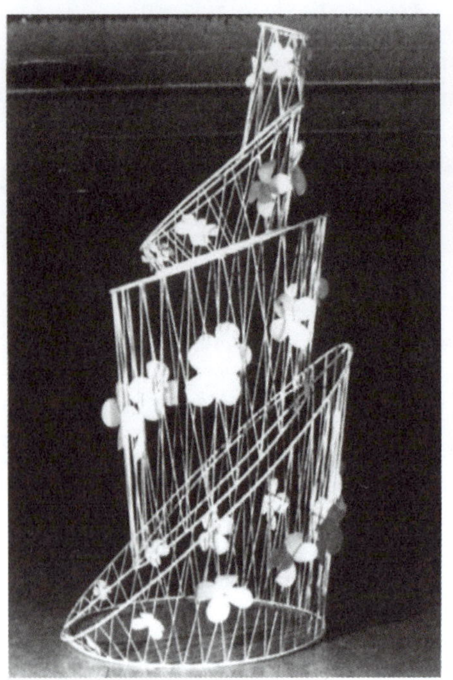

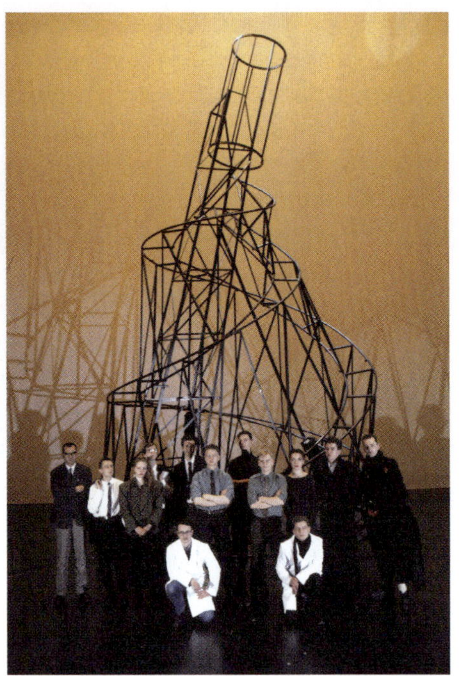

6.10. Aleksandar Saša Bukvić, *Wedding Cake à la Tatlin*, Sarajevo, 1986. Image courtesy of the artist.

6.11. A group portrait of NSK members in front of the model of Tatlin's Tower from the Scipion Nasice Sisters Theatre production *Krst pod Triglavom* [Baptism under Triglav], Ljubljana, 1986. Photograph by Marko Modic. Image courtesy of Moderna Galerija, Ljubljana.

words of Aleš Erjavec, what followed was a detached presentation of the "conflict between the church and the main character and his beloved, exposing the incessant power play between the state (or church) and the individual, whether an artist or a free spirit."[58] In *Baptism under Triglav*, IRWIN's "retro-principle" was enforced through the eclectic use of works by other artists, reinterpreted within a markedly Slovenian context. Ultimately, they recontextualized the symbols of historical avant-gardes to establish an authentic Slovene art, proclaiming: "There exists Greek, German, French art and not art in itself. Our art will be the better the more Slovenian it will be."[59] Given this commitment to "Slovenian" culture, it is not surprising that the Slovenian government chose to financially support this theater spectacle—the most expensive in Yugoslavia to date, costing over 30 million dinars—and allocated it the largest convention center in Ljubljana.[60] This was, after all, the time when the Slovenian youth organizations' ideas about civil society were gaining support from their elders, who had their own political interests. As Yugoslavia's economy continued to spin out of control and deadlock began to set in, *Baptism under Triglav* was financed in a republic where politicians were increasingly campaigning against all manifestations of federal power and expenditure, and Slovenia's economic options with neighboring markets were multiplying.

Compared to the Scipion Nasice Sisters Theatre's "retro-garde" performance, Zvono's projects seem considerably less sophisticated and politically agile. Yet, while Zvono's approach did not share the majority of the criteria implicit in IRWIN's "retro-principle," their work similarly imported historical motifs to validate the local cultural climate, and aimed to establish "an idea which emerged from this region," "totally unique, authentic and indigenous to this area."[61] In all of Zvono's performances and actions there is an overarching sense of the carnivalesque (or "folk humor"), defined by Bakhtin as a type of performance that is fundamentally communal, creating a situation in which diverse voices are heard and interact to break down conventions and enable genuine dialogue.[62] In Bakhtin's frequently cited words, the carnivalesque

> does not know footlights, in the sense that it does not acknowledge any distinction between actors and spectators.... Carnival is not a spectacle seen by the people; they live in it, and everyone participates because its very idea embraces all the people.... During carnival there is a temporary suspension of all hierarchic distinctions and barriers among men and of certain norms and prohibitions of usual life.[63]

In a city that was for decades seen as being incapable of offering anything substantial to the wider Yugoslav cultural community, Zvono fostered an art that was "modern" in its engagement and modes of display, but also "local" in its understanding of its audience. Setting themselves the goal of encouraging ordinary people to engage with contemporary art, and guiding Sarajevo to develop an actual feeling for art, they wanted art to have the same kind of visibility and influence that popular culture had locally. In the words of Bukvić:

> Just as soap, jeans, and the new records of Šemsa Suljaković [a popular Bosnian folk singer] are all advertised on television, and like people need frozen desserts, shampoo, or Marinko Rokvić [a Serbian folk singer], I think that they also need art. That's why for our retrospective exhibition we recorded an advertisement which isn't far from the video of a rock group. Since our primary objective is the same—to climb to the top of the pyramid. The only difference is in our areas of activity.[64]

By disseminating their ideas through video and television, Zvono were the first group of artists in Bosnia to open a space for new and unconventional media in the sphere of visual arts. In 1986 they carried out their most ambitious public action—*Sport i art* [Sport and Art]—in collaboration with TV Sarajevo. During a football game between FK Sarajevo and Dinamo Zagreb at the Koševo Stadium, the artists dressed up in the uniforms of the home team and dashed out onto the stadium field. They proceeded to set up their easels on the pitch, applying a few extra brushstrokes to completed paintings, and finally ran around the stadium track with their canvases lifted triumphantly over their heads, like trophies. For fifteen minutes, the shouts and cries of over twenty thousand stunned football fans, which could not clearly be deciphered as either approval or indignation, resonated through the stadium. Through a daring and fearless gesture, the artists had succeeded in transforming a football match into a communal art event. The action was filmed and later broadcast on television.

In a sense, *Sport and Art* alluded to the disproportionate way that sport and art were treated, echoing the SC Gallery's last issue of its *Newspaper*, which was ironically dedicated to sport (because "it is easier to gather money for sports," while the lack of special "monographs or 'collected works' is compensated for by newspapers and magazines that provide detailed and extensive daily reports from sports fields").[65] Zvono chose to challenge these social hierarchies directly, in situ. In a city with a strong affection for sport, having been host to the Winter Olympics (the first to be organized in a socialist country) two years prior to the event, Zvono had found the most effective means to make their voices as artists heard. *Sport and Art* shows the degree to which Zvono engaged with video and

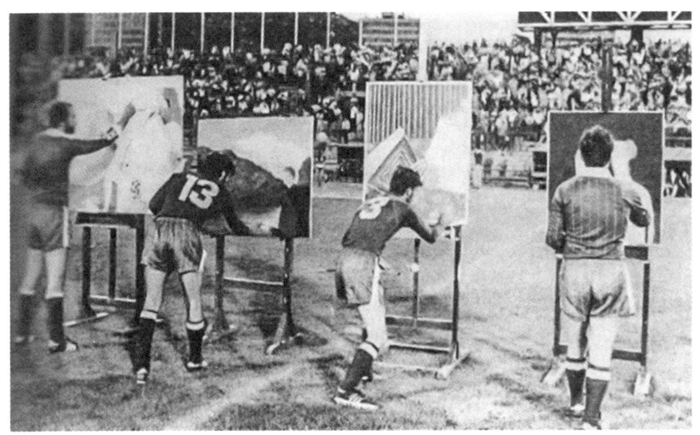

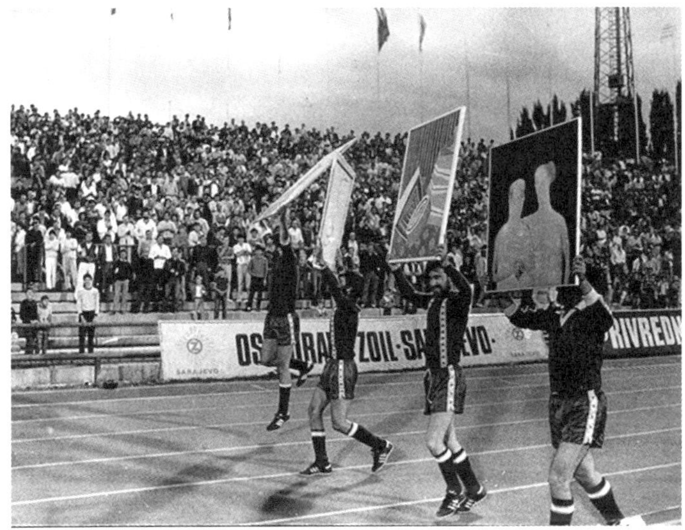

6.12. and 6.13. Zvono, *Sport i art* [Sport and Art], Sarajevo, 1986. Images courtesy of Aleksandar Saša Bukvić.

performance in an entirely fresh way, one that emerged organically from the spirit of the city in which they were practicing.

While Zvono employed media and methods that were by no means new, as they had been common in the global art scene for a long time, the group did pave the way for a new sensibility that was vital for later generations of artists in Bosnia and Herzegovina. As Miljenko Jergović elaborated: "If nothing else, thanks to Zvono, no one today is bothered or shocked with what younger artists are doing in Sarajevo."[66] Zvono exhibited the most radical behavior seen in the postwar art of Bosnia and Herzegovina up to that time: "It [was] as if these artists set out from the supposition that everything that didn't actually happen in our history of modern art can be compensated for in one furious, panther-like, gesture."[67]

"LONG LIVE THE ELECTRIFICATION OF THE VILLAGE!"

By the mid-1980s, Zvono had become one of the leading art collectives in Yugoslavia. Known throughout the entire federation, their presence was significant in paving the way for Sarajevo's cultural visibility. Yet they were not alone in countering the domination of other cultural centers. Instead, their activities paralleled other subcultural phenomena that were simultaneously occurring in Sarajevo, including the city's famous New Primitives.[68] As with Zvono's "new artistic sensibility," the New Primitives emerged as a self-organized subcultural group that were inspired by their immediate sociocultural environment. The movement's initial impetus was in reaction to the complacent imitation of Western cultural trends in the city. According to Gregor Tomc, the New Primitive argued that "if Americans have T-shirts with 'enjoy Coca-Cola' logos, why can't we have the same t-shirt with a picture of *burek* and the logo 'enjoy *burek*' below."[69] So the New Primitives ate *ćevapčići* instead of hamburgers, drank plum brandy and not whisky, and wore shirts from Elegant of Srebrenica instead of Lacoste T-shirts.[70] As Elvis J. Kurtović, the father of New Primitivism, explained, "The movement has emerged out of pure sociological analysis of the Jalijaš [Sarajevo's 'felons without a cause']."[71] It was modeled on the people "who gather on the corners of Sarajevo streets, are always in groups of ten or so, always walk together, and are not afraid of anyone"; the New Primitives "call each other 'friend' and shout slogans like 'long live electrification of the village,' not being embarrassed by their primitive roots. They have neighborly warmth, deep humanness [sic] and immediacy in communicating with others. They detest the West except for their *gastarbeiter* brothers, hate Western singers, actors, and politicians."[72]

The movement's name was suspended between mock reactions to two contemporary cultural developments: New Romanticism in global pop music and, more locally, Ljubljana's Neue Slowenische Kunst. Set between these two cultural currents, New Primitivism was, on the one hand, a clear reference in opposition to the staged artificiality of the New Romantics, and, on the other, an emphasis on the stereotypes encountered in many jokes about Bosnians and Slovenians: the former portrayed as unrefined, dim-witted, and open-hearted, and the latter understood as stiff, serious, and distant. While NSK, and particularly Laibach, had incorporated quasi-fascist iconography (which resembled that of the first generation of British punks) to produce the first authentic cultural phenomenon in Slovenia in the 1980s, the New Primitives wanted to demystify the city's national complex, which was driven in part by misconceptions of it by other cultural centers. Though clearly very divergent phenomena, according to Nermina Zildžo, both were based on an exaggeration of aspirations as a means of understanding the official cultural situation—the New Primitives confronting Sarajevo's "Eastern guilt," and NSK unveiling Slovenia's repressed "Germanic frustrations."[73] According to Nele Karajlić, one of the most famous musicians associated with the movement, the only difference between New Primitivism and NSK was the fact that "'old primitivism' existed, while the 'old slowenische kunst' never had."[74] Speaking in retrospect, Kurtović similarly explained:

> I didn't invent New Primitivism. At the time I thought something like this: I walk down the street and I see a guy who is into New Romanticism, and there is someone else right behind him dressed simply dreadfully.... We have a name for the first one, but what do we call the other one? I just gave a name to an already existing subcultural group—the New Primitives.[75]

While Kurtović insisted that the movement was just an exaggerated celebration of local cultural traits, its veneration of local customs was always executed with an element of irony. Consisting mostly of rock musicians, this subcultural segment came from Sarajevo's most urban district, Koševo, and was predominantly drawn from educated, middle-class families. As children, they had listened to rock music and were able to afford electric instruments. Still, they came into contact with the more "traditional" culture of their working-class neighbors, and were equipped with both the necessary cultural distance and sympathy for the "traditional." As one anonymous observer explained: "Although Elvis does not identify with the people he depicts, he has a great love for them. He does not adopt their axiology and as a result never himself becomes primitive. He is a New Primitive. He refuses to succumb to any cheap effect and is disgusted at the thought of subordinating to the masses. He is a 'populist elitist.'"[76]

Being a "populist elitist" presupposed that one revitalized the existing local mentality, while escaping local stereotypes of degeneracy. It meant rendering the "local" as a focus of popular culture for a new generation of Sarajevan youth. Driven by a group of people "with an urban mentality, without complexes of rural origins," New Primitivism began with the premise that if Sarajevo and Bosnia at large did not possess any (significant) popular-cultural past, inventing one rested on taking over the entire history of Western pop-rock music and interpreting it as "Bosnian" and, more specifically, "Sarajevan" pop-rock history.[77] The most significant band of the movement was Zabranjeno Pušenje [No Smoking], whose debut album, *Das ist Walter* [This is Walter], of April 1984 served as a declaration of the New Primitives' celebration of the local. Appropriating the last line from *Walter Defends Sarajevo*, the album's title cast Walter—the force of resistance, and the spirit of the whole city—as an expression of local authenticity, with the record's cover featuring a panoramic view of the city. The album's biggest hit was a version of Johnny Cash's song "Folsom Prison Blues," titled "Zenica Blues," which told the story of a man who was given a twelve-year prison sentence for murder in the city of Zenica, just north of Sarajevo. The song's significance rested on the fact that it engaged with themes previously unknown in Yugoslav rock music—murder and a murderer's fate, told through a sincere and direct language. Zabranjeno Pušenje played straightforward rock, while their lyrics spoke of their marginalized friends using the local slang. As the former lead singer known as Dr. Nele Karajlić said of the band in 1989: "Zabranjeno pušenje is a band of the first New Primitive calibre.... It is the first precise shot from Sarajevo since Gavrilo Princip.... If Maxim Gorky were alive today, he would play guitar in Zabranjeno pušenje."[78]

The general spirit of the New Primitives was driven by a liberation from foreign influence. Fueled by an apparent anti-intellectualism, it sought to base itself on the spirit of the ordinary Bosnian, and located itself outside of the cultural mainstream. The movement was credited with introducing the jargon of Sarajevo's *mahalas* [neighborhoods]—brimming with slang and Turkish loan words—to the wider Yugoslav public scene. It overcame the environment in which it originated and was accepted throughout Yugoslavia in an unprecedented manner. As Jergović observes, it was "a general cultural emancipatory movement that was supposed to rid the Bosnians of their eternal inferiority complex toward Zagreb and Belgrade."[79] Manipulating the prejudices toward Bosnians, in the words of Meliha Husedžinović: "It succeeded in throwing out the long-term cultural colonization of Bosnia and Herzegovina in practically one stroke."[80]

THE NEW PRIMITIVE ART OF JUSUF HADŽIFEJZOVIĆ

In 1984, the artist Jusuf Hadžifejzović arrived in Sarajevo in the midst of its new creative spirit.[81] Entering the shared physical and spiritual space of the Zvono Group—the Zvono Bar—he brought with him a set of completely different analytical and theoretical issues, and a different sociological dimension for reassessing the artist's role and function in society. Hadžifejzović had previously studied at the Sarajevo Secondary School for the Arts between 1971 and 1976. After leaving the city, he had tried to take advantage of everything the international art scene had to offer—studying at Belgrade's Academy of Fine Art (where he was active in the circle of artists associated with the SKC Gallery), followed by postgraduate studies from 1982 to 1984 at the National Fine Arts Academy in Düsseldorf in the class of Klaus Rinke. Already during his education in Belgrade, the artist had shown interest in analytical or "primary" painting. By the end of the 1970s, however, his main activity was rooted in performance and a special type of installation, which he called the "depot." In his "depots," Hadžifejzović exhibited and arranged works that had been kept in the vaults and storage of official cultural institutions, often omitted from public view for political reasons. In the words of Bojana Pejić, the artist intended to systematically air the museums' "dirty laundry."[82] Referring to museum storages, the "depot" series—each named after the city in which it took place—was intended to expose the operations of Yugoslavia's state-financed art system, and to examine the local economic and political situations. Taking on the role of archaeologist, Hadžifejzović employed his "depots" to examine storage procedures and consequently "detect" the identity of places.

In 1984, Hadžifejzović realized his first ever "depot" at Sarajevo's city hall, where he exhibited the wooden boxes used to pack works by Yugoslav artists when they represented the country abroad. In addition to the artists' names, the labels on the boxes also contained the names of ambassadors in nonaligned countries. Taking the art museum as a political, rather than cultural, center of distribution, Hadžifejzović revealed how artists were manipulated by political elites, placing this subservient relationship on display. Those items instrumentalized for political ends, such as the boxes, were placed beside objects that belonged to individuals. On the marble columns of the city hall's reception area, the artist taped bread, vegetables, his own clothes, stones, and a chair. On one of the hall's plinths he exhibited a loaf of bread, stabbed with several cooking knives, piercing through the crust into the dough's soft core. According to Belgrade critic Ješa Denegri, in the monumental and enduring city hall Hadžifejzović wanted to "showcase the ephemeral fruits of nature and handmade products, as codes not to be rationally

NEW PRIMITIVE ART JUSUFA HADŽIFEJZOVIĆA

predmeti kao što su glasačke kutije, uvezani »službeni listovi«, tube za diplome, prozorsko okno umrljano žbukom, crvene krpe, gipsani odljevci velikih očiju, komadi ugljena... u autorovoj postavi predstavljaju bastardnu formu između religioznih i političkih inscenacija.

Duže je već izvjesna pojava neobičnih kulturnih zbivanja u glavnom gradu Bosne i Hercegovine. Na području rock glazbe javljaju se atraktivna ostvarenja, da bi se u posljednjih nekoliko godina dogodila prava provala identiteta i samosvijesti. Riječ je, naravno o pojavi »novog primitivizma«, a posebno o »Zabranjenom pušenju«, grupi koja u svojoj agresivnosti i lucidnosti naglašava domaću rustikalnost, sadržaje i žargon. Robusnosti i ekstrovertiranosti rocka, oni su pridružili robusnost vlastite naravi, ponosno ističući njenu neprilagođenost: sevdah-sentiment uz brzopletost čaršije, istočnjačku inerciju, karakteristični patriotizam, specifičnost jezičnog idioma, ukratko lokalni »primitivizam«. Naravno, ta se afirmacija lokalnog genija ne odvija bez određene distance; u protivnom se ne bi radilo o fenomenu koji ima moć takvog prodora i sposobnost uznemiravanja. Oni su ambasadori »primitivizma«, ali ne i ignoranti: oni barataju medijem, posjeduju znanje kao i rafinirani osjećaj za parafrazu. Upravo sposobnošću integracije postojećih modela, s vlastitom osjećajnošću i temom oni uspijevaju iznenaditi novošću. Drugi bitni element ovog duhovnog trenda je Kusturičin film. Mada bi bilo previše mehanički podvesti njegova ostvarenja pod jednostavnu sintagmu »novog primitivizma« (i inače, čitav je taj termin previše lakonski, sam po sebi ironičan mada ne i neadekvatan) neosporno je da se suštinski radi o manifestaciji istog duha. Lokalna je intonacija (karakter, životni stil, humana boja) uvjerljivošću svog motiva uspjela uspostaviti dominaciju nad upotrebljenim poznatim modelima iz filmske povijesti. Kusturica je modele Felinija, Formana ili Vigoa prepoznao kao općeljudski izraz, a ne kao trade mark jednog podneblja i njegovog pojedinog interpreta. Upravo tako, on uspijeva izolirati jednu općenitu dimenziju u kontempliranju lokalnog mentaliteta i zbivanja kroz internacionalne obrasce. Rezultat je živi autentični organizam, kojeg svijet prepoznaje i s kojim je u stanju snažno komunicirati.

Na području plastičkih umjetnosti, ekvivalent sa takvom vitalitetu sve donedavno nije uočavao. Naime, Sarajevo se kao kulturni centar na likovnom području, proteklih decenija pokazalo gluhim za burna neoavangardna događanja koja su dimala Ljubljanom, Zagrebom, jedno vrijeme i Splitom, kao i Beogradom i Novim Sadom. Sarajevska je likovna scena u to vrijeme obilježena stilskim pastišerstvom starinskog tipa. Estetiziraju se elementi pop-arta, konceptualnih i srodnih umjetnosti, a prisutna je i specifična varijanta nesporazuma s upotrebom bizarnih i renesanse. Riječ je o, unatoč preozbiljnim pretenzijama, devalviranju matičnih stilskih obrazaca čije se ikonografske pojavnosti svode na ukrasnu funkciju lišene prvotnih značenja. Udivljenju renesansno-dalijevskom tehnikom pridružio se šarm

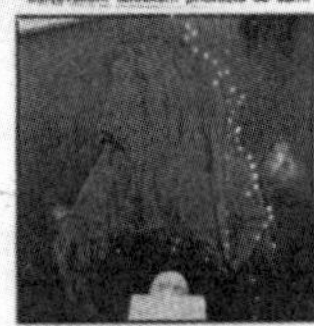

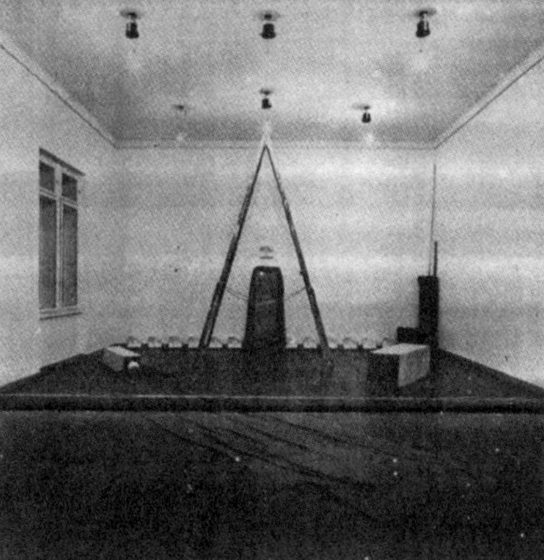

BORIS CVJETANOVIĆ

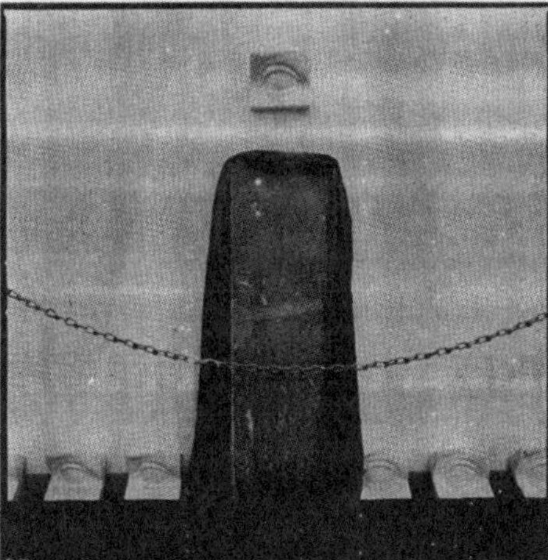

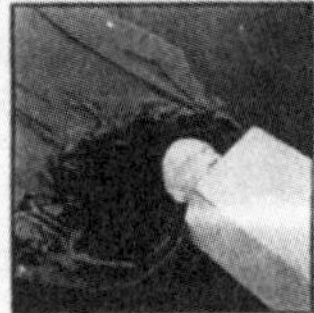

popartističkih slova, konceptualističkih sekvenci i krojačkih grafikona, sve protkano temperanim enformelističkim mrljama. Čitava ta slikovna gungula rezultirala je fiktivnim hermetizmom, i prizemnim patosom, a nerijetko i najordinarnijim, mada ekskluzivnim i, društveno, ekstremno valoriziranim kičem.

Istina, takvi se dekorativni konglomerati javljaju i u drugim sredinama, ali u Sarajevu dominiraju bez mladenačke alternative (s izuzetkom usamljenih kasnih pojava Rothku podobnih apstrakcija i primarnog slikarstva). Štoviše, te se kombinirane poetike, po ugledu na profesore, šire i na mlađe generacije slikara i grafičara, studenata, prije petnaestak godina osnovane sarajevske Akademije. Tek se prije nekoliko godina na tom području počinju primjećivati znaci živosti i gibanja. Mladi slikar Jusuf Hadžifejzović s nekoliko svojih kolega počinje unutar prostora Collegium artisticum organizirati izložbe kolega iz Zagreba, Beograda i drugih gradova. Na taj način entuzijazmom nekolicine (umjetnicima gostima, domaćini iz privatnog džepa financiraju putne troškove) sarajevska se likovna scena »internacionalizira« i obogaćuje. U samom Sarajevu se pojavljuju mladi autori drugačijeg opredjeljenja i svjetonazora: uz Jusufa tu su Saša Bukvić, grupa »Zvono«...

Jusuf je 1980. završio slikarstvo na beogradskoj akademiji, a zatim do 1982. boravi u Düsseldorfu na postdiplomskom studiju u klasi profesora Rinkea. Nakon toga živi i radi u Sarajevu. Već na svom školovanju na akademiji Jusuf je pokazivao interes za primarne postupke u slikarstvu, a zatim za prostorne zahvate uz akcije i performanse u kojima se sam pojavljuje kao akter događanja i dio ambijenta. Iako se u posljednje vrijeme uz ostalo opet bavi slikanjem ono što je posebno zanimljivo kao novost vezana za kulturni sarajevski fenomen su njegovi prostorni aranžmani-instalacije. Posljednja takva instalacija pod nazivom »Zenica-depo« izvedena je u Zenici i Zagrebu, u prostoru Proširenih medija. Predmeti od kojih je Jusuf sastavio tu izložbu-ambijent nisu umjetnički artefakti, niti predmeti u neposrednoj vezi s umjetnošću. Ipak, ti su predmeti pronađeni u skladištu galerije u Zenici. Na taj je način autor pomoću zatečenih stvari, koje su nosioci određenih značenja, progovorio o ustanovi u njoj samoj, njenim vlastitim jezikom i jezikom mjesta (Zenica) koje živi svojim specifičnim životom. Umjetnik, dakle, provodi svojevrsno razotkrivanje profanog i političkog »bekgraunda« institucije unutar njenog reprezentativnog prostora. Predmeti kao što su glasačke kutije, uvezani »Službeni listovi«, tube za diplome, prozorsko okno umrljano žbukom, crvene krpe, gipsani odljevci velikih očiju, komadi ugljena..., u autorovoj postavi predstavljaju bastardnu formu između religioznih i političkih inscenacija. Tako nas umjetnik podsjeća na zajedničke elemente (prividnih) suprotnosti sakralnog i svjetovnog.

Uloga umjetnika se u ovom slučaju svodi na prostorno aranžiranje već postojećih elemenata; on te elemente postavlja u odnos koji im omogućuje da sami što autentičnije progovore o sebi i mjestu na kojem se nalaze. Tako animirani, oni svojom formom, tragovima upotrebe, dizajnom, simboličnim nabojem, pričaju lokalnu priču.

Suštinski isti postupak primijenio je Jusuf i u svojim intervencijama u interijerima sarajevske Vijećnice. I tamo je unio predmete koji po svom karakteru tom prostoru ne pripadaju. Na mramorne stupove Vijećnice fiksirao je kruh, povrće, odjeću... Zabadao je ugljen, metalne strugotine, grančice i noževe u svježe tijesto...

Pored mnogih mogućih značenja, kao osnovno se nameće autorova potreba i htijenje da podsjeti na prizemnu stvarnost, elementarni život, bazične materijale i predmete, tako da ih unosi u one prostore koji su rezervirani za rafinirane prerađevine i zbivanja. U toj se dakle gesti dade očitati volja za demistifikacijom zvaničnog prostora u koga se unosi sirovi pejzaž neuljepšane svakodnevice. To proletersko prizemljivanje reprezentativne fikcije je krajnje pozitivni moralni čin, kreativni apel za uvažavanje elementarne moći kao i nesavršenstva.

Po svoj je prilici školovanje u Düsseldorfu ostavilo traga u Jusufovim plastičkim sklonostima. Interes za grube, neprerađene materijale karakterizira i tamošnje istaknute umjetnike kao što su npr. Beuys, pa i sam Jusufov profesor Rinke. Istu oporost, kao i zgusnutu atmosferu gamiranu političkim simbolima, nalazimo i u suvremenom njemačkom slikarstvu, naročito kod Jorga Immendorfa. Ugođaj »Zenica-depoa«, uz ostalo, može asocirati i na melankoliju i dekadentnu estetiku apokaliptičnih prizora s prošlogodišnjeg venecijanskog bijenala...

Sve su to mogući elementi jednog eklektičkog principa »kulturne memorije« koja u stvaralačkoj konzekvenci čvrsto prijanja uz topografiju domaćeg tla i duše.

Jusuf kao i ranije spominjani glazbeni i filmski radnici poznaju svijet, ali posve svjesno i djelatno izbjegavaju čeznutljivo, i s puno balkanskog kompleksa, utapanje u njemu. Naprotiv, oni nastoje ostvariti punu legitimnost svog, sudbinski dodijeljenog lokalnog genija.

ANTUN MARAČIĆ

22. STRANICA SL. BROJ 912 – 9. I. 86.

deciphered or understood, but to be experienced and felt sensually."[83] Within the hall's transcendent setting, Antun Maračić wrote, the artist wanted to remind visitors of the "ground reality, elementary life, basic materials and subjects, in spaces reserved exclusively for refined events."[84] He wanted to demystify the official space and introduce the raw landscape of an unvarnished everyday, in order to enact a proletarian grounding of a political establishment's "representative fiction."[85] Introducing the basic necessities associated with an ordinary person, Hadžifejzović's depot tarnished the "official" image of Yugoslav society. The Sarajevo city hall—a monument to "proper" society—was infiltrated with icons derived from the immediate sociocultural context, which had previously been marginalized under the "official cultural" program.

Acting as a "reexamination of identity," Hadžifejzović's depot was in itself a "New Primitive" gesture, functioning outside the "circles of influence" that determined local cultural production.[86] In the following year, the artist organized a "New Primitive dinner" at the Youth House Theatre. Sponsored by the Youth House, the happening was executed by the "disciples" of New Primitivism, including Kurtović and Bukvić, among others. Supplied with food and drink, they came onto the stage and set up a table, while guests, who had paid a fairly substantial sum to attend the performance, entered the room. As Bukvić described the event: "A lot of people gathered to watch us eat and chat, probably expecting us to begin throwing bones and cakes at each other. I can imagine the darkest night they experienced, when after an hour and a half, we bowed to the audience, and left."[87] The "New Primitive Dinner" was just another humorous validation of the local, presenting an everyday scene from Sarajevo within the domain of art. Examining the status of art and culture in Sarajevo, it let self-consciousness and self-reliance take the stage.

6.14. Antun Maračić, "New Primitive Art Jusufa Hadžifejzovića," *Studentski List* (Zagreb), no. 912, 9 January 1986, 22.

"THE MIRACLE OF MIRACLES": YUGOSLAVIA'S *DOKUMENTA*, 1987 AND 1989

Arising from the initially imperceptible presence of a small café, both Zvono and Hadžifejzović paved the way for two of the most significant exhibitions of contemporary art in the former Yugoslavia, the *Jugoslovenska dokumenta* [Yugoslav Documents]. Beginning in 1984, Bukvić, Hadžifejzović, and Sarajevan painter Radoslav Tadić organized a series of independent exhibitions of Yugoslav artists at the Collegium Artisticum, in an attempt to introduce the Sarajevo public to the work of fellow artists from across the federation.[88] Driven by an "uncompromising orientation towards the most recent tendencies in art," they launched the idea of organizing a large Yugoslav exhibition, whose predominant aim would be to show all of the country's "progressive trends in contemporary art."[89]

According to Hadžifejzović, "people thought that we were megalomaniacal in attempting to establish such a manifestation."[90] But by working on a voluntary basis, the three artists managed to secure the Collegium Artisticum as an exhibition space. Granted the 6,000-square-meter space of the gallery, the trio invited artists and critics from throughout the federation to participate in the event, which opened on 11 May 1987. Despite the fact that there wasn't even enough money to cover the expenses of a catalogue or a poster, 140 artists from across the federation were still willing to participate, contributing work "speaking in the most diverse plastic art tongues, including video art, performance, installation, etc." The "enthusiastic amateurism of three young artists" had developed into the greatest art event of its kind in Yugoslavia.[91]

While it was the largest exhibition of contemporary art in Yugoslavia to date, *dokumenta* did have two noteworthy local predecessors: Ljubljana's *Biennale grafike*, first staged in 1955, and the SKC Gallery's April Meetings, which had ceased to exist after the sixth manifestation in 1977. Established in the same year as Documenta in Kassel, the *Biennale grafike* sought to link the "East and West by the bridge of art" in a manner that would "underline the same active nonengagement that coincides entirely with our conception of international relations."[92] In line with its declared aim, the *Biennale grafike* directly connected its purpose to political developments because it had been established as an explicit materialization of Tito's nonaligned politics, as the key founder and long-term director of the biennial, Zoran Kržišnik, later revealed.[93] Not only was *Biennale grafike* in some respects defined by its political use value to the Yugoslav state, but its goal of establishing and supporting the "democratization" of culture was also somewhat compromised by the fact that it was arranged through the distribution of prizes.[94] As art historians Anthony Gardner and Charles Green have explained, the prizes' "persistence meant that supposedly 'objective' assertions of quality remained, contradicting the egalitarianism and transversality underpinning the biennial's politics of democratization and its 'active non-engagement' in geopolitical partitions."[95]

In contrast, *dokumenta* was a regionally oriented art fair, seeking to rehabilitate the contemporary art scene of Yugoslavia. It served as a precedent for future exhibitions in that it was organized not by cultural staff working through self-managing interest communities, but by three artists who had diligently fostered and sustained networks of communication with their counterparts throughout the federation. Rather than foregrounding competition between artists from different countries and cultures—most obviously through the awarding of prizes to specific artists (which in Venice had often resulted in "bitter and jealous rivalries as much as arbitrary determinations of 'quality'")—*dokumenta* wanted to give artists the opportunity to compare their works with the works of their neighbors. It wanted to establish artistic cooperation among its participants, along with alternative models of cultural exchange.[96] Moreover, as a large and regional manifestation, it attempted to offer Yugoslav artists broader visibility within the global art scene. As Hadžifejzović wrote in *dokumenta*'s catalogue:

> It would be of the utmost importance for Yugoslav art and its artists if we could have one big exhibition, with works of the highest quality, for if we want to become a part of the great European or world art scene, we must invest a sort of "chip," as one would say in the game of poker. Only then could we begin to "play," we are nothing but kibitzers now. To put it plainly, just imagine if we in Yugoslavia had a kind of international art exhibition, for which we could freely choose the works of foreign and Yugoslav artists, with the assumption that this exhibition is organized continually and with high artistic criteria.[97]

This "alternative attempt to do something new in Yugoslav art" sought to aid local artists who lacked support from official art institutions to "[get] out of the country," in a locale "not short of either artists or galleries," but one lacking in "funds to be invested in them, and the adequate criteria for the distribution of these funds."[98] The event's title itself was a playful reference to Documenta in Kassel, to which only a handful of artists had been invited. Speaking in retrospect, Hadžifejzović explained, "While the German government dedicated 17 million deutschmarks to the event in Kassel, demonstrating how much they valued contemporary art, the Yugoslav Ministry of Culture did not grant the Sarajevo exhibition a single dinar."[99] Filling this gap, *dokumenta* introduced a common all-Yugoslav program, the purpose of which was to place Yugoslav artists, and the country in general, on an equal footing with the European scene. Its significance was based on the fact that it was a "gathering of [artists, writers, and publics] from all over Yugoslavia, and one of the rare occasions where art moved from standard [gallery] spaces to huge halls."[100]

Emphasizing the vibrancy of Yugoslavia's contemporary art scene through a transcultural event, *dokumenta* stood in stark contrast to the period of profound political instability in which it first emerged. In 1987, according to many, the "systemic character of the Yugoslav crisis was made so evident that any good hope of a partial solution to the country's troubles ha[d] been buried for good."[101] Already at the beginning of the 1980s, as discussed in the previous two chapters, the League of Communists had faced its greatest economic crisis in history, along with a restive population, rising unemployment, and an explosive situation in Kosovo, which had undergone a state of emergency in 1981. The deteriorating internal social situation was further exacerbated by changes in the external environment, which were steering political battles over economic and constitutional reforms. By 1983, Yugoslavia was facing an accumulated foreign debt, mainly to the IMF and to Western banks, that had reached $20 billion. In the summer of 1987, Yugoslavia's economic rating finally hit zero, after the Agrokomerc scandal erupted in the northwestern part of Bosnia surrounding the city of Bihać. Employing over thirteen thousand people, Agrokomerc was a food-processing conglomerate that went bankrupt after it was discovered that its director was financing the enterprise through a series of promissory notes issued to Yugoslav banks. According to one journalist from Belgrade's *Danas* [Today], the scandal had exposed the political instabilities that lay behind the "Sarajevo school of media charm"—occurring in the republic that was assumed to be the strongest link in the "chain of the federation.... Agrokomerc had shaken everything."[102] For others, the affair was simply synonymous with the collapse of Yugoslav self-management. Dubbed a "scandal," Agrokomerc was in fact just a symptom of years of economic instability and declining living standards, both of which were fueling social tensions and massive unrest, while nourishing an emerging ethnonationalist authoritarian populism.

In *dokumenta*'s catalogue, Nermina Zildžo drew explicit parallels between the motivation behind the exhibition's organization and Yugoslavia's pressing economic crisis. In her words: "Their [the organizers'] feeling that contemporary art has somehow been ignored is emphatically stressed by this exhibition, entitled *Yugoslav Documents*: the name reminds me, by coincidence, of the measures introduced by the government for the Yugoslav economy, caused by a similar dissatisfaction with current events."[103] The "dissatisfaction," as she subtly referred to it, was the serious decline in social support for both the League of Communists and trade unions. This decline was resulting in the emergence of aggressive nationalist forces in the shape of intellectuals, mainly with backgrounds in the humanities, putting forward alternative solutions, not so much to socialism as to the very existence of Yugoslavia. In October 1986, the Serbian Academy of Arts and Sciences published its *Memorandum*—a document mixing references to the real fractures in Yugoslavia's economic and political system with a conspiracy theory claiming that other republics were responsible for the frustrations of Serbs. The *Memorandum* alleged that Serbia had been divided into three parts and been burdened with the entire federation's development, a resentment linked to the revisions of the 1974 constitution.[104] In response, the intellectuals from the academy proposed finding a solution outside the Yugoslav state that would essentially entail creating a Serbian nation along the lines of an ethnic map, which would claim most of southern and eastern Croatia; all of Bosnia, Montenegro, and Macedonia; and Serbia, with its autonomous regions of Vojvodina and Kosovo. A couple of months later, Ljubljana's journal *Nova revija* published a special edition on the "Slovene National Interest," which highlighted the need for Slovenia to find an "alternative solution to the national crisis" by abandoning the federation; consequently, their conclusions were not far from those of the Serbian Academy.[105]

In 1987, the newly elected Serbian communist leader Slobodan Milošević embraced the arguments of the Serbian Academy, exploiting the discontent of Serbs in other republics, building on their resentments, supporting their claims (such as for the reduction of regional autonomy), and encouraging mass demonstrations. Making full use of the economic disaster and the lack of power in the political elites in Montenegro and Vojvodina, Milošević exploited popular demonstrations to oust the leaders of these two regions, and soon afterward those of Kosovo too.[106] Milan Kučan, the president of Slovenia, challenged Milošević's aggressive strategy aimed at amending the constitution. But Kučan was unable to foster the political alliances necessary to isolate Milošević, and reacted to Serbia's challenges by isolating himself and moving closer to the separatist ideals of many intellectuals within his own republic. The different positions on how to reorganize the country's institutions soon became irreconcilable. While Milošević was proposing the centralization of power, Kučan insisted on a further reduction in the power of the federal institutions and a confederal arrangement in which Slovenia would have a privileged position. In the context of a gravely eroded party and a diminishing sense of federal unity, the willingness to cooperate on a common future was severely impeded, with Milošević's rise to power striking the most destructive and irreversible blow to Yugoslavia's cohesion.[107]

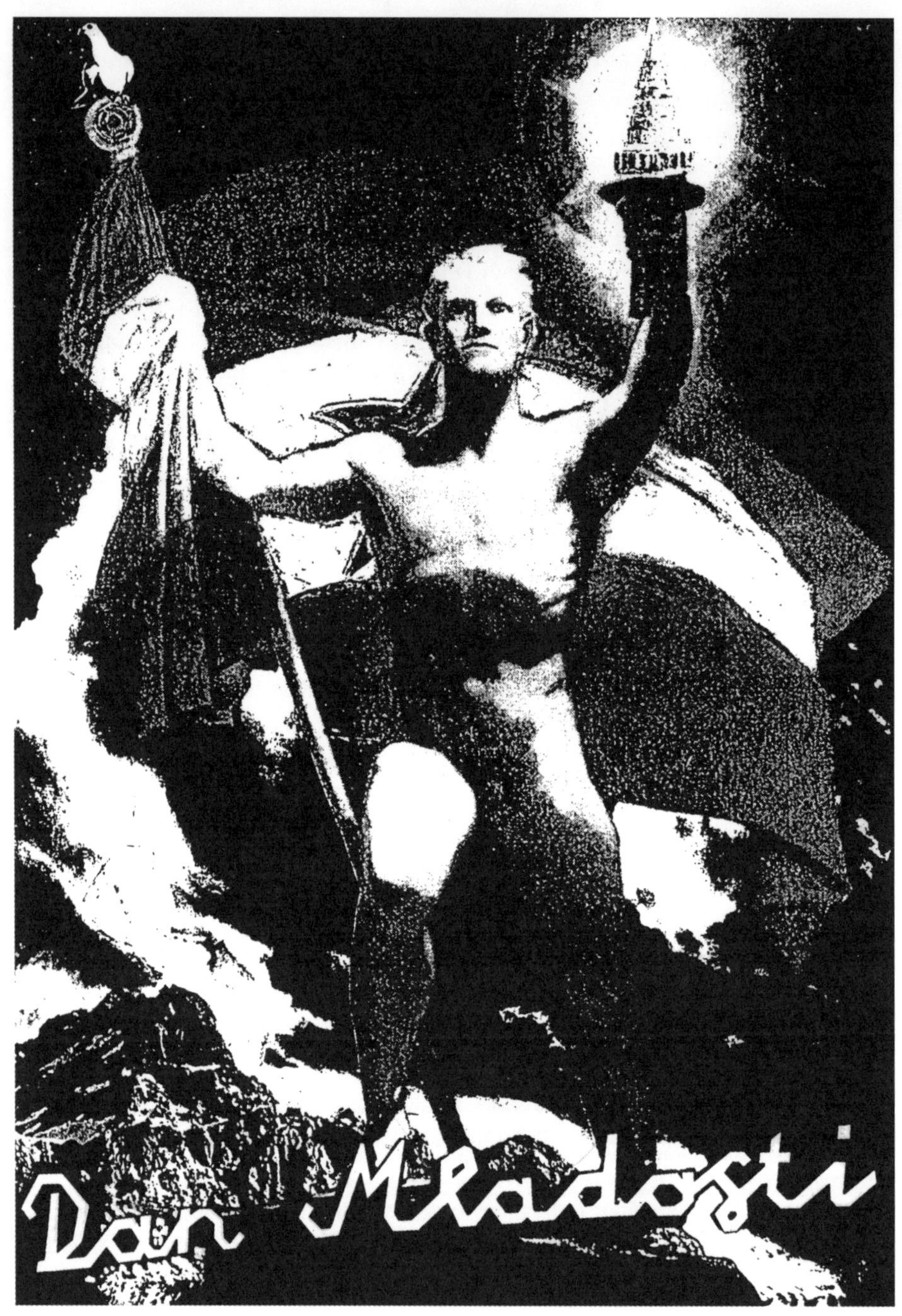
Dan Mladosti

In February 1987, a few months before *dokumenta*, the so-called Poster Scandal was symptomatic of an atmosphere increasingly driven by nationalist calls for the reassessment of the Yugoslav contract. Ljubljana's Novi Kolektivizem [New Collectivism], the design section of the Neue Slowenische Kunst, won the state-run competition for the visual concept for Youth Day, one of the major socialist festivals in Yugoslavia. Part of the concept was a proposal for a poster, which was supposed to be distributed and displayed all over the country. The proposed poster by Novi Kolektivizem, which showed a naked young man with a cone-shaped baton in one hand, and the Yugoslav flag in the other, was accepted by a Federal Youth Day Committee. But after being published in newspapers, someone in Belgrade discovered that it was an exact copy of a Nazi Kunst work by Richard Klein entitled the *Third Reich* and published in A. J. P. Taylor's book *From Sarajevo to Potsdam* (1966); the only difference between the two images was that the Nazi insignia had been replaced by Yugoslav symbols, combined with an unrealized design for the "Slovenian Acropolis" by the architect Jože Plečnik.[108] The poster was perceived as an attack on both the state and the Yugoslav National Army. On the front pages of the final weekend issue of the Sarajevo daily *Oslobođenje* [Liberation], one headline read "The Serpent Egg of New Collectivism," along with an additional caption above the headline lamenting "Is this even possible!," which meant to criticize the nerve of the artists as well as the selection committee that approved the poster.[109] Writing retrospectively, Marina Gržinić described the affair in the following way:

> New Collectivism had inverted Nazi symbols and changed them into socialist symbols: the swastika on the original poster was replaced by a star, and so on. The most cynical point of all was not the inversion of symbols, but, as was pointed out in numerous analyses, the complete identification of the Federal Jury with the poster's visual ideology—the Federal Jury had initially selected the poster designed by New Collectivism as the most appropriate one. Once their "mirroring" of the communist imagery with the transvestite Nazi symbolism (the latter being, so to speak, the obscene hidden supplement to the former) was revealed, the communist power machine tried, although without success, to put the group in jail.[110]

6.15. Novi kolektivizem [New Collectivism] (NK), *Youth Day*, a rejected poster proposal, 1987. Image courtesy of NSK archive.

Certainly, Gržinić's analysis offers a compelling interpretation of the scandal, now ingrained in historical accounts as a crucial moment in Yugoslavia's alternative art scene. Yet, while Novi Kolektivizem's poster submission was frequently perceived as a heroic attempt to expose the federal jury's true inclination to "fascist symbolism," one could also conclude that the selection of a poster designed by a young and unknown Slovenian group spearheading a new artistic movement was, in some respects, a recognition by the jury of "alternative" art, which had at the time gained a significant amount of respect from the cultural elite of the Slovenian republic.[111] In a way, then, Novi Kolektivizem's gesture sprang from its effective devaluation of the social and moral keystones of the dissolving socialist system, while adapting to the advancing of new social realities, highlighting, in the words of Miklavž Komelj, the "Eastern 'authoritarian tradition' and 'ideological past' for the sake of arguing for the necessity to become incorporated into the Western [capitalist art] system."[112] Branislav Jakovljević has provided an even more nuanced account of the affair, pointing out that by 1987 and at the peak of the NSK, "the ideological facade of Yugoslav socialism was [so] badly scarred by years of political and economic crisis [that] the fact that the poster scandal could be presented as totalitarian was actually a sign of the emergence of a new ideological order that was as invisible as it was effective."[113]

While Novi Kolektivizem was reflecting on, and adapting to, the country's swiftly deteriorating social climate, *dokumenta* was gathering together Yugoslavia's contemporary art scene in a single exhibition venue to stimulate broader, "regional" forms of cooperation. At this time, the largest threat impeding interethnic relations in Yugoslavia was the breakdown of a sense of community (which, at the time, received almost no explicit attention in the press), along with the breakdown of communication across republican borders and nationality groups. By advocating a form of engagement motivated by the spirit of "Yugoslavism," *dokumenta* was a clear counterpoint to the nationalist and xenophobic currents dissolving the distinctly Yugoslav fabric of a socialist community in crisis. It was no coincidence that it emerged in Sarajevo, the most "Yugoslav" city, in the sense that it was considered the most harmoniously multicultural, with several different cultural communities cohabiting in its milieu.

Two years later, in 1989, the Collegium Artisticum played host to the even more ambitious second *Jugoslovenska dokumenta*. Running on ever-decreasing finances, the exhibition's realization rested almost exclusively on the enthusiasm and dedication of Hadžifejzović and Tadić. An exhibition catalogue was printed to coincide with the event, its cover consisting of a vibrant pink ground splattered with purple dots. The cover's composition could not have been farther from the image of a country in a crisis—its playful abstract forms established an emancipatory potential, at a moment when culture was being manipulated to serve particular nationalist interests. With very little money to spend, Hadžifejzović nevertheless managed to secure a billboard outside of the city's Olympic Stadium, and replicated the minimal motif of the catalogue's vibrant cover on small, individual photocopied sheets, aligned together to produce a large, commanding, abstract image.

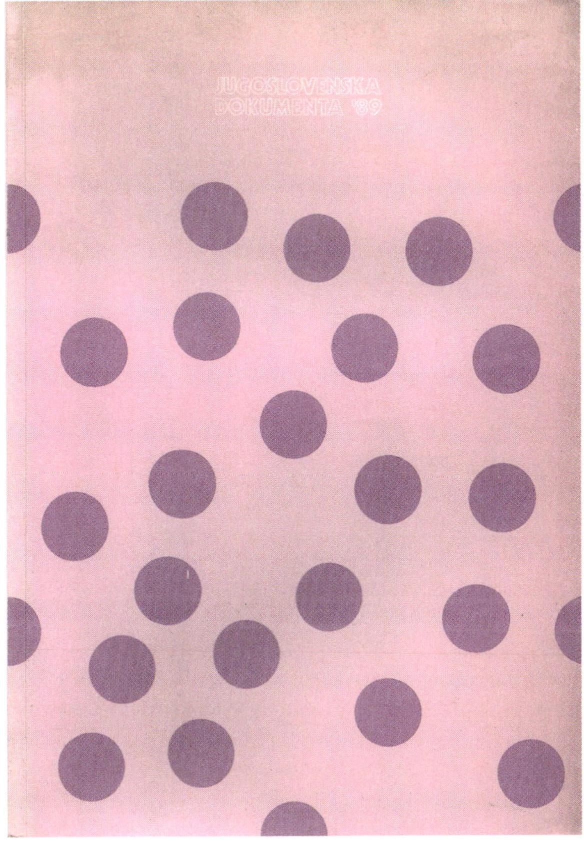

6.16. Front cover of exhibition catalogue for *Jugoslovenska dokumenta*, Sarajevo, 1989. Image courtesy of Jusuf Hadžifejzović.

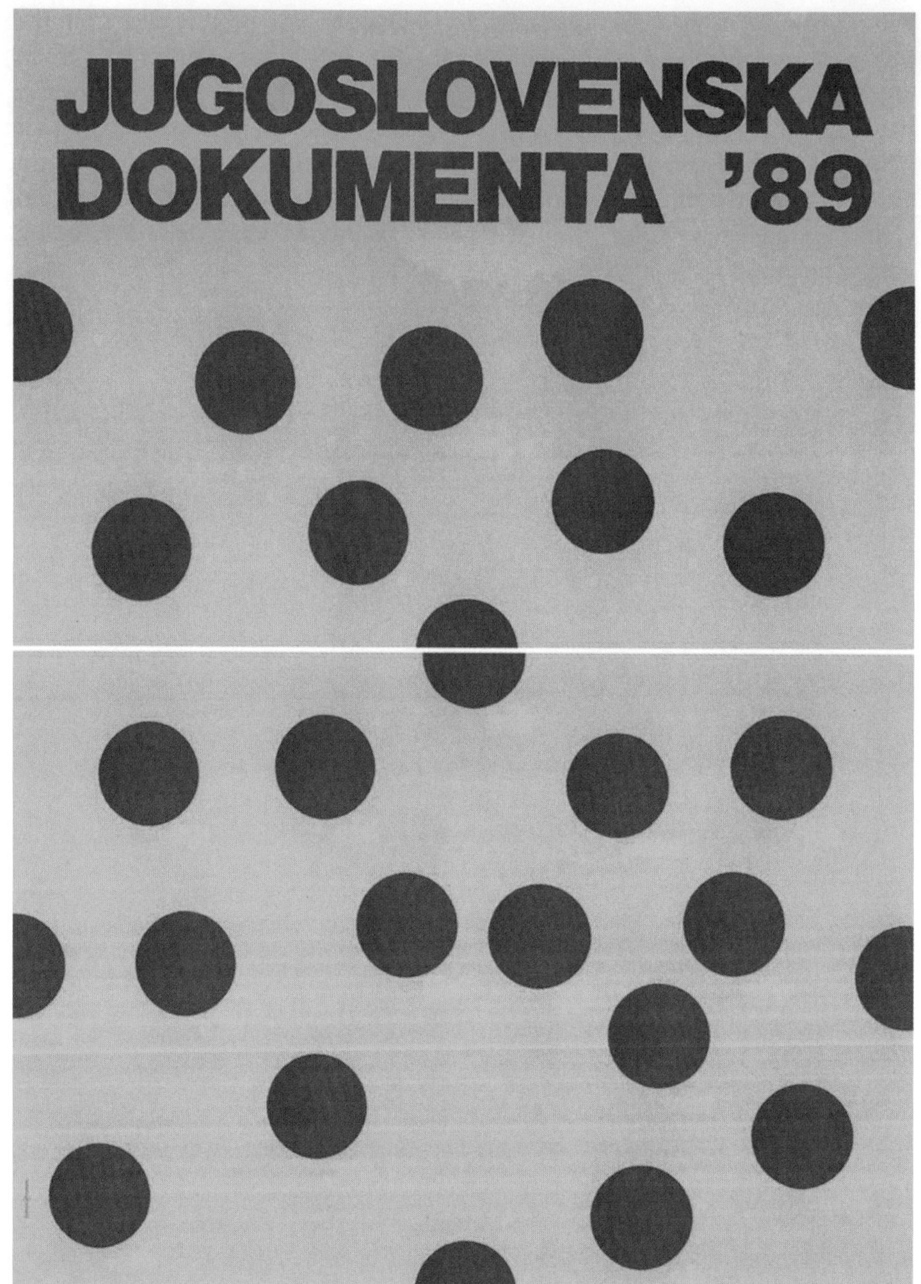
JUGOSLOVENSKA
DOKUMENTA '89

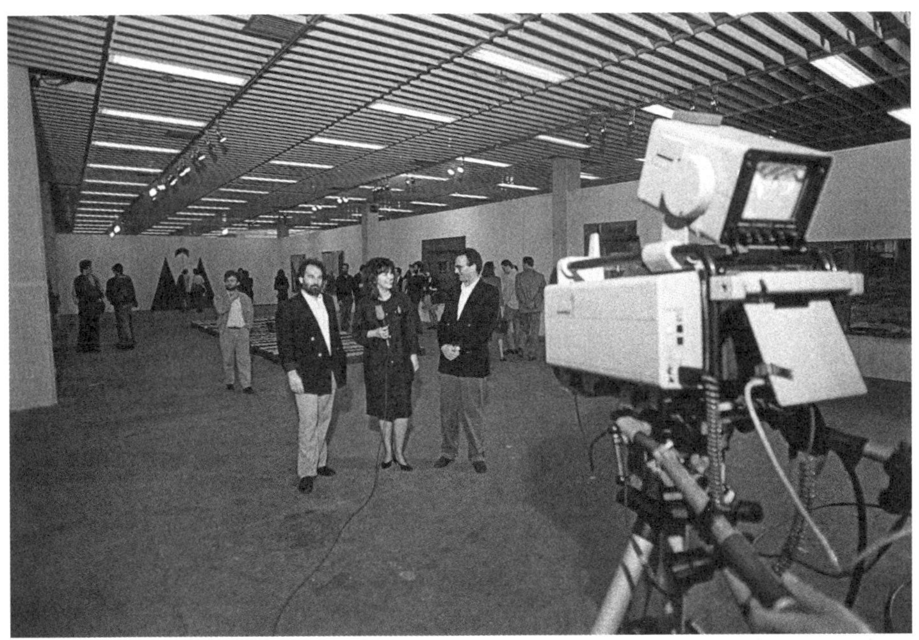

6.17. Poster for *Jugoslovenska dokumenta*, Sarajevo, 1989. Image courtesy of Jusuf Hadžifejzović.

6.18. Jane Štravs, *Jugoslovenska dokumenta '89*, Olimpijski Centar "Skenderija," Sarajevo, 1989. Image courtesy of Jane Štravs.

following pages

6.19. Jane Štravs, group portrait of artists participating in *Jugoslovenska dokumenta '89*, Sarajevo, 1989. Image courtesy of Jane Štravs.

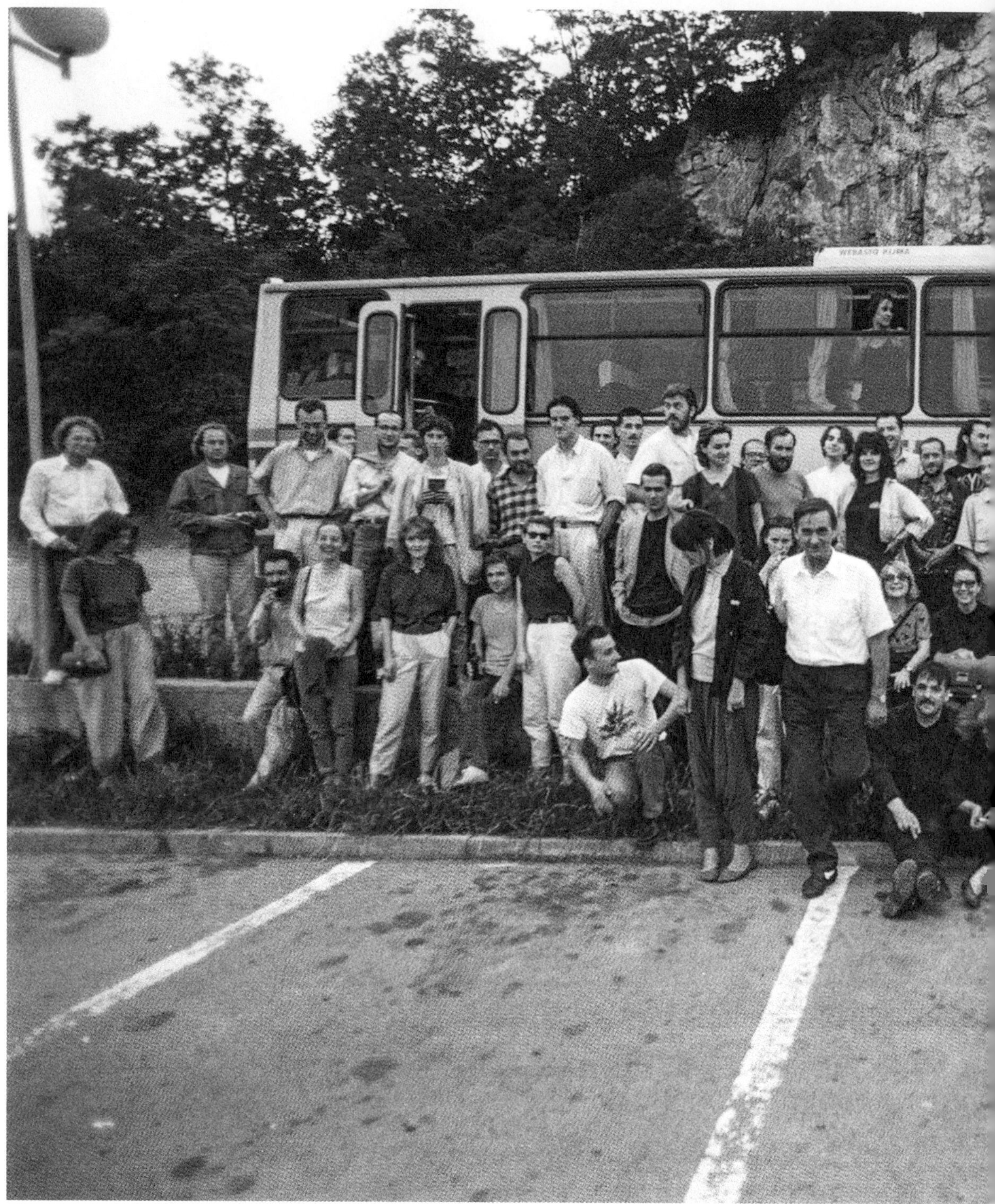

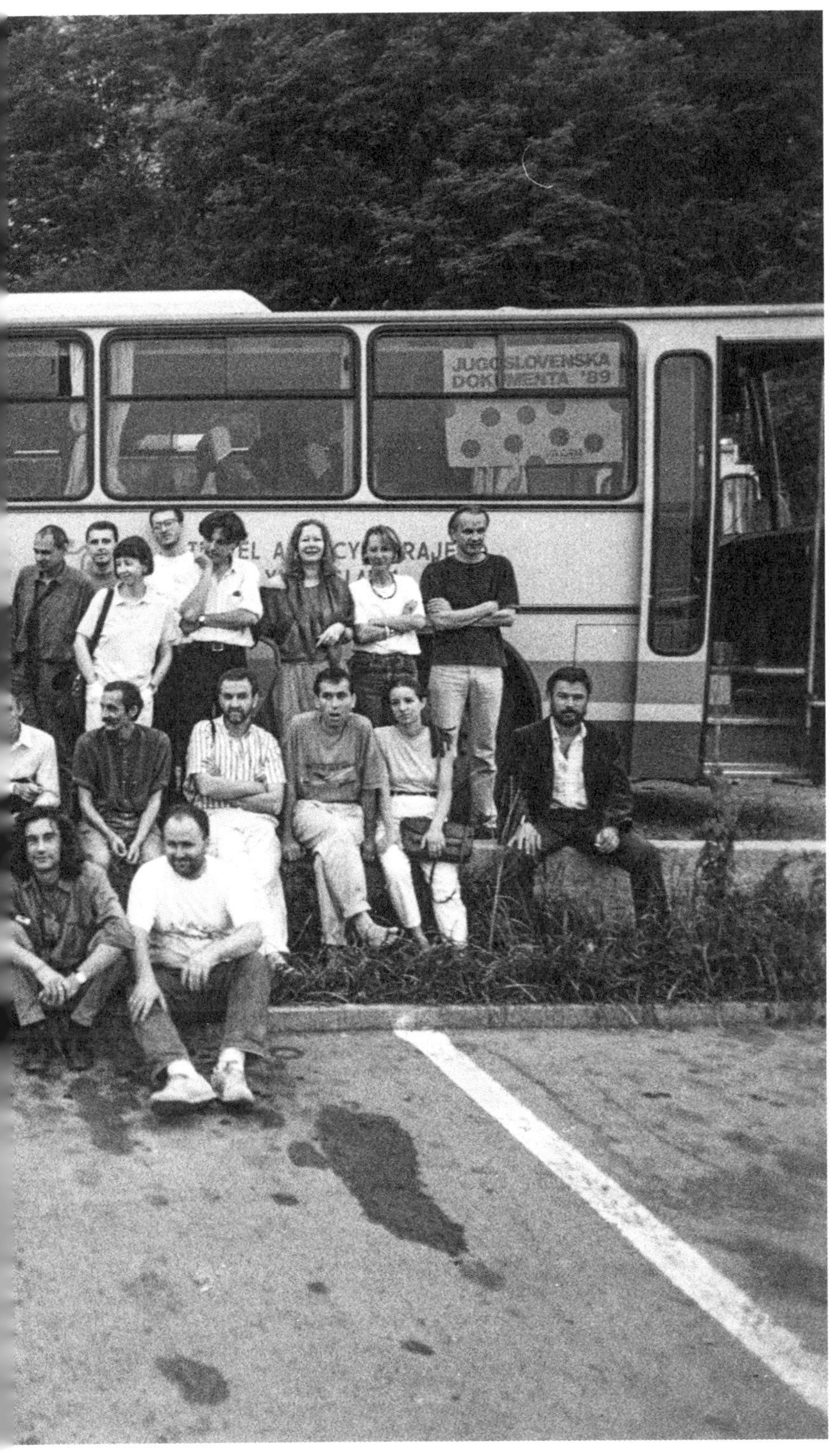
JUGOSLOVENSKA
DOKUMENTA '89

The second *Yugoslav dokumenta* opened on 1 July 1989, just a few weeks before Kosovo and Vojvodina would be stripped of their status as autonomous regions. Its opening commenced at midnight to ensure that only an audience that was truly dedicated to contemporary art attended, as trams in the city only operated until that time. Reportedly, over five thousand people attended.[114] At the end of the opening, buses waited outside the Skenderija Olympic center, leaving for the cities of other republics. According to Hadžifejzović, he distributed the catalogue to several people at the 1990 Venice Biennale—including, among others, Achille Bonito Oliva and Robert Rauschenberg—to expand awareness of the exhibition, and thereby pursue its aspirations for international recognition.[115]

Having grown in scale and recognition, *dokumenta* was beginning to establish the foundations necessary to become an internationally recognized art event, with the 1991 edition even envisioned in those terms.[116] But the progress of *dokumenta*'s development and the creative will from which it first emerged were interrupted precisely by the forces that it was seeking to counter. The 1991 *dokumenta* never took place because of the war that broke out after Slovenia and Croatia declared independence, on 25 June 1991, and which spread to Bosnia and Herzegovina in April of the following year.

With the aim of not only dismantling Yugoslavia but also preventing it from ever being recreated, the war in Bosnia and Herzegovina was from the start waged with only one aim—the complete destruction of the republic.[117] Once a symbol of reconciliation, cooperation, and coexistence between diverse cultural, ethnic, and religious communities, and by the end of the 1980s representing the capital of Yugoslavia's contemporary art scene, Sarajevo, as an ethnically mixed city, experienced some of the most violent fighting, remaining under siege for four years.

Fighting for a united contemporary art scene, *dokumenta* marked not only the end of a traumatic decade but also the last phase of "Yugoslav" art in general.

CONCLUSION

"It appears to me today," wrote Želimir Koščević toward the end of January 1990, "that all of us were a little too idealistic."[1] In an essay published amid Yugoslavia's dawning disintegration, he noted with deep regret that "we were mistaken in our assessment of the real potential of Yugoslav art, as regards politics, to speak of our reality, whatever it is, using its own language."[2] He proceeded to list an extensive range of issues that, as it turned out, the New Art Practice was incapable of addressing: "Repression, lies, nationalism, human rights, the one-party system, differences and similarities, the destruction of the environment, poverty, corruption, alcoholism, kitsch culture and cultural policy at home and abroad, false prophets and saints, or the moral crisis, or Zenica, Kosovo, Krško, Celje, Bor."[3]

Reading Koščević's remorseful words today, it is almost impossible not to interpret them from the perspective of the world in which we now live. All across the globe, we are witnessing a rise in repression, lies, and nationalism coming in with the sharp drift to the right that was set in motion by the neoliberal economics, globalizing capital, and neoconservative politics of the 1980s. Rejection, xenophobia, and anti-internationalism form the core of an emboldened populist right, which bears at present the faces of a vast cohort of people across the world—including the likes of Donald Trump, Jair Bolsonaro, Boris Johnson, Nigel Farage, Marine Le Pen, Viktor Orbán, Vladimir Putin, Recep Tayyip Erdoğan, Benjamin Netanyahu, Narendra Modi, and Rodrigo Duterte. Much like the leaders who came to prominence during Yugoslavia's violent disintegration, what these leaders have in common are policies favoring protectionism and neonationalism, appealing to many because they seem to offer refuge against the damaging effects of neoliberal deregulation and global trade. Their rise to power reveals that Yugoslavia may in fact have been an early warning sign of how political orders collapse under the international pressures of economic liberalization and austerity measures. And what Yugoslavia, in turn, tells us about the conflicts that are currently brewing globally is how the symptoms of this collapse very often first surface on a cultural level.

Following Yugoslavia's disintegration, academics sought to explain why there was never a strong sense of a Yugoslav identity in the country with that name.[4]

Arguably, there was never a strong identification with "Yugoslavism" because ruling communist elites and, more importantly, leading intellectuals never had enough cultural and political imagination to envision such a construct.[5] Throughout the country's existence, Yugoslavia's national cultures remained sheltered by complex legislation, and protected by funding from their constituent republics. By contrast, the New Art Practice emerged independently of any party or state cultural policies, because its proponents did not appear as representatives of their respective nations and republics; they were either individuals or self-organized collectives. But from the 1960s onward, particularist discourses dominated over the supranational concept of Yugoslavia. This is exactly what the philosopher Radomir Konstantinović identified in his four-hundred-page-long philosophical essay *Filozofija palanke* [Philosophy of Provincialism], published in 1969.[6] Konstantinović was a prophetic reader of the developments around him in Belgrade in the 1960s, observing the superficial status of "democratization" and "internationalization" in his local surroundings. His book gave a completely new meaning to the old word "palanka," roughly translated as the spirit of a market town mentality. As the writer Dubravka Ugrešić has eloquently summarized:

> The *palanka* is not a village or a city, it is somewhere in between the two. The *palanka* is a deterritorialized and decontextualized place, everywhere and nowhere, a state of mind.... The *palanka* experiences itself as cast-off, forgotten, time left out of historical time, and then it bemoans its bitter fate, while at the same time turning this accused destiny into its privilege. Being closed and forgotten means being safe, while beyond, outside the circle of the *palanka*, rules the dangerous chaos of the wide world. Autism, rigidity, petrification, a constant readiness for defense, a strong tribal awareness, infantilism, formulaic patterns of thought, fear of the unknown, fear of change, an apology for purity, innocence and simplicity, the hermetic, a cult of the dead, security, normativity, conservatism, the static, anti-historicism—are only a few of the features typical of the world of the *palanka*.[7]

Konstantinović expressed the secret fears of a provincial mind, its unspoken resentments, and its punishment of difference. In the words of Eda Čufer: "He saw the self-destructive and paranoid tendencies of Serbia in the 1960s, and was amongst the first to see what they would lead to in the 1990s: the completion of Belgrade's transformation of itself from metropolis to village."[8]

Of course, Belgrade's self-destructive transformation "from metropolis to village" was typical of many places throughout the world which, pressured to enter a world economy dominated by the West, succumbed to the values of unbridled competition and descended into violent barbarism. Its transformation in the 1990s speaks to how globalization and nationalism are congruent, as well as how they continue to function as forces that are both separate and synchronous—like two sides of the same coin—working together to undercut the development of any alternative and radical internationalism from below. In Yugoslavia, it was the absence of internationalist and self-managed alternatives that facilitated the turn toward provincialism, tribalism, and essentialist identities. As Koščević himself noted with much sorrow, the New Art Practice was ultimately powerless in the face of such forces, which in the end allowed Yugoslavia's successor states to territorialize and ethnicize the rights of ownership and national rights. Simply put, its practitioners never saw the future for Yugoslav society that they envisioned.

Despite its considerable efforts, the New Art Practice failed to foresee or combat the looming bloody conflicts or the material and moral dispossession that accompanied Yugoslavia's violent disintegration. But it did, as I hope this book has shown, nevertheless provide a powerful platform on which different cultural phenomena blended and communicated with one another. As the final episode of Yugoslavia's art scene in Sarajevo, *Jugoslovenska dokumenta*, reveals, even in the midst of the final acts of the federation's dissolution, individuals and collectives associated with the country's contemporary art scene continued to step out of national frames in order to pursue a supranational cultural field. Tracing further back to the rich histories of Yugoslavia's Students' Cultural Centers and more generally self-organized collectives again discloses the manner in which its New Art Practice scene constituted both a regional and international cultural space. In the words of Ješa Denegri,

> [the Yugoslav art space] lasted, with gradual changes, throughout the entire period of the existence of the common state, creating—this is becoming quite transparent today—an intensive and stimulating working environment (in the spheres of exhibition and various other forms of cooperation) in which the majority of its actors felt themselves to be simultaneously members of their narrower or broader national culture and members of the international and universal currents of contemporary art.[9]

Throughout this book, the wider significance of Denegri's definition of the "Yugoslav art space" is undeniably present. Although the individual narratives presented here have been predominantly structured through the lenses of the former Yugoslavia's capitals (due to the transcosmopolitan nature of the New Art Practice), I hope that this study has highlighted the clear limitations of isolating narratives exclusively in their respective national units. From OHO's presence in the majority of Yugoslavia's republics, Novi Sad's Youth Tribune's multilingual press, the SKC Gallery's April Meetings, artists from the SKC Gallery collaborating with Podrum and the Group of Six Authors and vice versa, the significant impact of both Belgrade's and Zagreb's conceptual art scenes on Ljubljana's "alternative," the exhibiting of the New Art Practice in Sarajevo's Collegium Artisticum, and finally *Jugoslovenska dokumenta*—it is clear that it was the porosity of boundaries, and the hugely intertwined network of cultural exchange this implied, that enabled Yugoslavia's art scene to flourish. Clearly, the "Yugoslav" art scene was an inherently "Yugoslav" phenomenon because it emerged within an atmosphere in which interactions between the various art centers of the federation were vital. These are histories that cannot and should not be contained and segregated through a strictly nationalist approach. Rather than homogenizing the multivalent cultures of Yugoslavia, adopting a "federalist" lens serves to strengthen each individual entity, revealing a vital field of intellectual experience and a vibrant common ground.

This desire to build a mutually respectful and equitably distributed cultural space which cuts across ethnonationalist divides certainly resonates with many of us today. Over the last few decades, the art world has become increasingly international, even global. In fact, art's power has never been greater, in the sense that contemporary art is created and viewed everywhere. And yet, as a system of production and circulation, contemporary art is, as Terry Smith has put it, "as real as it gets when it comes to capital's effects."[10] It is not surprising, then, that as contemporary art continues to parallel the intense soaring of global wealth inequality, we seek refuge in the art production of the mid-1960s to the 1970s, and that this remains the most exhaustively discussed period in postwar art. Nor is it unusual that, in the background of receding welfare states—when cutbacks almost seem inevitable and a kind of permanent economic state of emergency has become normalized—the Yugoslav project and its powerful symbolism of anti-imperial struggle, its experimental culture, and its independent path to socialism has once again captured the imagination of international audiences. But precisely because the Yugoslav "third way" has once again revealed its imaginative potential, we must be wary of falling for a nostalgia that sentimentalizes the Yugoslav project and glosses over its complex gains and losses. At the same time, we should avoid taking on an entirely melancholic and defeated outlook, and instead take stock of both the hopeful idealism and striking contradictions that defined socialist Yugoslavia. In other words, we must, as I hope this book has done, master a narrative that critically assesses its "successes" and "failures," while avoiding the inclination toward fatalist and linear views.

Translated to the case of Yugoslavia's Students' Cultural Centers, one might indeed be driven to concede that these spaces were "marginalized institutions," "artistic ghettoes," or even a form of "reservation freedom." Yet, as compelling as such disillusioned outlooks are, they deprive the New Art Practice of its political relevance and ultimately disregard the significance of these spaces—the environments they fostered, the networks of sociability they facilitated—in nurturing some of the world's most significant artists and art collectives in the second half of the twentieth century. For it was clearly the presence of these institutions that resulted in a rich and diverse history of alternative art practices.

And it is here that the generative potential of studies on socialist Yugoslavia lies—not in accounts of defeat and disillusionment, but in real experience, the actors of which were the peoples of a multinational federation, with evolving subjective identities shaped by relations of tension, or, as this book has shown, by the proximity which was created. Simply put, if the New Art Practice is to hold any relevance for us today, it is in its determined efforts to foster a political horizon for the subject and community beyond the nation-state, and in its imagining of alternatives that seemed, particularly for Yugoslavia at that time, otherwise impossible to contemplate. And if self-management is to have any meaning in our increasingly barbarous world, it will be in the form of an emancipatory project by which individuals have the right and responsibility to participate in the management of everything that concerns them—from education to work, be it manual or intellectual, cultural or service-related. It will take on relevance in models of self-organization seeking to create networks of common struggle—against discrimination, racism, and the rule of financial elites; against rights that are dependent on income, which affect in particular women, sexual and racial minorities, youth, the old, and immigrants.[11] As a phenomenon that emerged from the more progressive elements of Yugoslav self-management precisely when its promises of equality and social justice were being compromised, the New Art Practice invites us to imagine what shape this emancipatory project might take.

NOTES

INTRODUCTION

1 I am referring here to Antonio Gramsci's famous quotation about "mobid symptoms," popularized by Slavoj Žižek, who paraphrased the original statement as: "The old world is dying, and the new world struggles to be born: now is the time of monsters." See, for example, Slavoj Žižek, "A Permanent Economic Emergency," *New Left Review* 64 (July–August 2010), 95.

2 Marijan Susovski, foreword to *The New Art Practice in Yugoslavia, 1966–1978*, ed. Marijan Susovski (Zagreb: Galerija Suvremene Umjetnosti, 1978), 3.

3 Ibid.

4 Bojana Pejić, "Yugoslavia: Body-Based Art: Serbia and Montenegro," in *Body and the East: From the 1960s to the Present*, ed. Zdenka Badovinac (Ljubljana: Moderna Galerija, 1999), 72.

5 Jelena Vesić, introduction to *Political Practices of (Post-)Yugoslav Art: Retrospective 01*, ed. Jelena Vesić, Zorana Dojić, Ivana Bago, and Dušan Đorđević Mileusnić (Belgrade: Prelom Kolektiv, 2010).

6 Ibid.

7 Ana Janevski, "As Soon as I Open My Eyes I See a Film: Experiments in Yugoslav Art in the 60s and 70s," in *As Soon as I Open My Eyes I See a Film*, ed. Ana Janevski (Warsaw: Museum of Modern Art, 2008), 27.

8 Blake Stimson, "The Promises of Conceptual Art," in *Conceptual Art: A Critical Anthology*, ed. Alexander Alberro and Blake Stimson (Cambridge, MA: MIT Press, 1999), xxxix.

9 Bojana Pejić, "Serbia: Socialist Modernism and the Aftermath," in *Aspects / Positions: 50 Years of Art in Central Europe, 1949–1999*, ed. Lóránd Hegyi and Achim Hochdörfer (Vienna: Mumok, 1999), 120.

10 Benjamin H. D. Buchloh, "Conceptual Art 1962–1969: From the Aesthetic of Administration to the Critique of Institutions," *October* 55 (Winter 1990), 140–143.

11 Miško Šuvaković, "Conceptual Art," in *Impossible Histories: Historic Avant-Gardes, Neo-Avant-Gardes, and Post-Avant-Gardes in Yugoslavia, 1918–1991*, ed. Dubravka Djurić and Miško Šuvaković (Cambridge, MA: MIT Press, 2003), 218.

12 See Igor Zabel, "Art and State: From Modernism to the Retroavantgarde," in Zabel's *Eseji I* (Ljubljana: Založba /*cf, 2006), 319–325.

13 Ibid.

14 Pejić, "Serbia," 117.

15 Ibid.

16 Šuvaković, "Introduction: Art and Politics," in *Impossible Histories*, 11.

17 Ivana Bago and Antonia Majača, "Dissociative Association, Dionysian Socialism, Non-Action, and Delayed Audience: Between Action and Exodus in the Art of the 1960s and the 1970s in Yugoslavia," in *Removed from the Crowd: Unexpected Encounters I*, ed. Ivana Bago, Antonia Majača, and Vesna Vuković (Zagreb: BLOK/ Delve, 2011), 302; Dunja Blažević, "Who's That Singing over There? Art in Yugoslavia and After ... 1949–1989," in *Aspects / Positions*, 88.

18 These include the solo exhibitions of Sanja Iveković (1976) and Mladen Stilinović (1980) at the GSU Zagreb, and the solo exhibition of Marina Abramović (1975) at the Salon MSU Beograd.

19 Ivana Bago and Antonia Majača, "Spit in the Eye of Truth (Then Quickly Close Your Eyes before It)," *Život umjetnosti: časopis o modernoj i suvremenoj umjetnosti i arhitekturi* 83, no. 2 (2008), 133.

20 Pejić, "Body-Based Art," 73.

21 Pejić, "Serbia," 119.

22 Ljiljana Kolešnik, "Conflicting Visions of Modernity and the Post-war Modern Art," in *Socialism and Modernity: Art, Culture, Politics 1950–1974*, ed. Ljiljana Kolešnik (Zagreb: Muzej Suvremene Umjetnosti, 2014), 157.

23 Miško Šuvaković, "Students' Cultural Centers as Reservations," in *SKC and Political Practices of Art*, ed. Prelom Kolektiv (Belgrade: Museum of Yugoslav History, 2008), 85.

24 Reiko Tomii, *Radicalism in the Wilderness: International Contemporaneity and 1960s Art in Japan* (Cambridge, MA: MIT Press, 2016), 11.

25 To date, the most engaging scholarship on the New Art Practice has framed it in relation to Belgrade's student demonstrations of June 1968, the most noteworthy of which is Branislav Jakovljević's *Alienation Effects*—a work that is both sensitive and observant of the changing tides of Yugoslav self-management. See Branislav Jakovljević, *Alienation Effects: Performance and Self-Management in Yugoslavia, 1945–91* (Ann Arbor: University of Michigan Press, 2016).

26 Terry Smith, *Art to Come: Histories of Contemporary Art* (Durham: Duke University Press, 2019), 4.

27 I am referring here to Stilinović's famous work from 1992, *An Artist Who Cannot Speak English Is No Artist*. Regularly featured on websites such as e-flux, the work consists of a banner made of pink silk with the title phrase stitched on with spindly black letters and a red accent on the word "no." Conveyed through what looks like a home-made protest banner, the statement "An artist who cannot speak English is no artist" is often read as a pointed aphorism on the dominance of the English-speaking art world over less visible regions.

28 Smith, *Art to Come*, 4.

29 Goran Đorđević, "International Strike of Artists," in *3+4 Časopis Studenata istorije umetnosti* (Belgrade, 1980); reprinted in Prelom Kolektiv, *SKC and Political Practices of Art*, 28–39.

30 Ivana Bago, "A Window and a Basement: Negotiating Hospitality at La Galerie des Locataires and Podroom—The Working Community of Artists," *ARTMargins* 1, no. 2–3 (June–October 2012), 116–146; *Grupa šestorice autora*, ed. Janka Vukmir (Zagreb: Soros Center for Contemporary Art, 1998).

31 A small booklet published by ŠKUC in 1988, and featuring a chronology of the gallery's activities in its first ten years of existence is one key exception. See *Galerija ŠKUC Ljubljana, 1978–1987*, ed. Marina Gržinić (Ljubljana: ŠKUC, 1988), and *NSK from Kapital to Capital: Neue Slowenische Kunst—an Event of the Final Decade of Yugoslavia*, ed. Zdenka Badovinac, Eda Čufer, and Anthony Gardner (Cambridge, MA: MIT Press, 2015).

32 See *The Heritage of 1989: Case Study: The Second Yugoslav Documents Exhibition*, ed. Ana Mizerit and Adela Železnik (Ljubljana: MSUM, 2017).

CHAPTER 1

1 "Sixth Congress of the National Youth Organisation of Yugoslavia" (September 1965), translated in Ralph Pervan, *Tito and the Students: The University and the University Student in Self-Managing Yugoslavia* (Nedlands: University of Australia Press, 1978), 15.

2 Ibid., 6.

3 See Darko Suvin, *Splendour, Misery and Possibilities: An X-Ray of Socialist Yugoslavia* (Leiden: Brill Books, 2019), 163; and Vladimir Unkovski-Korica, "Workers' Councils in the Service of the Market," *Europe-Asia Studies* (November 2013), 108–134.

4 Hans Deiter Seibel and Ukandi G. Damachi, *Self-Management in Yugoslavia and the Developing World* (London: Macmillan, 1982), 180–182; and Nada Novaković, *Propadanje radničke klase: Materijalni i društveni položaj radničke klase Jugoslavije od 1960 do 1990 godine* (Belgrade: Institut Društvenih Nauka, 2007), 163.

5 François Fejtö, *Histoire des démocraties populaires* (Paris: Seuil, 1979), 127–129.

6 Dušan Bilandžić, *Historija Socijalističke Federativne Republike Jugoslavije* (Zagreb: Školska Knjiga, 1978), 171.

7 It has frequently been claimed that these economic improvements were less a result of workers' self-management than of the scale of foreign economic aid. This claim is unfounded, given that economic aid totaled an amount that was roughly equivalent to the output of a single firm. See Catherine Samary, *Yugoslavia Dismembered* (New York: Monthly Review Press, 1995), 62.

8 For more information on this period, see A. R. Johnson, *The Transformation of Communist Ideology: The Yugoslav Case, 1945–1953* (Cambridge, MA: MIT Press, 1972).

9 See Suvin, *Splendour, Misery and Possibilities*, 255.

10 See records of the Seventh Congress of the League of Communists of Yugoslavia (Ljubljana, 22–26 April 1958), translated in The International Society for Socialist Studies, *The Programme of the League of Yugoslav Communists* (London: Aldgate Press, 1959).

11 Ibid.

12 "Izveštaj redakcije za likovno-izložbenu djelatnost Studentskog centra" (Zagreb), 27 November 1962, in *Galerija studentskog centra: 1961–73*, ed. Želimir Koščević (Zagreb: Galerija SC, 1975), 27. Unless otherwise noted, all translations to English are my own.

13 Opened in 1954, the year in which the final blow to socialist realism was struck with Miroslav Krleža's speech at the Congress of Artists, the Gallery of Contemporary Art swiftly became home to the influential group of artists and architects EXAT 51, which actively promoted an alliance of applied artists with a constructive impulse. For an account of Yugoslavia's short-lived experiment with socialist realism, see Bojana Videkanić, "Yugoslav Post-war Art and Socialist Realism: An Uncomfortable Relationship," *ARTMargins* 5, no. 2 (2016), 3–26.

14 Dubravko Horvatić, quoted in Koščević, *Galerija studentskog centra: 1961–73*, 33.

15 Ibid.

16 Armin Medosch, *New Tendencies: Art at the Threshold of the Information Revolution (1961–1978)* (Cambridge, MA: MIT Press, 2016), 7.

17 Matko Meštrović, "Ideologija novih tendencija" (1963), translated in *A Little-Known Story about a Movement, a Magazine, and the Computer's Arrival in Art: New Tendencies and Bit International, 1961–1973*, ed. Margit Rosen (Cambridge, MA: MIT Press, 2011), 117.

18 Želimir Koščević, "Oblikovanje grada—alternativi i problemi," *Razlog* (Zagreb), no. 2, 1964.

19 Želimir Koščević in conversation with Zvonko Maković, "Bezobrazno nas ignoriraju," *Studentski list* (Zagreb), Autumn 1971; translated from Koščević, *Galerija studentskog centra: 1961–73*, 154.

20 Ibid.

21 Želimir Koščević, "Predgovor," *Hit Parade* (Zagreb: Galerija SC, 1967), reprinted in *Galerija studentskog centra: 1961–73*, 45.

22 Ibid.

23 S.R., "Od dogmatizma do vandalizma," *Telegram* (Zagreb), 29 October 1967, 3.

24 Ibid.

25 Koščević, "Predgovor," 45.

26 Ibid.

27 S.R., "Od dogmatizma," 3.

28 Ibid.

29 Ibid.

30 Ibid.

31 "Hit Parade," *Večernji list* (Zagreb), 23 October 1967, 7.

32 Želimir Koščević, "We Succeeded in Creating a Beautiful and Instructive Thing That's Inevitably Been Irredeemably Lost, but Such is Life," *Newspaper Galerija Nova* (Zagreb), no. 18 (December 2008), 16.

33 Ibid.

34 Koščević, *Galerija studentskog centra: 1961–73*, 11.

35 S.R., "Od dogmatizma do vandalizma," 3.

36 Ibid.

37 "HIT-PARADA," *Borba* (Belgrade), 24 October 1967.

38 Ibid.

39 See Vladimir Unkovski-Korica, "Self-Management, Development and Debt: The Rise and Fall of the 'Yugoslav Experiment,'" in *Welcome to the Desert of Post-Socialism: Radical Politics after Yugoslavia*, ed. Srećko Horvat and Igor Štiks (London: Verso, 2015), 34.

40 See Susan Woodward, *Socialist Unemployment: The Political Economy of Yugoslavia, 1945–1990* (Princeton, NJ: Princeton University Press, 1995).

41 "Foreign Investments in Yugoslavia Discussed," Radio Free Europe Research, 23 March 1973, Open Society Archives, quoted in Ante Batović, *The Croatian Spring: Nationalism, Repression and Foreign Policy under Tito* (London: I. B. Tauris, 2017), 19.

42 See Ksenya Gurshtein, "Part 1: The OHO Group, 'Information,' and Global Conceptualism avant la lettre," *POST: Notes on Modern and Contemporary Art around the Globe*, MoMA New York, 25 August 2016, https://post.at.moma.org/content_items/850-part-1-the-oho-group-information-and-global-conceptualism-avant-la-lettre.

43 Lucy R. Lippard, "Escape Attempts," in *Six Years: The Dematerialization of the Art Object*, ed. Lucy R. Lippard and John Chandler (New York and London: Praeger Publishers, 1973); reprinted, with a new introduction (Berkeley: University of California Press, 1997), xix.

44 Ješa Denegri, "Primjeri konceptualne umjetnosti u Jugoslaviji," *Život umjetnosti* 15–16 (1971), 151.

45 See Igor Zabel, "A Short History of OHO," in *East Art Map: Contemporary Art and Eastern Europe*, ed. IRWIN (London: Afterall, 2006); Miško Šuvaković, *The Clandestine Histories of the OHO Group* (Ljubljana: Zavod P.A.R.A.S.I.T.E., 2010), 45; and Ksenya Gurshtein, "An Experimental Microcosm on the Edge of East and West," in *L'Internationale: Post-War Avant-Gardes between 1957 and 1986*, ed. Christian Höller (Zurich: JRP-Ringier, 2012).

46 Tomaž Brejc, "OHO as an Artistic Phenomenon, 1966–1971," in *The New Art Practice in Yugoslavia, 1966–1978,* ed. Marijan Susovski (Zagreb: Galerija Suvremene Umjetnosti, 1978), 14.

47 Piotr Piotrowski, *In the Shadow of Yalta: Art and the Avant-Garde in Eastern Europe, 1945–1989* (London: Reaktion Books, 2001), 189.

48 "Galerija studentskog centra objavljuje i raspisuje," *Novine GSC* (Zagreb), no. 5 (1969), 20.

49 Davor Matičević, "Predgovor," in *Inovacije u hrvatskoj umjetnosti sedamdesetih godina*, ed. Marijan Susovski (Zagreb: Galerija Suvremene Umjetnosti, 1982), 96.

50 Zvonko Maković, "Sanja Iveković," *Novine GSC* (Zagreb), no. 17 (March 1970), 51.

51 Želimir Koščević, "Aspekti ambijentalizacije prostora," *Život umjetnosti*, no. 13 (1971), 57, translated in Maja Fowkes, *The Green Bloc: Neo-Avant-Garde Art and Ecology under Socialism* (Budapest: CEU Press, 2015), 122.

52 Ibid.

53 Željka Čorak, "Razbroj zbroja—'Suma 680' izložba Slobodana Dimitrijevića u galeriji studentskog centra," *Telegram* (Zagreb), no. 502 (12 December 1969).

54 Davor Matičević, "Ozbiljnost igre: povodom izložbe 'Suma 680' Braco Dimitrijevića," *Studentski list* (Zagreb), no. 15 (November 1969).

55 Braco Dimitrijević, "Eksperiment komunikacija 1," *Novine GSC*, no. 12 (November 1969), 32.

56 Braco Dimitrijević, "Čovjek i čovjek stvaralac, vizija osjećanje, stvaranje i djelo," *Novine GSC*, no. 12 (November 1969), 33.

57 Claire Bishop, *Artificial Hells: Participatory Art and the Politics of Spectatorship* (London: Verso Books, 2012).

58 For a nuanced interpretation of how artists from the Eastern Bloc engaged with political circumstances through nonpolitical means, see Klara Kemp-Welch, *Antipolitics in Central European Art: Reticence as Dissidence under Post-Totalitarian Rule (1956–1989)* (London: I. B. Tauris, 2014).

59 Karl Marx, quoted by Josip Broz Tito, *Workers Manage Factories in Yugoslavia* (pamphlet, Belgrade), 26 June 1950, 4–43.

60 Benjamin H. D. Buchloh, "Michael Asher and the Conclusion of Modernist Sculpture," in *Neo-Avantgarde and Culture Industry: Essays on European and American Art from 1955 to 1975* (Cambridge, MA: MIT Press, 2000), 10.

61 For more information on this show, refer to Julia Bryan-Wilson's searching analysis in *Art Workers: Radical Practice in the Vietnam War Era* (Berkeley: University of California Press, 2011).

62 Maković, "Sanja Iveković," 51.

63 Filip Kovačević, "Marcuse in Yugoslavia" (unpublished PhD dissertation, University of Montenegro, 2003).

64 The *Praxis* journal was founded by a group of Belgrade and Zagreb philosophers and sociologists that gathered at the Korčula Summer School, demanding "a ruthless criticism of all that exists." See Gajo Petrović, "Čemu Praxis?," *Praxis 1* (1964), 4.

65 Herbert Marcuse, "The Realm of Freedom and the Realm of Necessity: A Reconsideration," *Praxis International* 5 (1969), 20–25, http://www.marcuse.org/herbert/pubs/60spubs/69praxis/69praxis7pagePDF.pdf.

66 Jaleh Mansoor, *Marhsall Plan Modernism: Italian Postwar Abstraction and the Beginnings of Autonomia* (Durham: Duke University Press, 2016), 149.

67 Ibid.

68 Samary, *Yugoslavia Dismembered*, 65.

69 Suvin, *Splendour, Misery and Possibilities*, 95.

70 Ibid, 95–96.

71 Announcement featured in *Večernji list* (Zagreb), 27 June 1969, 4.

72 Želimir Koščević, "Izložba žena i muškaraca," *Novine GSC*, no. 8 (June 1969), 29.

73 Ibid.

74 Ibid.

75 As observed by Ivana Bago, "Dematerialization and Politicization of the Exhibition: Curation as Institutional Critique in Yugoslavia during the 1960s and 1970s," *Museum and Curatorial Studies Review* 2, no. 1 (Spring 2014), 14.

76 Koščević, "Izložba žena i muškaraca," 29.

77 See Batović, *Croatian Spring*, 122.

78 Goran Trbuljak, "Ne želim pokazati ništa novo i originalno," *Novine GSC*, no. 30, November 1971, 117.

79 Bago, "Dematerialization and Politicization," 8.

80 Alexander Alberro, *Conceptual Art and the Politics of Publicity* (Cambridge, MA: MIT Press, 2003), 5.

81 Lippard, "Postface," in *Six Years*, 263.

82 Ibid.

83 Želimir Koščević, "Poštanske pošiljke," *Novine GSC*, no. 35 (March 1972), 135.

84 Želimir Koščević, *Ispitivanje međuprostora* (Zagreb: Centar za Kulturnu Djelatnost Saveza Socijalističke Omladine, 1978), 133. Translated in Ivana Bago, "The City as a Space of Plastic Happening: From Grand Proposals to Exceptional Gestures in the Art of the 1970s in Zagreb," *Journal of Urban History* 44, no. 1 (2018), 34.

85 As quoted in Bago, "The City as a Space."

86 Boris Bučan and Davor Tomičić, "Akcija 'Total': nacrt dekreta o demokratizaciji umjetnosti (s obrazloženjem)," *Novine GSC*, no. 22 (April 1970), 81.

87 Ibid.

88 Ibid.

89 Ibid.

90 Ibid.

91 See Ellen Turkish Commisso, *Workers' Control under Plan and Market: Implications of Yugoslav Self-Management* (New Haven: Yale University Press, 1980), 109; see also Suvin, *Splendour, Misery and Possibilities*, 235.

92 Stipe Šuvar, *Sociološki presjek jugoslavenskog društva* (Zagreb: Školska Knjiga, 1970), 165, quoted in Suvin, *Splendour, Misery and Possibilities*, 53.

93 "Akcija Total," *15 Dana: Časopis za kulturu i umetnosti*, no. 8–9 (November/December 1970), 8.

94 Marcus Tanner, *Croatia: A Nation Forged in War* (New Haven: Yale University Press, 1997), 185.

95 See Steven L. Burg, "Republican and Provincial Constitution Making in Yugoslav Politics," *Publius* 12, no. 1 (Winter 1982), 131–153; *Deseta sjednica CK SKH 1970*, ed. Milovan Baletić and Zdravko Židovec (Zagreb: Savez Komunista Hrvatske, Centralni Komitet, 1970); Batović, *Croatian Spring*, 135.

96 Jill Irvine, "The Croatian Spring and the Dissolution of Yugoslavia," in *State Collapse in South-Eastern Europe*, ed. Lenard J. Cohen and Jasna Dragović-Soso (West Lafayette, IN: Purdue University Press, 2007), 159.

97 Batović, *Croatian Spring*, 136.

98 Ibid.

99 Tanner, *Croatia*, 152.

100 Davor Matičevic, introduction to *Mogućnosti za 1971* (Zagreb: Galerija Suvremene Umjetnosti, 1971), 3.

101 Ibid.

102 Ibid.

103 Sanja Iveković, "'Žive skulpture i medijske interakcije': Razgovarale Nataša Govedić i Suzana Marjanić," *Zarez* (Zagreb) 101, no. 27 (March 2003), 12–14.

104 Matičevic, "Predgovor," 12.

105 Sanja Iveković, "Feminism, Activism and Historicisation: Sanja Iveković Talks to Antonia Majača," *N.paradoxa: International Feminist Art Journal* 23 (January 2009), 6.

106 Davor Matičević, "Uvod," in *Sanja Iveković: Dokumenti, 1949–1976*, ed. Davor Matičević (Zagreb: Galerija Suvremene Umjetnosti, 1976), n.p.

107 Branislav Dimitrijević, "In-Between Utopia and Nostalgia, or How the Worker Became Invisible on the Path from Shock-Worker to Consumer," in *Nostalgia on the Move*, ed. Mirjana Slavković (Belgrade: Museum of Yugoslav History, 2017), 34.

108 Bilandžić, *Historija Socijalističke Federativne Republike Jugoslavije*, 394, translated in Patrick Hyder-Patterson, *Bought and Sold: Living and Losing the Good Life in Socialist Yugoslavia* (Ithaca, NY: Cornell University Press, 2011), 303.

109 E. C., "Bućan Art," *Večernji list* (Zagreb), 20 November 1973, 11.

110 As noted by Lina Džuverović, "Boris Bućan," *Tate Online*, September 2015, https://www.tate.org.uk/whats-on/tate-modern/exhibition/ey-exhibition-world-goes-pop/artist-biography/boris-bucan.

111 Sanja Iveković, discussion with Suzana Milevska, *Open Institutions* (Zagreb), 23 January 2011, accessed 15 September 2015, http://zagreb.openinstitutions.net/2011/01/ivekovic-milevska-art-and-invisible-labour-political-critique-activism/.

112 As observed by Dennison Rusinow, "Crisis in Croatia: Part I: Post-Mortems after Karadjordjevo" (DIR-4-'72), *American Universities Field Staff Reports: Southeast Europe Series* 19, no.4 (June 1972), 16.

113 Batović, *Croatian Spring*, 236.

114 Quotations are from, respectively, Dennison Rusinow, *The Yugoslav Experiment, 1948–74* (Berkeley: University of California Press, 1977), 292, and Tanner, *Croatia*, 194.

115 Željka Čorak, "Predgovor," *6. zagrebački salon—Prijedlog* (Zagreb: Galerija Suvremene Umjetnosti, 1971).

116 As described by Bago in "City as a Space of Plastic Happening," 30.

117 Rene Hollos, "Pismo," *Studentski list*, no. 17 (25 May 1971), reprinted in *Novine GSC*, no. 28 (June 1971), 107.

118 Ibid.

119 Želimir Koščević, "Hollos I," *Novine GSC*, no. 28 (June 1971), 107.

120 Ibid.

121 Zvonko Maković, "Hollos II," *Novine GSC*, no. 28 (June 1971), 108.

122 Ibid.

123 Sekreterijat za komunalne poslove građevinstva i saobraćaj, "Šesti zagrebački salon, Zagreb," 10 June 1971, reprinted in *Novine GSC*, no. 28 (June 1971), 110.

124 Vinko Srhoj, *Grupa Biafra 1970–1978* (Zagreb: Art Studio Azinović, 2001), 62; Fowkes, *The Green Bloc*, 124.

125 Koščević, "We Succeeded," 14.

126 Ibid., 16.

127 Ibid., 17.

128 Lenin, quoted by Tito, *Workers Manage*.

129 American consulate in Zagreb, quoted in Batović, *Croatian Spring*, 188.

130 Rusinow, "Crisis in Croatia," 16.

131 Cvijeto Job, quoted in Dennison Rusinow, "Reopening of the 'National Question' in the 1960s," in *State Collapse in South-Eastern Europe*, 141.

132 Savka Dabčević-Kučar, quoted in Tanner, *Croatia*, 199.

133 Josip Broz Tito, speech at Karađorđevo, 2 December 1971, quoted in Batović, *Croatian Spring*, 213.

134 Ibid.

135 Irvine, "Croatian Spring," 168.

136 Goran Trbuljak, "Referendum," *Novine GSC*, no. 38 (September 1972), 154.

137 Samary, *Yugoslavia Dismembered*, 52.

138 Vladimir Gudac, *Novine GSC*, "The Last Number" (December 1975), n.p.

139 Ibid.

140 Ibid.

141 Koščević, *Galerija studentskog centra*, 12.

CHAPTER 2

1 Photographs of *Action Heart-Object* were featured in Klaus Groh's seminal *Aktuelle Kunst in Osteuropa*—the first Western European survey of contemporary art from the geographic region of Eastern Europe. See Sanja Kojić Mladenov, *Bogdanka Poznanović: Contact Art* (Novi Sad: Muzej Savremene Umetnosti Vojvodine, 2016), 44; and Klaus Groh, *Aktuelle Kunst in Osteuropa* (Kölin: DuMont-Schauberg, 1972), n.p.

2 The 1954 Novi Sad Agreement is translated in Robert D. Greenberg, *Language and Identity in the Balkans: Serbo-Croatian and Its Disintegration* (Oxford: Oxford University Press, 2008), 187.

3 In many ways, this flourishing was connected to Yugoslavia's unfettered political decentralization after the ousting of Secret Police Chief Aleksandar Ranković in 1966. For more information, consult Steven L. Burg, *Conflict and Cohesion in Socialist Yugoslavia* (Princeton, NJ: Princeton University Press, 1983), 52.

4 Judita Šalgo, "Tribina mladih: otvorena—zatvorena," *Index: List studenata Vojvodine*, 21 October 1970, 7.

5 Ibid.

6 Ibid.

7 Ibid.

8 Miško Šuvaković, "Kulturna emancipacija i interventno prevodilaštvo Dejana Poznanovića," in *Bogdanka i Dejan Poznanović: Umetnost, mediji i aktivizam na kraju moderne*, ed. Miško Šuvaković (Novi Sad: Muzej Savremene Umetnosti, Vojvodina, 2011), 41.

9 *Rok: časopis za književnost i estetičko ispitivanje stvarnosti*, no. 1, ed. Bora Ćosić (Belgrade: Direkcija, 1969), n.p.

10 Rastko Močnik, "Edicija OHO," trans. Dejan Poznanović, in *Rok*, n.p.

11 OHO Katalog, "Jabuka," first published in *Tribuna*, 24 April 1968, reprinted and translated by Dejan Poznanović in *Rok*, n.p.

12 OHO Katalog, "Ritual," *Rok*, n.p.

13 Igor Zabel, "A Short History of OHO," in *East Art Map*, ed. IRWIN (London: Afterall, 2006), 413.

14 Mirko Radojičić, "Activity of Group KÔD," in *The New Art Practice in Yugoslavia, 1966–1978*, ed. Marijan Susovski (Zagreb: Galerija Suvremene Umjetnosti, 1978), 38.

15 Milenko Mataković in interview with Beti Žerovc, "The OHO Files: Interview with Milenko Matakovič," *ARTMargins Online*, 24 August 2011, http://www.artmargins.com/index.php/interview-with-milenko-matanovi.

16 As observed by Maja Fowkes, *The Green Bloc: Neo-Avant-Garde and Ecology under Socialism* (Budapest: CEU Press), 69.

17 For a detailed account of the events underpinning the crisis, see Burg, *Conflict and Cohesion*, 88–100.

18 Tomaž Brejc, "OHO as an Artistic Phenomenon, 1966–71," in Susovski, *New Art Practice*, 15.

19 Marko Pogačnik in interview with Beti Žerovc, "The OHO Files: Interview with Marko Pogačnik," *ARTMargins Online*, 27 July 2013, http://www.artmargins.com/index.php/interview-with-marko-poganik.

20 Ibid.

21 Quoted in Maja Breznik, "Urban Theatre: The OHO Group Happenings, 1966–69," *M'Ars* (Moderna Galerija, Ljubljana), no. 3–4 (1995), 69.

22 Tomaz Šalamun, "Why I Drew the Line" (Novi Sad, 1969). A translation of Šalamun's poem and a reenactment of his Novi Sad action by Samo Gosarič are available on Vimeo, accessed 8 June 2020, https://vimeo.com/2428834.

23 Brejc, "OHO," 15. In his 1969 *An Essay on Liberation*, Herbert Marcuse deployed the term "new sensibility," which Brejc also used in the same year to describe OHO's first large exhibition, *Pradedje* [Great-Grandfathers], at Zagreb's Gallery of Contemporary Art. See Herbert Marcuse, "The New Sensibility," in *An Essay on Liberation* (Boston: Beacon Press, 1969), 23–48.

24 Radojičić, "Activity of Group KÔD," 38.

25 Ibid.

26 Lucy Lippard and John Chandler, *Six Years: The Dematerialization of the Art Object* (Berkeley: University of California Press, 1997).

27 Marcuse, *Essay on Liberation*, 37.

28 Radojičić, "Activity of Group KÔD," 40.

29 Miroslav Mandić, "Galerije," *Index: List studenata Vojvodine*, 21 October 1970, 7.

30 Ibid.

31 Harold Rosenberg, "The American Action Painters" (1952), in *Art in Theory, 1900–1990: An Anthology of Changing Ideas*, ed. Charles Harrison and Paul Wood (Oxford: Blackwell Publishers, 1992), 583.

32 George Maciunas, letter to Tomas Schmit of January 1964, published in Caroline Tisdall, *Joseph Beuys* (New York: Guggenheim Museum, 1979), 84.

33 Ibid.

34 Slavko Bogdanović, "UMETNOST (DANAS); UMETNIK (STVARALAC), UČESNIK (AUTOR)," handwritten text, published in *Grupa KÔD, GRUPA (Ǝ, Grupa (Ǝ -KÔD: Retrospektiva*, ed. Miško Šuvaković (Novi Sad: Muzej Savremene Umetnosti, Vojvodina, 1995).

35 As Slavko Bogdanović revealed in email correspondence with the author, 24 November 2017. According to Tišma, such conflicts of interest were emblematic of the tension between the "old" and the "new"; see Jadran Boban, "Kralj šume u transu rock'n'rolla—razgovor sa Slobodanom Tišmom," *Zarez* (Zagreb) 146 (2005).

36 Radojičić, "Activity of Group KÔD," 44.

37 See Želimir Žilnik, in New Media Center_kuda.org, *Omitted History* (Novi Sad: Daniel Print, 2007), 64.

38 Šalgo, "Tribina mladih: otvorena—zatvorena," 7.

39 "Šta će biti sa Tribinom mladih?," *Index: List studenata Vojvodine* (Novi Sad), 11 November 1970.

40 Ibid.

41 Ibid.

42 Gal Kirn, "From the Primacy of Partisan Politics to the Post-Fordist Tendency in Yugoslav Self-Management Socialism," in *Post-Fordism and Its Discontents*, ed. Gal Kirn (Maastricht: Jan Van Eyck Academie, 2010), 264.

43 Milovan Đilas, *The New Class: An Analysis of the Communist System* (New York: Frederick A. Praeger, 1957).

44 *1958 Program of the League of Communists of Yugoslavia*, quoted in Dejan Jović, *Yugoslavia: A State That Withered Away* (West Lafayette, IN: Purdue University Press, 2003), 74.

45 Ibid.

46 Đilas, *The New Class*, 81.

47 Savez Komunista Srbije (SKS), Predsedništvo, *Aktivnost Saveza komunista Srbije u borbi protiv nacionalizma* (Belgrade: Komunist, 1972), 103–104; translated in Burg, *Conflict and Cohesion*, 102.

48 Josip Broz Tito, quoted in *Borba*, Belgrade, 16 April 1971; translated in Burg, *Conflict and Cohesion*, 129.

49 Ibid.; Đilas, *The New Class*.

50 Radojičić, "Activity of Group KÔD," 41.

51 Ibid.

52 The chronology of events at Novi Sad's Youth Tribune has been amassed in Gordana Đilas and Nedeljko Mamula, *Tribina Mladih: 1954–1977* (Novi Sad: Kulturni Centar Novog Sada, 2004).

53 Radojičić, "Activity of Group KÔD," 44.

54 These disqualifications were collected and quoted in Hrvoje Turković, "Farsa oko novosadske tribine mladih," *Studentski list* (Zagreb), no. 4–5 (16 February 1971).

55 "Izložba psovke," *Novosti* (Belgrade), 30 January 1971.

56 Ibid.

57 Ibid.

58 Turković, "Farsa," n.p.

59 See Gal Kirn, "On Yugoslav Market Socialism Through Živojin Pavlović's *When I Am Dead and Pale*, 1967," in *The Cultural Life of Capitalism in Yugoslavia: (Post)Socialism and Its Other*, ed. Dijana Jelača, Maša Kolanović, and Danijela Lugarić (London: Palgrave Macmillan, 2017), 145.

60 "Izložba psovke."

61 Rade Bojanović, "Lucifer and the Lord," *Praxis International* (Zagreb), no. 3–4 (1971), 374.

62 Turković, "Farsa," n.p.

63 Josip Broz Tito, quoted in *Kako ostvarujemo dogovor: posle XVII sednice Predsedništva*, ed. Savo Martinović (Belgrade: Komunist, 1971), 32.

64 Sava Dautović, "Zakuska političkih uvreda," *Vjesnik* (Zagreb), 2 March 1971. In a recent video interview, Rešin Tučić spoke of how he had "talked against [the] local government structure. When Makavejev heard what I was saying, Žilnik and he came to me and said 'tell them you were drunk,' and I said, 'I wasn't drunk, I meant to say that.'" Video interview owned by New Media Center_Kuda.org (Novi Sad), 2006.

65 Miroslav Antić and Pero Zubac, "Žurnal Miroslava Antića; Neki feler u mladima," *Dnevnik* (Novi Sad), 23 February 1971.

66 Ibid.

67 Dautović, "Zakuska."

68 Želimir Žilnik, "Žilnik demantuje," *Dnevnik* (Novi Sad), 24 Feburary 1971.

69 Ibid.

70 Ibid.

71 Referred to in Dautović, "Zakuska," and more recently corroborated by Vujica Rešin Tučić, in an interview with Peđa Vranešević, "Čemu umetnost," *Vreme*, no. 1159, 21 March 2013, http://www.vreme.com/cms/view.php?id=1105012.

72 Although Yugoslav communists never explicitly supported the communist reformers under the leadership of Alexander Dubček, Tito's visit to Prague on 9–10 August 1968 made the Kremlin suspicious that Czechoslovakia might follow Yugoslavia's individual path to socialism. For a more detailed discussion of Yugoslavia's relationship with the Soviet Union at this time, see Vladimir Unkovski-Korica, *The Economic Struggle for Power in Tito's Yugoslavia: From World War II to Non-Alignment* (London: I. B. Tauris, 2016); and Ragna Boden, "Soviet World Policy in the 1970s: A Three-Level Game," in *The Crisis of Socialist Modernity*, ed. Marie-Janine Calic et al. (Göttingen: Vandenhoeck & Ruprecht, 2011), 184–204.

73 On the last day of the 17th Session of the Presidium of the LCY, 30 April 1971, Soviet Party Secretary Leonid Brezhnev phoned Tito to enquire about Yugoslavia's "internal situation that he qualified as 'very important,'" and applauded the party's "initiative and the strenuousness to give the correct answer to all enemies of socialism." Later, in September, Brezhnev even made a visit to Yugoslavia, and the Soviet press coverage of the event referred to the existence of conflict and opposition to socialism from domestic forces in the federation. See "Note for Comrade Veljko Mićunović's Personal Use," Arhiv Jugoslavije (AJ), Kabinet Predsednika Republike (KPR), fond 837, I-5-b, 1971 (SSSR), translated by Milorad Lazić and available on the Wilson Center's Digital Archive, https://digitalarchive.wilsoncenter.org/document/175844.

74 Dautović, "Zakuska."

75 This allusion was revealed more recently by Rešin Tučić and Vranešević, "Čemu umetnost." Godina's *Zdravi ljudi za razonodu* is available on Youtube with English subtitles, accessed 23 March 2020, http://www.youtube.com/watch?feature=player_embedded&v=C-Jga-bb48M#!.

76 Grupa za nove umetnosti "Februar," "Otvoreno pismo jugoslovenskoj javnosti" [Open Letter to the Yugoslav Public], published in *Student* (Belgrade), 23 February 1971. Bogdanović's unpublished letter, "Dear Jaša," also mentions it was published in Ljubljana's student paper, *Tribuna*. See Slavko Bogdanović, "Dragi Jaša," published in Šuvaković, *Grupa KÔD*.

77 Dautović, "Zakuska."

78 Herbert Marcuse, "Repressive Tolerance" (1965), in Robert Paul Wolff, Barrington Moore Jr., and Herbert Marcuse, *A Critique of Pure Tolerance* (Boston, MA: Beacon Press, 1969), 95–137.

79 Zvonko Maković, "Kad li će procvjetati tikve," *Tjedni list omladine*, February 1971, 26.

80 Dragoslav Mihailović, *Kad su cvetale tikve* (Novi Sad: Matica Srpska, 1968).

81 For information on the book's reception, see Jasna Dragović-Soso, *Saviours of the Nation: Serbia's Intellectual Opposition and the Revival of Nationalism* (Montreal: McGill-Queen's University Press, 2002), 23–24.

82 S. Božović, "'Februar' osuđen u Martu," *Novosti* (Belgrade), 4 March 1971.

83 Ibid.; Branko Andrić, "'Februar' je prestao da postoji još u januaru," *Index*, 24 February 1971.

84 Andrić, "'Februar.'"

85 Ivan Kuvačić, "Contemporary Forms of Mental Violence," in "Power and Humanity Issue," *Praxis: A Philosophical Journal* (Zagreb), no. 1–2 (1970), 130–135.

86 Ibid.

87 These accusations were unfounded, given that two of Neoplanta's most important directors, Želimir Žilnik and Dušan Makavejev, had emerged from the amateur film clubs of Belgrade and Novi Sad, and that the company had, in accordance with its founding self-management principles, provided a technical base and film education for inexperienced film workers. For more information, consult Agnė Rimkutė, "Negotiating Self-Management While Producing Films: Yugoslav New Wave and Neoplanta

Film Studio in 1966–1972" (unpublished MA dissertation, Central European University, Budapest, 2014).

88 Slavko Bogdanović, "PROGRAM ČASOPISA 'L.H.O.O.Q.'" (Bosut, Novi Sad, 1971), reprinted in Šuvaković, *Grupa KÔD*, 76.

89 Benjamin H. D. Buchloh, "Allegorical Procedures: Appropriation and Montage in Contemporary Art," *Artforum*, September 1972, 43.

90 Radojičić, "Activity of Group KÔD," 45.

91 Bogdanović, "PROGRAM," 76.

92 Grupa za nove umetnosti "Februar," "Otvoreno pismo."

93 Slavko Bogdanović, "Posle dugog vremena," handwritten, Bosut, Novi Sad, 20 January 1972, reprinted in Šuvaković, *Grupa KÔD*, 77.

94 George Schöpflin, *Politics in Eastern Europe: 1945–1992* (London: Blackwell Publishers, 1993), 179.

95 Dušan Bjelić and Miroslav Mandić, "Droga i revolucija: narkomani svih zemalja ujedinite se!," *Zrenjanin*, 27 May 1971; reprinted in Šuvaković, *Grupa KÔD*.

96 In one line, *L.H.O.O.Q.* asks, "What do you think about the measures against drugs in Yugoslavia?," to which Dušan Bjelić responds: "those are representative measures and extreme tendencies of a handful of radical extremists who, together with Ranković, have made an atomic bomb." Ibid.

97 Miroslav Mandić, "Pesma o filmu," *Új Symposion* (Novi Sad), 76+77, September 1971. Dušan Makavejev's film *WR*, discussed in this essay, was financed by Neoplanta Film and Telepol, a Bavarian TV company, both working in the international market. Although it was not officially banned, the film was not publicly screened in Yugoslavia until 1987. It also prompted Makavejev's dismissal from the Communist Party and his emigration to Paris.

98 Mandić, "Pesma o filmu."

99 B. Mirosavljević, "Zabrana zbog laži i uvreda," *Novosti* (Belgrade), 11 December 1971.

100 "Neprihvatljive tendencije," *Novosti* (Belgrade), 15 December 1971.

101 Ibid.

102 According to Bogdanović's letter to Jaša Zlobec, Bogdanović, "Dragi Jaša," 1971, reprinted in Šuvaković, *Grupa KÔD*, 74.

103 Schöpflin, *Politics*, 179. As Bogdanović noted, "twelve existing copies of *L.H.O.O.Q.* [were] altogether enough for one illegal newspaper." See Bogdanović, "Posle dugog vremena," 77.

104 Bogdanović, "Dragi Jaša," 74.

105 Ibid.

106 Ibid. For more information on the ousting of the Serbian liberal leadership, see chapter 3.

107 Emil Rojc et al., *Deseti kongres SKJ: Dokumenti* (Belgrade: Komunist, 1974), 387.

108 Responding to news from his colleagues at Belgrade University, Noam Chomsky described these developments as the "new line's return to a crude form of ideological indoctrination, and the abandonment of all former sophisticated ideas of creating new socialist consciousness through dialogues or struggles of opinion and patient persuasion." Noam Chomsky, "The Repression of Belgrade University," *The New York Review of Books*, 7 February 1972.

109 Bogdanović, "Dragi Jaša," 74.

110 Ibid.

111 Ibid.

112 Slavko Bogdanović, "Pesma underground Tribina Mladih," in "Underground Issue," *Student* (Belgrade), 16 December 1971.

113 Ibid.

114 Vladimir Unkovski-Korica, "Self-Management, Development and Debt: The Rise and Fall of the 'Yugoslav Experiment,'" in *Welcome to the Desert of Post-Socialism: Radical Politics after Yugoslavia*, ed. Srećko Horvat and Igor Štiks (London: Verso, 2014), 42.

115 Bogdanović, "Pesma underground."

116 Ibid.

117 Josip Broz Tito, in a closed meeting with the Serbian leadership on 9 October 1972, printed in *NIN*, 15 April 1973, 39–50, translated in Burg, *Conflict and Cohesion*, 175.

118 Dušan Makavejev, interview by Christian Braad Thomsen, video recording, Denmark, 1972, quoted in Rimkutė, "Negotiating Self-Management," 91.

119 Kuvačić, "Contemporary Forms," 130.

120 Slobodan Tišma, video interview owned by New Media Center_Kuda.org (Novi Sad), 2006.

121 This connection has already been observed by Branka Ćurčić, in "Less of a Cultural Patrimony—More of an Actualisation of Past Practices of Cultural Dissent," paper presented at "Evaluating and Formative Goals of Art Criticism in Recent (de)Territorialized Contexts," AICA Press conference, Skopje, 29 May 2009.

122 See Boban, "Kralj šume."

123 See Luis Camnitzer, Jane Farver, Rachel Weiss, and László Beke, *Global Conceptualism: Points of Origin, 1950s–1980s* (New York: Queens Museum of Art, 1999).

124 Bogdanović, "Pesma underground."

125 Denegri, "Prisećanje na rad grupe OHO," *Polja: časopis za književnost i teroiji*, no. 190 (December 1974), 20. In the exhibition catalogue for the 1978 OHO retrospective at Ljubljana's Students' Cultural Center, Tomaž Brejc explained that OHO's decision to stop exhibiting on the "threshold of their greatest success" was because they never "belonged to the 'art system' dictated by the art market and exhibition policies in the late sixties." See Tomaž Brejc, *OHO, 1966–1971* (Ljubljana: Študentski Kulturni Center, 1978).

CHAPTER 3

1 Nebojša Popov, *Društveni sukobi izazov sociologiji: "Beogradski Jun" 1968* (Belgrade: Službeni Glasnik, 2008), 36–37.

2 Živojin Pavlović, *Ispljuvak pun krvi: Dnevnik '68* (Belgrade: Službeni Glasnik, 2008), 29.

3 For a more thorough treatment of events in Belgrade in 1968, consult Branislav Jakovljević, "Human Resources: June 1968, *Hair*, and the Beginning of Yugoslavia's End," *Grey Room* 30 (Winter 2008), 38–53, and his *Alienation Effects: Performance and Self-Management in Yugoslavia, 1945–91* (Ann Arbor: University of Michigan Press, 2016).

4 See Ralph Pervan, *Tito and the Students: The University and the University Student in Self-Managing Yugoslavia* (Nedlands: University of Australia Press, 1978). For a global contextualization of "Belgrade's 1968," consult Boris Kanzleiter, "1968 in Yugoslavia: Student Revolt between East and West," in *Between Prague Spring and French May: Opposition and Revolt in Europe 1960–80*, ed. Martin Klimke, Jacco Pekelder, and Joachim Scharloth (New York and Oxford: Berghahn, 2011), 84–100.

5 Media Centar Sarajevo, *Demonstracije u Sarajevu* (Sarajevo, 1968), VHS; quoted in Madigan Fichter, "Yugoslav Protest: Student Rebellion in Belgrade, Zagreb, and Sarajevo in 1968," *Slavic Review* 75, no. 1 (Spring 2016), 108.

6 Hrvatski Državni Arhiv (HDA), Policijska Uprava Zagreb (PUZ), Studentska Događanja (SD)/2, Informacije Leci Prijave u Vezi Studentskih Dogadaja (IL) (Inspector Zdravko Parag, "Informacija," 6 June 1968); quoted in Fichter, "Yugoslav Protest," 108.

7 Kemal Kurspahić, "Moja '68': Poziv na ljudski, pravedeniji, bolji svet," in *Šezdeset osma—Lične istorije*, ed. Đorđe Malavrazić (Belgrade: Službeni Glasnik, 2008), 202; translated in Ljubica Spaskovska, *The Last Yugoslav Generation: The Rethinking of Youth Politics and Cultures in Late Socialism* (Manchester, UK: Manchester University Press, 2017), 43.

8 Nebojša Popov, *Sukobi*, 66; quoted in Jakovljević, "Human Resources," 43.

9 Untitled statement from the Law Faculty of Belgrade University, 4 June 1968, in "Dokumenti," 87–89; HDA, PUZ, SD/2, IL (Mirko Petričec, "Izvještaj," June 6, 1968); quoted in Fichter, "Yugoslav Protest," 110.

10 Untitled statement from the Philosophy Faculty, 5 June 1968, in "Dokumenti," 156; quoted in Fichter, "Yugoslav Protest," 111.

11 HDA, PUZ, SD/2, IL (Zdravko Parag, "Informacija," 5 June 1968); "Proglas sa mitinga solidarnosti u Sarajevu," 5; quoted in Fichter, "Yugoslav Protest," 115.

12 "Akciono-politički program," *Student*, special issue 2 (1968), 1–2.

13 Ibid.

14 Ibid.

15 Student Action Committee, "Political Action Program," Belgrade, June 1968, translated in Sarah Zabić, "Praxis, Student Protest and Purposive Social Action: The Humanist Marxist Critique of the League of Communists of Yugoslavia, 1964–1975" (unpublished MA dissertation, Kent State University, 2010), 79.

16 Jakovljević, "Human Resources."

17 Nebojša Popov, *Danas*, 21 June 1988, 72, translated in Jasna Dragović-Soso, *Saviours of the Nation: Serbia's Intellectual Opposition and the Revival of Nationalism* (Montreal: McGill-Queen's University Press, 2002), 28

18 Ješa Denegri, "Art in the Past Decade," in *The New Art Practice in Yugoslavia, 1966–1978*, ed. Marijan Susovski (Zagreb: Galerija Suvremene Umjetnosti, 1978), 7.

19 Stevan Vuković, "Troubles with Reality, or Who Was to Carry the Burden of Self-Management," in *As Soon as I Open My Eyes I See a Film: Experiments in Yugoslav Art in the 60s and 70s*, ed. Ana Janevski (Warsaw: Museum of Modern Art in Warsaw, 2011), 49.

20 "Programming Principles of Belgrade's Students' Cultural Center," 1971; translated in *SKC and Political Practices of Art*, ed. Prelom Kolektiv (Belgrade: Museum of Yugoslav History, 2008), 65.

21 *Istorija*, 3 April 1971, reprinted in *Ovo je studentski kulturni centar: Prvih 25 godina*, ed. Slavoljub Veselinović (Belgrade: Students' Cultural Center, 1996), n.p.

22 "Programming Principles," 65.

23 Božidar Zečević, "Talason ili mala istorija zavere," in Veselinović, *Ovo je*, 19.

24 Ibid.

25 *Tribuna SKC-a*, 1971; reprinted in Veselinović, *Ovo je*, 29–30.

26 Nikezić, quoted in Sabrina P. Ramet, *The Three Yugoslavias: State-Building and Legitimation, 1918–2005* (Bloomington: Indiana University Press, 2006), 244.

27 "Programming Principles," 65.

28 Raša Todosijević, quoted in Dejan Sretenović, "Art as a Social Practice: Time, World, and Raša Todosijević," in *Thank You Raša Todosijević*, ed. Dejan Sretenović (Belgrade: Muzej Savremene Umetnosti, 2002), 3.

29 Ibid.

30 See MoMA's press release for "The Museum of Modern Art to Exhibit American Art in Belgrade," 18 June 1956, accessed 2 June 2020, https://www.moma.org/momaorg/shared/pdfs/docs/press_archives/2093/releases/MOMA_1956_0074_64.pdf.

31 See, for example, Eva Cockroft, "Abstract Expressionism: Weapon of the Cold War," *Artforum* 15, no. 10 (June 1974), 39–41.

32 For a detailed analysis of the exhibition and its significance in Yugoslavia, consult Branislav Dimitrijević, "'Iron Curtain Raiser': An Exhibition of American Modern Art in Belgrade and Its Relation to 'Socialist Modernism' and 'Socialist Consumerism' in SFR Yugoslavia in the 1950s," in *Different Modernisms, Different Avant-Gardes: Problems of Eastern European Art after World War II*, Kumu Art Museum Autumn Conference, ed. Sirje Helme (Tallinn, Estonia: Kadrioru Kunstimuuseum, 2009), 313–342.

33 Veljko Petrović, quoted in Predrag J. Marković, *Beograd izmedju istoka i zapada, 1948–1965* (Belgrade: Službeni List, 1996), 421.

34 Their prominence was in part connected to the exhibitions shown at the city's Museum of Contemporary Art, founded in 1965 under the initiative of the established painter Miodrag B. Protić.

35 In 1953, the Commission for International Cultural Relations also organized Le Corbusier and Henry Moore shows, along with exhibitions on Dutch painting from 1850 to 1950, including the work of Mondrian and Van Doesburg; work and folklore portrayed in Belgian art in the nineteenth and twentieth centuries; French tapestries from midcentury to present day; and English watercolors and drawings. The continuity with prewar art developments was further sealed with an exhibition titled *Seventy Paintings and Sculptures from 1920–40*, organized in 1951 in the ULUS [Udruženje Likovnih Umetnika Srbije, or Association of Fine Artists of Serbia] Gallery in Belgrade. See Ješa Denegri, *Srpska umetnost 1950–2000* (Belgrade: Orion Art, 2013).

36 Jelena Vesić has described this arrangement as an "ambivalent combination of *horizontal* and *vertical* forms of organization," making the SKC both a state institution of culture and "the site of spontaneous, occasionally subversive gatherings of heterogeneous communities of artists, intellectuals, and political activists." See Jelena Vesić, "The Student Cultural Center (SKC) as the Art Scene," in *Parallel Chronologies: An Archive of East European Exhibitions*, http://tranzit.org/exhibitionarchive/essays/jelena-vesic/.

37 As Jakovljević has noted, although Blažević modeled the SKC's activities on London's Institute for Contemporary Art (ICA), its organization "was profoundly informed by the Yugoslav experience of self-management.... While each SKC as a state-funded institution had an administrative staff that interfaced with outside political institutions and funding bodies, internally, the artists and art historians associated with the gallery enjoyed full artistic autonomy, which led to a modular and coordinated structure of decision-making." See Branislav Jakovljević, "The Howling Wilderness of the Maladaptive Struggle in Belgrade in New York," *ARTMargins* 7, no. 2 (June 2018), 24.

38 Richard Demarco, *Eight Yugoslav Artists: Edinburgh Arts 73: Marina Abramović, Radomir Damnjan, Nuša & Srečo Dragan, Neša Paripović, Zoran Popović, Raša Todosijević, Gergely Urkom* (Edinburgh: Richard Demarco Gallery, 1973), n.p.

39 Ibid.

40 Dunja Blažević "Who's That Singing over There? Art in Yugoslavia and After ... 1949–1989," in *Aspects / Positions: 50 Years of Art in Central Europe, 1949–1999*, ed. Lóránd Hegyi and Achim Hochdörfer (Vienna: Mumok, 1999), 89.

41 Gergelj Urkom, in *Oktobar '72*, ed. SKC, exh. cat. (Belgrade: SKC Galerija, 1972). Translated in *Impossible Histories: Historic Avant-Gardes, Neo-Avant-Gardes, and Post-Avant-Gardes in Yugoslavia, 1918–1991*, ed. Dubravka Djurić and Miško Šuvaković (Cambridge, MA: MIT Press, 2003), 561.

42 Jasna Tijardović, "Marina Abramović, Slobodan Milivojević, Neša Paripović, Zoran Popović, Raša Todosijević, Gergelj Urkom," in Susovski, *The New Art Practice in Yugoslavia, 1966–1978*, 59; Ješa Denegri, "Drangularijum," *Drangularijum*, exh. cat.

(Belgrade: SKC Galerija, June 1971), n.p. Duchamp's readymades were not in fact exhibited in Yugoslavia until 1984. See *Marsel Dišan: izbor tekstova* (Belgrade: Muzej Savremene Umetnosti, 1984).

43 Gergelj Urkom, in *Drangularijum*.

44 Raša Todosijević, in ibid.

45 Ibid. For a gender-based analysis of Todosijević's work at this time, see Jasmina Tumbas, "Decision as Art: Performance in the Balkans," in *Performing Arts in the Second Public Sphere*, ed. Katalin Cseh-Varga and Adam Czirak (Basingstoke: Palgrave Macmillan, 2018), 184–201.

46 Bojana Pejić, in *Drangularijum*.

47 Ibid.

48 Ibid.

49 Raša Todosijević, interview with the author, Belgrade, May 2012.

50 Ibid.

51 Ibid.

52 Raša Todosijević, "'Art Is the Basis, Beer Is the Basis, Beans Are the Basis'—The Belgrade Art Scene of the 1970s, Early Performances and Short Stories on Art: An Interview with Hans Ulrich Obrist," *Spike Magazine* (Brighton, UK), 2008, 78.

53 "Izložba umesto protesta," *Politika ekspres* (Belgrade), October 1972, 10.

54 Ibid.

55 Ibid.

56 Dunja Blažević, introduction to *Oktobar '72*, ed. SKC, exh. cat. (Belgrade: SKC Galerija 1972), n.p.

57 Ibid.

58 Jasna Tijardović, "Notes on Education in Art as Personal/Public Activity in Belgrade's Art Scene of the '70s," Belgrade (1975), accessed 10 March 2013, http://radical.temp.si/2011/07/notes-on-education-in-art-as-personal-public-activity-in-belgrade-art-scene-in-seventies-by-jasna-tijardovic/.

59 Dobrica Ćosić, "Kritika vladajuće ideološke koncepcije u nacionalnoj politici," *Stvarno i moguće* (Ljubljana/ Zagreb), 1982, 29; quoted in Dragović-Soso, *Saviours of the Nation*, 39.

60 Ibid.

61 Dobrica Ćosić, in Slavoljub Djukić, *Čovek u svom vremenu: Razgovori sa Dobricom Ćosićem* (Belgrade: Filip Višnjić, 1989), 209; quoted in Dragović-Soso, *Saviours of the Nation*, 41.

62 Dragović-Soso, *Saviours of the Nation*, 38.

63 For information on the reactions of various Serbian intellectuals to the political and economic decentralization of the 1960s, see ibid.

64 Josip Broz Tito, taken from the report in *NIN*, 15 April 1973, quoted in Steven L. Burg, *Conflict and Cohesion in Socialist Yugoslavia* (Princeton, NJ: Princeton University Press, 1983), 174.

65 Savez Komunista Srbije, Centralni Komitet, *Izveštaj o aktivnosti Saveza komunista Srbije i radu Centralnog komiteta izmedju Šestog i Sedmog kongresa* (Belgrade: Komunist, 1974), 18; see Burg, *Conflict and Cohesion*, 178.

66 Richard Demarco, *Eight Yugoslav Artists*, n.p.

67 Marina Abramović, "Interview with Achille Bonito Oliva," in Achille Bonito Oliva, *Encyclopaedia of the World: Artists' Dialogues, 1968–2008* (Rome: SKIRA, 2010), 290.

68 Richard Demarco, *Pages Magazine* (1971), quoted in "Strategy: Get Arts," *Palermo Restore*, https://web.archive.org/web/20110727223624/http://www.eca.ac.uk/palermo/history_strategy_get_arts.htm.

69 Alistair Mackintosh (1973), quoted in *Joseph Beuys*, ed. Caroline Tisdall (New York: Guggenheim Museum, 1979), 192.

70 Ibid.

71 Ibid., 196.

72 Benjamin H. D. Buchloh, "Beuys: Twilight of the Idol, Preliminary Notes for a Critique," *Artforum*, January 1980; reprinted in *Joseph Beuys: Mapping the Legacy*, ed. Gene Ray (New York: D.A.P.; Sarasota, FL: John and Mable Ringling Museum of Art, 2001), 210.

73 Raša Todosijević, interview with the author, Belgrade, May 2012.

74 Zoran Popović and Jasna Tijardović, "A Note on Art in Yugoslavia," *The Fox* 1 (1975), 49.

75 Ibid., 50.

76 Ibid.

77 Ibid.

78 Sanja Iveković, "Feminism, Activism and Historicisation: Sanja Iveković Talks to Antonia Majača," *N.paradoxa: International Feminist Art Journal* 23 (January 2009), 6.

79 Michael Corris and Andrew Menard, letter to *Left Curve: Art and Revolution*, no. 5 (1975), 98.

80 Studentski Kulturni Centar, *Prošireni mediji: I i II Aprilski susreti* (Belgrade: SKC Galerija, 1974), n.p.

81 Ibid.

82 Studentski Kulturni Centar, *Prošireni mediji: III Aprilski susret* (Belgrade: SKC Galerija, 1974), n.p.

83 Matko Meštrović, in ibid.

84 Jasna Tijardović, "The 'Liquidation' of Art: Self-Management or Self-Protection?," *The Fox* 3 (1976), 97.

85 Tomić had already encountered Beuys in 1970 through Lucio Amelia, a well-known gallery owner from Naples and large promoter of Beuys, and was supposed to come to Belgrade in the same year but was absent due to his participation in Documenta 5. Biljana Tomić, email correspondence with the author, May 2012.

86 Lutz Becker, "Art for an Avant-Garde Society: Belgrade in the 1970s," in *East Art Map: Contemporary Art and Eastern Europe*, ed. IRWIN (London: Afterall, 2006), 395.

87 Ješa Denegri, in SKC, *Prošireni mediji*, n.p.

88 Ješa Denegri, *Studentski kulturni centar kao umetnička scena* (Belgrade: SKC, 2002), 9, translated in Jelena Stokić, "Beuys's Lesson in Belgrade," *Post: Notes on Modern and Contemporary Art around the Globe*, MoMA, New York, 25 November 2014, http://post.at.moma.org/content_items/554-beuys-s-lesson-in-belgrade.

89 Kristine Stiles, "Between Water and Stone: Fluxus Performance, A Metaphysics of Acts," in *In the Spirit of Fluxus*, ed. Elizabeth Armstrong and Simon Anderson (Minneapolis: Walker Art Center, 1993), 70.

90 Joseph Beuys, quoted in *The Art of Participation: 1950s to Now*, ed. Rudolf Frieling and Boris Groys (San Francisco: MoMA, 2008), 95.

91 Joseph Beuys, Colloquium in Berlin, 26–27 April 1974, in *Art into Society—Society into Art: Seven German Artists: Institute of Contemporary Arts, London, 30 October–14 November 1974* (London: ICA, 1974), 17.

92 Stokić, "Beuys's Lesson in Belgrade." For Shkëlzen Maliqi, a philosopher from Kosovo, however, Beuys had failed to grasp the fundamentals of the utopian philosophy of Hegel and the revolutionary thought of Lenin. In short, Maliqi accused Beuys of not being the socially engaged artist he purported to be, and of making mere "plastic-art philosophy." See Sezgin Boynik, "Cultural Roots of Contemporary Art in Kosovo," in *New Public Spaces: Dissensual Political and Artistic Practices in the Post-Yugoslav Context*, ed. Radical Education Collective (Maastricht: Jan Van Eyck Akademie, 2009), 219.

93 Raša Todosijević, interview with the author, Belgrade, May 2012.

94 Raša Todosijević, in SKC, *Prošireni mediji,* n.p.

95 Briony Fer, *The Infinite Line: Re-Making Art after Modernism* (New Haven: Yale University Press, 2004), 160.

96 Peggy Phelan, "The Ontology of Performance: Representation without Reproduction," in *Unmarked: The Politics of Performance* (London: Routledge, 1997), 150.

97 Todosijević, "Statement," *Drangularijum*, n.p.

98 Todosijević, "Art Is the Basis," 79.

99 Raša Todosijević, "Interview with Andrew Gibbons," in *FRA-YU-KULT: Fraction of Yugoslavian Culture*, ed. Jozo Pejić and Jadran Adamović (Široki Brijeg: Muzej Široki Brijeg, 1990), 161.

100 Buchloh, "Beuys," 206–207.

101 Ibid., 201.

102 Marina Abramović, unpublished interview, quoted in Blažević "Who's That Singing over There?," 93.

103 Bojana Pejić, "Bodyscenes: An Affair of the Flesh," in *Marina Abramović: The Artist Body: Performances 1969–1998* (Milan: Charta, 1998), 33.

104 Achille Bonito Oliva, in SKC, *Prošireni mediji*, n.p.

105 Barbara Reise, in ibid., n.p.

106 In 1979, Goran Đorđević noted a similar condition in his response to the *Works and Words* exhibition at the De Appel Foundation Amsterdam. See Jelena Vesić, "Works and Words—Early Critiques of the Discourse of East European Art," *Parallel Chronologies: An Archive of East European Exhibitions*, accessed 28 March 2020, http://tranzit.org/exhibitionarchive/works-and-words-early-critiques-of-the-discourse-of-eastern-european-art/.

107 Joseph Kosuth, "1975," *The Fox* 2 (1975), 95.

108 Popović and Tijardović, "A Note on Art," 52.

109 For more information on Popović and Tijardović's collaboration with New York's Art & Language, refer to Robert Bailey, *Art & Language International* (Durham: Duke University Press, 2016).

110 Corris and Menard, letter to *Left Curve*, 97.

111 Ibid.

112 Transcript of Art & Language Seminars, Belgrade, October 1975, Michael Corris Archive, Getty Research Institute, Los Angeles, CA.

113 Ibid.

114 Corris and Menard, letter to *Left Curve*, 98.

115 Ibid.

116 Jelena Vesić, "SKC (Student Cultural Center) as a Site of Performative (Self-)Production: *October 75*—Institution, Self-organization, First-person Speech, Collectivization," *Život umjetnosti* 91 (2012), 35.

117 Dunja Blažević, "Art as a Form of Ownership Awareness," *Oktobar '75* (Belgrade: SKC Gallery, 1975); translated in Prelom Kolektiv, *SKC and Political Practices*, 7.

118 Zoran Popović, "For a Self-Managing Art," *Oktobar 75*; translated in Prelom Kolektiv, *SKC and Political Practices*, 17.

119 As Bojana Pejić has observed: "It is needless to mention that the professors teaching the 'main' media of painting and sculpture were all men. The usual academic hierarchy of media existing in these institutions was happily matched with gender hierarchies." See Bojana Pejić, "Proletarians of All Countries, Who Washes Your Socks?," in *Gender Check: Femininity and Masculinity in the Art of Eastern Europe*, ed. Bojana Pejić (Vienna: Museum Moderner Kunst Stiftung Ludwig Wien, 2009), 25. Despite the many laws for equality in the family and at work passed in Yugoslavia after the Second World War, women continued to be employed primarily in manufacturing, especially in the low-income textile industry, and then in culture and education, health and social welfare, and catering and trade. With the encroachment of market reform from the mid-1960s, many women were pushed out of full-time employment. Those who

did work were legally equal, but often burdened with housekeeping and therefore paid less on average. For an engaging analysis of how women artists in Yugoslavia addressed these inequalities, refer to Bojana Pejić's essay "The Morning After: Plavi Radion, Abstract Art and Bananas," *n-Paradoxa* 10 (2002), 75–84.

120 Jasna Tijardović, letter to Michael Corris, 23 March 1975, Getty Research Archive.

121 Student Action Committee, "Political Action Program," 9.

122 Tijardović, "The 'Liquidation' of Art," 98.

123 Ibid.

124 Ibid.

125 Zoran Popović, transcript of Art & Language Seminars.

126 Branislav Dimitrijević, "Neke uvodne napomene o radu Gorana Đorđevića u periodu 1974–1985: a posebno u vezi sa njegovim delovanjem u okviru beogradskog Studentskog kulturnog centra," *Prelom* (Belgrade) (Spring–Summer 2006), 151.

127 Group 143, "Group 143—Unity," in Susovski, *New Art Practice*, 70.

128 Branislav Dimitrijević, "Altered Identities: Goran Đorđević as an Artist; SKC as an Institution," in *Prelom*, no. 8 (Fall 2006), 243.

129 For a gender-based interpretation of the action, see Tumbas, "Decision as Art," 189–190.

130 As already noted by Branislav Dimitrijević, "Thank You Raša Todosijević: A Retrospective Exhibition of Raša Todosijević, Museum of Contemporary Art—Belgrade," *Springerin Online*, no. 4 (November 2002), https://springerin.at/en/2002/4/danke-rasa-todosijevic/; Joseph Kosuth, "Art after Philosophy," *Studio International* (New York), 1969.

131 Ibid.

132 Kosuth, "1975," 87.

133 Mel Ramsden, "On Practice," *The Fox* 1 (1975), 83.

134 Ibid.

135 SKC, *Art, Irony, Etc.*, exh. cat. (Belgrade: SKC Gallery, 1977), n.p.

136 Ibid.

137 Ibid.

138 Ješa Denegri, "Goran Đorđević," in Susovski, *New Art Practice*, 63.

139 Goran Đorđević, in Prelom Kolektiv, "Story on Copy: An Interview with Goran Đorđević," *Prelom: Journal for Images and Politics* 8 (Fall 2006), 255.

140 Goran Đorđević, *International Strike of Artists*; reprinted in Prelom Kolektiv, *SKC and Political Practices*, 29.

141 Hans Haacke, in ibid., 32.

142 Lucy Lippard, in ibid., 34.

143 Goran Đorđević, invitation card to *Against Art* exhibition (Belgrade: SKC Gallery, January, 1980).

144 Goran Đorđević, quoted in Slobodan Mijušković, "Goran Đorđević. Original i kopija," *Moment* (Belgrade) 2 (1985), 9.

145 Ibid.

CHAPTER 4

1 Bogdan Denitch, *The Legitimation of a Revolution: The Yugoslav Case* (New Haven: Yale University Press, 1976), 27–28. As noted in Darko Suvin, *Splendour, Misery and Possibilities: An X-Ray of Socialist Yugoslavia* (Leiden: Brill Books, 2019), 276.

2 Dennison Rusinow, *The Yugoslav Experiment, 1948–74* (Berkeley: University of California Press, 1977), 346–347.

3 Mladen Stilinović, "Living Means Never Having to Attend Court: Interview with Branka Stipančić," in *Mladen Stilinović—Artist at Work (1973–1983)*, ed. Alenka Gregorič and Branka Stipančić (Zagreb: Mladen Stilinović, 2010), 35.

4 Edvard Kardelj, *Pravci razvoja političkog sistema socijalističkog samoupravljanja* (Belgrade: Komunist, 1977), 120–121.

5 Ibid., 34.

6 Branislav Jakovljević, *Alienation Effects: Performance and Self-Management in Yugoslavia, 1945–91* (Ann Arbor: University of Michigan Press, 2016), 202.

7 Ibid.

8 Suvin, *Splendour, Misery and Possibilities*, 238.

9 Branka Stipančić, "Auction of Red: A Look at the '70s," in *Mladen Stilinović—Sing!*, ed. Branka Stipančić (Budapest: Ludwig Museum, 2011).

10 CEFFT was headed by Dimitrije Bašičević Mangelos, a pioneer member of Croatia's proto-conceptual collective Gorgona, who had to seek permission from the authorities for the Group of Six Authors to perform their Exhibition-Actions on the street.

11 Reactions to *Exhibition-Action* on Republic Square, translation in Ivana Bago and Antonia Majača, "Spit in the Eye of Truth (Then Quickly Close Your Eyes before It)," *Život umjetnosti: časopis o modernoj i suvremenoj umjetnosti i arhitekturi* 83, no. 2 (2008), 123.

12 In Gordana Brzović and Kristina Leko, *Grupa šestorice autora*, documentary film, Zagreb, 2002.

13 Julie Mostov, "Democracy and Decisionmaking," in *Yugoslavia, A Fractured Federalism*, ed. Dennison Rusinow (Washington, DC: Wilson Center Press, 1988), 108.

14 Kardelj, *Pravci*, 95.

15 Steven L. Burg, *Conflict and Cohesion in Socialist Yugoslavia* (Princeton, NJ: Princeton University Press, 1983), 346.

16 Group of Six Authors, *Izložbe-akcije / Exhibition-Actions* (Zagreb: Centar za Film, Fotografiju i Televiziju, 1977), n.p.

17 Ibid.

18 Sven Stilinović, in Suzana Marjanić, "Razgovor sa Svenom Stilinovićem," *Zarez* (Zagreb), 8 February 2007, http://www.zarez.hr/clanci/razgovor-sa-svenom-stilinovicem.

19 Ibid.

20 Mladen Stilinović, in *Zoran Popović: Film bez naziva* (Zagreb: Centar za Film, Fotografiju i Televiziju, 1978), n.p.

21 Mark Thompson, *A Paper House: The Ending of Yugoslavia* (London: Vintage Books, 1992), 39.

22 Jasna Tijarović, in *Zoran Popović: Film bez naziva*, n.p.

23 Marijan Susovski, foreword to *The New Art Practice in Yugoslavia, 1966–1978*, ed. Marijan Susovski (Zagreb: Galerija Suvremene Umjetnosti, 1978), 3.

24 Nena Baljković, "Group of Six Authors, Zagreb," in Susovski, *New Art Practice*, 35.

25 Ibid.

26 Goran Đorđević, quoted in Slobodan Mijušković, "Goran Đorđević. Original i kopija," *Moment* (Belgrade) 2 (1985), 9.

27 Boris Demur, quoted in interview with Mladen Stilinović and Demur, "Do kad će mame hraniti umjetnike?," *Polet* (Zagreb), 31 January 1979.

28 Ibid.

29 Ibid.

30 Josip Depolo, "Nedopušteni pritisci," *Večernji list* (Zagreb), 13 January 1979.

31 Ibid.

32 Mladen Stilinović, quoted in "Do kad će mame."

33 Sanja Iveković, "Razgovor," *Prvi broj* (Zagreb: Radna Zajednica Umjetnika Podrum, 1980), 1.

34 Ibid.

35 As noted by Ivana Bago in "A Window and a Basement: Negotiating Hospitality at La Galerie des Locataires and Podroom: The Working Community of Artists," *ARTMargins* 1, no. 2–3 (June–October 2012), 121.

36 Mladen Stilinović, in *Prvi broj*, 1.

37 See Dejan Jović, *Yugoslavia: A State That Withered Away* (West Lafayette, IN: Purdue University Press, 2003), 143.

38 Sanja Iveković, discussion with Suzana Milevska, *Open Institutions* (Zagreb), 23 January 2011, accessed 15 September 2015, http://zagreb.openinstitutions.net/2011/01/ivekovic-milevska-art-and-invisible-labour-political-critique-activism/.

39 Ibid.

40 See Bago, "Window and a Basement," 139.

41 *Prvi broj*, 3.

42 Ibid.

43 RZU Podrum, letter to Općinske i udruženje samoupravna interesa zajednica kulture grada Zagreba, Zagreb, 16 January 1979.

44 Bago, "Window and a Basement," 137.

45 "Razgovor," *Prvi broj*, translation in ibid., 137.

46 Ibid.

47 Ibid.

48 Ibid.

49 Ibid.

50 Ibid.

51 Ibid.

52 Sanja Iveković and Dalibor Martinis, "Pismo za članove RZU Podroom-a," Zagreb, 26 February 1980.

53 Mostov, "Democracy and Decisionmaking," 109.

54 Kardelj, *Pravci*, 60.

55 Jakovljević, *Alienation Effects*, 208.

56 Kardelj, *Pravci*, 11.

57 Jović, *Yugoslavia*, 145.

58 Jakovljević, *Alienation Effects*, 205.

59 Iveković and Martinis, "Pismo za članove."

60 Bago, "Window and a Basement," 143.

61 "Razgovor," *Prvi broj*, 1.

62 Ibid.

63 Ibid.

64 As detailed by Bago, "Window and a Basement," 141.

65 Jović, *Yugoslavia*, 143.

66 Branko Horvat, *Jugoslovensko društvo u krizi: kritički ogledi i prijedlozi reformi* (Zagreb: Globus, 1985), 37, quoted in Suvin, *Splendour, Misery and Possibilities*, 262.

67 Marie-Janine Calic, *Geschichte Jugoslawiens im 20. Jahrhundert* (Munich: Beck, 2010), 279–280, quoted in Suvin, *Splendour, Misery and Possibilities*, 297.

68 "Razgovor," *Prvi broj*, 1.

69 Bago, "Window and a Basement," 129.

70 Vesna Bojičić, "The Disintegration of Yugoslavia: Causes and Consequences of Dynamic Inefficiency in Semi-Command Economies," in *Yugoslavia and After*, ed. David A. Dyker and Ivan Vejvoda (London: Routledge, 1996), 34.

71 Ljiljana Kolešnik, "Conflicting Visions of Modernity and the Post-war Modern Art," in *Socialism and Modernity: Art, Culture, Politics, 1950–1974*, ed. Ljiljana Kolešnik (Zagreb: Muzej Suvremene Umjetnosti, 2014), 174.

72 Ibid.

73 Mladen Stilinović in conversation with Sabina Sabolović, "I've Got Time," in *Mladen Stilinović: Artists' Books 1972–2006*, ed. Branka Stipančić (Istanbul: Platform Garanti Contemporary Art Center; Eindhoven: Van Abbemuseum, 2007), 52.

74 Vlado Martek, "Journal-Catalogue *Maj '75*," *Novine Galerija Nova* (Zagreb), no. 18 (December 2008), 21.

75 Ibid.

76 Susan Woodward, *Balkan Tragedy: Chaos and Dissolution after the Cold War* (Washington, DC: Brookings Institution Press, 1995), 52–57.

77 Ibid., 46.

78 Ibid.

79 Ibid.

80 From 1974 to 1978, the annual investment rate grew by 12.7 percent annually. See Jović, *Yugoslavia*, 172.

81 Ibid.

82 Audrey Helfant Budding, "Nation/People/Republic: Self-Determination in Socialist Yugoslavia," in *State Collapse in South-Eastern Europe: New Perspectives on Yugoslavia's Disintegration*, ed. Lenard J. Cohen and Jasna Dragović-Soso (West Lafayette, IN: Purdue University Press, 2007), 100.

83 Stilinović, "Living Means Never Having to Attend Court," 27.

84 Mladen Stilinović quoted in Marina Gržinić, "Mladen Stilinović: Strategies of the Cynical Mind," *Mladen Stilinović: Exploitation of the Dead*, ed. Branka Stipančić and Tihomir Milovac (Zagreb: Muzej Suvremene Umjetnosti, 2001), 29.

85 See Branka Magaš, *The Destruction of Yugoslavia: Tracking the Break-Up, 1980–92* (London: Verso, 1993), 151.

CHAPTER 5

1 Arhiv Republike Slovenije (ARS), Fond Edvard Kardelj, box 126, doc. 6599, Informacija s 14. seje predsedstva CK SKS o varnostnih razmerah in delovanju opozicijskih sil v SR Sloveniji; quoted in Aleš Gabrič, "Cultural Activities as Political Action," in *The Repluralization of Slovenia in the 1980s: New Revelations from Archival Records*, ed. Leopoldina Plut-Pregelj (Washington, DC: Henry M. Jackson School of International Studies, 2000), 16.

2 Ibid.

3 Ibid.

4 Ibid.

5 Article 166 of the 1974 Constitution, quoted in Ljubica Spaskovska, *The Last Yugoslav Generation: The Rethinking of Youth Politics and Cultures in Late Socialism* (Manchester, UK: Manchester University Press, 2017), 66.

6 Franc Šali, *Kulturna pot ZK Slovenije* (Ljubljana: Komunist, 1987), quoted in Gabrič, "Cultural Activities as Political Action," 17.

7 Ibid.

8 Gregor Tomc, "The Politics of Punk," in *Independent Slovenia: Origins, Movements, Prospects*, ed. Jill Benderly and Evan Kraft (London: Palgrave Macmillan, 1994), 119.

9 Taja Vidmar-Brejc, "Interview with Alenka Pirman," ŠKUC website, accessed 11 April 2020, http://www.galerijaskuc.si/taja-vidmar-brejc/.

10 Ibid.

11 Ibid.

12 Tomc, "Politics of Punk," 120.

13 Ibid., 128.

14 Vidmar-Brejc, "Interview with Alenka Pirman."

15 "No-Man's Children," *Delo* (Ljubljana), 17 November 1981.

16 Marina Gržinić and Aleš Erjavec, *Ljubljana, Ljubljana: Osemdeseta leta v umetnosti in kulturi* (Ljubljana: Mladinska Knjiga, 1991), 90.

17 Darko Štrajn, "Black-and-White Shock in Trbovlje (1981)," translated in *NSK: From Kapital to Capital*, ed. Zdenka Badovinac, Eda Čufer, and Anthony Gardner (Cambridge, MA: MIT Press, 2015), 28.

18 Reported in *Politika* (Belgrade), 24 and 26 June 1980, and a biography of the new premier in *Politika*, 17 July 1980, quoted in Steven L. Burg, *Conflict and Cohesion in Socialist Yugoslavia* (Princeton, NJ: Princeton University Press, 1983), 343.

19 Ibid.

20 Ibid.

21 Trbovlje Youth Alliance, "Letter to *Mladina*," mid-December 1980, translated in Gržinic and Erjavec, *Ljubljana*, 92.

22 Ibid.

23 Laibach, TV Tednik Interview, 1983, Youtube, posted 20 February 2007, https://www.youtube.com/watch?v=xz_PhMpFR9U.

24 Gržinic and Erjavec, *Ljubljana*, 92.

25 Interview with ŠKUC Gallery directors, *Studentski list* (Zagreb), 16 April 1981.

26 Dušan Mandić, in ibid.

27 Marina Gržinić, "Interview with Alenka Pirman," ŠKUC Gallery website, http://www.galerijaskuc.si/marina-grzinic/.

28 Aleš Erjavec, "NSK, New Slovene Art: Slovenia, Yugoslavia, Self-Management, and the 1980s," in *Postmodernism and the Postsocialist Condition*, ed. Aleš Erjavec (Berkeley: University of California Press, 2003), 155.

29 For a detailed account of the 1981 demonstrations, consult Julie A. Mertus, *Kosovo: How Myths and Truths Started a War* (Berkeley: University of California Press, 1999), 17–93.

30 Branka Magaš, *The Destruction of Yugoslavia: Tracking the Break-Up, 1980–92* (London: Verso, 1993), 3.

31 Ibid.

32 Dušan Mandić, "Pogovor s člani RZU Podrum," *Galerija ŠKUC izdaja* (Ljubljana), October 1981.

33 Gržinić, "Interview."

34 For an account of Laibach's early exhibitions at the ŠKUC Gallery, refer to Barbara Borčić, "The ŠKUC Gallery, Alternative Culture, and Neue Slowenische Kunst in the 1980s," in *NSK: From Kapital to Capital*, 299–319.

35 Alexei Monroe, *Interrogation Machine: Laibach and NSK* (Cambridge, MA: MIT Press, 2005), 107.

36 See Magaš, *Destruction of Yugoslavia*, xxi.

37 Laibach, "Interview," *Džuboks*, 1982, translation from Laibach website, accessed 3 June 2020, http://www.laibach.org/interviews-1980-to-1985/. The *Džuboks* interview from 1982 was not published until the following year in the group's self-published zine *The Instrumentality of the State Machine*, 1983.

38 As noted by Monroe in *Interrogation Machine*, 107.

39 Ibid.

40 Branislav Jakovljević, *Alienation Effects: Performance and Self-Management in Yugoslavia, 1945–91* (Ann Arbor: University of Michigan Press, 2016), 267.

41 Laibach, "TV Tednik Interview."

42 Ibid.

43 Barbara Borčić, "Video Art from Conceptualism to Postmodernism," 2003, http://www.gama-gateway.eu/uploads/media/Video_Art_in_Yugoslavia_B_Borcic.pdf, 17.

44 France Popit, quoted in Tomc, "Politics of Punk," 120.

45 Zlato Šetinc, quoted in ibid.

46 Ibid.

47 See *Punk pod Slovenci*, ed. Neža Malečkar and Tomaž Mastnak (Ljubljana: Univerzitetna Konferenca ZSMS, Republiška Konferenca ZSMS, 1985), 485–489.

48 Ali Žerdin, "Kratki kurz zgodovine panka," in *Punk je bil prej, 25 let punka pod Slovenci*, ed. Peter Lovšin, Peter Mlakar, and Igor Vidmar (Ljubljana: Cankarjeva Založba / Ropot, 2003), 38.

49 Igor Vidmar, *Uzurlikzurli e-zine*, accessed 5 June 2010, http://members.iinet.net.au/~predrag/vidmar.html.

50 Ibid.

51 Tomc, "Politics of Punk," 121.

52 Ibid., 131.

53 Barbara Borčić, Aina Šmid, and Marina Gržinič, "Odnos vladojče ideologije do subkulture," *Galerija ŠKUC izdaja* (Ljubljana), December 1981.

54 Ibid.

55 Tomaž Mastnak, "Civil Society in Slovenia: From Opposition to Power," *Studies in Comparative Communism* 23, no. 3+4 (Autumn/Winter 1990), 309.

56 Marina Gržinič and Zemira Alajbegović, "Ljubljanska subkulturna scena," in *Problemi* (October–November 1983), 26, translated in David Crowley, "The Future Is between Your Legs: Sex, Art and Censorship in the Socialist Federal Republic of Yugoslavia," in *Monuments Should Not Be Trusted*, ed. Lina Džuverović (Nottingham, UK: Nottingham Contemporary, 2015).

57 As argued by Crowley, "Future Is between Your Legs."

58 In the Cultural Plenum of 1981 [O kulturni politiki 1981], translated in Tomc, "Politics of Punk," 121.

59 Slavoj Žižek, editorial in *Problemi* (1981), no. 205/206; translated in Helena Motoh, "'Punk Is a Symptom': Intersections of Philosophy and Alternative Culture in the '80s Slovenia," *Synthesis Philosophica* 54 (February 2012), 291.

60 Ibid.

61 Susan Woodward, *Balkan Tragedy: Chaos and Dissolution after the Cold War* (Washington, DC: Brookings Institution Press, 1995), 63.

62 Ibid.

63 *NIN*, Belgrade, 25 April 1982, 8. Quoted in Jasna Dragović-Soso, *Saviours of the Nation: Serbia's Intellectual Opposition and the Revival of Nationalism* (Montreal: McGill-Queen's University Press, 2002), 69.

64 Dušan Mandić, "Die Welt ist Schön," *Galerija ŠKUC izdaja* (Ljubljana), October 1982.

65 Ibid.

66 Dimitrij Rupel, "Slovenia's Shift from the Balkans to Central Europe," in *Independent Slovenia*, 186.

67 Tomc, quoted in Spaskovska, *Last Yugoslav Generation*, 116.

68 Jakovljević, *Alienation Effects*, 203.

69 György Konrád, *Antipolitics: An Essay* (London: Harcourt, 1984), 229.

70 Ibid., 230–231.

71 Nikolai Jeffs, "FV and the Third Scene, 1980–90," in *FV: Alternative Scene of the 80s*, ed. Breda Škrjanec (Ljubljana: MGLC, 2008), 403.

72 Zemira Alajbegović, "Mladinska Subkultura: Disco FV—No Future, No Escape," *VIKS*, ŠKUC-forum izdaja (Ljubljana), no. 1 (November 1983).

73 Igor Vidmar in *Mladina*, 1983, translated in Alajbegović, "The Frozen Time—The Eighties, ŠKUC-Forum, FV Video, and Others," in *Videodokument: Video Art in Slovenia, 1969–1998; Essays*, ed. Barbara Borčić (Ljubljana: SCCA, 1999), 40.

74 Slavoj Žižek, "Ideologija, cinizem, punk" (1984), translated in *NSK: From Kapital to Capital*, 111.

75 Dušan Mandić, "Come, Come Close to Me, I Tell You Man You Will See," translated into Serbo-Croatian in *3+4 Časopis studenata istorije umetnosti* (Belgrade), 1984.

76 Dušan Mandić, quoted in Marina Gržinić, "Graffiti as a Subversion of Slovenian Cultural Space," translated in *NSK: From Kapital to Capital*, 92.

77 The group's first name initially established a link to Marcel Duchamp, who started to use the name Rrose Sélavy (Rose—c'est la vie) as a female pseudonym in 1920. "C'est la vie" also implied a reference to FV's unabbreviated name, "C'est la guerre!" At the time, IRWIN's members were Marko Kovačič, Dušan Mandić, Andrej Savski, Bojan Štokelj, Roman Uranjek, and Borut Vogelnik.

78 The exhibition's full title was *Back to the USA: Pattern & Decoration, New Image, New Wave, New Expressionism, Graffiti; American Art of the Seventies and Eighties.*

79 IRWIN, "Back to the USA," *Galerija ŠKUC izdaja*, 1984, reprinted in Slovenian in *Do roba in naprej: Slovenska Umetnost 1975–85*, ed. Igor Španjol (Ljubljana: Moderna Galerija, 2003), 130.

80 Ibid.

81 Ibid.

82 Catherine Wood, "Back to the USA, Replayed," in *NSK: From Capital to Kapital,* 322.

83 IRWIN, "Back to the USA."

84 Cindy Sherman, quoted in Calvin Tomkins, "Her Secret Identities," *The New Yorker*, 15 May 2000, 78.

85 Gržinić, "Interview."

86 For more information, see Božo Repe, "The Introduction of Political Parties and Their Role in Achieving Independence," in *The Repluralization of Slovenia in the 1980s*, 39.

87 Rastko Močnik, "The Vagaries of the Expression 'Civil Society': The Yugoslav Alternative," *L'Internationale Online*, 21 June 2014, https://www.internationaleonline.org/research/real_democracy/6_the_vagaries_of_the_expression_civil_society_the_yugoslav_alternative.

88 Tomaž Mastnak, "Civil Society and Fascism," in *NSK: From Kapital to Capital*, 285.

89 Ibid., 284.

90 Močnik, "The Vagaries of the Expression 'Civil Society.'"

91 Gržinić and Erjavec, *Ljubljana*, 89. The Scipion Nasice Sisters Theatre was founded in Ljubljana in October 1983 by Eda Čufer, Dragan Živadinov, and Miran Mohar, and lasted for four years.

92 Ibid.

CHAPTER 6

1 For an incisive analysis of the impact of Yugoslavia's economic decentralization in the 1960s on the "national question," refer to Vladimir Unkovski-Korica, *The Economic Struggle for Power in Tito's Yugoslavia: From World War II to Non-Alignment* (London: I. B. Tauris, 2016), and Hilde Katrine Haug, *Creating Socialist Yugoslavia: Tito, Communist Leadership and the National Question* (London: I. B. Tauris, 2012).

2 It should be noted here that Yugoslavia's federal arrangement often served the interests of the less-developed republics. Modern-day North Macedonia, for example, attained nationality and republican status for the first time after the end of the Second World War. The poorest and least developed republic, it benefited enormously from the federal redistributive policies and security guarantees that Yugoslavia provided. Similarly, Montenegro, the smallest republic, profited from the country's federal subsidies program and enjoyed an influence in Yugoslavia that was disproportionate to its size and economic weight. It is for this reason that leaderships in Macedonia and Montenegro were more pro-Yugoslav and less nationally oriented than any others throughout the postwar period. It is also why they tended to be more conservative and dogmatic. For more information, see Michael Palairet, *Macedonia: A Voyage through History*, vol. 2 (Newcastle upon Tyne: Cambridge Scholars Publishing, 2015); Nada Boškovska, *Yugoslavia and Macedonia before Tito: Between Repression and Integration* (London: Bloomsbury Academic, 2017); Kenneth Morrison, *Montenegro: A Modern History* (London: I. B. Tauris, 2009).

3 Many of Bosnia's enterprises were, however, "political" factories, and founded as a result of a central investment fund's strategic decisions. Arms factories, for example, were built in central Bosnia, so that the republic could serve as a "fortress" should Yugoslavia be invaded. This investment followed the broader tendencies of socialist economic planning, which decreed that industrial centers should be constructed in underdeveloped areas. Although admirable in theory, this approach was often less viable in practice. See Gerard Toal and Carl T. Dahlaman, *Bosnia Remade: Ethnic Cleansing and Its Reversal* (Oxford: Oxford University Press, 2011).

4 For more information, consult Audrey Helfant Budding, "Nation/People/Republic: Self-Determination in Socialist Yugoslavia," in *State Collapse in South-Eastern Europe: New Perspectives on Yugoslavia's Disintegration*, ed. Lenard J. Cohen and Jasna Dragović-Soso (West Lafayette, IN: Purdue University Press, 2007), 91–129.

5 For more information on the Sarajevo Documentary School and its film production in the 1960s and 1970s, see Benjamin Halligan, "Idylls of Socialism: The Sarajevo Documentary School and the Problem of the Bosnian Sub-Proletariat," *Studies in Eastern European Cinema* 1, no. 2 (2010), 197–216.

6 Robert J. Donia, *Sarajevo: A Biography* (London: C. Hurst, 2006), 254; Dalibor Mišina, *Shake, Rattle and Roll: Yugoslav Rock Music and the Poetics of Social Critique* (Oxford: Routledge, 2016), 152.

7 For statistics, consult Nicholas R. Lang, "The Dialectics of Decentralization: Economic Reform and Regional Inequality in Yugoslavia," *World Politics* 27, no. 3 (April 1975), 314.

8 Susan Woodward, *Socialist Unemployment: The Political Economy of Yugoslavia, 1945–1990* (Princeton, NJ: Princeton University Press, 1995), 60.

9 Miljenko Jergović, *Naci bonton* (Zagreb: Duireux, 1998), 48–49.

10 Nermina Zildžo, "Sječam se ...," in *Sarajevski New Primitivs* (Sarajevo: Umjetnička Galerija Bosne i Hercegovine, 1990), 24; translated in Dalibor Mišina, "'Anarchy all over Baščaršija': Yugoslavia's New Socialist Culture and the *New Primitives* Poetics of the Local," *Journal of Historical Sociology* 26, no. 2 (June 2013), 174.

11 Miladin Lazović, "Kome 'Zvono' zvoni? Bravardžiluk, kujundžiluk, slikardžiluk," *U.Nov* (Sarajevo), 27 August 1986, n.p.

12 Ivo Andrić was a renowned Yugoslav author who won the Nobel Prize in Literature in 1961 for his novel *The Bridge on the Drina*. Much of his writing dealt with life under Ottoman rule in his native Bosnia. Nirma Moranjak-Bamburać, "Prema problemu kulturnog sinkretizma u Bosni i Hercegovini," *Dijalog* (Sarajevo) 2–3 (1988), 97–122.

13 Azra Begić, "Uvod," in *Umjetnost Bosne i Hercegovina 1974–1988* (Sarajevo: Art Gallery of Bosnia and Herzegovina, 1984), 12.

14 This was also the case in Yugoslavia's other less developed regions. The Museum of Contemporary Art in Skopje, Macedonia's capital, was established in 1967, but only through a gesture of solidarity by the international art world following the catastrophic earthquake of 1963. The city's Faculty of Fine Arts was founded years later, in 1980, which enabled artists to train locally for the first time, although students were forbidden from showing their work before graduation. In Kosovo, there was an art high school in the city of Peja, but most artists continued their education in the academies of Belgrade, Ljubljana, Zagreb, and Sarajevo. It was not until 1974 that a Faculty of Arts was established at the University of Priština, along with the Art Gallery of Priština, both of which facilitated a more independent art scene in Kosovo. Montenegro had its own University established in 1974, followed by the creation of the Montenegrin Academy of Arts and Sciences in 1976 and a solely Montenegrin media. As in Bosnia and Herzegovina, it is reasonable to assume that these developments came out of Yugoslavia's political decentralization, especially following the 1974 constitutional amendments.

15 V. Radusinović, "Neobičan ispit zrelosti," *Borba* (Belgrade), 25 July 1989.

16 Aleksandar Adamović, "Notes on the Contemporary Art of Bosnia and Herzegovina," in *Yugoslav Documents '87* (Sarajevo: Olimpijski Centar "Skenderija," Galerije Grada Sarajeva, 1987), n.p.

17 Ibid.

18 Antun Maračić, "New Primitive Art Jusufa Hadžifejzovića," *Studentski list* (Zagreb), no. 912 (9 January 1986), 22.

19 Suzana Milevska, "Mapping the 1980s Art Scene in Macedonia in Inverse Perspective," in *The Eighties through the Prism of Events, Exhibitions, and Discourses in Slovenia and Yugoslavia*, ed. Igor Španjol (Ljubljana: Moderna Galerija, 2017).

20 Ibid.

21 Shkëlzen Maliqi, "How Art Modernized in Kosovo," in "Balkart," special issue, *Kosovo 2.0*, no. 6 (Fall/Winter 2013), 24–36.

22 Ibid., 31.

23 For information on how nationalist tendencies surfaced in Serbian modernist painting, for example, including in the work of Belgrade modernist painter Petar Lubarda, refer to Jelena Vesić, "Politics of Display and Troubles with National Representation in Contemporary Art," *Red Thread* 1–3 (2009–2011), 8–17.

24 For more information, consult Meliha Husedžinović, "Aspects and Positions of Art from Bosnia-Hercegovina, 1949–1999," in *Aspects / Positions: 50 Years of Art in Central Europe 1949—1999*, ed. Achim Hochdörfer (Vienna: Museum Moderner Kunst Stiftung Ludwig, 1999), 109–144.

25 Ibid., 110.

26 Prostor-forma's statement is translated in Husedžinović's essay "Aspects and Positions," 110. For more information about the art collectives preceding Zvono, see Irfan Hošić, "Zvono prije 'Zvono,'" *Vizura: Časopis za savremene vizualne umjetnosti, likovnu kritiku i teoriju* (Sarajevo), no. 3–4 (October 2008), 92–99.

27 Adamović, "Notes on the Contemporary Art."

28 Studentski Kulturni Centar, *Prošireni mediji: I i II Aprilski susreti* (Belgrade: SKC Galerija, 1974), n.p.

29 Aleksandar Saša Bukvić, in Lazović, "Kome 'Zvono' zvoni?"

30 These events were spearheaded by a 1978 exhibition at the Collegium Artisticum called *Art in Yugoslavia 1970–78*, which was described as the "most important exhibition of the year" by the Serbian newsmagazine *NIN*. See Bojana Piškur, "Yugoslav Documents Exhibition(s)," in *The Heritage of 1989: Case Study: The Second Yugoslav Documents Exhibition*, ed. Ana Mizerit and Adela Železnik (Ljubljana: MSUM, 2017), n.p.

31 Zorica Vlačić, introduction to *Yugoslav Documents '87*, n.p.

32 Aleksandar Saša Bukvić, "Ne dozvoljavam da se 'Zvono' zaboravi," *Radio Slobodna Evropa*, 12 August 2011, http://www.slobodnaevropa.org/content/bukvic_ne_dozvoljavam_da_se_zvono_zaboravi/24325037.html.

33 Z. Milanović, "Čašica umjetnosti," *Naši dani* (Sarajevo), May 1979.

34 Niazid Ahmić, "Vidimo se u 'Zvonu,'" *Naši dani* (Sarajevo), 23 December 1981.

35 Dževdet Tuzlić, "Šmek Montmartrea," in *Bife galerija Zvono* (Sarajevo: Café-Gallery Zvono, 1985), n.p.

36 Ibid.

37 Nermina Zildžo, quoted in Aida Salketić, "Konstrukcija alternativnog galerijskog prostora na primjeru kafea Zvono" (unpublished MA dissertation, Philosophy Faculty, Sarajevo, 2014), 91.

38 Bukvić, "Ne dozvoljavam."

39 Bukvić, quoted in Salketić, "Konstrukcija alternativnog," 79.

40 Nermina Zildžo, quoted in Salketić, "Konstrukcija alternativnog," 91. Two years later, Skopje experienced the awakening of its own subculture through a similarly small gesture: the opening of the teashop "Gallery 7." Located near the Faculty of Fine Arts in the city's Old Bazaar, and named by the late painter Mustafa Asim, Gallery 7 quickly became, in the words of one frequent visitor, "Skopje's Cabaret Voltaire." In Milevska's view, it provided a unique space for local students and unemployed thinkers to exchange ideas and to work collaboratively, outside of state-financed institutions. This is also why it became the principal meeting place for Zero—the first art group in Macedonia to engage with new media and contemporary art practices such as video, performance, installation, happenings, murals, and public art. Zero was also the first group to embrace an "open, collective and participatory structure," although as Milevska noted, it maintained certain hierarchies within its membership, usually defined according to age, length of membership, and gender. For more information, see *Zero: Retrospective 1984–2009*, ed. Vladimir Veličovski (Skopje: Mala Stanica, 2009); and "Gallery 7—Space/ Event/ Knowledge—Ongoing Collaborative Archive, 1984–," in the frame of the project *Tailor-Made Knowledge Pavilion*, curated by Suzana Milevska, Festival AKTO 7, 2012.

41 Zildžo, quoted in Salketić, "Konstrukcija alternativnog," 91.

42 Davor Matičević, "A View of the Eighties: The Eighties—The Way to Remember Them," in *Jugoslovenska dokumenta 1989* (Sarajevo: Olimpijski Centar "Skenderija," Galerije Grada Sarajeva, 1989), 42.

43 Bukvić, "Ne dozvoljavam."

44 Ibid.

45 Bukvić, in Lazović, "Kome 'Zvono' zvoni?"

46 Sadko Hadžihasanović, quoted in Salketić, "Konstrukcija alternativnog," 73.

47 Ljiljana Kolešnik, "Conflicting Visions of Modernity and the Post-war Modern Art," in *Socialism and Modernity: Art, Culture, Politics, 1950–1974*, ed. Ljiljana Kolešnik (Zagreb: Muzej Suvremene Umjetnosti, 2014), 174.

48 Bukvić, in Lazović, "Kome 'Zvono' zvoni?"

49 Sanja Iveković, "Feminism, Activism and Historicisation: Sanja Iveković Talks to Antonia Majača," *N.paradoxa: International Feminist Art Journal* 23 (January 2009), 6.

50 Bukvić, in Lazović, "Kome 'Zvono' zvoni?"

51 Meliha Husedžinović, "Bosnia and Herzegovina," in *Body and the East: From the 1960s to the Present*, ed. Zdenka Badovinac (Ljubljana: Moderna Galerija, 1999), 40.

52 Pavle Pavlović, "Šareno zvona zvone," *Studio* (Sarajevo), August 1986.

53 Sava Stepanov, "Suočeni s vremenon," *Odjek* (Sarajevo), November 1986, 19.

54 Aleksandar Saša Bukvić, in Z. Kostović, "'Zvono' budi uspavane," November 1986.

55 Bukvić, in Lazović, "Kome 'Zvono' zvoni?"

56 Branka Vujanović, "Nepretenciozna filozofija igre i spontanosti—Likovna grupa 'Zvono' u galeriji 'Tate Liverpool,'" *Zmijski jezik*, 11 November 2013.

57 Claes Oldenburg, "I am For ... (Statement, 1961)," reprinted in *Art in Theory: 1900–1990*, ed. Charles Harrison and Paul Wood (London: Wiley-Blackwell, 1992), 744.

58 Aleš Erjavec, "NSK, Neue Slowenische Kunst—New Slovenian Art: Slovenia, Yugoslavia, Self-Management, and the 1980s," in *Postmodernism and the Postsocialist Condition: Politicized Art under Late Socialism*, ed. Aleš Erjavec (Berkeley: University of California Press, 2003), 165.

59 IRWIN, in *Neue Slowenische Kunst* (Ljubljana, 1984), 87; quoted in Erjavec, "NSK, Neue Slowenische Kunst," 162.

60 Darko Hudelist, "Pokret sa jelenskim rogovima," *Start* (Zagreb), 19 April 1986; quoted in Jakovljević, *Alienation Effects*, 272.

61 Sadko Hadžihasanović, in Salketić, "Konstrukcija alternativnog," 73.

62 Mikhail Bakhtin, introduction to *Rabelais and His World*, translated by Helene Iswolsky (Bloomington: Indiana University Press, 1984).

63 Ibid., 7.

64 Bukvić, in Lazović, "Kome 'Zvono' zvoni?"

65 Vladimir Gudac, *Novine GSC* (SC Gallery, Zagreb), The Last Number, December 1975, n.p.

66 Miljenko Jergović, in Salketić, "Konstrukcija alternativnog," 61.

67 Husedžinović, "Aspects and Positions," 111.

68 Nermina Zildžo, "Burying the Past and Exhuming Mass Graves," in *East Art Map: Contemporary Art and Eastern Europe*, ed. IRWIN (London: Afterall, 2006), 147.

69 Gregor Tomc, "We Will Rock YU: Popular Music in the Second Yugoslavia," in *Impossible Histories: Historic Avant-Gardes, Neo-Avant-Gardes, and Post-War Avant-Gardes in Yugoslavia, 1918–1991*, ed. Dubravka Djurić and Miško Šuvaković (Cambridge, MA: MIT Press, 2003), 460.

70 Ibid.

71 Z. Petrović, "Primitivci," *ZUM Reporter* (Sarajevo), 20 November 1984, 59; translated in Mišina, "Anarchy," 179.

72 Nele Karajlić, quoted in Snježan Lalović, "Bunker u Ljubljani," *ZUM Reporter* (Sarajevo), 24 November–1 December 1983, 70; translated in Mišina, "Anarchy," 180.

73 Zildžo, "Sječam se," 4.

74 Nebojša Grujičić and Jovana Gligorijević, "Smisao nadrealizma dr. Neleta Karajlića," *Vreme* (Belgrade), no. 1144 (6 December 2012), 52.

75 Emir Kurtović, quoted in Tomc, "We Will Rock YU," 460.

76 Ibid.

77 As observed by Mišina, "'Anarchy,'" 197.

78 Nele Karajlić, in Tomc, "We Will Rock YU," 461.

79 Miljenko Jergović, "In the Name of Love," *Ogledalo* (Sarajevo), early 1990s, cited in *Jedinstvena Bosna i Hercegovina*, blog, 8 October 2008, http://haler.blogger.ba/arhiva/2008/10/08/1831190.

80 Husedžinović, "Aspects and Positions," 110.

81 The growing role of the city's National Art Gallery, and particularly curator Nermina Zildžo, in supporting a younger generation of artists should also be factored into this "new creative spirit." Important exhibitions organized at the National Gallery and the Collegium Artisticum in these pivotal years include the *May Exhibition of Youth*, Collegium Artisticum, 1984; *Sklop u stranu*, Studio umjetničke galerije BiH, Sarajevo, 10–22 September 1985; *Videosusreti '85*, Skenderija 1–6 March 1985; *Umjetnosti-kritika usred osamdesetih*, Collegium Artisticum (realized under the patronage of the Yugoslav section of AICA), 7–28 February 1986; and *Ružičasti nihilizam*, Studio umjetničke galerije BiH, 6–20 October 1987.

82 Bojana Pejić, "Jusuf Hadžifejzović, Kunst-Werke, Berlin," *Artforum* 32, no. 2 (October 1993), 109.

83 Ješa Denegri, quoted in Željko Jerman, "Zagrebački Zenica depo," *Studentski list* (Zagreb), no. 908, 12 December 1985.

84 Maračić, "New Primitive Art," 22.

85 Ibid.

86 Husedžinović, "Aspects and Positions," 110.

87 Bukvić, in Lazović, "Kome 'Zvono' zvoni?"

88 See Nermina Zildžo, "Yugoslav (Intervening) Documents," in *Yugoslav Documents '87*, n.p.

89 Ibid.

90 Jusuf Hadžifejzović, interview with the author, Sarajevo, March 2015.

91 Zildžo, "Yugoslav (Intervening) Documents."

92 Miha Košak, "Avant-Propos," in *10. Biennale grafike*, ed. Zoran Kržišnik (Ljubljana: Moderna Galerija, 1973), n.p.

93 As already noted by Anthony Gardner and Charles Green in "Biennials of the South on the Edges of the Global," *Third Text* (London) 27, no. 4 (2013), 442–455; see also "Interview with Zoran Kržišnik" by Beti Žerovc, The 29th Biennial of Graphic Arts, Ljubljana, September 2007, https://29gbljubljana.wordpress.com/history/interview-with-zoran-krzisnik/.

94 Zoran Kržišnik, introduction to *10. Biennale grafike*, n.p.

95 Gardner and Green, "Biennials of the South," 447.

96 Ibid., 445.

97 Jusuf Hadžifejzović, in Zildžo, "Yugoslav (Intervening) Documents."

98 Davor Matičević, "On Conscious and Unconscious Vagueness," *Yugoslav Documents '87*, n.p.

99 Jusuf Hadžifejzović, quoted in Zdenka Badovinac, "An Exhibition about an Exhibition," in *Dediščina 1989 / The Heritage of 1989*, ed. Ana Mizerit and Bojana Piškur (Ljubljana: Moderna Galerija, 2017), n.p. In the words of Zdenka Badovinac, these artists declared, in typical "Sarajevan style," that if they could not "go to Documenta, then Documenta must come to them." See Ibid.

100 Matičević, "A View of the Eighties," 43.

101 Branka Magaš, *The Destruction of Yugoslavia: Tracking the Break-Up, 1980–92* (London: Verso, 1993), 105.

102 Milan Jajčinović, *Danas*, 12 July 1988, 22; translated in Neven Andjelić, *Bosnia-Herzegovina: The End of a Legacy* (London: Frank Cass, 2003), 64. For more information, consult Harold Lydall, *Yugoslavia in Crisis* (Oxford: Clarendon Press, 1989), and Magaš, *Destruction of Yugoslavia*.

103 Zildžo, "Yugoslav (Intervening) Documents."

104 For more information, see Jasna Dragović-Soso, *Saviours of the Nation: Serbia's Intellectual Opposition and the Revival of Nationalism* (Montreal: McGill-Queen's University Press, 2002), 181.

105 *Prispevki za slovenski nacionalni program* [Contributions to the Slovenian National Program], *Nova revija* (Ljubljana) 57 (January 1987).

106 The resort to extralegal means in the so-called anti-bureaucratic revolution by the Milošević regime marked a break in the possibility of establishing a new constitution by legal means across Yugoslavia. For more information, consult V. P. Gagnon, *The Myth of Ethnic War: Serbia and Croatia in the 1990s* (Ithaca, NY: Cornell University Press, 2004).

107 As argued by Haug in *Creating Socialist Yugoslavia*, 347.

108 As observed by Jakovljević, *Alienation Effects*, 33.

109 Nagorka Idrizović, "Zmijsko jaje 'Novog kolektivizma,'" *Oslobođenje* (Sarajevo), 28 February 1987, 1–5; translated in ibid., 33.

110 Marina Gržinić, "Neue Slowenische Kunst," in *Impossible Histories*, 254.

111 For Komelj, these events revived the totalitarian model, while ignoring why this desire for freedom surfaced only in the mid to late 1980s. See Miklavž Komelj, "Function of the Signifier 'Totalitarianism' in the Constitution of the 'East Art' Field," in *Retracing Images: Visual Culture after Yugoslavia*, ed. Daniel Šuber and Slobodan Karamanić (Leiden: Brill, 2012), 71.

112 Ibid., 74.

113 Jakovljević, *Alienation Effects*, 275.

114 Hadžifejzović, interview with the author, March 2015.

115 Ibid.

116 *Večernje novine* [Evening Newspaper] projected that by 2000, *dokumenta*'s significance would be equal to that of Documenta in Kassel and the Venice Biennale. Enrico Comi, then editor of the Italian magazine *Spazio Umano*, provided in-depth coverage of the exhibition in one of the issues. The 1991 exhibition was also to have a parallel event in Milan.

117 For a thorough analysis of the war in Bosnia and Herzegovina, consult Steven Burg and Paul Shoup, *The War in Bosnia-Herzegovina: Ethnic Conflict and International Intervention* (London: M. E. Sharpe, 1999).

CONCLUSION

1 Želimir Koščević, "Modeli u zraku," *Moment* (Belgrade) 18 (April–June 1990), 57–58; translated in *On Normality: Art in Serbia, 1989–2001*, ed. Branislava Anđelković, Branislav Dimitrievič, and Dejan Sretenović (Belgrade: Muzej Savremene Umetnosti, 2009), 11. It is interesting to note that toward the end of his text, Koščević acknowledges that IRWIN were excluded from the "context of this critical observation."

2 Ibid.

3 Ibid.

4 See Dejan Djokić, *Yugoslavism: Histories of a Failed Idea, 1918–1992* (Madison: University of Wisconsin Press, 2003).

5 Dejan Guzina, "Socialist Serbia's Narratives: From Yugoslavia to a Greater Serbia," in "Studies in the Social History of Destruction: The Case of Yugoslavia," special issue of *International Journal of Politics, Culture, and Society* 17, no. 1 (Fall 2003), 91. For the most comprehensive cultural study of the lack of effort spent on building a single collectivist national culture in Yugoslavia, see Andrew Watchel, *Making a Nation, Breaking a Nation: Literature and Cultural Politics in Yugoslavia* (Palo Alto, CA: Stanford University Press, 1998).

6 Radomir Konstantinović, *Filozofija palanke* (Belgrade: NOLIT, 1969).

7 Dubravka Ugrešić, "The Spirit of the Kakanian Province," in *After Yugoslavia: The Cultural Spaces of a Vanished Land*, ed. Radmila Gorup (Palo Alto, CA: Stanford University Press, 2013), 133.

8 Eda Čufer, in correspondence with Dušan Bjelić, in Dušan Bjelić, "Introduction: Blowing up the 'Bridge,'" in *Balkan as Metaphor: Between Globalization and Fragmentation*, ed. Dušan Bjelić and Obrad Savić (Cambridge, MA: MIT Press, 2002), 13.

9 Ješa Denegri, "Inside or Outside 'Socialist Modernism'? Radical Views on the Yugoslav Art Scene, 1950–1970," in *Impossible Histories: Historic Avant-Gardes, Neo-Avant-Gardes, and Post-Avant-Gardes in Yugoslavia, 1918–1991*, ed. Dubravka Djurić and Miško Šuvaković (Cambridge, MA: MIT Press, 2003), 172.

10 Terry Smith, *Art to Come: Histories of Contemporary Art* (Durham: Duke University Press, 2019), 324. For some refreshing perspectives on issues related to contemporary art and globalization, refer to *Curating after the Global: Roadmaps for the Present*, ed. Paul O'Neill, Simon Sheikh, Lucy Steeds, and Mick Wilson (Cambridge, MA: MIT Press, 2019).

11 As noted by Catherine Samary, *Decolonial Communism, Democracy, and the Commons* (London: Merlin Press, 2019), 52.

BIBLIOGRAPHY

Adamović, Aleksandar. "Notes on the Contemporary Art of Bosnia and Herzegovina." In *Yugoslav Documents '87*. Sarajevo: Olimpijski Centar "Skenderija," Galerije Grada Sarajeva, 1987.

Ahmić, Niazid. "Vidimo se u Zvonu." *Naši dani* (Sarajevo), 23 December 1981.

"Akcija Total." *15 Dana: Časopis za kulturu i umetnosti*, no. 8–9 (November/December 1970), 8–9.

Alajbegović, Zemira. "The Frozen Time—The Eighties, ŠKUC-Forum, FV Video, and Others." In *Videodokument: Video Art in Slovenia, 1969–1998; Essays*, edited by Barbara Borčić, 37–50. Ljubljana: SCCA, 1999.

Alajbegović, Zemira. "Mladinska Subkultura: Disco FV—No Future, No Escape." *VIKS* (Ljubljana), no. 1 (November 1983).

Alberro, Alexander. *Conceptual Art and the Politics of Publicity*. Cambridge, MA: MIT Press, 2003.

Anđelković, Branislava, Branislav Dimitrievič, and Dejan Sretenović. *On Normality: Art in Serbia, 1989–2001*. Belgrade: Muzej Savremene Umetnosti, 2009.

Andjelić, Neven. *Bosnia-Herzegovina: The End of a Legacy*. London: Frank Cass, 2003.

Andrić, Branko. "'Februar' je prestao da postoji još u januaru." *Index*, 24 February 1971.

Antić, Miroslav, and Pero Zubac. "Žurnal Miroslava Antića; Neki feler u mladima." *Dnevnik* (Novi Sad), 23 February 1971.

Bago, Ivana. "The City as a Space of Plastic Happening: From Grand Proposals to Exceptional Gestures in the Art of the 1970s in Zagreb." *Journal of Urban History* 44, no. 1 (2018), 26–53.

Bago, Ivana. "Dematerialization and Politicization of the Exhibition: Curation as Institutional Critique in Yugoslavia during the 1960s and 1970s." *Museum and Curatorial Studies Review* 2, no. 1 (Spring 2014), 7–37.

Bago, Ivana. "A Window and a Basement: Negotiating Hospitality at La Galerie des Locataires and Podroom—The Working Community of Artists." *ARTMargins* 1, no. 2–3 (June–October 2012), 116–146.

Bago, Ivana, and Antonia Majača. "Dissociative Association, Dionysian Socialism, Non-Action, and Delayed Audience: Between Action and Exodus in the Art of the 1960s and the 1970s in Yugoslavia." In *Removed from the Crowd: Unexpected Encounters I*, edited by Ivana Bago, Antonia Majača, and Vesna Vuković, 251–309. Zagreb: BLOK/Delve, 2011.

Bago, Ivana, and Antonia Majača. "Spit in the Eye of Truth (Then Quickly Close Your Eyes before It)." *Život umjetnosti: časopis o modernoj i suvremenoj umjetnosti i arhitekturi* 83 no. 2 (2008), 110–141.

Bailey, Robert. *Art & Language International*. Durham: Duke University Press, 2016.

Baletić, Milovan, and Zdravko Židovec. *Deseta sjednica CK SKH 1970*. Zagreb: Savez Komunista Hrvatske, Centralni Komitet, 1970.

Baljković, Nena. "Braco Dimitrijević—Goran Trbuljak." In *The New Art Practice in Yugoslavia, 1966–1978*, edited by Marijan Suskovski, 29–33. Zagreb: Galerija Suvremene Umjetnosti, 1978.

Baljković, Nena. "Group of Six Authors, Zagreb." In *The New Art Practice in Yugoslavia, 1966–1978*, edited by Marijan Suskovski, 34–35. Zagreb: Galerija Suvremene Umjetnosti, 1978.

Batović, Ante. *The Croatian Spring: Nationalism, Repression and Foreign Policy under Tito*. London: I. B. Tauris, 2017.

Becker, Lutz. "Art for an Avant-Garde Society: Belgrade in the 1970s." In *East Art Map: Contemporary Art and Eastern Europe*, edited by IRWIN, 390–400. London: Afterall, 2006.

Begić, Azra. "Uvod." In *Umjetnost Bosne i Hercegovine 1974–1988*, 11–16. Sarajevo: Umjetnička Galerija Bosne i Hercegovine,1984.

Bilandžić, Dušan. *Historija Socijalističke Federativne Republike Jugoslavije*. Zagreb: Školska Knjiga, 1978.

Bishop, Claire. *Artificial Hells: Participatory Art and the Politics of Spectatorship*. London: Verso, 2012.

Bjelić, Dušan. "Introduction: Blowing up the 'Bridge.'" In *Balkan as Metaphor: Between Globalization and Fragmentation*, edited by Dušan Bjelić and Obrad Savić, 1–22. Cambridge, MA: MIT Press, 2002.

Blažević, Dunja. "Art as a Form of Ownership Awareness." In *Oktobar '75*. Belgrade: SKC Gallery, 1975. Translated in *SKC and Political Practices of Art*, edited by Prelom Kolektiv, 7. Belgrade: Museum of Yugoslav History, 2008.

Blažević, Dunja. "Who's That Singing over There? Art in Yugoslavia and After ... 1949–1989." In *Aspects / Positions: 50 Years of Art in Central Europe, 1949–1999*, edited by Lóránd Hegyi and Achim Hochdörfer, 85–100. Vienna: Museum Moderner Kunst Stiftung Ludwig, 1999.

Boban, Jadran. "Kralj šume u transu rock'n'rolla—razgovor sa Slobodanom Tišmom." *Zarez* (Zagreb) 146 (2005). http://slobodantisma.blogspot.com/2010/03/kralj-sume-u-transu-rocknrolla.html.

Boden, Ragna. "Soviet World Policy in the 1970s: A Three-Level Game." In *The Crisis of Socialist Modernity*, edited by Marie-Janine Calic et al., 184–204. Göttingen: Vandenhoeck & Ruprecht, 2011.

Bogdanović, Slavko. *Inventar discernacije*. Belgrade: Orion Art, 2018.

Bogdanović, Slavko. "Pesma underground Tribina Mladih." In "Underground Issue," *Student* (Belgrade), 16 December 1971.

Bogdanović, Slavko. "PROGRAM ČASOPISA 'L.H.O.O.Q.'" (Bosut, 1971). Reprinted in *Grupa KÔD, GRUPA (Ǝ, Grupa (Ǝ-KÔD: Retrospektiva*, edited by Miško Šuvaković. Novi Sad: Muzej Savremene Umetnosti Vojvodine, 1995.

Bogdanović, Slavko. "UMETNOST (DANAS); UMETNIK (STVARALAC), UČESNIK (AUTOR)." In *Grupa KÔD, GRUPA (Ǝ, Grupa (Ǝ-KÔD: Retrospektiva*, edited by Miško Šuvaković. Novi Sad: Muzej Savremene Umetnosti, Vojvodina, 1995.

Bojičić, Vesna. "The Disintegration of Yugoslavia: Causes and Consequences of Dynamic Inefficiency in Semi-Command Economies." In *Yugoslavia and After*, edited by David A. Dyker and Ivan Vejvoda, 28–47. London: Routledge, 1996.

Borčić, Barbara. *Celostna umetnina Laibach: Fragmentarni pogled*. Ljubljana: Založba *cf, 2013.

Borčić, Barbara. "The ŠKUC Gallery, Alternative Culture, and Neue Slowenische Kunst in the 1980s." In *NSK: From Kapital to Capital*, edited by Zdenka Badovinac, Eda Čufer, and Anthony Gardner, 299–319. Cambridge, MA: MIT Press, 2015.

Borčić, Barbara. "Video Art from Conceptualism to Postmodernism." 2003. http://www.gama-gateway.eu/uploads/media/Video_Art_in_Yugoslavia_B_Borcic.pdf.

Borčić, Barbara. "Yugoslav Border Scenes—Fragments." In "Art Is Stronger than Death," special edition of *Likovne Besede* no. 21–22 (November 1992).

Borčić, Barbara, and Marina Gržinić. "ŠKUC i njegova likovna produkcija." *3+4: Časopis Studenata Istorije Umetnosti* (Belgrade), 1984: 5.

Borčić, Barbara, Aina Šmid, and Marina Gržinič. "Odnos vladojče ideologije do subkulture." *Galerija ŠKUC izdaja* (Ljubljana), December 1981.

Boynik, Sezgin. "Cultural Roots of Contemporary Art in Kosovo." In *New Public Spaces: Dissensual Political and Artistic Practices in the Post-Yugoslav Context*, edited by Radical Education Collective, 212–220. Maastricht: Jan Van Eyck Akademie, 2009.

Božović, S. "'Februar' osuđen u Martu." *Novosti* (Belgrade), 4 March 1971.

Brejc, Tomaž. *OHO, 1966–1971*. Ljubljana: Študentski Kulturni Center, 1978.

Brejc, Tomaž. "OHO as an Artistic Phenomenon, 1966–1971." In *The New Art Practice in Yugoslavia, 1966–1978*, edited by Marijan Susovski, 13–17. Zagreb: Galerija Suvremene Umjetnosti, 1978.

Breznik, Maja. "Urban Theatre: The OHO Group Happenings, 1966–1969." *M'Ars* (Moderna Galerija, Ljubljana), no. 3–4 (1995), 12–19.

Bryan-Wilson, Julia. *Art Workers: Radical Practice in the Vietnam War Era*. Berkeley: University of California Press, 2011.

Brzović, Gordana, and Kristina Leko. *Grupa šestorice autora*. Documentary film, Zagreb, 2002.

Bućan, Boris, and Davor Tomičić. "Akcija 'Total': nacrt dekreta o demokratizaciji umjetnosti (s obrazloženjem)." *Novine GSC*, no. 22 (April 1970), 81.

Buchloh, Benjamin H. D. "Allegorical Procedures: Appropriation and Montage in Contemporary Art." *Artforum*, September 1972, 43–56.

Buchloh, Benjamin H. D. "Beuys: Twilight of the Idol, Preliminary Notes for a Critique." *Artforum*, January 1980, 35–43. Reprinted in *Joseph Beuys: Mapping the Legacy*, edited by Gene Ray, 199–211. New York: D.A.P.; Sarasota, FL: John and Mable Ringling Museum of Art, 2001.

Buchloh, Benjamin H. D. "Conceptual Art 1962–1969: From the Aesthetic of Administration to the Critique of Institutions." *October* 55 (Winter 1990), 105–143.

Budding, Audrey Helfant, "Nation/People/Republic: Self-Determination in Socialist Yugoslavia." In *State Collapse in South-Eastern Europe: New Perspectives on Yugoslavia's Disintegration*, edited by Lenard J. Cohen and Jasna Dragović-Soso, 91–129. West Lafayette, IN: Purdue University Press, 2007.

Bukvić, Aleksandar Saša. "Ne dozvoljavam da se 'Zvono' zaboravi." *Radio Slobodna Evropa*, 12 August 2011, http://www.slobodnaevropa.org/content/bukvic_ne_dozvoljavam_da_se_zvono_zaboravi/24325037.html.

Burg, Steven L. *Conflict and Cohesion in Socialist Yugoslavia*. Princeton, NJ: Princeton University Press, 1983.

Burg, Steven L. "Republican and Provincial Constitution Making in Yugoslav Politics." *Publius* 12, no. 1 (Winter 1982), 131–153.

Calic, Marie-Janine. "The Beginning of the End—The 1970s as a Historical Turning Point in Yugoslavia." In *The Crisis of Socialist Modernity: The Soviet Union and Yugoslavia in the 1970s*, edited by Marie-Janine Calic, Dietmar Neutatz, and Julia Obertreis, 66–86. Göttingen: Vandenhoeck & Ruprecht, 2011.

Camnitzer, Luis, Jane Farver, Rachel Weiss, and László Beke. *Global Conceptualism: Points of Origin, 1950s–1980s*. New York: Queens Museum of Art, 1999.

Chomsky, Noam. "The Repression of Belgrade University." *New York Review of Books*, 7 February 1972.

Cockroft, Eva. "Abstract Expressionism: Weapon of the Cold War." *Artforum* 15, no. 10 (June 1974), 39–41.

Commisso, Ellen Turkish. *Workers' Control under Plan and Market: Implications of Yugoslav Self-Management*. New Haven: Yale University Press, 1980.

Čorak, Željka. "Predgovor." *6. zagrebački salon—Prijedlog*. Zagreb: Galerija Suvremene Umjetnosti 1971.

Čorak, Željka. "Razbroj zbroja—'Suma 680' izložba Slobodana Dimitrijevića u galeriji studentskog centra." *Telegram* (Zagreb), no. 502 (12 December 1969).

Corris, Michael, and Andrew Menard. Letter to *Left Curve: Art and Revolution*, no. 5 (1975), 97–100.

Ćosić, Bora. *Rok: časopis za književnost i estetičko ispitivanje stvarnosti*. Belgrade: Direkcija, 1969.

Crnković, Gordana P. "Vibrant Commonalities and the Yugoslav Legacy." In *After Yugoslavia: The Cultural Spaces of a Vanished Land*, edited by Radmila Gorup, 123–134. Stanford, CA: Stanford University Press, 2013.

Crowley, David. "The Future Is between Your Legs: Sex, Art and Censorship in the Socialist Federal Republic of Yugoslavia." In *Monuments Should Not Be Trusted*, edited by Lina Džuverović, 32–44. Nottingham, UK: Nottingham Contemporary, 2015.

Ćurčić, Branka. "Less of a Cultural Patrimony—More of an Actualisation of Past Practices of Cultural Dissent." Paper presented at "Evaluating and Formative Goals of Art Criticism in Recent (de)Territorialized Contexts," AICA Press conference, Skopje, 29 May 2009.

Dautović, Sava. "Zakuska političkih uvreda." *Vjesnik* (Zagreb), 2 March 1971.

Demarco, Richard. *Aspects '75*. Edinburgh: Richard Demarco Gallery, 1975.

Demarco, Richard. *Eight Yugoslav Artists: Edinburgh Arts 73: Marina Abramović, Radomir Damnjan, Nuša & Srečo Dragan, Neša Paripović, Zoran Popović, Raša Todosijević, Gergely Urkom*. Edinburgh: Richard Demarco Gallery, 1973.

Demur, Boris, and Mladen Stilinović. Interview. "Do kad će mame hraniti umjetnike?" *Polet* (Zagreb), 31 January 1979: 8–9.

Denegri, Ješa. "Art in the Past Decade." In *The New Art Practice in Yugoslavia, 1966–1978*, edited by Marijan Suskovski, 5–12. Zagreb: Galerija Suvremene Umjetnosti 1978.

Denegri, Ješa. "Drangularijum." In *Drangularijum*. Exhibition catalogue. Belgrade: Studentski Kulturni Centar, June 1971.

Denegri, Ješa. "Goran Đorđević." In *The New Art Practice in Yugoslavia, 1966–1978*, edited by Marijan Suskovski, 63. Zagreb: Galerija Suvremene Umjetnosti 1978.

Denegri, Ješa. "Inside or Outside 'Socialist Modernism'? Radical Views on the Yugoslav Art Scene, 1950–1970." In *Impossible Histories: Historic Avant-Gardes, Neo-Avant-Gardes, and Post-Avant-Gardes in Yugoslavia, 1918–1991*, edited by Dubravka Djurić and Miško Šuvaković, 170–208. Cambridge, MA: MIT Press, 2003.

Denegri, Ješa. "The Language of Art and the System of Art." *Oktobar '75*. Belgrade: SKC Gallery, 1975. Translated in *SKC and Political Practices of Art*, edited by Prelom Kolektiv, 13–14. Belgrade: Museum of Yugoslav History, 2008.

Denegri, Ješa. *Nova umetnost u Srbiji, 1970–1980: Pojedinci, grupe, pojave*. Belgrade: Muzej Savremene Umetnosti, 1983.

Denegri, Ješa. *Osamdesete: Teme srpske umetnosti*. Novi Sad: Svetovi, 1997.

Denegri, Ješa. *Pedesete: Teme srpske umetnosti (1950–1960)*. Novi Sad: Svetovi, 1993.

Denegri, Ješa. "Primjeri konceptualne umjetnosti u Jugoslaviji." *Život umjetnosti* 15–16 (1971), 151.

Denegri, Ješa. "Prisećanje na rad grupe OHO." *Polja: časopis za književnost i teroiju*, no. 190, (December 1974), 20–21.

Denegri, Ješa. *Razlozi za drugu liniju: Za novu umetnost sedamdesetih*. Novi Sad: Marinko Sudac/ Muzej Savremene Umetnosti Vojvodine, 2007.

Denegri, Ješa. *Sedamdesete: Teme srpske umetnosti*. Novi Sad: Svetovi, 1996.

Denegri, Ješa. *Šezdesete: Teme srpske umetnosti (1960–1970)*. Novi Sad: Svetovi, 1995.

Denegri, Ješa. *Srpska umetnost 1950–2000*. Belgrade: Orion Art, 2013.

Denegri, Ješa. *Studentski kulturni centar kao umetnička scena*. Belgrade: Studentski Kulturni Centar, 2002.

Denitch, Bogdan. *The Legitimation of a Revolution: The Yugoslav Case*. New Haven: Yale University Press, 1976.

Depolo, Josip. "Nedopušteni pritisci." *Večernji list* (Zagreb), 13 January 1979.

Đilas, Gordana, and Nedeljko Mamula. *Tribina Mladih: 1954–1977*. Novi Sad: Kulturni Centar Novog Sada, 2004.

Đilas, Milovan. *The New Class: An Analysis of the Communist System*. New York: Frederick A. Praeger, 1957.

Dimitrijević, Braco. "Čovjek i čovjek stvaralac, vizija osjećanje, stvaranje i djelo." *Novine GSC*, no. 12 (November 1969), 33.

Dimitrijević, Braco. "Eksperiment komunikacija 1." *Novine GSC*, no. 12 (November 1969), 32.

Dimitrijević, Branislav. "Altered Identities: Goran Đorđević as an Artist; SKC as an Institution." *Prelom: Journal for Images and Politics* 8 (Fall 2006), 241–247.

Dimitrijević, Branislav. "A Brief Narrative of Selected Art Events in Serbia 1948–2001." In *East Art Map*, edited by IRWIN, 287–297. London: Afterall, 2006.

Dimitrijević, Branislav. "In-Between Utopia and Nostalgia, or How the Worker Became Invisible on the Path from Shock-Worker to Consumer." In *Nostalgia on the Move*, edited by Mirjana Slavković, 30–41. Belgrade: Museum of Yugoslav History, 2017.

Dimitrijević, Branislav. "'Iron Curtain Raiser': An Exhibition of American Modern Art in Belgrade and Its Relation to 'Socialist Modernism' and 'Socialist Consumerism' in SFR Yugoslavia in the 1950s." In *Different Modernisms, Different Avant-Gardes: Problems of Eastern European Art after World War II*, Kumu Art Museum Autumn Conference, edited by Sirje Helme (Tallinn, Estonia: Kadrioru Kunstimuuseum, 2009), 313–342.

Dimitrijević, Branislav. "Neke uvodne napomene o radu Gorana Đorđevića u periodu 1974–1985: a posebno u vezi sa njegovim delovanjem u okviru beogradskog Studentskog kulturnog centra." *Prelom* (Spring/Summer 2006), 148–155.

Djokić, Dejan. *Yugoslavism: Histories of a Failed Idea, 1918–1992*. Madison: University of Wisconsin Press, 2003.

Donia, Robert J. *Sarajevo: A Biography*. London: C. Hurst, 2006.

Đorđević, Goran. "International Strike of Artists." *3+4 Časopis studenata istorije umetnosti* (Belgrade), 1980. Reprinted in *SKC and Political Practices of Art*, edited by Prelom Kolektiv, 28–39. Belgrade: Museum of Yugoslav History, 2008.

Dragović-Soso, Jasna. "Rethinking Yugoslavia: Serbian Intellectuals and the National Question in Historical Perspective." *Contemporary European History* 13, no. 2 (2004), 170–184.

Dragović-Soso, Jasna. *Saviours of the Nation: Serbia's Intellectual Opposition and the Revival of Nationalism*. Montreal: McGill-Queen's University Press, 2002.

Dyker, David. *Yugoslavia: Socialism, Development and Debt*. London: Routledge, 1990.

Džuverović, Lina. *Monuments Should Not Be Trusted*. Nottingham, UK: Nottingham Contemporary, 2015.

E. C. “Bućan Art.” *Večernji list* (Zagreb), 20 November 1973, 11.

Erjavec, Aleš. “NSK, New Slovene Art: Slovenia, Yugoslavia, Self-Management, and the 1980s.” In *Postmodernism and the Postsocialist Condition: Politicized Art under Late Socialism*, edited by Aleš Erjavec, 135–174. Berkeley: University of California Press, 2003.

Erjavec, Aleš. “The Three Avant-gardes and Their Context: The Early, the Neo, and the Postmodern.” In *Impossible Histories: Historic Avant-Gardes, Neo-Avant-Gardes, and Post-Avant-Gardes in Yugoslavia, 1918–1991*, edited by Dubravka Djurić and Miško Šuvaković, 36–63. Cambridge, MA: MIT Press, 2003.

February Group for New Art (Grupa za nove umetnosti “Februar”). “Otvoreno pismo jugoslovenskoj javnosti.” *Student* (Belgrade), 23 February 1971.

Fejtö, François [Ferenc]. *Histoire des démocraties populaires*. Paris: Seuil, 1979.

Fichter, Madigan. “Yugoslav Protest: Student Rebellion in Belgrade, Zagreb, and Sarajevo in 1968.” *Slavic Review* 75, no. 1 (Spring 2016), 99–121.

Fowkes, Maja. *The Green Bloc: Neo-Avant-Garde Art and Ecology under Socialism*. Budapest: CEU Press, 2015.

Gabrič, Aleš. “Cultural Activities as Political Action.” In *The Repluralization of Slovenia in the 1980s: New Revelations from Archival Records*, edited by Leopoldina Plut-Pregelj, 16–35. Washington, DC: Henry M. Jackson School of International Studies, 2000.

Gardner, Anthony, and Charles Green. “Biennials of the South on the Edges of the Global.” *Third Text* (London) 27, no. 4 (2013), 442–455.

Greenberg, Robert D. *Language and Identity in the Balkans: Serbo-Croatian and Its Disintegration*. Oxford: Oxford University Press, 2008.

Groh, Klaus. *Aktuelle Kunst in Osteuropa*. Kölin: DuMont-Schauberg, 1972.

Group of Six Authors (Grupa Šestorice Autora). *Izložbe-akcije / Exhibition-Actions*. Zagreb: Centar za Film, Fotografiju i Televiziju, 1977.

Grujičić, Nebojša, and Jovana Gligorijević. “Smisao nadrealizma dr. Neleta Karajlića.” *Vreme* (Belgrade), no. 1144 (6 December 2012).

Gržinić, Marina. *Galerija ŠKUC Ljubljana, 1978–1987*. Ljubljana: ŠKUC, 1988.

Gržinič, Marina. “Graffiti as a Subversion of Slovenian Cultural Space.” Translated in *NSK: From Kapital to Capital*, edited by Zdenka Badovinac, Eda Čufer, and Anthony Gardner, 92–95. Cambridge, MA: MIT Press, 2015.

Gržinić, Marina. “Interview with Alenka Pirman.” ŠKUC Gallery website, accessed 11 April 2020, http://www.galerijaskuc.si/marina-grzinic/.

Gržinić, Marina. “Mladen Stilinović: Strategies of the Cynical Mind.” In *Mladen Stilinović: Exploitation of the Dead*, edited by Branka Stipančić and Tihomir Milovac. Zagreb: Muzej Suvremene Umjetnosti, 2001.

Gržinič, Marina, and Zemira Alajbegović. “Ljubjlanska subkulturna scena.” *Problemi* (October–November 1983), 26.

Gržinić, Marina, and Aleš Erjavec. *Ljubljana, Ljubljana: Osemdeseta leta v umetnosti in kulturi.* Ljubljana: Mladinska Knjiga, 1991.

Gudac, Vladmir. "The Last Number." *Novine GSC*, December 1975.

Gurshtein, Ksenya. "An Experimental Microcosm on the Edge of East and West." In *L'Internationale: Post-War Avant-Gardes between 1957 and 1986*, edited by Christian Höller, 230–238. Zurich: JRP-Ringier, 2012.

Gurshtein, Ksenya. "Part 1: The OHO Group, 'Information,' and Global Conceptualism avant la lettre." *POST: Notes on Modern and Contemporary Art around the Globe,* MoMA New York, 25 August 2016, https://post.at.moma.org/content_items/850-part-1-the-oho-group-information-and-global-conceptualism-avant-la-lettre.

Guzina, Dejan. "Socialist Serbia's Narratives: From Yugoslavia to a Greater Serbia." In "Studies in the Social History of Destruction: The Case of Yugoslavia." Special issue, *International Journal of Politics, Culture, and Society* 17, no. 1 (Fall 2003), 91–111.

Halligan, Benjamin. "Idylls of Socialism: The Sarajevo Documentary School and the Problem of the Bosnian Sub-Proletariat." *Studies in Eastern European Cinema* 1, no. 2 (2010), 197–216.

Harrison, Charles, and Paul Wood. *Art in Theory, 1900–1990*. Oxford: Blackwell Publishers, 1992.

Haug, Hilde Katrine. *Creating Socialist Yugoslavia: Tito, Communist Leadership and the National Question*. London: I. B. Tauris, 2012.

"HIT-PARADA." *Borba* (Belgrade), 24 October 1967.

"Hit Parade." *Večernji list* (Zagreb), 23 October 1967, 7.

Hoare, Marko Attila. *The History of Bosnia: From the Middle Ages to the Present Day*. London: Saqi, 2007.

Horvat, Branko. *Jugoslavensko društvo u krizi: kritički ogledi i prijedlozi reformi*. Zagreb: Globus, 1985.

Hošić, Irfan. "Zvono prije 'Zvono.'" *Vizura: Časopis za savremene vizualne umjetnosti, likovnu kritiku i teoriju* (Sarajevo), no. 3–4 (October 2008), 92–99.

Husedžinović, Meliha. "Aspects and Positions of Art from Bosnia-Hercegovina, 1949–1999." In *Aspects / Positions: 50 Years of Art in Central Europe 1949—1999*, edited by Achim Hochdörfer, 109–144. Vienna: Museum Moderner Kunst Stiftung Ludwig, 1999.

Husedžinović, Meliha. "Bosnia and Herzegovina." In *Body and the East: From the 1960s to the Present*, edited by Zdenka Badovinac, 40–45. Ljubljana: Moderna Galerija, 1999.

Hyder-Patterson, Patrick. *Bought and Sold: Living and Losing the Good Life in Socialist Yugoslavia*. Ithaca, NY: Cornell University Press, 2011.

Ilić, Marko. "'Made in Yugoslavia': Struggles with Self-Management in the New Art Practice." *ARTMargins* 8, no. 1 (February 2019), 6–30.

Ilić, Marko. "'A Taster of Political Insult': The Case of Novi Sad's Youth Tribune." *Third Text* 32, issue 4, no. 153 (July 2018), 530–545.

International Society for Socialist Studies. *The Programme of the League of Yugoslav Communists*. London: Aldgate Press, 1959.

Irvine, Jill. "The Croatian Spring and the Dissolution of Yugoslavia." In *State Collapse in South-Eastern Europe*, edited by Lenard J. Cohen and Jasna Dragović-Soso, 149–178. West Lafayette, IN: Purdue University Press, 2007.

IRWIN. "Back to the USA." *Galerija ŠKUC Izdaja*, 1984. Reprinted in Slovenian in *Do roba in naprej: Slovenska Umetnost 1975–85*, edited by Igor Španjol, 130–133. Ljubljana: Moderna Galerija, 2003.

Iveković, Sanja. "'Žive skulpture i medijske interakcije': Razgovarale Nataša Govedić i Suzana Marjanić." *Zarez* (Zagreb) 101, no. 27 (March 2003), 12–14.

"Izložba psovke." *Novosti* (Belgrade), 30 January 1971.

"Izložba umesto protesta." *Politika ekspres* (Belgrade), October 1972, 10.

Jakovljević, Branislav. *Alienation Effects: Performance and Self-Management in Yugoslavia, 1945–91*. Ann Arbor: University of Michigan Press, 2016.

Jakovljević, Branislav. "The Howling Wilderness of the Maladaptive Struggle in Belgrade in New York." *ARTMargins* 7, no. 2 (June 2018), 17–41.

Jakovljević, Branislav. "Human Resources: June 1968, *Hair*, and the Beginning of Yugoslavia's End." *Grey Room* 30 (Winter 2008), 38–53.

Janevski, Ana. *As Soon as I Open My Eyes I See a Film*. Warsaw: Museum of Modern Art, 2008.

Jeffs, Nikolai. "FV and the Third Scene, 1980–90." In *FV: Alternative Scene of the 80s*, edited by Breda Škrjanec, 352–353. Ljubljana: MGLC, 2008.

Jergović, Miljenko. *Naci bonton*. Zagreb: Duireux, 1998.

Jerman, Željko. "Zagrebački zenica depo." *Studentski list* (Zagreb), no. 908, 12 December 1985.

Johnson, A. R. *The Transformation of Communist Ideology: The Yugoslav Case, 1945–1953*. Cambridge, MA: MIT Press, 1972.

Jović, Dejan. *Yugoslavia: A State That Withered Away*. West Lafayette, IN: Purdue University Press, 2003.

Kanzleiter, Boris. "1968 in Yugoslavia: Student Revolt between East and West." In *Between Prague Spring and French May: Opposition and Revolt in Europe, 1960–80*, edited by Martin Klimke, Jacco Pekelder, and Joachim Scharloth, 84–100. New York and Oxford: Berghahn, 2011.

Kardelj, Edvard. *Pravci razvoja političkog sistema socijalističkog samoupravljanja*. Belgrade: Komunist, 1977.

Kemp-Welch, Klara. *Antipolitics in Central European Art: Reticence as Dissidence under Post-Totalitarian Rule (1956–1989)*. London: I. B. Tauris, 2014.

Kirn, Gal. "From the Primacy of Partisan Politics to the Post-Fordist Tendency in Yugoslav Self-Management Socialism." In *Post-Fordism and Its Discontents*, edited by Gal Kirn, 253–304. Maastricht: Jan Van Eyck Academie, 2010.

Kirn, Gal. "On Yugoslav Market Socialism through Živojin Pavlović's *When I am Dead and Pale*, 1967." In *The Cultural Life of Capitalism in Yugoslavia: (Post)Socialism and Its Other*, edited by Dijana Jelača, Maša Kolanović, and Danijela Lugarić, 139–158. London: Palgrave Macmillan, 2017.

Kolešnik, Ljiljana. "Conflicting Visions of Modernity and the Post-war Modern Art." In *Socialism and Modernity: Art, Culture, Politics, 1950–1974*, edited by Ljiljana Kolešnik, 107–180. Zagreb: Muzej Suvremene Umjetnosti, 2014.

Komelj, Miklavž. "Function of the Signifier 'Totalitarianism' in the Constitution of the 'East Art' Field." In *Retracing Images: Visual Culture after Yugoslavia*, edited by Daniel Šuber and Slobodan Karamanić, 55–80. Leiden: Brill, 2012.

Konrád, György. *Antipolitics: An Essay*. London: Harcourt, 1984.

Konstantinović, Radomir. *Filozofija palanke*. Belgrade: NOLIT, 1969.

Košak, Miha. "Avant-Propos." In *10. Biennale grafike*, edited by Zoran Kržišnik. Ljubljana: Moderna Galerija, 1973.

Koščević, Želimir. "Aspekti ambijentalizacije prostora." *Život umjetnosti*, no. 13 (1971), 55–62.

Koščević, Želimir. *Galerija studentskog centra: 1961–73*. Zagreb: Galerija Studentskog Centra, 1975.

Koščević, Želimir. "Hollos I." *Novine GSC*, no. 28 (June 1971), 107.

Koščević, Želimir. *Ispitivanje međuprostora*. Zagreb: Centar za Kulturnu Djelatnost Saveza Socijalističke Omladine, 1978.

Koščević, Želimir. "Izložba žena i muškaraca." *Novine GSC*, no. 8 (1968–1969), 29.

Koščević, Želimir. "Modeli u zraku." *Moment* (Belgrade), no. 18 (April–June 1990), 57–58.

Koščević, Želimir. "Oblikovanje grada—alternativi i problemi." *Razlog* (Zagreb), no. 2 (1964).

Koščević, Želimir. "Poštanske pošiljke." *Novine GSC*, no. 35 (March 1972), 135.

Koščević, Želimir. "Predgovor." *Hit parada*. Zagreb: Galerija Studentskog Centra, 1967.

Koščević, Želimir. "We Succeeded in Creating a Beautiful and Instructive Thing That's Inevitably Been Irredeemably Lost, but Such Is Life." *Newspaper Galerija Nova* (Zagreb), no. 18 (December 2008), 13–17.

Koščević, Želimir, in conversation with Zvonko Maković. "Bezobrazno nas ignoriraju." *Studentski list* (Zagreb), Autumn 1971.

Kosuth, Joseph. "1975." *The Fox* 2, (1975), 87–96.

Kovačević, Filip. "Marcuse in Yugoslavia." Unpublished PhD dissertation, University of Montenegro, 2003.

Kurspahić, Kemal. "Moja '68': Poziv na ljudski, pravedeniji, bolji svet." In *Šezdeset osma—Licne istorije*, edited by Đorđe Malavrazić, 202. Belgrade: Službeni Glasnik, 2008.

Kurspahić, Nermina. "Likovna grupa Zvono, Sarajevo." In *Zvono*. Sarajevo: Foto-Kino Savez, Novi Sad, 1985.

Kuvačić, Ivan. "Contemporary Forms of Mental Violence." In "Power and Humanity Issue." *Praxis: A Philosophical Journal* (Zagreb), 1–2 (1970), 130–135.

Laibach. "Interview." *Džuboks*, 1982. Translated and available online, accessed 21 April 2020. http://www.laibach.org/interviews-1980-to-1985/.

Laibach. *LAIBACH: The Instrumentality of the State Machine*. Ljubljana: Galerija ŠKUC Izdaja, 1982.

Laibach. *10 Items of the Covenant*. Published on the invitation for the *Ausstellung! Laibach Kunst* exhibition, ŠKUC Gallery, Ljubljana, 28 April 1982. Translated and available online, accessed 21 April 2020. http://www.laibach.org/data/10-items-of-the-covenant/.

Laibach. TV Tednik Interview, 1983. https://www.youtube.com/watch?v=xz_PhMpFR9U.

Lang, Nicholas R. "The Dialectics of Decentralization: Economic Reform and Regional Inequality in Yugoslavia." *World Politics* 27, no. 3 (April 1975), 309–335.

Lazović, Miladin. "Kome 'Zvono' zvoni? Bravardžiluk, kujundžiluk, slikardžiluk." *U.Nov* (Sarajevo), 27 August 1986.

Leplat, Fred, and Catherine Samary. *Decolonial Communism, Democracy, and the Commons*. London: Merlin Press, 2019.

Lippard, Lucy R. *Six Years: The Dematerialization of the Art Object*, edited by Lucy R. Lippard and John Chandler, vii–xxii. New York and London: Praeger Publishers, 1973; reprinted, with a new introduction by Lucy Lippard, Berkeley: University of California Press, 1997.

Lovšin, Peter, Peter Mlakar, and Igor Vidmar. *Punk je bil prej, 25 let punka pod Slovenci*. Ljubljana: Cankarjeva Založba / Ropot, 2003.

Magaš, Branka. *The Destruction of Yugoslavia: Tracking the Break-Up, 1980–92*. London: Verso, 1993.

Majača, Antonia. "Feminism, Activism and Historicisation: Sanja Iveković Talks to Antonia Majača." *N.paradoxa: International Feminist Art Journal* 23 (January 2009), 5–13.

Maković, Zvonko. "Hollos II." *Novine GSC*, no. 28 (June 1971), 108.

Maković, Zvonko. "Kad li će procvjetati tikve." *Tjedni list omladine*, February 1971, 26.

Maković, Zvonko. "Sanja Iveković." *Novine GSC* (Zagreb), no. 17 (March 1970), 51.

Malečkar, Neža, and Mastnak, Tomaž. *Punk pod Slovenci*. Ljubljana: Univerzitetna Konferenca ZSMS, Republiška Konferenca ZSMS, 1985.

Maliqi, Shkëlzen. "How Art Modernized in Kosovo." In "Balkart." Special issue, *Kosovo 2.0*, no. 6 (Fall/Winter 2013), 24–36.

Mandić, Dušan. "Come, Come Close to Me, I Tell You Man You Will See." *3+4 Časopis studenata istorije umetnosti* (Belgrade), 1984.

Mandić, Dušan. "Pogovor s člani RZU Podrum." *Galerija ŠKUC Izdaja* (Ljubljana), October 1981.

Mandić, Dušan. "Die Welt ist Schön." *Galerija ŠKUC Izdaja* (Ljubljana), October 1982.

Mandić, Dušan. *Die Welt ist schön = Svet je lep = The World Is Beautiful*. Ljubljana: Mestna Galerija, 2014.

Mandić, Miroslav. "Galerije." *Index: List studenata Vojvodine*, 21 October 1970, 7.

Mansoor, Jaleh. *Marhsall Plan Modernism: Italian Postwar Abstraction and the Beginnings of Autonomia*. Durham: Duke University Press, 2016.

Maračić, Antun. "New Primitive Art Jusufa Hadžifejzovića." *Studentski list* (Zagreb), no. 912 (9 January 1986), 22.

Marcuse, Herbert. *An Essay on Liberation*. Boston: Beacon Press, 1969.

Marcuse, Herbert. "The Realm of Freedom and the Realm of Necessity: A Reconsideration." *Praxis International* 5 (1969), 20–25.

Marcuse, Herbert. "Repressive Tolerance," 1965. In Robert Paul Wolff, Barrington Moore Jr., and Herbert Marcuse, *A Critique of Pure Tolerance*, 95–137. Boston: Beacon Press, 1969.

Marjanić, Suzana. "Razgovor sa Svenom Stilinovićem." *Zarez* (Zagreb), 8 February 2007. http://www.zarez.hr/clanci/razgovor-sa-svenom-stilinovicem.

Martek, Vlado. "Journal-Catalogue *Maj '75*." *Novine Galerija Nova* (Zagreb), no. 18 (December 2008), 21.

Mastnak, Tomaž. "Civil Society and Fascism." In *NSK: From Kapital to Capital*, edited by Zdenka Badovinac, Eda Čufer, and Anthony Gardner, 280–289. Cambridge, MA: MIT Press, 2015.

Mastnak, Tomaž. "Civil Society in Slovenia: From Opposition to Power." *Studies in Comparative Communism* 23, no. 3+4 (Autumn/Winter 1990), 305–317.

Mastnak, Tomaž. "From Social Movements to National Sovereignty." In *Independent Slovenia: Origins, Movements, Prospects*, edited by Jill Benderly and Evan Kraft, 95–109. New York: St Martin's Press.

Matičević, Davor. Introduction to *Mogućnosti za 1971*, edited by Davor Matičević, 3–4. Zagreb: Galerija Suvremene Umjetnosti, 1971.

Matičević, Davor. "On Conscious and Unconscious Vagueness." In *Yugoslav Documents '87*. Sarajevo: Olimpijski Centar "Skenderija," Galerije Grada Sarajeva, 1987.

Matičević, Davor. "Ozbiljnošt igre: povodom izložbe 'Suma 680' Braco Dimitrijevića." *Studentski list* (Zagreb), no. 15 (November 1969).

Matičević, Davor. "Predgovor." In *Inovacije u hrvatskoj umjetnosti sedamdesetih godina*, edited by Marijan Susovski. Zagreb: Galerija Suvremene Umjetnosti, 1982.

Matičević, Davor. "Uvod." In *Sanja Iveković: Dokumenti, 1949–1976*, edited by Davor Matičević. Zagreb: Galerija Suvremene Umjetnosti, 1976.

Matičević, Davor. "A View of the Eighties: The Eighties—The Way to Remember Them." In *Jugoslovenska dokumenta 1989*, 39–45. Sarajevo: Olimpijski Centar "Skenderija," Galerije Grada Sarajeva, 1989.

Medosch, Armin. *New Tendencies: Art at the Threshold of the Information Revolution (1961–1978)*. Cambridge, MA: MIT Press, 2016.

Medosch, Armin. "Overcoming Alienation / New Tendencies (1961–1973)." In *L'Internationale: Post-War Avant-Gardes between 1957 and 1986*, edited by Christian Höller, 285–296. Zurich: JRP-Ringier, 2012.

Mertus, Julie A. *Kosovo: How Myths and Truths Started a War*. Berkeley: University of California Press, 1999.

Mihailović, Dragoslav. *Kad su cvetale tikve*. Novi Sad: Matica Srpska, 1968.

Mijušković, Slobodan. "Goran Đorđević. Original i kopija." *Moment* (Belgrade) 2 (1985), 9–11.

Milanović, Z. "Čašica umjetnosti." *Naši dani* (Sarajevo), May 1979.

Milevska, Suzana. "Mapping the 1980s Art Scene in Macedonia in Inverse Perspective." In *The Eighties through the Prism of Events, Exhibitions, and Discourses in Slovenia and Yugoslavia*, edited by Igor Španjol. Ljubljana: Moderna Galerija, 2017.

Miller, Nick. "Yugoslavia's 1968: The Greater Surrender." In *Promises of 1968: Crisis, Illusion and Utopia*, edited by Vladimir Tismaneanu, 227–239. Budapest: Central European Press, 2011.

Mirosavljević, B. "Zabrana zbog laži i uvreda." *Novosti* (Belgrade), 11 December 1971.

Mišina, Dalibor. "'Anarchy all over Baščaršija': Yugoslavia's New Socialist Culture and the *New Primitives* Poetics of the Local." *Journal of Historical Sociology* 26, no. 2 (June 2013), 169–199.

Mišina, Dalibor. *Shake, Rattle and Roll: Yugoslav Rock Music and the Poetics of Social Critique*. Oxford: Routledge, 2016.

Mladenov, Sanja Kojić. *Bogdanka Poznanović: Contact Art*. Novi Sad: Muzej Savremene Umetnosti Vojvodina, 2016.

Močnik, Rastko. "Edicija OHO." Translated into Serbo-Croatian by Dejan Poznanović. In *Rok: časopis za književnost i estetičko ispitivanje stvarnosti*, no. 1, edited by Bora Ćosić. Belgrade: Direkcija, 1969.

Močnik, Rastko. "The Vagaries of the Expression 'Civil Society': The Yugoslav Alternative." *L'Internationale Online*. 21 June 2014. https://www.internationaleonline.org/research/real_democracy/6_the_vagaries_of_the_expression_civil_society_the_yugoslav_alternative.

Monroe, Alexei. *Interrogation Machine: Laibach and NSK*. Cambridge, MA: MIT Press, 2005.

Moranjak-Bamburać, Nirma. "Prema problemu kulturnog sinkretizma u Bosni i Hercegovini." *Dijalog* (Sarajevo) 2–3 (1988), 97–122.

Morrison, Kenneth. *Montenegro: A Modern History*. London: I. B. Tauris, 2009.

Mostov, Julie. "Democracy and Decisionmaking." In *Yugoslavia, A Fractured Federalism*, edited by Dennison Rusinow, 105–119. Washington, DC: Wilson Center Press, 1988.

Motoh, Helena. "'Punk Is a Symptom': Intersections of Philosophy and Alternative Culture in the '80s Slovenia." *Synthesis Philosophica* 54 (February 2012), 285–296.

"Neprihvatljive tendencije." *Novosti* (Belgrade), 15 December 1971.

New Media Center_kuda.org. *The Continuous Art Class: The Novi Sad Neo-Avantgarde of the 1960s and 1970s*. Novi Sad: Daniel Print, 2006.

New Media Center_kuda.org. *Omitted History*. Novi Sad: Daniel Print, 2007.

Novaković, Nada. *Propadanje radničke klase: Materijalni i društveni položaj radničke klase Jugoslavije od 1960 do 1990 godine*. Belgrade: Institut Društvenih Nauka, 2007.

O'Neill, Paul, Simon Sheikh, Lucy Steeds, and Mick Wilson. *Curating after the Global: Roadmaps for the Present*. Cambridge, MA: MIT Press, 2019.

Palairet, Michael. *Macedonia: A Voyage through History*. Vol. 2. Newcastle upon Tyne: Cambridge Scholars Publishing, 2015.

Pavlović, Pavle. "Šareno zvona zvone." *Studio* (Sarajevo), August 1986.

Pavlović, Živojin. *Ispljuvak pun krvi: Dnevnik '68*. Belgrade: Službeni Glasnik, 2008.

Pejić, Bojana. "Balkan for Beginners." In *Primary Documents: A Sourcebook for Eastern and Central European Art since the 1950s*, edited by Laura Hoptman and Tomáš Pospiszyl, 325–340. Cambridge, MA: MIT Press, 2002.

Pejić, Bojana. "Bodyscenes: An Affair of the Flesh." In *Marina Abramović: The Artist Body: Performances 1969–1998*, 26–40. Milan: Charta, 1998.

Pejić, Bojana. *Gender Check: A Reader*. Vienna: Verlag, 2010.

Pejić, Bojana. "Jusuf Hadžifejzović, Kunst-Werke, Berlin." *Artforum* 32, no. 2 (October 1993), 109–110.

Pejić, Bojana. "The Morning After: Plavi Radion, Abstract Art and Bananas." *N-Paradoxa* 10 (2002), 75–84.

Pejić, Bojana. "Proletarians of All Countries, Who Washes Your Socks?: Equality, Dominance, and Difference in Eastern European Art." In *Gender Check: Femininity and Masculinity in the Art of Eastern Europe*, edited by Bojana Pejić, 19–29. Vienna: Museum Moderner Kunst Stiftung Ludwig Wien, 2009.

Pejić, Bojana, "Serbia: Socialist Modernism and the Aftermath." In *Aspects / Positions: 50 Years of Art in Central Europe, 1949–1999*, edited by Lóránd Hegyi and Achim Hochdörfer. Vienna: Museum Moderner Kunst Stiftung Ludwig, 1999. http://www.c3.hu/ican.artnet.org/ican/texted92.html?id_text=57.

Pejić, Bojana. "Yugoslavia: Body-Based Art: Serbia and Montenegro." In *Body and the East: From the 1960s to the Present*, edited by Zdenka Badovinac, 79–96. Ljubljana: Moderna Galerija, 1999.

Pejić, Bojana, and David Elliott. *After the Wall: Art and Culture in Post-Communist Europe*. Stockholm: Moderna Museet, 1999.

Pervan, Ralph. *Tito and the Students: The University and the University Student in Self-Managing Yugoslavia*. Nedlands: University of Australia Press, 1978.

Petrović, Gajo. *Čemu Praxis?* Zagreb: Praxis, 1972.

Phelan, Peggy. *Unmarked: The Politics of Performance*. London: Routledge, 1997.

Piotrowski, Piotr. *In the Shadow of Yalta: Art and the Avant-Garde in Eastern Europe, 1945–1989*. London: Reaktion, 2001.

Piškur, Bojana. "Yugoslav Documents Exhibition(s)." In *The Heritage of 1989: Case Study: The Second Yugoslav Documents Exhibition*, edited by Ana Mizerit and Adela Železnik. Ljubljana: Moderna Galerija, 2017.

Piškur, Bojana, Ana Janevski, Jurij Meden, and Stevan Vuković. *This Is All Film: Experimental Film in Yugoslavia*. Ljubljana: Moderna Galerija, 2010.

Popov, Nebojša. *Društveni sukobi izazov sociologiji: "Beogradski Jun" 1968*. Belgrade: Službeni Glasnik, 2008.

Popović, Zoran. "For a Self-Managing Art." *Oktobar 75*. Belgrade: SKC Gallery, 1975. Translated in *SKC and Political Practices of Art*, edited by Prelom Kolektiv, 7. Belgrade: Museum of Yugoslav History, 2008.

Popović, Zoran. *Zoran Popović: Film bez naziva*. Zagreb: Centar za Film, Fotografiju i Televiziju, 1978.

Popović, Zoran, and Jasna Tijardović. "A Note on Art in Yugoslavia." *The Fox* 1 (1975), 49–52.

Prelom Kolektiv. "Story on Copy: An Interview with Goran Đorđević." In *Prelom: Journal for Images and Politics* 8 (Fall 2006), 249–268.

Radna Zajednica Umjetnike. *Prvi broj*. Zagreb: RZU Podrum, 1980.

Radojičić, Mirko. "Activity of Group KÔD." In *The New Art Practice in Yugoslavia, 1966–1978*, edited by Marijan Susovski, 38–47. Zagreb: Galerija Suvremene Umjetnosti, 1978.

Radusinović, V. "Neobičan ispit zrelosti." *Borba* (Belgrade), 25 July 1989.

Ramet, Sabrina P. *The Three Yugoslavias: State-Building and Legitimation, 1918–2005*. Bloomington: Indiana University Press, 2006.

Ramsden, Mel. "On Practice." *The Fox* 1 (1975), 66–83.

Repe, Božo. "The Introduction of Political Parties and Their Role in Achieving Independence." In *The Repluralization of Slovenia in the 1980s: New Revelations from Archival Records*, edited by Leopoldina Plut-Pregelj, 36–57. Washington, DC: Henry M. Jackson School of International Studies, 2000.

Rimkutė, Agnė. "Negotiating Self-Management While Producing Films: Yugoslav New Wave and Neoplanta Film Studio in 1966–1972." Unpublished MA dissertation, Central European University, Budapest, 2014.

Rojc, Emil, et al. *Deseti Kongres SKJ: Dokumenti*. Belgrade: Komunist, 1974.

Rosen, Margit. *A Little-Known Story about a Movement, a Magazine, and the Computer's Arrival in Art: New Tendencies and Bit International, 1961–1973*. Cambridge, MA: MIT Press, 2011.

Rupel, Dimitrij. "Slovenia's Shift from the Balkans to Central Europe." In *Independent Slovenia: Origins, Movements, Prospects*, edited by Jill Benderly and Evan Kraft, 183–200. London: Palgrave Macmillan, 1994.

Rusinow, Dennison. "Crisis in Croatia: Part I: Post-Mortems after Karadjordjevo." (DIR-4-'72), *American Universities Field Staff Reports: Southeast Europe Series* 19, no. 4 (June 1972), 1–20.

Rusinow, Dennison. "Reopening of the 'National Question' in the 1960s." In *State Collapse in South-Eastern Europe*, edited by Lenard J. Cohen and Jasna Dragović-Soso, 131–148. West Lafayette, IN: Purdue University Press, 2007.

Rusinow, Dennison. *The Yugoslav Experiment, 1948–74*. Berkeley: University of California Press, 1977.

S.R. "Od dogmatizma do vandalizma." *Telegram* (Zagreb), 29 October 1967, 3.

Šalgo, Judita. "Tribina mladih: otvorena—zatvorena." *Index: List studenata Vojvodine*, 21 October 1970, 7.

Šali, Franc. *Kulturna pot ZK Slovenije*. Ljubljana, Komunist, 1987.

Salketić, Aida. "Konstrukcija alternativnog galerijskog prostora na primjeru kafea Zvono." Unpublished MA dissertation, Philosophy Faculty, Sarajevo, 2014.

Samary, Catherine. *Yugoslavia Dismembered*. New York: Monthly Review Press, 1995.

Savez Komunista Srbije (SKS) Predsedništvo. *Aktivnost Saveza komunista Srbije u borbi protiv nacionalizma*. Belgrade: Komunist, 1972.

Schöpflin, George. *Politics in Eastern Europe: 1945–1992*. London: Blackwell Publishers, 1993.

Seibel, Hans Deiter, and Ukandi G. Damachi. *Self-Management in Yugoslavia and the Developing World*. London: Macmillan, 1982.

Sekreterijat za komunalne poslove građevinstva i saobraćaj. "Šesti zagrebački salon, Zagreb," 10 June 1971. Reprinted in *Novine GSC*, no. 28 (June 1971), 110.

Sher, Gerson S. *Praxis: Marxist Criticism and Dissent in Socialist Yugoslavia*. Bloomington: Indiana University Press, 1977.

Smith, Terry. *Art to Come: Histories of Contemporary Art*. Durham: Duke University Press, 2019.

Spaskovska, Ljubica. *The Last Yugoslav Generation: The Rethinking of Youth Politics and Cultures in Late Socialism*. Manchester, UK: Manchester University Press, 2017.

Sretenović, Dejan. *Thank You Raša Todosijević*. Belgrade: Muzej Savremene Umetnosti, 2002.

Srhoj, Vinko. *Grupa Biafra 1970–1978*. Zagreb: Art Studio Azinović, 2001.

"Šta će biti sa Tribinom mladih?" *Index: List studenata Vojvodine* (Novi Sad), 11 November 1970.

Stepančić, Ljiljana. "The Poster Scandal: New Collectivism and the 1987 Youth Day" (1994). Reprinted in *IRWIN Retroprincip 1983–2003*, edited by Inke Arns, 44–48. Frankfurt: Revolver, 2003.

Stepanov, Sava. "Suočeni s vremenon." *Odjek* (Sarajevo), November 1986, 19.

Stilinović, Mladen. "Living Means Never Having to Attend Court: Interview with Branka Stipančić." In *Mladen Stilinović—Artist at Work (1973–1983)*, edited by Alenka Gregorič and Branka Stipančić, 26–37. Zagreb: Mladen Stilinović, 2010.

Stimson, Blake. "The Promises of Conceptual Art." In *Conceptual Art: A Critical Anthology*, edited by Alexander Alberro and Blake Stimson, xxxviii–lii. Cambridge, MA: MIT Press, 1999.

Stipančić, Branka. "Auction of Red: A Look at the '70s." In *Mladen Stilinović—Sing!*, edited by Branka Stipančić. Budapest: Ludwig Museum, 2011.

Stipančić, Branka. *Mladen Stilinović: Artists' Books 1972–2006*. Istanbul: Platform Garanti Contemporary Art Center; Eindhoven: Van Abbemuseum, 2007.

Stipančić, Branka. "This Is Not My World." In *Grupa šestorice autora*, 101–104. Edited by Janka Vukmir. Zagreb: Soros Center for Contemporary Art, 1998.

Stojanović, Svetozar. *Between Ideals and Reality: A Critique of Socialism and Its Future*. Oxford: Oxford University Press, 1973.

Stojanović, Svetozar. "The June Student Movement and Social Revolution in Yugoslavia." In "Power and Humanity Issue." *Praxis: A Philosophical Journal* (Zagreb), 1–2 (1970), 94–155.

Stokić, Jelena. "Beuys's Lesson in Belgrade." *Post: Notes on Modern and Contemporary Art around the Globe*, MoMA, New York, 25 November 2014, http://post.at.moma.org/content_items/554-beuys-s-lesson-in-belgrade.

Štrajn, Darko. "Black-and-White Shock in Trbovlje (1981)." Translated in *NSK: From Kapital to Capital*, edited by Zdenka Badovinac, Eda Čufer, and Anthony Gardner, 28–32. Cambridge, MA: MIT Press, 2015.

Studentski Kulturni Centar. *Art, Irony, Etc.* Exhibition catalogue. Belgrade: Studentski Kulturni Centar, 1977.

Studentski Kulturni Centar. *Drangularijum*. Exhibition catalogue. Belgrade: Studentski Kulturni Centar, 1971.

Studentski Kulturni Centar. *Moment 1–2, Biliten studentskog kulturnog centra*. Belgrade: Studentski Kulturni Centar, 1973.

Studentski Kulturni Centar. *Oktobar '72*. Exhibition catalogue. Studentski Kulturni Centar, 1972.

Studentski Kulturni Centar. *Prošireni mediji: I i II Aprilski susreti*. Belgrade: Studentski Kulturni Centar 1974.

Studentski Kulturni Centar. *Prošireni mediji: III Aprilski susret*. Belgrade: Studentski Kulturni Centar, 1974.

Susovski, Marijan. Foreword to *The New Art Practice in Yugoslavia, 1966–1978*, edited by Marijan Susovski, 3–4. Zagreb: Galerija Suvremene Umjetnosti, 1978.

Susovski, Marijan. "Inovacije u Hrvatskoj umjetnost sedamdesetih godina." In *Inovacije u Hrvatskoj umjetnosti sedamdesetih godina*, edited by Boris Kelemen. Belgrade: Muzej Savremene Umetnosti, 1982.

Susovski, Marijan. "The Seventies and the Group of Six Authors." In *Grupa šestorice autora*, edited by Janka Vukmir, 12–23. Zagreb: Soros Center for Contemporary Art, 1998.

Šuvaković, Miško. "Art as a Political Machine: Fragments on the Late Socialist and Postsocialist Art of Mitteleuropa and the Balkans." In *Postmodernism and the Postsocialist Condition*, edited by Aleš Erjavec, 90–134. Berkeley: University of California Press, 2003.

Šuvaković, Miško, ed. *Bogdanka i Dejan Poznanović: Umetnost, mediji i aktivizam na kraju moderne*. Novi Sad: Muzej Savremene Umetnosti, Vojvodina, 2011.

Šuvaković, Miško. *The Clandestine Histories of the OHO Group*. Ljubljana: Zavod P.A.R.A.S.I.T.E., 2010.

Šuvaković, Miško. "Conceptual Art." In *Impossible Histories: Historic Avant-Gardes, Neo-Avant-Gardes, and Post-Avant-Gardes in Yugoslavia, 1918–1991*, edited by Dubravka Djurić and Miško Šuvaković, 210–245. Cambridge, MA: MIT Press, 2003.

Šuvaković, Miško. *Grupa KÔD, GRUPA (Ǝ, Grupa (Ǝ-KÔD: Retrospektiva*. Novi Sad: Muzej Savremene Umetnosti Vojvodine 1995.

Šuvaković, Miško. "Introduction: Art and Politics." In *Impossible Histories: Historic Avant-Gardes, Neo-Avant-Gardes, and Post-Avant-Gardes in Yugoslavia, 1918–1991*, edited by Dubravka Djurić and Miško Šuvaković, 210–245. Cambridge, MA: MIT Press, 2003.

Šuvaković, Miško. *Istorija umetnosti u Srbiji XX vek—Prvi tom: Radikalne umetničke prakse*. Belgrade: Orion Art, 2010.

Šuvaković, Miško. "Students' Cultural Centers as Reservations." In *SKC and Political Practices of Art*, edited by Prelom Kolektiv, 85–87. Belgrade: Museum of Yugoslav History, 2008.

Šuvar, Stipe. *Sociološki presjek jugoslavenskog društva*. Zagreb: Školska Knjiga, 1970.

Suvin, Darko. *Splendour, Misery and Possibilities: An X-Ray of Socialist Yugoslavia*. Leiden: Brill Books, 2019.

Tanner, Marcus. *Croatia: A Nation Forged in War*. New Haven: Yale University Press, 1997.

Thompson, Mark. *A Paper House: The Ending of Yugoslavia*. London: Vintage Books, 1992.

Tijardović, Jasna. "The 'Liquidation' of Art: Self-Management or Self-Protection?" *The Fox* 3 (1976), 97–99.

Tijardović, Jasna. "Marina Abramović, Slobodan Milivojević, Neša Paripović, Zoran Popović, Raša Todosijević, Gergelj Urkom." In *The New Art Practice in Yugoslavia, 1966–1978*, edited by Marijan Susovski, 59–63. Zagreb: Galerija Suvremene Umjetnosti, 1978.

Tijardović, Jasna. "Notes." *Oktobar '75*. Belgrade: SKC Gallery, 1975. Translated in *SKC and Political Practices of Art*, edited by Prelom Kolektiv, 11. Belgrade: Museum of Yugoslav History, 2008.

Tijardović, Jasna. "Notes on Education in Art as Personal/Public Activity in Belgrade's Art Scene of the '70s." Belgrade, 1975. Accessed 10 March 2013. http://radical.temp.si/2011/07/notes-on-education-in-art-as-personal-public-activity-in-belgrade-art-scene-in-seventies-by-jasna-tijardovic/.

Tito, Josip Broz. *Workers Manage Factories in Yugoslavia.* Pamphlet, Belgrade, 26 June 1950, 4–43.

Toal, Gerard, and Carl T. Dahlaman. *Bosnia Remade: Ethnic Cleansing and Its Reversal*. Oxford: Oxford University Press, 2011.

Todosijević, Raša. "Edinburgh Statement." In *Art, Irony, Etc.* Exhibition catalogue. Belgrade: Studentski Kulturni Centar, 1977.

Todosijević, Raša. "Interview with Andrew Gibbons." In *FRA-YU-KULT: Fraction of Yugoslavian Culture*, edited by Jozo Pejić and Jadran Adamović. Široki Brijeg: Muzej Široki Brijeg, 1990.

Tomc, Gregor. "The Politics of Punk." In *Independent Slovenia: Origins, Movements, Prospects*, edited by Jill Benderly and Evan Kraft, 113–134. London: Palgrave Macmillan, 1994.

Tomc, Gregor. "We Will Rock YU: Popular Music in the Second Yugoslavia." In *Impossible Histories: Historic Avant-Gardes, Neo-Avant-Gardes, and Post-War Avant-Gardes in Yugoslavia, 1918–1991*, edited by Dubravka Djurić and Miško Šuvaković, 442–465. Cambridge, MA: MIT Press, 2003.

Tomii, Reiko. *Radicalism in the Wilderness: International Contemporaneity and 1960s Art in Japan*. Cambridge, MA: MIT Press, 2016.

Trbuljak, Goran. "Ne želim pokazati ništa novo i originalno." *Novine GSC*, no. 30 (November 1971), 117.

Trbuljak, Goran. "Referendum." *Novine GSC*, no. 38 (September 1972), 154.

Trifunović, Lazar. *Enformel u Beogradu*. Belgrade: Umetnički Paviljon "Cvijeta Zuzorić," 1982.

Tumbas, Jasmina. "Decision as Art: Performance in the Balkans." In *Performing Arts in the Second Public Sphere*, edited by Katalin Cseh-Varga and Adam Czirak, 184–201. Basingstoke: Palgrave Macmillan, 2018.

Turković, Hrvoje. "Farsa oko novosadske tribine mladih." *Studentski List* (Zagreb), no. 4–5 (15 February 1971).

Tuzlić, Dževdet. "Šmek Montmartrea." In *Bife galerija Zvono.* Sarajevo: Café-Gallery Zvono, 1985.

Ugrešić, Dubravka. "The Spirit of the Kakanian Province." In *After Yugoslavia: The Cultural Spaces of a Vanished Land*, edited by Radmila Gorup, 289–306. Palo Alto, CA: Stanford University Press, 2013.

Ulrich Obrist, Hans. "'Art Is the Basis, Beer Is the Basis, Beans Are the Basis'—The Belgrade Art Scene of the 1970s, Early Performances and Short Stories on Art: An Interview with Hans Ulrich Obrist." *Spike Magazine* (Brighton, UK), 2008. Accessed 5 June 2020. http://old.spikeart.at/en/a/magazin/back/Portrait_Rasa_Todosijevic.

Unkovski-Korica, Vladimir. *The Economic Struggle for Power in Tito's Yugoslavia: From World War II to Non-Alignment*. London: I. B. Tauris, 2016.

Unkovski-Korica, Vladimir. "Self-Management, Development and Debt: The Rise and Fall of the 'Yugoslav Experiment.'" In *Welcome to the Desert of Post-Socialism: Radical Politics after Yugoslavia*, edited by Srećko Horvat and Igor Štiks, 21–45. London: Verso, 2015.

Unkovski-Korica, Vladimir. "Workers' Councils in the Service of the Market." *Europe-Asia Studies* (November 2013), 108–134.

Veličovski, Vladimir. *Zero: Retrospective 1984–2009*. Skopje: Mala Stanica, 2009.

Veselinović, Slavoljub. *Ovo je studentski kulturni centar: Prvih 25 godina*. Belgrade: Students' Cultural Center, 1996.

Vesić, Jelena. Introduction to *Political Practices of (Post-)Yugoslav Art: Retrospective 01*, edited by Jelena Vesić, Zorana Dojić, Ivana Bago, and Dušan Đorđević Mileusnić. Belgrade: Prelom Kolektiv, 2010.

Vesić, Jelena. "Politics of Display and Troubles with National Representation in Contemporary Art." *Red Thread* 1–3 (2009–2011), 8–17.

Vesić, Jelena. "SKC (Student Cultural Center) as a Site of Performative (Self-)Production: *October 75*—Institution, Self-organization, First-person Speech, Collectivization." *Život umjetnosti* 91 (2012), 30–53.

Vesić, Jelena. "The Student Cultural Center (SKC) as the Art Scene." *Parallel Chronologies: An Archive of East European Exhibitions*. Accessed 28 March 2020. http://tranzit.org/exhibitionarchive/essays/jelena-vesic/.

Vesić, Jelena. "Works and Words—Early Critiques of the Discourse of East European Art." *Parallel Chronologies: An Archive of East European Exhibitions*. Accessed 28 March 2020. http://tranzit.org/exhibitionarchive/works-and-words-early-critiques-of-the-discourse-of-eastern-european-art/.

Videkanić, Bojana. "Yugoslav Post-war Art and Socialist Realism: An Uncomfortable Relationship." *ARTMargins* 5, no. 2 (2016), 3–26.

Vidmar-Brejc, Taja. "Interview with Alenka Pirman." ŠKUC website, accessed 11 April 2020. http://www.galerijaskuc.si/taja-vidmar-brejc/.

Vilić, Nebojša. "Glossary of Art Terms: Macedonian Case." In *Aspects / Positions: 50 Years of Art in Central Europe, 1949–1999*, edited by Lóránd Hegyi and Achim Hochdörfer. Vienna: Museum Moderner Kunst Stiftung Ludwig, 1999.

Vinterhalter, Jadranka. "Umetničke grupe—Razlozi okupljanja i načini rada." In *Nova umetnost u Srbiji, 1970–1980: Pojedinci, grupe, pojave*, edited by Ješa Denegri, 14–23. Belgrade: Muzej Savremene Umetnosti, 1983.

Vlačić, Zorica. Introduction to *Yugoslav Documents '87*. Sarajevo: Olimpijski Centar "Skenderija," Galerije Grada Sarajeva, 1989.

Vranešević, Peđa. "Čemu umetnost." *Vreme*, no. 1159, 21 March 2013, http://www.vreme.com/cms/view.php?id=1105012.

Vujanović, Branka. "Nepretenciozna filozofija igre i spontanosti—Likovna grupa 'Zvono' u galeriji 'Tate Liverpool.'" *Zmijski jezik*, 11 November 2013.

Vukmir, Janka. *Grupa šestorice autora*. Zagreb: Soros Center for Contemporary Art, 1998.

Vuković, Stevan. "Troubles with Reality, or Who Was to Carry the Burden of Self-Management." In *As Soon as I Open My Eyes I See a Film: Experiments in Yugoslav Art in the 60s and 70s*, edited by Ana Janevski, 43–63. Warsaw: Museum of Modern Art in Warsaw, 2011.

Watchel, Andrew. *Making a Nation, Breaking a Nation: Literature and Cultural Politics in Yugoslavia*. Palo Alto, CA: Stanford University Press, 1998.

Wood, Catherine. "Back to the USA, Replayed." In *NSK: From Kapital to Capital*, edited by Zdenka Badovinac, Eda Čufer, and Anthony Gardner, 319–325. Cambridge, MA: MIT Press, 2015.

Woodward, Susan. *Balkan Tragedy: Chaos and Dissolution after the Cold War*. Washington, DC: Brookings Institution Press, 1995.

Woodward, Susan. *Socialist Unemployment: The Political Economy of Yugoslavia, 1945–1990*. Princeton, NJ: Princeton University Press, 1995.

Zabel, Igor. "Art and State: From Modernism to the Retroavantgarde." In Igor Zabel, *Eseji I*, 319–325. Ljubljana: Založba /*cf, 2006.

Zabel, Igor. "A Short History of OHO." In *East Art Map: Contemporary Art and Eastern Europe*, edited by IRWIN, 410–432. London: Afterall, 2006.

Zabić, Sarah. "Praxis, Student Protest and Purposive Social Action: The Humanist Marxist Critique of the League of Communists of Yugoslavia, 1964–1975." Unpublished MA dissertation, Kent State University, 2010.

Žerovc, Beti. "The OHO Files." *ARTMargins Online*, 24 August 2011. https://artmargins.com/the-oho-files-preface/.

Zildžo, Nermina. "Burying the Past and Exhuming Mass Graves." In *East Art Map: Contemporary Art and Eastern Europe*, edited by IRWIN, 141–152. London: Afterall, 2006.

Zildžo, Nermina. "Sječam se …" in *Sarajevski New Primitivs*. Sarajevo: Umjetnička Galerija Bosne i Hercegovine, 1990.

Zildžo, Nermina. "Yugoslav (Intervening) Documents." In *Yugoslav Documents '87*. Sarajevo: Olimpijski Centar "Skenderija," Galerije Grada Sarajeva, 1987.

Žilnik, Želimir. "Žilnik demantuje." *Dnevnik* (Novi Sad), 24 Feburary 1971.

Žižek, Slavoj. Editorial. *Problemi*, no. 205/206 (1981).

Žižek, Slavoj. "Ideologija, cinizem, punk" (1984). Translated in *NSK: From Kapital to Capital*, edited by Zdenka Badovinac, Eda Čufer, and Anthony Gardner, 96–113. Cambridge, MA: MIT Press, 2015.

Žižek, Slavoj. "A Permanent Economic Emergency." *New Left Review* 64 (July–August 2010), 85–95.

Žižek, Slavoj. "Why Are Laibach Not Fascists?" (1993). In *Primary Documents: A Sourcebook for Eastern and Central European Art since the 1950s*, edited by Laura Hoptman and Tomáš Pospiszyl, 285–286. Cambridge, MA: MIT Press, 2002.

INDEX

Note: Page numbers followed by "f" indicate figures.

Abramović, Marina
  background, 143
  in *Kino beleške*, 153
  Rhythm 5, 142, 143, 145f
  Rhythm 10, 129, 131f
  at SC Gallery, 122
  Umetnost mora biti lepa—Umetnik mora biti lep (Art Must Be Beautiful—Artist Must Be Beautiful), 154f
Adamović, Aleksandar, 255, 257
Africano, Nicholas, 245
Ahmić, Niazid, 259
Alajbegović, Zemira, 240–241, 242–243
Alberro, Alexander, 42
Alijević, Mustafa, 259
Alpine symbolism, 219, 223
Alternativa slovenski umetnosti (An Alternative to Slovene Art), exhibition, 210
Andrić, Branko, 79
Andrić, Ivo, 255
Antić, Miroslav, 94
Aprilski susreti (April Meetings), 12, 135–143, 136f, 137f, 144f, 173, 257, 282, 297
Art
  democratization of, 87
  invisible, 109–114
  against the new art, 158–166
  and politics, 135, 152–153
  without a market, 146–148
Art & Language, group, 146–150, 147f, 149f, 155, 158, 198
ART EVENT (Edinburgh, 1973), 129
Art Workers' Coalition (New York), 161
Associated Labor Law of 1976, 187
Ausstellung! Laibach Kunst, exhibition, 219
Back to the USA, exhibition, 245–250
Bago, Ivana, 42, 197
Baljković, Nena, 174, 183, 184
Banja Luka, 256
Barr, Alfred, 225
Basic organization of associated labor (BOAL), 187, 193
Becker, Lutz, 153
Begić, Azra, 255, 257
Belgrade. *See also* SKC Gallery; Studentski Kulturni Centar
  in 1971, 114
  artists, 133, 135, 148
  Beuys visits, 138
  Group of Six Authors in, 177
  International Theatre Festival 6, 129
  as metropolis and village, 296–297
  Museum of Contemporary Art, 127
  Political Action Program, 116–117
  university, 115
Benjamin, Walter, 233
Beuys, Joseph
  on artists, 141
  Buchloh on, 142
  in Edinburgh, 129–130
  and *Josephine Beuys*, 133, 134f
  lectures, 129, 132f, 138
  performance of *Celtic (Kinloch Rannoch) Scottish Symphony*, 133
  social idealism, 138–139
  at Third April Meeting, Belgrade, 136f, 137f
  Twelve Hour Lecture: A Homage to Anacharsis Cloots, 129, 132f
  work, 133–134
Biafra, 60
Biennale des Jeunes, Paris, 44
Biennale grafike, 282

Bilandžić, Dušan, 54
Bishop, Claire, 30
Bitenc, Brane, 233
Bitka u Neretvi (The Battle of Neretva), 259
Blažević, Dunja, 120, 121, 122, 152, 155
"Art as a Form of Ownership Awareness," 150
BOAL. *See* Basic organization of associated labor
Bogdanović, Slavko
Apotheosis to Jackson Pollock, 83
ART (TODAY); ARTIST (CREATOR); PARTICIPANT (AUTHOR), 84
and Grupa KÔD, 79
on Novi Sad, 103
"Pesma underground tribina mladih Novi Sad" (Underground Song for the Youth Tribune, Novi Sad), 104f, 105f, 108
proposal for *L.H.O.O.Q.* magazine, 100
"Song," 107, 110
Stripa o grupi KÔD (Comic about the Group KÔD), 101, 102f
Zakovana knjiga (Riveted Book), 89, 90f
Bojanović, Rade, 93
Bonito Oliva, Achille, 143, 146, 294
Borčić, Barbara, 215
Borofsky, Jonathan, 245, 246
Bosman, Richard, 245
Breakstone, Jill, 148
Brecht, George, 73
Brejc, Tomaž, 27, 75, 79
Brotherhood and Unity, ideology of, 178
Bućan, Boris
Akcija total (Total Action), 45, 46f, 47f, 49, 51
Art (According to Coca-Cola), 55, 55f
Bućan Art series, 54–56
Laž (Lie), 56, 56f
SC Gallery and, 45
Buchloh, Benjamin H. D., 142
Bukvić, Aleksandar Saša, 259, 260, 267, 281
before joining Zvono, 269, 271
organization of independent exhibitions, 282
sculptures at street exhibition on Vase Miskina, 264f
Wedding Cake à la Tatlin, 271, 272f
Bull, John, 133
Buren, Daniel, 129
Burliuk, David, 45

Cabanne, Pierre, 73
Café-Gallery Zvono, 255–260, 258f. *See also* Zvono, group
Campaign for Nuclear Disarmament, 228
Čanadanović, Mirko, 98, 103
Caravan of Friendship (Belgrade, 1968), 115
Center for Film, Photography, and Television, 174
Četrti Reich (Fourth Reich), band, 228
Četvorica (Group of Four), 256
Chandler, John, 82
Čizmić, Sead, 260
Clark, Lygia, 33
Collegium Artisticum, 257, 282, 288, 298
Communist Alliance, Novi Sad, 87
Communist Party, 16
Conceptualism, 37–44, 129–135, 184, 223
Congress of Self-Managers (1971), 93
Čorak, Željka, 59
Corris, Michael, 148, 150, 155
Ćosić, Bora, 72
Ćosić, Dobrica, 127
Croatia
in 1971, 95
constitutional amendments, 128
as "sullen republic," 65
Croatian Mass Movement, 61, 67, 103, 128, 214
Croatian spring, new art in, 57–61
Čufer, Eda, 296

Dabčević-Kučar, Savka, 50, 61
Damnjan, Radomir, 143
Danas, newspaper, 284
Dautović, Sava, 98
"Decree No. 1 on the Democratization of Art," 45

De Kooning, Willem, 121
Dellabernardina, Drago, 74, 75f
Demarco, Richard, 129, 133
Demur, Boris, 173, 184
Denegri, Ješa, 25, 117, 138, 279, 297
Denitch, Bogdan, 167
Depolo, Josip, 185
Đilas, Milovan, 88, 89
Dimitrijević, Braco
Casual Passerby I Met at 1:15 pm, 4:23 pm, and 6:11 pm in Zagreb, 1971, 60–61, 62–63
in SC Gallery newspaper, 28, 30
Slika Krešimira Klike (Painting by Krešimir Klika), 31f
Suma 680, 28, 29f, 30
Dimitrijević, Branislav, 54, 156
Disco FV, 240, 243, 247
Dom Omladine (Youth House), 94, 129, 259
Đorđević, Goran, 269
Against Art, show, 161
Glasnici apokalipse (Harbingers of the Apocalypse), 165f, 166
International Strike of Artists, 12, 160–162
Kako kopirati Mondrijana (How to Copy a Mondrian), 270f
Kratka istorija umetnosti (A Short History of Art), 161–162, 164f
on New Art Practice, 184
organization of exhibition in his apartment, 166
Drangularijum, exhibition, 122–126, 123f, 125f
Drča, Čedomir
THE END (time-based action, with Tišma), 109, 110, 114
Primeri nevidljive umetnosti (Examples of Invisible Art), 111f, 112f, 113f, 114
withdrawal from public art, 109
Dubček, Aleksander, 40
Duchamp, Marcel, 73, 133
Džuboks, magazine, 223
Eight Yugoslav Artists, exhibition, 129
Erjavec, Aleš, 273
European Economic Community, 40
European modernism, 121
"Exhibition-Actions," 174, 177, 253

February Group, 94–100
Federal Executive Committee, 172
Federal General Investment Fund, 251
Federal People's Assembly, 16
Fejtö, Ferenc, 15
Fer, Briony, 140–141
Fluxus movement, 83–84
Fox, The, journal, 135, 146, 147f, 148, 155
Fund for Accelerated Development, 251
FV 112/15, theater group, 240

Galerija ŠKUC izdaja, 228, 230f
Galerija Studentskog Centra, Zagreb. *See* SC Gallery
Galić, Mladen, 19
Gallery of Contemporary Art, Zagreb, 18, 27
Gardner, Anthony, 282
Gavranović, Biljana, 260
Gego (Gertrud Louise Goldschmidt), 33
Geister, Iztok, 24
Gioconda, La (*Mona Lisa*), 100
Godard, Jean-Luc, 57
Godina, Karpo
Zdravi ljudi za razonodu (Healthy People for Fun), film, 95, 96f, 97
Gogh, Vincent van, 121
Gorky, Arshile, 121
Gramsci, Antonio, 1, 155
Green, Charles, 282
Gregorič, Miloš, 245
Group of Six Authors
in Belgrade (1976), 177
collaboration with Popović on *Untitled Film*, 179
Đorđević's disillusionment with, 184
Maj '75, 198, 206

money in the work of, 201
organization of, 174–175
and RZU Podrum, 167–206
SKC Gallery collaboration with, 297
Zvono and, 263
Grupa 143 (Group 143), 156, 157f
Grupa KÔD
Bogdanović among founders of, 79
decoding, 79–86
"democratization" of art, 87
dismissal from *Index*, 89
Javni čas umetnosti (Public Art Class), with Trbuljak, Mandić, and Mandić, 84f, 86f
Radojičić, *Estetika* (Aesthetics), 81f
Grupa za Nove Umetnosti "Februar" (February Group for New Art), 95f
Gržinić, Marina, 215, 228–229, 247, 287, 288

Haacke, Hans, 161
Hadžić, Kemal, 260
Hadžifejzović, Jusuf
Jugoslovenska dokumenta (Yugoslav Documents), 282
"New Primitive Dinner," 281
writing in *dokumenta* catalogue, 283
Hadžihasanović, Sadko, 260, 261
Hesse, Eva, 33
Hit-Parada (Hit Parade), exhibition, 19–24
destruction of, 21, 22f, 23
opening at SC Gallery, 20f, 21, 22f
reviews in newspapers, 23–24
Hollos, Rene, 59
Horvatić, Dubravko, 18
Huizinga, Johan, 28
Husedžinović, Meliha, 256, 278

Ilyich, Vladimir, 109
Index: Magazine of the Students' Association of Vojvodina, 79, 81, 82, 83, 87, 89
Information, exhibition (MoMA), 25
Informel painting, 21
International Strike of Artists, 12, 160–162
Invisible art, 109–114
IRWIN, 243
Back to the USA, ŠKUC Gallery, 244f
in *Baptism under Triglav*, 273
FV scene and exhibition space, 245
replica of Tatlin's *Monument to the Third International*, 271
Iveković, Sanja, 53–54, 185, 187, 189
on art and politics, 135
Bez naziva (Untitled), 34–35f
as Canada's visiting artist, 194
and Podrum, 191–195, 218–219
Prolaz (Passage), 51, 52f, 53f
studio, 185
Untitled Environment, 33
on Yugoslavia new generation of artists, 265
Ivkov, Boško, 108
Izložba žena i muškaraca (Exhibition of Women and Men), 37, 38, 39f, 40, 44

Jakovljević, Branislav, 117, 173, 193, 194, 225, 288
January Group, 89, 92, 93–94
Kako smo (How We Are), 92f
Jeffs, Nikolai, 240
Jergović, Miljenko, 254, 276, 278
Jerman, Željko, 173
Moj prostor (My Space), 195, 196f
Ovo nije moj svijet (This Is Not My World), 179, 181f
studio, 198
Job, Cvijeto, 61
Jugoslovenska dokumenta (Yugoslav Documents), 282–294, 297
in 1984, 282
in 1987, 284–285, 287
in 1989, 288–289, 294
cover of exhibition catalogue, 289f, 290f
group portrait of artists, 292–293f
poster for, 291f
as regionally oriented art fair, 283

Kaj je alternativa? (What Is the Alternative?), conference, 240–244
Kamensky, Vasily, 45
Kantardžić, Narcis, 260
Karajlić, Nele, 277, 278
Kardelj, Edvard, 172, 173, 175, 193, 198
Klein, Richard, 287
Klein, Yves, 178
Klika, Krešimir, 60
Knez, Dejan, 215, 216
  Artist Condition I, 217f
Kocijančić, Janez, 79
Kolešnik, Ljiljana, 198, 263
Komelj, Miklavž, 288
Konrad, György, 238
Konstantinović, Radomir, 296
Kosanović, Dragan, 92
Koščević, Želimir, 23, 28, 38, 60, 295
  "Ideas" or objects, 19–20
  on New Art Practice, 297
  and SC Gallery, 18, 44, 45
Kosovo
  conservative forces in, 218
  "developmentalist" approach, 253
  national movement in, 127
  visual arts in, 256
Kosuth, Joseph, 146, 158
Kožarić, Ivan
  Prizemljeno sunce (Grounded Sun), 58f, 59, 60
Koželj, Marinela
  contribution to SKC exhibition, 124
  Todosijević and, 129, 140, 158
Križnar, Naško, 24
Krvavac, Hajrudin, 253
Kučan, Milan, 285
Kuduz, Ante, 19
Kurspahić, Kemal, 115
Kurtović, Elvis J., 276, 277
Kusama, Yayoi, 261
Kuvačić, Ivan, 99

Lacan, Jacques, 239
Laibach, 210–227
  Black Cross, 212f
  The Deadly Dance, 213f
  installation at ŠKUC, 223
  Metalec (metal worker), 219
  organigram, 224f, 225
  Rdeči revirji (Red Districts), concert, 210
  TV tednik interview, 226f, 227
Landseer, Edwin, 219
League of Communists, 172, 173, 178, 179, 235, 251, 252, 284
League of Communists of Croatia (LCC), 50, 57, 65, 69
League of Communists of Serbia (LCS), 120, 127, 128, 249
League of Communists of Slovenia, 207
League of Communists of Vojvodina, 103
League of Communists of Yugoslavia (LCY), 16, 88, 99, 103, 107, 108, 120, 198
Left Curve, magazine, 148, 150
L.H.O.O.Q., magazine, 100–101, 103
Lippard, Lucy R., 25, 82, 161–162, 164f
Ljubljana. *See also* ŠKUC Gallery
  Zvezda Park, 74, 75f
Lozano, Lee
  General Strike Piece, 160

Maciunas, George, 73, 83, 84
Mackintosh, Alistair, 133
Magaš, Branka, 223
Magritte, René, 215, 216
  Maj '75, magazine, 198–199
  Issue B, 200f
  Issue Đ, 199
Makavejev, Dušan, 101, 109, 172
Maković, Zvonko, 59, 98
Malevich, Kazimir, 210
Maliqi, Shkëlzen, 256
Mandić, Božidar
  Javni čas umetnosti (Public Art Class), 84f, 86f
Mandić, Dušan, 215, 233, 238
  album design, 239f
  Cindy Sherman, 248f
  Cross, 237f

graffiti work, 242–243, 243f
invitation postcard for *Back to the USA*, 246f
Portrait of a Private in the Barracks, 236f
reproduction of Đorđević's *Harbingers of the Apocalypse*, 245–246
Untitled, 244f
Die Welt ist Schön (The World Is Beautiful), 233, 236f, 237f
Mandić, Miroslav, 79, 83, 100–101, 103
and *Javni čas umetnosti* (Public Art Class), 84f, 86f
"Song on Film: Sonnet or Fourteen Stanzas," 101
Mandić, Vladimir, 84f
Mansoor, Jaleh, 36
Maračić, Antun, 255, 280f, 281
Maračić, Jovan, 259
Marc, Davorin, 210
Marcuse, Herbert, 33, 36
Marinović, Žarko, 119
Martek, Vlado, 173, 195, 199
Martinis, Dalibor, 185, 187, 191, 192, 193, 194, 195
Mastnak, Tomaž, 229, 249
Matanović, Milenko, 74, 75f
Matica Hrvatska, 57, 60, 65, 88
Matica Srpska, 88
Matičević, Davor, 27–28, 54
Matisse, Henri, 121
Mayakovsky, Vladimir, 45
McShine, Kynaston, 25
Medosch, Armin, 18
Menard, Andrew, 148
Meštrović, Matko, 18–19, 135, 138
Mihailović, Dragoslav, 98
Kad su cvetale tikve (When the Pumpkins Blossomed), 98–99
Milevska, Suzana, 257
Milivojević, Era, 122
Milošević, Slobodan, 285
Mladina (Youth), journal, 210, 214, 242
Močnik, Rastko, 249
Modern Art in the United States, exhibition, 121
Mogućnosti za 1971 (Possibilities for 1971), exhibition, 51
Molnar, Marijan, 187, 189
Monroe, Alexei, 225
Moranjak-Bamburać, Nirma, 255
Morris, Robert, 32–33
Motherwell, Robert, 121
Mullican, Matt, 245

National Liberation Struggle, 178
National Youth Organization of Yugoslavia, Sixth Congress (1958), 15
Nedeljski dnevnik (Weekly Diary), 227
Neoplanta Film Company, 95, 99–100
Neue Slowenische Kunst (NSK), 250, 272f, 277
New Art Practice, 1–14, 174, 179, 256
Collegium Artisticum and, 257
Depolo and, 185
Đorđević on, 184
Koščević on, 297
Mandić and, 242
and Novi Sad, 114
origins of, 24–25
and Sarajevo, 255, 256
Tijardović on, 183
work affiliated with, 225
world markets and, 24
New French Fine Art, exhibition, 121
New Left, 27
New Primitivism, 276–278
New Tendencies, 18–19, 21, 135
Newton, Helmut, 219
Nez, David, 74, 75f
Nikezić, Marko, 120, 128
Nova revija (journal), 238, 249, 285
Novi kolektivizem (New Collectivism) (NK), rejected poster proposal for Youth Day, 286f, 287, 288
Novine Galerije SC (SC Gallery newspaper), 17f, 28, 30, 37, 40, 59, 65, 66f, 67
Novi Sad, 68, 99, 103, 109, 110. *See also* Youth Tribune
January Group in, 93–94
Katolička Porta Square, 76, 82

Municipal Youth League, 87
New Art Practice in, 114
and OHO, 25, 74–79
Novosti, newspaper, 101
NSK. *See* Neue Slowenische Kunst
Nuremberg Kunsthalle, 25

OHO, group, 24, 25, 27, 207–209
Brejc on, 27, 75
Izložba cipela (Exhibition of Shoes), 25, 26f
Jabuka (Apple), 72
manifesto, 72
Mount Triglav, 74–76, 75f
in Novi Sad, 74–79
Ritual, 72
Rok and "reistic" approach, 73
Summer Projects, 76, 78
Oldenburg, Claes, 271
Organization for Direct Democracy, 138
Oslobođenje, newspaper, 287
Otok, Goli, 98
Otroci Socializma (Children of Socialism), band, 233, 238

Palach, Jan, 73
Palanka, 296
Pankrti (Bastards), band, 208–209
Parade, film, 172
Paripović, Neša, 122
"Parquet salon," 82, 89
Pavlović, Pavle, 265
Pejić, Bojana, 122, 126, 143, 279
Pengov, Jure, 225
"People's militia," 227–228
Perović, Latinka, 120, 128
Petrović, Veljko, 121
Phelan, Peggy, 140
Picasso, Pablo, 121
Piotrowski, Piotr, 27
Plečnik, Jože, 287
Podrum. *See* Radna Zajednica Umjetnika (RZU) Podrum
Pogačnik, Marko, 76
at the Academy of Fine Arts, 24
Bočice (Flasks), 25, 27, 28
Project: Water Oozing from the Lower into the Upper Bucket on a Woolen Yarn, 77f, 78
Poinsot, Jean-Marc, 44
Polet, magazine, 184, 185
Political insult
decoding Grupa KÔD, 79–86
going "underground," 94–109
January's messages of insolence, 87–94
OHO in Novi Sad, 74–79
translating the new art practice, 69–73
Politika ekspres, newspaper, 127
Polja, magazine, 71, 72, 89, 94, 108
Pollock, Jackson, 83, 121
Popit, France, 227
Popov, Nebojša, 117
Popović, Zoran, 146, 156
and Art & Language group, 148
at *ART EVENT*, 129
"Art in Serbia/Yugoslavia," 147
"For a Self-Managing Art," 152–153
gathering with artists at the gallery, 122
"GIVE ME YOUR MONEY," 202f
invitation to *Harbingers of the Apocalypse*, 166
in *Maj '75*, 199, 202f
Untitled Film and collaboration with Group of Six Authors, 179, 183
"Populist elitist," 277–278
Poštanske pošiljke (Postal Packages), exhibition, 44
Poznanović, Bogdanka, 74
Akcija srce-predmet (Action Heart-Object), 69, 70f, 78
Poznanović, Dejan, 72
Prapradedovi (Great-Great-Grandfathers), exhibition, 76, 79
Praxis, journal, 93, 99
Problemi, journal, "Punk" issue, 231f, 232, 238, 241

Prostor-forma (Space-Form), group, 256
Prvi broj (First Issue), publication, 187–192, 188f, 190f, 192f
Punk, 227
Socialist Youth Alliance definition of, 232
Žižek acceptance of, 232

Radio Free Europe, 24
Radna Zajednica Umjetnika (RZU) Podrum, 185–198, 218–219
members, 186f
"podroom," 191
and *Prvi broj*, 187–192, 188f, 190f, 192f
salvaging self-management, 206
SKC Gallery collaborates with, 297
space in, 194–198
Radojičić, Mirko, 82
Apotheosis to Jackson Pollock, 83
as culture editor of *Index*, 79
Ramsden, Mel, 158, 166
Ranković, Aleksandar, 36–37, 50
Rauschenberg, Robert, 294
Rdeči revirji (Red Districts), concert, 210
Ređep, Draško, 100
"Red University–Karl Marx," 115
Reise, Barbara, 146
Reism, 25, 27
Renger-Patzsch, Albert, 233
"Republican particularism," 88
Rešin Tučić, Vujica, 89
Rok, magazine, 72, 73, 73f
Rosenberg, Harold, 83
Rothko, Mark, 121
Rupel, Dimitrij, 238
Rusinow, Dennison, 167
RZU Podrum. *See* Radna Zajednica Umjetnika (RZU) Podrum

Šalamun, Tomaž, 78, 79, 177
Marking the Line to Petrovaradin, 78f, 79
Šalgo, Judita, 71, 74
Šampion, Ljuba, 98
Sarajevo, 251–294. *See also* Café-Gallery Zvono; Zvono, group
and *Jugoslovenska dokumenta*, 282–294, 297
and New Art Practice, 255
Youth House, 259
Savski, Andrej, 245
SC Gallery, Zagreb
by 1975, 67–68
Akcija total (Total Action), 46–47f
artists at, 27, 32
Bućan exhibitions, 46–47f, 54–56, 55f, 56f
city's cultural scene and, 18
"Draft Degree on the Democratization of Art," 49–50, 51
exterior of, 17f
Koščević and, 18, 45
Mogućnosti za 1971 (Possibilities for 1971), exhibition, 51
origins of, 15–19
"*Ovo nije moj svijet* (This Is Not My World)," slogan in front of, 179
Poštanske pošiljke (Postal Packages), exhibition, 43f
Schneemann, Carolee, 166
Schöpflin, George, 100
Scipion Nasice Sisters Theatre, 250, 271, 273
Krst pod Triglavom (Baptism under Triglav), 271–273, 272f
Self-management, 175
Serbian Academy of Arts and Sciences, 285
Memorandum, 285
Serbian Literary Cooperative, 127–128
Šetinc, Zlato, 227
Sherman, Cindy, 245, 247
Šibenik, Ljerka, 19
Šimičić, Darko, 199
"Ovaj rad govori nešto o meni" (This work says something about me), 203f
SKC Gallery, Belgrade, 115–166. *See also* Studentski Kulturni Centar
Abramović five-pointed star, 142–143
Aprilski susreti (April Meetings), 12, 135–143, 136f, 137f, 144f, 173, 257, 282, 297
artists at, 128–129

Art's Condolence Book, 160
Beuys and, 133, 138
Corris on, 150
"Cultural Imperialism," 148
Đorđević, *Against Art* show, 161
Drangularijum, exhibition, 122–126, 123f, 125f
Exhibition-Actions, 174–177
exterior, 118f
founding principles, 120
Group of Six Authors, collaboration with, 297
Grupa 143 at, 156, 157f
nonhierarchical operation, 121
Oktobar '72, event, 126–129
Oktobar '75, event, 150, 151f, 152–153, 155–156, 185, 193, 263
self-management, 155
Umetnost, ironija itd. (Art, Irony, etc.), exhibition, 160
ŠKUC Gallery, Ljubljana
and *Alternativa slovenski umetnost*i (An Alternative to Slovene Art) exhibition, 210
Ausstellung! Laibach Kunst, exhibition, 222f, 238
Back to the USA, exhibition, 245–250
bastardizing OHO, 207–209
Galerija ŠKUC izdaja, newspaper, 220–221f, 230f
Harbingers of the Apocalypse, exhibition, 215
Kaj je alternativa? (What Is the Alternative?), conference, 240–244
Laibach at, 223
openings, 233
Mandić's work at, 233
revisiting the New Art Practice, 218
Todosijević lectures at, 216f
Die Welt ist Schön, exhibition, 238, 239
Working Community of Artists at, 218
Slovene Culture Day, 207–208
Slovenia
Alpine symbolism in, 219, 223
punk in, 227
return to repression, 214
Woodward on, 232–233
Slovenian Central Committee, 233
Smith, Terry, 298
Socialist modernism, 121
Socialist Youth Alliance (Zveza Socialistične Mladine Slovenije, or ZSMS), 207, 208–209, 214
State Security Apparatus, 36
Stilinović, Mladen, 174, 178, 191
Ađo voli Stipu—Stipa voli Ađu, 167–169, 168f, 170f
Aukcija crvene (Auction of Red), 181f
on censorship, 187
cover of *1 Maj 1975*, 170f
interview in *Polet* magazine, 184
Kraljica (2) (Queen (2)), 179, 182f
1 Maj 1975 (1 May 1975), 171f, 198, 199
Moje / tvoje (Mine | Yours), 175–176, 176f, 179
O radu (On Work), 201, 204–206, 205f
"Pljuni to iz usta" (Spit that out of your mouth), 202f
in Zagreb, 167, 173
Stilinović, Sven
Akcija s toalet papirom (Action with Toilet Paper), 177, 180f
forming the Group of Six Authors, 173
Stipančić, Branka, banners, 167, 168f, 169
Strategy: Get Arts, exhibition, 133
Štravs, Jane, 290f, 292–293f
Student, newspaper (Belgrade), 107, 116
Studentski centar (Students' Center, or SC), 16
Studenski Grad (Student City), Belgrade, 115
Studentski Kulturni Centar (SKC), Belgrade, 117, 119, 120, 121–122. *See also* SKC Gallery
artistic experimentation, 128
artists working through, 135
Beuys lectures at, 138
collaboration between artists, 122–123

exterior, 118f
foundation of, 114
Yugoslavia's new artists connected with, 265
Studentski list, newspaper (Zagreb), 59, 93, 281f
Susovski, Marijan, 183
Šutej, Miroslav, 19
Šuvar, Stipe, 48
Suvin, Darko, 37
Szombathy, Bálint, 106f, 107

Tadić, Radoslav, 282
Taylor, A. J. P., 287
Telegram, newspaper (Zagreb), 23, 28
Thompson, Mark, 183
Tijardović, Jasna, 146, 148, 183
collaboration with Popović, 147
in *The Fox*, 135, 155–156
at Museum of Contemporary Art, Belgrade, 127
Tišma, Slobodan
THE END (time-based action, with Drča), 109, 110, 114
and Grupa KÔD, 79, 80f, 82, 83
Primeri nevidljive umetnosti (Examples of Invisible Art), 109–110, 111f, 112f, 113f, 114
Rasporedite predmete prema priloženoj legendi (Arrange the Subjects According to the Signs of the Legend), 89, 91f, 92
reason for not publishing until 1995, 110
Tito, Josip Broz, 32, 61, 65, 89, 109
after split with Stalin, 142
at the Congress of Self-Managers (1971), 93–94
death of, 198, 211, 254
on high profile of Serbs, 50–51
LCS leadership and, 128
Mandić text about, 101, 103
students' vision and, 117
Tjedni list omladine (Weekly Youth Newspaper), 98
Todosijević, Raša, 126, 133, 139, 141, 158, 215
at *ART EVENT*, 129
at the *Harbingers of the Apocalypse*, 166
Josephine Beuys, 134f
as key artist in the SC Gallery, 120–121, 122
lecture at the ŠKUC Gallery, 216f
list of keywords in English, 140
Marinela, plava natkasna sa flašom, stolica za maleckog Kaldera (Marinela, Blue Night Table, Chair for Little Calder), 125f
Odluka kao umetnost (Decision as Art), 129, 131f
Pijenje vode—inverzije, imitacije, i kontrasti (Drinking Water: Inversions, Imitations, and Contrasts), 139f, 140, 141
at Sixth April Meeting, 160
Was ist Kunst, Marinela Koželj?, 158, 159f
Tolnai, Ottó, 100
Tomc, Gregor, 209, 276
Tomić, Biljana, 74, 138
and Grupa 143, 156
at the SKC Gallery, 122
Tomičić, Davor
Akcija total (Total Action), 45, 46f, 47f, 49, 51
Trbovlje, 210–215
Trbuljak, Goran, 83, 126
conceptual art, 42
Javni čas umetnosti (Public Art Class), 84f, 86f
Ne želim pokazati ništa novo i originalno (I Do Not Wish to Show Anything New or Original), 41f
Referendum, 64f, 65, 67
solo exhibition at SC Gallery, 40
Tribuna, magazine (Novi Sad), 103
Tribuna, newspaper (Ljubljana), 25, 72
Tripalo, Miko, 50, 61
Turković, Hrvoje, 93
TV tednik (TV Weekly), 225

Udovički, Svetozar, 100
Ugrešić, Dubravka, 296
Új Symposion, magazine, 71, 100, 101–102, 108–109
Unkovski-Korica, Vladimir, 107
Uranjek, Roman, 245
Urkom, Gergelj, 122, 143
  at *ART EVENT*, 129, 130f

Valter brani Sarajevo (Walter Defends Sarajevo) (film), 253
Vertov, Dziga, 153
Vesić, Jelena, 152
Vidmar, Igor, 228, 240–241
Vidmar-Brejc (Vidmar), Taja, 25, 208, 209
Vjesnik, newspaper, 97–98
Vlasta, Delimar, 198
Vogelnik, Borut, 245
Vojvodina, Association of Students, 87
Volunteer Youth Brigade, 115
Vučemilović, Fedor, 174

Weiner, Lawrence, 166
Whitney Museum of Modern Art, 32
Wood, Catherine, 245
Woodward, Susan, 232, 253
Workers' self-management, 16
Working Community of Artists, 187, 189, 195, 197, 218, 263
World Bank, 40
WR: misterije organizma (Mysteries of the Organism), film, 101

Youth League, 89, 99, 101, 103
Youth Salon, 184, 185
Youth Tribune, Novi Sad, 71–109, 297
  and February Group, 94–100
  founding of, 71
  and Grupa KÔD, 79–86
  and *Index*, 88
  January Group at, 89
  as official property of the youth organization, 107
  OHO exhibition at, 74, 78
  performance of *Action-Heart Object* in, 69
  "Pesma underground tribina mladih" (Underground Song of the Youth Tribune), 107
  Új Symposion, 71, 100, 101–102, 108–109
  Youth Tribune, 71, 84f
Yugoslavia
  in 1960s, 40, 88–89
  in 1965, 23–24
  in 1970s and 1980s, 201
  after Second World War, 251
  as contractual federation, 172–173
  culture in, 152
  in December 1971, 65
  economic condition, 93
  events of 1968, 117
  prewar, 15
  purges in political life, 93–94
  in state of crisis, 128

Zabel, Igor, 73
Zabranjeno Pušenje, band, 278
  Das ist Walter (This Is Walter), 278
Zagreb. *See also* SC Gallery
  artists in, 135
  political crisis of 1971, 61
  Sixth Zagreb Salon, 57–58, 59
  Stilinović at, 167, 173
  university, 16
  Working Community of Artists, 263
  Zakmardijev passage, 51
Zajednica, Radna, 190f
Zdravi ljudi za razonodu (Healthy People for Fun), film, 95, 96f, 97
Zečević, Božidar, 119
Zildžo, Nermina, 254, 260, 277, 284
Žilnik, Želimir, 87, 94
Žižek, Slavoj, 1, 232, 242
Zlobec, Jaša, 103, 107, 108
Zubac, Pero, 94
Zvono, group, 260–276. *See also* Café-Gallery Zvono
  Akcija Mondrian (or *Passage through Painting*), 269, 270f

fostering modern and local art, 274
Group of Six Authors and, 263
Izlog (Shop Window), 268f
Obitelj na vikendu (Family on the Weekend), 265–266, 266f
Sport i art (Sport and Art), 274, 275f
street exhibition on Vase Miskina, 262f